THE OLD REGIME AND THE REVOLUTION

ALEXIS DE TOCQUEVILLE

THE OLD REGIME
AND THE
REVOLUTION

VOLUME TWO

Notes on the French Revolution and Napoleon

EDITED AND WITH AN
INTRODUCTION AND CRITICAL APPARATUS BY
François Furet and Françoise Mélonio

TRANSLATED BY
Alan S. Kahan

THE UNIVERSITY OF CHICAGO PRESS
CHICAGO AND LONDON

FRANÇOIS FURET (1927–1997) was the leading French historian of the Revolution and, according to the *New York Times,* "one of the most influential French thinkers of the post-war era." FRANÇOISE MÉLONIO is the editor of Gallimard's critical edition of Tocqueville's works. ALAN S. KAHAN is associate professor in the Department of History at Florida International University and author of *Aristocratic Liberalism.*

The University of Chicago Press, Chicago 60637
The University of Chicago Press, Ltd., London
© 2001 by The University of Chicago
All rights reserved. Published 2001
Printed in the United States of America
10 09 08 07 06 05 04 03 02 01 1 2 3 4 5

ISBN: 0-226-80533-6 (cloth)

The French text on which this translation is based has been licensed to the University of Chicago Press by Éditions Gallimard and is protected by French and international copyright laws and agreements. Pléiade Collection, © Éditions Gallimard. The University of Chicago Press gratefully acknowledges a subvention from the government of France, through the French Ministry of Culture, Centre National du Livre, in support of translating this volume.

The Library of Congress has cataloged vol. 1 as follows:

Tocqueville, Alexis de, 1805–1859.
[Ancien régime et la Révolution. English]
The Old Regime and the Revolution / Alexis de Tocqueville ; edited and with an introduction and critical apparatus by François Furet and Françoise Mélonio ; translated by Alan S. Kahan.
p. cm.
Includes index.
ISBN 0-226-80529-8 (cloth : alk. paper).
1. France—History—Revolution, 1789–1799—Causes. I. Furet, François, 1927– . II. Mélonio, Françoise. III. Title.
DC138.T6313   1998
944.04—dc21   97-43814
CIP
ISBN 0-226-80533-6 (vol. 2)

∞ The paper used in this publication meets the minimum requirements of the American National Standard for Information Sciences—Permanence of Paper for Printed Library Materials, ANSI Z39.48-1992.

Contents

✻

BOOK TWO

Notes Excerpted from Tocqueville's Papers concerning

the History of the Revolution

Translator's Foreword

With this, the second volume of Alexis de Tocqueville's *The Old Regime and the Revolution: Notes on the French Revolution and Napoleon,* this translation is complete. Most of the issues for a translator to address have already been discussed in the Translator's Foreword to the first volume. Nevertheless there are a number of questions relevant to this volume which merit discussion.

One issue relates to the organization of the material compared to the French edition published by Gallimard in the Pléiade series. As in volume one, in this volume the French text's "critical apparatus" and "historical notes" have been combined under a common rubric as "Notes and Variants." The section in this volume titled "Excerpts from Tocqueville's Research Notes" is included in volume one in the French version. With the exception of a few brief passages, listed below, this material was shifted to volume two in the translation in order to keep the first volume as short and inexpensive as possible for classroom use. The passages that, because of their intimate connection with the text, were retained in volume one, were integrated into the "Notes and Variants" to that volume. They are found on pp. 339–40, "Mémoire"; pp. 358–59, "Growing Inequality . . ."; pp. 371–72, "How the constitution . . ."; p. 380, "The Tax of the Tenth"; pp. 399–401, "It Was Not the Government's Flaws . . ."; and pp. 411–13, "Government Inquiry . . .".

The translation of volume two departs from the practice of volume one in one respect. In the first volume, Tocqueville's paragraphing was occasionally adjusted in order to avoid multiple very short paragraphs that might shock the English-language reader. Here, where the writing in question is not a finished literary product intended by both Tocqueville and the translator to be read with the greatest possible ease and pleasure, but notes and drafts reproduced in order to give the greatest possible insight into Tocqueville's thinking, the original paragraph structure has been retained throughout.

It is a pleasure to be able to thank all those who have contributed to this volume. The National Endowment for the Humanities supported this translation through a Translation Grant in 1995–96, and Florida International University granted me a leave of absence to make use of it. The University of Chicago Press, whose best traditions are represented by my editor, Mr. John Tryneski, has encouraged and supported my work throughout. I would also like to thank the Press's anonymous readers, whose comments and suggestions have improved this volume, as well as Prof. Lois Hinckley of the University of Southern Maine and my colleague Prof. Hugh Elton of FIU, who provided translations of Tocqueville's Latin. I owe a particular debt to Prof. Françoise Mélonio, coeditor of the French edition, who has been an unfailing source of erudition and encouragement. Most of all, I owe thanks to my wife, Sarah Bentley, for her continuing help and patience with a project that has been going on for a very long time.

The memory of François Furet has been a continuing inspiration.

Alan S. Kahan
May 2001

Tocqueville's Workshop

François Furet and Françoise Mélonio

The Work in Progress

When Tocqueville finished *The Old Regime and the Revolution* in February 1856, he wrote to his English translator about what was at stake in his next work: "It will make the Revolution with its unique character emerge from what [the first volume] contained, and if I am not mistaken it will display the general movement inside and outside France. When this Revolution has finished its work, it will show what that work really was, and what the new society which has come from that violent labor is, what the Revolution has taken away and what it has preserved from that old regime against which it was directed."[1] From this project, interrupted by death, there remain only three thick bundles of notes and sketches, written between 1850 and 1858, of which the oldest were summarily reclassified in 1856. Bibliographical lists and references to quotations adjoin almost-finished chapters and jumbled analyses of documents. The heterogeneity of these bundles has made dating them difficult, but the reader will be more conscious of the coherence of the ideas than their fragmentation. This is because Tocqueville always asked himself the same question: he wanted to understand the Revolution "from its beginning until the fall of the Empire,"[2] and in so doing to illustrate the genealogy of democratic despotism. The work would denounce the "palpable absurdity" of "giving the title democratic government to a government where political freedom is not to be found."[3] This was already the goal of *Democracy in America* in 1840. Thus it is not at all surprising that in 1856 Tocqueville shifted some much earlier writings to the files of this final

1. Tocqueville to Reeve, 6 February 1856, in *Oeuvres complètes* (hereafter cited as *OC*), v. 5, t. 1, edited by J.-P. Mayer (Paris, 1961–), p. 161.
2. Tocqueville to Hubert, 7 March 1854, *OC*, v. 14, p. 295.
3. See p. 163.

work: the parallel between the English revolution of 1689 and the revolution of 1789 written in 1841; the reception speech at the Academy of 1842, which was his first meditation on the Empire; and finally some notes on the movement of the Revolution initially intended for *The Old Regime.*[4] The files of the unfinished book on the Revolution are the tombstone of Tocqueville's thought.

The oldest stratum of documents in the files relates to the period from the end of the Thermidorian Convention to the Empire. In December 1850 Tocqueville had planned to write a book on the ten years of the Empire in the manner of Montesquieu, a "considerations on the causes of the greatness and decline of Napoleon." For Tocqueville this was the means of understanding the march of the Second Republic towards the Empire by analogy. In the six months which followed the coup d'état [of 1851—Trans.], he established a bibliography. We find a numbered list of 198 titles of works preserved in the Bibliothèque Nationale: pamphlets published under the Directory, the Consulate, or the Empire; memoirs of Mme. Campan, Marshal Ney, etc.; books like the *Considérations sur la France* by Joseph de Maistre; recent works like the *Histoire de la Révolution française* by Michelet. Tocqueville also examined specialized catalogues, collected notes written for his use by his learned friends, anticipated visits to those of his circle who were leading servants of the Empire, such as Mathieu Molé and Etienne Pasquier. In the beginning of the year 1852, he plunged himself into memoirs of the Convention and the Directory in order to understand the spirit of the times. In February he read the memoirs of Lafayette, then those of Mallet du Pan, of Thibaudeau, and of Fiévée, whom he had known in the thirties. In May, at the Imperial Library, he examined the pamphlets of the Directory (Year III–Year VIII). From all of this he drew elements of a history of public opinion. But opinion for Tocqueville was never enough to tell the truth about passions, practices, or mores. To all these writings he therefore joined a close reading of administrative documents, where he could simultaneously scrutinize the strategy of power and the resistance of men; in April at the National Archives he examined documents from Year IV;[5] in May the register of the Directory's deliberations (Year V–Year VII), the file of the Interior police, the ministers' correspondence. After which, during the summer, like all good society, he headed for the country. It was in the

---

4. These notes are grouped in a folder "to the chapter on the progress of France under Louis XVI."

5. Tocqueville to Beaumont, 22 April 1852, *OC,* v. 8, t. 3, p. 41.

calm of his château, in July and August 1852, that Tocqueville began to write. French politics was no encouragement; Tocqueville felt the need to give himself an appetite for writing. This is why he did not begin with the end of the Convention, which he had just studied, but with the preparation for 18 Brumaire, which he analyzed in the two chapters now found in book three: "How the Republic Was Ready to Accept a Master" and "How the Nation, While No Longer Republican, Had Remained Revolutionary." This was the moment which presented the greatest analogy with the fresh experience of the coup d'état. Tocqueville also gave himself the bitter pleasure of understanding the present and of skewering despotism's henchmen with an avenging pen: "one or two chapters are already drafted [. . .]," he wrote to Kergorlay on 22 July. "I have not begun the book with what ought to be its beginning. I started it at the place to which the notes I gathered in Paris chiefly related and where I felt the most desire to write. For the difficulty is to get started, and in order to get started, one must follows one's imagination a little. What I have written forms the picture of the period which preceded 18 Brumaire, and the state of mind which brought about that coup. I have naturally found again many characteristics which are well known to me, for despite great differences there are many similarities between the time of which I am speaking and that which we have just been through."[6] At that time, however, Tocqueville had already changed the object of his research. Since April 1852 he had begun to ask himself about the paradoxical memory which the French retained of the Revolution: they venerated its egalitarian principle and jealously defended its social conquests, without having any real attachment to political freedom. The experience of 1848–51 had just repeated the proof offered by the Directory. Tocqueville therefore turned towards the study of the old regime in order to understand the roots of this unique political psychology. A note of December 1852 marks the change: "I return to the library Thibaudeau's memoirs on the Consulate, without having read them; to take up again when I come back to this period." The files relating to the Empire contain only rare gleanings after 1852, picked up by chance at meetings and from readings: notes on articles in the *Revue des deux mondes*,[7] from conversations, isolated ideas such as the parallel between the Roman Empire and the Napoleonic Empire written in January 1853, or a long note of 27 March 1853 on conscription under

6. Tocqueville to Kergorlay, 22 July 1852, *OC*, v. 13, t. 2, pp. 243–44.
7. Notes on Vielcastel in 1855, on the life of Stein in 1856.

the Empire. It was only in 1856 that Tocqueville took up this file again. He seems to have then envisaged devoting a third volume[8] to the Empire, with nothing remaining from this project but the material assembled here under the title of book three.[9]

From 1852 to 1856, therefore, Tocqueville put off the study of the events of the Revolution and the Empire to work on the old regime. The work that he undertook nevertheless prepared for this study. Book one of *The Old Regime,* which analyzed the Revolution's general character, constituted the beginning of the great work. With broad strokes Tocqueville painted the description of public opinion in Europe at the end of the eighteenth century which he would later take up in detail in the opening chapter of his book on the Revolution [our volume two—Trans.].[10] Above all, from the outset in 1856 he defined the Revolution as an event of the greatest symbolic and cultural importance, although the rest of the book limited itself to examination of the social conditions which gave the French an unbounded taste for general ideas. Lamartine concluded from it that Tocqueville misunderstood the philosophical greatness of the Revolution, which in Lamartine's eyes constituted its mystery. After the publication of *The Old Regime* in 1856, Tocqueville devoted all his efforts to studying just this mystery. He concentrated on the actors' speeches, in order to understand through them the dynamic of social demands and the interlacings of ideas and events. *The Old Regime* presented itself as the picture of a society; *The Revolution* as the account of the excitements

8. See his letter to Reeve, 6 February 1856, *OC*, v. 6, t. 1, p. 161.

9. *Book 3 thus consists of the two chapters "How the Republic Was Ready to Accept a Master" and "How the Nation, While No Longer Republican, Had Remained Revolutionary" mentioned above, as well as selections from Tocqueville's research notes. Book 1 covers the period 1787 to May 1789, and book 2, the rest of 1789 with brief mentions of 1790–99.—Trans.*

10. The first chapter of the unfinished book was thus prepared without discontinuity between 1853 and 1857. See Tocqueville's letter to Bunsen of 2 January 1853, *OC*, v. 7, p. 328: "I am applying myself at this moment to studying the circumstances which accompanied the beginnings of our revolutions, or rather of our revolution, for there is only one, which still continues and is not ready to end. I seek to return myself to the period of its birth and get a clear idea of the first impressions, the first ideas, suggested to foreigners by the still hazy sight of this great movement. I would like to rediscover the trace of the various judgments which were made about it from outside, during the years 1787, 1788, '89, '90, '91, and '92, by the important men of the times, the writers, statesmen, rulers; what they thought about it in advance, what conclusions they drew from it or thought they were able to make about it for their own country; the influence that they attributed to it over the general course of affairs in Europe, the profit that they thought could be drawn from it." It was to Bunsen that Tocqueville owed his first interest in Schiller, Klopstock, Arndt, and Droysen. At Bonn in 1854, Tocqueville gathered documentation which he completed in 1857 by correspondence with the Swiss historian Monnard, the German historian Leopold von Ranke (see *OC*, v. 7), and Mrs. Austin and Chancellor of the Exchequer Lewis, English people to whom the Germanic world was well-known (see *OC*, v. 6).

and frenzies of opinion. To this inquiry Tocqueville devoted a little more than three years, from June 1856 until his final departure from his Norman château on 28 September 1858 for Paris and then Cannes, where he would die.

To write a history of revolutionary ideology implies a recourse to sources other than the government archives exploited before 1856, and consequently new difficulties of which Tocqueville was very soon conscious: "Since my goal is much more to paint the movement of the feelings and ideas which successively produced the events of the Revolution than to recount the events themselves, it is much less historical documents that I need than writings in which the public mind manifested itself at each period, newspapers, pamphlets, private letters, administrative correspondence," he wrote on 6 October 1856.[11] The chief difficulty was evidently the immensity of the documentation: "For the old regime, the problem was the absence of sufficient and certain ideas; in the first period of the Revolution, the problem comes from the immense multitude of writings published by contemporaries. To read everything is impossible; to choose, dangerous."[12] To the problem of choosing was added the confusion of a history still afire. For Tocqueville, the history of the Revolution was practically a history of present times. "The object which I want to represent is still so close to my eye that the proportion between the different parts which compose it is difficult to establish," he wrote on 20 September.[13]

Having determined his method and his sources, Tocqueville needed to establish a periodization of the Revolution in order to organize his readings. In 1853 he had sketched a plan in five chapters:[14] the general spirit of the Revolution; the Republic internally; the Republic externally; the Directory; 18 Brumaire. In 1856, when he wrote a "general view of the subject,"[15] he still envisaged a history which would finish in lingering on the portrait of Napoleon. On 1 September he asked Duvergier "how and where to best study the known facts, ideas, and passions of the period which extends from '89 to the Directory."[16] In October he decided, in his "plan of work," "to concentrate all my studies on the space which extends from 1788 to 10 August," and specified to Maury, the assistant librarian of

11. Tocqueville to Lewis, 6 October 1856, *OC,* v. 7, pp. 406–12.
12. Tocqueville to Duvergier, 1 September 1856, *OC* (Beaumont), v. 6, p. 335.
13. Unpublished letter to Freslon, 20 September 1856.
14. See p. 375.
15. See. p. 27.
16. 1 September, *OC* (Beaumont), v. 6, p. 331.

6

INTRODUCTION

the Institute: "In order to be able to finish my task, I am forced to divide it into *periods*. The period with which I naturally ought to start, and which in fact concerns me at this moment, is that which extends between 1 January 1787 (to choose an exact date) and 20 June 1789, that is to say until the Tennis Court Oath. The Revolution announced itself at that time in a thousand ways: by the struggle of the royal court with the parlements; by the assemblies of notables; through the reforms of all kinds attempted by the crown itself: finally by the question of the Estates-General which was debated everywhere, the form of convocation, the rules which they ought to follow." [17] At this time, Tocqueville had thus defined the subject of what was going to constitute book one: the period from 1787 to the meeting of the Estates-General on 5 May 1789, with some reflections on the following months. We may be astonished at the point of departure. Tocqueville had already made a general judgment on the reform of 1787 in *The Old Regime*. Furthermore he hesitated and thought about beginning with 14 July 1789, before resolving on a continuous narration of the events of 1787 and 1788 in order to understand, no longer as in *The Old Regime* the Revolution's global significance but its forms, no longer the why of the Revolution but the how.

Tocqueville's correspondence allows us to follow the research accomplished between July 1856 and December 1857, when Tocqueville began to write book one. Tocqueville did not leave Normandy, except for a brief research trip to Paris from April to June 1857, followed by a stay in London from 19 June to 24 July to consult the British Museum's collection of revolutionary pamphlets. This seclusion, far from book collections and archives, seems unsuited to an historian's work: it had personal reasons. Mme. de Tocqueville, neurasthenic, only felt comfortable in the country; Tocqueville himself, coughing blood, tired and discouraged by public misfortunes, preferred solitude. He has described in a melancholy tone his existence as an unhappy writer in the morning and a peasant in the afternoon: "I wake up very diligently at six o'clock in the morning," he writes to Beaumont, 21 December 1856, "and I conscientiously shut myself up in my office until lunchtime. I do almost nothing there, and I spend the rest of the day resting . . . As an excuse I tell myself that at the moment I have hardly any of the books or other documents here which would be necessary for my work. But would I work if I had them?" [18] Ampère has left us a more cheerful description of this sleepy château life: read-

17. Unpublished letter, 13 October 1856.
18. *OC*, v. 8, t. 3, p. 453. See also the letter to Mme. de Circourt of 5 December 1857, *OC*, v. 18, p. 428.

ings aloud of newspapers or travel accounts, billiards, walks, or vaudeville shows broke the dryness of the work of writing.[19] Let us not conclude too quickly from this testimony that Tocqueville would be diverted from primary sources in order to give in to the ease of writing a philosophical history. After 1856, as before, he was not at all concerned with erudition as such. But the research to which he proceeded was nonetheless considerable: he had acquired the collected acts of the assemblies and many pamphlets, and the employees of the Imperial Library were so obliging as to send him hundreds of revolutionary pamphlets in Normandy. A former minister who was furthermore a famous academician had the power to transport the Bibliothèque Nationale as well as the Institute's library to the countryside.

On 1 September 1856, Tocqueville wrote to Duvergier that he had already studied "the acts of the Constituent Assembly and the debates to which those acts gave rise inside and outside." In the months which followed he examined the pamphlets grouped in the present series Lb of the Bibliothèque Nationale.[20] This source was still little used, for lack of a catalogue. In order to study the old regime, Tocqueville had known how to find one of the pioneers of archival work in Tours; in 1857 he similarly had the intelligence to use the competence of Bordier, who in 1855 had published a first catalogue of the "Archives of France," and who sent Tocqueville the still unpublished continuation of his notes.[21] There remained the official documents to read in order to understand the link between the passions of public opinion and the discourse of power: from April to June 1857 Tocqueville installed himself at the château de Chamarande, in the south of the Paris region, from which he could easily reach the national archives to consult the correspondence of the royal household, documents relating to the second Assembly of Notables, to the electoral assemblies of 1789, and the documents on Dauphiny to which his attention had been drawn by the scholar M. Rochaz. In June, on the advice of one of his former colleagues in parliament, also an historian, Duvergier de Hauranne, Tocqueville left Paris for London. For a politician excluded from public affairs since the coup d'état, and isolated in his own country, the voyage offered great satisfactions to his self-esteem. Celebrated by London society, Tocqueville returned to Cher-

19. Ampère to Tocqueville, 10 February (for January) 1857, *OC*, v. ii, p. 361.
20. See a list of these documents in an unpublished letter to Ravenel of 25 January 1857, BN manuscripts.
21. See E. G. Ledos, *Histoire des catalogues des livres imprimés de la Bibliothèque nationale* (Paris, 1936).

bourg as an official guest of Her Majesty aboard a vessel of the British navy, to the astonishment of the Norman population. But in return the profit for the historian was very little. The pamphlets of the British Library not being catalogued, Tocqueville only picked up odds and ends from his hasty examination. He fell back on the State Papers Office. As a favor Lord Clarendon, the minister of foreign affairs, authorized him to consult the diplomatic correspondence of 1789–93, still closed to the public. Tocqueville drew from it the conviction that contrary to received opinion, the English had not played any Machiavellian role in the course of a Revolution whose importance they had not in the least understood.[22] Although after his return he asked for copies of documents, particularly from 1788 and 1789, we find in the written chapters hardly any traces of these too-quickly-examined documents, which furthermore would have been chiefly useful for writing the history of the revolutionary wars.[23]

In September 1857 Tocqueville had amassed enough documentation to undertake the indexing.[24] The work in fact was already very advanced, for the research notes, from which selections may be read in the chapter appendixes, are often drafts more than lists of citations. Tocqueville never hid himself behind his documents. With him there is none of that humility affected by historians of the end of the nineteenth century. To the pamphlets or newspapers he applied a uniform reading method which the headings of the paragraphs exhibit without dissimulation: "1792 in 1788," "radicalism of the moderates" . . . this radicalism, which Tocqueville called the revolutionary disease, he tracked everywhere—"this is the most original way to tackle the subject," he wrote. Everyone was struck with this disease: the writers of the cahiers, Volney, Condorcet, Brissot, Sieyès, and even a Roederer or a Mounier, however liberal and Anglophile, and "alone among the reformers of this period in having in advance an idea of what he wanted to do and having seen the consequences of his ideas." The notes and drafts are structured around a principal line of research, the search for the circumstances of the meeting of Rousseau and the Revolution. Tocqueville here meditates on the collusion between the affirmation of the rights of the individual and the cult of absolute power. The result is that in preparing for the account of the beginnings of the Revolution, he already sought to explain the Terror.

After re-reading and indexing which allowed him to survey in a single glance the years 1787 and 1788, Tocqueville wrote seven chapters in less

22. Tocqueville to Beaumont, 25 July 1857, *OC*, v. 8, t. 3, p. 491.
23. See *OC*, v. 6, t. 1, pp. 239–41.
24. In January 1858 Tocqueville took more notes on the struggle with the parlements in 1787.

than two months, from December to mid-January. Starting from a picture of the state of mind in Germany in 1787 (chapter one) then in France (chapter two), he followed chronology: the crisis of the monarchy, from the struggle with the parlements in July '87 to their re-establishment in September '88 (chapter three); the brutal fall in popularity of the members of the parlements that same month of September (chapter four); the struggle around the types of representation from September 1788 to the elections of March 1789 (chapter five); the writing of the cahiers (chapter six). The book ends at the sublime moment of the meeting of the Estates-General on 5 May 1789, to which all of chapter seven is devoted, the climax of the liberal phase of the Revolution, when time seemed suspended before the nation rushed into servitude. Tocqueville reported to Beaumont on 12 January 1858, that "all the pieces which compose [the first book] are in their places."[25] In fact we only have the structure of the seven chapters. Tocqueville wrote them almost entirely without notes, which leads to some confusions, for example between the parlementary crisis of November 1787 and that of May 1788. In the margin the recurrent mention "citations here" shows that the writing was to be supplemented. But this incompleteness has the advantage of making us "see the work in progress."[26] Tocqueville concerned himself chiefly with highlighting the "fundamental ideas" and with underlining the global significance of the revolutionary movement. Also, it was not without repugnance that he returned to the narrative, which risked blurring the lines: "the difficulty and danger of what I am doing here is that I cannot go into the account of events enough to interest the reader in the facts, and yet the little that I do go into the narrative slows the progression of the idea," he writes about chapter three. In passing from description of the old regime to narration of the Revolution, he did not imitate the models of the great historical narratives of Thiers, Michelet or Henri Martin. He set out in quest of a new poetics. The account should make intelligible the revolutionary dynamic which shortened time. And for that an "animated description" was required, "to write a short but animated story," "to describe very briefly," and "to show in brief" the collapse of old institutions. The shortened narrative gives the furious haste of the Revolution.

In January 1858 Tocqueville undertook book two, which was to lead from the meeting of the Estates-General to the end of the Constituent Assembly, 30 September 1791. For this book he did not have time to do

25. *OC*, v. 8, t. 3, p. 478.
26. Tocqueville to Ampère, 9 August 1857, *OC*, v. 11, pp. 385–86.

more than accumulate notes and broadly trace a plan: a first chapter on
the crisis until 14 July; a second chapter, whose outline was established in
December 1857, which was to lead from 14 July to the end of the Constituent Assembly, although the notes that have been preserved concern only
the taking of the Bastille and the uprisings of the countryside which followed; finally chapter three on "What Made the Revolution Victorious
Externally," a chapter planned since 1853 but whose place and arrangement were never decided. The method of work hardly changed. Installed
in his Norman château, except for a brief stay in Paris from March to
May 1858, Tocqueville still privileged pamphlets and memoirs, inasmuch
as the Revolution was first of all a cultural break that could only be understood by taking the discourse of the actors seriously. To the works of
French publicists he joined the testimony of foreigners, Americans, Swiss,
or Germans. Again on 11 November 1858, installed at Cannes, where he
would die, Tocqueville asked Beaumont for memoirs of 1788 and 1789.
The stay at Paris had allowed him to understand the other end of the
chain; after the pamphlets, which gave the state of public opinion, he
looked for the discourse of power: at the national archives, in March and
April 1858, Tocqueville thus went through the government files relative to
the pays d'état and the registers of the ministry of the Royal Household;
at the Imperial Library in April and May, the official correspondence between Bailly and Necker, Bailly and Lafayette and Gouvion, the files of
the city of Paris.

Almost nothing in the files of book two relates to post-1789. Thus we
do not know what Tocqueville would have written about the Legislative
Assembly, although he had drawn up bibliographical lists and gathered
various printed materials on the Assembly's work. On the Convention
there remain only the old notes from the years 1851–52. Would he have
emphasized the Terror? In 1852 in his notes on Mallet du Pan he thought
it was possible "to speak about this period in passing," since 1792 seemed
to him already present in 1788. It is probable that he would not have limited himself to this brutal affirmation of continuity, to which his ideas are
often reduced. The final research notes demonstrate a new perplexity in
the historian. Doubtless Tocqueville was tired, often sick with a stomach
ailment; he regretted the youthful speed with which he once composed
Democracy in America in his little room at Verneuil. But the slowness of
the writing, its difficulty, the doubts, also relate to the nature of the revolutionary event. Tocqueville wrote to his wife in April 1858 that "unfortunately, I still don't find any ideas to illuminate my path. [. . .] Lost amidst
an ocean of papers whose banks I cannot see [. . .] what is most difficult

in my subject is conceiving clearly what it consists of and understanding it."[27] A letter to Kergorlay of 16 May 1858 explains the theoretical reasons for this discouragement:

> The successive changes which take place in the social state, in the institutions, in the mind and the mores of the French as the Revolution proceeds. There is my subject. In order to see this clearly, up to the present I have found but one means, that is in some way to live each moment of the Revolution with its contemporaries by reading, not what has been said about them or what they themselves have said since, but what they themselves said then and, as much as possible, what they really thought. The little writings of the times, personal correspondence . . . have, for attaining this goal, still more utility than the assemblies' debates. By the course I pursue I attain the goal I set myself, which is to put myself successively in the milieu of the times. But the process is so slow that I often despair. Yet is there an alternative?
>
> Furthermore, there is something particular about this illness of the French Revolution which I sense without being able to describe well, or analyze its causes. It is a *virus* of a new and unknown kind. There have been violent Revolutions in the world; but the immoderate, violent, radical, desperate, bold, almost insane, and yet powerful and effective character of these revolutionaries does not have any precedents, it seems to me, in the great social agitations of centuries past . . . Independently of all that can be explained about the French Revolution, there is something in its spirit and its actions which is inexplicable. I sense where the unknown object is, but despite my best efforts I cannot lift the veil which covers it. I grope for it as if through a curtain which prevents me from either really touching it or seeing it.[28]

In order to understand the work of ideas in the test of events, Tocqueville entered, despite himself, into the interminable hermeneutics of revolutionary discourse. The last notes thus leave us as a testament the project of a history of the Revolution as a messianic ideology.

The Revolution as Ideology

Since we only know the material of volume two through drafts, it would appear difficult to bring out how new and how consistent Tocqueville's interpretation of the Revolution is. At first glance the drafts do not present a Tocqueville unknown to us: from the very first plans of 1850 to the autumn of 1858 they manifest the unity of a thought haunted by the threat of a new democratic despotism. But the approach is new. It is no longer

---

27. *OC*, v. 14, pp. 633 and 637.
28. *OC*, v. 13, t. 2, pp. 337–38.

a question, as before 1856, of examining the meaning of the Revolution, but its modalities. In 1850 Tocqueville had proposed writing a philosophical history of the greatness and decline of the modern French in the manner of Montesquieu—"I speak about history and do not tell it," he wrote again in 1857.[29] But in the course of his inquiry, he discovered, as if despite himself, that the mystery of the event could only be approached through the minutiae of chronology. From which comes the narrative structure of his new work: a book one that leads in seven chapters from the parlementary struggle in 1787 to the meeting of the Estates-General on 5 May 1789; a book two that leads in three files of drafts from 14 July to the end of the Constituent Assembly.

Throughout volume two, passing from description to narrative, Tocqueville still more than in *The Old Regime* gives a role to "circumstances," and first of all to the economic situation: he evokes at length, following the press and government archives, the food shortage of the winter of 1788–89. "Providence, which doubtless wished to present the spectacle of our passions and misfortunes to the world as a lesson, allowed there to come to pass, at the moment when the Revolution began, a great food shortage and a phenomenal winter."[30] In fact the account resembles a lament over the misfortunes of the times in the poetic manner of Agrippa d'Aubigné more than an economic analysis: "The air was frigid, the sky empty, dull and grey. This accident of nature ended up giving people's feelings a sharp and violent character . . ." Economics was a dimension of human life which never interested Tocqueville, except through its interference with politics. The food shortage entered his field of research because it radicalized discontent with regard to the king, although it was not its chief cause. In this sense, Tocqueville concludes, "this accident of nature was a great political event."[31] The error of the English economists hostile to the Revolution, like Sir Francis d'Ivernois, was precisely in believing that the Revolution could be interpreted according to the laws of economics, that it could be defeated by financial strangulation, when what gave it its strength was on the order of the symbolic. The economy thus never had more than the weight of a secondary cause in the general movement of the Revolution. Similarly, individuals had no more than the historical role which the Revolution's internal dynamic gave them. Tocqueville gathered some elements for portraits: Mirabeau, Sieyès, Lafayette, above all Napoleon, who fascinated him. But

29. See below, p. 35.
30. See below, p. 65.
31. See below, p. 65.

none of these ever had more than the role conceded by circumstances, or rather by the dynamic proper to revolutions. At the beginning of a revolution one follows principles, and the revolution devours all those whom it has successively adored. At the end, lassitude puts power within the range of an ambitious coup. Napoleon was superbly the man of the hour.[32] Thus neither economic fluctuations, nor individuals, nor plots, whose lack of weight Tocqueville shows, allow one to explain the revolutionary radicalization, although these external "circumstances" gave it the harshness of its character.

All the art of the narrative therefore consists of highlighting a dynamic internal to the Revolution, whose irresistible strength Tocqueville describes with metaphorical force: the great events are links of a chain,[33] springs in a machine, the Revolution is an illness without a cure. Causes and effects thus seem to engender one another without a break, in this gloomy history which leads from absolutism to radicalism and then to Caesarism with growing precipitation.

In volume two this dynamic of revolutionary demands starts with the vacuum of power. In the first three chapters of book one, Tocqueville's "chief object" is to show "the momentary union of classes and its immediate effect which is the impotence of absolute power."[34] "A kind of fever of dissolution reigned."[35] *The Old Regime* had already shown the abasement of the aristocracy by the absolute monarchy. The book on the Revolution shows the "paralysis" and setting aside of the nobility before its expulsion. For Sieyès, notes Tocqueville, the aristocrats are the Algerians of France, badly tolerated foreigners whose generosity attracted no recognition whatsoever, neither in 1788 when they led the combat against the king, nor on 4 August when they sacrificed their privileges. What was new in 1787 and 1788 was therefore not the powerlessness of the nobility, it was the dissolution of the monarchy itself, and of the whole authority of the state. Nothing similar had been seen before or since, for the later revolutions of 1830 or 1848 had not destroyed a centralization solidly established since Napoleon and consequently were nothing but brief shocks. This unheard-of vacuum of power was visible as early as the administrative reform of 1787, which was a "first revolution." From the crisis of the winter of '88–'89 on, it was much worse: Tocqueville notes the "setting aside" of the king and his government. Thus centralization was sus-

32. See below, p. 208.
33. Tocqueville to Beaumont, 26 December 1850. *OC,* v. 8, t. 2, pp. 343–44.
34. See below, p. 50.
35. See below, p. 408.

pended, power abandoned by the traditional authorities. The members of the parlements and then the deputies of 1789 had no other choice than to attempt to salvage absolute power and occupy this empty space. The history of the Revolution is first of all the history of the successive attempts to appropriate the vacant space of power, and their failure. The predominance of the legislative organ of the nation over the executive, which was distrusted for fear that it would become a monarchy, made government impossible. The Constituent Assembly, the Convention, and the Directory were all characterized, although in different forms, by "an anarchy tempered by violence" and the inability to overcome popular violence and class struggles.

These class struggles, silent for a brief moment in the enthusiasm of 1788–89, very quickly became the motor of the revolutionary dynamic: Tocqueville, it has been said, does not make class struggle the primary cause of the Revolution. In this he breaks with liberal tradition. According to Tocqueville, 1789 was not the end of the long struggle of the Third Estate against the privileged, but the result of the despotic education of the nation, which made the peaceful satisfaction of the republican desire for freedom impossible. If the struggle between classes was not the *cause* of the revolutionary explosion, it was in return soon "the real and fundamental character" of the revolutionary process. In 1788 the hatred between classes was hidden by the heat of the struggle against the common enemy: the king rendered this last service to the nation, in creating its unity against his person. Still the union was not perfect. The nobility rose up first because it had the republican desire for freedom, but also because it was the chief victim of the rise of absolutism.[36] The bourgeoisie, "long accustomed to obey," and furthermore favored by the monarchy against the aristocracy, remained very timid. It awaited the return of the parlements in September 1788 and the campaign leading up to the elections to affirm its specific demands, before being outflanked in turn by the lower classes as early as 14 July 1789. After that date, notes Tocqueville, all revolutions have the "same mechanics, the same procedures: the middle classes heat up, excite, put in motion the lower classes, support them morally and push them further than the middle classes want to go."[37] We are very far here from the bourgeoisie as the spearhead of emancipation. Certainly this analysis of the changing demands and the conflict of interests was not completely new: Benjamin Constant in *De l'usurpation* had

36. See below, p. 46.
37. Draft from file 44.

noted that "in all violent struggles, interests run right behind exalted opinions, like scavenger birds follow armies ready to fight hatred."[38] For Tocqueville the conflict of interests in itself alone was nevertheless insufficient to explain the increasing demands. England or the United States managed the clash of class interests without revolution. In France the increase of demands found in the appropriation of an absolute sovereignty the means of its revolutionary deployment. Chapter five of book one is wholly a meditation on the absence in France of "the very idea of a moderate and balanced government, that is of a government where the different classes which make up society, the different interests which divide it are counterweights, where men weigh not only as units, but by reason of their property, their patronage, their interest in the general good." England and the United States illustrate the pacifying virtues of moderation analyzed by Montesquieu. The Revolution preferred Rousseau and the cult of absolute sovereignty: "At the beginning, people spoke only of better balancing powers, better adjusting class relations; soon they walked, they ran, they threw themselves into the idea of pure democracy. At the beginning, it was Montesquieu who was cited and commented on; in the end, only Rousseau was spoken of. He became and he was to remain the sole teacher of the Revolution in its youth."[39]

The Revolution was therefore chiefly a cultural revolution: a new understanding of power that Tocqueville designated by the recurring expression "radicalism." One measures here the distance from his point of view in *The Old Regime*. In 1856 Tocqueville had shown the illusion of the revolutionaries who imagined they were writing on a blank slate. Writing the history of the Revolution, Tocqueville looked for how the ideas of the revolutionaries became political forces. Doubtless men do not know the history they are making. But one cannot understand that history without studying the history they thought they were making. From which a change in the economy of sources: Tocqueville had sought to understand absolutism in its administrative archives. Later he scrutinized revolutionary culture in novels, pamphlets, newspapers, or memoirs. He read them en masse and without great regard for the nature of the documents: seeking to understand the "general mores of the times," he examined the novels of Jacobi, where one went "to daily shed torrents of tears in the imagination," as well as a fashion journal, and the scholarly treatises of Roederer and Mounier. Of no import, too, the writer's talent: the "bad

38. Benjamin Constant, "De l'usurpation," in *De la liberté des modernes*, Paris, 1980. 194.
39. See below, p. 57.

writing" which betrayed average opinion was even better. In this pile of texts, what he discovered was the appearance of the real spirit of the Revolution, which he dated from September 1788. He found then, even among the moderates, "the revolutionary and despotic idea that all individual rights are necessarily contrary to the common good and must be destroyed," even among a Péthion, a Brissot, a Mounier. Even in the cahiers. The interpretation here is doubtless too strong; Tocqueville let himself be carried away by the teleological illusion which made him find "'92 in '88." The pamphlets of 1788 and the cahiers were still wrapped up in the mental universe of absolutism, but it is true that they opened the way to the class war for power through the forms of representation.[40] Tocqueville thus has the merit of showing how revolutionary ideology was formed in the electoral battle and the struggle for appropriation of sovereignty. From these radical passions, the Convention then made a system, in creating "the politics of the *impossible;* the theory of folly, the cult of blind audacity,"[41] "one of the most unusual, most active, and most contagious illnesses of the human mind."[42]

In this sequential progress of the Revolution, which leads from violent anarchy to Caesarism, it seems that there was never anything but a burst of enthusiasm amidst a continuity of misfortunes. But how to make a History from so many misfortunes, and distinguish revolutionary "journées" and distinct phases? We often classify the historians of the Revolution, from left to right, according to the point of departure they assign for the Revolution going off course. The most radical reject even the idea of a going off course and accept the Revolution as a whole; the doctrinaires and liberals oppose the liberalism of 1789 to the terrorism of 1793; the conservatives, behind Burke, hate the Revolution from its birth. Sometimes Tocqueville seems close to Guizot and the liberals, when he distinguishes "various phases of the beginning of the Revolution in France: aristocratic and liberal then demagogic and egalitarian."[43] But if 1792 is already in '88, and if the radicalism of '88 is the inverted image of absolutism, the Terror is no longer anything but a lugubrious necessity, the Revolution is no longer the coming of a new world, and it is vain to distinguish phases in it. Why then does Tocqueville think of the Revolution as an unheard-of symbolic event? What constitutes the event for Tocqueville is the sudden and unforeseeable irruption of freedom. There are

40. See François Furet, *Penser la révolution* (Paris, 1978), pp. 61–69.
41. See below, p. 213.
42. See below, p. 218.
43. Undated folder, file 45.

"sublime" moments when man imagines he can tear himself loose from fate and found a new society. This is true of 5 May 1789, the date of the meeting of the Estates-General, on which Tocqueville lingers for a whole chapter at the end of book one. Time seemed suspended: "at this solemn moment, each person stopped and considered the greatness of the enterprise" . . . "this first spectacle was short, but it had incomparable beauty. It will never depart from human memory."[44] In a "sublime élan," the barriers between the aristocracy and the bourgeoisie disappeared, "hearts" united. After this blossoming moment of a foundation which did not know it was an illusion, book two shows the return of class divisions and the despotic tradition: 14 July 1789 is the "first manifestation in the facts of the dictatorship of Paris, already established in mores and in governmental habits; a dictatorship that is the mother of revolutions to come."[45] On 6 October, it is worse. The Assembly abdicates before the lower classes of Paris: "this event [is] one of the most unfortunate of the Revolution."[46] The Constituent Assembly's return to dictatorship did not exclude, however, a few more sublime leaps of freedom: 4 August 1789 is a "tempest of disinterest" although fear was mingled with enthusiasm among the privileged, and the Third Estate contented itself with profiting from the generosity of the nobility and the clergy. Finally, 14 July 1790, the Fête de la Fédération, is for the union of the bourgeoisie and the lower classes what the election to the Estates-General had been for the nobility and the bourgeoisie. But this concord, sincere as it was, was nothing but a "mirage." The emotion, in part feigned, was born of the persistent disturbance of souls more than from a new élan. After which, in book three, Destiny takes over. The Terror, which Tocqueville intended to treat only "in passing," innovated little: the crowds had been educated in ferocity by the barbarism of the punishments of the old regime.[47] 18 Fructidor and 18 Brumaire are only the solemn declaration of a return to servitude begun much earlier. There remains the fact that in the Terror itself, there is still a sublimity of horror where a perverted freedom manifests itself. "Only the absurd can make men make such efforts." "Violent and sublime," the masses of the Convention still aspire to freedom in their folly of radical destruction. In this sense, there is in the Terror something exorbitant, which in fact makes it something very different from the unconscious heir of absolutism. The history of the Revolution written by

44. See below, p. 68.
45. See below, p. 135.
46. See below, p. 156.
47. See below, p. 138.

Tocqueville thus oscillates between two interpretations: the first, which remains dominant, makes him inscribe the Revolution in the long-term of old-regime centralization, as in the work of 1856, at the risk of eliminating the specificity of the event and making all periodization impossible. The second defines the Revolution as a symbolic break, whose sublimely bold as well as radical and desperate character Tocqueville highlights. But he only perceives this break in the leaps of freedom or exceptional moments, in a sublime politics which is debased during the Constituent Assembly and then perverted under the Convention. As a result he did not succeed in elaborating a history of the revolutionary dynamic.

It is possible to analyze Tocqueville's writings as a work of tragedy.[48] The dramatic metaphor is furthermore recurrent in his writing: for Tocqueville it is a question of looking for the character of each "unique act" "in this strange play whose ending is still unknown to us."[49] The Revolution is a tragedy whose characters imagine that they are masters of their destiny when they succumb to that modern form of fatalism which is historical determinism. The prouder the ambition, the crueler the fall. But the final catastrophe does not disqualify the attempt. It is even the tactic of despotic regimes like the Directory to mock the sublimely generous spirit of those who had falsely believed they had razed servitude to the ground. The history of the Revolution written by Tocqueville does not have the satirical platitude of Taine, for whom the revolutionary ideology of rights stems from sentimental foolishness. There is in the Revolution something like the mystery of grace, which Tocqueville ascribes to the most hidden part of the French national temperament. Neither the English like Burke, nor Americans like Hamilton or Washington, can understand these "strange extremes" of the sublime which escape "the general study of human affairs."[50] In this sense the history written by Tocqueville, like that of Michelet, is a sort of national autobiography, although infinitely darker. In 1789 the French—and they alone—still have a primitive savagery which makes them great, even in their mistakes.[51] The chosen children of history even in their exemplary misfortune, it is not certain that they have retained their virtues afterwards. Apparently the revolution of 1848 is a revolution of 1789 which is beginning

48. Hayden White, *Metahistory: The Historical Imagination in Nineteenth-Century Europe* (Baltimore, 1973), demonstrates this for *Democracy in America*.
49. See below, p. 186.
50. Tocqueville to Corcelle, 27 June 1851, *OC*, v. 15, t. 2, pp. 222–23.
51. See below, p. 200.

again. Tocqueville multiplies the parallels between pre-Fructidor and pre-
2 December, the Club de Clichy and the rue de Poitiers. But "Alas! That
those who are born at the end of a long revolution little resemble those
who began it."[52] In 1789 people preferred principles to business, and even
"women, amidst their petty household tasks, sometimes dreamed about
the great problems of existence."[53] In 1851 the private prevailed over the
public, and people "concentrated more and more on the contemplation
of petty daily business." From the great Revolution to 1851 one slid,
according to Tocqueville, from the sublime to sentimentalism, from the
bloody Terror to silently murderous deportation, from the genius of the
Uncle to the ability of the Nephew [Napoleon I and III—trans.]. From
one revolution the other: Tocqueville had begun his work by comparing the French Revolution with the revolution of 1848 and those of the
United States and England. From these comparisons, in the end the
French Revolution emerged incomparable.

Note on the Manuscript

At his death on 16 April 1859, Tocqueville left an unfinished work. His
wife appealed to Gustave de Beaumont, who rapidly carried out the publication of excerpts from the manuscripts.

Beaumont first published two chapters on the Directory in the first volume of *Oeuvres et correspondance inédites d'Alexis de Tocqueville* (Paris,
Michel-Lévy Frères, 1861). In the introductory note to the volume, dated
May 1860, he announced his intention of limiting himself to this, while
underlining the enormous quantity of notes accumulated by Tocqueville:
"In order to publish one volume, he wrote ten, and what he put in the
rubbish as a study made only for himself, for many others would have
been a text completely ready for publication. His studies on the physiocrats and notably on Turgot, his notes on the cahiers of the Estates-
General, his observations on Germany and on several German publicists, his studies on England, etc., etc., are so many completely finished
works. But who would dare give the public what he himself did not judge
worthy of publication, and offer as books what he would only consider
supporting documents for his book? How to present, prolix and diluted,

52. See below, p. 381.
53. See below, p. 31.

that thought which he never showed in any but a concise form, and which he put all his skill into condensing?" (p. 90).

Beaumont was to change his mind, and a little later undertook a publication of *Oeuvres complètes* with Michel-Lévy Frères. In it are found not only the two chapters on the Directory already published (volume five, 1866), but also new documents, in volume eight, *Mélanges: Fragments historiques et notes sur l'Ancien régime, la Révolution et l'Empire; voyages; pensées; entièrements inédits* (1865). In this volume Beaumont presented seven "unpublished chapters of the work intended to be the continuation of the book on the old regime and the Revolution" that Tocqueville drafted about the period preceding the meeting of the National Assembly (pp. 55–148); some "notes and ideas relating to the work *The Old Regime and the Revolution*" on the Marquis de Mirabeau and Turgot (pp. 149–68); and some "notes and ideas relative to a work on the Revolution whose title was not yet decided" that focused on the period extending from the Constituent Assembly to the Empire (pp. 169–225).

In 1953 a new edition based on the manuscripts was published by André Jardin, in the *Oeuvres complètes d'Alexis de Tocqueville* (*OC,* v. 2, t. 2), under the title *L'Ancien régime et la Révolution: Fragments et notes inédites sur la Révolution.* This edition presented the two chapters written on the Directory and the seven draft chapters on the years 1787–1789; some extracts from the research notes on the old regime, the Revolution, the Consulate, and the Empire; and a set of diverse reflections. The texts, carefully transcribed, are much more numerous than in Beaumont's edition. The present edition supplements, based on the manuscript, the edition made by André Jardin.

The manuscript, preserved in Tocqueville's personal archives, is divided into two groups. One file (44) contains 46 folders with covers handwritten by Tocqueville, four folders with covers in Beaumont's handwriting, and some dispersed papers. The documents, of which many relate to the Empire, are disparate: notes on printed texts or archives, pages of bibliography, plans . . . The folders are not numbered, and the pages are not subject to any consistent pagination.

Two files (45A and B) contain folders of notes, plans, and drafts for the work on the Revolution, folioed and filed in handwritten covers by Tocqueville:

Folder "A.A. Vague intellectual disturbances that preceded the Revolution. Examined," containing notes on the state of mind outside France (Perthes, Forster, the Illuminati), in folios numbered 1–34.

Folder "1788. Various works on this year. Folder B.B.," containing notes on the assemblies of notables, the struggle of the parlements, and the pamphlets of 1787, in folios numbered 1–52.

Folder "D.D. 1787, 1788, and 1789. Dauphiny," containing folios numbered 7–39.

Folder "1789. From 1 January until the meeting of the Estates-General. E.E. Examined," and, on an under-cover, "1789. Between 1 January and the meeting of the Estates-General," containing notes on the preparations for the Estates-General and the writings of Fauchet and Sieyès, in folios numbered 1–65.

Folder "Y. Y. Various notes to examine before giving a *title* to the cahiers. Examined," containing twenty-seven pages of general reflections without consistent pagination.

Some pages of "fumblings," or successive drafts of plans, filed in six handwritten covers.

Finally, for each of the seven chapters written on the years 1787–89 there is an index referring to the folders of notes, a rough copy, a handwritten paginated manuscript written in one column with notes and marginal additions, and a copy by Beaumont.

Two handwritten covers contain the text of the two chapters on the Directory in folios, with many cross outs, and are inscribed in ink on the front side of the page: "How the Republic Was Ready to Accept a Master. Good pages for a chapter of the second volume of the work on the Revolution"; and "How the Nation, While No Longer Republican, Had Remained Revolutionary."

THE OLD REGIME AND THE REVOLUTION

Book One

THE OUTBREAK OF
THE REVOLUTION

CHAPTER ZERO

Plans

Original Idea, Overall Perspective, First General Feelings about the Subject

To reread sometimes to put myself back on the main trail of my ideas (1856).

My subject is:

1) The true depiction of the man,* more extraordinary than great, whom I take for my subject, and who it seems to me has not, up to now, been described with accuracy or depth. The new side of my subject.

Everything which shows his thoughts, his passions, finally his true *self,* should attract my special attention.

2) The help he received from the conditions and opinions of his time.

3) The means he used.

But what I want to depict above all, through him and because of him, is the great Revolution in which he played such a leading role. [I want] to judge the Revolution and describe it with a freer mind than those who have spoken of it up to now, profiting from the light shed on it as it endures; this can be great and original, if it is well done.

I also want to describe the French character amidst this general revolution, this phase of humanity: what this Revolution took from the national character, what the national character added to it. A new point of view, if I bring to it the freedom of mind of which I am capable, above all today when, disinterested in my time and my country, I have no passions which lead me to embellish or alter, and no longer have any desires except to find the truth and portray it.

Tentative Ideas (November and December 1856)

I think that in the first part of the history of the Revolution, which is the part about which the most has been written, as little time as possible

---

* The individual referred to is, of course, Napoleon Bonaparte. In this piece Tocqueville seems to be thinking in terms of his original project of writing a biography of Napoleon.—Trans.

should be spent on sketching the facts and details. I would lose myself in the immensity. But which general traits, which general questions to choose?

What place to assign to individuals? They certainly played a great role in this first moment.

Louis XVI; above all the court; Mirabeau.

My mind is drowned by details and cannot draw the fundamental ideas out of them.

I will not escape from the details if I want to write the story of that first period, even philosophically, and if I attempt anything more than a few considerations. But which ones?

Why did Reform turn so quickly into Revolution?

How was real or apparent agreement replaced by the most violent division? How could the Revolution have been made by a riot? Paris. How could the lower classes have suddenly become so furious, and the leading power?

Why the powerlessness of individuals? Why was civil war impossible?

The first thing to paint is that first period, which lasts from the meeting of the Estates-General up to the fall of the Bastille and the formal establishment of the Constituent Assembly. From that moment the Revolution is made.

This is the beginning and the most difficult part of the whole book. It is on this narrow space that I must concentrate all my attention at first. I will do nothing good *a priori,* but perhaps from looking at the details the fundamental ideas will be born.

For this first period, to choose the issues which will end up in the formal establishment of the Constituent Assembly.

Based on this to judge the work of that assembly. Disentangle what was fundamentally right, great, lasting in its works, then show how nevertheless it failed and did everything wrong. This is a crucial part of my work.

Apparent unanimity; good intentions; common love of freedom. First picture.

When I get to the analysis and judgment of the Constituent Assembly's work, the horizon clears: show on the one hand the greatness, the honesty, the beauty of its principles; on the other hand the lack of practical wisdom which ended up disorganizing everything.

How we suddenly fell from the old regime into the Revolution.

At the beginning perhaps pose this question first: Could the old regime have fallen without the Revolution?

CHAPTER ONE

The Intense and Shifting Agitation of the Human Mind at the Time of the Revolution's Outbreak

How during the Ten or Fifteen Years Which Preceded the French Revolution the Human Mind Became Agitated throughout Europe

Throughout Europe, during the ten or fifteen years preceding the French Revolution, the human mind surrendered itself to bizarre, irregular, and incoherent movements such as had not been seen for centuries. These were symptoms of a new and extraordinary sickness which would have greatly frightened contemporaries if they had been able to understand them.

The idea of the greatness of man in general, the omnipotence of his reason, the unlimited extent of his intellectual abilities, penetrated all minds and filled them; with this proud notion of humanity as a whole there was combined an unnatural contempt for the particular time in which they lived and the society of which they were part.

People were simultaneously immensely proud of humanity and exceptionally humble with respect to their own time and country. Throughout the continent the instinctive love and so-to-speak involuntary respect that, in general, people of all times and countries feel for their own institutions, for their traditional mores, for the wisdom or virtue of their ancestors, was hardly ever encountered any longer among the educated classes.

Everywhere people spoke of nothing but institutions' weaknesses, their incoherence, the absurdities and vices of contemporaries, society's corruption, its rottenness.

Quotations about the Disgust for the Times

The Idea of Disgust for the Times Closely Linked to the Vague Idea of a Coming Change, Without Even Imagining the Time and Shape of the Change

All this can be seen in novels. In that extremely insipid philosophical novel by the title of *Woldemar,* written by Jacobi around 1780, which despite its immense absurdities made a very great impression then, because its absurdity was that of the times, everything is full of diatribes against the present and predictions of a coming catastrophe:

"To me the present state of society looks like a dead and stagnant sea, and that is why I would favor any kind of flood, even of barbarians, to flush out this pestilential marsh and uncover the virgin earth."

The listener, Hornich (who is the straight man, the butt of the novel), expresses his great alarm at hearing this, and in fact with reason. I think that the author would have been more frightened himself if he had really believed in the coming of the barbarians.

Further on: "We live amidst the wreckage of forms and institutions, a monstrous chaos which presents the image of corruption and death everywhere."

This was written in a pretty country house, by a rich man who held an open literary salon, where people passed their time endlessly philosophizing, becoming tender, stimulating themselves, sensitizing themselves, daily shedding torrents of tears in their imagination.

Nothing shows better to what extent all the eccentricities of a leisured, restless, literary society were spread throughout Europe (the passion for philosophizing, analyzing feelings, making distinctions, sensibility, heated style). This book exaggerates with all the heaviness and clumsiness of a German setting all the defects of the contemporary French mind.

It was not the sovereigns, the ministers, the bureaucrats, in short those who in various ways controlled the details of human affairs, who recognized that one was heading towards some great social change. The idea that one could govern differently, and destroy what was so old and replace it with something that didn't yet exist except in a few writers' minds; the thought that the order in front of one's eyes could be overturned in order to establish a new order amidst anarchy and destruction: all this seemed an absurd illusion to them. For them the possible did not extend beyond the gradual improvement of the existing situation. In the bureaucratic correspondence of the period it is interesting to see able and foresighted administrators make their plans, adjust their measures, and expertly plan ahead for how they will use their power in a future time when the government they serve, the law they apply, the society in which they live, and they themselves will no longer exist.

It is the usual mistake of the people we call prudent and practical to go on judging according to the rules men whose precise purpose is to destroy and change those rules. But in times when passion begins to gain control over the conduct of human affairs, it is less what people of experience and knowledge think that deserves attention than what fills dreamers' imaginations.

It must not be believed that this sort of horror of one's own time and country which had so strangely seized hold of almost all our continent's inhabitants was a superficial and passing feeling. Ten years later, when the French Revolution had inflicted on Germany all kinds of violent transformations accompanied by ruin and death, even then, one of these Germans who had . . . thinking about the past, exclaimed in a confidential outpouring: "That which once was, is destroyed. What new construction will be raised on the ruins? I do not know. What I can say is that the most horrible thing of all would be if from this time of terror, the old time with its apathy and its ruined forms were reborn. You don't perform the play by going back to the first act. Go on, then!"—"Yes," replies his interlocutor (a noble), "the old facade must fall."

The ten or fifteen years which preceded the French Revolution were, in almost all of Europe, times of great prosperity. Everywhere the useful arts were developing; material needs increased; the industries and commerce which took on the task of satisfying these needs extended and improved in all ways. It seems that since human life was becoming busier and more materialistic, the human mind ought to have turned away from the abstract studies which have man and society for their object, and concentrated more and more on the contemplation of petty daily affairs. This is seen only too often in our own day. But at that time it was the contrary which happened. In all of Europe, almost as much as in France, people philosophized, they theorized, throughout the educated classes. Even those whose habits and business are normally most foreign to these kinds of ideas took them up passionately as soon as they had the time. In the most commercial cities of Germany, in Hamburg, in Lübeck, in Danzig, traders, industrialists, and merchants met among themselves after their daily labors, in order to discuss the great questions relative to human existence, the human condition, happiness. Women, amidst their petty household tasks, sometimes dreamed about the great problems of existence.

One would have said that everyone wanted to escape from their own individual concerns in order to occasionally concern themselves only with the great interests of humanity.

Just as in France literary pleasures occupied an immense place in the busiest lives, and just as in the capital cities the publication of a book was an event in the smallest town. Everything was a subject of interest, everything was a subject of emotion. It seemed that there were treasures of passion stored up in souls that were only looking for an opportunity to be distributed.

A traveler who had been around the world attracted general attention.

When Forster, one of Cook's companions, returned to Germany in 1774 he was received with great excitement. There was no town so small that he was not celebrated. People pressed around him, wanting to hear his adventures from his own mouth; but above all people wanted to hear talk of the unknown countries he had visited and the mores of the new men among whom he had recently lived. People asked if savage simplicity was not worth more than all our riches and arts; their instincts worth more than our virtues.

A certain excommunicated Lutheran pastor named Basedow, a sort of caricature of Luther, ignorant, quarrelsome, and a drunkard, imagined a new school system which ought, he said, to change the ideas and mores of his contemporaries. He preached it in language that was vulgar but fervent. His purpose, he took care to announce, was not only to reform the Germans, but the human race. To do so, it was sufficient to follow a simple and very easy method, with whose help all men were going to become educated and virtuous without difficulty. Immediately Germany was moved: sovereigns, ministers, nobles, bourgeois, magistrates, free cities came to the reformer's aid. The greatest lords and ladies modestly wrote to Basedow to ask his advice. Mothers of families hurried to put his books into their children's hands. Throughout Germany the old schools founded by Melanchthon were abandoned. The college destined to instruct these reformers of humankind was finally founded under the name of the Philanthropion; for a moment it enjoyed wide fame, then disappeared. The excitement vanished, leaving everyone shaken and confused. That such a man could produce such effects would be inconceivable if we did not know that the power of innovators in revolutionary times comes much less from themselves than from what, often by chance, they encounter in the crowd's soul.

We know that on the eve of the French Revolution Europe was honeycombed with bizarre associations and secret societies which were entirely new or had long been forgotten. The disciples of Swedenborg, the Martinistes, the Freemasons, the Illuminati, the Rosicrucians, the People of Strict Observance, the adepts of Mesmerism, and so many others which were only variations on these.

At their beginning several of these sects had in view only the particular interests of their members. But then everyone wanted to concern himself with the destiny of the human race. At their birth most of these sects were purely philosophical or religious; all turned together then to politics and were soon absorbed by it. The means differed, but all proposed the regeneration of society and the reform of government as their common aim.

Doctors tell us that during epidemics all particular illnesses end up presenting some of the symptoms of the reigning malady. The same phenomenon produced itself then in the intellectual world.

Another thing which is well worth noting: one lived then at a time when science, by becoming more exact and more certain, discredited the miraculous, when the inexplicable easily seemed false, when reason claimed to replace authority in everything, replacing the imaginary with the real and faith with free inquiry. The mass of minds walked down this path; however, most of the sects I just spoke of at some point touched on the invisible. All ended up in the chimerical in more ways than one. Among them, some nourished themselves on the mystical imagination; others thought that they had found the secret for changing some of the laws of nature. At that time there was no enthusiasm which was impossible, no dreamer who couldn't make himself heard, nor any imposter who couldn't find credence. Nothing shows better than this the troubled disturbance which then characterized the human mind, which was like a traveler in a hurry who can't find his train, running here and there, and sometimes, instead of going on, suddenly retracing his steps in a rush.

It Was Above All among the Upper Classes That the Illuminati Were Recruited

In our day it is poor workers, lowly artisans, ignorant peasants who usually fill the secret societies. At the time of which I speak there were found in them only sovereigns, great lords, capitalists, traders, intellectuals. In 1786, when the secret papers of the Illuminati were seized from their leader Weishaupt, several extremely anarchist principles were revealed: private property was pointed out as the source of all evil, absolute equality was advocated. In these same archives of the sect the list of members was found: only the most renowned names of Germany were there.

Many contemporaries, unable to see the general causes which produced this strange social upheaval that they witnessed, attributed it to the action of secret societies. As if any given conspiracy could ever explain the sudden destruction of all existing institutions!

The secret societies were certainly not the cause of the Revolution, but they must be considered one of the most visible signs of its approach.

America

It would be wrong to think that the American Revolution did not give birth to much sympathy outside France; its sound echoed to the ends of Europe; everywhere it seemed like a signal. Professor Steffens, who, thirty years afterward, took such a large part in the uprising of Germany against France and finally fought for Germany arms in hand all the way to Paris, tells us in his memoirs that in his childhood, his father, a doctor at Elsinore, told his very young children the events of the American War when he returned home one evening (Heinrich must then have been seven or eight years old):

> I was already sufficiently aware of the importance of the American War to be interested with all my soul in a people who so bravely defended their freedom . . . I still remember vividly what happened at Elsinore and in the harbor the day when the peace which assured the triumph of freedom was signed. It was a beautiful day, the harbor was full of ships from all nations. Since the previous evening we had been awaiting the dawn with the greatest impatience. All the ships had put on their dress clothes, their masts were decorated with long pennants, everything was covered with flags; the weather was calm, there was no wind except for what was needed to flutter the pennants and spread the flags; the firing of cannon, the cheers which were shouted by the crews assembled on the ships' bridges made the day into a holiday. My father had invited some friends to dinner; there they celebrated the Americans' victory and the triumph of the freedom of peoples; with that joy mingled some vague presentiments of the great events which were going to come out of that triumph. It was the gentle and brilliant dawn of a bloody day. My father wanted us to feel political freedom. Against the usual custom of his household, he had us come to table; he wanted to find a way to make us really understand the importance of the event which we were witnessing, and had us drink a toast with him and his guests to the health of the new republic.

Among the men who, in the most obscure corners of old Europe, felt so moved when they learned what a little people of the new world had done, none yet understood the event's importance. There were few who could understand what caused such deep emotion within their own hearts; but all were moved and all heard the faraway sound as a sign; what it prophesied, people didn't yet know. It was like the voice of John the Baptist crying from the wilderness that new times were coming.

Do not look for the particular causes of the individual facts which I have just described; they were all merely different symptoms of the same social disease. Everywhere the old institutions and the old powers were no longer adapted to the new situation and people's new needs. From this came that strange discomfort which made it appear even to the great and the upper classes that their situation was unbearable. From this came that universal idea of change which occurred to all minds without anyone seeking it, even though no one yet imagined how things could change. An internal movement without any source seemed to shake society's whole public life at once, and even shook each man's individual ideas and habits on their foundations. People felt they couldn't hold on any more. But people were ignorant of the direction in which they were going to fall. All Europe presented the spectacle of an immense mass swaying back and forth before hurtling forward.

CHAPTER TWO

How This Vague Agitation of the Human Mind Suddenly Became a Real Passion in France, and What Form It First Took
(war on absolute power, notables)

In the year 1787, this vague agitation of the human mind that I have just described, which had long stirred all Europe without any fixed direction, in France suddenly became an active passion with a set goal.

But, strange thing! At first this goal was not the one the French Revolution would eventually reach; and the men who felt this new passion first and foremost were those whom the Revolution would later devour.

Indeed, in principle it was not equal rights that seemed to be intended, but rather political freedom. The French who were first affected, who shook society and started the Revolution, did not belong to the lower classes, but to the upper. Before descending to the lower classes, this new hatred for the old absolute power and the old arbitrariness first seized the nobles, the priests, the magistrates, the most privileged of the bourgeois. In fact it reached all those who were the leaders of the state after the master, who more than others possessed the means to resist him and the hope of acquiring a share of his power.

The Notables

I will not describe how, in 1787, Louis XVI's financial difficulties led him to call together the princes of the blood and the leading members of the nobility, clergy, and upper bourgeoisie, and submit the financial situation to this Assembly of Notables. I am speaking about history, not retelling it.

Henry IV had already used this method of putting off the Estates-General and giving his wishes a sort of public sanction in the nation's absence; but times had changed. In 1596, France was coming out of a long revolution, it was exhausted from its efforts and distrusted its strength; it was looking only for rest and asked of its leaders nothing but the appearance of deference. At that time the Notables made France forget about the Estates without any difficulty. In 1787, the Assembly of Notables immediately recalled to mind the image of the Estates-General.

In the time of Henry IV, the classes whom he called on and consulted were still society's masters; they could therefore limit the movement they created and support the monarchy just as they could have resisted it then. These same classes under Louis XVI held only the trappings of power; we have seen that they already had lost its substance forever. They were like hollow bodies, striking in appearance, but easy to break with a single blow. They could still arouse the people, but they were already incapable of directing them.

Since this great change had occurred gradually and silently, no one recognized it clearly yet. The chief interested parties did not know that it had taken place; their enemies themselves doubted it. The whole nation had been kept away from its own affairs, and had only a murky view of itself.

The Notables Act in Opposition; Opinion Lends All Its Weight to Them

As soon as they met, the notables forgot that they were nothing but the sovereign's delegates, chosen by him to give advice and not lessons, and acted like the country's representatives. They asked for accounts, censured actions, attacked most of the measures whose execution they had simply been asked to facilitate. Their help was wanted: their opposition was encountered.

The Government Vainly Tried to Flatter Democratic Passions; Public Opinion Was Against It

Immediately public opinion was aroused and put all its weight on their side. People spoke, people wrote in their favor. There then appeared the unusual sight of a government trying to become popular by proposing measures favorable to the country's interests, without being able to stop being unpopular, and an assembly fighting it with the support of the public.

The government proposed to reform the salt tax, which weighed so heavily and often so cruelly on the lower classes. It wanted to abolish the corvée, reform the taille, and eliminate the vingtième from which the upper classes had succeeded in partially exempting themselves. In place of these old taxes, abolished or reformed, the government proposed a land tax established on the same basis as our current real estate tax. It pushed back to the frontier the internal customs barriers which harmed trade and industry. Finally, alongside and almost in place of the intendants who administered each province, the government tried to create an elective assembly which would be charged not only with supervising the conduct of business but in most cases with running affairs.

All these measures were in accord with the spirit of the times; all these measures were rejected or delayed by the notables. However it was the government which was unpopular and the notables who had the voice of the public on their side.

Afraid that he had been misunderstood, the minister Calonne explained in a public document that the effect of the new laws would be to relieve the poor of part of the weight of taxes and put that burden on the rich. This was true, and he stayed unpopular. "Priests," he says in another place, "are above all citizens and subjects. They ought to submit to paying taxes like everyone else. If the clergy have debts, let them sell some of their property to pay them." This was to attack the public on one of its most sensitive sides. The public didn't seem to notice a thing.

To the reform of the taille, the notables objected that it could not be done without adding a surcharge on the other taxpayers and in particular on the nobility and clergy, whose privileges in matters of taxation were already reduced to nothing. Against the abolition of internal customs duties, they peremptorily put forward the prerogatives of certain provinces that needed to be treated with special consideration. If they strongly approved of the creation of provincial assemblies in principle, they nevertheless wanted to keep the three orders separate in these little local bodies instead of mixing them, and insisted that a noble or a clergyman should always preside: "For," said several committees, "these assemblies would tend towards democracy if they were not directed by the superior wisdom of the higher orders."

Yet the notables retained their popularity to the end. Still more, their popularity continually increased. They were applauded, spurred on, supported. They resisted: they were pushed on to the struggle with loud cries. And the king, hastening to dismiss them, thought he was obliged to thank them.

It is said that several of the notables were themselves astonished by this public favor and sudden power.

They would have been still more astonished if they could have foreseen what was going to happen. For what they fought with popular approval, these new laws that they rejected or delayed, were based on the very principles that the Revolution was going to make triumph; it was precisely the traditional institutions through which they opposed the government's proposed innovations that the Revolution was going to demolish.

What made the notables popular was not the form of their opposition, it was their opposition itself. They criticized the government's abuses, censured its waste, asked it to account for its expenses. They spoke of the country's constitutional laws, of the fundamental principles which limited the unlimited power of the king and, without exactly calling on the nation to take care of its own affairs in the Estates-General, they constantly revived the idea.

That was enough.

For a long time the government had already been suffering from a disease which is the usual and incurable disease of powers which have tried to command everything, to foresee all and do all. The government had become responsible for everything. However divided people were on the subject of their complaints, they therefore freely united in blaming the government for them; but what previously had only been a general mental inclination became a universal and impetuous passion. All the hidden sorrows, created by the incessant friction of ruined institutions whose debris wounded ideas and mores in a thousand ways, all the restrained anger fed by class divisions, contested status, ridiculous or oppressive inequalities, all turned against the government. For a long time these passions had looked for a way to make themselves known. A road was opened, and they rushed down it blindly. It was not their *natural* way, but it was the first which presented itself. Momentarily, therefore, hatred of despotism seemed to be the only passion of the French, and the government appeared as the common enemy.

CHAPTER THREE

How the Parlement Overturned the
Monarchy with the Help of Precedent

(the struggle of the parlement against the court,
from the end of the first meetings of the
Notables until September 1788)

Feudal government, amidst whose ruins France still lived, had been a
mixture of despotism, violence, and great freedom. Under its laws,
actions had often been constrained, but words were almost always proud
and independent.

The kings had always exercised legislative power, but never without
limits. In France, when the great political assemblies ceased, the parlements partly took their place in this regard. Before the parlements officially entered on the books the new laws made by the kings, they gave
their opinion and made their objections to the sovereign.

The origin of this usurpation of part of the legislative power by the
judiciary has been the subject of much research. It must be sought solely
in the general mores of the time, which could not accept or even conceive
of a secretive and absolute power with which obedience could not even
be discussed. The institution was not at all planned. It arose spontaneously and necessarily from the ideas and habits of the kings themselves as
well as those of their subjects.

The law, before being put into effect, was therefore brought before the
parlement. The royal agents explained its principles and its advantages;
the magistrates discussed it; everything happened publicly and openly,
with the manliness which characterized all medieval institutions. Often it
happened that the parlement sent deputies to the king several times to
ask him to change or withdraw his law. Sometimes the king came in person; he allowed his own law to be subjected to loud and violent debate in
front of him. But when he had finally expressed his will, everything returned to silence and obedience; for the magistrates recognized that they
were only the first officers of the sovereign, his representatives, charged
with informing and not with constraining him.

The Independent Constitution of the Parlement

In 1787, people merely followed these old royal precedents. The old machine of government was put back into motion, but it was soon realized that it had a new motor, one of an unknown kind, which was going to break it rather than make it work.

The king, following custom, brought the new edicts before the parlement and the parlement, in accord with custom, remonstrated.

The king responded, the parlement insisted. Things had happened like this for centuries and the nation had occasionally heard this kind of political discussion between the sovereign and the magistrates passing over its head. This discussion had been interrupted for a while only during the reign of Louis XIV. What was new was the subject of the debate and the nature of the arguments.

This time the parlement asked that before registering the new laws, it should receive as justificatory evidence all the financial accounts, what would have been called, when France had a government which could breathe freely, the communication of the budget. Since the king correctly refused to thus turn over the entire government to an irresponsible body without any mandate, and to share legislative power with a court, the parlement declared that the nation alone had the right to agree to new taxes and asked that it be assembled.

This was to capture the people's very heart, but to hold it for only a moment.

The arguments which the magistrates made in support of their demands were no less new than the demands themselves: the king being only the administrator and not the owner of the public fortune, the representative and chief official of the nation, not its master, sovereignty resided only in the nation itself; the nation alone could decide its chief business; its rights did not depend at all on the sovereign's will; these rights took their origin from the nature of man, they were as indestructible as nature.

The king having exiled the parlement, the parlement in its declaration said that the freedom to act and to speak was an inalienable right of man, and could not be taken away without tyranny except following the regular forms of law.

It must not be thought that the parlement presented these principles as innovations; on the contrary it very industriously derived them from the depths of the antiquity of the monarchy. The parlement's decrees bristle with historical citations often reproduced in barbarous medieval

Latin. It is a question only of capitularies, old royal ordinances, decrees, of precedents which come out of the shadows.

It is a strange sight to see newborn ideas surrounded and as it were swaddled in these old languages.

It was an old tradition in the monarchy that the parlement in its remonstrances could express itself with a kind of manly frankness bordering on rudeness. The parlement was in the habit of making a lot of noise to get very little. Its words therefore usually went beyond its intentions, and it was allowed a sort of exaggeration in its speech. The most absolute sovereigns had permitted this license in language for the very reason that the parlement was powerless; since they were sure of being obeyed and of keeping the parlement tightly bound within its limits, it was left the consolation of speaking freely. Furthermore, in this very stable society, it was a sort of serious comedy which was performed before the country. But this time the play had changed and the audience was different.

The parlement extended this old freedom to a license which had no historical precedent, for a new fire burning at the bottom of hearts inflamed its language without its even being aware of it. I dare say that among the governments of our day, which, however, are almost all more or less based on the sword, there is not one which could allow itself to be attacked in such a way without its proposals and its ministers falling.— Put quotations here.

This language would seem inconceivable if this had been the first time it was spoken. But all that was done then was to repeat more violently what had already been said on the same subject so many times before. Since, in the old monarchy, most taxes were levied on behalf of particular individuals who had bought them on lease and by their agents, people had been accustomed for centuries to consider taxes nothing but certain men's profits, not common resources. Taxes were therefore freely treated as hateful exactions; their flaws were recognized, their weight was exaggerated; those who raised them were often spoken of as public thieves who enriched themselves from everybody's misery. The government itself, which had given the tax-farmers the rights that they possessed, hardly expressed itself any differently. It seemed that the tax-farmers' business didn't concern the government and that the government was only concerned with avoiding the blame which surrounded its agents.

Therefore the parlement said it was only following the usual custom— quotations—and thus repeating what had already been said a hundred times. The play was the same. But the audience had become larger and the uproar, rather than stopping as usual within the limits of the classes whose privileges made them little affected by taxes, this time was so loud and repeated so often that it penetrated down to those who suffered most from taxes, and began to fill them with fury.

The parlement and the king could agree on only one point: the edict which created new local authorities called provincial assemblies.

When one thinks of the importance of this law, and of the strange revolution which it created in the entire old constitution of society and government, one cannot be too astonished at the agreement which was reached on this occasion between the two oldest powers of the monarchy, one to present it, the other to accept it. Nothing can make us better understand to what extent, in this country where everyone, even women, passed their time debating politics, the real science of human affairs was unknown, and how the government, in plunging the nation into this ignorance, had ended up making itself ignorant.

—Here in a very rapid analysis show in passing how the edict on provincial assemblies ended up destroying the entire old European political system from top to bottom, and suddenly substituted a democratic republic for what remained of the feudal monarchy, substituted democracy for aristocracy, republic for monarchy.—

I do not judge the value of the change, I only say that it was a matter of an immediate and radical change of all the old institutions, and that if the parlement and the king together chose this path deliberately, it was because neither one saw where they were going: they joined hands in the dark.

If the parlement used new arguments to establish its ancient rights, the government employed arguments no less new in defense of its old prerogatives.

—Here gather together all that I will find in the responses of the king, the ministers, even the works published by their friends among the officials, that most tends to arouse the rich against the poor, the unprivileged against the privileged, the bourgeois against the noble . . . Then say:—

It seems, in short, that the parlement and the king had arranged their roles in order to instruct the people more quickly and easily. One taught them about the vices of royalty, and the other about the crimes of the aristocracy.

While people thus discussed the very principles of government, the daily work of administration threatened to stop; money was lacking. The parlement had rejected the tax measures; it refused to authorize loans. In this extremity the king, seeing that he could not win over the parlement, wanted to try force: he went to the parlement, and before commanding obedience had the edicts discussed again before him.

—Paint this session in very much abridged form, even limit myself, I think, to presenting the principal truths that the king allowed to be said to his face for eight hours.—

However, after having thus allowed his most recognized and least feared rights to be contested before him, the king attempted to exercise one of the most contested and least popular of them. He himself had opened the orators' mouths; he wanted to punish them for having spoken. Then occurred the scene most apt to give a benevolent power the appearance of tyranny.

Two men had made themselves particularly known by the boldness of their speeches and their revolutionary attitude: Goislard and d'Eprémesnil. A few days after the royal session, they were to be arrested. Warned, they fled their homes and went to the parlement, then about to begin its session. They dressed themselves in their robes and lost themselves among the crowd of magistrates who composed that large group. Soldiers surrounded the Palace of Justice, occupied the entrances, and forced the doors. The Viscount d'Agout, who commanded the soldiers, went into the great hall alone. The entire parlement had assembled there in its most solemn form and was holding session. The number of magistrates, the venerable age of the court, the solemnity of their robes, the gravity of mores, the extent of their powers, the very majesty of a place so full of all the memories of our history . . . made the parlement then the most august and most respectable object that there was in France, after royalty.

How the Oldest Government in Europe Took It Upon Itself to Teach the People to Defy the Majesty of the Most Ancient Institutions, and to Violate the Most Revered of the Old Powers in Their Very Sanctuary

The officer was at first forbidden to enter the assembly. He was questioned about his errand. He responded with a voice simultaneously gruff and uncertain that he came to arrest two members of the court; he asked that they be pointed out to him. The parlement remained silent and motionless. The officer left, then returned, then left again. The parlement was still silent and motionless; it neither resisted nor surrendered.

Night fell. The soldiers lit their fires around the Palace as if outside a place under siege. A crowd of people surrounded them without pressuring them. The crowd was disturbed without yet being threatening and limited itself to considering from afar, by the gleam of the campfires, this sight that was so strange and so new in the monarchy.

Things continued like this until the middle of the night, when d'Eprémesnil finally got up. He thanked the parlement for the efforts which it had made to save him, he did not want to abuse it any longer . . . He commended the public welfare and his children to them; and, descending the steps to the courtyard, he gave himself up. One would have said that he was leaving that place only to mount the scaffold; he was indeed to mount the scaffold, but in another time and under another government. The only remaining witness of this strange scene has told me that on hearing d'Eprémesnil, tears burst out from all sides. It seemed as if Regulus was leaving to be shut up in the barrel full of spikes that they were preparing for him at Carthage. The Marshal de Noailles sobbed; alas! how many tears were soon going to be shed for higher destinies! These sufferings were doubtless without cause, but not feigned. For in the first days of a revolution, the magnitude of emotions always goes far beyond that of events, just as at the end they fall short of attaining them.

After having thus struck down the parlement's leaders, it remained only to reduce it to impotence. Six edicts then appeared simultaneously.—Analyze them perhaps in a few words to show that they were not bad in themselves; still more, that they realized several of the most important and most useful reforms made by the Revolution. We had not yet reached the time when democracy could pardon despotism anything in return for order and equality.—In a moment the whole nation was on its feet.

We know that France was divided into thirteen judicial provinces, each of which was based on a parlement. All these parlements were absolutely independent of one another, all equal in prerogatives, all equally provided with the ability to debate the lawmaker's orders before submitting to them. This will seem natural if one thinks back to the era when the majority of these courts of justice had been founded. The various parts of France then differed so much from one another by interests, intellect, habits, mores, that the same legislation could not be applied to all of them at the same time. The law was usually particular to each province. It was natural that in each province there was a parlement charged with examining it. Since then, the French had become more similar and laws more uniform, but the power to scrutinize them had remained divided.

When, therefore, an edict of the king had been accepted in one part of France, it could always be contested or applied differently by the twelve others. This was certainly the law but it was no longer the practice. A kind of tacit agreement had been made, for people are ordinarily wiser than the law. The provincial parlements contested only regulations which were particular to the province, and most often accepted general laws without discussing them, or after the Parlement of Paris had accepted them. But this time each one wanted to make itself known by a particular resistance amidst the common resistance.

Among the different edicts, a given clause accepted at Paris was rejected by the province, that which the province accepted being opposed at Paris, and the government, struck simultaneously from all sides by all kinds of enemies with all types of weapons, looked in vain for a spot where it could strike down resistance with a single blow.

But what was remarkable was not so much the simultaneity of the attacks, but the common spirit of resistance. Each one of the thirteen courts took a slightly different course, but they were all heading for the same place at the same time. The remonstrances which were then published are enough to fill several volumes. I have found the same ideas in almost the same words everywhere.

All demand . . .

—Here citations or at least a succinct analysis.—

Listen to the uproar which emanates from all the magistrates spread out over the surface of France simultaneously; you will think you are hearing the confused noise of a crowd; listen attentively to what they say: it is a single man.

The union of all the parlements was not only the means of the Revolution, it was its sign [that a revolution had already taken place—Trans.]. It presumed that the nation was already united amidst the multitude of institutions which still seemed to divide it into a thousand parts; that none of these parts had a separate life any longer, but that the entire nation already lived a common life, obeyed the same interests, followed the same ideas, was alike.

—Perhaps after having shown the multiple and united actions of the parlements, which struck from all sides at once with only one aim in view, show how this judicial riot was more dangerous for the government than all other riots, even military rebellion, because it turned against the government the regular, civil, and moral power which is the government's usual tool. One occasionally represses with the army's help for a day, but one defends oneself daily with the courts. Furthermore, the disorder and elimination of the courts were enough in themselves to create a situation in which regular government could not be sustained.

—How one of the consequences of this kind of resistance was less the harm the courts themselves did to authority than the harm which they *allowed to happen*. They established, for example, the worst of all freedoms of the press, that which does not come from a right that has been conceded, but comes from the nonexecution of the laws and the paralysis of the right to repress excesses.

—Freedom of assembly: it permitted the members of each order to momentarily lift the barriers which separated them internally and to unite in common action. The same for the different orders between themselves. Start from here to show all the orders in each province attacking the king's absolute power, each in its own way.

—Then continue thus:—Little by little they all ended up joining the struggle, but not at the same time or in the same way.

It was the nobility which entered first and most boldly into the common struggle against the king's absolute power.

It was in place of the nobles that absolute government had established itself: it was the nobles who were the most humiliated and inconvenienced by that obscure delegate of the royal power who, under the name of "intendant," daily came to settle the pettiest local matters without them and often in spite of them; it was from the nobility that there came forth several of the writers who were most forceful against despotism. Almost everywhere the new ideas had found their chief supporters among the nobles. Independently of their particular grievances, the nobility were carried along by the common passions which at first blamed the government for so many of the varied grievances created by the ruinous situation of society; and what was very noticeable was the nature of the nobles' attacks. What they complained of was not at all that their particular political privileges were being violated, but that the common law was trampled on, the freedom of the press chained, the liberty of persons threatened, the provincial estates abolished, the Estates-General suspended, the nation put in tutelage, and the country deprived of the government of its affairs.

During this first epoch of the Revolution, when war had not yet been declared between classes, the language of the nobility was in all respects similar to that of the other classes, except that it went further and took a haughtier tone. The nobles' opposition had republican traits. These were the same ideas and as it were the same passions inspiring prouder hearts, souls more used to looking directly and more carefully at the great ones of the earth.

—Here gather all the facts belonging to the period which precedes the withdrawal of the ordinances and show what I have just said *in the no-*

bility's actions: their meetings, their writings, the mildness with which the nobility led the soldiers against the riots. Finally show the nobles of Brittany ready to arm the peasants to fight against royal power! Then take up again:—

The Opposition Was Hardly Less Lively or Less General among the Clergy, But They Limited Themselves to More Restrained Language and Spoke in a Discreet Tone

The clergy's opposition was no less firm, although more discreet. It naturally took the particular form of that group. The first member of the Parlement of Paris who was arrested for the rudeness of his demands was an abbé (?).

—Try to describe well the particular character of this clerical opposition, what is special about its language and acts; show the particular appearance of the clergy in this passion, the speeches made before the parlements, particularly at Troyes, the orders of the bishops, the assembly of the clergy which *I think* is in this period.—

—*Course of ideas:*

1. *The bourgeoisie at first timid and undecided. Proof of this.*

2. *Tempted to accept the benefits and favors offered by the government; quotations.*

3. *Finally became inspired, but with its own motivation. Advances quickly, but always covered by the passions of the other classes, pushed by an internal motivation which it does not reveal.*—

At the beginning the bourgeoisie was timid and indecisive. The government counted chiefly on the bourgeoisie to support it in its troubles without stripping the government of its old rights; it was the bourgeoisie's particular interests, its passions, that the government had above all kept in view in its reforms. Long accustomed to obedience, at first the bourgeoisie only engaged in resistance fearfully; it still was accommodating (citations everywhere) . . . the bourgeoisie still flattered power while resisting it, recognized the government's rights while contesting their use. It showed itself in part tempted by the government's favors and ready to accept absolute power provided that it was given its share.

—Here what concerns the tribunals which agreed to become courts.—

Even in the places where it marched in the lead, the bourgeoisie never dared go alone: it advanced as if under the shelter of the upper classes. It marched as if under cover, sharing the fury which inspired the upper classes, but above all full of a passion which was particular to itself and whose expression it withheld, which had already become heated inside without being revealed.

Then, as the struggle went on, the bourgeoisie became emboldened, inspired, moved ahead of the other classes, took the lead role and did not leave it until the lower classes themselves mounted on stage.

—Here paint this picture according to the facts. I am led to believe that, in this first part of the struggle, the upper classes (whether of the robe or the sword) were always very far ahead of the bourgeoisie in language and action. It is only when it was a question of the meeting of the Estates-General, when the issue of classes was opened, that the bourgeoisie moved, as I have said, to front stage and took over the leading role. Up until then, it had followed more than it led (see, however, the episode in Dauphiny where, it seems to me, even during this first moment of the struggle it was the bourgeoisie which was in the lead, without, however, ever daring to march alone). The bourgeoisie mostly profited from the passions of the upper classes in order to obtain concessions, rather than inflaming them . . . —

In this first period of struggle, no traces of class war. A single visible passion, a common passion: war on power, spirit of opposition.

—Lively and animated picture of this spirit which breathes throughout, in small as well as great matters, which is attached to everything, which takes all forms, even those which disfigure it.—

In order to fight against authority, some base themselves on whatever remains of old local freedoms.

Some demand an old privilege of their class, certain outdated rights of their profession, in order to safeguard themselves against power. Others want some ancient prerogatives of their body. In their ardor to attack authority, people armed themselves using all the weapons to be found, even those which fit their hand least well. It might have been thought that the purpose of the coming revolution was not the destruction of the old regime, but its restoration. Even for the individuals who are themselves carried along by these great social movements, it is very difficult to distinguish which is the great motor among the causes which moves them! Who would have said that what made people demand so many traditional rights was the very passion that would irresistibly lead them to abolish them all!

—Thus the nobility (whether of the robe or the sword) led the battle. The clergy, at least some priests, fought. The bourgeoisie was at first hesitant and divided, then carried along, but by separate passions which remained hidden. A chorus of opposition among the educated classes; opposition taking all forms.—Do a continuation on the lower classes.—

Now, amid this upper-class tumult, let us listen a little to the sound of the storm which was beginning to whip up the waves of the masses.

No sign that I can see, from the distance where we are, shows me that the rural population was yet aroused. The peasants silently went about their business. This vast part of the nation was mute and seemingly invisible. In the towns themselves, the lower classes showed themselves little moved by the emotion of the upper classes and at first remained indifferent to the commotion going on over their heads. But as soon as they began to become interested, one sees that they were inspired by a previously unknown spirit.

I have said in another part of this work that under the old regime nothing was more frequent than riots; authority was at the same time so strong and so . . . that it freely let these passing upheavals take their course. But France had arrived at a point where even old things only happened with new features, riots just like everything else.

—Here study the facts; show those nighttime shouts, those burnings in effigy, the unexpected resistance, something violent, cruel, savage, which reveals itself.

Paris, which can barely be held down by 100,000 men, was then held in check by the watch (define it). This time, the watch was not enough.—

At the sight of an opposition so new and so widespread, the government at first showed itself surprised and worried rather than beaten. It tried all its old weapons one after another, it made new ones, but this time in vain: warnings, *lettres de cachet,* exiles; employing enough violence to irritate, never pushing it far enough to make people afraid. Furthermore you cannot make an entire people afraid. The government sought to arouse the passions of the lower classes against the rich, the bourgeoisie against the nobility, the lower courts against the upper. This was to take up the old game; this time it played in vain. The government named new judges, most of the new judges refused to judge. It offered favors or money; people were still too impassioned to be bribed. It sought to distract public attention, public attention remained fixed. No longer able to stop or even limit the freedom of the press, the government wanted to make the press serve its designs: at great expense it published many little writings in its support. Its defense was hardly read and people fed themselves on the thousand pamphlets which attacked it.

Finally an incident happened which precipitated the crisis.

The Parlement of Dauphiny had resisted like all the others, had been attacked like all the others. But nowhere had the cause it defended found more unanimous support and more active defenders. While in most of the other provinces the different classes made war on the government separately and independently, in Dauphiny they united formally as a political body and prepared themselves to resist. Dauphiny had had estates for centuries. Some nobles, clergy, and bourgeois, spontaneously meeting at Grenoble, dared to convoke these provincial estates which had not met since . . . They invited the nobility, the clergy, and the Third Estate to meet as provincial estates in a château situated at . . . and called Vizille, to give anarchy the appearance of being according to the rules.

—Since I must give this importance to the events in Dauphiny, study them well, even their underside. Thus, it seems to me that at the assembly of Vizille hardly any nobles were found except those whose right to participate in the estates was at least doubtful; the kind whose liberalism was mixed with a kind of relatively democratic spirit.

But of the clergy, I think that at Vizille there were hardly any but parish priests, that is those ecclesiastics who would not have been admitted (doubtless) to the old estates.

Take care, in making these fine distinctions, not to lose from view the chief object which I want to highlight, namely the momentary unity of classes and its immediate effect: the impotence of absolute government.

Know Vizille well, its appearance, its position. A château of Lesdiguières, a great *feudal* château. (Try to see paintings of Vizille or Vizille itself if possible.)

Tell the story of this assembly as well as I can after having reread the notes I took on it. Then say:—

The assembly of Vizille produced a prodigious effect on all France. It was the last time that something that happened outside Paris exercised great influence on the general destiny of the country.

The government feared that what had been dared in Dauphiny would be imitated everywhere. It finally despaired of defeating the resistance which opposed it and declared itself beaten. Louis XVI dismissed his ministers, abolished or suspended his edicts, recalled the parlements.

The parlements returned to their seats less as men amnestied than as victors. In accepting their recall, they rejected the conditions that had been placed on them. This time Louis XVI, given the situation things had reached, is not to be blamed for having backed down; one should only wonder at the prodigious number and greatness of the mistakes he had

had to commit to get there. If he gave up absolute power it was because everything was then lacking for him to defend it. He could not shelter himself behind the laws, his own courts were against him, he could not prevail by material force, the leaders of the army lent themselves to his plans only with repugnance. In the old France, furthermore, absolute power had never had a brutal appearance. It was not born on the battle-field; it had never been upheld by force or arms. It was essentially a civil despotism which was founded not on violence but on art. The kings would not have been able to create this uncontrolled power except by dividing the classes, isolating each one in the midst of the prejudices, jealousies, and hatreds which were peculiar to it, so that they never had to deal with more than one class, and were able to lean on it with the full weight of all the others.

It was enough for the French who made up these different classes to lower for a moment the barriers that had been built up around them, to see each other and agree to resist in common, even for only a single day, in order for absolute power to be at their mercy. The day that they agreed, absolute power had to be defeated, and in fact it was.

The assembly of Vizille was the material sign, visible to all, which an-nounced this new union and showed what its effect could be. And it was thus that an event which happened in the depths of a little province in a corner of the Alps was decisive for all of France, and that a particular incident suddenly became the chief fact.

CHAPTER FOUR

How the Parlements, Just When They Thought They Were Masters of the State, Suddenly Discovered They Were No Longer Anything

When royal authority had been defeated, the parlements at first thought that they were the ones who had triumphed. They re-turned to their seats less like those pardoned than like victors, and thought they had only to enjoy the fruits of victory.

The king, abolishing his edicts which had established new sovereign judges, had ordered that at least the verdicts that they had already ren-dered should be respected. The parlements declared void the cases which had been judged without them; they made the insolent magistrates who had dared aspire to replace them appear before them, and rediscovering in these new circumstances the old language of the Middle Ages, they "marked their infamy." Throughout France the king's friends were punished for having obeyed him and learned, by an experience they would never forget, that safety was no longer to be found on the side of obedience.

But where this change was felt above all was in Paris.

The intoxication of these magistrates is easy to understand. Never had Louis XIV in all his glory been the object of more universal adulation, if one can call the excessive praise that real and disinterested passion is willing to give by that name.

—Here put all the titles that were given them: senators, heroes, etc. . . .—

When the Parlement of Paris was exiled to Troyes [August–September '87], every group came, one after another, to offer their homage at the parlement's feet, as if it had been the sole sovereign of the country.

—"What has happened to them plunges us into suffering and consternation . . . They are generous citizens, virtuous and compassionate magistrates . . ."

The officials of the Troyes Mint: "Our descendants will know that this Temple (the Palace of Justice) became the sanctuary of your oracles (the place where you render your decrees); they will know that their ancestors were witnesses of your patriotic decisions." (I doubt it!)

"In all French hearts you deserve the name of fathers of the country . . . You console the nation in its hardships . . . Your actions are the sublime acts of energy and patriotism. How sweet it is to sacrifice oneself for the country like you . . . The parlement is an august senate . . . The principles it supports are the fundamental principles of the monarchy . . . The nation's voice acknowledges the councilors of the parlement as its fathers . . . We render homage to your patriotic virtues and ornament your heads with the civic crown . . . All the French think of you with veneration and emotion."

The Church itself came to compliment them. The chapter of the cathedral church of Troyes: "We have seen with as much pain as the other orders of the state . . . this universal national mourning, yourselves stripped of your duties, taken from the bosom of your families . . . All these things were a shameful sight for us, and, as long as these august walls resound with the sounds of public suffering, we will carry back to our sacred temple our own suffering and our wishes." (In ordinary language: as long as people come to the Palace of Justice to compliment you we will pray for you and your cause in our churches . . .)

"We will follow you, covering you with blessings, we will no longer hide our veneration and our love behind the compliments of hospitality. Country and religion solicit for you a lasting monument for what you have just done."—

The University itself came in robes and square bonnets to nasally pronounce its compliments in bad Latin:

—Illustrissimi senatus princeps, praesides insulati, senatores integerrimi [chief of the most illustrious senate, presidents of the courts of the Ile-de-France, impartial judges—Trans.]: We join in the general feeling and testify to you the strong feelings of admiration excited by your heroic patriotism, and the constancy with which you defend the people's interests . . . We once appreciated only the military valor which made legions of heroes abandon their homes . . . Today we see the heroes of peace in the sanctuary of justice . . .

The nation looks upon you with enthusiasm. You are under the eyes of a Europe made attentive and moved by the spectacle that you offer it . . .

The Palace which once resounded to your oracles (the Palace of Justice) since your departure has heard only the cries and groans of the citizens. The nation will raise altars to this august senate, peace has its heroes like war . . . They are the fathers of the country who have brought truth into the royal palace and pleaded the people's cause there . . . Like those generous citizens Rome honored when, victors over the state's enemies, they paraded before the eyes of their fellow citizens, you will enjoy a triumph (the king had just withdrawn the new taxes) which will guarantee you an immortal memory.

It was impossible for a judicial body that suddenly found itself plunged into the delights of political popularity not to become intoxicated. The first president responded to all these addresses in a few words, like a king: he assured those who had spoken of the court's good will.—

In several provinces the arrest or departure of the magistrates had brought about riots. In all the provinces, their return brought almost insane demonstrations of popular joy. For, in France, there are hardly any great emotions which are not mingled with a little absurd exaggeration, nor great successes which do not degenerate a little into ostentation.

—Chiefly what happened in Dauphiny and at Bordeaux. The scene in Bordeaux would be excellent if it could be vividly portrayed, naturally and yet clearly. But how to really get across the comedy of that crowd climbing over the carriage that blocked the door of the house and pursuing the first president even at home?—

Barely a few days later, the noise ceased, the enthusiasm fell, there was solitude around them. Not only did the parlements fall into indifference, but all the grievances that had ever been held against them, the very ones that the government had tried in vain to use against them, were raised against them.

They had been treated as legislators, fathers of their country; now people didn't even want them as judges any more.

—Here put all the criticisms that were made of them then.—

The fall was sudden and terrible above all for the Parlement of Paris.

—Paint the isolation, the impotence, the despair, the sadness so well reproduced in Pasquier's memoirs, the royal government's disdainful vengeance, the expulsion of d'Eprémesnil, their astonishment, their inability to comprehend . . . They asked each other how to understand this . . . —

These magistrates didn't see that the flood which had borne them up was the very same flood which submerged them. How many times in my own life have I seen with my own eyes a sight like what I have just painted!

—Develop the reasons for this.—

Originally, the parlement had consisted of jurists or lawyers whom the king chose from among the most able of their profession. Merit opened the greatest honors of the magistrature to men born in the most humble conditions. Along with the Church, the parlement was then one of those powerful democratic institutions which were born and implanted in the aristocratic soil of the Middle Ages and introduced a kind of equality there. Later the kings, in order to make money, thought of selling the right to judge. Then the parlement was filled with a certain number of rich families who considered the national administration of justice as their special privilege. Soon they wanted to enjoy it solely among themselves and excluded everyone else from it, obeying that peculiar impulse which seemed to push each particular group to become more and more a small, closed aristocracy at the same time that the nation's ideas and mores made society tilt more and more towards democracy. Rules that would never have been accepted in feudal times prescribed that only nobles be accepted in the high courts of justice.

There was assuredly nothing more contrary to the accepted ideas of the time than a judicial caste rendering justice by itself after having purchased the right. For a century no institution had in fact been more often and more severely criticized than the venality of offices.

The courts, whose organization was indefensible, had, however, one rare merit that the best-constituted courts created in our own day do not possess. These courts were independent. They rendered justice in the sovereign's name, but not according to his wishes. They obeyed no other passions but their own. After all the intermediate powers which could balance or temper the unlimited power of the king had been flattened, the parlement alone remained on its feet.

The parlement could still speak when everyone was silent; it could keep a stiff back for a while when everyone else had long been forced to bow. Thus one saw it become popular as soon as the government ceased to be. And when the hatred that despotism inspired momentarily became an ardent passion and a common feeling among all the French, the parlement seemed the only road that remained for the country's freedom. All the defects that had been most criticized in it seemed to be political safeguards of a kind; one sheltered behind its very vices. Its hegemonic spirit, its pride, its prejudices were the weapons the nation used.

But, as soon as absolute government had been definitively defeated, and the nation no longer had any need of a champion, the parlement suddenly became once again what it had been before: an old, deformed, and discredited institution inherited from the Middle Ages, and it immediately returned to the place that it had occupied in public hatred. To destroy it, the king had only to let it win.

CHAPTER FIVE

How the Revolution's Real Spirit Suddenly Showed Itself as Soon as Absolutism Had Been Defeated

(from September 1788 up to the elections)

For a moment, the bond of a common passion held all classes together. As soon as this bond was relaxed, they separated; then the real figure of the Revolution, which up until then had been veiled, suddenly revealed itself.

As soon as the king had been defeated, it became a question of knowing who would profit from the victory. The Estates-General having been obtained, who was going to dominate in that assembly?

The king could no longer refuse to call the Estates-General, but he retained the power to choose their form, the Estates-General not having met for 160 years. Furthermore, they were no longer anything but a vague memory. No one knew exactly how many deputies there ought to be, the relationship between the orders, the form of elections, the manner of deliberating. The king alone could say. He didn't say anything.

A unique idea on this subject came to Cardinal de Brienne, the king's prime minister, and he made his master take a decision that was unparalleled in all history. The cardinal considered it a matter for historical research whether the number of voters ought to be limited or unlimited, the assembly large or small, the orders separate or united, equal or un-equal in rights, and as a result an edict of the Royal Council ordered all local authorities and official organizations to make inquiries about the holding of the old Estates-General and about all the forms which were followed there. The cardinal added: "His Majesty invites all scholars and other educated people of his kingdom, and particularly those who are members of the Academy of Inscriptions and Belles-Lettres, to address all information to the Chancellor and report on this question."

This was to treat the country's constitution as an academic exercise and make it a topic for a competitive examination.

This appeal was immediately heard. France was flooded with writings. All the local authorities deliberated about what they should respond to the king, all the individual groups made demands, all classes thought of their special interests and sought to find in the ruins of the old Estates-General the forms which seemed most likely to guarantee them. Everyone wanted to give his opinion, since France was the most literary country in Europe, and as this was the period when literature clothed the passions of the times in the heavy garments of erudition.

The class struggle, which was inevitable but which would naturally have started only in the Estates-General itself, in an orderly way, on a limited field and with reference to particular questions, thus found limit-less scope and was able to nourish itself on general ideas. It soon took on a character of exceptional boldness and unheard-of violence, which the hidden state of feelings makes comprehensible, but for which [nothing] had prepared people.

The Movement of Ideas, the Movement of Passions

Between the time when the king abdicated his absolute power and when elections started, [around five months] passed. During this space of time, there were almost no changes in the facts, but the movement which led French ideas and feelings towards the total subversion of existing society accelerated, and in the end became extremely rapid.

At first people were only concerned with the constitution of the Estates-General, and thick books of raw erudition, where one tried to reconcile the Middle Ages with contemporary views, were hastily pro-duced. Then the question of the old Estates-General faded, the jumble of old precedents was tossed aside, and people looked in an abstract and general way for what the legislative power ought to be. Ideas became more comprehensive as people went on; it was no longer just the constitution of the legislature which was in question, but of all power; people attempted to shift not only the form of government, but the very basis of society. At the beginning, people spoke only of better balancing powers, better adjusting class relations; soon they walked, they ran, they threw themselves into the idea of pure democracy. At the beginning, it was Montesquieu who was cited and commented on; in the end, they only spoke of Rousseau. He became and he was to remain the sole teacher of the Revolution in its youth.

The idea of government was simplified: numbers alone made law and right. All politics was reduced to a question of arithmetic. The roots of everything to come implanted themselves in ideas. There is almost not a single opinion professed during the Revolution which does not appear in one of [these writings], not one of the works of the Revolution which is not announced and often surpassed . . .

—Citations—

The government itself had asked to be discussed; it could no longer limit the argument.

At the same time, the same movement leading ideas led passions with furious speed towards the same goal. In principle, the nobility was criticized for wanting to push its right too far. Towards the end, it was denied that the nobility had any right. At first people wanted to share its power; soon they didn't want it to have any power. Not only shouldn't the nobles be masters, they hardly had the right to be fellow citizens: they were foreigners who had imposed themselves on the nation and whom the nation was finally rejecting . . .

—Citation from Sieyès—

Perhaps for the first time in the history of the world, we see upper classes who are so separated and isolated from all the others that they can be counted and set aside like the doomed members of a flock; middle classes who do not try to mingle with the upper classes, but on the contrary try with jealous care to preserve themselves from any contact with them: two symptoms which, if anyone had been able to understand them, would have announced to everyone that an immense Revolution was going to happen, or rather had already been made . . .

The writings which attacked the privileged were innumerable, those which defended them so few that it is pretty hard to grasp what was said in their favor. In the midst of the noise made by the multitude, it might seem surprising that the attacked classes found amongst themselves or elsewhere so few and such weak defenders when they held most of the important posts and owned a large part of the land, whereas after they were defeated, decimated, and ruined so many eloquent voices have pled their cause. This can be understood if one thinks of the extreme confusion into which this aristocracy fell when the rest of the nation, after having for a while marched alongside it, suddenly turned on it furiously. With surprise the aristocracy recognized its own ideas in the ideas which were used to attack it. The ideas with whose aid people tried to annihilate it were the very basis of its own thought. What had been its intellectual amusement during its leisure became a terrible weapon against it.

Like its adversaries, in fact, the aristocracy freely believed that the most perfect society would be one where natural equality was best approximated; where merit alone, and not birth and fortune, would classify men; to the aristocracy the most legitimate government seemed to be the general will expressed by a numerical majority. If interests differed, ideas were the same, and everyone knew about politics only what they had read in books, the same books. The only thing missing for these nobles to make the Revolution was to be commoners.

Thus, when the aristocracy saw that they had suddenly become the object of so many attacks, they found themselves singularly hampered in their own defense. None of them had ever thought about what position to take in order to justify their privileges in the eyes of the people. None had considered what must be said to show how only [an aristocracy] can preserve the people from the oppression of royal tyranny and the misery of revolution, so that privileges which seem to benefit only those who possess them are the best guarantee that can be found to assure the peace and well-being even of those who do not have any of them—they were ignorant of this. All these arguments, which are so familiar to classes which have long experience with public affairs and understand the science of government, were new and unfamiliar to them. They were reduced to speaking of the services which their ancestors had rendered six hundred years before—here arguments taken from the writings of the times—. They relied on old titles which went back to a hated past. They claimed to be the only ones who knew how to use weapons and who were able to maintain traditional military courage. Their language was often so arrogant because they were in the habit of being first; however, they were ill at ease because they themselves doubted their right . . .

The discussions which the royal edict provoked, after having run through the entire circle of human institutions, in the end finished by concentrating on two points—which in practice summarized the object of the struggle:

In the Estates-General which were about to meet, should the Third Estate have more representatives than each of the other two orders, so that the number of its deputies would equal the number of deputies of the nobility and clergy combined?

Should the orders thus constituted vote together or separately?

At the time the doubling of the Third Estate and the three orders voting in common in the same assembly seemed to be things less new and less important than they really were. Little facts both old and contemporary hid their novelty and importance.

For centuries the provincial estates of Languedoc had been composed this way and voted this way, without any effect except to give the bourgeoisie a greater part in public affairs without making it dominant, and to create common interests and easier relations between the bourgeoisie and the other two orders. Rather than dividing the classes, it had brought them closer together.

The king himself seemed to have already pronounced in favor of this system, for he had just applied it on a small scale in the provincial assemblies which the recent edict had established in all the provinces which didn't have estates. It could still only be barely perceived, without full recognition, how an institution which in a province had only modified the region's old constitution was bound to suddenly and violently upset the old constitution from top to bottom the day people tried to apply it to the whole state.

It was evident that the Third Estate, when equal in numbers to the other two orders in the nation's general assembly, was going to predominate; not just participate in affairs, but take absolute control of them; for it marched united against two groups divided not only against each other, but within themselves: one class with the same interests, the same passions, the same purpose; the others with separate interests, different purposes, and passions often opposed.

The Third Estate had the current of public passions for it, the others had it against them; this external pressure on the assembly could not fail to exercise a very great influence on it. It kept the members of the Third Estate together, and on the contrary detached from the nobility and clergy those who sought reputation or wanted to clear themselves a new route to power. In the estates of Languedoc one usually saw some bourgeois abandon their group to vote with the nobles and bishops because the old strength of the aristocracy, still dominant in mores and ideas, weighed on them. Each bourgeois of the estates of Languedoc in a sense felt the weight of the whole aristocracy of France. Here it was the opposite which was sure to happen, and the Third Estate could not fail to have a majority, even though the number of its deputies was equal.

The Third Estate's action in the assembly would necessarily be not merely dominant, but violent; for in the assembly it would encounter everything which can excite men's passions. To make people with opposite opinions live together is already difficult. But to enclose within the same walls completely formed political bodies, each fully organized, each having its own origin, its past, its own procedures, its esprit de corps, and put them there separately, confronting one another while working together in the same place to set limits on each other's rights, to force them to speak to each other constantly without intermediaries, this was to prepare not for a discussion, but for a war.

Now this majority, which inflamed its own passions and those of its opponents, was all powerful, since it alone was going to make the law. Nothing could stop it or even slow it down, since nothing was left to limit it except a royal power that was already disarmed, which could not fail to bow under the pressure of a single assembly leaning on it from a single point of view.

This was not to change the balance of power gradually: it was to suddenly overturn it. This was not to make [the Third Estate] share in the aristocracy's exorbitant rights; it was to make omnipotence pass immediately into different hands. It was to deliver the direction of public affairs to a single passion, a single interest, a single idea. It was to make not a reform, but a revolution.

Mounier, who alone among the reformers of this period seems to have had in advance an idea of what he wanted to do, and to have seen the logical consequences of his ideas, Mounier, who in his definitive plan of government took care to divide powers, was favorable to this meeting of the three orders in assembly and gave his reason for it candidly: "that above all it is necessary to have an assembly which will destroy what remains of the old constitution, of special rights, of local privileges: but this is what an upper chamber composed of nobles and clergy would never do."

In any case it would seem that the doubling of the Third Estate and the vote of the three orders in common were inseparable questions. For what good would it be to increase the number of deputies from the Third Estate, if the Third was going to deliberate and vote separately?

The government intended to separate these questions.

M. Necker, who then directed the king's wishes and momentarily served as the whole nation's idol, was one of those minds who never see the final consequences of any of their ideas, and who always remain halfway through their plans; one of those who never know how far they are going, because they direct themselves not according to their own ideas, but according to the ideas that they see passing one after another through other people's minds.

It cannot be doubted that Necker wanted both the doubling of the Third and the vote of the three orders in common. It is highly probable that the king himself leaned to the same side. What had just defeated the king was the aristocracy. It was the aristocracy which had defied him from the closest position, which had raised the other classes against royal authority and led them to victory. The king had felt its blows, and he did not have a sufficiently piercing [eye] to understand that the aristocrats were going to be forced to defend him, and that his friends were going to become his masters. Like his minister, the king leaned therefore to constituting the Estates-General as the Third Estate wanted.

But Necker and the king did not dare go that far. They stopped halfway, not because of a clear view of the dangers, but because of the vain clamor ringing in their ears. What man or class who occupied a high position has ever seen the moment when it is necessary to lower oneself in order to avoid being thrown off?

The question of numbers was decided in favor of the Third Estate and that of the common vote left undecided. Of all the courses to take, this was assuredly the most dangerous.

It is true that nothing serves better to nourish despotism [than] class hatreds and jealousy. In truth, it has happened that way. But only on the condition [that] those hatreds and envies are no more than quiet and bitter feelings, enough to prevent men from helping each other and not strong enough to make them fight each other. There is no government which will not fall in the violent impact of classes once they have begun to clash.

It was very late to try to maintain the old constitution of the Estates-General, even while improving it. But this bold resolution was supported by old practice, tradition was in its favor, and one kept the instrument of the law in one's hands.

To simultaneously grant the doubling of the Third and the vote in common was doubtless to make a revolution, but it would have been to make it oneself; and while ruining the ancient institutions of the country with one's own hands, to soften their fall. The leading classes would have been prepared in advance for an inevitable fate. Feeling the weight of royalty press on them at the same time as that of the Third Estate, they would have understood their impotence from the beginning.

Instead of senselessly fighting to keep everything, they would have fought not to lose everything.

In Dauphiny, it was the assembly of the provincial estates which chose the representatives of the three orders [to the Estates-General—Trans.] by a common vote. This assembly was composed of the three orders, each order having been elected separately and representing only itself. But the deputies to the Estates-General were elected by the assembly as a whole: in this way each nobleman had some bourgeois as constituents, and each bourgeois some nobles; and the three deputations, while remaining separate, thus became in a sense homogeneous. Perhaps the orders thus represented would have been able, if not to dissolve their divisions in a common assembly, at least to act without clashing too violently.

But one must not attribute too much power to these particular procedures of the lawmaker. It is men's ideas and passions, not the mechanics of the law, which determine human affairs.

Whatever method had been chosen then to form and regulate the nation's assemblies, it must be thought that war would have broken out violently between classes. The hatreds which divided them were already too inflamed for them to want to march together, and royal power was already too weak to force them. But it must be recognized that no one could have done any more than what was then done to make their combat immediate and deadly.

See if by premeditated design, intelligence, and art anyone could have succeeded better in making such a deadly plan as was then made by incompetence and lack of foresight! The Third Estate had been given the opportunity to become bold, to get used to combat, to count itself. Its fervor had increased beyond measure and the weight of its mass had been doubled. Then, after allowing it to hope for everything, it was left with everything to fear. In a sense victory had been put before its eyes, but hadn't been given to it. It had only been invited to take it.

After having allowed the two classes five months to mature and refresh their old hatreds, to take up again the whole long tale of their grievances, and inspire themselves against each other to the point of fury, finally they were confronted with one another and for the subject of their debate given the question which included all others, the only one where it seemed they could decide, once and for all, all their quarrels.

What strikes me most is less the genius of those who served the Revolution while wanting it than the exceptional stupidity of those who made it happen without wanting it to.

When I think about the French Revolution, I am astonished at the event's immense size, its fame which spread to the ends of the earth, its power which has moved more or less all peoples.

I then consider the court which had such a part in the Revolution; I see there the most ordinary pictures which can be found in history: thoughtless or incompetent ministers, debauched priests, idle women, bold or greedy courtesans, a king who had only useless or dangerous virtues. I see, however, that these petty personalities facilitate, push, accelerate this immense event. More than accidents, they become almost prime causes; and I admire the power of God, for whom such short levers are enough to put in motion the entire mass of human societies.

CHAPTER SIX

How the Writing of the Cahiers Made the Idea of a Radical Revolution Sink Deeply into the Minds of the Lower Classes

What is most striking in the imperfect institutions of the Middle Ages is their diversity and their sincerity. They march straight to their goal and give all the freedoms that they seem to promise. Deception is not found there any more than is art.

At the time when the Third Estate had been called to take part in the nation's general assemblies, it had been given an unlimited right to express its complaints and bring forward its requests.

In towns which were to send deputies to the Estates-General, the entire population was called to give its advice about the abuses to eliminate and the requests to make. Independently of the towns' general assemblies, where business was publicly discussed and decided, each Estate was called to express its grievances and its requests. Each individual furthermore had the right [to complain]. The means were as simple as the political procedure was bold. Up to the sixteenth century one still saw in the towns (in Paris itself), a large chest to which all individuals came [to throw their complaints]. All the varied demands were put into order and a report was created, which, under the humble name of grievances, expressed with unlimited freedom and often with exceptionally sharp language the complaints of each and every individual. The social and political constitution of that time was so solid on its foundations that this kind of popular inquest on its abuses and vices did not risk shaking it at all: it was not in the least a question of changing the principle of the laws, but of modifying their practice, not of breaking royal power and the aristocracy but only of returning them to their proper bounds. Furthermore, what was then called the Third Estate was not at all the lower class, nor even the rural middle class (these were considered to be represented by their lords and, if the deputies of the Third spoke for them, it was without consulting them), it was the inhabitants of a few towns. One could leave these urban people complete freedom to express their grievances because they were not in a position to obtain what was due them by force; they were left the unlimited use of democratic freedom without inconvenience because everywhere else the aristocracy reigned uncontested. In truth the societies of the Middle Ages were nothing but aristocratic bodies that contained only (and this in part is what made their greatness) little fragments of democracy.

In 1789 the Third Estate, which was to be represented in the Estates-General, was no longer composed of only the urban bourgeoisie as it had still been in 1614, but of twenty million peasants spread over the entire surface of the kingdom. These peasants had never before been concerned in public affairs; political life for them was not even a particular memory from another age, it was a novelty in all respects, so that while they thought they were doing the same thing as three hundred years before, people were actually doing the opposite.

However, on a given day, the bells of every rural parish in France assembled all the inhabitants on the public square, at the church door. There, for the first time since the beginning of the monarchy, they set to composing what was still called, as in the Middle Ages, the cahier of the grievances of the Third Estate.

In countries where political assemblies are elected by universal suffrage, there is no general election which does not affect a people down to its foundations, if the freedom to vote is not a lie. Here, it was not only a universal vote, but universal deliberation and inquiry. And what was discussed was not at all a particular custom, a local matter. Every Frenchman was asked, as a member of one of the most numerous nations on earth, what he had to say against all the laws and customs of the country. I think that such a sight had never before been seen on earth.

All the peasants of France therefore set themselves, at the same time, to search out and tell each other what they had had to suffer, what they had just cause to complain about. The spirit of the Revolution, which influenced the bourgeois of the towns, immediately spread itself through a thousand channels into this agricultural population, which was thus affected in all its parts at the same time, opened to all impressions from the outside, and it penetrated to the bottom. But the spirit of the Revolution was not entirely the same there. It took a particular form in the countryside, one more appropriate to those whom it came to inspire. In the towns it was a matter above all of acquiring rights, in the countryside they concerned themselves above all with satisfying needs. All the great general and abstract theories which filled the minds of the urban middle classes took on concrete and definite smaller forms in the countryside.

When these peasants came to ask each other what they had to complain about, they didn't concern themselves at all with the balance of powers, guarantees for political freedom, the general rights of man and the citizen. They stopped first at some objects that were closer and more particular to them, from which each one had recently suffered. One man thought of the feudal dues which had taken half his grain that year; another of the corvée which had forced him to give his time without pay yesterday. This one remembered the lord's pigeons which had devoured his grain before it had sprouted, that one the lord's rabbits which had grazed on his budding crops. To the extent that they inspired each other by the detailed recital of their wrongs, it seemed to them that all these various evils came less from institutions than from a single man who still called them his subjects, although he had long ago ceased to govern them; who had only privileges without obligations, rights without duties, and who of his political rights kept only the right to live at their expense; and they more and more agreed to consider him the common enemy.

Providence, which doubtless wished to present the spectacle of our passions and misfortunes as a lesson to the world, allowed there to come to pass, at the moment when the Revolution began, a great food shortage and a phenomenal winter. The harvest of 1788 was insufficient, and during the first months of the winter of 1789 the cold raged with unheard-of severity; a freeze similar to what is felt in Europe's extreme north froze the ground to a great depth. For two months all France disappeared under a thick layer of snow like the steppes of Siberia. The air was frigid, the sky empty, drab, and gray. This accident of nature gave people's feelings a sharp and violent character. All the grievances that they might have had against the laws and those who applied them were felt more bitterly amidst the sufferings imposed by cold and poverty. The misery that came from everywhere sharpened all jealousies and envenomed all hatreds.

And when the peasant left his barely lit fireside, leaving a cold house and a starving family to go with some of his fellows and criticize their situation, he didn't have a hard time finding something: it seemed to him that it wasn't difficult to find a cause for all his troubles and that it would have been easy for him, if he had dared, to point a finger at their author.

CHAPTER SEVEN

How for a Moment, When the National Assembly Was About to Meet, Hearts Were Joined and Spirits Raised

Two questions above all had divided classes: the doubling of the Third Estate and the vote in common. The first was decided; the second postponed. This great assembly that everyone individually had considered the only means of realizing their hopes, that everyone had demanded with the same fervor, was going to meet. The event had long been expected; it had remained doubtful up until the last minute. Finally it happened. People felt that they were passing from preparation to work, from words to deeds.

At this solemn moment, each person stopped and considered the greatness of the enterprise: they were close enough to action to see the import of what they were about to do and to understand the effort that was going to be necessary.

Nobles, priests, bourgeois, all clearly recognized that it was not simply a question of modifying this or that law, but of revising them all, of introducing a new spirit, of changing and rejuvenating all institutions and, as they said then, of regenerating France. No one yet knew exactly what was going to be destroyed, what was going to be created; but everyone felt that immense destruction was going to happen, so that immense constructions could be built.

But ideas did not stop there. No one doubted that the destiny of the human race was involved in what we were preparing to do.

Today, when the hazards of revolution have humbled us to the point that we believe ourselves unworthy of the freedom which other nations enjoy, it would be difficult to imagine how far our fathers' pride extended. When we read a writer of those times, we are astonished at the immense opinion that the French of all classes had of their country and their race, of the calm and simple confidence with which they put "French" for "men." Among all those reform projects which burst forth at the time when the government seemed to put the constitution up for an academic competition, there were almost none which deigned to imitate what was going on abroad. It was not a question of taking lessons, but of furnishing new examples. The very nature of the political ideas which filled all minds, ideas which seemed applicable to all peoples, favored this view. Therefore there was no Frenchman who wasn't convinced that he was not only going to change the government of France, but introduce new principles of government into the world, destined to change the entire face of human affairs. There was no Frenchman who did not believe he had in his hands, not the destiny of his country, but the very future of his species.

If this feeling was exaggerated it was not wrong. And indeed we were finally going to start on the task. From up close one saw its greatness, its beauty, its risks. This clear and distinct view succeeded in seizing the imagination of all the French, and delighted them. In the presence of this immense object, there was a moment when thousands of men seemingly became careless of their own particular interests in order to concern themselves only with the common task. It was only a moment; but I doubt if anything like it has ever been encountered in the life of any people.

The educated classes then had nothing of that fearful and servile nature which revolutions have since given them. They had long since ceased to fear the royal power and they had not yet learned to tremble before the lower classes. The greatness of their plan succeeded in making them bold. The desire for material well-being which was going to end up mastering all other desires was then nothing but a lesser and impotent passion. The reforms accomplished had already disturbed private life; people were resigned to it. The inevitable reforms to come could not fail to change the situation of thousands of men; people hardly thought about that. The uncertainty of the future already slowed the movement of commerce and paralyzed industry, the economic activity of the humble [was] suspended or disturbed. The distress and suffering did not extinguish fervor. All individual hardships dissolved and disappeared, in the eyes of the very people who endured them, in the immense greatness of the common enterprise.

The passions which had just put the classes into such violent confrontation seemed to die down at that hour when, for the first time in two centuries, they were going to act together.

All had demanded the return of the great assembly which was being born with the same fervor. Everyone individually had seen in the meeting of [this] great body the means of realizing their most cherished hopes. These Estates-General, called for with such a unanimous and tumultuous voice, were to meet at last: a common joy filled all these hearts that were so disunited and brought them together a moment before they separated from one another forever.

People Embraced Each Other before Being Reconciled

At this moment the dangers of disunity suddenly struck all minds. People made a supreme effort to agree. Instead of looking for where they differed, they tried to concentrate on what they wanted in common:

To destroy arbitrary power, to put the nation back in possession of itself, to assure the rights of every citizen, to make the press free, individual liberty inviolable, to soften the laws, strengthen the courts, guarantee religious toleration, destroy the hindrances to commerce and industry, this is what they all wanted. They reminded each other of it; they congratulated each other about it. People spoke of what united them, they were silent about what still divided them. Fundamentally people didn't agree at all, but they sought to persuade themselves that they were going to agree; people reconciled without explaining themselves.

—Put here all the facts which can shed light on this.—

I do not believe that at any moment in history, at any place on earth, a similar multitude of men has ever been seen so sincerely impassioned for public affairs, so truly forgetful of their interests, so absorbed in contemplation of a great plan, so determined to risk everything that men hold most dear in their lives, to strive to lift themselves above the petty passions of their hearts. This is the common basis for the passions, the courage, and the devotion from which came forth all the great actions which were going to fill the French Revolution.

This first spectacle was short, but it had incomparable beauty. It will never depart from human memory. All foreign nations saw it, applauded it, were moved by it. Don't try to find a place in Europe so out of the way that it wasn't seen and where it didn't give rise to hope and admiration. There was none. Among the immense crowd of individual memoirs which contemporaries of the Revolution have left us, I have never seen one where the sight of these first days of 1789 did not leave an indelible trace. Everywhere it communicated the clarity, the intensity, the freshness of the emotions of youth.

I dare say that there is only one people on earth which could present such a spectacle. I know my nation. I see only too well its errors, its faults, its weaknesses, and its hardships. But I also know what it is capable of. There are enterprises which only the French nation is able to conceive, magnanimous resolutions which only it dare take. Only France could one day wish to embrace the common cause of humanity and *want* to fight for it. And, if it is subject to great falls, it has sublime impulses which suddenly bring it up to a level that no other people will ever attain.

APPENDIX TO CHAPTERS THREE, FOUR, AND FIVE
1787, 1788, and 1789 in Dauphiny

*T**ocqueville grouped his notes on this subject, which were taken after June 1857, in Folder DD of File 45B. These notes, which were used in the writing of chapters three through five, are presented here in the chronological order of the events described in 1787 and 1788. The year 1789 was not the subject of any personal analysis by Tocqueville.*

1787

Regulation Issued by the King on 4 September 1787 for the Establishment of a Provincial Assembly in Dauphiny*

The king chose twenty-eight persons, fourteen from the privileged, fourteen from the Third Estate. These twenty-eight persons chose twenty-eight others, still in the same proportions, in all fifty-six persons. Votes were counted *by head.*

The doubling of the Third and the vote by head prescribed by the king himself and his ministers a year before Necker. Thus we see that the doubling of the Third and the vote by head were not Necker's invention at all, nor a consequence to which people were led at the end of 1788. It was an idea that was put into circulation and applied as early as 1787, by the king and Loménie [de Brienne—Trans.].

This immense concession did not prevent the king and the ministers who made it from being violently unpopular, and the parlement which rejected it from being supported fanatically by the people. What is no less noteworthy is that the minister who made (perhaps without realizing it) a concession to the Third Estate so immense that it could not fail to make the Third Estate absolutely master of affairs in a little [while], this minister was the object of the people's execration, and the parlement which opposed the application of a law so democratic for the times was the object of the fanatic applause of that same people.

---

* Tocqueville examines in succession: the local assemblies; the department assemblies; the provincial assemblies.—Eds.

The doubling of the Third and the vote by head had existed in the estates of Languedoc without having led, ostensibly at least, to the exclusive domination of the Third Estate, and this could create illusions. But what could give the first two orders hegemony in an assembly where they did not have the numerical majority was the absence of open struggle between classes. This open struggle, with the classes counted, including their different subgroups; a wind of revolution which blew from the direction of the lower classes and made them more and more a power which necessarily would push some aristocrats over to the side of the Third Estate, while previously tradition, respect, influence, and power had instead drawn some bourgeois into the hands of the nobility and clergy: all these were new circumstances, which, I repeat, could not fail to turn the pretended equality of the orders into the controlling hegemony of the Third Estate in any assembly.

Remonstrance by the Parlement against This Regulation, 6 October 1787

Antidemocratic tendency of the remonstrances. The parlement criticized the regulation because, among other things, it would suffice for an individual to pay a tax that was *personal,* not based on real property, in order to be a voter; because according to the regulation tithe-holders, other ecclesiastics, and all nonresident inhabitants, nobles or commoners, who usually owned the largest properties in the village community, would be forced to submit to the discretion of the rural inhabitants as to the amount of their contribution to the tax; because the legal jurisdiction of the barons would be almost eliminated and the lords deprived of a large part of their judicial powers; because the obligation to be *resident* in the countryside in order to participate in the local assemblies in which the other assemblies were chosen would have the effect that in a few years the clergy would only be represented by village priests, almost all of whom were hired substitutes for the officeholders, the lay lords would be represented by their local agents, and the large noble or commoner landowners by local notaries or simple laborers.

Abandonment of the countryside proved by the edict. —To cite when I get to showing how the landowners lacked roots, no longer theoretically and in general as in volume one, but in practice and in particular cases through facts; for, says the remonstrance, there are almost no abbés or tithe-holders who live in the countryside, and there are very few lords who live on their lands, and all the owners of any considerable amount of land make their home in the towns where their rank and their tastes call them.

Passages. Still more noteworthy because this is said by members of the same order, incidentally and without thought of blame. [. . .]—

Brochure Published at Grenoble in 1787 for the Purpose of Combating the Conduct of the Parlement Which Refused to Allow the Provincial Assemblies to Be Established, Titled "Dialogue on the Provincial Assemblies of Dauphiny."

Regulation on provincial government of 1787. Changes the country's entire constitution. It strips bare the nobility and the lower classes simultaneously. [. . .] I see in the pamphlet cited above that the rural communities in Dauphiny held assemblies often; that everyone could vote, while the new regulation created a municipal council and a property franchise for voters. The author very much approves, saying that up to then the rich man had no more authority than the poor man in the assemblies of the community. The new regulation for Dauphiny reduced those who could participate to 11,000, from a number which might previously have been as high as 300,000.

Thus the author finds a conservative and aristocratic advantage in this reform.

It is true that within these new rural municipal councils, elected by property-owning voters, the power of the lord and the priest disappeared. Thus this modest provincial reform created an entire revolution, taken from ideas foreign to the old society and realizing in advance the new society, through a regulation whose implications no one, but above all the king who made it, recognized to their real extent. [. . .]

1788

7 June 1788. Riot at Grenoble. First Bloody
Riot of the Revolution.

[. . .] *How the parlements created a lower class that supported them in the towns where they were resident, so that when they were attacked, although they were an aristocratic body, one always had to deal with a popular movement.*

This is clearly seen in a request to the king drafted by the forty-one corps and communities of the town of Grenoble, where it is said: "The ruin of Grenoble is assured if the edicts are maintained, if the parlement's jurisdiction is reduced to the edict's narrow limits. All that sustains the population of Grenoble, all that gives the artisans, the merchants, the means of subsistence, is the consumption of the numerous businessmen, the magistrates who live here, the strangers who come here from all parts of Dauphiny for trials . . . To what deplorable fate would the petitioners not be brought if almost all the trials which were taken to Grenoble were now retained by the local courts?" [pp. 3–4] . . . That is to say, if the court was brought closer to the parties. Never has local egoism been more frank. It is thus that the lower classes, in rebelling on behalf of and with the privileged, first learned the art of rising up to destroy those very privileges.

Traditions from the Middle Ages invoked by the enemies of all tradition for this particular interest. In another report based entirely on old feudal laws from the Middle Ages, one goes so far as to affirm that Dauphiny is not really part of France, and that the king reigns there as dauphin and not as king.

Feudal justice strongly defended by the Grenoble city government. The dispositions of the edict reduced the lords' judicial powers to almost nothing, and took away from them all the dignity of their fiefs. The edict damaged the lords' property. It usually forced the parties to a lawsuit to go to more expensive courts.

Oh, the admirable suppleness of political passions! The judicial powers of the lords violently and shamelessly defended by the bourgeois of the towns.

All the communities of Dauphiny follow the lead given by Grenoble on 14 June. Even though the king, by letters patent, had formally forbidden any assembly relating to his edicts, all the communities of Dauphiny met in the most public, most calm, in appearance the most legal manner to name deputies to the provincial general assembly called by the town of Grenoble.

In these deliberations the nobility and clergy appear with the Third Estate almost everywhere. The towns assemble the general council to which are usually added nobles and clergy (almost all local priests). The rural areas form separate assemblies of deputies, who name deputies to the general assembly.

Nowhere lower-class assemblies. At this period action entirely concentrated in the upper classes. All the movement's action was concentrated in the upper classes alone. In all the assemblies one saw only nobles, clergy, bourgeois appear. Everywhere the lower classes appeared only through *deputies,* not a single general meeting of the population. All deliberations were signed, printed, and sent to the intendant absolutely as if it was a matter of an ordinary and legal measure. But all this was done in flagrant violation of letters patent which had just been published. Complete anarchy. Strange mixture of patience and violence on the part of power. The intendant limited himself to writing the communities a reassuring letter to calm them down. But of orders to cease and measures of repression, none.

Between the Edicts of 8 May and the Reestablishment of the Parlements,
Pamphlet by Barnave ["Spirit of the Edicts Registered by Force at the Parlement
of Grenoble on 10 May 1788," June, 1788]

This pamphlet, which betrays the rhetorical exaggeration of youth (the author was twenty-six years old), and sometimes the library and the imitation of Montesquieu, made a great impression in the province, at once went through three editions, and was the subject of a decree by the superior court. It has both the liveliness and the inflamed violence of the age. It preaches insurrection and is only very slightly respectful of the king. For the times, it is very violent.

A single spirit reigns here: hatred for despotism. To struggle against it, all weapons seem good to the author. He criticizes the best things in the edicts with the same force as the bad ones.

But what is interesting above all in Barnave is the manner in which he speaks of things which a year later he contributed so much to destroy.

He criticizes in the edict "*the spirit of innovation* so deadly when it is despotic and hasty" (p. 13), "the annihilation of feudal justice pronounced in an ironic and insulting form" (ibid.).

"They take part of their jurisdiction from those majestic tribunals invested with the nation's confidence, the objects of foreigners' admiration. These bodies raised above vile considerations by the glory of their origin, by the greatness of their prerogatives . . ." (p. 15).

"O ministers of religion [. . .] proclaim today political freedom. [. . .] You received from the veneration of our fathers (Barnave was a Protestant) the right to form alone the first order of the state. You are an integral part of the French constitution and you must protect it" (p. 21). "You, illustrious families, . . . the monarchy has not ceased to flourish under your protection . . . You have created it at the price of your blood, on several occasions you have saved it from foreigners, defend it now against its internal enemies, assure for your children the brilliant advantages that your fathers transmitted to you. [. . .] It is not under the sun of slavery that we honor the names of heroes" (ibid.).

There follows a warm appeal for the union of all classes and all interests against despotism.

It is necessary, I think, to use this pamphlet. First of all because the name of Barnave will make it shine and also because in itself it perfectly marks the *character of the moment.*

We sense in several philosophical phrases about the natural equality of men, in some particular details, the democratic ideas which are at the base of the writer's mind, so to speak, and the democratic passions which disturb the bottom of his heart. But, as an immediate and superficial impression, I believe in Barnave's sincerity at the time he wrote; and if the struggle could have gone on, perhaps this common hatred of tyranny which inspired all classes would have ended up making them forget their grievances and unite. But that was not possible.

Problem particular to force when it attacks the courts. Surely nothing more *prosecutable* than this pamphlet and its author. One can say that no constituted government could allow such a thing. The author was known. The government, pushed to the end of its tether, for a moment possessed the will to be violent and was. But its problem was to have as its chief adversary the courts, that is the tool with whose aid governments triumph over their opponents. To defeat the courts, the government had disorganized them and, disorganized, it could no longer use them. At war with the courts the government had no recourse against the violence of the press except arms.

[Pamphlets Aroused by the Assembly of Vizille, 21 July 1788]

A pamphlet, probably dictated by the authorities or emanating from some noble of Dauphiny, titled "The Plot Revealed," sought to ridicule this assembly, and notes that the so-called order of the nobility was composed mostly of nobles of recent date, of ennobled men, and met at the home of the marquis Périer. He was a bourgeois (I think) who had bought the marquisate of Vizille. It says also that the so-called order of the clergy (this is more probable) was composed of salaried curates and a few canons of the town of Grenoble, the real leaders and aristocracy of the clergy all being absent.

"Twenty against One; or, A Decree Proposed to the Third Estate," a Work on the Assembly of Vizille

Premature attempt to unite the cause of power with that of democracy and to make all the antiaristocratic and anticlerical passions of the latter serve the former.

Very interesting specimen of this attempt which would be the Revolution's long-term result.

This pamphlet, which was probably written at the instigation of the government and with its money (it states that the parlement paid for all the writings and flooded the province with pamphlets in its favor), breathes the most violent passion against the nobility and seeks to encourage this passion in the lower classes by all means.

Its purpose is to make the Third Estate believe that the opposition movement comes from the aristocracy, that it is in the aristocracy's sole interest, that in joining the opposition the Third Estate acts like a fool and that it would do much better to join the government which is working on its side. (The time when this language would become all-powerful in several parts of Europe had not yet arrived.) [. . .]

Way in which one defended the government while admitting all the abuses, but blaming the nobility for them.

Pretty good description of a regiment under the old regime. Here is a good, well-drilled regiment. Who is the colonel? Monsieur the Marquis of X, a young man of twenty, of great merit. The major is a well-known lord with excellent connections. Among the officers, there is not one who is not a knight of Malta. The nobles have great difficulty leading their troops in such complicated maneuvers, in maintaining good order in the ranks . . . They give all these burdens to that man who is half officer, half soldier, who under the name of adjutant is the mainspring of the machine which you admire. In this case, it seems to me that neither this man nor his colonel are in their proper place.

This is still more or less the situation in English regiments except that the noble is replaced there by the rich man and twenty-year-old colonels are no longer found.

First idea of the armies which conquered Europe. The author proposes forming regiments where one could not be an officer except after proving that one was a commoner; he thinks that these regiments could well be worth more than all the others.

Antiaristocratic passions created by social contact. Who is that good-looking man who seems educated, intellectual, with good manners? . . . Nothing. A lawyer, a doctor. Who is that little hunchback whose mind is as twisted as his body, ignorant and insolent? That is a perfect man, he is the son of Count X.

It is for having supported the cause of the people against the parlement that all this uproar has occurred (true in part): If the aristocracy had thought of fighting the abuses erected into privileges, the magistrates would have been docile. They say that they are the defenders of the people. The new laws (the May edicts) are all favorable to the people and against the aristocracy. *True.* It is for this reason that the parlementary nobility and others attack them.

Violence against nobles. Let clerical positions, judgeships be opened up for competitive examinations . . . I am wrong, it is not necessary to want to exclude the nobility from everything.

Appeal to the Third Estate to support the government.

The Third Estate ought to shout their cry of gratitude in opposition to the shouts of the rebelling aristocrats.

Instead of this the Third Estate is letting itself be seduced by the nobles' blandishments, forgetting that the noble is like the hedgehog who sheds his spines to look for what he needs, but then covers himself again and pricks from every side.

The inhabitants of the town of Grenoble are betraying the cause of the Third Estate. The Third Estate ought to declare that it views with indignation these seditious conspiracies attacking the sovereign. The assembly of Vizille has been held by some nobles and a handful of commoners yoked to their cart (this is unbelievable)! From afar this assembly seemed like something; up close it is nothing. The order of the nobility, missing its chief members, was above all composed of younger sons without money and without substance and recently ennobled men. On that day people were not choosy. Anyone was a noble who wanted to be. As for the deputies of the Third Estate, the chief towns were not represented: Valence, Gap, Montélimar did not send anyone. Those who came were false deputies elected by local assemblies composed of five or six cousins and friends.

At the end the author obliged despite himself to join the antidespotic current of the times.

What has happened is a fight between usurped and legitimate authority. That the constitution gives the king the right to make the laws and execute them . . . That it is necessary for the Third Estate to maintain the king's sacred authority which he uses on their behalf. That, however, the king must be begged to convoke the Estates-General as he has promised, and to prevent the influence of the nobility from corrupting the choices of the Third Estate.

[The Last Estates of Dauphiny]
Letter Written to the King by the Three Orders of the Province of Dauphiny, Assembled at Romans on 14 September 1788.

I do not know how the orders had been assembled. I have only seen their letter. It is signed in the name of the orders by the archbishop of Narbonne, the president ex officio, I believe, of the estates, and by Mounier, secretary.

This letter, although expressing itself in polite formulas, is still written in an animated and quite tart style. It expresses itself at length on the evil of the May edicts, on the odiousness of the conduct committed then, in these times when we have seen honor and patriotism publicly persecuted (it is an archbishop who is writing this to the king), private interests attacked, the bankruptcy of the finances completed . . . [p. 5].

It asks for the complete reestablishment of the parlements, the revocation of all measures against them, the prompt meeting of the Estates-General.

In this document one does not yet see class struggle sprouting, nor war against the past. On the contrary (through an imitation of England that was unique to Mounier, doubtless the piece's author) the new freedoms asked for are attached to the idea of similar ancient freedoms that have been lost. Bad things are said of feudalism here, but from it is derived, a little fictively, *a magnificent constitution, a king as legislator, a court which is the supreme organ and depositary of the laws, a national assembly in which essentially resides the right to consent to taxes and to accept laws* [p. 3]. All this smells of importation, it is not really *indigenous,* and possessed no basis in the state of hearts and minds.

Account of the Celebrations at Grenoble on 12 and 20 October 1788 on the
Return of the Parlement [Anonymous Brochure, 1788]

On 18 September, the news of Lamoignon's fall was announced at Grenoble.

The courier was led in triumph through the whole town, covered with caresses and cheers. The women who could not hug him hugged his horse. That evening, the whole town illuminated spontaneously; a dummy representing the minister was burned; another dummy representing the superior court of Valence (which had obeyed the edicts of 8 May) was thrown into the gutter. On 29 August, the news of the dismissal of the archbishop of Sens had already been received. All the streets were filled, people congratulated one another, hugged each other. [. . .]

The first president of the parlement, (M. de Bérulle) arrived on 12 October. The whole town was in commotion; the volunteer companies turned out to fetch him. The first company of grenadiers, in scarlet uniforms, the second of chasseurs, in green uniforms, then a third in sky-blue uniforms.

M. de Bérulle, better welcomed than a king, could not make his way across the province. The whole population in arms accompanied him;

at every stop people made speeches to him. [. . .] He passed beneath triumphal arches, from whose tops crowns were thrown. Cannons were fired. [. . .]

At the reopening of the parlement (20 October) there were still more demonstrations. It is an endless description of triumphal arches, ingenious displays, magnificent illuminations. [. . .]

All the groups, all the corporations paraded before him, offering great praise. The first president, in the parlement's name, responded to everyone like a king, briefly, with dignity, making each one aware of the greater or lesser degree of satisfaction or displeasure caused by the memory of what he had done since 8 May; he assured some of his protection, others of his good will.

Was the Capitol ever so close to the Tarpeian Rock?

Letter Written to the King by the Three Orders of Dauphiny Assembled at Romans, on 8 November 1788

This second letter is entirely about the format to give the Estates-General. It is again signed by the archbishop of Vienne and by Mounier.

The letter does not mention what discussion and voting preceded it. It asks for the doubling of the Third Estate, the vote by head.

(In the name of the three orders): the reason to double the order of the Third Estate is not just because they are the majority, the Third Estate is the portion of your subjects who pay the most taxes and possess the most wealth [p. 9].

Although the wonderful institutions of the past are no longer spoken of and on the contrary one speaks of *the rights of nature,* the letter is grave and moderate in its terms. It is less removed from public spirit than most documents of this kind, without class struggle.

Mounier, who wrote it, really wanted to leave the old privileged groups a large place in the constitution. But how could he believe that he would succeed by making them vote together in a single chamber where the majority would obviously be on the side of the Third Estate?

End of 1788. "Observations on the Letter of the Estates of Dauphiny to the King of 8 October (sic) *1788" (Anonymous)*

In this letter the estates had asked for: 1) an assembly more numerous than the preceding ones; 2) the doubling of the Third Estate; 3) the vote by head on all questions.

The pamphlet is one of the very rare productions of this period which is against these three points. It is very firm, very peremptory, and was doubtless very little read. It proves very well:

1) That an assembly of more than six hundred members will be an ungovernable anarchy; 2) that the doubling of the Third Estate has as a necessary consequence the vote by head.

That if numbers and collective wealth ought to be the rule for representation, the Third Estate is as eighteen out of twenty compared to the other two orders and its doubling is illogical. That by limiting itself to doubling, if one votes by head on all questions, the infallible result will be to always [give] the Third Estate the majority, for it is rare for the nobility and the clergy to be unanimous in defense of the same privilege while the Third Estate is unanimous in attacking it.

That the infallible result of this arrangement will be the annihilation of the first two orders and the alteration of the entire old constitution of the monarchy.

What is interesting is that instead of asking whether there are not several interests which ought to be represented among a people, whether the various elements which compose society do not need to be held in a kind of balance . . . all the reasons given later on or in other places to support two chambers or the inequality of representation, [instead] of that, I say, he only bases himself on the acquired rights of the clergy and the nobility, on tradition, on precedents . . . These are all arguments without power over his audience and his time.

The real and powerful reasons that one could give to support his opinion are not even in his head, nor, it would seem, in those of any of his contemporaries.

Excerpt from the Registers of the Estates of Dauphiny, Assembled at Romans, 9 December 1788

This piece is also signed by Mounier. It states that the estates persist in their desire for the Third Estate to have as many members as the other two orders combined and that voting at the Estates-General should be by head.

In this piece we see how political passions had continuously increased during the preceding six months. How democratic and revolutionary passion had taken the place of liberal passion. How lively the struggles between classes were, even in the groups where they seemed to be least important at the time.

This excerpt from the transcript is a plea in favor of a single assembly (something pretty unusual in a piece signed and written by Mounier). He notes with justice that the comparison with England is not applicable, because in England "the citizens are not divided into several classes, all interested in the abuses which are particular to them." In France to separate the different orders into several chambers would be "dangerous" . . . [pp. 2–3].

If the French are unfortunately separated into several classes with different rights, which makes it more difficult to reach agreement among several chambers, why does Mounier not see that this same cause will necessarily bring about a rapid, radical, and violent revolution if these classes are united in a single assembly which will necessarily at one stroke make law in the interest of a single class?

It must be recognized that it was difficult then to see clearly why that class would necessarily be dominant, even in an assembly in which it would make up only half.

General Observation

I often see the *Revolution of 1788* spoken of in these pamphlets, and this was in fact already a revolution and one which fully deserved that title until that of 1789.

In Dauphiny municipal offices were not held by virtue of an office one owned; they were all elective [p. 21], which explains how the municipal governments took the lead in the movement almost everywhere.

In Dauphiny landownership is very divided, above all at that time ("Observations on the Principles of the Constitution of the Estates of Dauphiny" [p. 28]). In all this contemporary polemic (not only in Dauphiny but elsewhere) I see foreigners cited very little. Sometimes England, almost never the United States.

In Dauphiny the taille was real and not personal, which means that the nobles were not at war with the Third Estate on this point too, as in many other regions, and only had to concede equality on a smaller number of points [p. 33].

APPENDIX TO CHAPTER FIVE

1788

The Radicalization of Ideas: On the Convocation
of the Estates General [September–November 1788]

*"The Monitor," Published during the Parlement's Moment
of Triumph in September 1788*

This pamphlet still seems inspired by the spirit that reigned during the struggle. It is still inspired by the great services rendered by the parlement and still considers the establishment of political freedom the chief goal to be pursued. It is still liberal rather than democratic and revolutionary. Above all it leaves out the quarrels between classes in order to try to unite them all against despotism. [. . .]

Condorcet and Brissot given as the authors of this pamphlet. What makes this pamphlet really remarkable and worth quoting is that it is attributed to Condorcet and Brissot. It contains absolutely nothing revolutionary, it is purely liberal, very firm, but very moderate and without anything excessive. If it is in fact by Condorcet and Brissot it proves:

1) What a rapid change there was in public opinion in a very short time.

2) How men are quickly changed by circumstances, by revolutions, violently thrust not only beyond the ideas that they had had at first, but in a direction actively hostile to those ideas.

*"On the Conditions Necessary for the Estates-General to be
Legal," by Volney [Published at Rennes, 5 November 1788]*

I think that this work is by the famous Volney. He writes with a style that is vigorous, cutting, and clear. Everything one can imagine that is the most radical. A completely revolutionary mind reigns here.

One must act only by virtue of abstract principles: natural law; the social contract. France does not have a constitution. Its laws are only absurd old customs to which no obedience is due.

The author does not deign to return to the science of old facts except to prove that everything is founded on violence and war, and to make this go back to the conquest of Gaul by the Franks.

Everything must be done anew, except the monarchical form and heredity within the reigning house.

The vote should be universal, not even property is necessary to exercise it. One should not take any account of the present territorial divisions, but divide France into equal electoral districts: the only fear is that the rich will have too much influence on elections; those who are too closely dependent on them must be excluded from voting.

Certainly only a single assembly is necessary, where votes will be counted by head; this assembly *can* do everything and ought to change everything; for everything is full of abuses. But this assembly does not bind the nation, which can always reject its work if it is not content: "if the results of the Estates-General are good, we will legalize them by adopting them; if they are bad, we will make them illegal by rejecting them" [p. 29]. It is the people who are the legislator, the king does nothing but accept their will.

Throughout this writing we see the strange combination of a remnant of fear and a boldness which already gives the feeling that victory is certain. The deputies who are going to be elected can do everything. For two years fortune has done everything to put power in their hands (p. 37).

"On Representation in the Estates-General," 8 November 1788, by Roederer

This pamphlet is remarkable above all because it treats the question solely through philosophical reasoning, as if it were a question of an ideal society to be created. It is from the principles of nature that the author chiefly derives his arguments, and then from the abstract books of Locke, Rousseau, and Montesquieu. In general he only accepts Montesquieu with reservations and while fighting him, but Rousseau is evidently his inspiration. He never deviates from the idea of the *social pact* and representation *by numbers*. He rejects the ideas of Turgot, who wanted to admit only landowners to assemblies, declaring that the rest were mere passengers in the state and not citizens.

He rejects Montesquieu's idea that in a balanced monarchy it is necessary for the role that the principals have in legislation to be proportionate to the advantages that they have in the state, otherwise the common freedom will be their slavery, and they will have no interest in defending it. Not only does he want there to be no division of orders in the Estates-General, but he would like for there to be none in the elections. He glimpses that in present society it is no longer the lords but the rich, who are found among all orders, who ought to be the counterweight to the lower classes. But he does not derive any consequences from this idea, since he wants a single assembly, with everyone eligible to be elected and everyone a voter.

The tax privileges of the nobility denied by Roederer. It is quite interesting and amusing to see Roederer led by the need to support one of his
radical theses to argue that the real privileges of the nobility with regard
to taxation are immensely exaggerated. [Nothing] shows better the kind
of disorder which existed in minds, left each to their own fantasies and
pushed together only by common passions. [. . .]

"The Convocation of the Estates-General," by Lacretelle

It seems that this brochure had a certain influence. Although moderate in
its terms and respectful towards individuals, it is no less forcefully *radical*
and *revolutionary* in its conclusions, and nothing shows better the violence of the times than to see such thoughts and such language *in a fool*
as benevolent and well-intentioned as Lacretelle. He is full of condescen-
sion and even of a sort of admiration for insurrections when they are well-
intentioned.

As with Roederer, all the arguments are taken from natural law, the
rights of man, pure metaphysics with regard to government. Everything
which does not come from this seems not merely false to this author, but
so absurd that he does not even know how it can be fought. As with
Roederer it seems like it is a question of the constitution of an ideal
people, and that the past, interests, old influences are not even perceived.
What is surprising is that I see absolutely *no one* argue about the principles of this question. Thirty years before, there would have been arguments. Montesquieu had defended them, or at least discussed them; no
one in 1788 can conceive of them any more, even those interested in them;
they dare not support them for reasons of political expediency. The ideas
of Rousseau are a flood which has momentarily submerged this whole
part of the human mind and the human sciences.

As a consequence of this, all the while saying that reasonable prerogatives of the orders should be respected, Lacretelle reasons as if there
ought not to be any kind of order or class, as if it were only a question
of having everyone represented as completely as possible, the *numerical*
majority being the rule. He seems to a accept a certain property qualification for the vote; one might say that he glimpses the utility of having two assemblies; but what he doesn't understand is that there could
be two orders each respectively possessing a veto, and he shows clearly
that if the king wants to maintain this form, the Third Estate should refuse to vote.

The Revolutionary and Republican Mind before 1789;
1792 in 1788: Péthion, "Warning to the French" (One Volume, Without Publisher's
Name; Large, in Duodecimo)

This book does not have the author's name, but it is attributed by Quérard, doubtless correctly, to Péthion.

The date would be very useful to fix. It was started and finished at least in part, as the author says, during the king's last struggle against the parlements, between their suspension and their forced reestablishment. The end was written after this great popular victory, also after Necker's entry into the ministry and while the notables were discussing the form of the Estates-General, whose convocation was then certain.

All these different phases are visible in the text when it is read carefully and with good knowledge of the events of the times.

Real revolutionary spirit of 1792 in 1788. Character of the piece. Up to the present, and above all during this period which extends from the beginning of 1787 up to September 1788, I have seen books where revolutionary passions proper hardly appear, or are only found in the state of vague and almost involuntary desires, or at least taking many precautions with the existing facts and above all the monarchy; passionate inexperience rather than complete and radical systems set out in advance.

Péthion's work, where I find the revolutionary spirit proper without dilution or constraint, a system completely formulated and not retreating before any consequence, [is] very interesting in this respect.

Not even verbal respect for royalty and even the king. As we are still in the Revolution's first period (p. 165), when freedom yet held center stage and the hatred of despotism was still (in appearance at least) the dominant passion, Péthion's book is imprinted with this passion above all. But it is in a fashion peculiar to it. No respect for the monarchy as an institution. Kings are nothing but the nation's agents, agents who are always revocable. He does not propose to abolish the monarchy, but we see that his passion goes that far, he clearly says as much. He is a republican and full of the general principles which served as text for the American Revolution. These principles are found diluted in all the minds of the time. But here they are substantially compact, and English freedom inspires pity in him.

He does not express even a word of sympathy for Louis XVI, and often outrageous words escape him (which is still unique).

Contempt for the past. It goes without saying that the idea of connecting what one wants with what has been, of making even a list of the laws, the customs, *the very contracts* which might hinder what he calls the Reformation, that this idea seems not only unacceptable, but profoundly ridiculous.

Love of unity. In the France that he wants to reform, everything ought to be similar and indistinguishably uniform between provinces. Legislation ought to be absolutely the same in all parts of France.

Single legislative body. He certainly accepts as a concession *to fact* that the Estates-General will be composed of people from the three estates (with the doubling of the Third, of course, and vote by head as is explained in the supplement), but what he does not want at any price are separate assemblies, and above all at any price *two*.

More democratic than the Americans. Things are done this way in America, it is true. But on this point the Americans are not to be admired. Further, the evil is less great in America, the two chambers of the legislature being composed of persons of the same class. But to unite an aristocracy in one chamber like the English is the height of absurdity.

Boldness and insolence of individual reason above facts. What characterizes this man's mind is the boldness and insolence with which, without hesitation or the shadow of a doubt, he pits his individual reason against the facts and the experience of the only free nations of his time (p. 166).

He would like the legislative power given to this assembly. What he would prefer is that the Estates-General too form only a single assembly, exercising executive as well as legislative power. According to him only this would be rational. However, he would be willing to accept, as a compromise, that the executive and legislative powers remain divided; but then, he refuses the king the right of veto; he wants the assembly to be permanent; he rejects as a revolting absurdity the idea that the king can dissolve the assembly (note that one didn't even know yet then if there were going to be any Estates-General whatsoever).

He is not a centralizer in the contemporary sense. At that period of the Revolution people were centralizers involuntarily, through the basis of their system and through their ideas, but by intention universally decentralizers. Throughout all these ideas, simultaneously revolutionary and favorable to despotism, are notions favorable to decentralization; he wants to entirely abolish the intendants, to put all local administration in the hands of local assemblies (subject, it is true, only to the legislative power), absurd machinery, but proof that men, even the revolutionaries and demagogues of those times, had not yet conceived the ideal of political freedom combined with bureaucratic despotism which is adored by those of our day. They were led towards administrative centralization through the basis of their ideas and their system. But this was without realizing it; by intention they were still more decentralizers than any man of our time.

The influence of the United States replaces that of England. As long as the Revolution was led by the privileged, who marched without knowing very well where they were going, and who violently pushed the cart off its track without putting it on its true and natural slope, it was the example of England which was chiefly dominant. The word Anglomania was created. Those who marched after them, and headed towards the real goal where affairs and the great currents of thought were going, those people imitated the United States, it was the United States which filled their minds.

The real originality of the French of this time and the insolence of their individual reason. But in truth there was never any spirit of imitation of foreign nations. Foreign examples were able to inspire certain passions, suggest ideas and arguments, but the spirit of this time was original, people wanted to do something new, French; people intended to do something different and better than anyone else. The confidence of the French in themselves, in their superiority, in their reason, was limitless: a major cause of their admirable élan and of their enormous mistakes.

Greatness of the goal which they have in mind. False greatness making people do really great things. Péthion declares with imperturbable aplomb, as early as this text of 1788, that there is only one rational way for men to govern themselves; that this way is rationally clear to everyone; that the same institutions are equally applicable everywhere and to all peoples; that everything which is not this rational government, however old it may be, should be destroyed and replaced by this ideal which first the French, [and then] the entire human species must end up adopting. If these views are exaggerated, superficial, false, one cannot deny that their greatness was of a nature to elevate people to an uncommon height, to fill them with immense passions, to make them violent and sublime. Deprive the French of those days of their false ideas, and you will immediately make them lose part of their élan; this élan even becomes incomprehensible. Only the absurd can make men make such efforts.

Revolutionary inspiration which does not begin until the second half of 1788. All the authors who write around the end of this year (p. 168), among others Péthion, note this sudden development of political passions, their spread, their new aspects during the final struggle between the parlements and the government, that is from August to about October.

Unpopularity of the provincial assemblies. Péthion, who highly approves of the system of provincial assemblies, notes that those which are working already excite great complaints, that they are not very popular, that often people miss the intendants' government (of which he is the absolute adversary, p. 191). He attributes this bizarre state of public opinion to the fact that these assemblies are not elected and that they are composed in their great majority of privileged persons. Above all, their unpopularity should be attributed to the great political [in]experience of the French of all classes at running small as well as large affairs, and their repugnance at being governed by a neighbor rather than a common master.

Unlimited freedom of the press. This book, in which the monarchy and all existing institutions are violently attacked, where republican institutions are almost openly requested, where it is declared that people must refuse to pay taxes and if necessary rebel if the complete overthrow of all the old laws is [not] obtained, this book is printed and distributed without any obstacle and everything indicates that the beautiful binding is from the king's offices.

Old love of the French for the king. "The Frenchman idolizes his masters and superstitiously blesses the chains he bears. At the least sign of generosity and public prosperity, his king is a God" (p. 36).

War on Montesquieu. He says of Montesquieu, after a pious invocation, that he only had the prejudices of his birth and rank, and that he wrote on the general laws of the world like an aristocrat and a member of the parlement (p. 62).

Freedom still holds first place in Péthion's mind. Fundamentally, with all his soul Péthion wants the overthrow of the entire old monarchy, and he adores equality. This is the base of his soul, but at the moment when he is writing, freedom is what most excites his passion: "freedom is the source of all good things" (p. 73).

He is bitter against the clergy without violence; he is radical with respect to the nobility but without anger against the nobles; it is against the government, the monarchy, that his fury boils; this comes from the time period.

When he writes the postscript, the whole struggle has been transported onto the terrain of classes, by the debate opened about the composition and regulation of the Estates-General; then he returns to the real fundamental principles of the Revolution, and cries out that if they do not want to let themselves be destroyed by the privileged, the Third Estate must range itself on the king's side, for, he says, "it is a great deal

better to be governed by one sovereign than by a hundred aristocrats"
(p. 253).

The Revolution's final conclusion pronounced as early as 1788. Here is
the Revolution's final conclusion: we will try to be free while becoming
equal, but we would a hundred times rather cease to be free than to remain or become unequal!

Ultraradical goal. Prudence still retained in practice. The nation cannot
attain perfection all at once: "If the nation wants to make the kingdom
elective (what a supposition for 1788! what boldness of mind in these
prudent words!) and its leaders removable, if it wants to eliminate all
distinctions, deprive the great of their marks of rank, annihilate all hereditary nobility, formidable alliances will immediately arise [against it—
Trans.]" (p. 83).

Complete contempt for acquired rights, for previous commitments. The
provinces uselessly invoke the old treaties that were made with them.
Agreements should only be executed when they are just and reasonable.
"The law does not accept civil contracts made in pain or illness, it should
not be different with political contracts" (p. 173). This was written in the
middle of 1788.

Not very favorable to irremovability from positions. He does not suggest
making judges elective and temporary, but he does not hide that this is
his theory (p. 186).

*Omnipotence of the Estates-General announced well before the Tennis
Court Oath.* "The Estates-General can do everything, they combine all
types of power in their hands" (p. 204). When the Estates are assembled,
the king is without any authority. "All the powers which the nation has
wished to confer upon him are legally suspended." In 1788!

Unlimited sovereignty of the people. Peoples are by inalienable right
"masters of the leaders they have chosen; they can change them if it seems
good to them; they can change, eliminate all powers and give government
the form they think most useful" (p. 211).

*Animosity against the monarchy in the text is rapidly replaced by ani-
mosity against the privileged.* This movement of opinion is shown in an
interesting way in the text, starting during the struggle of the parlements,
ending after their victory. In the text, there is violent animosity against
the government, ideas hostile to privileges, but good will towards the
privileged. In the postscript, no dislike for the monarchy, intense bitterness against the privileged, above all the clergy, infinitely less against the
nobility.

Rabaud-Saint-Etienne, "Consideration on the Interests of the Third Estate"
(End of 1788), Small Edition of 1826; Revolutionary Spirit of the Moderates

France has no constitution or what ought to be understood by a constitution. Like all the reformers of the time (regardless of their rank, birth or character, for that matter), Rabaud works in every way to demonstrate that France DOES NOT HAVE A CONSTITUTION, in other words, that there is nothing in existing institutions that is obligatory, nothing which has the character of a fundamental law, which cannot and should not be more or less changed in order to establish a completely new whole. Rabaud, whose language is very moderate with regard to individuals, is as radical as anyone else on this point. This in 1788!

The constitution is the monarchy. Like all the others, he is happy to admit that the monarchy is a constitutional institution, but this point clearly cannot be sustained amidst the general doctrine that nothing in the old order has solidity or real legality. Furthermore, what is a monarchical constitution when one says nothing about how it will be organized?

The republic advocated even though the constitution is monarchical. Like the others he is constantly pushed towards advocating republican institutions, all the while declaring that monarchical institutions are part of the constitution: "The republic," he says, "is a house where those who live in it take constant care of making daily repairs or adapting it to new needs. Monarchy is a house that one only repairs from time to time, rarely according its inhabitants' taste, and only when one is tired of hearing their cries" [p. 1].

Thus, only the house is in the constitution, and this house is very bad to live in. However, Rabaud shows an exalted love of the king; but in the long run what do feelings matter when logic and political passions continually run in the opposite direction.

Contempt for custom, individual rights, longevity. There is only one principle of state, it is the people's happiness; except for the monarchy, all the rest is only form and can be changed according to the nation's will. To justify the present laws, people say that they are old, "but the longevity of a law does not prove anything except that it is old . . . One bases oneself on possession, but past possession does not give any right to future possession . . . one bases oneself on history, but history is not the legal code" [p. 11].

View of the classes presently dominant, separate from the nation; a kind of superfluity which is not the nation. This way of seeing things is universal among writers: the nobility and clergy are never seen as part of the nation, as making up an integral and at least necessary part of the nation, if not the chief one. They are a sort of foreign body that can be extracted without damaging the rest. In all history I do not believe that there is any example of a similar division of classes and such a way (theoretically and before even starting on the work) of considering an aristocracy. "Mentally subtract," says Rabaud, "all the clergy, subtract even the nobility, you still have the nation. Subtract the Third Estate, there will no longer be any nation" [p. 28].

Reason alone to be consulted, independently of all past facts. This idea is found in Rabaud's mind as much as in any other text, although by his position he is a man of tradition: "Do not look at your ancestors' conduct," he says, "they did not have any principles and they were debased. Do not ask what they did, . . . consult only your common sense, and natural law whose principles never change" [p. 34].

Fury against the inequalities of the time leading Rabaud to combat, even in theory, all secondary bodies, and even all individual groups; to adore unity, uniformity, a single crowd, a single master. These ideas so essentially revolutionary, so democratic in the French fashion, and necessarily ending in despotism and servility, these ideas are the author's own thoughts and the great object of his book, even though four years later he will die for having said that he was tired of playing his part in a tyranny. All the seeds of servitude in his head, the love of freedom in his heart. The most lively passion that inspires this author is still much more visibly hatred of the nobility than love of freedom, at every turn Rabaud flatters the ambitious passions of the central power, showing what the king would gain in power by destroying all the individual groups which resist him; these groups have, it is true, the appearance of thus serving freedom, but fundamentally they are only defending their privileges, which are more to be feared than royal power.

Praise of the present conduct of the upper classes, amidst the most violent attacks against them. "Already," he says, "we have seen that in the handful of provincial governments that we have been able to establish, the bishops and the great interest themselves in the fate [of the lower classes], lower taxes . . ." [p. 40].

War on all intermediary powers. Montesquieu out of fashion. Intermediary powers are not in the nature of things; what need is there for an intermediary power between king and people? Provided that the people are well governed, of what use an intermediary body? In the primitive constitution of the monarchy "we only see one nation and one king, one body and one head" (p. 42).

It is impossible to better sow despotism while spreading freedom. In 1787 and in part of 1788 one still fought only against the common master; Montesquieu was in fashion, he filled all writings. After the final months of '88, he was fought to the death: it was no longer freedom which preoccupied people, he only taught how to be free, we were looking above all for how to become equal.

Fairly moderate when it comes to practice. As with many others, Rabaud's thoughts and reasoning go far beyond his present desires. After having said that any separate group was contrary to nature and dangerous, and that to a healthy mind nobility could only be personal, he is very willing to recognize that the hereditary nobility must be left its coats of arms, titles, and honorific privileges; to take from it only its privileges of exemption (p. 64).

The very fixed idea that the Third Estate is everything, made to lead, in a position and with the right to take power. One would be wrong to believe that this idea was born in the heat of the struggle; it predated the struggle. From 1788, for example, Rabaud among others produces it in many ways: "Remember," he says, "that you are the nation; [. . .] know your dignity . . ." (p. 100).

The revolutionary and despotic idea that all individual rights are necessarily contrary to the general good and should be destroyed, always present. This idea fills the text I am examining. It reigned alone in this generation's mind, I do not find anyone who contests it. The deeper and truer notion that there are many individual rights which not only are not opposed to the general good but which, by an influence more or less obvious and more or less indirect, create the general good; that it may even be for the general good not to destroy individual rights which are useless to it or even contrary to it, or at least that even those rights should not be harmed except with caution, this idea is absent. Yet what is more evident? To begin with the right of property, is it not one of those individual rights certain of whose effects can be very harmful? Nevertheless it is the basis of civilization, which is a great general good.

Question of Public Law: Should Votes Be Counted by Order or by Head? (Same Period, Same Volume)

Sudden and irresistible impulse given to minds after the king's defeat by the parlements and the certain coming of the Estates-General. This point, so important for painting the movement of minds, is highlighted by this passage (p. 107): "Three months have changed the nation. It is done, the nation is regenerated. I no longer speak to Frenchmen whom a long despotism had condemned to turn their rare wisdom towards pleasure or frivolous reading. We may be heading for another servitude, but we will never go back to the one we have left."

In fact, we were running towards another servitude in leaving the old one. Rabaud did not realize how well he spoke.

There can be no respectable interests other than the interest of the greatest number. Maxim of revolution and of tyranny. We speak, says Rabaud, with regard to the division of powers (p. 114), of the various interests which must be balanced; but it is an injustice to counterbalance the interest of all with the interest of a few. One of these interests is a right, the other a usurpation.

Danger of three powers or even two. The purpose of the whole little work by Rabaud that I am examining at this moment, like that of Mounier, was to prevent the vote by orders, through which the three orders would form three chambers, and also to prevent the two first orders forming an upper house. Rabaud's ideas are the same, less deep, less mature, perhaps less clearly expressed, and reducing themselves in sum to this:

What we want is to demolish the old institutional fabric; not just to attain this gradually, but to hurry and profit from the occasion which has finally offered itself to us to do this radically and at one blow. We do not want those who have an interest in defending all or part of that fabric to be able to stop us, or even slow us in our work. Therefore we only want a single legislative power, where we will have a certain majority.

I note:

1) That everything Rabaud says can be equally applied to the royal veto, although he does not speak of it, as well as to the veto of the nobility and the clergy.

2) That the very idea of a COMPROMISE is absent: an arrangement between the different interests, the old and the new, does not even present itself to his mind. It is a question of attaining a certain ideal constitution; everything that might be an obstacle, in former institutions or in the men who represent them, must be set aside as illegitimate, and deprived of any ability to defend itself.

It is true that one makes a revolution thus; but that you can found something free or even durable this way I deny.

3) It should not be astonishing that the meaning of the doubling of the Third Estate and the vote by head thus being so clearly defined in advance,

the nobility and clergy resisted. One may be of the opinion that they deserved to be destroyed at any price, but to wish that they had not tried to avoid destruction is absurd. It is astonishing that so many of their members so easily agreed.

4) If the vote in common had to be adopted, it is regrettable that it was not done everywhere the way it was done in Dauphiny, that is that the deputies of each order were not chosen by all the orders: this would have favored cooperation. But to have the deputies of each order chosen by that order itself and then to put all these deputies together was to make cooperation visibly impossible, the most violent struggle certain, and to doom one group to permanent and inevitable oppression by the other.

5) Finally, it must be recognized along with Mounier and Rabaud that the situation and the constitution of classes in France differed so profoundly from what they were in England that division into two or three chambers made government almost impossible among us, while it favored it among the English. And yet I BELIEVE that in the long run, with patience and a spirit of compromise, we would have ended up, through the beneficial effects of freedom, of publicity, of common discussion, bringing the nobility and the clergy little by little to cede most of their prerogatives and allow themselves gradually to be pulled towards the Third Estate. But extremely difficult and very doubtful.

Justice rendered to the nobles and priests. The needs of the discussion lead Rabaud to say, which is exaggerated but contains much truth (p. 137): "One single thing could divide the three orders, that is the privileges of tax-exemption. But this subject of discord no longer exists, and after the generous declaration by a large part of the nobility, by the peers of the kingdom, by the nobility of Dauphiny, of Guyenne, of Languedoc and of Roussillon, the instigators of trouble would try in vain to persuade us that we are enemies."

Why then therefore take such great precautions so that these good friends cannot hinder us?

[The Struggle between Classes: The Report of the
Princes of the Blood, December 1788]

Report of the Princes of the Blood presented to the King. At the end of the second Assembly of Notables.

These princes were: the Count of Artois, the Prince of Condé, the Duke of Bourbon, the Duke of Enghien, and the Prince of Conti (we know that the Duke of Orléans at the head of his committee had asked for the doubling of the Third Estate).

This report was a great event. It gave the signal for class war and immediately made it more violent. It identified the princes with the threatened and suspect classes. It made the heads of the nobility join the resistance and opened the way which soon led to the emigration of the nobility.

Threatening tone. The report lets it be understood that if the doubling of the Third Estate and the vote by head is granted, the nobility might well abstain or resist. This was to really understand the situation.

Haughty tone. In this report the princes give all the other nobles the example of that haughty tone and self-glorification that the nobility had not used even in former times when it was more sure of its real power.

Insulting concession. "That the Third Estate cease to attack the rights of the first two orders, rights no less ancient than the monarchy and as unalterable as its constitution, that the Third Estate limit itself to soliciting the reduction of taxes with which it may be overburdened: then those of the first two orders [. . .] could through generous feelings renounce the prerogatives which have a monetary interest for their purpose, and consent to bear public burdens in the most perfect equality" [pp. 9–10]. Thus, they maintained all the humiliating and wounding inequalities. And as for the one that was onerous, the inequality of taxation, even in renouncing it they still found a way to irritate those to whom they made such an important concession. This whole piece is virtually the *archetype* of all the ridiculous, dangerous, or imprudent speeches and feelings that some of the French nobility have not ceased to imitate.

"Plan for a Response to the Report of the Princes of the
Blood," from December '88, by the abbé Morellet

This is a response in fairly moderate form to the Report of the Princes.

It clearly states here that a great nation has need of a monarchical government, but that it can perfectly well exist without a nobility and without a clergy.

This shows well where minds had already arrived.

Uncertainty left to the end on the question of the vote by order or by head. It is evident that the Third Estate, by asking so strongly and so unanimously to have as many deputies for itself as the nobility and the clergy, understood that they would vote by head, because without that the question of numbers would not have been very important. However, through a sort of prudence and compromise which parties often have, even in the midst of their most lively passions, they at first avoided bringing up this inevitable consequence and above all avoided following it rigorously.

"In electing two deputies," says Morellet, "the question still remains undecided. It remains possible for the assembled nation to decide itself whether these two deputies will have but one vote or whether they will have two votes" [p. 24]. The princes had spoken of "generosity," which might lead the nobility to consent to equality of taxation. To this insultingly phrased concession, Morellet responds, as it was easy to foresee, that it is not generosity to give what is strict justice and that one cannot refuse to do so [p. 41].

"Modest Observations on the Report of the Princes Made in the Name of Twenty-Three Million French Citizens," by the abbé Brizard, 22 December 1788 (50 Pages)

A pamphlet more bitter in its irony than the preceding, similar in everything else. It says that the most sacred of our institutions is the *National Assembly* [p. 7] (not the Estates-General). We see that the formula of the Tennis Court Oath was not unprecedented and that the idea that it represented already existed in everyone's mind.

In general shows clearly how the passions of class and all the *ideas* which were attached to them are suddenly displayed in their entirety and have leapt to their final consequence, as soon as this debate is begun. Proof that everything was prepared in this respect, although we had not yet turned to it.

"Report for the French People." December, 1788 [. . .]

Definition of freedom. We must agree on this word: freedom is often the desire to command and make oneself free vis-à-vis the sovereign, in order to be a despot vis-à-vis the Third Estate (p. 34). This passage is interesting in that it is already a reaction against the liberal movement which had just united all classes and already shows the true democratic idea of freedom, or rather the true feeling of our democracy for freedom. True freedom, says the author, is a government in which all parties are in their place. In less ambitious terms, the desirable freedom is the equality of everyone. [. . .]

Real passions of the Third Estate, according to the author. You fear, he says to the nobles, that the Third Estate is going to demolish your privileges. It will take care not to do so. It wants to share them. The difficulty is not to convoke the Third Estate, but to find the real one. Everyone is burning to leave it.

This was to reason based on English facts and passions and not French ones.

[The Battle of the Privileged among Themselves—
End of 1788—Beginning of 1789]

*"Report to the King in Favor of the French Nobility by a
Patrician Friend of the People," by the marquis Gouy d'Arsy (A Pamphlet of
Thirty-four Pages in Octavo; Time of Printing: Between the Triumph
of the Parlements and the End of 1788)*

Combination of revolutionary ideas and caste spirit. This marquis, of whose history I am ignorant, is full of all the ideas of the times. The nobles are above all citizens. He calls the Third Estate the *most useful* order [p. 6]. He is for the doubling of the Third Estate and the vote by head. This does not at all prevent him from making an emphatic eulogy of the nobility and above all from being infinitely attached to its remaining very much apart. Which he expresses in these words: let us be forever united and never combined. (What a jumble of impractical and contradictory ideas in the lightweight minds who, without any experience, start practicing politics!) [. . .]

Battle of the privileged among themselves. What is characteristic in this miserable little pamphlet is the violent hatred that this aristocrat shows for the clergy. From the height of his philosophy he judges them with great contempt. Three-quarters of priests are useless; celibacy makes them dangerous. They should not form a special order and in any case they should have no more than half the deputies of the nobility and a third those of the Third Estate, and it is to be believed that the Estates-General will take some of their property from them (p. 15). [. . .]

*"Exclusive Right of Curates" [to the Tithes of Their Parishes; or,
Letter to M. de Gr . . .], by a Curate of Anjou (Eighty-three Pages; Author
Unknown; Period: Before the Opening of the Estates-General)*

Work evidently written by a priest. Seriously written in erudite and moderate language. Interesting to show how divisions worked within the clergy and would have brought about internal war there if the common persecution had not reunited everyone. [. . .]

*Irritation of the curates against the other classes composing the clergy.
Deep and strong divisions within the clergy.* The author seems a very sincere Christian. He is very attached to the interests of the order and rejects

with force the idea that its properties can be taken away. But he is no less unhappy with the bishops and above all with the canons and monks who have enormous wealth while the curates who are the real administrators of the church by divine institution mostly die of hunger. [. . .]

The purpose of the whole book is to prove that it is the other orders of the clergy who have stolen the tithes they own from the curates, and have unjustly taken them for themselves. "Is it for the general good of the Church that chapters have as many as sixty or eighty people receiving stipends, and that they offer each of them four to five hundred pistoles, and that the cloistered find the same opulence in retreats closed to all superfluities of luxury and benefits of wealth? That benefices that do not take care of people and nourish the indolence and useless existence of a crowd of lazy beneficiaries without any duties and that they accumulate them on their heads . . . while the hardworking and useful workers remain not only reduced to the most humiliating mediocrity, but even to the sad condition of being beneficiaries of public charity" (p. 74)?

In another place: "that we be allowed to break the irons with which the greed of the rich holder of benefices keeps us chained" (p. 83).

What is remarkable is that this is said by a man who seems to be a very good priest and who seems hardly affected by the political passions of the times. [. . .]

"Salutary Warning to the Third Estate by a Savoyard Jurist" (Sixty-three Pages; Author Unknown; Period: Immediately before the Elections to the Estates-General)

This pamphlet made a certain impression, for I have often seen it cited. It is in fact written in a biting style which summarizes the ideas and passions of the moment in a picturesque manner.

Violent diatribe against the clergy and nobility. [. . .] "On the common base of original equality nature alone can raise and mark out difference." . . . "Do not hesitate to let that sweet and terrible word equality be heard" . . . (p. 53). One could not hear a more revolutionary cry. About which it must be noted:

1) That once the crowd's mind has seized on such maxims and nourished itself on them, the Revolution is inevitable. From the moment such questions are turned over to the crowd they are inevitably resolved. Individual rights are only defensible before an intelligent, educated, and attentive audience, or in silence (this is so true that the author himself states that a very short time before these public expositions the majority of the members of the Third Estate would not have dared to think that things could and should be different than they were).

2) That the form that aristocracy and inequality had taken in France was absolutely unsustainable, of a nature to push minds towards the most excessive doctrines and to explain and in part justify the demagogic passions of the times.

Ultrarepublican principles and immoderate flattery of the monarch. Rapid about-face by the parties: during the first ten months of 1788 the Third Estate with the nobility and the clergy against the king; during the last two the Third Estate with the king against the clergy and the nobility.

[The Beginning of 1789: On the Estates-General]

"What Is the Third Estate?" by Sieyès

Period. The author says that this text was written at the end of 1788, during the deliberations of the notables, and published in January 1789.

A real battle cry. A specimen of the violence and radicalism of opinions, even before the struggles that are said to have provoked violence and radicalism.

Sieyès himself states that he is ahead of general opinion. But he leads it.

This text, which was famous (it immediately went through three editions and sold three hundred thousand copies) and, in a certain respect, worthy of its fame, breathes the most violent, the most congenitally Revolutionary spirit, and goes beyond the state of mind of the moment when it appeared; or rather it led minds to the consequences of ideas they already had, and gave form and color to passions which existed in seed or in development in all hearts.

The whole soul and imagery of the Revolution in Sieyès's writing. The violent class hatreds which act as the Revolution's axis, the natural daring of innovators, the boldness of their false logic, the absolute absence of any consideration for existing interests, rights, facts . . . all this, which in larger or smaller doses was already to be found everywhere in the writings of the times, here is combined and highlighted so well that this book can be considered the best specimen of the Revolution's spirit before the Revolution, and of the violence of theories and passions even before the struggle.

The Third Estate forms a complete nation. This idea, which I have already noted in a large number of writings, is formulated here in detail and with the rigorous force of mathematical reasoning which follows its logic to the end.

Not only are the nobility and clergy useless, they are harmful. Not only not serving any purpose but a hindrance. But what is more particular to Sieyès is not going so far as to say that the Third Estate by itself alone is the entire nation and the rest foreign bodies, but that the nation would do better without these foreign bodies than with them: "What is the Third Estate? A whole that is shackled and oppressed. What would it be without the privileged orders? A free and flourishing state. Nothing can work without the Third Estate, everything would go infinitely better without the others" (p. 10). The order of the nobility is a burden on the nation, it is not part of it.

One realizes that the nobility and clergy were not of the opinion that they ought to let themselves be exterminated. Is it extraordinary that the nobility and clergy, hearing the applause of all France for such things, were not disposed to let those who said them or applauded them legislate alone!

Emigration to some extent excusable. We rightly condemn the act which led the nobility to leave the country and form a separate nation abroad. But it must be recognized that perhaps it had never before happened, among any people at any time, that a whole class of citizens was thus outlawed in advance, and so to speak chased from the land before they had left it.

The nobility is a caste without function, without utility. A very true aspect (p. 12). All that Sieyès says is very true. It is very clear that the nobility, in the situation in which it found itself, and at the point to which the nation had come, was a caste without function and without utility. And it is this truth so vigorously expressed which is Sieyès's merit and created his success. But what was false was:

1) To overlook that this abnormal fact was so old, so well-rooted, related to so many other respectable facts, and itself so worthy of respect for its antiquity, that mother of law, that instead of making the nobility disappear all at once, it had to be demolished gradually.

2) If in fact caste is in itself a bad institution, and furthermore useless, the system of the purely numerical majority is no less so. Some influence of traditions, of principles, in a word an aristocratic element, is a very necessary part of a free government, above all in an inexperienced free government, and this caste, gradually reduced to no more than an aristocratic party, the aristocracy, was a precious resource for France that it was very harmful to destroy. Finally, it was not true that the Third Estate was a complete nation; or, at least, that reduced to itself it could create a free and stable order of things.

Nobility attached to the right of conquest. To arouse the passions of the Third Estate and to make the nobility more and more of a foreign nation amidst the French people, Sieyès links all its rights to conquest, as if that conquest had happened yesterday: "Why don't we send back to the Franconian forests all these families who retain the insane claim of being the descendants of the conquerors' race?"(p. 11). "The nation, thus purged, could console itself for no longer being composed of any but Gauls and Romans."

After having exalted pride and hatred, a pretense of exaggerated fears. Even when the Third Estate was equal to the two other orders, it was still to be feared that the others would dominate it, since they controlled all the jobs and favors. The Third Estate is like a vast waiting room, where, always busy with what the masters are doing or saying, people think of nothing but the means of pleasing them (p. 31).

The nobility not only a foreign people, but a barbarous enemy people in the heart of the French nation. Compared to the Algerians. In order to prove that the Third Estate cannot be allowed to vote for anyone outside its ranks, he says: "If it were question of a congress of maritime nations to regulate the freedom or security of navigation, do you believe that Genoa or Livorno would choose its ministers plenipotentiary from the Barbary pirates?"

The aristocrats are the Algerians of France (p. 40).

Fury in expression as well as in feeling. Abusive freedom of the press. Assuredly a country where different classes of citizens are allowed to insult one another in this fashion is a country which is close to civil war if the strengths of the different classes are balanced, to violent revolution if they are unequal.

Generous efforts of part of the nobility in favor of the Third Estate. What should be noted is that Sieyès himself was named [a deputy to the Estates-General—Trans.] by the Third Estate.

"It is a remarkable thing that the cause of the Third Estate has been defended with more force and readiness by ecclesiastical and aristocratic writers than by the nonprivileged themselves" (p. 68).

A precious confession and one which proves that this nobility had, amidst its abuses and vices, a certain vigor and a certain greatness that ought to have been preserved for the nation and not sent away to the Franconian forests.

The nobility's abandonment of their tax privileges noted by Sieyès. Sieyès notes that this abandonment had been offered by the notables, by the peers and in many districts by the nobility in general, and that this point can be considered won (p. 72).

The bad mood in which this abandonment puts him. Efforts to prevent it from extinguishing hatred. Sieyès cannot hide the bad mood that this abandonment puts him in. He needs a nobility as egoistic and unreasonable as possible. "It was not on this subject," he says, "that the notables were asked for their advice." The nobility thus wants to lull the Third Estate to sleep (p. 73). The nobility furthermore does not renounce anything except what it can no longer keep. The gratitude with which these renunciations were received was quite ridiculous and even dangerous. One thus seems to recognize that there was a right which it was permissible or possible to keep.

The needs of the moment make Sieyès reduce the tax privileges to little. As long as the nobility seemed to want to retain its tax privileges, they were, with reason, made the chief complaint. After the nobility abandons them, Sieyès assures us that what the nobility surrendered had very little value because in reality the nobility already paid taxes through its tenants (he goes so far as to say, on p. 84, that the elimination of the taille would be monetarily advantageous to the nobility). Very good to recall.

All the privileges which remain to the nobility after it has renounced those of taxation. Furthermore, tax privileges abandoned, how many others remain to the nobility! Here (p. 78) Sieyès makes a list of all the privileges of the nobility beyond those of taxation. Almost all of them consist of easier access to government positions. In fact the leading families of England could be criticized for this today.

The love of government positions already the great motive of revolutions. We perceive that it is above all with this that Sieyès hopes to move the whole Third Estate, the love, the habit of, and the need for government jobs being already very widespread in France. Sieyès said elsewhere (p. 7) that nineteen-twentieths of the jobs were already in the hands of the Third Estate. But it was only with great difficulty that they arrived at the highest and best paid.

Inde irae! [The source of anger.—Trans.]

Constitution of England. Fear that we will imitate it. In general fear of compromise. We must take care not to imitate the constitution of England, which is still half barbarous, little in conformity with true principles. We can do much better. Above all we must guard against the system which consists of making an upper house out of the superior clergy and higher nobility while putting all the other clergy and nobles into the lower chamber and making them eligible for election by the Third Estate (p. 88).

In general everything that might tend to bring the classes together, to become a matter for compromise . . . makes him very fearful. It is war, and in consequence of this, the absolute and unlimited triumph of his theory that he demands.

Ultrarepublican and democratic theory of Sieyès. From all that Sieyès says here it follows that, according to him, the numerical majority, without any distinction among voters, ought to make the law; that sovereignty resides only in the majority; that there can be no contract between the majority and anyone else, either class or ruler, because outside the majority there are none but removable *agents* with whom one cannot negotiate; that the constitution can and must be changed according to the will of this majority in convention . . . fundamentally very close to the basic ideas of the American constitutions, above all as they have evolved since.

Boldness of philosophical pride. "The principles that I have just described are certain," says Sieyès; "all social order must be renounced or they must be accepted" (p. 124).

The nobility accused of arousing the lower classes. Since the agitation of the lower classes was beginning to alarm some people, Sieyès implies that perhaps it is the aristocrats who are starting it in order to frighten the king (p. 135). Those were some very clever aristocrats, who were having their own castles burnt out of party spirit!

Battle cry: appeal for a definitive division. No, it is no longer the time to work for conciliation between the parties. The nobility have dared to pronounce the word *secession.* How fortunate it would be for the nation if this separation were made permanent, this very desirable secession! How easy it would be to get along without the privileged! How difficult it will be to make citizens out of them (p. 137)!

Aristocrats: Montesquieu an aristocrat. "No more aristocrats should be the rallying cry of all the nation's friends" (p. 141). "This aristocracy which hides its power for evil behind the imposing authority of the aristocrat Montesquieu" (p. 141).

He rejects the idea of having the representatives of each estate elected by everyone. This idea, which had been applied in Dauphiny, and which could be considered an acceptable compromise and would necessarily have led very quickly to the absorption of the whole nation into a common mass, is carefully rejected by Sieyès (p. 145).

The consequence that society must be thrown to the ground and rebuilt anew boldly accepted. "I recognize that these truths are embarrassing in a situation which has not been created under the auspices of reason. What do you want? Your house is only artificially maintained with the aid of a forest of props placed without taste and without plan. Unless you want to prop up each part as it threatens to fall down, you have to reconstruct the whole thing" (p. 146).

The idea even of the common vote and the combination of the orders at the Estates-General declared insufficient. Only the Third Estate should be there, forming a National Assembly. No alliance between the three orders at the Estates-General is possible. They cannot vote together either by order or by head, since they represent different persons or enemies. It is necessary that the national will be *one* and it cannot be one as long as there are three representations. You can thus have three nations making a single wish but you will never have *one* nation, one representation, one common will (p. 146). These principles are among those which must be accepted or else all social order must be given up.

Furthermore the Third Estate is more cautious than he. The author recognizes that his principles "will not be to the taste even of those members of the Third Estate most able to defend its interests" (p. 151).

For these he makes the concession that we begin by not applying his principles in their full rigor, even though they are all strictly just. Some concessions must be made to the times, if the Third Estate wants to regard itself for a little while longer as an order and not suddenly jar the prejudices of ancient barbarism (p. 154).

He foresees that these principles will appear extravagant. "I foresee that such principles are going to seem extravagant to most readers" (p. 169). So much were they in accord with the passions of the times that they would soon be applied to the letter.

Number of nobles and priests in 1789, according to Sieyès:

Clergy:

curates	40,000
vicars	10,000
bishops and canons	2,800
cathedral canons	5,600
benefice holders	3,000
clergy without benefices	3,000
monks	17,000
	81,400

(Monks and nuns have declined at an accelerating rate in the past thirty years, says the author.)

Nobility. The author takes the nobles of Brittany as the common measure because in Brittany, since all the nobles vote in the provincial estates, figuring out their number is easier than elsewhere.

In Brittany, 10,000 nobles out of a population of 2,300,000 individuals. Thus proportionately for the whole of France, 110,000 nobles of both sexes and all ages.

We see that this is very random. I am led to believe that the number of nobles was larger. But nevertheless Sieyès has a very scientific mind and in this respect is pretty worthy of faith (p. 50).

All politics reduced to a calculation of numbers. Thus, says the author, "compare the number of 200,000 privileged with 26 million souls and judge the result" (p. 53). Here is all politics reduced to a rule of proportion. This is very easy. How much superficiality under this pretended depth, and what ignorance of the true conditions for governing men beneath this pride in political infallibility.

Sieyès much more the enemy of the nobility than the clergy. We see throughout this text that Sieyès is the violent opponent only of the nobility, or at most of the part of the clergy which is full of nobles. He combats the privileges of the clergy, but without bitterness. He is very far from wanting to see it robbed; on the contrary, he makes clear the utility of having it paid in real estate. We know that he fought against the destruction of the tithe without compensation. What he is, to the point of being rabid, is the enemy of the nobility.

He complains that there is much more passion against the clergy than against the nobility. He states that people were much less hostile to the nobility than to the clergy, and he complains of this bitterly.

He remains a priest amidst his revolutionary passions. Not only does he remain a priest in his opinions on the Church. But we feel the priest in him even in the midst of his revolutionary passions; his inflexibility, his pride, his taste for metaphysics, his despotic nature . . .

"Continuation of the Writing Titled:
The Estates-General Convoked by Louis XVI" (Forty-one Pages)

Author. The catalog of the National Library gives Target (I would like to have proof of this).

Period. During the Notables at the end of '88 and the beginning of '89.

This writing is the continuation of another which is not found in the library. I have seen Target's pamphlets of this period quoted in many other writings of the times. I do not know if this is one of those in question. It seems to me that this brochure is very moderate to have had the success that it seems the writings of Target had.

The number of deputies based on interest and not on numbers. This is the only text in which I see the author glimpse that in matters of elections, it could well be prudent, even legitimate and natural, not to take numbers as the sole basis, but to adopt a sort of average resulting from numbers and the interest that one is seen to have in public affairs. This interest is manifested by the sacrifices one makes for public affairs in terms of taxes paid and by the conservative spirit which the possession of property brings. Such a simple idea as this, which experience would so naturally suggest, is expressed hardly anywhere except in this text. This, it is true, leads the author as surely as other doctrines to the doubling of the Third Estate so that he gives the substance to the reforming passions of the day, while according reason to the spirit of conservation and tradition. [. . .]

Argument against the imitation of England. Analogous to that already given by Mounier. When the constitution is completed and accepted, a legislative body in two or three branches can be good. It prevents danger-ous innovations. But when on the contrary the constitution must be fin-ished and a new order created, to give the right of absolute veto to the old interests is to reduce oneself to impotence.

Always the same chimera; we want to be absolute master for a time, after which we will accept counterweights.

If people had been sincere and experienced they would have known that aristocratic bodies, even armed with a legislative veto, when forced to hold out under the pressure of a national movement and under the fire of a free press, are often forced to retreat and not use their right of veto. They only still use it to moderate, not to stop movement. [. . .]

Observations on the Report to the King Made by M. Necker on 27 December 1788

A little brochure of sixty-one pages without the printer's name. Author unknown. *Period:* The time immediately preceding the elections.

One of the very small number of pamphlets in favor [*sic*] of the vote by head. Work of some ability and of unquestionable superiority over all the other brochures in its political reasoning.

The vote by head: the whole question is here. The question is very well posed. The author shows that everything is in the question of voting by head; that the doubling of the Third Estate is only a secondary question but that the vote by head is the constitution itself, and that it replaces a balanced monarchy and complex government with a simple government which excludes all secondary powers and which can produce only pure democracy or absolute power.

An incontestable truth but very useless in the state of the public mind.

The balance of powers perhaps impossible with powers constituted the way the nobility and Third Estate were then.

Further, if it is true that the coexistence of different bodies is necessary to the establishment of a monarchical government, and even to the establishment of a free state, it must be recognized that groups as essentially distinct as the Third Estate and the nobility, and as separate . . . could hardly coexist, and that at the point we had reached, it was very difficult to make them work together reasonably well.

Incredible incapacity and imprudence of Monsieur Necker in the report of 27 December '88. This made perfectly plain in this text.

1. The Third Estate, through desire for popularity, recognized as the sole source of wisdom.

2. A horrible depiction of the state of the peasants and all that the rich owe them, at a time when a peasant uprising was so close.

2. [*sic*] The will of the Third Estate officially considered the national will, that is the king himself removing the nobility and the clergy from the nation, as in the revolutionary pamphlets already analyzed.

3. In general the historical viewpoint that the Third Estate is the monarchy's real support is retained when new facts have made it false.

4. Finally, *supreme* mistake, the question of the vote by head, rightly given as the chief question, discussed from the Third Estate's point of view and in such a way as to arouse the hopes and passions of the Third and yet not *decided.* This was the worst of all imaginable courses of conduct. If the king had clearly rejected voting by head in advance, it would have been more difficult for the commons to demand it. If the king, in advance, had commanded the vote by head, it would have been very difficult for the privileged to hope to fight against the current. The Revolution would have been made, but with more chance of mildness and for peace of mind.

But to give people hope for the vote by head and yet not authorize it was to arouse the Third Estate to attack and to permit the privileged to resist. In other words, to suddenly turn reform into violent revolution.

Division of the clergy encouraged. This text also clearly shows that the electoral law, published after this report, was intentionally created in such a way as to make curates the clergy's chief representatives, and to create an internally disorganizing struggle between the bishops and their flock.

This did not have great consequences because the attacks against the clergy in general soon strengthened anew the internal links within this group, and the struggle against the enemies of the Church soon made the different orders of the clergy forget their internal differences.

But if things had followed their natural course, it is probable that great disorder would have occurred within the body of the Church of France, a disorder which was only prevented by the general disorder of the entire nation.

*Works of Mounier; Interesting to See Revolutionary Passions and Ideas
in Men Who Were Not Revolutionaries; "New Observations on the Estates-General"
(Period Preceding the Elections to the Estates-General) [March]*

Aristocracy worse than despotism. The despotism of a single man is a thousand times preferable to aristocratic despotism (p. 198).

Hatred of provincial privileges, of the provincial aristocracy, among the very people whom they had served most and best. Despite the admirable role which Dauphiny had just played, and the attachment that had been shown there for provincial rights; despite the leading and honorable role that Mounier had just played in this first act of the Revolution, he is no less the enemy of all provincial privileges. From the moment that it is no longer a question of the means for making the Revolution, but of the results to get from it, he wants nothing less than to make a blank slate of all separate existences (same contempt for tradition, for the effectiveness of memories, for old things . . . as with revolutionaries of another kind).

He doesn't exactly want centralization but what leads to it. It is true that in his opinion about local government he wants to leave great power to localities . . . but by destroying everything which could facilitate resistance and even life in the old provincial institutions, he unknowingly prepared not the destruction of provincial privileges, but the extinction of all local life. What he asked for, within the limits that he asked for it, was just: it seems he only wanted to take away from the provinces some rights which belonged to sovereignty, like voting taxes . . . and he was right. But for lack of knowing exactly what they wanted and what was possible, men, even the most prudent men of the times, through logic always went far beyond the goal they intended to reach.

Violent class divisions which succeeded their common struggle. "But what, therefore, is the cause of this frightening mistrust which seems to inspire the nobility, the clergy, and the Third Estate at this moment? In slavery they did not complain of being strangers to government. We speak of freedom and here they are to acquire more strength, not as parts of the nation, but as orders, as separate groups" (p. 207).

Mounier just as opposed to the nobility as others, although in his province he had had so much to praise in them. Although Mounier in particular had had before his eyes in his province a nobility as disinterested and enlightened as it is possible to hope for, and greater than which had never been seen in any country, he is no less full of violent passion against the nobility in general than others, and this again leads him farther than his own ideas. For fundamentally it is not the aristocracy proper that he absolutely rejects, but only *caste;* but his reasoning works against the aristocracy, for he violently opposes Montesquieu's system of intermediary powers and the necessity of those powers in a free country and a balanced monarchy.

Old liberal and even democratic forms of the feudal monarchy. What made these forms harmless. I know nothing more liberal and in certain respects more democratic than the system of grievances and cahiers of the old Estates-General, since in this situation the least inhabitant of a village, as well as the lord, was called to take part in a sort of grand inquest and to publicly discuss without fear all abuses from which he might suffer. Mounier tells that even in the towns (in Paris itself) a great chest had been set up where all individuals came to throw in their grievances. This had even been regularized by an edict of the Council of 1576 (p. 226).

What made this public participation in public affairs, even by the least individual, inoffensive, this sort of universal inquest on abuses, this attention focused by all who could complain on their grievances, was the unquestioned and dominant power possessed by the aristocracy at the very time when this *ultrademocratic* institution was in force, as if isolated in the midst of the constitution; and the recognized solidity of the existing political system where no one even thought of disputing the bases of political society, which even in the imagination could not be replaced. But at a time when the aristocracy was as weak as it was hated, when not only were the bases of political society in question, but when nothing excited the imagination more than reform, such a method was the best possible to make the Revolution happen and even to give it an ultrademocratic character on the spot, since it had the effect of stirring up the masses from the very first, and down to their greatest depths.

The idea that the assembly to be named ought to have unlimited power to change everything, as familiar to Mounier as to the greatest revolutionaries. In the chapter on the deputies' powers [chapter 26] (p. 225), we see that even before the meeting of the Estates-General Mounier put no mental limits on what they might do and gave them not only the ability to remedy particular abuses, but the unlimited right to do anything new in any respect. He was pushed by those passions and that inexperience spoken of above to give them the power to do what he certainly did not want them to do, and to push the Revolution a hundred times further than where he wanted it to stop.

As with the other revolutionaries, the idea that nothing from the past was important or obligatory, that nothing from the past had the character of law, which he expressed by this phrase: France has no constitution. The idea that there is a whole past that has rights, political habits, customs which are really laws even though unwritten, which one should only alter with caution, which have created real rights which should be taken into account, that change must come gradually, without making a complete break between what has been and what one wishes there to be, this concept which is the very idea of a practical and regular political freedom is as absent from Mounier's mind as from those of the most violent revolutionaries who will soon appear. The only difference between him and them is that in place of the old he wants to put something more reasonable and less radical than they. This will be seen better below.

Mounier wants a single assembly, legislation by the majority, the immediate elimination of old influences in the creation of laws as much as others do. But he only wants all this as preparation for something else. Mounier is one of the most ardent supporters of the doubling of the Third Estate and the vote by head. However, he clearly lets it be understood that this is transitional, an arm of the revolution, not a definitive institution. We see clearly that he wants an assembly of this kind in order to destroy all that remains of the old constitution, all the special rights, all the local privileges, but not in order to make it part of the machinery of the future government of France.

An upper house composed of the nobility and the clergy would prevent this result forever. He is very much in favor of two houses, but after the Revolution, not before.

A single chamber is necessary, one where the Third Estate will have the dominant power to make, on the spot, the constitution France lacks. Never a legislative power composed of two branches, one of which would represent only the old society, which needed to be thoroughly reformed if not destroyed, and the other, only the opposing tendency. Never would such a legislative body make the radical and above all rapid changes which were needed. Two chambers will in fact be very necessary, but only when the great changes have been made, when the new constitution is finished, when it is only a question of providing for the ordinary business of government. Then a legislative body with two heads and whose two parts are not of different natures is in fact necessary to assure the maturity of laws, beneficial deliberation in creating legislation, and the stability of legislation already passed.

Thus the sum of Mounier's ideas is very clearly expressed: what he wants as the final government of France is very close to what was established in 1814 and continued from 1830 to 1848. All the ideas expressed on this matter by Mounier show a mind which had thought about political questions a great deal, which had breadth and as much soundness as one can have when one has not been able to acquire any experience other than from books and solitary thought. Like the others, Mounier lacks practical experience. He does not know that a single assembly is subject to the irresistible force of a single class or a single party; that while it is excellent for making a revolution, it is very poor at stopping that revolution at a given point. The radical change that Mounier desires not only in the law, but in the status of individuals and, so to speak, in the existence of the entire established social and political order, is never made without a revolution, above all when at the same time that one wants to make such a radical change, one wants to make it quickly. Finally, what he wanted to make happen needed several of the things he wanted to destroy before it had happened: a secure society, the existence of an aristocracy, tolerance at least for old beliefs . . . supports without which we were reduced to an unstable and precarious freedom and often to equality in servitude.

It was feared that with the doubling of the Third Estate and the vote by head, the nobility and the clergy would still be dominant. It is so difficult to measure in advance the real effects of laws, that even among the effects which in hindsight seem to have been inevitable, there are none which beforehand are not unforeseen or disputed. We see Mounier devote a chapter to combating the fears of those who thought that, even with the doubling of the Third Estate and the vote by head, the nobility and the clergy would still dominate the assembly. How can we be astonished that the nobility had crazy illusions about their importance and strength when their opponents had them? Their error was not due to the particular nature of the institution, but to the general state of society and minds, a clear view of which is not within everyone's capacity. In the Middle Ages or even in the fifteenth century, the orders had in fact sometimes been able to voice their opinion by head, without the first two orders losing their hegemony, even though together they did not have any more votes than the Third Estate. This, I think, could perhaps still have been seen even in the sixteenth century. It would already have been very doubtful in the seventeenth century and obviously false in the eighteenth. When the nobility and the clergy enjoyed their former situation or retained the greater part of it, they dominated society before they got to the assembly, and at the assembly itself their influence was far from being circumscribed by their numbers. Each one of their members weighed far more than his vote alone. Furthermore, the Third Estate, who voted with them, did not even have the idea of taking their place; it complained about certain of their rights, not against the idea that they had rights. In 1789 each noble and each priest weighed in the assembly only by his vote, and the general current of thought was not merely to limit their powers and rights, but to destroy them. This reason alone, independently of secondary causes, should not have left any doubt that the first two orders, even if equal to the Third Estate when combined, would necessarily be defeated in all important struggles.

Plan of Conduct for the Deputies of the People to the Estates-General of 1789 (One Volume in Octavo, 268 pages)

Author: Brissot de Warville; *Period:* April 1789, after the elections or when they were finishing before the first meeting of the Estates-General.

Brissot had lived in England and returned from America. Traces of these two facts are found throughout this text.

Of all that I have read up to the present this is the writing which most directly bears the imprint of the American Revolution. Almost all his general principles and their application have this origin.

This text has this dual character:

1) It is more moderate in the means of execution Brissot gives than many other writers of the same period, and than his subsequent conduct would lead one to suspect. He insists on the idea that one must *proceed slowly.* He doesn't want the orders to separate from one another at all. He shows a certain spirit of conciliation, at least with regard to the speed of operations: "Reforms, in order to be wise and lasting," says the author, "cannot be made after a few tumultuous debates. By hurrying them, the evil will only be palliated, the abuses will soon be reborn . . . When I speak of effecting the destruction of the distinction between orders," he says, "this is not immediate, it is not for the Estates-General of 1789" [p. 3, part 4].

2) Purely democratic and republican principles are the end towards which the author is openly heading. [. . .] The strict right of the Third Estate, according to the author, would be to consider the nobility and clergy merely as two corporations foreign to the nation, which ought to have no vote. But he recognizes that almost everywhere the Third Estate seems disposed to some compromises, that it wants harmony and will buy it with sacrifices. "The lower clergy almost everywhere forms a kind of league to ex-

clude bishops, commendatory abbés, and canons from the deputation. In many regions, the clergy prefers curates. In the same way the lesser nobility allies against the great" (p. 24).

Notion of two chambers. Way in which Brissot understands it. Brissot had seen in England, and above all in America, the utility of two chambers. He himself had advocated this system in a previous work. He is of the small number of those who dare to speak of it. He absolutely rejects the idea of an upper house and a lower house. But he would like the Estates-General to separate themselves into two chambers equally divided among the three orders combined (p. 33). The little bit of practical experience that he had acquired in England and in America makes him suspect that a single chamber is too quick and necessarily turbulent when it is numerous—he had just seen the bad effects of the single assembly in Pennsylvania, and he says so (p. 58). [. . .]

Attack on the English constitution. The author had admired it several years previously. But, since then, he had been to America and furthermore was carried along by the current of contemporary French ideas, which rolled towards the Revolution. He therefore declares that "it is to want to dishonor the most beautiful monument reason has ever created (the constitution of the United States) to say it is like the English constitution, which is a gothic construction, creviced, falling in ruins, which only sustains itself by means of foreign props" (p. 47).

Homage rendered to Louis XVI. Brissot wants to end up with the elimination of royal power. He only believes in the rights of the people. But there is no hostility in this book for the king, Louis XVI, whom he would however condemn to death . . . The author declares that for the present it is expedient to leave the king the veto. This is better to start out with. "The people have been so habituated to despotic forms that the sudden passage to entirely free forms would be dangerous, even to them" [p. 109].

The nature of Brissot's moderation. Violence of the moderates. All of Brissot's system of moderation is here. He demonstrates that kings are nothing but the passive agents of the people, that they should be under its control; that the nobility and clergy are merely foreign corporations, who have no other rights than to petition the nation; that all special rights are absurd, inimical, and should be destroyed from top to bottom in order to attain the creation of a democratic and republican society.

After having so clearly shown all the existing powers and groups that they can be pulverized and absolutely abolished, he is happy to agree not to kill them on the spot. As if such a compromise could be accepted by anyone, either by those whose rights one established without completely putting them into effect; or by those whose right to live one disputed but whom one agreed not to kill immediately.

Brissot, instead of wanting, like most of his companions, to extend the powers of the Estates-General that had just been elected, sought rather to limit them. In general Brissot, contrary to other authors of the same opinion, limits more than he extends the sphere of the Estates-General: he only wants to give them what is indispensable to make them master and leave the great reforms to be made to a *Convention* which alone would have the right to rework the whole French constitution. [. . .] Brissot's temperance does not come from moderation at all, but on the contrary from the radicalism of his ideas. He mistrusts the Estates-General such as they will be composed even if the vote by head is accepted; he does not think that they will go as far as he wants towards making a revolution. Furthermore, the pure theory of *conventions,* which he found in the United States, carries him along. Finally, he is not a deputy to the Estates-General, a reason that I should have put first.

In France the success of revolutionaries goes beyond their hopes. What is not particular to our Revolution, but which is seen there more than in any other, is that success almost always goes beyond what was hoped and sometimes beyond what was desired by the leaders. This is part of the democratic nature of this Revolution and of the sudden character of the French, as difficult to stop as to start; so that the difficulty one has to make them start a revolution misleads one about the difficulty one will have in making them push on suddenly to the end. [. . .]

The most dangerous imitators of the United States are those who have not been there. In general one notes that if the sight of the United States suggested to Brissot all kinds of revolutionary ideas that were inapplicable to France, it also gave him certain conservative notions that many of his companions did not have. The system of two chambers, a nonpermanent legislative body . . . The worst imitators were those who had taken from the United States the abstract principles of their constitution without having understood the necessity of certain conservative applications of these principles which had been made in America. [. . .]

Book Two

NOTES EXCERPTED
FROM TOCQUEVILLE'S
PAPERS CONCERNING
THE HISTORY OF
THE REVOLUTION

CHAPTER ZERO

[Plans]

October 1856

Work Plan

To concentrate all my studies on the period from 1788 to 10 August [1789—Trans.]

To read various kinds of documents about this period:

1. Legislative documents.
2. Newspapers.
3. Pamphlets of the time.
4. Books published since then about this period.
5. Finally, when I will be in Paris, the manuscript documents: the elections of 1789, the correspondence with the authorities or of the authorities among themselves, the work of the local assemblies . . .

When I have made notes on all these different texts, make an appendix of these notes like the one I made before starting to write the first volume.

1. The country's disposition at the time when the Estates-General met. Characteristics: What did everyone agree about? Good intentions. Revolution begun with fewer bad feelings than any other. Sign of this? How was this produced? How it can be explained? To penetrate deeply into what happened then within each class. What moved them; what they thought, wanted, hoped, feared . . .

In order to find all these things and paint them truly:

1. The collection of the archives: cahiers, correspondence by the minister and with the minister.

2. If it exists, other official correspondence of this time between the government and its agents.

2. [*sic*—Trans.] Try to find how to show how these excellent intentions, this apparent agreement, naturally turned into deep divisions and terrible passions at the first contact with the facts.

3. Once into the Constituent Assembly, show the accuracy of its general views, the true greatness of its plans, the generosity, the loftiness of its feel-

ings, the admirable combination of the desire for freedom and the desire for equality that it displayed . . . Its clumsiness, its practical ignorance making so many good intentions, so many just views, end up . . . in an impossible government, an anarchical and powerless administration, and finally in the general disorganization from which came the Terror.

CHAPTER ONE

[From the Meeting of the Estates-General until the Fall of the Bastille]

[The Crisis of the Winter of 1788–1789]

Notes on the "Journal de Paris"

Extreme cold—hardships of the last months of 1788 and the first days of 1789. We see only depictions of misery and suffering in the first issues of this newspaper.

Interruption of work. On 13 January, the archbishop of Paris, in a pastoral letter, says: "think of so many poor families ruined by the interruption of work, think of the high cost of bread . . . the poor inhabitants of the countrysides whose priests do not know how to alleviate the most urgent needs . . ." [13 January, p. 57].

Thaw. The thaw does not finally come until around 15 January [24 January, p. 115].

Violence of the Freeze. Communication between Calais and Dover entirely interrupted by ice. All the ports closed because of ice. Around the coasts of England the sea frozen far out. The basin of the port of Marseille entirely frozen [15 January, p. 65]. The Rhone frozen from one end to the other, people cross by coach [24 January, p. 115]. Thirty-one December, −17.5 degrees Réaumur.

Little poems and New Year's gifts for the ladies . . . going on amidst the ice and hardship and tumult of the approaching Revolution. "Most minds, during the year 1788," says the issue of 1 January, "were turned towards subjects foreign to poetry" [p. 1]. This doesn't in the least prevent the newspaper from abounding in little poems throughout the whole month of January.

Floods. The disaster brings immense floods throughout the whole Loire valley [24 January, p. 111].

Regulation of 24 January 1789 for the elections. This regulation, which I have been looking for for a long time, is found here [6 February, pp. 163–64].

Financial privileges. Abandonment of these privileges. Unity of the orders in the elections. On many days one finds in this newspaper news of scenes of this kind: St. Jean D'Angely ([5 March, p.] 296); Mâconnais ([10 March, p.] 315; one finds among the secretaries who write up this retreat of the nobility the name of Lamartine); Clermont in Beauvaisis ([13 March, p.] 328); seneschalship of Lyon ([24 March, p.] 380); district of Chartres ([25 March, p.] 384); Berry ([26 March, p.] 388). The Duke of Charost speaking in the name of the nobility: "We say to you today in the name of the nobility what formerly M. de Mesmes said in the name of the Third Estate: We are all brothers. [. . .] In order to paint for you the sweet emotion that the members of our order felt when your deputies assured us of your fraternal feelings, we attest to you once again our fraternal feelings for you, and every occasion to assure you of them will be a new joy for us," Beauvais ([27 March, p.] 392); the seneschalship of Auvergne: "The annals of our history," says the transcript of the Third Estate, "do not present any more beautiful patriotic movement than that which the nobility led yesterday in the assembly of the Third Estate, which, in mingling all hearts, indestructibly inscribed all rights there. The generous abandonment of financial privileges was so much the more felt by the Commons as the aristocracy did not hide that wealth, unlike generosity, was not the fief of the old nobility of Auvergne" [19 March, p. 399]; Chaumont ([30 March, p.] 403); Villers-Cotterets, idem; district of Châtillon ([31 March, p.] 407).

A subscriber writes to the paper: "when your newspaper made the cries of love and fraternity raised among the three orders ring everywhere": district of Senlis ([1 April, p.] 411). District of Orléans ([3 April, p.] 423).

Vermandois ([4 April, p.] 427). 674,500 individuals in the district. *Spirit of the clergy.* An abbé le Duc, spokesman; the cathedral resounding with applause; he spoke of "that pure and sacred fire that was suffocated by a vile egoism [. . .] and that a new Lycurgus has rekindled. [. . .] O you whom general esteem is going to proclaim our representatives to the nation's *consistory* . . . may our property be sacred, our persons free . . ." (p. 427).

The nobility everywhere making little tables of the rights of man. District of Blois: the nobility says, "The purpose of all social institutions is to make as happy as possible" all citizens. "Happiness should not be reserved for a small number of men" ([5 April, p.] 431).

District of Mantes. The nobility agrees to pay all taxes, to accept the Third Estate alongside them in all jobs. Forez, 14 towns, 302 villages: scenes of fraternity. In order not to insult the nobility, the Third Estate does not ask for admission to jobs at all . . . The nobility asks on behalf of the Third Estate what the Third had had the delicacy not to ask for ([12 April, p.] 463).

District of Péronne ([14 April, p.] 471).

Special electoral rules for Paris. Found here [18 April] (p. 493). Dates: 28 March 1789, 13 April 1789. Electoral qualification: six livres in capital. Electoral division of Paris into sixty districts. Further, everyone can put anything which he thinks ought to be part of the cahier of the Third Estate in a book which is provided. A locked box in the great hall of the Hotel de Ville in which everyone can deposit daily all reports, projects for the cahiers [21 April] (p. 504).

Spirit of the Three Orders at the Elections. District of Château-Thierry (p. 503).

Famine of '89. The government sets the example of violent and arbitrary measures against the rich. A decree of the Council of 23 April 1789 in which the king invites the landowners and tenant farmers not to abuse the difficult circumstances. He invites them to use their claims moderately . . . He authorizes the intendants to force those who have wheat in their granaries to take it to market: authorizes home inspections as a result ([28 April, p.] 535).

Spirit of the Three Orders at the Elections. The clergy of Paris renounces its tax privileges ([29 April, p.] 539). The same for the nobility of Paris ([3 May, p.] 559).

Freedom of the Press. Censorship. 6 May 1789. Decree of the Council which maintains censorship for all periodicals ([8 May, p.] 584).

First Fumblings of the Third Estate. Inexperience of the Assemblies. In this newspaper, during the first eight days, we see the Third Estate meet in the chamber of the Estates-General, disperse, fumble, speak at random, thrown into extreme uncertainty and showing the greatest inexperience of assemblies ([20 May, p.] 635).

Tax privileges. Renunciation of privileges before the crisis. One after another we see first the chamber of the clergy (19 May) then that of the nobility (23 May) officially renounce their tax privileges as soon as they are constituted ([22 and 23 May, pp.] 643 and 649).

Public sessions. We see that from the beginning, two thousand spectators attend the meetings [4 June] (p. 699).

"Journal historique et politique de Genève": 1789

The passion which pushes towards unity uses the diversities of the Middle Ages as weapons. The town and community of Cahors ask that the province of Quercy have an assembly of estates separate from that of Rouergue. 9 December '88. Issue of 3 January '89 [p. 36].

Commercial Crisis. It is written in the newspaper, 31 December '88: "For several days I have been in the city of Lyon, I am struck by the decline of its trade and its manufactures" . . . Some of these effects are ascribed to the commercial treaty with England [3 January, p. 40].

Unprecedented hardship of the winter. The frost began on 24 November '88 and lasted without interruption until the beginning of January. The thermometer went down to 18 degrees Réaumur [10 January, pp. 106, 109].

Union of classes. On 26 January, the clergy, the nobility, and the Third Estate of the town of Châteauroux unanimously decree that they are in favor of the vote by head. The nobility and clergy solemnly renounce financial privileges. Issue of 7 March '89 [p. 33].

Tax privileges. Renunciation. Declaration of the nobility of Burgundy addressed to the lower classes: the nobility declares that it formally renounces all financial distinctions and commits itself to share all taxes present and future with them.

I think this declaration was preceded by a very lively struggle between the nobility and the bourgeoisie over the question of the doubling of the Third Estate. Thus, the declaration was made *to the people* [7 March, p. 37].

It was reported from Paris on 8 April '89: "In all the districts whose resolutions up to the present are known, the clergy and the nobility are united in the desire for an equality of taxation and for the cessation of financial exemptions" [11 April, pp. 79–80].

District of Caen.—The clergy renounces all tax privileges, the order of the nobility accepts "to bear taxes in perfect equality and everyone proportionate to his wealth" [7 March, pp. 83–84].

Idem, the order of the nobility of Colmar and Sélestat; the nobles of Provence possessing fiefs [18 April, p. 127].

Persistence in privilege. The nobles of the Generality of Alençon have a majority against. But the day after, the most *qualified* want to protest and the majority agrees that the issue be left up to the wisdom of the Estates-General [18 April, p. 127]. I see that a majority of the nobles of the district of Rouen persisted. But 107, at whose head I see the name of Blangy, protested that they never wanted to separate their status as gentlemen from that of citizen and that they asked for nothing but the most complete equality in matters of taxation [16 May, p. 140].

Examples of provocative measures taken by the government of the old regime with general approval. On 23 April '89, a decree of the Council which permits one to force landowners to bring their wheat to market; allows judges to verify how much wheat everyone possesses . . . This is preparation for the law of the maximum and all the tyrannical measures of the Convention [2 May, p. 30].

Paris elections. They expected to divide 6,000 nobles into 20 assemblies. There were only 900 of them.

It had been assumed that the 60 district assemblies of the Third Estate would have 60,000 members; the total did not exceed 12,000 [2 May, p. 33].

Financial privileges of the bourgeois. All the bourgeois of Paris possessing buildings in the suburbs were exempt from the taille for those buildings. M. Des Essarts, in one of the municipal assemblies, declared that he renounced this privilege. At once several bourgeois of Paris hurried to follow this example [2 May, p. 36]. I have not seen very many of these renunciations of privileges previously made by the bourgeois. Less frequent than for the nobles.

Debate of the Estates-General apropos of the verification of powers. I find a detailed journal of everything which happened at the opening of the Estates, the formal speeches made, by the king, by the chancellor, by M. Necker, the discussion about the verification . . . day by day in this newspaper starting from issue 18, p. 168.

[The Beginnings of the Constituent Assembly]

With Regard to the Election of the Constituent Assembly

Make clear how the attempt to reproduce the ancient Estates-General produced the most dangerous modern assembly which can be imagined. How a body was formed that was separate from all the great lay and ecclesiastical landowners, under the pretext of making separate chambers for them, how the Third Estate found itself forced to choose outside the ranks of landowners and among the ranks of lawyers. And then how the great landowners were set aside or only appeared in the assembly with a discredited mandate. It resulted from this that the power to make laws fell almost exclusively into the hands of those who did not have the conservative spirit that property gives, which had never been seen before and has never been seen since.

If, in principle, one had wanted to create only a single assembly where everyone could be elected, one must think that many noble or clerical landowners would have been elected in the countryside, which would have created a much less dangerous assembly.

Why the Constituent Assembly included more lawyers than had ever been found in any political assembly. It had been elected to represent one class alone and not a nation, and in that class there were still only a few landowners and furthermore political life existed only in the towns. The agricultural class invisible.

See if there are not as many lawyers, proportionally speaking, in the political assemblies of America, which would tend to make one think that the large number of lawyers comes from the constitution of democratic societies more than from any particular reason.

Struggle between the Orders before 14 July According to the Correspondence of the Deputies of the Commons of Anjou

This collection is composed of reports which were occasionally sent to Angers where they were printed. Among the deputies who wrote the reports are found Larevellière-Lepeaux (who then signed himself M. de Lepeaux) and Volney.

The king more popular among the Third Estate than among the other orders. At the king's entry during the Te Deum at Versailles on 4 May (during the procession): "at the monarch's arrival," says the correspondence, "an extraordinary cry of 'Long live the King' from the commons alone," repeated several times . . . (p. 13).

Vote in common, at least for the verification of powers, seems to follow from the chancellor's language. The chancellor finished by adjourning the three orders until the next day in the chamber of the Estates (p. 16). Check if this has meaning.

Perplexity, inexperience of the Third Estate at the first sessions. Although the same feeling then inspired all members, which in large assemblies is the most solid guarantee of order, the inexperience and novelty of the situation made the assembly a free-for-all during the first sessions; everyone spoke at once, people acted without any purpose, they didn't know what forms to follow, people did not know one another; the great talents had not yet taken leadership of the movement. Mounier was there called M. Mounier Dauphinois, M. Malouet de l'Auvergne, Barnave was called Barnabé, Robespierre, Robert-Pierre (p. 234). He was already admired but his exact name wasn't known (p. 27). On the other hand, men who would remain unknown afterwards were remarked upon at the beginning. The deputies of Anjou and Mirabeau in the *Courrier de Provence* (p. 4) note the great oratorical talents and beautiful speeches of a M. Populus, whose name I have not found in any biography.

Despite this the assembly already felt its omnipotence. Despite this confusion, the assembly is already all-powerful, by the unity of its feelings and the current of public opinion which supports it and which it feels beneath its feet.

The Tennis Court Oath in all minds, announced six weeks before it took place. On 9 May, the deputies of Anjou report to their constituents: we will employ for a few days "all means of conciliation capable of bringing the privileged orders to unite with the order of the Third Estate, and afterwards, having exhausted these means, we will constitute ourselves as the National Assembly" (p. 25).

Thus it was not the course of the struggle which pushed minds beyond the point where they intended to go. People wanted to go that far in advance, and everyone knew it.

These beginnings of an inexperienced assembly have something childish and weak about them. But what made it great, strong, and virtually irresistible in the midst of its fumblings was that people fumbled to find the path to follow, not to know where they wanted to go.

What ended up making the Third Estate irresistible was its isolation. This, which seems paradoxical, is strictly true. In all this first part [of the Revolution—Trans.] we see complete unity existing throughout the Third Estate; because class interest, class relations, similarity of position, the uniformity of past griefs, group discipline kept the most dissimilar minds firmly together and made them march in step, even the ones who later on would agree least about conduct and the goal to attain. People were still above all of their class before being of their [individual—Trans.] opinion. Isolation would have been a weakness if the class outside the assembly had been as weak. It was an immense strength in the circumstances of the times and after the changes which had taken place in society.

Taste for costumes. Futility of large, lazy assemblies. Mirabeau's opinion. In the midst of the most serious matters on 25 May, there was a deputy struck by the problem of participating in the meeting without special clothing, who wanted to have the assembly deliberate on this great subject. Mirabeau booed him and covered him with ridicule.

Scramble of men until a majority and a minority within the Third Estate had been sketched out. On 10 July we still see pell-mell in the commission chosen to present the king the threatening address that we know, Mirabeau, Robespierre, Barnave, Péthion, de Sèze, Tronchet . . .

Imperative mandates which hinder the members of the nobility most inclined to meet in common. I see (p. 358) [11 July] M. de Lafayette who seems to appear in the general assembly for the first time (at least I haven't seen his name among the minority of the nobility who had joined [the Third Estate—Trans.] before the king's letter). M. de Lafayette declares that his mandate does not allow him to vote, but that he can speak, and as a result he proposes the Declaration of the Rights of Man.

Orderly and disorderly character of the lower classes of Paris when rioting. The idea that they have become another people. A mirage which appears in every revolution. From 14 July, we see these traits appear. "In the midst of the tumult, those imprisoned for ordinary crimes were going to escape; the people opposed the escape, saying that criminals were not worthy of mingling with the creators of freedom . . . If, among the armed men, someone committed some baseness, he was immediately led to prison by his comrades" (p. 375) [13 July]. This is particular to our French lower classes.

One concludes from this: "We have been able to make some observations during these disorders which give reason to believe that a change has occurred in the part of the people known under the name of the populace, such that the love of freedom inspires it more than the love of license" [13 July, p. 375]. One still strongly perceives here the contempt of the upper classes for the lower classes, and recognizes the transition which is going to lead people to treat this same lower class *known under the name of the populace* as the most respectable power and the most legitimate representation of France.

Lafayette obscure during the period of struggle for the verification of powers. From the Assembly of Notables until 11 July we no longer see Lafayette's name appear. We know that he had been sent to the Estates-General as a deputy of the nobility with an imperative mandate against the vote in common. During the struggle over the verification of powers we do not see that he stood out among the dissidents within the nobility. He does not appear in the protest made by the minority of that body. On [. . .] we do not see his name among those nobles who joined the Third Estate before being forced by the king. In the first meetings, he is

among those who declare themselves able to speak, but not to vote. Only
on 11 July do we see him appear to present a project for the Declaration
of the Rights of Man, which immediately makes him prominent. On 15
July he is chosen to go to Paris at the head of a deputation of forty members to bring the good words of the king and to reestablish public peace.
He speaks at the Hôtel de Ville in the name of this deputation and he is
elected colonel-general of the National Guard by acclamation.

How success and being carried away hid the horror of crimes. The first
time that the deputies report to their constituents the murder of M. de
Launay, they call this frightening news ([p.] 377). The day after, describing how M. Bailly has been named mayor, they add laconically: in place
of M. de Flesselles, "punished with death the day before for the crime of
treason" ([16 July, p.] 390).

Administrative anarchy in Paris after 14 July.

Day-by-day Account of the Struggle According to the
Correspondence of the Deputies of Anjou

Different phases of the struggle. Correspondence of the deputies of Anjou.
At first people met without knowing what to do, without even wanting to
give themselves a provisional government. Some wanted to limit themselves to being good neighbors; others wanted signs of life to be given by
inviting the other orders to meet. One ended by asking for conferences
and by naming commissioners to take part in them (19 May).

26 May. This conference led to nothing. The clergy showed only more
tendency to look for an expedient and arrive at a compromise.

28 May. (Thus three weeks have passed before the king tries to intervene.) The king wants the conferences to be repeated in the presence of
guards and commissioners whom he will name. In the letter that he writes
regarding this to the chamber of the Third, he calls the Estates-General
the National Assembly that I have summoned, an expression which entered (doubtless involuntarily) into the idea that the Third Estate had already put forward: that there was only one assembly and not three (p. 64).

The nobility and the clergy accept eagerly. There was long debate in
the chamber of the Third before agreeing and at the same time a deputation to the king was adopted.

These new conferences went on for a long time without leading anywhere. For eight days the Third asked for an audience from the king without being given one.

Independently of the great fundamental dispute, the nobility pecked at the Third Estate over trifles. The nobility contests the name of *commons,* it does not want to sign the transcripts of the sessions.

3 June. On this day, Bailly is named doyen (people did not want to say president because it was felt that the assembly had not been constituted).

5 June. I see in the account of this day: "a member renewed the motion made so many times to constitute ourselves as the National Assembly" (p. 103).

This goal was present in all minds and constantly pointed at by impatient minds; but we see that up to the present the assembly hesitated to take this extreme measure and recoiled when it was a question of definitively engaging in the route which led to it.

5 June. This day M. Necker, in the king's name, proposes a compromise to the commissioners of the three orders:

1) That each order verify the powers of its members.
2) That in case of dispute commissioners of the three orders be called.
3) That if these cannot agree the king will pronounce.

The clergy agrees entirely, the nobility with reservations.

6 June. Commissioners from the Third Estate are finally received by the king. This conference is spent in compliments. Speaking to the king, the Third Estate calls itself the commons, and the king responds: the representatives of the Third Estate.

8 June. Malouet formally proposes that they constitute themselves as the *representatives of the commons,* refuses to go so far as to constitute a National Assembly.

10 June. The conferences continue without any chance of result. Sieyès proposes to declare that there is no longer anything to discuss, to send to ask the other two orders one last time to join the commons in the common hall during the day. Otherwise things will proceed without them, while leaving them the ability to come take their place when they wish.

12 June. The Third Estate, after having this day made its last appeal to the nobility and the clergy, remains in session waiting for them until nine o'clock at night. Then the roll is called for the absent clergy and nobility, and then they proceed to call the roll of the Third Estate.

13 June. Arrival of three curates of Poitou coming individually to verify their powers. The one who speaks in their name says: "We come, preceded by the torch of reason, led by love of the public good, to place ourselves beside our fellow citizens" (we see that these curates were more of their time than of their church). Received with applause. It is the stone which detaches itself from the arch.

14 June. Several other curates present themselves.

15 June. The powers of the deputies present having been verified, Sieyès makes an oath to declare themselves the *assembly of the verified deputies of the nation,* and to start legislative work, without any veto by another order being able to stop them.

Long discussion to decide what title to take.

This continues on the sixteenth. In the evening when people want to come to a vote, sixty or eighty opponents violently demand postponement until the next day. Already in this session speakers participate in a violent manner. One calls those who want adjournment *traitors.* A member of the minority makes an address to the spectators without being able to make himself heard (p. 168). After several hours of tumult, adjournment is pronounced. Thus, even amidst the isolated Third Estate, there was a minority, if not very numerous at least very determined, which would have allowed the other two orders, even with the common vote, to balance the victory or at least to slow the movement and absorb it.

17 June. It is on this day that the assembly decisively constitutes itself as the *National Assembly* by 491 votes to 90. This phrase, so natural, "national assembly," furnished by an obscure deputy; Sieyès and Mounier had not found it. Barely constituted, the Assembly names its executive committee, retaining the existing members, and decides to provisionally authorize the levy of taxes, declaring that they can no longer be levied if it is dissolved.

Next they adjourn for two days until Friday the nineteenth.

This seems like a great mistake at such a critical moment.

But their opponents do not profit from this.

19 June. Session entirely taken up by internal arrangements. As if they had the most incontestable existence and despite a letter from the king which spoke only of the three orders and the Third Estate.

Meeting of the clergy. On the same day, this decisive event took place: the chamber of the clergy decided by 148 votes to 137 that they should unite with the Third Estate in the common hall. Although several bishops were among the 148, the motion was carried by the curates. Also the public cried out: "Long live the good curates" (p. 180). More than a thousand coaches from Paris were waiting for the decision. This act of the clergy made the king's opposition, already so late, very difficult.

20 June. Tennis Court Session. The deputies find the doors locked, meet in the Tennis Court, and swear never to separate; they adjourn until the following Monday. Again the government lets a day go by without an assembly.

We know that the closure of the room had as pretext and perhaps for cause (since one had to do with such miserable minds), a royal session which was supposed to be held and required preparations. One cannot imagine a smaller and more maladroitly chosen entrance for one of the greatest accidents of history. The body's wounded vanity was added to all the other passions which already inspired it. Also, we see only *one* opponent to the Tennis Court Oath, even though the assembly was extremely numerous.

22 June. Same attitude by power, a mixture of incomplete violence and disdain. The assembly again presents itself in vain at the doors of the common hall. The Tennis Court is judged too small. The Church of the Friars is refused by the monks. The assembly so to speak *wanders* around Versailles, until it takes refuge in the Church of St. Louis. It is there that the 150 members of the clergy, with some bishops at their head, come to join the Third by virtue of the decision taken by the order on 17 June. Nothing better shows the irresistible movement of the moment than to see these curates and bishops not even wait until the incident is settled, the announced royal session held, and go to the common hall despite the royal proclamation that all meetings should be suspended.

Moreover, one should remember that the habit of considering the king's will nonexistent and continuing to assemble when he had ordered separation was a habit of long standing with the parlements, and for a year had become, with impunity, the habit of everyone and all groups, nobles, provincial assemblies (see Dauphiny). The only difference, what causes the glance of history to stop here, is the greatness of the theater and the immensity of the consequences. At the same session at the Church of St. Louis two deputies from the nobility arrive. As early as 18 or 19 June a considerable minority had protested against the majority that wanted to remain apart.

23 June. Royal session where the king annuls everything which has taken place, as if it were a question of a decree of the parlement and of a *lit de justice.* He leaves ordering that everyone separate immediately. The nobility and some of the clergy leave. The Third Estate remains.

It is then that the Marquis de Brézé comes and that Mirabeau says, according to the correspondence ([p.] 209): "The assembly has decided not to disperse unless constrained by force." The assembly adjourns after having declared that it persists in its preceding decrees and having voted that its members were legally inviolable.

Constitution of the Estates-General made late. In this session the king gives a real constitution to the Estates-General and a program of operations to follow. If this had been done two months before, it is certain that things would have gone along this path for a while, and the inevitable Revolution, I think, would have been produced a little differently, and without the fiery impetuosity which was imprinted on it by the premature class struggle.

24, 25, and 26 June. The royal power, ardently contested, had recourse to mischief-making, to parliamentary tricks: the deputies were allowed to enter the common hall, but the doors which led to the other orders were closed and above all foreign spectators were excluded ([pp.] 230ff.). The assembly, irritated and excited and not struck down by these light pressures by authority, more and more took the attitude of master. It objected violently to these constraints. It threatened to move elsewhere. Despite the king's order, the majority of the clergy came to join them. A minority of the nobility presented itself.

The assembly appeared in public, calmed the lower classes of Versailles through commissioners, received in its midst and let itself be harangued by the deputies of the voters of Paris, made ovations to M. Necker, who publicly thanked it.

Every minute some dissident deputies of the nobility and the clergy arrived individually.

27 June. The minority of the nobility and the clergy which up to then had publicly adhered to what the king had ordered in the session of 23 June were required by the king to violate his order and go to the assembly, which they did with poor grace on the twenty-seventh. They are treated as brothers, despite their defeated attitude, and the lower classes make great cries of joy. Intoxication of the lower classes. The French guards dance in the courtyard of Versailles ([p.] 255). Illuminations, fireworks.

From 30 June to 8 July. The assembly receives addresses, enters into direct communication with petitioners who receive the honors of the session; it intervenes with the king in favor of the French guards liberated by the people of Paris whom the assembly blames very gently. It allows M. de Clermont-Tonnerre to say that all its members are an integral part of the sovereign . . . For the rest, it mostly takes internal measures, but no great action.

8 July. Motion by Mirabeau who, interrupting the agenda, asks for an address and a deputation to the king against the approach of troops.

9 July. Plan of the address, written and presented by Mirabeau, received with transports of joy by the great majority of the assembly, says the correspondence ([p.] 313). This address, which is [publicized—Trans.] everywhere, takes the haughtiest and even the most threatening tone.

On the same day Mounier, in the name of the committee on the order of work, presents a work program and a constitution that must be read to get an idea of the theoretical and inexperienced character of this great revolution. Mounier, who was one of the most prudent and the most experienced of the assembly, deduced a plan of work in which all the parts follow one another absolutely like a thesis in philosophy. All government must have for its sole purpose the maintenance of the rights of men . . . from which it follows that they must first of all be defined in an abstract way . . . then . . . (p. 319).

10 July. The day passes in choosing the members charged to bear the address and in the verifications of powers.

11 July. Saturday—The king's response, brief and dry. He refuses to withdraw the troops and threatens to move the Estates-General to Noyon or Soissons.

The assembly cannot arrive at any conclusion on a new measure to take and, to keep itself busy, has some debate over internal regulations.

M. de Lafayette proposes a plan for a Declaration of the Rights of Man which receives lively applause.

12 July. Sunday, at nine o'clock in the morning, Necker's dismissal is learned of. Deputies assemble around six in the evening, but in such small numbers that no decision can be taken.

13 July. The next day the assembly meets. The events of Paris unfold. Some deputations of voters arrive. A deputation is sent to the king to offer to send sixty deputies to Paris to reestablish order and promise the withdrawal of the troops. Dry and somewhat disdainful response by the king: your presence at Paris would not do any good.

The assembly replies by *unanimously* declaring that the present ministers and advisers of the king, whoever they are, are responsible for the evils which are going to occur.

Troops continue to arrive at Versailles.

Quasi-unanimity of resistance at this time in the National Assembly. Growing confidence of the Assembly at the greatest moment of crisis. What is striking in this correspondence is to what degree there still persisted the current which in 1788 had led all the orders to resist. We still see hardly any opposition show itself in the National Assembly, the strongest measures are taken unanimously; the names of the future victors and vanquished are mixed. Even more, the correspondence says that nobles who until then had been dissidents came to join the National Assembly: "in a few more days," write the deputies, "the Assembly will only be inspired by a single spirit, at least in the principal object" (p. 374).

We see in fact, on 16 July, all the nobles and priests who up to then had attended without voting declare that in these circumstances they think they ought to go beyond the narrow theory of the mandate. When, on 16 July, the Assembly snubs the parlement, all the dukes and peers and members of the parlement, even D'Eprémesnil, like Duport, vote with the Assembly.

What again is very striking is the confidence of this assembly which grows even during the crisis itself, at the time when it seems most threatened; "events are more sad than desperate," write the deputies (13 July, p. 372). The idea that the Revolution is inevitable, whatever the evolution of the struggle, is universal: "the constitution will be made, or we will be no more," says Clermont-Tonnerre. "The revolution will be made even if we are no more," adds Lafayette [p. 374]. "We are persuaded of this truth," write the deputies. And what gives them this belief in part are the new adhesions of dissidents brought by the gravity of the situation (p. 374).

15 July. The king comes in person, on foot, into the National Assembly to which he has just surrendered; he calls it, for the first time, not the Estates-General but the National Assembly. This speech, moreover, is touching and by that saves the situation from shame.

The king himself invites the Assembly to act as intermediary between the government and Paris. The Assembly names a deputation of forty members to go to Paris. In this deputation are found Bailly and Lafayette. Lafayette speaks at the Hôtel de Ville and is elected by acclamation colonel-general of the militias. Bailly is elected mayor in the same way.

The Assembly immediately becomes the government. The Assembly, even before 14 July, already took the attitude of a government. It received deputations, people sent it a multitude of addresses in which it was treated as such. After 14 July, it fully assumes executive power; it is the Assembly that Lafayette and Bailly ask for permission to accept, the latter the position of mayor, the former that of colonel-general of the militias (p. 391). The Assembly asks for the dismissal of ministers and (what is still more executive) the nomination of M. Necker. Marshal de Broglie announces to it that the army is withdrawing. Finally, the king charges the Assembly to recall M. Necker. From this moment on the Assembly sits almost without interruption, night sessions becoming the rule.

The nobles and the priests who have not yet voted declare themselves ready to do so. 16 July. All the members of the nobility and the clergy who had attended the sessions without voting, because they were hindered by the imperative mandate, declare that they are ready to vote. Declaration followed by great applause (p. 394).

The parlement treated as a secondary power by the Assembly. This same day, the sixteenth, the parlement having charged its first president to go in person to the king and thank him for all that he had done for the reestablishment of order, and to *inform* the National Assembly how much its conduct was approved, the Assembly disdainfully responds that it would have been more touched by this compliment if the first president had come to make it in person (p. 396).

17 July. The Assembly, although in session, does nothing, a large part of the Assembly having followed the king to Paris, rather more as a safeguard than as an honor (p. 398).

The habits of the monarchy facilitating these usurpations by the Assembly. None of the things the Assembly did were novelties, their roots were found in old habits which had prepared minds for them. Thus, only a few assemblies had been permitted, but in those which were allowed, such as those of the judicial bodies or the estates . . . it was the habit to speak in the presence of the public, to give audiences, to receive addresses, to use exaggerated language, to act within an unclear limitation of duties and to constantly intermingle powers; it is only the result produced by all this that is new. For those who saw the present and did not know the future, the acts of the Assembly did not appear as unusual and as revolutionary as they do to us; many things which have since become infallible signs of revolution did not yet have that character. All the assemblies of estates had, for example, received deputations, addresses, and been in direct communication with the public.

The Assembly suddenly completing, after 14 July, becoming the government, the sovereign. All the great bodies come in person to render it their homage; the Court of Finance (21 July), the Tax Court, that of Accounts, the Grand Council which is made to speak standing ([p.] 414) finally the parlement comes to pay the homage of their feelings of respect and admiration (p. 471).

The parlement had done the same thing at Troyes, a year before, and would have also substituted itself for the sovereign, if it had been able to do so like the National Assembly.

The Assembly writes directly to M. Necker to beg him to return ([p.] 412). It sends delegates to act in localities, for example to calm the lower classes at Saint-Germain and to save some unfortunates ([p.] 413).

Classical anachronism. In these circumstances, it was proposed as early as July, following the Roman example, to award a civic crown to members who had saved a poor devil, which was accepted by acclamation. Note that this crown was given to a bishop ([p.] 414).

Perplexity, slackness of the Assembly in the presence of anarchy and popular crimes—20 July and the days following. The Assembly, victorious with the aid of the lower classes, finds itself unusually embarrassed and weak when faced with the crimes of the same lower classes. Even amid their greatest excesses the Assembly spares the irregular forces which have just saved it. We see the Assembly wasting its time counting ballots, receiving deputations and addresses, debating question of rules, while all around it the lower classes are cutting off people's heads and lynching. The horrible murders of Foulon and of Bertier de Sauvigny cannot even *reach* it.

The Assembly wants to limit the fire and is afraid to extinguish it: "The movement of fiery passions must be tempered, without suffocating a *salutary upheaval.*" These instructions sent by the deputies of Anjou to their constituents ([p.] 427) show the very bottom of their hearts.

It is only on the twenty-third that Lally-Tollendal proposes to make a timid address to the people to recommend moderation to them. Even this address waits several days without being able to come to a vote. All words which announce vigor are taken out of it. Mirabeau and Barnave want to eliminate it. It is then that the latter pronounces the famous words: "this blood . . ." which afterwards made him so unhappy.

On 25 July no vote had been taken on it. The volume stops here. This is the greatest fault, one could say the great crime of the Constituent Assembly; from this day on it was destined to obey and not to command; the lower classes of Paris became the sovereign. Power had only spent a moment with the Assembly before passing to them. The Assembly had immense moral authority, it seemed unanimous, it influenced the nation on all sides; if it had felt its strength and its weight, it would have simultaneously opposed royalty and the lower classes and kept the direction of the Revolution in its hands. Assuredly the majority wanted to, but it lacked the clear view of the consequences of events that is given by the experience of popular revolutions, and the sureness of hand given by long practical political experience. It lacked organized and disciplined forces like the very class which it represented, and did not at all resemble that English parliament of 1688 which, at the same time as it deposed King James, forbade the lower classes to discuss questions before it had decided on them itself, which made a revolution and did not permit riots.

[General Remarks]

Show well and highlight this first Revolution of Paris, the model of all others. The same mechanism, the same procedures: the middle classes heat up, excite, put in motion the lower classes, support them morally, and push them further than the middle classes want to go.

What would be very important to know is what was going on in the councils of the king and the court from the opening of the Estates-General until 14 July. Afterwards, the external movement controlled everything. But at this time much depended on what happened at court. Where is this side of the question explained? It should be in some memoirs. But which?

There must be many interesting memoirs about this decisive moment, among others those of M. Necker.

CHAPTER TWO

[From the Fourteenth of July to the End of the Constituent Assembly]

Plan of the Chapter (December '57)

How it was suddenly discovered for the first time that Paris was master of France—the fall of the Bastille (1).

How the nobility suddenly realized that it was only an officer-corps without an army—the uprising of the rural lower classes after the taking of the Bastille (2).

What the Principles of '89 Are (3)

1. Slide over the quarrel among the orders, although its details are little known, in order to get to the taking of the Bastille, not to tell the story but to show what is announced in the chapter heading. For contemporaries, it was the victory of the Revolution of '89. For us, who see the event from seventy years further on, it is the first actual manifestation of the dictatorship of Paris, already established in mores and governmental habits; a dictatorship that is the mother of revolutions to come.

Try to find in government correspondence some facts which show the *passivity* of the provinces before Paris rose.

2. If possible have all kinds of administrative details on this point. But where and how? Everything was already so disorganized in the provinces and the government that I do not know who made reports and to whom.

3. Examine the Constituent Assembly's whole system of laws, bringing out this double character: liberalism, democracy, which will bring me bitterly back to the present.

[The Taking of the Bastille]

[Notes on the Pamphlets in the Bibliothèque Nationale, May 1858]

The king does not guard Paris and refuses to allow the bourgeoisie there to arm themselves as in all other towns. This follows from the response made by the king to the National Assembly on 13 July. The situation Paris had been allowed to reach is truly astonishing. Paint it well. Show how 14 July was over before it started, the revolution finished before breaking out. [. . .]

Generous and thoughtful characteristics among some good-for-nothings. This, which is seen so often in all our great popular movements, is well illustrated at the taking of the Bastille: I see some pamphlets which tell how these same French guards who had just been won over with wine, girls, and promises of all sorts, refused all kinds of cash payment and a higher salary. Our whole revolution is full of these emotions which suddenly raise men above their level and let them fall back a moment later. [. . .]

Violence and ferocity of language which follows victory. Among others I find a pamphlet, written by the lower classes themselves, entitled "The Hunt for Stinking, Ferocious Beasts." This pamphlet asks that the queen, the princes of the blood, and a large number of men and women of the court or who hold public office, named individually, that this one's head be cut off, that one be strangled, this one sent to a convent for ex-whores, another be hung and strangled . . . almost always death or the galleys. If this was a joke never has a more atrocious one been made, and one more characteristic of what was going to follow. I think that nothing parallel has ever been written and read in another revolution, and I note that this state of extreme fury followed a very easy victory, one which had not been preceded by any violence. In the pamphlets full of savage fury which then appear, I note that the clergy is attacked with still more rage than the nobility, even though the majority of the clergy had joined the Third Estate.

Unique insensitivity of the educated classes towards the first horrors. It is not only these horrible writers who speak of the first cruelties of 14 July with insensitivity. I read some pamphlets where nothing is spoken of but the union of citizens, concord, love for the king, true political idylls in which is found the following, speaking of M. de Launay: he suffered the punishment which he deserved and he paid for what he owed with his head. Speaking of M. de Flesselles: the head of this monster, carried through all the streets of the capital, has intimidated the scoundrels who might be tempted to imitate him. There must have been something in this old regime, so mild and gallant, which prepared these atrocious mores. Seek it out. [...]

Absence of political feeling. A revolution with a popular character cannot establish anything permanent. I find nothing of this feeling. There are aristocrats who are struck with terror and fury by the event. There are their enemies who are full of admiration and enthusiasm. I do not see any political intellect who, while wanting to profit from the event, sees its consequences, and realizes that the revolution, thus amputated and delivered to the popular masses of a great city, is a blind and unknown force (a new fact in modern history) which no one can govern. Nothing of those English of 1688, keeping London quiet with the same hand that overthrew James II.

Enthusiasm for the king half real, half fake. The usual spectacle during revolutions. In the pamphlets which teem after 14 July, many still breathe fury against the king's advisors and the aristocracy. But none attack the king himself and most are overflowing ["overflowing" in English in the original—Trans.] with expressions of love, when on 17 July the king appears in Paris without a guard. For those who have experience of people's temperament during a revolution, it is easy to see here a base of tender feelings left by the traditions of the monarchy (however a base already very eroded, there was little support left), combined with that passion which suddenly turns parties towards love for the men who agree with their momentary views and interests. It is a passion which in revolutionary times very often creates illusions in those who are its object, who persuade themselves that it is they whom the crowd really adores, while in reality the crowd only adores its own ideas, for which by chance you are momentarily the instrument.

Good account of the taking of the Bastille. The best account of the event that I have found is in an anonymous pamphlet published three days after the event and titled "Paris Saved; or, Detailed Account of the

Events Which Have Taken Place at Paris from Sunday, 12 July, until the Following Friday" (thirty-four pages). [. . .] The Bastille taken, Paris remained in the greatest uncertainty until the next day, without any government, believing that at any moment the royal army was going to attack. It was then, says the author, that people had the idea of pulling up the cobblestones and began to do it [p. 20].

Cowardice of the defeated.

On Wednesday morning people learned of the retreat of the troops, the king's approach to the Assembly, and the Assembly's deputation to Paris with Bailly and Lafayette at its head. People then turned to joy and confidence. Bailly was named mayor by acclamation and Lafayette captain-general [p. 16].

We see then, as always since, the cowardice of the defeated. The archbishop of Paris singing a Te Deum at Notre Dame over the still-warm corpses of the officers and cavalry who had been massacred. The clergy has always acted like this. They support governments while compromising them. If they fall, they sing the Te Deum for their conquerors.

It is remarkable that during all this anarchy and this abandonment of Paris, the parlement, still in existence, is as if dead. Not only doesn't it do anything but no one seems to think about it any more, even to attack it. It is dead.

Bloody temperament. A pamphlet titled "National Judgment" (a few days after the taking of the Bastille), where the princes who have emigrated are condemned, as well as a crowd of other persons, including some women, not only to death, but to tortures terrifying by their horror or their cruelty, worthy of the imagination of the sepoys. It is only a joke but how atrocious! And what might men who found pleasure in writing and even in reading such horrors do?

Imagination prepared by the tortures of the old regime. Further, all this is nothing but a more horrible imitation of the tortures of the old regime, and nothing shows better the influence of punishments on mores.

Almost immediately after the victory, the lower ranks of the army murmur against the upper. How the moderates set alight the fury. I see in a speech given by the abbé Fauchet, 31 August '89, in the Church of Sainte Marguerite in the presence of the workers of the Faubourg St. Antoine, that he complains that they are beginning to distrust their leaders, Bailly and Lafayette. The evident purpose of this speech is to persuade the workers to stay calm and use only legal means. But in order to give himself the necessary authority and make himself listened to, he begins by speaking language more inflamed and more hateful than anyone, without realizing that it is his fury and not his moderation which is communicated.

Interesting application of political jargon to religion. Jesus Christ is nothing but the divinity as fellow-citizen of the human race," says Abbé Fauchet. [. . .]

The upper bourgeoisie at first takes control of the movement. Hatred for government by one's neighbor. French vanity. What then makes ranks and military uniforms desirable above all. I see from several pamphlets published about the National Guard in August '89:

1) People complain that the rich bourgeois have managed to become all the officers, which seems to many people an unbearable aristocracy.

2) I see also with what ardor people sought these ranks. It seems that the new officers make a point of never being out of uniform or without their swords, even when they are not on duty, which was understandable at the time, when the sword and the epaulet were a privilege no one had yet tasted.

Free and civilian mores of Paris before the Revolution. The Revolution made military mores predominate throughout the continent. I see in one of these brochures that up until then it had been against custom to show oneself in uniform in Paris (as today in London). A general, says the brochure, would have blushed to show his uniform in Paris. What would the author say today!

Famine. The great incident due to general causes. I see from a pamphlet of 16 August that the most intense famine continued to reign in the environs of Paris, that the richest inhabitants of Versailles found it difficult to get their daily bread.

Unemployment, second great incident due to the same causes. I read in a pamphlet of August '89, I think, entitled "Letter from the People to M. Necker on the High Cost of Bread": "One speaks of the frightening hardships and famine which crush the suburbs of the capital above all, half of whose inhabitants have been out of work for a long time" [p. 5].

National workshops. It seems that the unemployed workers wandering around Paris and its surroundings had been gathered in the Montmartre area in order to engage in or pretend to engage in work, according to the law. I find in a pamphlet titled "Patriotic Measures of M. Lafayette with Regard to the Workers of Montmartre" that on 15 August '89, M. de Lafayette went among them to require those of them who were not from Paris to return to their homes and to threaten the others with the National Guard if they did not keep in order [p. 5].

He tells them that there are eighteen thousand of them. "Can one see without pain," he says, "that people leave the plow for work as useless as that of Montmartre which consists only of scratching the earth?" [p. 3].

Notes Taken from the Manuscript in the Imperial Library

The manuscript contains:

Certain parts of the correspondence of Bailly with M. Necker and others in 1789 and 1790, 1791 (1); and between Bailly and M. de Lafayette and M. de Gouvion (2).

Excerpt from the register of deliberations of the City Council since 8 October 1789 (3). This is the provisional council elected by the assembly of the commune in October 1789 and replaced by the permanent Council in August 1790. This Council had itself been preceded by an assembly of voters meeting spontaneously in July '89.

Excerpt from the register of deliberations of the City Bureau (4).

[1.] Correspondence of Bailly and Lafayette

Feeding of Paris. Famine. We see from the letters that Bailly writes to M. Necker and M. Necker to Bailly that at the beginning of August '89 nothing was less certain than the feeding of Paris; people there lived from day to day, at the mercy of small shipments which were often halted or detoured en route.

In order to get some wagons of grain, which people needed to survive, to the Paris market, on 20 August '89 we see M. Necker using a detachment of bailiffs commanded by a young prosecutor's clerk.

Universal anarchy. I see from a letter from Bailly (14 September) that the municipality of Troyes wants to have some works made in the Seine destroyed, in return for allowing trains of wood to go to Paris. These works were accused of harming local industries. Bailly cries out at the injustice of the proceedings and asks Necker to intercede. [. . .]

Hardship of Paris. 1 October '89, letter from Bailly to Necker: "I cannot picture for you the astonishing number of unfortunates who besiege us. Everything at Paris is in a state of idleness which makes one shudder. Most of the workers of this great city are reduced to complete inactivity. Everything presages a fate still more frightening for the winter because it strikes the poorest class . . ." He asks for charity workshops for eight thousand persons to be established.

Classical references in the secret correspondence. 13 November '89. We see Bailly, apropos of a man from Poissy who had saved a miller whom people wanted to hang, speak of the civic crown which would have been awarded in the good old days of Roman freedom. "Will we do less than the Romans?" This not in an official speech but in secret government correspondence. [. . .]

[2.] Correspondence of Bailly with M. Gouvion,
Major-General of the National Guard

Anarchy. Absence of power, of public security in Paris and its environs. It seems to result from all this correspondence that after the return of the king to Paris on 6 October '89, and the installation of the Constituent Assembly, there is a certain calm in Paris, despite the food shortage and the stagnation of commerce (but I am still not sure). The National Guard is in its first élan and it substitutes for the absence of a really obedient public security force. It furnishes detachments of cavalry to reestablish order far away. But, from the middle of 1790 until the middle of 1791, when the correspondence ceases, we see that every day there are fears of mobs, or else mobs to disperse or warn. Bailly and M. de Gouvion spend their time informing each other of seditious plans to forestall, acts of violence to repress. Contraband can no longer be forbidden, nor persons effectively protected; the Assembly itself is often afraid. Everything causes agitation, everything leads to violence. I do not see a single day which gives the idea of a society that is settled or even in the course of settling down. We see that the government no longer exists, and what is a marvel is that such a state could last for so long in the midst of a city where so many passions, so many hardships, so many vices and no real public security force are to be found. It must have been based on a fear of armed force which the mob still had. [. . .]

Charity workshops. We see in this correspondence the role, less than in 1848 but still very great, that the national workshops, then called more simply charity workshops, play in all the trouble. Gouvion shows uneasiness when people want to dissolve them in May 1791.

[3.] Excerpt from the Register of the City Council; Government
of Paris; City Council from 8 October '89 [. . .]

The bickerings of vanity amidst these great passions, a legacy from the old regime. I have already described above the violent warning given the honest Bailly because he wanted to review the National Guard by himself. This time (23 June 1790) it is the City Council which is indignant because not it, but the representatives of the commune, will preside over the fireworks of St. Jean, and it declares that it will not participate. See the dignity and pride well employed in such times!

Habits of the old monarchy contributing to revolutionary disorder. We see that inhabitants of the various quarters of Paris who have requests to make name deputies who are received by the municipal council. A great element of disorder that comes from the most orderly period of the monarchy. In the same way the Paris sections have several matters to settle as a deliberative assembly before they name the members of the municipal council. Also habits from the monarchy.

Control of the government after 14 July at first belongs to the moderates. The municipal body provisionally named by the sixty districts whose transcripts I am studying at this moment does not seem to me to have any violent revolutionary impulse. It seems to me to be composed of wealthy members of the bourgeoisie, very preoccupied with petty concerns of precedence like their predecessors.

They make very lively complaints against the intolerable license of the press and urgently solicit the National Assembly to make a law to regulate it.

Emotion caused by the ceremonies of the Federation. Mirage of concord. 14 July 1790. At the time of the Federation the transcripts are full of all kinds of testimonies, motions, speeches, which show the moment's extreme emotion and the effort everybody made to persuade themselves that there were no longer any divisions, that it was only a matter of embracing one another tenderly. Emotion in large part real, in part false, born from disturbed hearts and not from a calm understanding of the situation, which, after all, seemed to announce that the Revolution rather than being finished was going to *rush ahead.*

The Federation was for the union of the bourgeoisie and the lower classes what the election of '89 had been for the nobility and the bourgeoisie. [. . .]

Paris without a government, even when the Revolution was declared over. The king and the Assembly, and later the municipal administration, had established certain reserved platforms for ticket holders in the Champ de Mars. On the eve there was an uprising against this arrangement *contrary to equality;* the authorities of the sections had the criers proclaim that no attention would be paid to tickets, and the municipal assembly meeting in haste on the evening of the thirteenth declared in effect that the tickets were canceled and that the platform would be for everyone. [. . .]

Organization of the provisional municipality of Paris from August '89 to August '90.

I see that it was composed of three chief mechanisms:

1. *The Assembly of the Representatives of the Commune,* composed of 180 members, a body improvised, I think, in July 1789, which in certain cases exercised the highest local legislative power.

2. *The City Council,* composed of 60 members, including the heads of all the chief services. This is the municipal government proper.

3. Then finally the *City Bureau,* a sort of executive power composed of 20 members elected by the City Council and chosen from its members. [...] I see it occupied with details of execution and several purposes which are more like regulations, such as setting salaries, for example.

[4.] Excerpt from the Registers of the City Bureau [...]

The government of the city after 14 July belongs to the leading bourgeois and the moderates. The most emotional matters, those which could arouse popular passions, are only rarely discussed here. There is little discussion about the question of subsistence, the chief problem of the moment, nor even of the details of the police, the most delicate point of government.

The spirit of the body seems very moderate. One senses here rather the bourgeoisie which prepared the Revolution than the mores of the lower classes which made it. The upper classes are spoken of with respect here; people are extremely in favor of religious things (this outward respect by the well-mannered classes was shown even when they had ceased to be believers), thus one maintained an almoner charged with saying mass for the government every Sunday, who needed the fee for his masses in order to live. But after him, the position was to be eliminated. The same for the shows during Holy Week: the mayor can authorize them, but with a large portion of the receipts for the poor and only if the spectators ask him ...

Another trait which shows that it is the bourgeoisie of the old regime which governs is the bickering and susceptibility vis-à-vis the other bodies which make up the municipal government and the assembly of the commune; between the latter and the city bureau there is a quarrel which fails to lead to much.

The lower classes continue to remain the master of affairs. This is clearly seen among other things with regard to the demolition of the Bastille. The town had given the work to some contractors to do. The simple workers employed up until then disliked this bidding-out and agitated: given, says the transcript of the City Bureau, that riots should be prevented rather than repressed ... they seized a pretext to cancel the bidding and gave in to the workers.

[2. Uprising of the Rural Lower Classes]

Notes Taken from the Registers of the Minister of the Royal Household in 1789 (April 1858)

Famine. Its political effects. As time passes the agitation caused by the famine increases. Not only are there upheavals and riots in a hundred different places, but everywhere the inhabitants join together, whether to procure grain or forbid the export of grain, or to repress riots, or defend themselves from brigands. A flock of little irregular governments is formed alongside the general government. Great preparation for so many headquarters of revolutionary forces when 14 July transformed the subsistence crisis into a political crisis. [. . .]

Poitou. Brittany. What is striking in all the documents of this time is that the seeds of the special attitude of the western provinces are not to be found. Rather they seem, even the peasants, more advanced in the Revolution than all the others. The class war there seems more complete, people refuse to pay the tithe in the diocese of Léon. The same thing manifests itself in a lot of other places, says the minister. [. . .]

Anarchy. One constantly sees municipal officials stripped of their offices by the population and replaced. Some municipal officials have the correspondence of a subdelegate with the intendant sent to them, and only pass it on after having read it. In a thousand places there are upheavals under one pretext or another, troubles over grain, tumultuous attacks against houses or individuals. No precise direction, the tumultuous movements of an unsettled society. The old powers discredited or destroyed. The old governing classes half disarmed. The new ones not firmly in power; the old regime almost uprooted, still holding on by a finger, the new not yet established. Paint well this first moment of the Revolution, when the National Assembly had already destroyed the existing government or allowed it to be destroyed, without having yet rebuilt it. [. . .]

Paralysis of the nobility. In all this correspondence I see one or two attempts by provincial nobility to deliberate and protest, but so feeble and so aborted that one can say that there is not the least resolute attempt anywhere. Strange spectacle of death having preceded the fall.

Notes Made about a Folder Titled "Pays d'État," Various Subjects (Archives, April '58)

Riot at Lyon. 4 July '89. This riot began on 4 July '89, at the announcement of the Tennis Court Oath and the combining of the orders, I think.

At first, universal joy. Then, disorder of an almost entirely *interested* character, that is to say tollgates burnt, sales-tax registers destroyed, wine and all kinds of goods brought in by force without paying any tax.

No garrison: one sends to the surrounding garrisons to look for some soldiers, one appeals for volunteers: twelve hundred young men or knights of St. Louis appear; they are armed. They reestablish order. The lower classes abashed, seeing the Third Estate in arms against them, when they thought they would only have to fight the nobility.

The riot came chiefly from outside and was made by peasants.

We see that the means to calm the peasants was to write the curates so that they would read proclamations in the sermon.

From which we see:

1. To what degree the countrysides were without government and without political leaders.

2. How people were still in their old routines, wanting to use the forces of the old regime to calm the effervescence against that same old regime.

Famine, hardship, despair of the environs of Paris. War on wild game. The subdelegate of Enghien to the intendant (Bertier) of the Île-de-France: the hail of 13 July has completely destroyed the grain and wine harvests. The high price of bread, the food shortage have driven the peasant's heart to despair, as a consequence of which there is no one to hire labor. The lords and bourgeois, obliged to conserve their income, cannot hire anyone. There are therefore no resources, and the starving lower classes see no other means of subsistence than to look for all kinds of ways, even illegal ones, to find something to eat for the moment and to get rid of the rabbits which take a portion of their harvest . . . They ask that we give them bread or that we let them kill the rabbits.

Highlight this incident of the food shortage coming to crown the peasant's isolated and miserable situation.

Violent repression, amidst the most extreme weakness. In general one let things go or almost. I see in other places, chiefly in the distant provinces, some very summary death sentences combined with this enervation of authority: the remains of old habits. This seems to have very little effect, whether on those who order them, or on the fellows of those who suffer them, equally because of tradition. We understand the habit of killing, coming naturally from such a mild monarchy. [. . .]

Provincial troubles after the taking of the Bastille. '89: an effort by the bourgeoisie against those above and below.

The intendant of Champagne to M. de Saint-Priest, minister of the Royal Household: "[. . .] the extreme upheaval which began in my generality the very instant the news of the Revolution of Paris was spread. The uprising is general, in almost every town." . . . There follow numerous accounts of riots, in general all the establishments for indirect taxes are sacked, the registers burned, the agents mistreated . . .

"There is only, I think, one means of preventing many further misfortunes: the immediate establishment of a bourgeois militia composed of citizens of all orders and from which all journeymen and workers must indispensably be excluded."

We see in this piece and in many others of the same time that the lower classes often rise up against the bourgeois, and make the bourgeois very afraid. We see, in this first phase of the Revolution, the bourgeoisie making a great effort against those above and those below simultaneously.
[. . .]

Correspondence of the Deputies of Anjou: Attitude of the Provinces to 14 July 1789

We see that even before knowing the events at Paris, resistance was starting to be organized in the provinces. We read (pp. 329ff.) that in various towns of Anjou, Laval, Saumur, Angers, there are town assemblies, the formation of national guards. The inhabitants of Pont-de-Cé occupy the bridge militarily. Two thousand workers of the slate quarries put themselves at the disposal of the patriots of Angers. It is only after four days, on the eighteenth, that the events of the fourteenth are known there.

At *Grenoble,* on 15 July, before knowing the events of Paris, a meeting of people from all orders; an address to the Assembly full of revolutionary energy, signed at the head by clergy, nobles, more than three thousand persons ([p.] 402).

At Lyon, on learning of the departure of M. Necker, and upon the impact of the agitation of Paris, an assembly of all orders took place on 17 July. There people formally adhered to the National Assembly, and agreed that if it was dissolved they would not pay taxes. This is signed, among others, by the canons, counts of Lyon [p. 429].

But the majority of these movements and these urban agitations only began after people knew of the beginning, if not the end, of the insurrection at Paris. Note this well.

Some of the privileged still take part in the first effort at resistance. We read in a letter written by the deputies of Anjou (21 July; [p.] 427): "The people see with satisfaction some persons of quality joining with them in their patrols. Not only the honest bourgeois, but also men distinguished by their titles, their rank, and their birth, have asked for and accepted positions in the new militias."

Paint well this last dying effort of the great movement of the *whole* nation against despotism in '88.

[3. What the Principles of '89 Are]: Notes Taken on the "Journal des Débats et Décrets"

[1.] From 14 July until 6 October

The Assembly immediately seizes the government and takes the king's place. 20 July. A member [Freteau] says that "when an individual presents himself before the National Assembly, he appears before his legislators, and ought to have an attitude which expresses respect, . . . but that the great bodies which represent the king deserve *some* more regard" *[p. 223]*.

The Assembly's indignation against the crimes of the losers, contrasting with its indifference towards the crimes of the winners. The Assembly, which had remained cold during the slaughters in Paris, burst into flame when it was *furiously* informed that a councilor of the Parlement of Dijon had set off an explosion at the château de Quincey. The Assembly (session of 25 July, p. 254) orders its president to go to the king to testify to him to the horror and indignation with which it has been seized in learning of a crime so horrible, and demands action and tortures.

Note that at the same time, the Assembly heard the account of the horrors of which that same province was the theater, château burnings, etc. . . .

Report on the cahiers made to the Assembly on 27 July (p. 269). This report made by the Count of Clermont-Tonnerre includes only a very incomplete and pretty poor analysis of the cahiers. This is nevertheless interesting, because official.

Essentially decentralizing character of this first moment. "As for governing bodies or provincial bodies," says the report, "*all* the cahiers ask you for their establishment" (p. 272).

Violation of the privacy of letters pointed out with extreme severity. All object with indignation, says the reporter (p. 273), "against the violation of the privacy of the post, one of the most absurd and most infamous inventions of despotism."

The English obliged to disavow fomenting troubles. Letters from Lord Dorset, 26 July, containing an energetic denial (p. 284).

Provincial troubles after 14 July. 29 July. M. de Toulongeon says to the Assembly: [The town of—Trans.] Vesoul has been taken, three abbeys destroyed, eleven châteaux ruined . . ." (p. 295).

Apotheosis of M. Necker so close to his fall. Idem [29 July]: "M. Necker was announced," says the transcript, "and an attentive silence was replaced by a tumult of joy. He appeared . . . , he entered amidst long applause . . ." (p. 313).

Bourgeoisie of Paris as dominated by the lower classes as they had been by the king. Profiting from a moment of enthusiasm provoked by the return of M. Necker, the electors of the Hôtel de Ville decree a general amnesty, but the lower classes who do not wish to be deprived of their vengeance immediately begin agitation so formidable that the electors are obliged to withdraw their decree and excuse it. They had been all-powerful in pushing the lower classes to the attack, they are powerless to organize the victory (p. 329).

Discussion of the question of whether there will be a Declaration of Rights. Three days of discussion. Fifty-six orators listed, speeches written like treatises of abstract philosophy. 1 August: some bishops, several great lords speak in favor of a Declaration of Rights. The opposition, obscure men, often give excellent reasons (p. 341). It is proposed to say *duties* and rights. Refused (p. 354).

Inexperience of the Assembly. Ridiculous means it imagines to repress speakers' wordiness. 1 August—A speaker [Bouche] proposes to fix at five minutes the time during which one can speak, and this ridiculous motion is debated long after it has been rejected [pp. 345–46].

Night of 4 August. We see that the first cause of this memorable session was the almost universal uprising of the peasants against the châteaux. The event was the combined product, in proportions impossible to measure, of fear and enthusiasm; people were swept along by fear down the current of opinions which were at the base of every heart, even those of the privileged.

There is the cause, here is the occasion: on 3 August, prompted by the account of disorders, the Assembly decided on a proclamation "for the conservation and respect of property" (p. 351).

On the evening of the fourth, the committee charged with putting on paper the Assembly's idea proposed, by the voice of Target, a draft proclamation which declared that the old laws continued to exist and had to be respected until they were abolished, that taxes had to continue to be paid in the old way, that all customary payments in money and kind had to continue until ordered otherwise. Nothing yet announced the tempest of disinterest which was going to arise.

All the rest of the session has only the nobility and clergy as actors, the Third Estate remaining in the position of a chorus, supporting the actors with the shouts various emotions aroused from it.

It is the Viscount de Noailles who begins; correctly attributing the cause of the disorders to the passion of the lower classes against their material burdens, he proposes to immediately declare absolute equality of taxation, the redemption of all feudal dues, the abolition without payment of corvées and other personal servitudes.

He indicates the difference noted above, which at that time and ever afterwards remained the character of the Revolution: it was the *towns* which demanded a constitution; the *rural districts* demanded only the elimination of taxes and the lightening of feudal dues ([p.] 359).

The Duke d'Aiguillon supports the motion (p. 362).

The motion is welcomed with transports of inexpressible joy, says the transcript.

The bishop of Nancy proposes that this be applied to ecclesiastical property, the bishop of Chartres renounces hunting rights. "A multitude of voices was raised," says the transcript; "they came from the gentlemen of the nobility, uniting to consummate this renunciation immediately" (p. 365).

"All the clergy united and rose to join in, such a mass of applause and expressions of gratitude came from the commons that deliberations remained suspended for some time" (ibid.).

Some curates want to sacrifice their fees ([p.] 366; ibid.).

The Duke of Châtelet proposes the redemption of tithes, M. de Saint-Fargeau wants all decisions to take effect retroactive to 1 January '89.

The signs of emotional transport and the effusions of generous feeling in the Assembly become more lively and more inspired from hour to hour.

The archbishop of Aix asks for laws which will henceforth forbid any contractual clause having this [feudal—Trans.] character. There followed a moment of exhaustion. People no longer knew what was left to sacrifice.

Then the movement, which had upraised souls, also pushed them impetuously towards another point. See one after another all the deputies who come to sacrifice all provincial privileges, they push each other, they follow each other; people cut off their speeches in order to surrender their constituents' rights faster. They can't get to the podium quickly enough to submit their renunciations, they push each other, they cut each other off, they almost use force in order to get to the podium, which is like a place besieged.

The archbishop of Paris asks that a Te Deum be ordered and people leave at two in the morning. I do not think that in all history there has ever been anything more extraordinary than this scene, nor any single circumstance in which the French character was so highlighted.

Universal disorder. 7 August. The king's ministers come to officially announce that *order and the public peace are disturbed in almost all parts of the kingdom (p. 392). Properties are violated, incendiary hands have ravaged citizens' homes, the forms of justice are ignored and replaced by proscription.*

National workshops in Paris. Same day. M. Necker says to the Assembly: We have established special workshops around Paris, uniquely in order to give work to those who lack it. The number amounted to twelve thousand men who were paid twenty sous a day (p. 396).

Tithes merely declared redeemable during the night of 4 August, entirely abolished by surprise. During the night of 4 August, there had been no discussion of ecclesiastical property, and tithes had only been declared redeemable. Since people had strictly followed the principle that the final decree, which would give legislative form to the precipitate resolutions of that night, would not change anything except for editorial changes, one might think ecclesiastical property for the moment safe, and at least the principle of the tax represented by the tithe saved. But on 8 August, when the pressing needs of the treasury and the necessity of a loan to cover the daily deficit were shown by M. Necker, the Marquis de Lacoste (one of the men who make themselves much spoken of during the first moments of a Revolution, and then entirely disappear from the eyes of history), suddenly declared that the property of the clergy belonged entirely to the nation, and proposed eliminating the tithe ([p.] 406). This first idea had no results.

10 August. The question is taken up again, but only with regard to tithes. It is on this day that Sieyès makes a speech which I think is indisputable (p. 425), where he shows that eliminating the tithe instead of only declaring it redeemable is very simply to make a free gift to the big landowners. He calls on the principle, so strongly maintained by the majority against later regrets, that no one could go back on principles accepted during the night of 4 August in the final decree. But the principle, maintained by the passions of the majority, no longer stopped that majority when they were hindered by it.

11 August. Nothing was decided after Sieyès's speech. The affair ended that day with a scene of generosity, but one which this time has the air of being a little forced. First some curates, then, in the name of all the clergy, the archbishop of Paris, renounce tithes without any indemnity. In a sense they had just been summoned to do so (p. 428).

11 August. Drafting and final vote on the resolution of the night of 4 August (p. 432).

This decree, which completes the top-to-bottom overthrow of the old social and political constitution, is not even submitted for the king's approval; it was only brought to him in order for him to participate in the Te Deum with the Assembly. This does not prevent the decree from giving the king the title of Restorer of French Freedom (p. 444).

Declaration of the Rights of Man. A Declaration of the Rights of Man had already been proposed by M. de Lafayette, from before 14 July. Then another, I think, by Mounier.

13 August. A committee of five is named in order to prepare this declaration: the bishop of Langres, Tronchet, and Mirabeau, then two unknowns.

17 August. Mirabeau makes this report in their name (p. 453); the declaration is still more metaphysical and antilegislative than other versions. The Assembly spends almost two weeks (all France being in the most frightful anarchy and the public coffers empty) losing itself in the detour of this political metaphysics, in the midst of indescribably confused discussion. No one knowing what angle from which to take up the question, what to put in, what to take out from these abstract principles; one version is piled on another . . . The whole with very brilliant rhetoric, the subject uniquely lending itself to that and being, furthermore, marvelously adapted to the particular spirit of the times.

What must be well noted is to what degree this declaration established *freedom* still more than equality. Which shows well how the character of '89 is liberal, whatever the servants and the Cousins of today say about it [Tocqueville is referring to Victor Cousin (1792–1867), French philosopher and political thinker, and those of his ilk—Trans.].

18 August. Mirabeau's practical mind, from the second day on, makes an effort to get back to business. He proposes to put the writing after the constitution (p. 475); but he cannot carry the Assembly, which votes for a loan of eighty million in an hour, then plunges back into its cherished abstract theories.

It must not be concealed that it is through these discussions, which seem useless to us, that the Revolution entered the minds of the rest of the world, and that people worked to make the event European, not French. An idea half expressed by Mirabeau in his report (p. 457).

Destruction and reorganization of all the old judicial powers. Cold funeral oration for the parlements. Right in the middle of the interminable discussions on the abstract rights of man, the constitutional committee presents the section of its work on the judicial system (p. 457). It is the absolute, radical destruction of *all* existing authorities without exception, at the very moment when social links are being completely destroyed. Furthermore, the plan contains nothing but principles. They are the principles which have been followed since, except that the reaction against the judge went so far as to take the power of *interpretation* away from him, a strange sight in a country where judges had just made the Revolution.

"The nation has not forgotten," says this report (p. 464), "what is owed to the parlements: they alone resisted tyranny; they alone defended the nation's rights. We owe them gratitude; but it is not gratitude we can concern ourselves with to regenerate an empire. [. . .] Our judiciary was well constituted to resist despotism, but despotism no longer exists. This form of judiciary is therefore no longer necessary."

Interesting reasoning, given what we have seen so often since, and still see!

The Assembly so bold in theory troubled and hesitant as soon as Paris is spoken of. 31 August. Insurrectional movements in Paris are announced to the Assembly. The Assembly is asked to take measures, when the latest letters announce the reestablishment of calm. The Assembly refuses to deliberate (p. 552).

Troubles in Paris. The idea of the expedition of 6 October as early as August. 30 August. Sunday, 30 August, revolutionary motions had already been made at the Palais-Royal with regard to the veto. Heads got hot, "and that portion of the lower classes whose work does not allow time for thought was pushed to take the road to Versailles." They were only prevented because the roads which led there were militarily occupied by the National Guard ([vol. 2,] no. 3, p. 2).

The veto defended by Mirabeau. 1 September. It is in this session that Mirabeau argued as a statesman, in one of his most beautiful speeches, the thesis that the king's intervention in the making of laws is a necessary element, introduced in the people's interest and not the king's (no. 5, p. 5).

The Assembly, carried away, orders the printing [of this speech— Trans.], a measure which it cancels the next day.

Two-chamber system in the constitutional plan presented by the committee. We see that this idea of two chambers, although with very little support in the first moment which followed the struggle between the orders, managed however, thanks to Mounier and the manner in which the first constitutional committee had been composed, to reach the Assembly as a draft. Rejected, it is true, on 10 September by an immense majority: 89 to 849, 122 declaring that they have not heard the question (no. 17, p. 3).

Patriotic foolishness. 7 September. Some virtuous female citizens of Paris present themselves before the Assembly, are admitted and placed on stools at the barrier in order to offer their jewelry to the nation, no. 13, p. 5.

A little nine-year-old girl offers a gold chain and a gold thimble to the nation. The Assembly accepts with emotion (no. 26, p. 1). We find here, says the journal, the generous sacrifices that Roman ladies came to offer the Senate . . . *[no. 13]*.

All this foolishness being in conformity with the French mind of the times, and being born (ridiculous product) of real and deep passions, it produces great effects on minds and thus merits being judged seriously from the particular point of view of the times.

The suspensive veto accepted in principle. 11 September. It is on this day that the Assembly declared by a great majority that the king would have a veto and, by 673 to 325, that it would only be suspensive (no. 19, p. 4). The consequence of the veto, that is the question of how long it would be suspensive for, was only decided later.

How this discussion and several other causes prepared and brought about the insurrection of 5 October. This discussion about the veto, which went on for a long time, both on the tribune and in the press, with great publicity and great impact, profoundly influenced people. It affected all passions, since all the reforms that one might wish or fear could depend on the greater or lesser powerlessness of royal authority.

Other causes came to join it. The king's responses with regard to all the political and social reforms of the night of 4 August were ambiguous and full of restrictions. But above all the ferment of the lower classes of Paris, hungry, without work, miserable, already used to upheavals, in the hands of vicious leaders, and confident of their strength.

After 14 July, but above all after 6 October, we can say that the Assembly was no longer mistress of itself and that it governed and legislated under the more or less hidden tutelage of the people of Paris. The Assembly only acted when simultaneously *supported* and *dominated* by them; *supported* and *dominated,* words which contain the whole picture to be drawn.

Constitutional committee, not always the same. It seems that the constitutional committee changed every month. To the one which had proposed two chambers there succeeded, on 15 September (no. 24, p. 1) a committee composed of Sieyès, Target, Talleyrand, Rabaud-Saint-Etienne; [Le] Chapelier . . .

First arguments by the king about the reforms of 4 August, sensible and serious, but dangerous. Sanction for the decrees of 4 August had not yet been given. The Assembly had been aroused by this and had asked the king for a response. His first response, read at the session of 18 September (no. 29, p. 1) contained some observations and, regarding the tithes, some very sensible objections. The response seemed sincere, but could make people fear that the king wanted to go back on the reforms of 4 August. In such a matter, when one has allowed oneself to be brought to the brink of such a ditch, the most prudent course is to jump it all at once and without hesitation, and only afterwards to look for one's path.

The tithe, its official assessment. Effect of its destruction.

In this response the king assesses the tithe at sixty to eighty million a year. He notes, as Sieyès had already done, that to purely and simply abolish it means to give a gift of sixty or eighty million more in revenue to the owners of the land (no. 29, p. 3).

21 September. The king's second response, which gives its sanction with some reservations (no. 33, p. 2).

4 October. Third letter from the king. This one no longer seems sincere. It no longer seems to come from him, it seems to indicate all kinds of mental reservations of an alarming nature. It refuses to respond to the Declaration of the Rights of Man.

Horrible financial decline. 24 September. Report read by M. Necker to the session of this day where he draws a very alarming picture of the effects of the loss of credit and its reaction on commerce. There remain only 8 million in the treasury for the month of October.

Character of all revolutions, even those most in accord with the general wish, and least contested. The law which makes business prosper is so opposed to the effects of revolutions that even a revolution like that of '89, which was made with almost universal agreement, which almost the whole nation considered the source of all good, which took place almost without effort, without a change of sovereign, without a general convulsion, even such a revolution immediately dries up all the sources of trade and industry.

First idea of the division into departments. 29 September. We see the idea for this division appear in a plan by the constitutional committee for electoral districts only. It was a question of dividing France into eighty equal parts for voting purposes. Absolutely like American territories. This electoral territory was a department, the department was then an electoral district, just as today's electoral arrondissement is often different from the administrative arrondissement (no. 45, p. 1).

Address to the king by Mirabeau. 2 October (no. 51, p. 4). The Assembly sends an address to the king. Mirabeau writes it and gets applauded for what he says about the monarch's virtues; "feeling and truth," says the journal, "respectively gave it appeal and simultaneously touched the heart and the mind."

2. From 6 October to . . .

The growing storm at Paris has no echo in the Assembly. As early as 30 August the lower classes of Paris had wanted to move on Versailles. During the whole month of September, the discussion about the constitution, the unchained license of the press, above all the hardship and famine of Paris, so well described in Bailly and Lafayette's manuscript, prepared for the successful return of this plan. Only the combined effort of the *triumphant middle class* and the Assembly could have had a chance to stop it. As soon as the king, through his letter full of reticence about the reforms already made, and the demonstrations of the court, as impotent as they were hostile, made the middle class and the Assembly fear for their conquests, the compressed spring expanded without obstacle and the *journée* of 6 October took place. It was an event where one saw, as on 14 July, but much better, the middle classes and the Assembly simultaneously *supported* and *dominated* by the lower classes of Paris, who were called on or not rejected as defenders, and at the same time submitted to as masters.

No echo of the outside situation and the real passions of the moment are seen in the Assembly before 5 October. I have already noted this: until this day, one would have said an Assembly sure of itself and occupied solely with general affairs, or rather a society of philosophers dissertating on the principles of government.

The king's response of 4 October, which reached the Assembly on the fifth, finally aroused in it a great echo of the reaction outside. This response (no. 55, p. 2), combined above all with the banquet of the royal bodyguard, was in fact of a nature to excite the gravest suspicions. But the fear of what the king could do was excessive.

Mirabeau impetuously returns to his role of tribune as in the month of July. It is in this session of 5 October that Mirabeau makes that little speech, so violent, where he offers to denounce all the plots, if it is only declared that the person of the king is sacred (no. 55, p. 6).

In the discussion about the constitution we have seen that Mirabeau had shown himself more conservative than his party, whether because he hoped to become minister, or because his political genius overcame the passions and interest of the moment. His words about the necessity of the monarchy and the veto remain. But at the approach of 6 October, whether because he saw that the king had escaped from him and he was above all afraid for the Revolution, or because the torrent of revolutionary passions carried him away, we find him the same man who in July had shown himself past master of that revolutionary genius which consists of choosing the moment and the form most apt to raise storms.

The session ended with a vote which asked the king for his pure and simple assent to the Rights of Man (ibid., p. 7).

Night of 5 to 6 October. Read the notes I have made on the pamphlet by Mounier, who presided, about the disturbed and passive attitude of the Assembly during this night.

The Assembly, on the morning of the sixth, declares that it will follow the king to Paris. This decision was taken on Barnave's motion (no. 56, p. 3). This measure simultaneously completed the triumph and servitude of the Assembly.

This event one of the most unfortunate of the Revolution. I do not know if during the whole Revolution there was an event more fatal than that of 6 October; it was, it is true, easy to foresee. But this does not lessen the regret it must cause.

It completed the destruction of royal authority and put the Assembly into dependence on the lower classes of Paris, who had become the great political engine; it happened contrary to the wishes of the majority of the Assembly and of the country, perhaps *the first example* of this which was going to be seen so often. The horrible circumstances which accompanied it aggravated still more the basic fact.

The Assembly remained at Versailles for a fairly long time after the king's departure. Even though the Assembly had decreed that it would follow the king to Paris, various obstacles, above all the difficulty of finding a convenient meeting place, prevented it from leaving Versailles for a long time.

On 9 October the king officially recalled it to Paris (no. 60, p. 6).

A large number of deputies leave the Assembly. The transcripts state that a large number of deputies asked for their passports on one pretext or another. This kind of *desertion,* as those who stayed called it, alarmed the Assembly, which took measures to recall those who fled (no. 70, p. 1).

19 October. It is only on this day that the Assembly established itself at Paris, provisionally at first in the bishop's palace (no. 71, p. 1).

First direct attack made against the clergy's property by the bishop of Autun. It was during those ten days when the Assembly remained at Versailles that M. de Talleyrand gave form to what was floating in all minds and constantly came back in discussions: he proposed to use all the clergy's property for paying the state's debts (no. 62, p. 2 [10 October]).

Property of the clergy, its evaluation. He evaluates it at 150 million of income in bonds, 80 million in tithes, 70 million in real estate. He proposes to give the clergy a salary, from the 150 in bonds, of 100 million. The sale of the clergy's real estate ought to produce 2,100,000,000 calculated at thirty times the annual payment.

The Assembly completes its own servitude by remaining silent about the crimes of 6 October. Nothing more shameful in the Constituent Assembly's whole life than the cowardice with which that Assembly submitted. Its great majority was critical of what had just happened, and had not been less violated and humiliated than royalty by the event, but it silently passed over the crimes which had just been committed under its eyes and in part against [it].

The Assembly created to fight the king and the aristocracy, not the lower classes. The truth is that this Assembly had been created to resist the king, not the lower classes, and that in such a matter the feeling that presides over the birth of a political body dominates its entire life.

Martial law: first effort to halt the lower classes' violence. 21 October. It is only on 21 October that the Assembly, without referring to the past, takes a first step against the excesses of the lower classes by declaring martial law (no. 73, p. 11).

Upheaval at Paris during the whole month of October, the Assembly visibly terrified. This follows from all the discussions; their tone is troubled, hasty, and fearful.

Mounier, "Influence Attributed to the Philosophes . . .
on the Revolution" (1801, Tübingen)

The chief subject is the search for the immediate causes of the revolution. [. . .]

Mirabeau—his portrait. "He often told me his real opinions, and I have never known a man of a more enlightened mind, of a more judicious political doctrine, of a character more venal and of a heart more corrupt" (p. 101). Excellent in its simplicity. Worthy of a great painter.

A lot of revolutionaries moderates at the beginning. A large majority of the Assembly. "At the beginning," he says, "the voluntary or involuntary agents of anarchy did not number eighty in an assembly of eight or nine hundred persons" (p. 100).

He next cites many proper names of people whom he knew personally: *Barnave; Rabaud-Saint-Etienne,* very moderate and accused of being too moderate, moved into the violent party; *Thouret,* very moderate, Bailly, mild, timid and moderate, coming to the National Assembly with a draft constitution which left all sovereign power in the king's hands; *Barère* in a periodical essay showed very moderate principles; *Roland de La Platière,* before being such a zealous republican, had admired the Pope's government ("Italian Voyage," p. 105). Is this Mme. Roland's husband? Get the "Voyage."

All this interesting piece shows well what I have seen so many times in assemblies and what must be well painted: how in a few instants men are inspired, changed, transformed when they move from isolated struggles to common action, some voluntarily from interest, fear . . . a great number involuntarily, as the result of a sudden sympathetic excitement which surprises them, inspires them, and carries them along.

The Revolution could have been avoided by the union of Louis XVI with the plebeian element. Mounier is of the opinion that if Louis XVI, before the taking of the Bastille, had based himself frankly on the majority of the National Assembly, he would have prevailed over the nobility and the clergy, would have made himself followed by part of those two orders, and would have found sufficient support in the Assembly among all the people who were sensible and interested in order (p. 99).

A disposition to agree after the union of the orders and before the fall of the Bastille. Mounier affirms positively that this existed. "The majority of those who prepared the vicious constitution of 1791 were, before the taking of the Bastille, disposed to sign a general pacification" (p. 104). [. . .]

The Revolution avoidable, even after the Tennis Court Oath, according to Mounier. "Although the different classes had been allowed to mutually embitter each other, and their hatred and defiance had been excited with so much imprudence, the union of the three orders in a single assembly produced joy and general reconciliation, and the most distinguished men more than ever had moderate views" (p. 110). [. . .]

Severe judgment on the National Assembly by Mounier. After the taking of the Bastille, "the majority of the Assembly, dominated by a minority of the factious and the enthusiasts, and the cowardly men who joined out of fear of them, was forced to accept the justification of all the crimes" (page 111).

After 6 October, "my presence was useless in an Assembly where fear most often determined the majority of votes, which had become an instrument in the hands of a few imprudent or fanatical men" (page 114).

It should be well noted that Mounier, having deserted the Assembly at this period, was made more for tranquil times and to serve an established free government than for times of revolution, and is interested in saying that people there were no longer free.

1789: Pamphlets after 14 July

Mounier—"Considerations on Governments and in Particular on the Government Suitable for France"

This pamphlet was written, I think, between 14 July and 6 October, that is after victory had made the two parties which the Third Estate really contained appear, the one which wanted to push the Revolution to its ultimate limits, and the one which wanted to contain and stop it.

As soon as the lower classes enter the scene, the whole spirit of the political world changes. We see clearly that the arrival of the lower classes entirely changes the aspect of the political world: not only does it make the two parties of which I have just spoken appear, who would have more or less appeared without it, but it changes the relationship of these two parties; carrying one further than they wished to go, dominating them while pushing them; immediately giving the other not only inferiority, but the feeling of defeat, and suddenly making the Revolution something other than what it had been up to then.

In Mounier's tone there already reigns profound discouragement. He complains that after having been thought bold up to then, he appeared weak. I think, in fact, that he continued to want what France had wanted and still wanted, but a new force from then on was stronger than its representatives and than France itself.

Liberal spirit of the beginning. "The French people wants freedom." It is by this sentence, which he considered an incontestable axiom, that the pamphlet [begins]. Who would not have believed it then!

Danger of popular dictatorship already seen very clearly. It is already clear that the danger is no longer for freedom, but for royalty. What we can see in this pamphlet above all is how the inexperience of lower-class movements was suddenly overcome in many minds; although people had seen only the opening scenes which preceded, accompanied, and followed the taking of the Bastille, Mounier already speaks of popular dictatorship as he might have two years later.

Ignorance of the conditions of power in those very people who had most theorized about it. In this pamphlet, where the author's chief purpose is to prove the necessity of a strong executive power and to show the means of making it such, he removes even the proposal of laws, leaving only the veto (p. 29).

Mounier a declared supporter of two chambers, but only after the Estates-General. As if the single assembly from which he so justly see dangers as the legislative body was not still more dangerous as a constituent body! It is true that the violence of a single chamber, directed by a single passion, alone could make reforms as great and as destructive of the nobility and the clergy as those which everyone wanted, even Mounier. The error was to have imagined that in acting so quickly, in doing everything at once, in ignoring time, in not taking into account anything that was established, the same force that had helped you do these things was not your master, and that such changes could be made by discussion alone (p. 41).

The English constitution out of style. "A little while ago we professed the most extravagant admiration for the English constitution. Today we claim to despise it" [p. 37].

Mounier favorable to a hereditary peerage. Mounier realizes with rare perspicacity the advantages for freedom of heredity, and he has the courage to show them. But considering this cause as lost, he proposes, at least, a senate elected every six years by the provincial assemblies.

"Defence of M. Mounier's Conduct" [by Mounier—Trans.]

This pamphlet was written in Dauphiny after the author's return, that is at the end of October 1789.

Paris suddenly become a republic governing France. "I did not resist the feeling of joy in contemplating the triumph of freedom in the capital, and the destruction of the Bastille . . ." (in fact there is a writing by him, written at that time, which testifies to these feelings). "How much those feelings would have been mingled with bitterness if I had been able to foresee then . . . that all the old laws, all the institutions which protect public security, would suddenly be overthrown before they had been replaced by new laws. That Paris would become a republic, having an army completely at its command, disposing of the income from the taxes at its will, and of all that had previously been ruled by the government" (p. 15).

The fact that Paris dominated the Revolution from then on gave a new turn to all events, new interests, new passions, new views to all men, from the first making France something like the Roman world in the last days of the Republic, when an entire vast empire did nothing but follow the slightest movements of a single city.

Mirabeau's charlatanism. Mounier states, and I believe him without difficulty, that Mirabeau in his "Courrier de Provence" [his newspaper—Trans.] arranged and sometimes significantly changed the speeches that he had really made. It was probably in imitation of this example that Lamartine acted in the same way (p. 18).

Weakness of the Assembly. The Assembly put in servitude by the same blow as the king. Mounier rightly says that after 14 July, amid universal anarchy, if the Assembly had wanted to remain its own mistress it ought "to have promptly declared that all the old laws continued to remain in force and the courts in action, and asked the king to make them respected with all the forces at his disposal." But the Assembly was already no longer its own mistress, nor the real leader of events (p. 20).

Custom which dates from that time of putting one's name on a list to speak. Mounier already deplores that one puts oneself on the list several days in advance, that people only make major speeches (page 25).

Servitude of the Assembly. On 1 August, M. Thouret having been elected president, this nomination was violently attacked at the Palais-Royal; threats were made: M. Thouret offered his resignation and the Assembly accepted it (p. 27).

Oppression of thought in Paris. Mounier tells about wanting to print a speech that he had made in the Assembly on 5 September, against anarchy and the concentration of all powers; the printer to whom he went in Paris refused to print it for fear of the lower classes (p. 46).

Shameful servitude of the Assembly to the fishwives on the night of 5 to 6 October. During this night a troop of women and some miserable scoundrels who accompanied them entered the Assembly, mingled with the deputies, and forced them to withdraw. Mounier, who as president had been delayed with the king, returned and found a fishwife in his chair and others on the benches. He was obliged to speak at length with these jokers, to buy them some bread; "they told me to be very careful or I'd be strung up" (p. 75).

What assembly would ever have been able to lead a revolution after having been subjected to such scenes? Every assembly obeys the idea for which it was created. The Constituent Assembly of '89 had been sent to fight the aristocracy and despotism, it was full of vigor against those, but

[not] against anarchy, against which it was not prepared to struggle. On the other hand the Constituent Assembly of 1848, which was assuredly far inferior in all things to its predecessor, having been elected specifically to fight anarchy, acted much more bravely and more effectively in this part of its task. It was also *violated,* but it returned arms in hand and thus found in the event a cause of strength and not of [weakness]. It is rare that a man and almost impossible that an assembly can alternately make violent efforts in opposite directions. The spring that pushed it violently in one direction softened it in the other.

Abandonment of the king by the Assembly during the journées *of October.* A simultaneous lack of elevation and prudence. Useless effort by Mounier to lead it to the king. Review everything he says on this point, where he is the chief witness, if I want to paint this moment and this mistake (p. 83).

[General Remarks]

The French Revolution was made by virtue of general theories closely linked with each other and forming a single body of doctrine, a sort of political gospel where each principle resembled a dogma. The goal that was proposed inspired the French not only with enthusiasm, but to proselytize and make propaganda. Its doctrines were not only believed by them, but ardently preached, an entirely new thing in history.

* * *

Look in the debris of chapter seven (how spirits . . .) [How for a Moment, When the National Assembly Was About to Meet, Hearts Were Joined and Spirits Raised—Trans.] Set aside everything which was intended to show how at the beginning of the Revolution people wanted to make a society not only democratic, but free; not a military society, but a civil society. How people who would like to claim that this great movement of the Revolution had to end up in a kind of Roman society (in decline) minus domestic slavery, a small copy of the immense and detestable Roman Empire . . . And keep it for the chapter titled: What Should be Called the Ideas of '89.

* * *

Democracy. Democratic institutions. Various meanings of these words. Confusion which results from this.

What confuses the mind most is the use we make of these words: *democracy, democratic institutions, democratic government.* As long as we do not succeed in defining them clearly and agreeing on the definition, we will live in an inextricable confusion of ideas, to the great profit of demagogues and despots:

Some will say that a country governed by an absolute ruler is a *democracy,* because he governs through equal laws or amidst institutions which will be favorable to the condition of the lower classes. His government will be a *democratic government.* He will create a *democratic monarchy.*

But, the words *democracy, monarchy, democratic government,* in the true sense of those words, can only mean one thing: a government where the people play a more or less large part in the government. Their meaning is intimately linked to the idea of political freedom. To give the name "democratic government" to a government where political freedom is not found is to say a palpable absurdity, according to the natural meaning of the words. What has made people adopt these false or at the very least obscure expressions is:

1. The desire to give an illusion to the crowd, the phrase "democratic government" still having a certain success among them.

2. The real difficulty which people have when trying to express in a single word an idea as complicated as this: an absolute government, where the lower classes do not take any part in affairs, but where the classes above them do not enjoy any privileges and where the laws are made to favor the well-being of the lower classes as much as possible.

* * *

Why very similar principles and similar political theories in the United States led only to a change of government, but in France to the total subversion of society. An idea from which much can be drawn, but which I don't know where to put.

* * *

In our time people still attribute marvelous effects to this liberation of the soil, and there are many people among us who would willingly console themselves for the inhabitants' subjection by thinking that the land is free.

How and where to put some portraits of the leading personalities? Mirabeau, for example (see what Mounier says about him). Do a full-length portrait.

Perhaps do a chapter on the influence of men or rather on their impotence when they are not borne up by the tide, on the first period of the Revolution . . .

On the part that individuals played in the Revolution.

* * *

Powerlessness of a particular man or even of men at the beginning of the Revolution and as long as the Revolution's own impulsion lasted. One of the great characteristics of the Revolution. Highlight its causes well. A great and terrible sight.

CHAPTER THREE

What Made the Revolution Victorious Externally

[Plans]

The Revolution overflowing into Europe. Conquests. Their causes. The ease of making them.

A large chapter for which I do not yet know either the place or the organization (1856).

* * *

Enthusiasm, enchantment of all Europe after the taking of the Bastille and during the first period of the Constituent Assembly. Perhaps make this a separate chapter.

* * *

Chapter Three. What Made the Revolution Victorious Externally.

Movement of the Revolution externally.

Wars of the Revolution, the causes of their success. Special advantages of democratic armies when the democratic Revolution is in progress. The new world against the old world. Victory taken by surprise. Newness of the war to everyone. The Revolution's novelty more visible here than anywhere else. Propaganda. Europe ravaged and aiding its own devastation. Senile imbecility of sovereigns who are broken before having understood that something new is going on in the world.

Feeling of Foreigners at the Beginning of the Revolution

Sound and Echo of the Revolution Externally: Translation of the Memoirs of Heinrich Steffens, Was ich erlebte *["What I Experienced"—Trans.] (Volume One, Pages 362–[366])*

"I now arrive at an important moment of my life, the same moment which gave history a new turn, and which, after shaking all Europe, gradually made itself felt by the entire human race: the French Revolution.

"I was sixteen years old. My father returned home in a frenzy; he called his sons. Witnesses of his deep emotion, we anxiously awaited what he was going to tell us: 'Children,' he cried, 'how enviable you are! What happy and brilliant days are before you! Now, if each one of you does not create an independent position for himself, the fault will be yours alone. All the barriers of birth and poverty are going to fall; from now on the least among us is going to be able to compete with the most powerful, on the same footing and with equal weapons. I wish I were young like you! But my strength is exhausted, all kinds of hindrances which will no longer exist for you have limited me in every way. You must be very stupid and really contemptible if the enthusiasm of such a moment does not ravish you!' In saying these words, his emotion overcame him, and before being able to continue, he began to sob for a little while. Amidst the deep solitude in which we lived, we had not yet learned anything of the agitations which, in Paris, foretold a coming crisis; we therefore looked at our father with stupefaction, and without responding, waited for him to go on. He then told us, in broken words, about the scenes at the Palais-Royal, the immense enthusiasm which had seized the people, how this enthusiasm had overthrown all the obstacles the existing authorities had created, and finally how the Bastille had been taken, and the victims of despotism freed.

"A truly prodigious moment! It was not only the beginning of a revolution in France, but one which was beginning throughout Europe. It had it roots in millions of souls. [. . .] The Revolution was already made, deep within all free hearts, even where it did not break out. These first moments of enthusiasm, which were going to be followed by such a terrible future, in themselves had something pure and holy which will never be forgotten.

"A limitless hope filled my heart then. It seemed to me that my future took root in a new and more fertile soil. After a little while, my father brought us a piece written by a *Livonian,* who told about the first scenes of the Revolution, which he had witnessed. He had understood all the importance of this event, so remarkable in the history of the world. Like a flaming sword, the most ardent enthusiasm suffused his whole account, from the moment when Camille Desmoulins, mounting a table at the Palais-Royal, announced to the excited people that Necker, whom they then called their father, had been taken away from them, to the liberation of the prisoners of the Bastille; with him I participated in all the moving scenes which happened during that brief period. The great results which would come from these events filled me, elevated me, inflamed me. The future appeared hazy to me, but pure. From that moment on, I read the newspapers every day. I participated, although from very far away, in all the phases of the Revolution. My whole being received a new form from it . . .

"It is thus that, still a child and an enthusiast of the times, I left the quiet isolation of my first youth."

Notes on the Book Titled Briefe aus Paris zur Zeit der Revolution *["Letters from Paris during the Revolution"— Trans.], by J[oachim]-Heinrich Campe, Brunswick, 1790 (June–July '58)*

Enthusiasm of foreigners. Arriving at the frontier, he says: "The impressions I felt when I saw for the first time, on every hat and bonnet, on those of bourgeois, peasants, old men, children, priests, beggars, the French cockade, the symbol of the freedom they had conquered, cannot be described (p. 12). I would have happily embraced everyone we met."

Universal character of the Revolution felt instinctively by everyone. "It seemed to us that there were no longer any French; we ourselves had ceased to be Hamburgers and Brunswickers. All national differences had evaporated. These people had just reconquered the rights of the human species, and we were human" (ibid.).

Feeling of degradation in the army which, along with all the other reasons, must have encouraged soldiers to embrace the Revolution's cause. At Valenciennes he encountered the National Guard controlling the gates and acting as police. An army soldier appeared with his bayonet. "Take off the bayonet," cried the bourgeois, and the soldier obeyed instantly, just as the bourgeois would have obeyed before" (p. 13). Such a situation, in certain cases, unites the army and inspires it against the revolution, in others, it completes its disorganization and carries it along [with the revolution—Trans.].

The bourgeoisie mistress. Its resistance to the lower classes. Habit of summary executions and capital punishment on all sides. In arriving at the square of Valenciennes in the midst of this army of bourgeois conquerors, he sees two peasants who have been hung. They were two poor devils who the day before had gone with a crowd to do violence to a neighboring abbey (p. 14). If this bourgeoisie had remained mistress of the movement, it is evident that it would not have let the Revolution go where it went.

Unanimity of the movement. All classes at work. We see that what is most striking is the united agreement, the common agitation of all classes, the air of universal confidence and joy.

National cockade. Cause of its different colors. He gives the explanation which was given at that early time of the three colors: the blue represented the nobility, the red the Church, and the white the Third Estate. At which he point he tells (p. 23) of a coachman, who, upon seeing the cockade of his companion on the trip folded in such a way that the blue had almost disappeared under the white, said: "Look at the Third Estate pressing hard on the nobility."

A striking remnant of the idea of the three estates from which was born a cockade that was the symbol of the final destruction of the estates.

Everyone wearing a cockade. 7 and 8 August '89. Everyone, down to the little children, wore the cockade. He estimated that this might have cost 4 million thalers.

Overexcitement, which lent itself to everything and changed all habits. At Péronne, at sunrise, he finds all the youths playing ball, which surprised him greatly ([p.] 26).

At Senlis, the whole population promenaded in the streets, the men dressed in bright colors, all the women in blue. Joy, satisfaction, well-being was so strongly painted on all faces that the honest Campe felt his heart open, and he would have liked to jump out of the coach in order to mingle in this crowd which, seeing his emotion, smiled at him from all sides like friends and acquaintances.

Naive and boundless enthusiasm caused by the sight of Paris. His admiration, which already had few limits, went beyond all bounds in arriving at Paris ([p.] 29).

He cannot believe that he is in this city on which [the eyes] of the world are riveted, full of enthusiasm and astonishment, as on the central point of the greatest and most marvelous events in the world: "a public life in which Brutus and the Catos would have liked to take part . . . a people who had suddenly raised themselves to a height where the wide eyes of foreigners could barely follow them . . ." He could not thank Providence enough for having permitted him to witness such a sight; this spectacle ennobled, made one greater . . . He finished by modestly declaring to his correspondent that if he did not come back from Paris with an immense increase in his moral worth, it was because he was a bad student and wouldn't learn at school.

An event occurring among a foreign and faraway people causing such transports and such insane admiration, does this not show well the event's new and general character?

Universal happiness (in appearance); order amidst anarchy. Ease of gov-

erning without a government in the first month following the Revolution. Campe arrived at Paris at the beginning of August and stayed there a month.

What strikes him most is the sweet, happy, well-ordered appearance of the population. No disorder; a volunteer police force to which everyone hastens to give voluntary obedience. No bad language, no quarrels. The picture of the city perfectly governed without government. The French, as long as the heroic and warlike imagination lasts, freely supply this *trompe-l'oeil* to the spectator.

Gamins of Paris. The author is struck by admiration at seeing, he says, children, seized by the patriotism and enthusiasm for freedom which inflame their parents, arm themselves in their own way, provide themselves with flags and drums, go through the streets in great troops, and seem to take part in the maintenance of order and tranquility (p. 31).

The ancestors of the mobile guard of '48.

The Revolution Outside France: The Life of Perthes (1856)

Sluggishness, indifference of the majority of the German people, despite the inspiration of some, up to 1805 and 1806.

"If Perthes recognized with bitter indignation and profound pain," it is said in his *Life,* "the indifference with which after the Peace of Lunéville and the Decree of Ratisbon the men who were Germany's pride looked on the country's innumerable woes and the oppressor's arrogance, he was filled with anger when he saw Goethe's *Eugénie* appear." "A shame, a burning shame," Perthes writes to Jacobi in 1804, "on top of the dismemberment of our country which ought to torment our hearts. What do our most noble fellow citizens do? Instead of arming themselves and uniting their strength, courage and anger, everyone surrenders himself to his individual feeling and makes works of art. If one must despair of the salvation of a sinner who plays cards in order to avoid feeling remorse, if our leading citizens thus forget their troubles, how will our nation escape the fate of falling into the situation of a vile multitude spread over the earth without a fatherland?" (vol. 1, p. 164).

The sovereigns and even the journalists (1805) on Napoleon's side. Perthes saw with fear that most of the political leaders of Germany ranged themselves on Napoleon's side against England, and influenced the lower classes in this direction, mostly by popular writings. "By baseness, stupidity, fear or venality, our journalists (I name only Woltmann, Archenholz, Voss, and Buchholz), do the work of the tyrant and the great

nation" [France—Trans.]; it is in these words that Perthes opens his oppressed heart to Müller in a letter of 25 August 1805 (vol. 1, p. 165).

Universal Concern Which the French Revolution Causes in Europe.

He (Perthes) wanted to see humanity reach an ever-greater perfection,
and it is from this perspective that he considered the French Revolution,
whose sight threw him into great emotion (*Aufregung*). "I think," he
wrote to his uncle in 1792 (he was then twenty years old), "that humanity
is at this moment in a revolution (*Verwirrung*) from which it will emerge
shining to make a great step towards perfection . . . According to me,
being master of oneself is the true freedom of the individual, and if all
men knew how to be free in this way, civil freedom would soon follow
because we would no longer need an authority to constrain us. But such
a state of [things] will take centuries to arrive, and must the poor French
patiently suffer odious oppression until then? No, they do well to free
themselves and I rejoice, as a human being and as a citizen of the world,
in the progress of the French army; but as a German I can weep (and this
will bring us eternal shame, that constraint was necessary to bring us to
the side of good)." . . .

He thought that "if the sovereigns' efforts succeed in beating down the
peoples, a darkness like that of the Middle Ages will cover Europe again;
but this will not happen, for knowledge of all kinds has been spread
among all classes, and the spirit of freedom and of natural rights has
spread to the beggar's hut. For another thing, which of our masters will
have that heroic courage, that boldness, that presence of mind which
made the old tyrants remarkable amidst all their cruelties?" (vol. 1, p. 30).

Doubts about success. Perthes doubts whether the immediate consequences of the Revolution will be favorable: "I do not believe," he says,
"that we are yet able enough or good enough to be capable of delivering
ourselves entirely from despotism; the lower classes and the *Gelehrten*
[the educated—Trans.] speak of despots and aristocrats with outrage.
But if one of them comes to smile at them, they become base flatterers;
raise them, they themselves become worse aristocrats than those by birth"
(ibid.).

Pain caused by the horrors of '93. "I cannot," he writes in the spring of
1793, "look at the political world without pain: in France, a people captive to a furious folly; here, the unlimited oppression of tyrants" (vol. 1,
[p.] 31).

Hope in the Revolution and in perfectibility still persists. He adds: "Yet

I continue to believe that if the individual lowers himself, the human species gradually rises, but this begins to seem like a dream" (ibid.).

The general, human character of the Revolution strikes foreigners as
much as us. "Klopstock himself," says Perthes, "had hoped, thanks to the
Constituent Assembly, to see the degradation of man by war disappear:
he was wrong" (vol. 1, p. 58).

Intellectual movement of Germany strong but theoretical, philosophical,
as in France. We note throughout Perthes' youth, above all in his letters,
several of the same intellectual symptoms which marked the period preceding the Revolution in France, and which made that period one of the
greatest and most noble spectacles which humanity has ever presented,
despite the errors, vices, and faults of the times. There was a strong movement which pulled all men (above the lower classes proper) beyond the
petty interests and petty individual passions and events of the times, to
concern themselves with general truths, with the perfection and development of the species, with theories for the use of all humanity; the idea
of unlimited perfectibility through reason . . . "I thought until now," says
Perthes somewhere, "that the perfection of man derived only from the
greater or lesser power of his mind, and that in becoming very educated
he could become perfect" (vol. 1, p. 58). In the very heart of the commercial city par excellence, Hamburg, among the very people who participated in commerce, this intellectual activity and this taste for high
subjects of conversation, this passion for ideas reigned. Even when the
Revolution is already in fury (1794–1795), we see there men of letters,
philosophers, artists as well as merchants, concerned with the sciences,
the arts, above all with political philosophy. Eminent men of several kinds
meet; people are inspired, they fight over the terrain of the Revolution
with each other. One of them ornamented his study with portraits of
Mirabeau, Pichegru, of Charlotte Corday, and of his son who out of enthusiasm for the Revolution fought in the French army. One of the richest
citizens of Hamburg (Sieveking) brought all these elements together at
his country house and created a great center for this whole intellectual
movement. Around his wife, every night, seventy to eighty guests met,
among whom the greatest questions of the times and of all time were
discussed (vol. 1, p. 50).

All of this picture, so absolutely similar to what happened in France
before the Revolution, is characteristic of the period, of the society, very
great and original in itself; there is no parallel in any country whatsoever
in our time.

Unsystematic irreligious movement. What distinguishes the intellectual movement in Germany from France is that in Germany unlike France one does not see it linked to a regular war against religion. On the contrary one sees that in Germany religious feeling still fundamentally occupies souls.

The Revolution even makes some nobles enthusiasts. Example: the count Adam von Moltke, from a great family of Denmark or Holstein, which gave ministers to Denmark, was seized, says Perthes, by the first impressions of the French Revolution and for a long time belonged to its most ardent and purest partisans. After having visited the greater part of Europe and having experienced many rude assaults from life, he returned to a property he owned at Nütschau, which was small compensation for the loss of his family fief in Zealand, which had been taken from him. There, far from the world, but full of political passion, he tried to bear the hard times he went through with energetic resignation; content with only a few hours of sleep, he tried to calm the worries of his soul by serious and assiduous study of history. He had, says the author, *"eine herrliche Männergestalt mit edler Stirn und blitzendem Auge"* [a magnificent manly figure with a noble forehead and shining eyes—Trans.]. He was the friend of the young Niebuhr, who said that there was a lion in him (vol. 1, p. 137). A picture of the old feudal vigor put into the service of new ideas and passions.

How the enthusiasm for the French Revolution swept away all minds and made the Germans more French than German. Perthes was, when the Revolution broke out, seventeen years old (!) and he shared his contemporaries' enthusiasm in favor of those who fought against the old French monarchy. But when war broke out between France and the German Empire, his heart was on the German side, *contrary to most of the others.*

Indifference of the Germans towards the German Empire and unity. Where attachment to the Empire was still felt. It was neither in Austria, nor Prussia, nor any of the large territories which had a separate existence, that attachment for the Empire could be found during the last century, but in the counties or small principalities. There the representative of the Holy Roman Empire was still often called *our emperor,* people showed dependence with regard to it, more it is true by habit than because the Empire was judged strong and animated by an active life. Perthes, who was born in one of these little territories, became the enemy of the French as soon as they made war on the Empire (vol. 1, p. 136).

Jean de Müller. He linked himself in 1804 with Perthes, a political relationship. At this time, Müller traveled from Vienna to Berlin, where he had been appointed historian, and was linked with Gentz. He tried with the greatest ardor to unite Prussia and Austria against France. He published in this regard some *kühne und kräftige Aufsätze* (bold and powerful writings) to inflame German feeling and raise anger against the oppressor of Germany. Attracted by these writings, Perthes began a correspondence with Müller in 1805, "in this time when the old, the young, the rich, the poor, the strong and the weak, in sum all those who love the fatherland, freedom, law and order, should unite." To which Müller responds (p. 161), "Thank you, *edeldenkender Mann* [noble-thinking man— Trans.]! It is a great comfort (*Labsal*) to find such German feeling. Without having met you, I am your friend. The moment has come when all who think alike must unite fraternally for the work of national deliverance. Life no longer has any charm for me but this. Among those who think alike there is an internal language, an invisible fraternity which is recognized at every word. This fraternity to which you belong, my friend, is the salt of the earth. He who meets there immediately becomes my brother and my friend, more than many others whom I have known all my life" (vol. 1, p. 161).

As early as 1805, we see from a letter of Perthes, where Perthes reproaches him with despairing of the future, that Müller's mind began to surrender: "Your letter has disturbed me," Perthes says to him: "if men such as you despair of their time, what will become of us?"(vol. 1, p. 165).

1. The invasion of German life by literature as in French life immediately before the Revolution.

2. Transformation by experience and the test of revolutions. "It seems to me," adds Perthes in the same letter to Müller (1805), "that the preparation for something better is already visible among us. A vague but strong desire for a *Haltungspunct* [stopping-point—Trans.] is general. Many things are already destroyed: I will cite only the end of the time of word-scribbling (*papiernen Zeit*). Another twenty years of such literary coquetry (*Buhlerei mit der Literatur*), *solcher Verhätschelung geistiger Bildung, solcher Krämerei mit belletristischem Luxus* [such overindulgence in intellectual education, such trifling with literary luxury—Trans.], would have made us like our neighbors. Now the young feel that the fatherland is not at the service of literature, but the contrary. How many are already convinced that strength and virtue are not only born of moral theories (*moralischen Grundsätze*), but grow from an entirely different soil! In how many men does the idea spread that love and the free care of one's house and what is attached to it is worth more than general principles (*allgemeine Umfassung*), that a passionate patriotism is worth more than a cold cosmopolitanism."

Love of humanity replacing that for the country among the Germans.
During the time which preceded the Revolution, feeling for the fatherland had almost disappeared, to make way for a sentimental and sterile love for the human race (describe this well); "and religion also, although unbelief and indifference have put forth deep roots through the long-reigning abuses of theological principles, religion itself is taking more root every day . . . We suffer for the sins of our fathers; the last two generations worked with incredible levity to push us into the abyss" [p. 166].

Greatness of events. Changes of scene which strike and frighten the imagination. Effects that this produces on Jean de Müller. 1806. Foundation of the Confederation of the Rhine; final dissolution of the Holy Roman Empire: "The facts to which the world is witness," writes Müller to Perthes, "go beyond all political calculations. Nowhere does one see any help appear. God must withdraw a man or call forth a greater one, or bring about events until now unforeseen. I am filled with worry and terror; the scene becomes too somber. The Ancient of Days holds his court: the books are opened, nation and sovereigns weighed. What will be the result of that which we see? A new order is preparing itself, very different from the one supposed by those who are nothing but its blind instruments. That which is will not last. That which was can hardly return . . ." (vol. 1, p. 171).

A year after the battle of Jena, he writes: "I think of the prophet of days past who had recognized the signs that God wanted to do something new. Jeremiah saw that Asia and his own people were going to be delivered to the king of Babylon and he advised people to accept this fate. In this he did not forget either his people or their fundamental feelings. In the same way today, by the marvels of the year 1807, we see the nations imprisoned as in the net of the fisherman. From Cadiz to Danzig, from Ragusa to Hamburg, and soon on all sides, everything is the French Empire; must this endure seventy years like the Babylonian Empire, or seven hundred years like the Holy Roman Empire? Who can know?" (vol. 1, p. 173).

It is interesting to see: 1) How the imagination simultaneously pushed people like Perthes to the heroism of resistance, others like Müller to despair. 2) How a great mind, joined to a weak soul, sometimes serves to increase the weakness of the latter. The brilliant faculties of the one give reason and color to the cowardice of the other. The man who wrote these lines was already defeated at the bottom of his heart before the interview with Napoleon put him behind the victor's chariot.

The Holy Roman Empire intellectually bankrupt before being legally bankrupt. "There are few Germans," says Perthes in 1806, "who regret the destruction of the Empire. The majority, and among them some very sensible people, see with pleasure that there will no longer be any taxes to send to Vienna and Ratisbon, and think that Hamburg will continue to be Hamburg" (vol. 1, p. 171).

Philosophical mind of the eighteenth century, taste for philosophical discussion which continues even in the army of the Empire. Bernadotte. 1807: Hamburg is occupied. Bernadotte commands there. "There is much of Jacobi in his manners and his habits," says Perthes. "Like Jacobi, he likes to philosophize; at a grand dinner at Lübeck he discussed at great length the existence of God in whom he claimed not to believe. At the end, finding himself too closely pressed, he cried out: 'If God existed, how could I [be] at Lübeck!'" (vol. 1, p. 177).

Complete ruin of the old society in Germany. Birth of a new society, a clear and obvious result of the French Revolution. Vices of that society. Hatred which it inspired in Perthes through his hatred for Napoleon completely unforeseen up to then. A sort of recognition for Napoleon. Idea that he was a harsh but effective agent of Providence. "Who does not see," writes Perthes, "that a sort of renaissance in the state, in the Church, in morality, had become necessary for Europe? Who does not know the disorder, the petty spirit, the languor (*Erstorbenheit*) which reigned in the Holy Roman Empire? Among the individual states of Germany, there was not one which did not deserve to be destroyed, since there was not a single sovereign or a single people who wanted to live and die for all of Germany. From this universal weakness, from this egoistic languor, a force had to be born which would triumph over all, because nothing strong resisted it. Napoleon was and remains a natural necessity. He, power on earth, is such in himself, he only thinks of himself . . . To this man similar to a demon, God has abandoned the world, not so that the world will bow to this man, but in order that from the destructive force of evil the extinguished strength of good can be reborn, even at the price of the most frightful hardships" [p. 178].

Anything preferable to a return to the Old Regime. "That which was is destroyed; what new structure will be raised on the ruins, I do not know. What I can say is that the most horrible thing of all would be if, from this time of terror, the old time with its languor and its ruined forms should be reborn. God wants to lead us through pain and suffering to a new order of things. The play is not performed by going back to the beginning; forward, therefore! That which falls, falls because it cannot hold on. [. . .] Whoever, now, wants to make the wheel turn backwards is thinking only of his personal interest and of his comfort, but Providence can't be concerned with that." It must not be lost from sight that Perthes belonged to the middle classes and, while detesting the Revolution, had breathed its air.

"Yes," Stolberg reports to him at the same time, "the old leaf must fall; let us see the green finger of the new sprout" (vol. 1, pp. 177–79).

Pride in his race which persists in the German amidst his defeats. Gigantic idea they have of themselves, even when prostrate. "God counted particularly and above all on the German people for the great renovation, we Germans are a chosen people (in 1807), a people which represents all humanity and works on behalf of everyone. We have never been a purely national people. [. . .] Intellectual gifts of a general nature have never been lacking in us. We have devoted ourselves to the sciences for their own sake. Has not Germany long been an academy of sciences for all Europe? Everything which has been found elsewhere was discovered and thought of in Germany. For as long as we have been alive, we have lived not for ourselves, but for all of Europe . . ." [p. 179].

God has filled the hearts of all peoples with the same smoke, so that, thinking more of themselves than they really are, they think themselves obliged to do everything that they can.

The sovereigns more beaten down than the peoples. Nothing to expect from them. "Our sovereigns," writes Perthes after the Peace of Pressburg, "have sufficiently brought to light their egoistic cowardice and their submission to Napoleon. Our peoples are betrayed, we are surrendered to dishonor by our leaders. All feeling of the general good is extinct in the hearts of those who lead, who have power and give the tone to opinion. Salvation can only come from the peoples themselves" (vol. 1, p. 182).

Influence of the wife in political crises. Once excited, Perthes no longer throws a backward glance at himself: "Thanks to God," he says, "I have a wife who shares my way of feeling and who, when her husband needs all his courage, doesn't come to take it away from him" (vol. 1, p. 187).

Internal movements which take place among the German people. Cohesion. New union which is made under the pressure of Napoleon. Finding himself at Leipzig in 1809, Perthes writes: "You could not believe what unanimity reigns here (I imagine that this was at the time of the Fair). Never has all of Germany been united as at present" [p. 200].

After the battle of Wagram: "I cannot describe to you the degree of discouragement into which people have fallen; but the courage of despair is the neighbor of such a state, and it will come" (vol. 1, p. 200).

*How the Germans, divided among themselves in all ways, and by the
foreigner, preserve their intellectual unity through literature, the only thing
which remains common to them.* "If the Austrians, the Prussians, the inhabitants of the left bank of the Rhine, and the subjects of the Confederation of the Rhine lost the feeling that they all formed part of the
same nation, the reestablishment of political unity and of German independence would have become impossible. Yet at that time there no
longer remained to the Germans (after Wagram, 1809) any way but one in
which their nationality could freely develop itself without attracting the
eyes of the enemy's spies and without being crushed by violent force.
Literature, insofar as it remained literature, did not inspire any fear in
Napoleon (always the same mistake with men of action, even the greatest
and most open-minded; they are always full of contempt for ideas). For
the Germans however, for centuries, the true independent life of Germany found one of its most active strengths in literature. Through literature above all, Germany considered itself a single nation; this feeling of
intellectual independence and unity was doubtless insufficient to produce
political unity; but it could help it and be the cover under which hidden
hatred for the oppressor fortified itself. It could be a means of calling,
from all parts of this Germany torn into pieces, of uniting in an association under a form which would not excite suspicion, all men who had
remained German in their hearts; then, when the hour of deliverance had
struck, to make them act with weapons other than those of the intellect
(vol. 1, p. 201).

Perthes tried to found a review which would be a meeting point for
all Germans, in whatever country they already belonged to or had been
ceded to (vol. 1, p. 203): The German Republic of Letters still exists," he
wrote, "and can continue to exist, even though our sovereigns are defeated and the Holy Roman Empire is in shreds. [. . .] German publishing is today," he wrote, "the only existing link which covers the whole
nation. It is, in truth, our national institute, forced to develop itself and
characterizing almost alone our national particularities . . . Publishing
alone can save the German Republic of Letters . . . To do so is the purpose
of my life. I have friends in all Germany . . ."

Starting from here, Perthes founded a review (the *"Deutsche Museum"*) which would become the meeting place for all minds who had
remained German and would form a kind of secret freemasonry among
them. Perthes went everywhere to explain his plan to those who should
cooperate in it. To some he told his political purpose; to others he revealed only the literary goal: "An unsuspected association," he says (vol.

1, p. 207), "will thus be established among all the men who one day could be called on to become the leaders of our people. It will exist beneath the oppressor's eyes without his seeing it. Every member can, according to his situation and his importance, group around him a certain number of like-thinking men and, in this way, when the hour comes, a literary association can become a great political force."

State of the literary world at this time in Germany (1809). He in fact succeeded in uniting *Jean Paul, Rumohr* [who] promised to do some articles on old German art, *Wilken* on the customs of old Germany, *Feuerbach* on German law, *August-Wilhelm Schlegel* on German literature, *Friedrich Schlegel* on the particular literature of Austria, *Sailer* on the life of German Catholics, *Marheineke* (of Heidelberg) on German preaching, *Schleiermacher* on philosophy, *Planck* on the historical theology of Germany, *Schelling, Gentz.*

Goethe refused to do anything. Goethe refused to associate himself with the enterprise with that magisterial egoism which was characteristic of him: "I have," he wrote, "all kinds of reasons for concentrating, in order to be able to do, even in part, the things which I am already obliged to do; and since time is of such a nature that I freely let it pass before speaking of it or about it; pardon me therefore [. . .] and let me know some time how your enterprise is going" (vol. 1, p. 208).

Other German writers who participate: Adam Müller, Karl-Ludwig von Haller, Karl-Friedrich Eichhorn, Thibault, Savigny, Stolberg, Steffens, Arndt, Arnim, Fouqué, Görres, Franz Bender and *Brentano, Tischbein* and *Fiorillo, Schneffner* from Königsberg, *Schlippenbach* of Courland, *Lichtenstein, Grimm, Rühs, Heeren, Raumer, Rehberg* (the writer on the Revolution), old *Hegewisch* from Kiel.

Haller of Bern writes: "I consider your enterprise as coming from God" (vol. 1, p. 209). "We should never despair. The only means of struggle against the misfortune of the times is to introduce better principles and better feelings into the hearts and minds of men."

Duration of the "Deutsche Museum." This collection appeared in 1810, but disappeared shortly afterwards, Hamburg having become a French city and Perthes a French subject. "Your *Museum* has died," wrote a friend to Perthes, "but its spirit will live" (vol. 1, p. 217).

Effects of the French Revolution on Germany

Haüsser says in his history (*Deutsche Geschichte vom Tode Friedrichs bis zur Gründung des deutschen Bundes* [German History from the Death of Frederick to the Foundation of the German Confederation—Trans.],

2 vols., Berlin, 1855): "It is a remarkable fact that the shock of '89 passed over Germany almost without leaving a trace and that the great rupture (*Riss*) which took place in the whole constitution of the Empire, which we can consider an aftereffect of the Revolution, only took place in 1803. It is not less worth noting that this shock did not come from the masses, but from the sovereigns themselves. It was they who transported into the German constitutions the revolutionary ideas of aggrandizement and equality through violence, which had transformed feudal France since '89. Here, like there," says the author "one proceeded by force; a mass of individual rights had to bow before the new raison d'état of the public good; but, here like there, many vicious or outdated institutions were put aside, the division of the social body into a crowd of little parts was denounced; the circulation of blood, which the fractioning into so many little states clogged in a thousand ways, was greatly accelerated. In the reformed and enlarged groups of states, the same system of government as in France was introduced. The form of government which ran things in France, active, regular, aspiring to equality and unity, acclimatized itself in several German territories then, and it was equally active, imperious, revolutionary, without respect for historical or traditional things, equally full of the doctrine of the omnipotence of the state and the leveling dispositions of Bonaparte's French bureaucracy . . . The Reformation itself had not been as rude a blow to the Catholic Church and the Catholic clergy as these later changes. The fate of the nobility was intimately linked with the destruction of the ecclesiastical states: more than seven hundred members of the *Domstifter* [cathedral chapters—Trans.] lost their positions. As many relatives of the nobility destined for those places, therefore, were without resources for the future. What a blow, not only to the fortunes of the nobility, but still more for its constitution! To this was joined the reduction which the *Reichsgrafen* [imperial counts—Trans.] and the *Ritterschaft* [imperial knights—Trans.] suffered by the *Theilungsgeschäft* [partitions—Trans.], a reduction which rendered still more poignant the violences of the new sovereigns. The nobility and the towns, those ancient rivals, were joined in the same destiny . . .

The clergy, the nobility, the free cities therefore complained about this revolution. The secular sovereigns and their bureaucrats vaunted it as great progress. The mass of the nation approved it or was indifferent.

Haüsser says earlier that "what is proof of the sad condition of Germany was that the opinion of the peoples of the left bank of the Rhine

was in general favorable to union with France. From then on Joseph Görres (see his work of 1799, *Rechenschaft an seine Landsleute über seine Sendung nach Paris* [Report to His Countrymen about His Mission to Paris—
Trans.]) saw the return to the old regime as a horrible specter. He feared
'oppressive despotism,' he feared the introduction of the Church into the
state, where the civil power would be under the surveillance of priests
and would share with them the spoils of the simple . . . From union with
France he would hope on the contrary for the addition of a representation derived from the people, the liberation of the state from priestcraft
(*Pfaffheit*), the complete separation of political and religious institutions,
and immense progress for civilization and enlightenment."

Effects of the French Revolution on Its Greatest
Enemies, Voluntarily Produced by Them

In 1807 Baron vom Stein, the representative of the oldest German aristocracy, the most fiery enemy of France and French ideas, in order to be
able to raise and organize the Prussian people against us (the organized
forces of the state no longer being sufficient), made an ensemble of reforms which derived directly from the spirit of the French Revolution
(study them).

1) Law of 9 October 1807 which destroyed the nobles' privilege of alone
possessing estates. Serfs' attachment to the land is abolished. Everyone can
acquire and own land. In return the nobles are given the right to be involved with industry and commerce without losing their rank. Civil equality
is founded.

2) Appeal to the citizens to participate in local affairs. Municipal governments made elective with a property qualification for voters, but without any
distinction of birth nor of religion.

3) Rank in the army given to everyone according to merit.

Furthermore he tended completely towards the representative system.
Excerpt from the "Revue des deux mondes," 15 November 1852.

[Revolutionary Wars]

Military power, which persists amid the weakness of the internal government and the contempt the government inspires. Visible above all under
the Directory.

* * *

Why the armies remained energetic and full of ardor when the nation
ceased to be.

Civil society can subsist for a long time in the midst of anarchy, but that little artificial society which we call an army cannot. It dissolves as soon as its links separate. Thus a nation's army remains organized when the nation itself is no longer organized. Which alone would be enough to explain how all revolutions end up with military power.

*   *   *

A profound revolution in the manner of making war. New aspect of war, one of the great characteristics of the French Revolution. A large chapter on this point. See chapter of the "Mercure britannique" (vol. 2, p. 65).

Boldness, violence, and impudence natural to democratic governments, increased when they are revolutionary and, I add, French.

Coincidence of the vices of the mind of the man and those of the times. A disordered mind, in a revolutionary time. Reaction of each of these causes on the other.

The Revolution and the Emperor, perhaps a good title for the book.

The French Revolution and Napoleon.

One can succeed in things which need the qualities one has. But one only excels in things where one's flaws themselves are useful. This explains why the French are so superior in war to what they are in civil life and government and in general everywhere but on the battlefield.

*   *   *

What makes the French good at war.

It is a mistake to believe that the French succeed at war because they have a passion for it. They do not have an *a priori* passion for war (even though their imagination in itself, I think, is more pleased by war stories than that of any other people), they do not even have the taste for it. They greatly fear its consequences, are reluctant to make all the sacrifices which it demands, are frightened at the prospect of its dangers and hardships, and leave their village to go to the army only in tears. What makes them so good at war is a certain hidden agreement, of which they themselves are ignorant, between war and their faults and qualities. War is the theater where both show themselves most naturally and contribute equally to success.

*   *   *

Character of the Revolution's conquests. There then happened something analogous to what was seen at the birth of Islam, when the Arabs converted half the Earth while devastating it.

*   *   *

Struggles of Germany against France. It is the peoples who push the kings. The kings are tempted to see a revolutionary and subversive moment in the emotions and the fierce and noble passions which save them, and while trembling allow themselves to be saved.

This is well seen in the letters of Prince Metternich cited in the "Revue des deux mondes" of 1 January 1857, in an article titled "Uprising of Germany after the Russian War," by M. Armand Lefebvre.

Why all the plans of the Coalition failed until 1813 and succeeded then:

1. The old diplomacy which could not adapt to the novelty of the situation, where all individual advantages were secondary to the fall of the common enemy.

2. The élan of the peoples pushing the kings.

3. The victories themselves of the Republic and the Empire which had destroyed the little states and concentrated all political action in two or three hands.

Highlight this idea well and make people grasp this *disunity* of Europe which, with the *concentration* of public power in France, was the cause of the victories.

Finish this chapter on the wars of the French Revolution with England defending itself because it opposed a similar strength to French strength, a centralized government, an entire nation mobilized. It was not the sea which saved it; it was its spirit, its constitution, it was above all *freedom*. Great spectacle, freedom alone capable of fighting against the *Revolution*.

Where to put this chapter? It is great and perhaps new or at least full of novelties.

Before starting the story of Napoleon; it is with the Directory that the revolutionary wars proper end.

Book Three

NAPOLEON

[Plans]

Sorrento, December 1850—Napoleon.

What I would like to paint is less the facts themselves, however surprising or great they are, than the reasons behind the facts; less the different acts of Napoleon's life than Napoleon himself; that unique, incomplete, but truly *marvelous* being, whom one cannot closely examine without seeing one of the most interesting and strangest sights to be encountered in the universe.

I would like to show what Napoleon in his prodigious enterprise really took from his own genius, and how the situation of the country and the spirit of the times helped him. I want to make it seen how and why at that moment this indocile nation ran to servitude of its own accord; with what incomparable art Napoleon discovered in the Revolution's most demagogic works everything which was apt to despotism, and made it come forth naturally. Starting from his internal government, I want to contemplate the effort of this almost divine intelligence, coarsely employed to restrain human freedom; this perfected, wise, strong organization, such as the greatest genius in the midst of the most enlightened and most civilized century alone could conceive it; and, under the weight of that admirable machine, society repressed and suffocated, becoming sterile, the movement of intelligence slowing down, the human spirit drooping, souls growing narrower, the great men who cease to appear, an immense and flat horizon, where, in whatever direction one turns, nothing appears but the colossal figure of the emperor himself.

Arriving at his foreign policy and his conquests, I will try to paint the furious ride of his fortune across peoples and kingdoms; I would like to say how, here again, the strange greatness of his military genius was aided by the strange and disordered greatness of the times. What more extraordinary picture, if one knew how to paint it, of human power and weakness, than that of this impatient and mobile genius constantly making and unmaking his work himself, daily tearing out and replacing the limits of empires, and making nations and sovereigns despair, still less because of what he made them suffer than because of the eternal uncertainty in which he left them about what was left for them to fear. I would finally like to make clear the series of excesses and mistakes by which he led to his own fall; and, despite these mistakes and excesses, follow well the immense furrow that he left behind him in the world, not only as memory, but as influence and lasting action; what is dead with him, what remains.

And to finish this long picture, to show what the Empire means within the French Revolution, the place which this singular act should occupy in this strange play whose ending is still unknown to us.

Here are the great objects which I glimpse, but how to grasp them?

The memories; the silence.

*   *   *

To tell and to judge at the same time.

Tell first the way in which Napoleon seized power. What seemed extraordinary in this result of the Revolution. Facilities that he found in seizing power. Period of the French Revolution at which we had arrived.

Facilities which he found in constituting his power. The constitution which he gave it. Picture of the activity and the prodigious nature of his mind applied to administrative things, before describing the institutions created by him. Development of the changes which took place in Napoleon's character at the same time as his fortune increased, his power became irresistible, and he was delivered from the salutary safeguard of fear.

THUS, FIRST CHAPTER:

Taking of power. How? Why?

Picture of society such as the Revolution had made it, which facilitated such an event.

Force of the current not only towards order, but servitude. Middle class retaking power.

SECOND CHAPTER:

Napoleon become master. Details on his manner of work; his character as legislator. What he founded. Why?

Facility which he finds. What was new, what was old in his work. The anarchic Revolution ending up naturally with the greatest administrative centralization which had ever existed.

ANOTHER CHAPTER:

Development and progress of the civil government of the Empire. All safeguards removed. All freedoms taken away. Despotism becomes capricious. Suffocating atmosphere. Abasement of souls. Shuddering of minds. Numbness and sleep of the human spirit in the midst of all this great noise of victory.

Literature zero. Arts heavy. Administrative talent without genius; military capacity the same, without invention or greatness. An immense personality weighs on the world and crushes everything.

ANOTHER CHAPTER:

Change which happened even to the emperor's character at the same time as his fortune developed.

ANOTHER CHAPTER:

The emperor's foreign policy. How it is both true and false that he was constantly pushed irresistibly towards war.

Describe in summary form the chief diplomatic and political events of the reign.

The chief cause is in himself, a genius who doesn't know how to stop. Picture of this *furious course of his fortune* across territories, peoples, empires.

ANOTHER CHAPTER:

Don't go on at length about his battles. Take one campaign as an example, try to summarize it. Give the marvelous spectacle of this military genius in his natural element.

ANOTHER CHAPTER:

Fall of the Empire. Exhaustion of all resources. Weakening of all forces. Abuse of French nationality. Even the army tired.

ANOTHER CHAPTER (FINAL):

What the Empire was within the great drama of the French Revolution. What was only a passing event, what was durable. What it did, what it prepared.

ANOTHER CHAPTER:

How Napoleon brought out the despotic aspect of the Revolution's works. What he took from it, what he put aside. The clever and egoistic beginning that he made in his works and his tendencies.

ANOTHER CHAPTER:

How the course of fortune took him beyond his original plans and led him to attempt to combine old materials with new ones in his construction. The comedian, charlatan, petty, even vulgar side of the great man. In what way he betrayed the newly rich, the parvenu. His taste for the gaudy, false greatness, bombast, the gigantic.

Incoherence, absence of plan, mutability of his foreign policy.

Great cause of his fall: Europe was so defeated, the sovereigns so broken and so mediocre, that they would have submitted themselves to any enormity whose fixed and precise limits were known in advance. What reduced them to despair was less what they suffered than the perpetual uncertainty of their future and the frightening wait for something still worse.

Oppression of the defeated, while improving their condition and their laws. A partly inevitable result of the way in which Napoleon made war, partly caused by a false point of view on the need to use pillage to make the army fond of war. Result: the same peoples who most regretted his institutions or who have best preserved them and who have prospered afterwards because of him were the most ardent to fight him.

Character of his conquests different from those of all other conquerors: propagandist and warrior, preserving to a certain extent the propagandist character of the wars of the Republic. Violence combined with philosophy and the light of reason. There is something here of Napoleon and the nineteenth century together.

Bold, incoherent, unheard-of character of the enterprises of the emperor and his genius, coming not only from his nature, but from the time of upheaval, of extraordinary novelties, in which he lived, from the unforeseen, strange, unprecedented turn which human affairs had taken.

*   *   *

In order to fully study this history, it must be divided into compartments: war, government, literature.

Men to consult: Molé, Pasquier, Brévanne, d'Aunay, Mignet, Thiers.

Documents. Printed: the *Moniteur,* the *Bulletin des lois,* histories, memoirs. Manuscripts: The diplomatic documents, handwritten letters, unpublished memoirs.

*   *   *

What manuscript documents are necessary for the study of the Directory.

The documents of the ministry of police.

How did the government run or at least how did it not run? What gears were missing? Only in the files of the ministry of the interior and that of the police can this be learned.

What was the extent of and the means for the repression of banditry?

See, in the library, the engravings, the caricatures published at the time of the Directory. Hauréau.

Take care of having the work on the publications done. Hauréau.

Everything which is of a nature to throw light on Bonaparte's first period, his first opinions, his first writings, his character as it manifested itself before he came to power, must be brought out. His real conduct on 13 Vendémiaire, on 18 Fructidor, in Egypt, in a word on the whole period of his life before 18 Brumaire.

Part One

THE CONVENTION
AND THE DIRECTORY

CHAPTER ONE

How the Republic Was Ready to Accept a Master

If you want to look at one of the strangest periods ever encountered in the course of human history, consider the internal workings of this republic which made Europe tremble.

Its government, which had at its command perhaps the most powerful armies and the greatest generals who had appeared in the world since the Roman Empire, crept along painfully, constantly tottering, always ready to collapse under the weight of its flaws and vices. It was corroded by a thousand well-known ills and furthermore, despite its youth, it was subject to that nameless sickness which usually attacks only old governments, a kind of general weakness, of senile consumption, which can only be defined as the difficulty of existing. No one tried to overthrow it anymore, but the government seemed to have lost the strength to sit up in its chair.

After 18 Fructidor (give date), the Directory was armed with more power than any of the kings which the Revolution had overthrown had ever possessed. For it had become, in fact, an absolute sovereign, and in addition the heir of a revolution which had broken down all the barriers that laws, customs, and mores had previously opposed to the abuse and sometimes to the use of power. The press was silent. France provided the representatives it was told to, the local administrators had been replaced or were submissive; finally the legislature, humiliated and humbled, no longer wanted to do anything except obey orders.

However, the Directory was never able to run the country. It occupied the government, but it did not govern. It could never return normalcy to administration, order to the budget, or peace to the country. Its rule was nothing but anarchy tempered by violence. It did not know how to give anyone, even for a single day, the illusion of stability. The factions never

191

took it for an established government. They retained their hopes, and *above all* their hatreds.

The government itself was nothing but a faction, an exclusive faction, always worried and violent, the smallest and most despised of them all. It was a clique of regicides, composed almost entirely of second-rate revolutionaries who, having done nothing but tail along after great criminals or having committed only obscure crimes, had escaped from both the Terror and the reaction that followed. These people regarded the Republic as their protection. But fundamentally most cared about nothing but power and its pleasures. Skeptical and materialistic, they had kept nothing of their old selves but their former energy. It is remarkable that almost all the men who became demoralized in the course of that long Revolution still kept, along with the vices it had given them, something of that wild and uncontrolled courage which had helped them make it. Several times, in the middle of their difficulties and dangers, they planned and desired a return of the Terror. They wanted it after Fructidor, or tried to reestablish it after Prairial, but in vain. This gives rise to several noteworthy points.

At the beginning of a violent revolution, the laws, made in normal times, are more gentle than mores suddenly hardened by new passions. But as time passes, laws end up being harsher than mores, and gentle mores paralyze the laws. In the beginning, the Terror was created without, so to speak, the lawmaker getting involved; afterwards, the legislator often exhausted himself trying to recreate it. The cruelest laws of 1793 are less barbarous than some of those passed in 1797, '98 and '99. The law which deported journalists and representatives of the people to Guyana without trial, the law which authorized the Directory to imprison and deport at will any priests whom it considered dangerous, the graduated tax which, under the name of a forced loan, seized the entire income of the rich, and finally the infamous law of hostages, present a picture of perfected atrocity that the laws of the Convention itself had not possessed, and yet these laws could not bring the Terror back to life. In their conception of tyranny the men who proposed these laws had perhaps as few scruples, as much boldness, and maybe more intelligence than their predecessors; further, these laws were passed almost without debate, and applied without resistance. While most of the laws which had prepared and established the Terror were actively opposed, and aroused part of the country into rebellion, these laws were silently accepted. But they could never be fully put into practice and, what is most noteworthy, the same cause which facilitated their birth diminished their effect. The Revolution, in its long existence, had made the French so listless and blasé that neither astonishment nor active condemnation was left in them at the announcement of the cruelest and most violent laws. But this same mental depression made the daily application of such laws difficult. Public feelings no longer lent themselves to them; they opposed the rulers' violence with the passive but almost invincible resistance of the mass of the governed. The Directory exhausted itself.

It is true that this government, so fertile in the invention of revolutionary procedures, was exceptionally clumsy and inept when it came to organizing power. It never learned how to substitute a well-constructed governmental machine for the popular fervor which it lacked. In its hands tyranny always lacked tools, and the majority of its victims escaped for lack of agents ready to seize them. In short, the Directory was ignorant of that great maxim of famous despots, a maxim which we will soon see applied, that to make a people obedient and keep it that way, horrible laws that are not followed are worth less than mild laws which a perfected bureaucracy applies regularly, as if naturally, every day and to every one.

Towards the end of the Directory the Jacobin Club reopened. They took up once again their banners, their language, their slogans. For parties hardly change, and it is a remarkable fact that parties are more inflexible in their ideas and practices than the individual men who compose them. Thus the Jacobins repeated everything that they had done during the Terror but they were unable to revive it. The only effect of the fear they inspired was to make the nation in even more of a hurry to exit freedom.

The Directory, after having governed without opposition, almost without limits, in the fullness of power which the events of Fructidor had given it, intervening in everything, trying everything, seemed, towards the end of its career, in the month of June 1799 (30 Prairial Year VII), to collapse little by little, without meeting the least resistance. The same legislative body that it had decimated, partly reconstituted, and always treated as its servant, once again became master and returned to power. But soon the victor itself did not know what to do with its victory. Up until then the governmental machine had worked without rules; this time, it seemed to stop. It became clear that assemblies, which are excellent at both strengthening and limiting a government, are less able to run things than the most inept government.

Sovereign power was no sooner returned to the legislature than a kind of universal collapse spread throughout the country's administration. Anarchy spread from individuals to public officials. Without rebelling, everyone ceased to obey. It was like a disbanding army. Taxes, which previously had been collected poorly, were no longer collected at all. Draftees everywhere preferred to take up banditry rather than join the army. For a moment, it might have been thought that we were going to leave behind not merely the normal order of civilized society, but civilization itself. The safety of goods, the security of persons, the passableness of the roads were threatened. One must look at the correspondence of public officials with the government, as it still exists in fragments in the national archives, to get a picture of these problems. For, as a minister of the times remarked, "one ought to offer reassuring news in public accounts; but in the refuge where the government deliberates far from the public eye, everything must be said."

Here is the picture which France presented, found in one of these secret reports on the state of the Republic, this one from the minister of police, in the month of September 1799 (Fructidor, Year VII). It results that of the eighty-six departments which made up France proper (I leave out the conquered territories), forty-five were entirely given up to anarchy or civil war. Troops of bandits stormed the prisons, murdered the guards, and freed the prisoners; tax collectors were robbed, killed, or mutilated; municipal officials were slaughtered, landowners kidnapped, lands devastated, coaches robbed. Bands of two hundred, of three hundred, of eight hundred men wandered the country. Everywhere groups of draftees put up armed resistance to the authorities charged with inducting them; everywhere laws were disobeyed, in some places in order to follow one's passions, in others to follow one's religion. Some profited from the circumstances to rob travelers, others to ring the church bells so long rendered silent, or to parade the symbols of Catholicism through devastated cemeteries.

The means used to repress disorder were both violent and ineffective. These reports show that when a draft dodger would try to escape from the hands of the soldiers who were in charge of him, the soldiers often killed him as an example. The private homes of citizens were constantly entered forcibly for official inspection. Mobile columns, almost as disorderly as the bands that they pursued, roamed the countrysides, and for lack of pay and supplies held them for ransom.

Paris was docile, but uneasy. A thousand rumors of some great uprising circulated in the city. Some said that a great movement in favor of democracy would be mounted against the Directory; others thought that it would take place in favor of the royalists. A huge fire was supposed to give the signal. Someone had heard it said: it's crazy to pay debts, for a time is coming when all debts will be paid; soon there will be blood to shed. Such is the language of the reports. It is interesting to see the despair into which this universal confusion throws the agents who report it, the causes they give for it, the remedies they suggest. The citizens are in the greatest apathy, say some, public spirit is totally destroyed, say others. Some say: the bandits find refuge everywhere; others: the factions' plots and the impunity of crimes spread deplorable indifference in the hearts of patriots. Some make decrees against the *creators of fanaticism,* several ask for still more violent laws against émigrés, priests, and clergy. Most are astonished and find what is going on incomprehensible. This hidden illness which astonishes the Directory's agents, this internal and invisible sickness which thus makes all powers lapse, this was the state of minds and mores. France refused its aid to its government.

In long revolutions, it is easy to be wrong about the signs which announce the approach of great events, for these signs vary greatly according to the times. They even change their nature completely as the revolution goes on.

At the beginning, public opinion is active, alert, intolerant, presumptuous, and fickle; in decline, it is glum and tenacious. It seems that after having refused to tolerate anything, there are no longer any limits to what the public can bear; but people become irreconcilable while remaining obedient; each day the feeling of unhappiness increases, contempt becomes established, hatred sharpens amidst obedience. The nation no longer has the strength and energy to throw its government into the abyss, as it did at the beginning of the revolution, but it is unanimous in allowing it to fall.

This was France in 1799; it despised and detested its government, and obeyed it.

We were a sad sight then: everywhere France showed the traces of that kind of moral usury which is produced in the long run by the course of revolutions.

In truth all revolutions, even the most necessary ones, have had this effect for a while. But I believe that ours had it more than any other, and I do not know if one could cite from history a single event of this kind which contributed more to the well-being of the generations which followed, and more demoralized the generation which produced it. This was due to many things, first of all to the immense mass of property confiscated by the victorious factions. The French Revolution multiplied, in a way that had never before been seen in any people's internal quarrels, the number of disputed properties whose ownership was guaranteed by law, but which worried the conscience: those who sold these confiscated goods were not very sure that they had the right to sell them; those who bought them, the right to acquire them. Among both, it usually happened that laziness or ignorance kept people from having a very firm opinion on this crucial point. Furthermore self-interest always kept most people from examining it very carefully.

This put the souls of several million men in a difficult position.

During the great revolution which brought about the religious reformation of the sixteenth century, the only revolution which can be compared to the French Revolution, the goods of the Church were confiscated, but they were not put up for public auction. A small number of great lords took them. Among us, furthermore, it was not only the lands of the clergy but those of the majority of large proprietors, not the property of a corporation but the inheritance of a hundred thousand families which was divided up. Note too that one did not enrich oneself merely by the purchase, at ridiculous prices, of a multitude of confiscated lands, but also by the token repayment of an enormous mass of debts: a profit that was simultaneously very legal and very dishonest.

If I may push the comparison further, I find that the revolution of the sixteenth century shed doubt only on a certain portion of human opinions and disturbed established mores on only a few points: honesty, which among most men has its source of support much less in reason than in habit and prejudice, was only shaken. The French Revolution attacked political and religious beliefs simultaneously, the French Revolution wanted to reform the individual and the state at the same time, and it tried to change old customs, received opinions, and old habits in all ways and at once. This produced a universal earthquake in the moral world which staggered the conscience on every side.

But what demoralizes men most in long revolutions is much less the mistakes and even the crimes they commit in the fervor of their belief or their passions than the contempt they sometimes acquire for the same belief or the same passions which made them act in the first place. This is the time when, tired, disenchanted, disappointed, they finally turn against themselves and decide that they have been childish in their hopes, ridiculous in their enthusiasms, more ridiculous still and above all in their devotion. One cannot begin to imagine how the energy of the strongest minds is destroyed in this fall. Man is crushed by it, to the point that not only can one no longer expect great virtues of him, but one would say that he had become incapable almost of great evil.

Those who saw the French reduced to this state thought that they were from then on incapable of ever being able to make any great moral effort. They were wrong; for if our virtues must always worry the moralist, our vices must always leave him grounds for hope. The truth is that we never go deeply enough into either virtue or vice to be unable to change.

The French, who had loved liberty passionately in 1789, or rather had believed they loved it, no longer loved it in '99, without having attached their hearts to anything else. After they had attributed a thousand imaginary charms to freedom, they did not see its real qualities, they could only recognize its difficulties and dangers. In truth, for ten years they had hardly known anything but these. In a contemporary's vivid expression, the Republic had been nothing but an agitated servitude. At what other period of history had one seen the private mores of a great number of men thus violated, and tyranny penetrate more deeply into private life? What feelings, what actions had escaped constraint? What habits, what customs had been respected? The simple individual had been forced to change his days of work and rest, his calendar, his weights and measures, even his language. While he had to take part in ceremonies which seemed useless and ridiculous to him, he was forced to exercise in secret the worship he believed he owed God. He had to constantly break laws in order to follow his desires or his conscience. I do not know if anything like this could have been borne so long by the most enduring of nations, but there is no limit to our patience, nor to our rebelliousness, depending on the times.

On several occasions during the course of the Revolution, the French believed that they were about to successfully overcome this great crisis. Sometimes they counted on the constitution, sometimes on the assemblies, sometimes on the executive power itself. They had even thought, once or twice, of wanting to save themselves, which is always the last thing the French think of. All these hopes had been disappointed, all these attempts vain. The Revolution was not over. It is true that it no longer brought great novelties; but it continued to keep everything in suspense. In fact it was like a wheel spinning in the air, but which seemed like it would have to spin that way forever.

It is difficult to imagine, even today, into what extremes of fatigue, of apathy, of indifference or rather contempt for politics that people had been thrown by an effort so long, so terrible, and so futile. Several peoples have presented the same picture, but since each nation brings to a common situation the particularity of its nature, this time one saw the French put a kind of passionate joy and vivacity into thus abandoning themselves. Despairing of escape from their hardships, they tried not to think of them. The pleasures of Paris, writes a contemporary, are no longer interrupted for a moment by the crises which follow one another, nor by those which are feared. Never had theaters or public amusements been more crowded. It was said at Tivoli that things were going to be worse than ever, they called the fatherland "the sick one," and they danced. A banner has just been hung at the foot of the statue of liberty, a police report says, which reads: "Our government is like a mass for the dead: no Gloria, no Credo, a long Offertory, and at the end, no Benediction." [To paraphrase, ". . . no praise, no belief, lots of sacrifice, and no blessing at the end."— Trans.]. Never had fashion exercised an empire more extravagant and more fickle. A strange thing, despair had made all the frivolity of the old mores reappear. Only frivolity had taken on new characteristics: it had become bizarre, chaotic, and so to speak revolutionary; like serious things, pleasure had lost its rules and boundaries.

Political institutions are like religions, where worship usually long outlives belief. At the center of this nation, which no longer cared about freedom or believed in the Republic, where all the Revolution's fervor seemed extinct, it was strange to see the government persisting in all the revolutionary routines. In the month of May, it solemnly attended the festival of the sovereignty of the people; in spring, the festival of youth; in summer, that of agriculture; in autumn, that for the aged. On 10 August the government assembled public officials around the altar of the fatherland to swear fidelity to the constitution and hatred for tyrants.

François de Neufchâteau, minister of the interior in 1799, was chiefly concerned about the good conduct of civic festivals. At the very moment when foreigners threatened the territory of a France devoured from within by anarchy, the majority of his circulars are about this. He relied greatly on the shows, he said, to reanimate patriotism and all the private virtues. It is true that he was one of the stupidest intellectuals who ever got involved in politics.

Since no one wanted to take these ridiculous festivals seriously any more, a law had been made (17 Thermidor, Year VI) to require merchants, under pain of fine and imprisonment, to close their shops on the days they were celebrated, as well as on the *décadis* [every tenth day—Trans.], and to forbid under the same penalties any work taking place in public or in sight of public places on those same days. Since the word "citizen" had become a kind of insult (a kind of coarse word which no one wanted to use any more), these words had been posted in large letters in all public places: "here, we are honored by the title of citizen."

The revolutionary faction which held power had also retained in its official style all the Revolution's rhetoric. The last thing that a party abandons is its language, because, among political parties as elsewhere, the vulgar make the rules in matters of language, and the vulgar more readily give up the ideas they have been given than the words which they have finally learned. When one rereads the speeches of this time, it seems that nothing could be said simply any more. All the soldiers are warriors; the husbands, spouses; the wives, faithful companions; the children, pledges of love. Honesty was never spoken of, but always virtue, and one never promised anything less than to die for the country and for freedom.

What is even worse is that most of the orators who gave these speeches were themselves almost as tired, disenchanted, and cold as the rest; but that is the sad situation of great passions which long after they have lost their hold on the heart leave their mark on language. He who paid attention only to the newspapers might have thought himself in the midst of the nation most passionate for its freedom and most interested in public affairs. Never had the newspapers' language been more inflamed, never was their clamor more lively than at the moment when they were about to be silent for fifteen years. If you want to know the real power of the press, never pay any attention to what it says, but rather to the way people listen to it. Sometimes its passion announces its weaknesses and foretells its end. Its clamor and its peril often have the same cause. It shouts so loudly only because its audience has become deaf, and it is this public deafness which, one day, finally allows it to be silenced with impunity.

Although from then on the citizens remained estranged from the nation's affairs, it must not be believed that they were insensitive to the particular dangers that politics could subject them to. Precisely the opposite happened. Never perhaps have the French more feared the personal consequences of political events than at the moment when they no longer wanted to concern themselves with politics. In politics, fear is a passion which often grows at the expense of all others. People are easily afraid of everything when they no longer desire anything very strongly. The French, furthermore, have a kind of gay despair which often fools their master. They laugh at their problems, but that doesn't keep them from feeling them. The French were devoured by political worries right in the middle of their egoistic preoccupation with their own petty personal business and the giddiness of their pleasures; an almost unbearable anguish, an inexpressible terror, took possession of all minds.

Although the dangers which one ran in 1799 were, all in all, infinitely less great than those of the Revolution's first days, nonetheless they inspired a fear infinitely stronger and more general, because the nation had less energy, less passion, and more experience. In 1799 all the various ills which had crushed the nation over ten years gathered in its imagination to form the picture of the future, and after having thrown itself fearlessly and even without caution into the most terrible catastrophes, the nation trembled at the movement of its own shadow. One can note, in the writings of the time, that the most contradictory things were successively and often simultaneously feared: some men fear the abolition of property, others, the return of feudal dues. Often the same man, after having feared one of these dangers, almost immediately began to fear the other; in the morning a restoration, in the evening a return of the Terror. Many were afraid to show their fear, and it was only after the crisis of 18 Brumaire that one could judge, by the extent of their satisfaction and the excess of their joy, what an abyss of cowardice the Revolution had dug in those weakened souls.

However used to humanity's illogical fickleness we ought to be, it seems permissible to be astonished at seeing such a great change in a people's moral disposition: so much egoism after so much devotion, so much indifference after so much passion, so much fear after so much heroism, such great contempt for what had been the object of such violent desires and for what had cost so much. One must give up the attempt to explain such a rapid and complete change by the usual laws of the moral world. The character of our nation is so particular that the general study of humanity is not enough to understand it. It constantly surprises even those who have tried to study it in particular: a nation better endowed than any other with the capacity to easily understand extraordinary things and adopt them, capable of anything which only demands one effort, however great it may be, but unable to sustain itself very high for long, because it has only feelings and no principles. The most civilized of all the civilized peoples of the earth and yet, under certain circumstances, the people closer to barbarism than any of them; for what is proper to savages is to decide by the sudden impression of the moment, without memory of the past or idea of the future.

CHAPTER TWO

How the Nation, While No Longer Republican, Had Remained Revolutionary

The royalists, who saw that the nation had thus become disgusted with freedom, thought it was ready to return to the old regime. This is the mistake the defeated always make, believing that they are loved because their successors are hated, without realizing that it is much easier for people to remain faithful in their hatreds than in their loves. France, which no longer loved the Republic, remained deeply attached to the Revolution. This fact had so many consequences that it is appropriate to stop for a moment to examine it at length.

As time went by and the old regime receded, people became more stubborn about not wanting to return to it. It was an odd phenomenon: to the extent that it made the nation suffer, the Revolution seemed to become more dear to it.

From contemporary writings it can be seen that this surprised the Revolution's enemies more than anything else. When they compared the evils that the Revolution had made people endure with the attachment they retained for it, it seemed to them that France had gone crazy.

However, the same cause had these contradictory effects.

The Revolution had made people suffer more because the bad government that it had founded had lasted. The fact that the Revolution lasted gave roots to the new habits it created, and multiplied and diversified the interests which needed it. As the nation went on this was like the creation of so many barriers behind it, which made it more and more impossible to turn back.

Almost all the French had taken an active part in public life since the beginning of the Revolution, and had supported it by public actions. They felt themselves in some way responsible for the misfortunes that had followed. As these misfortunes continued and worsened, this responsibility seemed to grow. Thus the Terror gave many of the very people from whom it took its victims an invincible aversion for the reestablishment of a master who would have so many crimes to investigate and so many injuries to avenge.

Something similar is seen in all revolutions. The very revolutions which most torment a people make a restoration of the old situation almost unbearable, provided that they last.

Further, the Revolution had not oppressed everybody equally: some people had suffered little from it and, even among those who had borne its brunt, many had found some very precious gains mingled with the harm it caused. I think that the lower classes' standard of living declined much less than is commonly thought. At least they found great compensations among their hardships.

A prodigious number of workers having been sent to the armies, or having volunteered, the remaining workers in France were much better paid. Salaries rose despite all the public and private disasters because the working class shrank even more quickly than industry did.

Mallet du Pan, one of the greatest enemies of the Revolution, wrote in 1796: "Today the workers earn more than in 1790." Sir Francis d'Ivernois, who every year for ten years set out to prove to the English that France, exhausted by its hardships, had no more than six months to live, himself admitted in his last pamphlet in 1799 that since the Revolution salaries had increased everywhere, and that the price of wheat had declined.

As for the peasants, I do not need to remind anyone that they had acquired a lot of land at very low prices. For them at least the resulting profit was incalculable.

Everyone also knows that the Revolution abolished a multitude of burdensome or humiliating taxes, such as the tithe and the feudal dues known under the names of the corvée, the taille, the salt tax; some of these taxes were never reestablished and others only partially or only after the period of which we are speaking. Today it can hardly be calculated how unbearable many of these taxes seemed to the lower classes, whether because of their flaws or as a result of the ideas which were attached to them.

Finding myself in Canada in 1831, chatting with some peasants of French origin, I realized that to them the word "taille" had become the synonym for evil and misery. They said of a very bad event: "it's a real taille." The tax itself had not, I believe, ever existed in Canada; in any case, it had been abolished there for over half a century. No one remembered any more what it had consisted of, only its name remained in the language as an imperishable testimony to the horror which it had inspired.

What has not been sufficiently noted is the more indirect and irregular but not smaller profit that the Revolution gave a multitude of poor debtors. Debts properly speaking were never legally abolished, but in fact they were eliminated shortly after the establishment of paper money.

We know now that in many French provinces the number of small landowners was already very large before '89. There is reason to believe (this cannot be fully proved, however) that the majority of these small proprietors were very indebted, for it was they who then bore the chief tax burden. Even today, when the burden of public expenses weighs on everyone equally, they are still the most indebted.

The towns themselves were full of little fortunes in difficulty with debt, for France has always been a country of worried people where everyone always has more desires and more vanity than money.

Finally it must be noted that before the Revolution, as in our day, the class of tenant farmers was very numerous because our farms in general are very small.

The rapid depreciation of paper money was like a bonfire of all debts, a reduction of all rents to almost nothing.

Even the debts that were owed the state were never either completely or regularly repaid. The disorder of the times and still more the weaknesses of public administration were obstacles. The Republic's financial accounts show that no more than a quarter of the taxes that were maintained or the new ones that had been established could ever be collected. The state supported itself by means of assignats, requisitions in kind, and by the spoils of Europe. The assignats, M. Thibaudeau rightly says in his memoirs, whose discredit ruins the big landowner and the rentier, enrich the peasants and the tenant farmers (vol. 1, p. 54).

In 1795, that same Mallet du Pan whom I have already cited writes that the countryside enriches itself from the towns' misfortunes; they make fabulous profits. A sack of grain pays the farmer the price of the rent on his land. The peasants become calculators, speculators; they argue over the émigrés' property and don't pay any taxes. An intelligent foreigner who traveled through France during the same time writes in the account of his trip: "The real aristocracy of France today is the aristocracy of farmers and peasants."

It is true that the peasant thus relieved was often afflicted by civil troubles, the lodging of troops, or government requisitions; but these brief and limited events did not disgust him with the good that the Revolution had brought him. On the contrary, they made him more attached to his gains; one suffered from these evils as one suffers from hail and floods, which only make people more impatient for a normal season which will allow them to profit.

When we see how the authors of our first revolution acted in order to win the hearts of the rural population, through what substantial gifts they interested the small landowners and the poor, who were the large majority of the nation, in their work, despite the hardships and misfortunes of the times, one wonders at the naïveté of some present-day revolutionaries. They believe that it is easy to make a very civilized people patiently bear the discomfort inseparable from great political change by giving them freedoms instead of profits and spoils.

The bourgeoisie, which had started the Revolution, above all that of the towns, was the class which suffered most among the winners. Its members suffered more and its goods almost as much as the nobility itself. Its commerce was partly eliminated, its industry destroyed; all the little offices from which many of its members lived were abolished. But the same event that bankrupted it gave it hegemony. It already gave it political power and soon permitted it to put much of the public treasury at its sole disposal.

Furthermore, most of the changes that the Revolution had suddenly produced through the violent and chaotic exertion of its tyranny had been announced, advocated, and demanded throughout the whole length of the eighteenth century. They satisfied the reason and charmed the minds of those very persons whose interests they most harmed. The new things were blamed only for having cost too much. But the very price paid made some of them still more precious. Thus much had been suffered and feared, but there was still something which seemed worse than the suffering and present uncertainties, and that was a return to the previous situation.

A royalist writes during the famine of 1796: the people curse and complain about the Republic. But talk sense to them, tell them that they were happier before; they respond that the aristocrats want to make them ask for the king by means of fear and hunger, but that they'd rather eat cobblestones.

Certain clever people in our day have tried to rehabilitate the old regime. I note first of all that it is a bad proof of how good a government was when you only start to praise it upon ceasing to believe in the possibility of reestablishing it. As for me, I judge it not by what I think, but by the feelings the old regime inspired in those who experienced it and destroyed it. I see that throughout the whole course of such a cruel and oppressive Revolution, hatred for the old regime always surpassed all other hatreds in French hearts, and so rooted itself there that it survived its very object. From a momentary passion it has become a permanent national trait. I note that, during the most perilous vicissitudes of the last sixty years, the fear of a return of the old regime has always smothered all other fears in these fickle and worried minds. That's enough for me. For me, the test has been made and the system judged.

The impossibility of making the French return to the old order of things was, for that matter, recognized almost as soon as they had left it. Mirabeau pointed it out right away and several of the greatest opponents of the new institutions soon discovered it. I find what follows in a little brochure that M. de Montlosier published during the emigration (in 1796), which is perhaps the most remarkable work that that eccentric and energetic mind produced:

"The monarchy," he says, "has drowned under the weight of our rights and privileges which were based on it. We must sacrifice these rights and privileges in order for it to return to the surface. We are assured that everyone curses the Revolution; ah! I believe it. I only try to see if there isn't a difference between cursing the Revolution and wanting to reestablish the old order of things. France wants only its present situation and peace. No one wants to lose the fruit of his talents or of events. The generals in the army don't want to become privates again, the judges don't want to go back to being bailiffs, the mayors and presidents of departments don't want to return to being workers or artisans, the purchasers of our properties don't want to return them. It is done, the Revolution which all France curses has penetrated all France. We must enter into this mixture such as it is, find our place there, and persuade ourselves that we will not be accepted with all the trappings of our previous existence."

Most émigrés had very different ideas. The folly of the royalists outside France would seem inconceivable if one didn't know that they had been brought up on the futile prejudices of a powerless aristocracy and that they had lived a long time in exile.

The punishment of exile had had the cruel result that it made them suffer a great deal and taught them nothing. Somehow it *immobilized* the minds of those who endured it, kept them forever in the ideas that they had had or that were current when their exile began. For the émigrés, the new facts which had been created in the country and the new mores which had been established there did not exist. It was like the hands of a clock which remain fixed at the time when the clock stopped, however much time has since passed. It is said that this came from a particular process in the minds of certain exiles. I hold that it is the common disease of exile; few escape it.

Thus these émigrés lived in the imaginary enjoyment of their privileges long after they had been lost forever. They only thought about what they would do when they were again in possession of their lands and their vassals, without considering that those vassals were now making Europe tremble. What worried them most was not how long the Republic would last, it was that the monarchy would not be reestablished exactly the way it was before its fall; they detested the constitutional monarchists more than the terrorists, spoke of nothing but the just severity that they would exercise when they were masters, and, while waiting for their time to come, devoured one another; in a word, they left out nothing that would create hatred and contempt and make the French imagine an old regime even more hateful than the one which they had destroyed.

Caught between fear of these royalists and fear of the Jacobins, the majority of the nation looked for a way out. We loved the Revolution and feared the republican state which could bring either one of them back. One could even say that these two feelings mutually encouraged each other; because the French found certain advantages which the Revolution had given them very precious, they were all the more annoyed by the problem of a government which wouldn't let them enjoy their gains. Among all the advantages that they had acquired or obtained during ten years, the only one they were ready to abandon was freedom. They were ready to sacrifice this freedom that the Revolution had never more than promised them in order to finally obtain undisturbed enjoyment of the other goods that it had given them.

The political parties themselves, decimated, exhausted, and tired, wanted to be able to rest for a moment, under whatever kind of oppression, provided that it was exercised by a neutral and that it weighed on their rivals as much as on themselves. This stroke puts the finishing touch on the picture: when the great political parties begin to become lukewarm in their loves without lessening their hatreds, and finally arrive at the point of caring less about winning than about preventing the success of their opponents, one had better prepare oneself for servitude; the master is near.

It could easily be seen that this master could only come from the army.

It is interesting to follow, across the different phases of this long Revolution, the army's gradual march towards sovereign power. At the beginning, the army was dispersed by unarmed crowds, or rather dissolved itself in the rapid movement of public opinion. For a long time, the army seemed separate from what was going on internally; it was the people of Paris alone who at their pleasure made and unmade the army's leaders as well as the masters of France. However, the Revolution took its course. The passions that it had created ran down, the able men who had directed it in the assemblies died or retired, its government became gentler, the feelings that it had hardened became lax, anarchy spread everywhere. During this time the army organized itself, trained itself, made itself famous; great generals were made. In the army a common purpose was maintained, and common passions, when the nation no longer had any. The civilians and military constituted, in short, two completely different

societies, at the same time and among the same people. The links of one society were stretching while those of the other became tighter.

On 13 Vendémiaire (1795) the army, for the first time since 1789, took a role in internal affairs: it made the Convention prevail and triumph over the bourgeois of Paris. In 1797 (on 18 Fructidor), the army helped the Directory defeat not only Paris but the legislative body, or rather the entire country, which had chosen the legislature. On 30 Prairial (1799), it refused to support those same Directors, whom it blamed for its defeats, and they fell before the legislature.

Beginning 13 Vendémiaire one could no longer govern without the army. Soon after, one could only govern through it. This point having been reached, the army wanted to do the governing itself. These facts led to one another. Long before becoming the masters, the soldiers had taken on their tone and attitude. A Swiss who traveled through France in 1798, a great partisan of the Revolution and a great friend of the Republic, remarked with regret that during the public festivals anyone who saw the pride of the military parade, the power the soldiers exercised over the citizens, the arrogance with which they spurned them, would have thought that never during royal festivals had less regard been shown for the people.

The friends of the Republic who recognized this growing military influence reassured themselves by noting that the army had always demonstrated very republican feelings, and that it still seemed strongly moved by these feelings when the rest of the country no longer cared.

What they took for love of the Republic was above all love for the Revolution. Among the French the army was, indeed, the only class where all its members without exception had gained from the Revolution and had a personal interest in maintaining it. All the officers owed their rank to the Revolution and all the soldiers owed their chance at becoming officers to it. The army was, in truth, the Revolution in arms. When it still shouted with a kind of furor "Long live the Republic!" it was as a challenge to the old regime whose friends shouted "Long live the King!" Fundamentally the army didn't care at all about public freedoms. Normally, even among free peoples the soldier's entire public spirit consists of hatred for foreigners and love of the soil; still more strongly must this be so among a nation which has reached the point that we in France had then. Thus the army, like almost all the armies of the world, understood absolutely nothing of the slow and complicated gears of representative government; it detested and despised assemblies, understood only a strong and simple power, and wanted nothing but national independence and victories.

Everything being so well prepared for a new revolution, it must not be thought that anyone had a clear idea of what was going to happen. There are times when the world resembles one of our theaters before the curtain goes up. You know that you are going to watch a new play. You can already hear the preparations on stage; the actors can almost be touched, but they aren't seen and you don't know what the play will be. Thus, towards the end of 1799, the approach of a revolution was felt everywhere without anyone yet imagining what it could be. It seemed impossible to remain in the current situation, but it seemed equally impossible to leave it.

The content of all the correspondence of the times is this: the present situation can't last. Nothing more. The imagination itself was weary, we were tired of hoping and foreseeing. The nation, surrendering itself, terrified but sluggish at the same time, nonchalantly turned its eyes here and there to see if anyone was coming to help. One could certainly see that this savior must come from the army. Who would it be? Some thought of Pichegru, some of Moreau, others of Bernadotte.

"Retired to the countryside in the depths of the Bourbonnais [a region in central France around Moulins—Trans]," says M. Fiévée in his memoirs, "one thing alone reminded me of politics: every peasant that I met in the fields, vineyards, or woods took me aside to ask if there was news of General Bonaparte, and why didn't he return to France; nobody ever *asked for news* about the Directory."

APPENDIX

Tocqueville's Research Notes on the Convention and the Directory

The Terror

Various Notes

General fatigue. Indifference. Desire to stop and retrace one's steps. Feelings which long precede the moment when they reach the light of day. At the earliest this goes back to '91 or '92.

The nation's fatigue and desire for rest at any price date from much farther back than is thought. To the second chapter. I have reasons to believe that fatigue of the Revolution overtook the nation (above all the agricultural classes) much sooner than people think, and that from very early on the nation allowed things to happen more than it took the initiative. We find traces of this from the beginning of the Terror. See the writings of the times. See 13 Vendémiaire, which was assuredly produced by a national feeling. See 18 Fructidor, the unanimity which presided at the election of the second third, and the unanimity in the opposite direction which returned the Montagnard deputies after the elections had been canceled (the nation's incredible faculty of just letting things happen and everyone always following the same path like sheep; it is in the nation's gentleness itself that one must look for the origin of the great and energetic things done by the hands which mistreated it. Interesting and central problem! But how to lay it out well and resolve it?). It is equally evident that from a very early period the nation was passionately attached to the great results of the Revolution, so that disgust with the Revolution and attachment to its results were almost contemporary with its birth.

Unfortunate and almost ridiculous situation of those who were attached to the Revolution's purely political side, and who honestly thought the Revolution meant the Republic. Second chapter. To paint well, with the help above all of Thibaudeau and my own memories (for in this the two republics resemble each other), the unfortunate and almost ridiculous situation of the sincerely republican party, that honest third party, running after an ideal and ever receding republic, caught between those who wanted the Terror and those who wanted the monarchy, laboriously trying to make the republic survive without republicans. If ever it was permissible to laugh at good faith and honesty, this would assuredly be the time.

What explains the patience of the lower classes under the Terror, beyond the natural ease of submitting to authority once it seems the stronger, accepting everything from it, resigning oneself to it like death and hunger in the countryside, chief cause, a trait of character. What helps one understand how a government as violent, as despotic, and at the same time as irregular as that which reigned over France during the first period of the French Revolution could last so long is that under this bad government, the classes which usually overthrow governments, the lower classes proper, were in a situation infinitely better than one might believe. The class that was really suffering was the one which does not overthrow governments (and again even amid the class I call suffering there were still a multitude of individuals who profited from the Revolution, even under the Terror: purchasers of land, debtors who paid off their debts . . .).

* * *

Movement of the Revolution. The Terror.

Movement of the Revolution internally.

The Terror. Impossible elsewhere than in France with the characteristics that it had among us. A product of general causes that *local* causes pushed beyond all bounds. Born from our mores, from our character, from our habits, from centralization, from the sudden destruction of all hierarchy . . .

Its means, its real form, its powerful organization, its crushing unity amidst the disorder of all things and apparent anarchy.

Paint the general character of the periods which follow, the general movement of the Revolution across the reactions, the disenchantments, the fatigue, the boredom with assemblies and freedom; the growing dominance of military power; the military character which the Revolution took on more and more . . .

*   *   *

Why the French submitted so easily to the hardship and miseries of the Revolution. What prevented them from almost immediately returning to any kind of order.

Must I make this a separate chapter when I get to the Terror or before that? 1856.

The lower classes less unfortunate than is believed. What attached them to the Revolution, despite its rigors.

*   *   *

France, at the same time as it became more industrious, was not yet *industrial.* That this was not a country of industry, that is of large populations, which needed and believed they absolutely needed internal peace in order to live. Although very advanced in intellectual refinement and even, to a certain degree, in luxury, this was not a nation where everyone had the habit of comfort. Life was ornate but it lacked many of the little conveniences which become necessities to peoples, in our day, and make internal peace necessary to them *at any price.*

*   *   *

How the French were able to submit to the hardship and miseries of the Revolution so easily.

The French, much less manufacturers, much less businessmen, much less well-off, much less connected by their wealth to the wealth of the state, much less possessed by the desire for material well-being, much more concerned with ideas and feelings, much more uncouth and rude in their mores, more simple and manly in their habits than those of today.

*   *   *

Little industrial development in France. One of the causes of the Revolution. Very interesting point of view which can be considered in two ways.

1) The great side, which consists of showing how men were much less fearful of revolutions for this reason and much less controllable through the passion for material well-being.

2) As a proof that the passion for material well-being did not exist to the same degree as now.

Today industrial mores have become national mores.

* * *

France already industrial before the Revolution.

The facts relating to this question can be very useful to study from two points of view:

1. To show the already great movement of population and industrial population in the large cities, above all in Paris; which facilitated riots.

2. How industry (the needs which it created, the habits of heart and mind it suggested) was still little developed in France, which explains with what ease and for how long people submitted to the hardships of the Revolution.

One of the chief elements for learning the truth on this point is the book or report made in 1788 by M. de Tolosan, inspector of commerce.

* * *

Why the Revolution was able to last despite the financial situation, and did not perish for lack of money, despite predictions.

It is not the *financial* causes which must be discussed here, I would be poor at that. It is the general and political causes.

Much to take here from Mallet du Pan.

* * *

Why the Revolution did not and could not lead to civil war. This did not come from the small number or moral weakness of those who did not love it or wanted to fight it. No center of resistance, neither around certain men nor around local governments.

Why, on the contrary, the Revolution led to riots and why it was made by riots and surprise attacks.

* * *

Emigration.

This measure so new and so extraordinary, mass emigration, is explained by the equally new and equally extraordinary historical circumstance of an entire body of nobility which, planted for a thousand years, suddenly found itself so deprived of roots that it did not see any way to remain upright in its place. An entire upper class which could not find, in any of the other classes that made up the nation, a force of resistance with which it could combine, sympathy, common interests . . . which found itself like an officer corps against which the soldiers all open fire.

This is its condemnation and, in this particular case, its excuse. This could hardly have been found anywhere but in France, where, independently of the fact's general causes, there is a mental disposition which leads everyone to head for the same side following the blind inspiration of the moment, and where present interest or current passions made the isolation of the nobility still greater than the grievances people had against it.

*   *   *

The more or less violent and persistent hatred between classes was born not only from the more or less great vices of the social state which created them, but from the struggle which changed it (June 1858).

We see that in foreign countries where the aristocracy seems to have been as vain, as irritating, as abusive as in France, the hatred which it inspired and inspires is infinitely less bitter, less violent, less strong than among us, and we are astonished. We are not paying attention to this: What inflames, sharpens, exasperates, eternalizes the hatred that the aristocracy inspires, and the spite between classes, is not only the importance of the abuses, it is the duration and liveliness of the struggle to which they have led. A given aristocracy which slowly retreats under the pressure of time, or falls rapidly and violently under the blows of a foreign cause, or under the action of a power which simultaneously compresses all parties and makes the revolution without exciting war, an aristocracy of this kind, after its fall or even before its fall is completely over, excites less hatred, arouses less rancor, leaves behind a reputation much less bad than another aristocracy which, less abusive, did not perish or does not give way except amid long civil struggles. Also it is not, as I have said above, from the abuses alone of an aristocracy that one must ask for an account of the feelings that it leaves behind, it is again the fashion in which it has been changed or destroyed that must be considered.

An idea which does not lack either truth or depth, but which needs to be compressed in a shorter passage, more terse and striking, in order not to have the air of a commonplace, which it is not.

*   *   *

Fatal influence of the French Revolution. M. Vogt, urging (in September 1848) the Frankfurt Parliament to break with the great powers of Germany with regard to the peace of Malmö, cried out: "People are frightened of our position if the peace is rejected. Our situation will be that of France in '93; threatened like us from inside and outside, France based itself on the strength of the people, it created men, it made armies rise from the earth, and Europe was defeated. It was a Convention which did that; it is only a Convention which can reproduce those great things." The Convention which did so much immediate damage to contemporaries by its fury has done permanent damage by its examples. It has created the politics of the *impossible,* the theory of folly, the cult of blind audacity.

People do not see the particular circumstances in which France and Europe found themselves at that moment and which allowed the Convention to triumph, and people believe it is enough to try to do the impossible as it did, and try with insane violence and blind audacity, in order to succeed (20 June 1854).

Notes on Thibaudeau [Memoirs on the Convention and the Directory]

"The majority of the Convention was not any more terrorist than the majority of the nation. But not being able or not daring to disapprove, it kept a gloomy silence. The sessions formerly so long and so stormy were, for the most part, cold and quiet and did not last longer *than one or two hours.* It could not use the shadow of freedom which remained to it except on matters of little importance" (vol. 1, p. 48).

What is to be pictured is the dominance which always belongs to *minorities* in revolutionary periods; this mechanism of revolution always the same: the majority's state of mind which makes this tyranny of the minority possible and brings it about. [...]

"In entirely withdrawing from affairs I would have made myself uselessly suspect. The dominators did not find it bad that the members of the right wing kept, in their silence, the attitude of a defeated party, nor that what was inside people stayed there. But the Mountain would not have permitted a deputy, no matter how obscure, to give himself the air of being discontented by his inaction" (vol. 1, p. 70). Interesting as a physiology of the parties.

Letter written by a royalist to an émigré in 1794. [...] Among other things one finds here this sentence applicable to several other periods of the Revolution: *"there are no longer any men in France, there are only events,"* and this other sentence worthy of the most profound thought: "it is the Republic which will suffocate the Republic and the revolutionaries who will end the Revolution. It will happen like this or else it will never happen" (vol. 1, p. 100). [...]

What is visible, whose cause must be sought with care, is that the furious hatred against priests and religion is the strongest and last extinguished of the revolutionary passions. All chapter 12, page 106, shows it. We see that the last ones oppressed are the priests, that the persecution against them outlasted all others. The Terror, insofar as it concerned them, continued or recreated itself even through the Directory. The fury is greater and more persistent than even against the émigrés, although the émigrés were still in arms. [...]

After the elections of Year V the constitutionals were divided among themselves. The government was more revolutionary than the Councils and the nation. The armies were revolutionary out of hatred for royalty and assemblies. The Club de Clichy, a picture similar to what one could have made of the rue de Poitiers [vol. 2] (chapter 18, p. 170). [...]

War between the Directory and the Councils, which disorganized what little there was of government existing in France, the administrative machine being not yet mounted in such a way as to function almost by itself. Anarchy among the great powers brought about real anarchy in the services and the country. Difference from what we have seen in our time. [...]

Perfect analogy between what happened before Fructidor and what preceded 2 December 1851. Mockeries of the Councils. Plan to attack by the Directory. Violent men who are attracted to Paris. The sight of danger clear enough to alarm all those who are threatened, not enough to force them to unite in common action. Attempt at unity among them which fails. People want to wait until the Directors act unconstitutionally before acting that way themselves. While waiting, they are threatened, they are harassed by petty measures. Read the whole of chapter 22, volume 2, it is as if you are reading the history of the last six months. [...]

Perplexity of the true republicans. Caught between the terrorists and the royalists, entirely similar in their predicament to their perplexity in recent times and their despair between the Mountain and the Burgraves. Nothing is better painted in Thibaudeau's chapter about 18 Fructidor. Augereau takes personal responsibility for the security of the Councils. This is pure Saint Arnaud (p. 251). [...]

Deportations substituted for the guillotine. A means within the scope of violent powers acting amid gentle mores and tired nations. One thus kills without seeing blood or hearing the cries of the tortured (vol. 2, p. 319).

Difficulty of recreating the Terror. Desire of the victorious party in Fructidor to reestablish the Terror. Terror conceived and welcomed by them more systematically, one should note, and even more grandly and with more iniquity than by the terrorists of '93. Mass deportation of all nobles proposed (vol. 2, p. 319). [. . .]

Clothing. There was no formal dress during the whole terrible period of the Revolution. It was only when power fell into the Directory's miserable hands that people invented a splendid costume for the Directors, and after 18 Fructidor, when the legislative body allowed itself to be mutilated and debased, that people thought of a purple coat to cover it (vol. 2, p. 331).

Industrial ruin of France in this period. I find a small but unique proof of this: The impossibility of having coats for the legislative body made in France, the obligation to get them from England, despite the war. To complete the charade they are stopped by customs (vol. 2, pp. 331ff.). [. . .]

Bonaparte's attitude after the peace and before Egypt. Bonaparte's reception on his return from Italy. Loquacity of Barras. Brief and very obscure style of Bonaparte: "the organic laws of the Republic remain to be made, the era of representative governments begins" (vol. 2, p. 325).

He observes the parties, apparently joins none. He has connections with the Thermidorians, Barras, Tallien (become moderates by comparison with Sieyès); the Jacobins, who had a marvelous instinct for scenting their enemies, attack him (even though he had often served them); his compatriot Arena says that he is the man most dangerous to freedom (this is exactly what begins to help him: in revolutions opinion moves more quickly than certain men and what the latter continue to say as an insult is heard by the nation as praise). "Public opinion was favorable to him and gave him the means to dare all. We were tired of endless disruptions and, in order to rest, the nation threw itself into the arms of a man whom it believed strong enough to stop the Revolution and generous enough to consolidate its benefits" (vol. 2, p. 339).

Opinion, astonished by Bonaparte's inaction, envisaged every post for him. The Directory, tired of his presence, looked for any excuse to get him out of Paris. He, playing at disinterest and fatigue, only seemed to want rest and silently observed everything that was going on under his eyes (vol. 2, p. 341).

The Directory and he, two rival powers: it was necessary to fight or separate (ibid., p. 349). The idea of Egypt, which had often presented itself to his mind during the Italian campaigns, proved by his letters (ibid., p. 343).

Natural and invincible dominance that the executive power in France has over the legislative power as soon as revolutionary passions calm down. "At the Commission of Eleven" (which had prepared the constitution of the Year III), "we had looked at the balance of powers as a chimera, and while conferring great power on the Directory, we had given preeminence to the legislative body and taken all kinds of precautions in order to assure its independence against the enterprises of the executive power" (vol. 2, p. 337).

Which did not prevent 18 Fructidor a few months later and the almost complete subjection of the legislature. [. . .]

Notes on Mallet du Pan: "Organization, Resources of the Government of the Terror," Written in 1794

Better explained and even better depicted in chapter 1, volume 2, than I have ever seen it. This must be reread in order to understand well the mechanism of this prodigious dictatorship, its gears, its regular means of action, its principles, its rules, for it had them.

As for its financial resources, they can be summed up in this passage: "The Republic is richer and disposes of greater resources than all the sovereigns of the Coalition combined. For here it is the national wealth of an empire and the accumulation of wealth in that empire over a century which fight against the weak incomes of a few sovereigns" (p. 21).

He could have said: It is the struggle of capital against income, a combat in which capital must always triumph, if the struggle is short.

The Terror made by terror. This phenomenon is very vigorously depicted by Mallet du Pan (vol. 2, p. 56). He shows well, in a few words, which should be reread when I want to speak of this period in passing, the state of mind of these men who were at first led into atrocity by the hatred which they bore for the enemies of the Revolution, by the resistance of the latter, by the fear that the counterrevolution inspired in them. Who then, when these enemies were defeated, continued to commit atrocities from fear of the revolutionaries themselves; who, after having committed atrocity out of fear of their enemies, became more atrocious out of fear of their friends; who exaggerated the terror out of fear of being devoured by it; who killed in order not to be killed; who were condemned to remain dictators in order to stay alive and make eternal war on the human race because they would cease to live the day they returned to humane principles. [. . .]

Why the Committee of Public Safety could not want peace. Because there was identity between its means of authority and the means of public defense. "Without the war, no more pretext for extortions, for pillage, for forced enrollments, for requisition of all the fruits of the land and industry, for universal plundering. [. . .] War is a necessity for the Committee and only a Hottentot could be excused for thinking it possible to obtain peace from the Republic" (vol. 2, p. 59). [. . .]

The old governments of Europe in the face of the French Revolution. Their incapacity, their old routine, their old jealousies, their lack of concert, their slowness, their self-interested and superficial viewpoints; not realizing the greatness and novelty of the event, and not seeing first of all that for them it was a matter, not of aggrandizement, but of survival. "As long as the allies do not have [. . .] their Committee of Public Safety, whether it be a congress of plenipotentiaries armed with absolute and general instructions [. . .] empowered to give operations a direction as prompt as the circumstances, we will lose the fruits of the most expensive efforts" (vol. 2, p. 77).

Paint the old governmental Europe in the face of the novelty of revolutionary government. The Revolution fell amid this antique machine like an artillery shell, neither whose cannon nor gunners could be seen, smashing everything by its novelty, its unexpectedness, its strangeness as much as by its power.

Paint above all how the old governments and the Revolution being such, the latter could not fail to triumph. Never has success been due less to chance. Make this come out strongly.

The political parties at the end of the Terror (1794–1795). Pretty interesting analysis of this by the author. Their classification, their respective strengths (vol. 2, pp. 129ff.). Above all he depicts the constitutional party well, the party of the bourgeois and the rural landowners, the most numerous, condemned to nullity and dissimulation but having deep roots and ready to rush in on all sides the moment republican tyranny weakened. Better placed than any other to lead the Republic into a moderate monarchy. [. . .]

New and particular appearance of the French Revolution among the great human revolutions. Recognized somewhat vaguely, from its beginning, by some contemporaries, some individuals, rather than by sovereigns.

"What does not change is the *essence* of revolutionary doctrine. [. . .] It dominates in the governments, in the sections, in the clubs; the popular societies created in every city, every town or village, where the lower classes go every evening, are its depot and arsenal. [. . .] This is what that crowd of writers and ignorant reasoners who constantly describe the French Revolution as *local,* as produced by causes particular to France, as maintained by the need to resist foreign invasion, do not understand at all. [. . .] The revolutionary system is applicable to all nations. It has as its basis philosophical maxims proper to all climates and enemies to all governments. This antisocial theory is a veritable religion" (vol. 2, p. 134).

This is what must be well brought out and highlighted. The characteristic traits of the French Revolution, what *in truth* makes it a general and human event, or at the very least a European event, not particular and French; what distinguishes it from all other Revolutions; what made it, as he says, a new religion which spread beyond the interests of nationality, and among those very people whom it pillaged, massacred, oppressed, made despair. One of the most unusual, most active, and most contagious illnesses of the human mind. I am, on this side, on a road which must lead beyond commonplaces.

Impossibility of returning to the old regime. This is apparent from the earliest time of the Revolution. Why? Look for it. Mirabeau's imperturbable certainty on this point. See his letters. Opinion expressed in every way by Mallet du Pan, the irreconcilable enemy of the French Revolution. "It is as impossible," said the émigré Abbé de Pradt, "to remake the old regime as to build St. Peter's of Rome with the dust of the road" (vol. 2, pp. 142, 153). [. . .]

Material well-being of the peasants after the Terror, when the Towns were still suffering horribly. "Crushed under Robespierre, the countryside breathes now (July 1795), they enrich themselves from the hardships of the town, they make fabulous profits. A sack of wheat pays the farmer the price for the rent of a field. The well-off peasants have become calculators, speculators, purchasers of antique furniture, they dispute among themselves over the sales of the property of the émigrés, do not pay any taxes, congratulate each other daily over the abolition of the tithe and feudal dues, and will be, until this prosperity changes [. . .] happy enough with their condition to accept the Republic without a murmur. They *accept it without believing in it,* for while loving the present regime, they all think that one day we will return to some kind of king" (vol. 2, p. 154).

How realistic this portrait must be! Find out the condition of this class of peasant throughout the Revolution. They suffer from it less and profit from it more than any other class. A great cause which explains along with many other things the extreme tolerance of the nation amid times which seem to be and which really were frightful.

The terror caused by the émigrés, which prolongs the Revolution. [. . .] Failures and stupidities of the emigration. The royalists who remain in France are much more reasonable and much more disposed to conciliation although having suffered more. [. . .] A well-known phenomenon which makes it such that, in times of parties, the dissident is detested more than the enemy. A natural flaw of the human heart pushed to folly among the émigrés by a thousand particular flaws, a thousand special prejudices, the separation from the great national whole, life among themselves in foreign countries, and the despair of exile. Good to paint. [...]

Attachment of the lower classes to the Revolution. Mallet's correspondent tells him (vol. 2, p. 207; 1796): "The lower classes complain of their hardships, they curse the Republic, but speak reason to them, tell them that they used to be happy ... they respond that they don't want a master any more and that the aristocrats would like to make them ask for a king out of hunger and misery, but they would rather eat stones. They are still all anger."

"*The habit of poverty* and privation, the frightful situation in which the Parisians lived under Robespierre, makes them find their present situation bearable" (March 1796; vol. 2, p. 223). Robespierre had in effect lowered the bar of happiness so low, reducing it to the enjoyment of life itself, that he had rehabilitated ordinary tyrannies and common hardships.

The ability to suffer things that another people would not have suffered, to bear one's part in unbearable miseries, to immediately make it into a *habit:* this is less *human* than French. Analyze, explore, relating it to the particular times and the general temperament. [...]

How the Revolution took root through its duration, despite the duration of the misfortunes which it brought. "What frightens me above all, is that by prolonging the existence of the Republic we multiply the sales of confiscated properties. The mass of new owners increases, and when everything will be sold, who could despoil two million invaders?" (vol. 2, p. 225; April 1796).

Bonaparte: his lack of notoriety when he came on stage. Mallet, giving an account to one of his friends (April 1796) of the first French successes in Italy, and of what has taken place since the battle of Montenotte, doesn't even name the general. It is doubtful that he knew his name. Never did greater lightning ever come from greater darkness (vol. 2, p. 29). [...]

"Appearance of France and Paris a Year after the Terror" (1795)

An anonymous work, but by a man of much intelligence, titled *Recollections of My Last Trip to Paris. Printed in Year V of the Republic* (1796), but relating to Year IV (1795) a little after the Terror, at the time of 13 Vendémiaire.

The author seems to be a foreigner, Swiss, I think. He does not like the Revolution, has a taste for the delicate pleasures of the choice society that he frequented before the Revolution and which the Revolution destroyed. But he is cool-headed and does not seem to be inspired by party passion.

The majority of the nation allowing itself to be held in revolution rather than remaining revolutionary of its own will. "What I have most often met throughout my route, without taking any trouble to look for it, is the air of malaise, of unease, of fatigue, of discontent, combined with a great deal of indifference over the success or lack of success of the new order of things. Although this Revolution has had the unique merit of interesting, even of impassioning a prodigious number of men, surely more than any other, it is however a fact that the majority of the nation has remained neutral, and that it would have been still more so if the imperious necessity of circumstances and the terrible violence of revolutionary despotism had allowed it" (p. 55).

"Many of the new acquirers of national properties have become the object of hatred and contempt by all their neighbors, whether because those whose places they have taken are still missed, or because people know too well by what vile means they managed to get their hands on the property . . . I asked a coachman who was the present owner of that beautiful château: 'Eh! My lord, that is a man who used to have lice'" (p. 69).

The ravages of the Terror less general than is thought: a flood which destroyed everything in its path, but which did not go everywhere. "In certain respects I have found the part of France which I traveled through much changed; in others, I was astonished that it had changed so little. [. . .] There are regions where the Revolution has left almost no evil trace. I have been through villages, towns, perhaps even entire districts, where, submitting to the new forms without passion as without murmur," people have been able "to conjure the violences of tyranny and maintain peace and order." . . . "Many châteaux were pillaged and destroyed, but there were so many of them that those which still exist hardly allow the traveler to realize that their number has decreased. Along the whole of the long route which I have just traveled, I do not think I saw more than three or four destructions of this kind. Those which were least spared were the convents, the abbeys, the bell towers, and above all the crosses" (pp. 27ff.).

"The real aristocracy in France, the one about which everyone has the right to be indignant today, is the aristocracy of tenant farmers and workers . . . The greed of this new aristocracy must appear odious, its proceedings harsh and revolting . . . There is no despotism more oppressive, no avarice more pitiless than that of a tenant farmer drunk with his wealth; ask all those who have had the misfortune of living dependent upon him" (p. 48).

Appearance of Paris. He arrives there on 22 September 1795. The material aspect little changed. Embellished at a few points, the Chaussée d'Antin built. Desolation of the Faubourg Saint-Germain. Silence of Paris in the evening, at ten o'clock, after the plays: formerly this was almost the time for the most lively and brilliant movement; people ran to suppers, to entertainments. Today, from that hour on, the silence of the tomb, encountering a carriage is an event; rarely people on foot, besides the patrols . . . During the day, almost no private carriages, very few buggies even . . . [pp. 93–94].

Speculation, secondhand dealing universal: "The extent and activity of this universal speculation goes beyond any idea one can have from far away. You cannot step into the street without seeing it: almost all the fronts of houses, all the large passages have become as many furniture stores, used-clothes shops, shops for paintings, engravings . . . You will see almost everywhere the same display that formerly used to be seen only on the Saint-Michel bridge or under the pillars of Les Halles [the chief Paris food market—Trans.]. One would think that everything that used to be inside apartments had just been simultaneously exposed in the street. The capital of the world has the air of an immense secondhand clothes shop. One is tempted to believe that Paris is moving out . . . At every step, you meet people of both sexes, all ages, all ranks, carrying some package under their arms. This fury of secondhand dealing and speculation is kept up as much from excess of hardship as from extreme greed, from the unease inseparable from the wealth of the moment . . . The uncertainty and constant change in the common measure of all values is such [. . .] that people fear so much not selling and buying quickly enough that the most important transactions are made with a lightness which must be seen to be believed. There is a certain large house at Paris which was sold four times in two weeks, without any of the purchasers ever having seen it. [. . .] A man who would go out every day with his pockets full of paper money, without any plan except to buy everything he finds going cheap, could make an immense fortune in a little while. This is what several persons have known how to do: The Viscount of S. is one of them; he has one of the best stores in Paris, which does not prevent him from being the most resolute aristocrat in his opinions and his jokes . . . People speculate on the bread that is distributed to those who are provided with a card by the sections . . . [pp. 95–108].

"What strikes me most generally at Paris is a strange character of uncertainty, of displacement; on all faces an uneasy air, defiant, tormented, often even haggard. [p. 111] . . . It seemed to me that I saw again a cherished home, abandoned by its old masters, presently occupied by strangers, and strangers who did not feel at home there, who did not even seem to be sure of staying there. I saw the same things once again, but nothing seemed to me to be in its place, so to speak. What used to be inside was outside, what used to be in the courtyard and the attic or the antechamber was in the living room. All told, nothing was stable, nothing fixed, nothing seemed in its natural place." [pp. 115–16] . . . Many long moustaches, big swords over bourgeois clothes. Extravagance in women's make-up, which did not suit them well . . . women excessively adorned on the arms of real sans-culottes . . . women dressed with the utmost simplicity still distinguished by their bearing . . . old abbés, the remains of their gray hair tied in a knot . . . respectable old men obliged to walk on foot while their former tenants or domestics splash by them; swarms of those soldiers whose unheard-of success has threatened the universe with invasion, pale and tattered . . . these obscure men who from the height of the tribune seem to dictate laws to all of Europe, in the most dirty and neglected clothing, clothing which the tricolor scarf with gold fringes makes stand out, trying to undress themselves in the crowd and not always escaping the curses of passers-by . . . the ceremony of burial limited to a miserable bier covered by a tricolor cloth, carried by one or two men. It is no longer permissible to wear any sign of mourning . . . People circulate more freely than ever in the streets of Paris, except in all the neighborhoods surrounding the Convention and in a fairly wide circumference, extending from the Place Vendôme to the Carrousel, and from Saint-Roch to the Pont-Royal; in any of these streets one can pass only by means of privileged cards, the ordinary cards of the section being insufficient . . .

In the midst of such painful and sorrowful scenes, much luxury, much pride, much extravagance, much frivolity. "We can well torment Paris in every way, make it take on the attitudes most contrary to its desires, it still preserves the fiery activity which makes it live and that happy gaiety which amuses it and consoles it for everything" [p. 135]. Nothing seems less changed to me than the shows; never have so many plays attracted such a great audience (pp. 8off).

Book by B. Constant titled "On the Strength of the Present Government," 1796

Picture of certain royalists of the time, to generalize when I want to speak of this party:

"These men, simultaneously bitter and frivolous, insensitive but vindictive, consoled without having been softened, who had forgotten their love for their country without having pardoned it; who, distracted or compensated when they ran after pleasure, were seized again with regret when it was a question of motivating hatred" [p. 57].

"It is a thing infinitely more dangerous to make a revolution for virtue than to make a revolution for crime. When violent scoundrels violate the rules against honest men, we know that it is one more crime . . . But when honest men violate the rules against scoundrels, the people no longer know what is going on. The rules and the laws seem like obstacles to justice. They contract I don't know what habits, they build themselves I don't know what theory of equitable arbitrariness, which is the overthrow of all ideas," (ibid., pp. 100–101).

How true this is and even profound and furthermore well said! Useful to use when I paint the French mind at the end of the Directory and its causes. What is well worth noting is that the B. Constant who wrote these lines in 1796, in 1797 applauded 18 Fructidor, thus ranging himself in a practical way on the side of those less dangerous rascals who, in violating the laws, at least took care to violate them only against honest people!

"On Political Reactions," by the Same

An entire generation has been swallowed up by the Terror. Today we are caught between old men in their second childhood and badly brought-up children.

"We are led by an almost physical impulse far from both liberal ideas and revolutionary crimes."

Notes on the "Mercure brittanique," Mallet du Pan
[December 1798–December 1799]

Although this collection is very remarkable, above all at the approach of 18 Brumaire, there reigns here less freedom and serenity of judgment than in his correspondence with the sovereigns. We see that anger has won over the author and that he writes for an audience carried away by its anger against the French Revolution and France. Compared to other writ-

ers of the times, he is unusually moderate; from the point of view of absolute truth, he is very violent.

What we see best in this last work is the external conquering movement of the French Revolution in its different vicissitudes. At first, at the
end of 1798 and the beginning of 1799, the insolence and avidity of the
victorious Directory, the destruction of the Sardinian monarchy and
the kingdom of Naples, the occupation of Switzerland, the haughty language of the plenipotentiaries at Rastadt; the contempt, the horror that
the French government inspires in all those who are the Revolution's
enemies; the fear which dominates all these feelings. Europe is defeated
and bewildered, in despair of resisting the power of France anymore; the
irresistibility of France's armies; the patience and dejection of the great
cabinets, except the English cabinet; the persisting jealousies and cu-
pidities of the little powers, which still think only of profiting from the
dismemberment of Europe; the immobility of Prussia, the anger of the
peoples trampled and pillaged by France, which begins to dominate their
revolutionary sympathy (Lafayette's *Mémoires* also testify to this).

Then, towards the spring, when for the first time the Russians enter the
scene and the Austrians take up arms again, the defeats of France, their
enemies' joy mingled with astonishment, the contempt for French forces
as exaggerated as the crushing idea of them which people had had a little
while before, its enemies' hopes immediately going so far as the conquest
of the country. The peoples begin to respond to the appeal of the sovereigns, but much less than one might have hoped. The sovereigns themselves still fear the support that the people can give them almost as much
as their indifference, and only want men and money from them. Finally,
towards the summer, this revolutionary government of France that had
been thought powerless after having been judged omnipotent, reforms
its armies, crushes the Russians in Switzerland, carries the war back into
Germany and reestablishes the balance of the struggle without however
retaking lost Italy, and thus arrives at the winter when the Revolution is
transformed by 18 Brumaire and becomes uniquely military and conquering. [. . .]

Errors of political economy in matters of revolution and above all rela-
tive to the French Revolution.

The English economists, applying the general rules of their science to
the explanation of what was going on in France, Sir Francis d'Ivernois
among others, always ended up proving very scientifically that France
could no longer go on or wasn't going to be able to go on any more and
would be reduced to complete bankruptcy, weakness, and poverty. What

they were missing was an instrument to measure the new, unknown, and immeasurable force given by such a revolution. They reasoned like doctors who base themselves on the efforts a man can make in ordinary conditions when it is a question of what is possible for a man in convulsions. Those who argued from what France could do in normal circumstances or nearly normal circumstances fell into an identical error, and in general we can say that all great revolutions give rise to two great errors: first they make people misunderstand what they can do, deceiving in turn both their enemies and their friends.

"We will see," says Sir Francis d'Ivernois, "the most deplorable weakness follow this hot fever that the vulgar today still take to be a symptom of strength." New blunder ["blunder" in English in the original—Trans.]: the Revolution, by destroying acquired wealth, destroyed that which prevented the acquisition of wealth; in creating the activity and passions which devoured acquired property, it gave birth to the activity, passions, and needs which create property, so that France was never more industrious, more productive, and more rich than after this epoch which destroyed all the instruments of industry and production and all the wealth which they had produced (vol. 2, p. 339).

Revolution, a swift and strong illness, always serves the movement of industry. Only the chronic state of revolution slows it and often stops it. In the first case see even Spain, in the other the Spanish colonies.

French advantages in the struggle against Europe.

In a letter written by Frederick the Great to Voltaire in 1738 we see this judgment made in the middle of the weak reign of Louis XV: "The comparison you make highlights well the strength of the French and the weakness of the powers which surround them; it uncovers the reason for it and allows the mind [to pierce] down through the centuries which will follow us, to see there the continual growth of the French monarchy, emanating from a constant principle, always uniform, this power united under a despotic leader who by all appearance will one day swallow up his neighbors" (vol. 2, p. 371).

The comparative situation of France and Germany in fact permitted this forecast. The Revolution, which substituted itself for the despotic leader of whom Frederick spoke, and combined the despotic force which he already understood with the revolutionary force of which he had no idea, just missed executing his prediction sixty years later. But the shock which disorganized the Germany of Frederick and just missed swallowing it ended up renewing it and strengthening it, and it is to be thought that this great man would no longer hazard such a prophecy. [. . .]

*The peoples invaded by the French carried along at the beginning, rec-
ognized by Mallet.* The mass of bourgeois, of intellectuals, of well-off artisans were impassioned for the equality of ranks, and the poor for the
equality of wealth. All thought that the Golden Age was beginning. A
republican battalion appeared at the frontier, it electrified hopes. Brothers and friends came out from the universities, the counters, the shops,
and even the salons to welcome these philosophical warriors, who spoke
so well, as the benefactors of the human race; everywhere the sovereigns,
even in the ranks of their armies, encountered opposition or tepidness,
the bewitched or the uncaring. Were victories won? Peace became the
general cry. Was it defeat? Peace and again peace. [. . .] These shameful exclamations repeated themselves from the foot of the thrones to the
camps, from the châteaux to the monasteries, from the academies to the
workshops. Thus the general folly everywhere favored the Revolution,
whether from principle or from passion, by love of repose or love of
movement. That the war did not go well with such a public spirit is not
astonishing, that it did not lead to the total ruin of the states which bore
it, this is the miracle" (vol. 3, p. 91).

Mallet adds that all this enthusiasm gave way to contrary feelings. This
was true but not as much as he thought. Love for the Revolution still
struggled (in 1799) against the horror of its ravages at the bottom of the
souls of the populations pillaged and ravaged, and it required nothing
less than Bonaparte's long oppression to raise Germany as a whole and in
its depth. When [they] cried war on the French, some hidden fires still
burned from the French Revolution. [. . .]

On great social crises when they go on for a long time. For a people as
for an individual, impressions are made less by reason of the greatness or
the importance of the facts than by their number.

After having described the dethronement of Pope Pius VI and the odious violences perpetrated against him, Mallet adds: "Like so many others
this event passed by the fleeting awareness of Europe. In countries struck
by the Revolution, everyone thought only of bearing his own misfortunes
or avoiding new ones; elsewhere, pleasures followed one another as in the
most fortunate of times. This period was a carnival for most of those who
up until this moment had escaped France. People cried or they danced"
(vol. 3, p. 137). May '99. [. . .]

*The mirage which during the first periods of the Revolution made people
always see an individual as the cause of everything.*

"Because of a prejudice that experience has not yet destroyed, we always go back to mechanically attributing the vicissitudes of the Revolu-

tion and the Republic to such or such an individual who acquired a momentary importance. [. . .] From Mirabeau and the Duke of Orléans to Barras and Sieyès we have made the magic wand of revolutionary command pass from hand to hand . . . A week later the orator is booed, the minister sent back to his attic, the general eclipsed or disgraced without leaving behind any trace or any regret in his army. Every dogmatic revolution is founded on principles, it creates instruments, never leaders" (vol. 3, pp. 390[–91]).

The explanation which Mallet gives is good, but does not explain everything. It applies above all to the first period of what he calls dogmatic revolutions. As these go on, a new element enters in. Once fatigue and disgust are born, the influence of individuals makes itself felt, a man can become the master of a dogmatic revolution, above all if he respects its principle. What must further be noted is that at the beginning of revolutions of this kind, the greatest men can do nothing, and that on the contrary at the end a mediocre man can do everything, if circumstances favor him.

Because they didn't know these different laws the contemporaries of the beginning of the French Revolution always thought that a man was going to end it, and at the end, the most sensible men thought that it could not be ended by an individual, a mistake which singularly eased Bonaparte's establishment, everybody seeing him as a passing accident. Double *mistake* ["mistake" in English in the original—Trans.], into which Michaud fell, for example. A mistake about the exceptional value of the man, a mistake about the new and particular character of the illness. [. . .]

The evolution of 30 Floréal.

Towards the end of great revolutions the spirit of the times, constantly halted by fatigue, fear, slackness, is like a river which runs so slow and so deep that at every moment the least accident brings a few eddies to the surface. The spectators, seeing the object for a moment go in the opposite direction from the current, cry out at the marvel or think that the current is going in another direction than had been thought. Mistake. In the midst of these surface oscillations, the mass of water underneath slowly follows the slope which leads it towards the place where it can lie down and rest. [. . .]

Vain efforts to bring back the Terror after 30 Floréal. Growing atrocity of the laws and doctrines of the government amid the slackening of passions. Characteristics of the end of revolutions.

At the beginning of great revolutions, laws, made by and for a normal time, are milder than mores, which the violence of passions renders cruel. At the end, laws become harsher than mores, because the legislation and the habits of the legislators are formed amid those same violent passions which the public no longer possesses. In the first stage the Terror is, so to speak, made without the government taking part; in the second, the government exhausts itself trying to make it. By terror I mean the violence of an entire party. For the enormities which can be committed by the government itself can be as great and even greater at the end of revolutions than at the beginning; the governments retaining, if only in the interest of their security or their personal ambition, the taste for violence, the habit of using it, the contempt for men and rules that long usage of power during revolutions gives. Because the nation in its collapse no longer has astonishment or strong criticism for anything, no longer recognizes either precedent or a fixed doctrine, no longer imposes any limits on those who lead it, we see acts of unheard-of violence and boldness practiced amid general indifference. [. . .]

Violence of the newspapers, which does not decline and seems to grow amid the weakness of passions and the decline of the press's power, and which is never greater than on the eve of the destruction of the freedom of the press. Symptom of the end of revolutions. Obliged to shout ever more loudly as the listener becomes more deaf, and to strike the public mind in proportion as it becomes more inert. [. . .]

Paris amid the defeats of 1799.

It is amid this uneasy luxury and inopportune enjoyment that the horror of revolutions spreads best in dried-up and weakened hearts, and that these tired and futile souls conceive a more furious hatred for freedom than an energetic despot ever felt.

Try to depict well how at the end of revolutions the hatred for revolutions and for freedom grows, and reaches its maximum amid torpor and indolent obedience. The very signs of submission hide the greatest revolt of the heart and prove nothing if not that the horror of public agitation has reached the point of taking away even the desire to resist the state which creates it. [. . .]

Impression produced on the public [by 18 Brumaire].

What nations, like individuals, find most difficult to bear are not the evils they feel, but the ones they fear. A bad government which allows one to hope that it will get better will always be borne more easily than a good government which lets people fear a worse. Fear is a greater cause of revolutions than suffering.

[Analysis of Pamphlets, Year III–Year VIII]
Year III: 23 September 1794–22 September 1795

In general, recrimination against certain facts of the Terror. Accounts made by decimated communities or in their name. Defenses of the deputies proscribed on 31 May. If one wants anecdotes about the horrors of the Terror in the provinces, they abound. Here a father and his daughter arrested because their parrot cried "Long live the Emperor." There the son of a farmer, a child eight years old, who had a toy guillotine with which he spent the whole day cutting the heads off birds under the eyes of his father and mother.

Many pamphlets about the Convention's decree which required the election of two-thirds of its members. What is to be noted in these little writings is their freedom and violence against the Convention.

The general character of these publications (save a few exceptions): extreme violence against the men of the Terror. Violence no less injurious against the royalists and above all the priests and the nobles. Since, above all near the end of the Convention, the freedom of the press seemed complete, at least against the Convention, it is to be believed that the passion shown against the royalists was sincere or at least dictated by the current of opinion as it still was then.

Year III. Pamphlets not directly discussing politics.

Various very insignificant pamphlets from Year III. The majority are speeches at the openings of schools, little courses in morality or education. Here among other things one notes the following:

1) The hatred that the regime of the Terror inspired among the educated elite.

2) While they detest the crimes of the Revolution, the anti-Christian movement of the Revolution still carries them along. Political reaction had not become philosophical reaction for them. The irreligious, Voltairean, Encyclopedic impulse continues to push those who speak and write, while the movement is halted among the masses and an opposite movement is beginning. A frequent phenomenon in all revolutions, where those who have made the revolution ordinarily continue to speak and write in the same way a long time after the bulk of their audience has secretly and silently begun to change its opinion.

One overthrows a government by raising the masses against it with the aid of certain words. One continues to speak the same way more freely and more loudly still after the Revolution because one has become the government. The noise one makes deafens one to the effect which it produces; and when those who made so much noise are overthrown in their turn, they are astonished to see that there is hardly anyone who is still of their opinion.

Year IV: 23 September 1795–22 September 1796

Infinitely fewer publications than in Year III. Four boxes instead of eighteen or twenty. Is it that fewer were printed or fewer collected at the library? I don't know.

Some pamphlets almost overtly royalist; several violently terrorist. A return to these two extremes in certain minds. Religious preoccupations. Examination and criticism of the laws against priests. Pamphlets by priests who have taken the Constitutional Oath and by priests who have refused to take it. Retractions. In general, an effort by the former to be readmitted to the Church. [. . .]

What will be no less necessary than reading the political pamphlets of the times is to go through those which are not about politics, and the books, if it is the case that people published books in this period. See also the engravings and caricatures of the times. Is there a bibliographic work which will tell me about all the publications of this period?

Very interesting report from the minister of the interior to the Directory, 20 Pluviose, Year IV. To reread and copy, if I ever want to paint the state of France when leaving the hands of the Convention. General traits: disorder, universal brigandage, but above all in the regions of the west. Difficulty of finding citizens willing to accept municipal positions and even the positions of agents of the Directory, a multitude of resignations, some through fear, others because of apathy. No trace of the ardor of the first years of the Revolution. No more passion for great principles, indifference towards freedom and politics in general amid hatreds which, more and more, become violent. Roads almost impassable. Priests everywhere agitating the countrysides. Universal hardship. Agriculture ravaged by civil war and requisitions. The establishments for public education destroyed. Food shortages. At Paris, however, the shows always have full houses. The foreigners who flock, the cafes which multiply amid the universal distress. The peasants speak badly of the Revolution despite its immense benefits and make comparisons to its disadvantage. Reread. Copy.

[Year V]

Report of the Bishops Meeting at Paris by Citizen Grégoire, Bishop of Blois,
8 December 1796 (18 Frimaire, Year V)

Very interesting in order to learn the effects of the schism at this period. We see here the constitutional clergy's so painful and so critical position, exposed on the one hand to the ill-will and contempt of the government, above all of the terrorist party which was still mingled with it and which detested religion and in particular Catholicism in all its forms, and on the other hand to the virulent hatred and contempt of the nonjuring clergy, and of the faithful who regarded the latter as the only real priests.

The abbé Grégoire is full of invectives against the terrorists, of bitterness and recriminations against his nonjuring brethren. We see here the poverty of this unfortunate schismatic clergy, its few solid roots, its efforts, doubtless often honest, to take its mission seriously, the at least apparent successes that it obtained, its martyrs. We see here above all the frightful demoralization which must have resulted for the lower classes from the sight of these two clergies disputing souls with each other: the ones who were judged "intruders" protected by the state and masters of external religion; the others who were reputed faithful pursued; and, in the midst of all this, a government and a dominant party professing hatred and contempt for both of them, with the sole difference that the hatred was greater against the latter and the contempt more pronounced for the former.

Speech Read to the Constitutional Circle by Riouffe, Messidor Year V,
June 1797, Two Months before the Coup d'État of Fructidor

The Constitutional Circle was a rallying point opposed to the Circle of Clichy. This is the opening speech. We see here clearly how the Republicans had been abandoned by opinion; how the government of the Republic was impudently ridiculed by the *reactionaries* of the time and the armies of émigrés. We see here also the fears and furies of the party which feared and detested the counterrevolution. [. . .]

"With what horror we reject that infernal system which covered twenty-five thousand square leagues with scaffolds and threatened to swallow up twenty-five million men. O Terror, you who bury your dagger so deep in the heart of the nascent Republic, you whose effects have survived you in such a cruel way, monster composed of anarchy, robbery, tyranny and royalism, we doom you to the execration of the centuries"; in these times bordering on the Terror we see that the revolutionaries themselves had

not invented the systems of the clever minds of our day to justify or minimize the crimes of that period.

*Notes Taken on the Register of Deliberations of the Directory at the
National Archives, May 1852; Transcripts of the Directory*

Transcript of 28 Messidor, Year V (p. 83), which shows the internal scene
which signals the division existing within the Directory: Reubell, La Revellière, Barras on one side; Carnot, Barthélémy on the other. The meeting is opened by Carnot's proposition, made unexpectedly, to dismiss
four ministers as disagreeable to the majority of the Councils. Not only is
this proposition rejected by the three others (because there is no proof
that the ministers are in the minority in the Councils, and furthermore the
Councils have nothing to say about the choice of ministers), but also the
three others decide on the spot that the ministers for whose dismissal
Carnot had not asked will be dismissed, and they replace them, on the
spot, with their friends.

Transcript of 12 Thermidor, Year V (p. 133). Carnot, opposing the detachment of nine thousand men from the army of the Sambre and Meuse
that would send them to the west (a movement whose secret purpose was
to bring them to Paris to make the coup of 18 Fructidor), gives this reason, worthy of remembrance: experience has proven that one cannot have
troops travel in the interior of the Republic without half or two-thirds of
them melting away. The transcripts of Messidor and Thermidor are full
of often very insufficient traces of:

1) The deep division which existed between the three directors Barras, La
Revellière, and Reubell, and the two, Carnot, Barthélemy, and the constant
oppression of the latter by the former.

2) The active war, although very petty, between the majority of the Directory and the majority of the Council of Five Hundred. There are messages to
ask Barras's age, to know who made the cavalry advance towards La Ferté-
Alais (without ever being able to get to the source of the order), to know why
nine thousand men of the army of the Sambre and Meuse have been sent
towards the west.

After Fructidor, this war of pinpricks seems to stop. Until 17 Fructidor, nothing in the transcripts announces the approach of the crisis, if
not a certain number of reports made to the Directory by the minister
of police, signaling royalist maneuvers tolerated or encouraged by some
departmental administrations whom the Directory dismisses. On the
morning of the seventeenth, a last, equally insignificant meeting takes
place. The same day, *in the evening,* the session is continued. The Direc-

tory, reduced to three members, La Revellière-Lépeaux, Reubell, and Barras, declares itself in permanent session and makes a series of decrees in view of a royalist conspiracy, makes proclamations, decrees measures which, I think, are in all the histories. The permanent session is only lifted on the nineteenth. As early as the morning of the eighteenth, the grenadiers of the legislative body fraternize with the troops of the Directory and go to them to protest their devotion. A deputation is introduced to the Directors. The generous devotion of these brave soldiers, says the transcript, made tender tears run from all eyes (pp. 224–239).

Transcript of the twenty-fourth. Reception of two new Directors. Merlin de Douai, François de Neufchâteau. Each of these new Directors makes a speech. Merlin's speech, which has doubtless been published, is a real model of cowardly invective against the defeated, and of low and imprudent flattery towards the victors, whose talents and virtues he exalts. The talents of La Revellière and the virtues of Barras! This already stinks up his reign (p. 252).

The following sessions are full of dismissals pronounced against the central governments of departments, elected governments which the Directory replaces by men of its choice.

Hilarian Puget (I think this is de Barbantane's family name)
"To Republicans," Nivôse, Year V (December 1797)

One of those nobles whom the party of the Duke of Orléans had thrown into the Revolution and who speaks of Robespierre with more consideration than of revolutionaries of good blood. This pamphlet illustrates well the terror which the idea of counterrevolution caused such men. He feared the royalists still more than the terrorists. Make clear the antiroyalist fears and passions which preceded and brought about 18 Fructidor.

Year VI, 23 September 1797–23 September 1798.

Report by Citizen Grégoire to the National Council (Year VI)

This pamphlet is interesting for shedding light on the history of the *constitutional* Church of France. Its spirit, its actions, the spirit of its populations. We see here its violent persecution under the Convention, the number of its bishops who apostatized at that time, who died on the scaffold, who fled; the first attempt to revive it made by Grégoire in the midst of the Convention, rejected to cries of "Long live the Republic!" by the assembly, in the midst of the silence of the tribunes, accorded a little later under the pressure of opinion after a speech by Boissy d'Anglas. The government and the bureaucracy tolerate [the constitutional clergy— Trans.], but remain hostile through a very blind philosophical fury, for the clergy which is evidently compromised by the Revolution is the monarchy's enemy almost as much as the revolutionaries are.

Difficulties, passions of this Church. Violent hostility between the Church and the former clergy, despite the unctuous phraseology of the ecclesiastical style and the very ardent desire of the constitutional clergy to rejoin the see of Rome and the Universal Church. Its useless efforts in this direction; its attempts to organize itself as a church by a national council, an enterprise at first abandoned, as much because of the government's opposition as because of the clergy's lack of enthusiasm, it seems to me. The Council ends up by meeting at Paris on 15 August 1797 (28 Thermidor, Year VI).

Antireligious and above all anti-Catholic character retained by the Revolution.

Attempt to make a philosophical religion. *"Manual of Theophilanthropists"—Year VI (1798).*

Irreligious verses, little impious writings which continue to be published under the Directory, above all in the period before Fructidor, when the royalists and the clergy were raising their heads. See several of these writings which I have noted at the library, among others "The Epistle of a Catholic, Published by a Republican" (10 Messidor, Year V), "Dialogue between Pius VI and Louis XVIII" by Chénier . . .

Year VII, 23 September 1798 – 23 September 1799, and the first months of Year VIII

"On the System Followed by the Executive Directory towards the Cisalpine Republic," by Bignon, Ex-Secretary to the Embassy; Year VII, Fructidor (August 1799)

Interesting in more than one respect. We see here the succession of violence and pillaging through which this country had been disaffected:

1. The Directory, instead of respecting this new government created by it, treats it with the utmost contempt. First of all, through its ambassador Trouvé, it changes the constitution and the personnel of the executive and legislative powers. A little later, the commanding general Brune changes what Trouvé had done without the Directory's authorization: soon a new ambassador, Rivaud, reverses what Brune had done. Thus, in less than ten months, a constitution recognized by a treaty is three times overturned by the blun-

dering activity of the Directory or its agents, and all the authorities who should have emanated only from the people change at the whim of the caprices of these foreign powers.

2. The commanding generals retain, after the peace, the omnipotence that conquest had given them.

3. The contractors only furnish part of the supplies and the rest has to be taken by requisitions. The Bodin company, charged with providing rations, fodder, fuel, has exports of necessary goods forbidden in order to buy them for very low prices.

We also see clearly in this little text:

1. The powerlessness of the Directory, whether to know what is going on, or to make itself obeyed by its agents, or to have them punished when they disobey; a powerlessness highlighted by Brune's conduct.

2. That there already existed at Milan a party made up of Cisalpine fanatics, as well as of refugees from all over Italy, who dreamed only of Italian unity and the overthrow of all the states of the peninsula.

3. That the Directory not only feared this party and persecuted it, but was always afraid that the worthless government created by it would become too powerful and too independent. The result of all this is shown well in this passage: "It is felt that we worked only for ourselves, that our purpose was to hold under our tutelage peoples to which we had given a phantom existence, that in order to guarantee ourselves against their future emancipation, we forbade their growth, that we wanted slaves rather than friends. People shiver over our miscalculated ambition; people are irritated against it, people have tried to withdraw from it; and when our power was tottering, people made few efforts to support it because it only offered a new servitude, no less frightful than that which preceded it" [p. 8].

Demoralization of the Army of Italy and French character: "And just as a few months before we thought it was impossible for us to be beaten, then we almost thought it was impossible for us to win" [p. 41].

Notes taken on "Le Mois"

Le Mois is a journal devoted to literature, to fashion. It is a journal of fashion, a little more serious than its subject, fairly similar, although with a different temperament, to the journal *La Mode* of our times. Pays a little attention to politics.

The first issue is from Germinal, Year VII, March 1798.

[. . .] We see at several points in this little journal, which however was very favorable to 18 Brumaire, that at the beginning of that event people did not think they were being carried as far away from freedom as they were. In general Sieyès's constitution seemed a new form of freedom rather than its elimination.

Power of the *revolutionary* mind. Influence of this opinion on the First Consul which forced him to introduce into the constitution an article which permanently expelled the émigrés, although his point of view and his practice was to make them come back. A violence criticized by the journal, although it is very anti–old regime. But tired of violence, mores were softened by skepticism and political indifference.

The result of 18 Brumaire was not the *immediate* increase of trade. Confidence was only established slowly. Business activity was still paralyzed by the stagnation with which it had been struck for some time.

In general little business was done and those activities that people risked were very limited (p. 306). Frimaire Year VIII. [. . .]

The spirit which reigns in this collection chiefly devoted to women is the licentious, erotic, philosophical, and irreligious temperament of old-regime literature. The irreligious mind above all is violent here. It survives the revolutionary mind proper. For the authors of the journal, although very hostile to the old regime, are, however, very strong supporters of order and full of horror for the terrorists. However, among them the old spirit of Voltaire and Diderot is present in all its vivacity. This was evidently the general spirit of the literary class even though among all other classes the religious reaction that was going to lead to *The Genius of Christianity* [by Tocqueville's cousin Chateaubriand—Trans.] was evidently not only begun, but complete. A proof that if a people's literature taken over a long term can be said to represent the people's mind, this can be very false at a given moment, literature being made by men who have often learned their trade in a time previous to the one when they continue with it or when they practice it.

Many perspectives. All with a pretty good style. Few ideas in them. A verve which kills. A lot of futility, of searching for new words, of affected style.

As we approach the end of the Directory, during the last months preceding 18 Brumaire, all the symptoms of a crisis manifest themselves in this little journal like everywhere else. It shows it in its way of speaking about the stagnation of trade born from worry, from fears for the future, from political events, the misfortunes of the armies. Even fashion becomes sterile. We will no longer have any articles about fashion, says the journal at the end of Fructidor, until the crisis is over. Until then it is fear and worry which seem to have usurped rule over the amiable Frenchman.

Even in the little political articles scattered throughout this journal of literature and fashion we see this unhappy society which floats lost between the fear of terrorism and the fear of the old regime, no longer believing in what is, not knowing what could be, and ready to seize on the first government which will be neither the counterrevolution nor the terror.

Interesting Conversation between Molé, Rémusat, and Myself about the Revolution and the Times Which Followed It (3 April 1855)

Very interesting, as showing the general lines to follow, although relating particularly to the time which followed the Terror and chiefly useful when I get there.

Barante's book, said Rémusat, is, in sum, the most faithful thing which has been written about the French Revolution, the one which best tells about the events and actions of men, but the period's real life is not found there any more than elsewhere. The author understands everything, except the real passion. The bombast, the bad taste of the personalities always makes him think they are play-acting. The serious side escapes him. He cannot understand what there was of sincerity, of truth, of warmth amid all these exaggerations. M. Molé was of this opinion. That intimate truth, he says, is in fact missing from the work for those who have lived through those times; but I don't find it in any book. None of the historians of the Revolution have ever fully entered into the spirit of the times, and do not make me feel it in any of their writings. One would get a *better* idea of it by going through all the little writings of the times. There is above all a period which for me is more present than yesterday, that which followed the Terror, the time of the Directory. No history has given the least idea of it.

There just appeared, Rémusat went on, a book which makes the period of which you are speaking better known than any which I have read. It is *David's Studio,* by *Delécluze.* One could not imagine anything more lively and which better depicts that brief period. What most strikes me, added Rémusat, is to what degree that time, with all its inconsistencies, its vices, its chaos, was superior to our own on one point. People had real convictions; everyone followed his own convictions boldly, passionately, was concerned with them and not with the role they would make him play, thus doing the most eccentric, the most bizarre, sometimes the most ridiculous things, without intending to make themselves noticed. M. Molé said that this was perfectly true; that this description of the times was exact; that it had never been well done in a book, and that it was for this reason that reading any book on the Revolution had never given him an idea of the truth nor been able to accord with his own memories. No one, furthermore, had reproduced well the sight that the upper classes presented when the émigrés returned. For me that time has remained the most striking of my whole life. We had no idea of looking for the enjoyment of material well-being, we had no interest in business, no ambition, we lived only for the things of the mind, the intellectual pleasures of ideas, the cult of the arts. Never has the mind created more real equality between people of different ranks.

To go back to Delécluze's book, said Rémusat, it is very certain that just after the end of the Terror, despite the horror that David inspired, his talent transported all souls; my maid took me to see him pass. I knew three names: Bonaparte, Moreau, and David. It was an ardor and an enthusiasm of rebirth. That is so true, said M. Molé, that so and so (he named them), who had just lost their whole family on the scaffold, and hated the Terrorists with all the strength of their soul, nevertheless went to study in David's studio, and adored the painter.

We came to speak of Napoleon. No one has yet painted him as I knew him, said M. Molé. Thiers has not even approached him, continued Rémusat. He has written an admirable administrative history of the Empire; but the man himself, the reality of that strange being, escapes. Notably what no one has yet painted is Bonaparte, master of everything before knowing anything, learning everything at the same time as he governed everything; taking on all subjects in his conversations, even the things which were least familiar to him; delivering himself of all kinds of bold intellectual statements, finding pleasure in throwing himself down every path, always unexpected, startling, daring to say what he would never have dared say a few years later. This first dash of genius into the new and unknown, who has described it?

Then they cited as giving some true ideas about Napoleon *Roederer's* new book, the unpublished memoirs of the *Duke of Vicenza* [Caulaincourt—Trans.], then disgraced, unhappy; a very interesting work which M. Pasquier has read.

Part Two

THE CONSULATE
AND THE EMPIRE

Section One: Tocqueville's Research Notes on the Consulate

Information Given by M. Molé

A lmost nothing about this period. Thibaudeau's history is still the most instructive, the only book which has the *flavor* of the times. Above all with regard to Swiss affairs the First Consul's language is notably, as I myself know firsthand, absolutely accurate.

"I admit that I was dazzled and bewitched," M. Molé said to me, "by seeing such a rapid reconstruction of government. My youth concealed from me the resources for such a work that society offered then; this was my great mistake, I confess. Everything seemed to me as though it had been smashed, destroyed beyond recall. I did not imagine how anything could be reconstructed."

M. Molé added: "Moreover, if Napoleon has always seemed to me the most extraordinary man of genius, I have never, even during the time of my greatest infatuation with him, recognized real moral greatness in him" (which proves that one can judge well the value and merit of things which one does not possess oneself).

Paint this well while generalizing: astonishment, dazzlement of the spectators.

Events of 18 and 19 Brumaire and the Following Days
(This Is a Collection of Official Documents Collected and Published by
Rondonneau Immediately after the Event).

I note here:

1) The Ancients were called to order at eight o'clock in the morning by the commissioner-inspectors of the chamber presided over by Lemercier. *Cornet* read the report. *Regnier* seconded it.

In these two documents, whose style is coldly violent, embarrassed,

239

bombastic, tangled, people speak in obscure terms about a plot which is not explained. This reeks of lies and embarrassment. The movement's character and spirit (basically an anti-Jacobin movement) do not appear here. Among the reasons which should lead the assembly to leave Paris, Regnier notes the presence in that city of "a crowd of thieves and desperate scoundrels, vomited and thrown up among us from all parts of the globe by this execrably foreign faction which has caused all our misfortunes" [p. 5] (I thought this was the royalists, but I see now that people meant the agents of Pitt and Coburg).

The decree of transfer is voted. A proclamation to the French people as obscure and vague as the discussion. Bonaparte is introduced, says a few words in his style, although at its worst: brief, yet vague and incoherent; a long, general, and inflated sentence, awkwardly thrown in, without anything leading up to it or following it. Oath of fidelity and devotion to the Republic. In general everyone speaks of the Republic, everything is done to the cry of "Long live the Republic!" Everything proclaims that the enterprise was and above all seemed bolder and more difficult then than it seems to us. Furthermore, "Long live the Republic!" meant: "Long live the Revolution! No Royalist reaction!"

2) Session of 19 Brumaire at St. Cloud; Council of Five Hundred at 2 P.M.

These are the scenes we know. But what I didn't know was that the claim was not to have dissolved the Council of Five Hundred by force, but merely to have reestablished order, this assembly remaining [in existence—Trans.], and its majority meeting at nine o'clock in the evening of the same day, with its president, declaring first of all that Bonaparte and his troops have deserved well of the country.

Then Lucien makes a long speech, full of invective against the anarchists who, having violated the constitution a hundred times and preparing to violate it again, invoke it today. Good model of the only role there is to play when one is openly violating the law, which consists of taking the initiative to attack and insult those who think it wrong. A method as old as the world, which always succeeds when the mass to whom it is addressed is only looking for a pretext to help you.

Speech by Boulay. The constitution is the cause of all the evils. Necessity of having a more stable government and more able diplomacy in order to have peace. Individual security and property are poorly guaranteed. The principle of the sovereignty of the people is badly applied. Elections are not free. The public authorities are badly established. Bad organization, unstable, incoherent. The responsibility of power, a vain phrase. Bad government. In a word, he says, there is in France neither public freedom nor individual freedom; everyone gives orders, no one obeys, in sum there is only a phantom government.

He concludes that the executive power should be temporarily given to three consuls, and that the Councils should be adjourned, leaving two commissions to replace them and prepare a new constitutional organization.

On the general principles of the constitution, which are good: these are the principles of every republican government; the sovereignty of the people, the unity of the republic, the equality of rights, freedom, representative government.

[Speech] by Cabanis which supports him. In these speeches nothing shows that people want to give up freedom, and this crisis would resemble several that had preceded it, if we didn't know that we are at the end of a revolution and that Bonaparte is charged with profiting from the coup d'état: something Cabanis does not seem to have thought of when he cries out: "Equality, Freedom, Republic, cherished names, sacred names, all our wishes, all our efforts, all the powers of our souls belong to you; it is for you that we live, it is for your defense that we are ready to perish" [p. 42].

Without any doubt, among those who favored 18 Brumaire a very large number did not think they were being pushed into despotism and made the same mistake as Cabanis.

There follows a decree which:

1. Declares that there is no longer a Directory.

2. Expels sixty-one members from the national representation.

3. Creates a consular commission composed as we know.

4. Adjourns the legislative body until 1 Ventose, Year VIII (20 February 1800); during the adjournment, the members will continue to be paid.

5. [Decides] that before separating, each Council will name a commission of twenty-five members, which will decide *on the initiative* of the consuls on all urgent matters of police, legislation, and finances; they are further charged with preparing changes to the constitution, which changes should have as their purpose to consolidate, guarantee, and invariably to consecrate the sovereignty of the people, the republic, the representative system, freedom, equality, security, and property (who will do the final work is not said). Before separating, an address to the French is voted on Cabanis's motion. Read it.

Lucien then makes a speech where he says that freedom "has just reached the age of adulthood: from today onwards all the convulsions of freedom are over" (doubtless because the sick one was dead) . . . "Hear this sublime cry from posterity: if freedom was born at the Tennis Court of Versailles, it was consolidated at the Orangerie of Saint-Cloud . . . Long live the Republic!"

The consuls enter; they take an oath to the sovereignty of the people, to the Republic, to equality, to freedom, and to the representative system, and the session terminates amid a thousand cries of "Long live the Republic!" [p. 55].

3) During the morning meeting of the Five Hundred, there had been a meeting of the Ancients; here, those who had not been warned what to say beforehand complained; the opposition, having regained courage, showed itself. At half past four, Bonaparte entered. This awkward improvisation must be read to see this extraordinary genius succumb amid the difficulties in which ordinary minds drown when they want to speak in public; passions which lack the art of containing and expressing themselves and only see daylight through incoherent words; the idea, prepared in advance, which no longer leaves any trace in the mind of the one who wants to express it, except for the leading expressions which were supposed to summarize it but which remain isolated and obscure and out of proportion to those surrounding them; the embarrassment caused by interruptions and questions, which turns into anger, into violent language, into tangled thoughts; in sum, one of the greatest, most bombastic, and most maladroit jumbles (although full of tricks) which ever came out of a famous man's mouth.

After his exit, Lucien entered in his turn, in order to say that a factious minority armed with daggers dominated the Council of Ancients but that the majority agreed with the Council of Five Hundred.

4) Proclamation by Bonaparte after the events, warning by the minister of police. Circular from the minister of justice. In general, one of the most badly planned and badly executed coups d'état imaginable; succeeding through the omnipotence of the causes which brought it about, the state of the public mind, and the disposition of the army, still more the first perhaps than the latter two.

"The Last Good-Byes to the Victorious Bonaparte"
(Without Author's or Publisher's Name)

We know that this remarkable pamphlet is by Michaud. It bears the date May 1799. It is doubtless 1800 since it is written six months after 18 Brumaire during the Marengo campaign.

Remarks. A pretty well-expressed idea about this habit of exaggerated and bombastic style, which people had acquired from the sight of extraordinary events and amazing feelings. "The imagination of the French, struck by so many extraordinary images, for a long time remained in a sort of exaltation, and distanced them from that fortunate inclination of the soul which makes us look for the truth and gives us the ability to know it." To put ideas within the reader's grasp, one must, so to speak, elevate them above themselves. "On several subjects today the people, because they were credulous, have used up their credulity, and because for ten years they had faith in the most absurd stories, they have ended up no longer believing even the simplest things. This is what, even among the most independent writers, has created the need to exaggerate their accounts, to so to speak *overdo* their ideas; the distrustful public is always inclined to *discount* them, and one must consider oneself lucky when one succeeds in making them believe half what one wanted to prove" (p. 5).

Widespread contempt for men in general and for one's compatriots in particular created by revolutions which last a long time. Bonaparte put in chains a depraved nation which was no longer capable of any movement except that which nature gives a body it wants to disintegrate and in which it has sown the active seeds of corruption. England under Cromwell could picture itself in the image of a young and vigorous slave who had passions which the master could profit from. France under Bonaparte would perhaps be well represented in the form of a chained old Sybarite who brings those who reduce him to slavery only the contagion of his vices and his decay" [p. 142]. What a fall from the limitless pride of 1789 and the dogma of indefinite perfectibility.

Striking error by the author about the means which Bonaparte was going to use to govern. "The greatest of Bonaparte's errors is to have counted on ideas which have lost their charm to maintain his illegitimate power, on words which no longer have any meaning for the people. I know that today religion would be a lever less powerful than in Cromwell's time; but the vain display of philosophical maxims and liberal ideas cannot substitute for it" [p. 144].

It is striking to see Bonaparte accused of giving in to philosophical maxims and liberal ideas, at least if one does not give this name to the part of the Revolution's work which he had adopted but which was precisely that which entered least into what are usually called philosophical maxims and liberal ideas.

Bonaparte accused of addressing himself to the second-rate and contemptible portion of parties. "Bonaparte, despite his system of amalgamation, began by discontenting the republicans and the royalists" [p. 156] (that is he rejected the active and determined portion which would never have wanted to go along with his plans). "In order to shore up his authority he has had the imprudence to address himself only to that intermediary class of weak and characterless men, the most vile and most contemptible part of the nation, those men who do not have the courage to have an opinion and will have still less to defend the government; to those slaves accustomed to changes of master, who have smothered all the idols of the Revolution with their incense, who prostrate themselves today before the great Consul, and who tomorrow will be on their knees before his successor" (p. 47).

Charming expression invented by the mystic cowardice of the English, who were always inclined to adhere to the dominant power and support the established government: they called this "trusting in providence."

This whole little work is a parallel between the revolution which brought Cromwell to power and that which elevated Bonaparte, from which one concludes that it will be much more difficult for Bonaparte to keep his usurped power than it had been for Cromwell, and that there would be still more greatness in surrendering it, as Monk did, to the legitimate sovereign. This work proves how little people still knew Bonaparte when he had become master, how his *civil genius* was incompletely known, that people did not immediately see that it was a question of a completely new phase of the Revolution, which outside France Mallet du Pan saw so clearly. Finally, how some believed that it was only a question of *repairing* the Republic, others of establishing a brief tyranny, Bonaparte making his way through these false fears and false hopes.

Speech Made in the Temple of Mars by Lucien Bonaparte, Minister of the Interior, on 25 Messidor, Year VIII (14 July 1800), for the Anniversary of 14 July

Ten months after 18 Brumaire the brother's whole theory is found here; the old monarchy was corrupt and had to die. 14 July was a great day. Painting of the horrors and mistakes which made the Revolution go wrong.

18 Brumaire consecrates everything which was wanted on 14 July '89. It derives from it, is attached to it. The French no longer have what they hated, they have everything they wanted in making the Revolution, they have the real Revolution. Let us rejoice.

February 1852: Notes on the Memoirs of General Lafayette

That the Republic is not freedom. This has never been better proved than from 18 Fructidor to 18 Brumaire. "I myself declare," writes Lafayette (January 1798) "that although I like republics better than monarchies, I prefer freedom to the republic and I am very far from believing that free-dom exists at present in France" (vol. 4, p. 401). [...]

Hatred for the government, which is one of Bonaparte's strengths. Although people do not have confidence in his morality, although the memories of Vendémiaire are present in the minds of the Parisians, and although he has partisans rather than friends, people need a change so much, they are so tired of the present institutions, that it is enough to overthrow what exists to regain popularity. October 1799 (vol. 5, p. 138). [...]

Lafayette's judgment and feeling about Bonaparte.
In general we see that Lafayette saw 18 Brumaire with pleasure, that he had a liking for Bonaparte and that he would very freely have conceded him a presidency for life. He constantly held himself back from falling under the spell of this extraordinary man, who, however, by his qualities and his vices was so antipathetic to his nature.

Idea of the necessity of pomp, of show, of the exterior of strength. "An idea rare among great men and most deeply rooted in Bonaparte's mind. An idea grafted, I think, on the desire, the conception of his mind born in the lower parts of his soul." [...]

Conversations of Bonaparte with Lafayette. "You can disapprove of the government, find me a despot; it will be seen, you will see one day if I am working for myself or for posterity ... but after all I am the leader of the movement. I, whom the Revolution, whom you, whom all patriots have brought where I am; if I called in those people there (the émigré princes), it would be to deliver you all to their vengeance." "These feelings were so nobly expressed, he spoke so well of the glory of France, that I took his hand in telling him of the pleasure he caused me."

Filial feeling for the Revolution which one sees in Napoleon; the in-terest in maintaining it of all those who were responsible for that Revo-lution, if only as a *barrier* against the throne, which is well seen here (vol. 5, p. 178).

"I have always seen him express himself with the most friendly confi-dence on everything which related to our political interests or the glory of France, of which he spoke bewitchingly" (vol. 5, p. 190).

Moral greatness which always touches great minds, if only from time to time, even the corrupt, that they even grasp sometimes but never re-tain. I do not know if there has ever been a single great mind which never combined some great feeling in his acts.

Bonaparte's policy with respect to the Church. Precautions to take against the spirit of the eighteenth century.

To abase the Church and win it over. To compromise it against the old regime and with despotism, beneath his government, above the rest. Alliance with it against the liberal mind, the common enemy. "You will not complain," he told me, that "I put the priests below where you left them: a bishop will think himself very honored to dine with a prefect . . . you say to hell with holy water and so do I, but realize that it is important internally and externally to make the Pope and all those people declare themselves against the legitimacy of the Bourbons. I find this stupidity every day in the negotiations. The dioceses of France are still ruled by bishops in the pay of the enemy."

Speed with which the clergy agreed with Bonaparte's idea, not only to submit, but to kiss the yoke. Tirade of fairly eloquent bitterness by Lafayette on this point (read vol. 5, p. 183) finishing with the famous phrase: "with my prefects, my police, and my priests, I will always do what I want."

Bonaparte irritated by the hostility of the salons. His taste for them (vol. 5, p. 185).

Habits of the old regime, resentment of the parvenu amid this immense grandeur; superiority of Lafayette on this point because he was a great lord; a frank hatred unmingled with envy or attraction. [. . .]

Fear of freedom which pursued Bonaparte at the summit of his power. His efforts to compromise with Lafayette and to render useless to freedom all the men who had shone in its cause and who could serve him as a cover, his insistence on making the man of '89 a senator, his annoyance at refusal:

"You feel too active to want to be a senator?"

"It is not that, but I think that retirement is what is best for me."

"Good-bye, general Lafayette, very pleasant to have passed this time with you." "And he was already at the door of his rear office" (vol. 5, p. 192).

Corsican side of Bonaparte which must never be lost from sight. "An intelligent man depicted Bonaparte to me, a little after my arrival, as having something knightly about him. But let us understand each other, he added, this is not a French knight, it is a Corsican knight" (vol. 5, p. 192). [. . .]

How at the end of long revolutions parties are confused, desperate, tired, content themselves with little and freely nourish the most unfounded hopes, sometimes the most chimerical and often the most contradictory. A sort of imbecile credulity of old men or children which makes people hope for what they want. What is most useful to Bonaparte is to have been a stranger to the beginning of the Revolution, which did not take hope away from any of those who had fought for or against it.

He said to me: "The opponents of the Revolution have nothing to reproach me with. For them I am a Solon who has made his fortune" (vol. 5, p. 234).

He offered the Jacobins "the merit to have preferred the Republic to freedom, Mohammed to Jesus Christ, the Institute to the generals. People furthermore found him to their taste because of his respect for the Pope, the clergy, the nobles, because of a certain princely tone and for his court tastes" (ibid., p. 235).

Everyone indolently let himself be carried towards him because of the side of him they liked to look at, half-voluntarily, half-involuntarily ignoring all the others.

Fortunate circumstances which favored Bonaparte's elevation.

Luck of neutral powers who follow long and violent revolutions. All the party hatred turns into tolerance for them. They are loved not for the power which they exercise, but because of those whom they prevent from exercising power.

Section Two: Tocqueville's Research Notes on the Empire

When I get to the Empire, analyze this fabric well: the despotism of a single man resting on a democratic base; the most effective combination for bringing about, in accord with the times and the men, the most unlimited despotism, the despotism best supported by the appearance of legality and by an interest which is sacred, that of the greatest number, and at the same time the least responsible. This seems extraordinary in a government which takes its origin (at least supposedly) from popular election, and yet it is true. Here, comparison. Reminder of the Roman Empire. Study and summarize the nature of this government, its causes, its organization; how throughout it resembled the idea conceived by the emperor, and still further completed and realized by his nephew. Bring in here, through some examples (there must certainly have been some at the beginning of the Empire), the actions of legists inventing theories and philosophy for this power created by violence and force, the Troplongs.

Above all since the study of Roman law has spread, the example of all the nations of Europe has proved that there is no tyranny which lacks for lawyers any more than it lacks for executioners. These two races abound under the hand of a despot, and there is no usurper so mediocre that he does not find a jurist to prove that violence is right, tyranny order, and servitude progress.

Roman Empire; Its Analogies with the [Napoleonic—Trans.]
Empire, Product of the Revolution; Democratic Character of the Roman
Empire; Researches on the Principles and Mainsprings of That
Empire (To Use at the Beginning of the Empire)

Differences and similarities between the different revolutions which, in France and Rome, made people pass from freedom to despotism. On both sides democratic passions and democratic ideas exploited.

The same procedure: to govern in the people's name, but without the people; to represent numbers and govern through the elite; to satisfy the lower classes through the recognition that one represents them, by abolishing all the intermediate orders which humiliate them, by satisfying the feeling of envy and equality in the grossest form (everyone reduced to the same level of servitude); to satisfy the upper classes by assuring them of material order, the tranquil possession of their goods, their material well-being and enrichment through industry and government positions.

Difference. The Roman Revolution made an effort to attach itself to the past, and retained the names when it abolished the things. The French Revolution flattered itself that it made everything anew, and the despotism which emerged from it made the same claim *in part* itself. This is born from the difference in their points of departure.

At Rome, freedom was the habit; in France, it was despotism. Augustus, in taking away the substance of republican government, was obliged to leave its shadow. Bonaparte was not forced to take the same precautions. For one, it was a question of making the nation depart from its mores; for the other, of making it return to them.

Book to consult, although odiously partial in favor of the Empire: *History of the Romans under the Empire,* by Merivale. What among other things is striking in this book is to what point Augustus, and according to Merivale his first successors, while presenting themselves as the representatives of the Roman people and (this is more obscure) the champions of Democracy, exclusively used the aristocracy to govern (which they had, it is true, either created themselves or put into close dependence); the small part they left to popular action, the large part they gave the Senate, which not only helped them govern, but under Augustus at least still directly governed part of the Roman provinces (the most peaceful and those where no armies were found), so that the emperor appeared still more the founder of order than the destroyer of the aristocracy.

What is also worth noting in Augustus is the appearance of election and popular power which he still allowed to persist, all the while taking care to make it illusory and powerless. He substituted *paid* positions for the unpaid positions of the Republic and multiplied posts. [He created—Trans.] permanent armies, part of the army for the first time being garrisoned at Rome itself; the power of being perpetual imperator gave him all authority in the army, and allowed him to leave a semblance of aristocracy and democracy in the government. The tribunary power gave him inviolability, although the reasons for which inviolability had been established no longer existed; the censorial power permitted him to name senators; the priestly power put him at the head of religion. Finally, all the functions which the Romans had separated, to each one of which they had given, for the purpose which they had in mind, the omnipotence the state has in a Republic (where the short duration of positions and election allows arbitrariness, and even compensates by the greatness and vagueness of attributions for the weakness which a short and precarious authority gives each official), all the functions, I say, were *united in a single man and become perpetual in his hands.* Much more art and many more precautions taken by Augustus than by Napoleon or in our time in order to hide the establishment of despotism and smooth the transition.

Democratic appearance of the Roman Empire. Trajan did not want to permit associations of workers because, says Pliny, "neque enim secundum est nostri seculi morem" [this is not in accord with the customs of our time—Trans.] (Pliny the Younger, *Letters,* book ten). Trajan himself, the great and virtuous Trajan, after a century of uncontested imperial government, could not even allow workers to associate in order to help each other; and held to the maxim that before the sovereign, the unique representative of the Roman people, there should be none but isolated individuals!

Study this democratic monarchy of the Roman world. Great analogy: common servitude taking the place of common freedom, envy satisfied, some enjoyment of freedom. Equality before the master more dear to base and common souls than equality before the law, which allows permanent social inequalities to persist, and while safeguarding against oppression still obliges one to have respect.

Roman government: not one of the forms of democracy, as some people who don't know the value of the words they use, or don't want to give it to them, have basely or foolishly said, but one of the forms of government which democratic equality can lead men to most easily, and which the evil passions and perverse instincts which are born in equality can make them accept and even love.

Villemain remarks in the second lesson of his 1830 course on medieval literature that Cicero says in one of his letters (find out which) that when he was in the countryside he was astonished to see that all the peasants were for Caesar's party. He only realized this while chatting with them. Does one not think oneself in France! I read the following (January '53) in a very learned report to the Academy: when Roman freedom succumbed under the emperors' military force, Republican forms were retained, and authority passed into their hands without the old constitution being overthrown; in theory the supreme power resided in the people. In fact, Ulpian and Gaius, in saying that the will of the sovereign is law, explain this through the law which was passed at the beginning of every reign, and which, through the Senate, transmitted to the sovereign all the rights of the people (*quum omne jus suum populus in principem transferat*) [since the people transfers all its rights to the ruler—Trans.].

State Prisons: Conversation with M. de Brévannes (1 April 1852)

"I was among a very numerous class of auditors at the Council of State. We drew our assignments among the various ministries by lot, and my lot was chosen for the ministry of police, directed by the Duke of Rovigo. I was particularly recommended to him by one of his friends. One day he had me come to him and said to me: It is said that you fear neither solitude nor work and that you like to play chess a lot. I have an important mission for you. It is to go live for a while at the hostel of Mont Cenis. You will find there a prior who is a great chess player, and you can render a valuable service. I complained about this assignment, and asked what there was to do there. I finally understood that the work consisted of nothing less than giving accounts of the travelers who daily passed through this point of separation between France and Italy, to eat at the hostel's table where they ate, in a word, to play the role of a spy. I refused, but diplomatically, and I did not lose the minister's good will. Some time later he said to me: I have a new job to propose to you. By decree (a senatus-consultus, I think) the emperor has created eight state prisons. But several of his ideas have not been implemented. It is a question of regularizing this service and first of all of inspecting it. Do you want to take charge of this along with a doctor, M . . . ? This time, I accepted. We were supposed to begin by examining Vincennes, where it was thought that things ought to be better than elsewhere, and which we were to take to some degree as a model. We were supposed neither to visit the prisoners, nor even to inquire as to their names and history, but only to observe how things were in the administration of these places. Curiosity was so little allowed me that after three weeks, my traveling companion, Dr. M . . . , a friend of the Duke of Rovigo, confessed to me that he was secretly charged with observing me to see if I did not try to know too much. He asked me in turn if I had not been charged with some similar mission with respect to him; this was not the case.

"The emperor's idea, the Duke of Rovigo had told us, was that the state prisons should contain proper places for prisoners of all ranks. For finally, the emperor had added, imagine that I want to imprison either one of my brothers or my uncle in one of them. I intend them to be treated according to their rank, that they can find there a living room, a library, billiards . . .

"There was not time to make all these improvements to the system. When I made my trip at the end of 1811 or the beginning of 1812, there were prisoners in only five prisons, where, in general, they were all very badly off. The other prisons existed only on paper. The châteaux which had been designated did not even exist. It was thus with the prison of . . . (I have forgotten the name), in the department of Mont-Tonnerre. When we came to inspect it, we found that the château had already been destroyed when the decree was made. But, on the other hand, state prisoners were found in a crowd of ordinary prisons. We were not charged with inspecting them. I only had proof that there were very many of them.

"We thus began with Vincennes. At the very top of the donjon tower I found a Spaniard who was treated with great respect. He had some books, a flute, some paints, a family of pigeons that he raised in a nook. But I later learned that this was the famous Palafox captured at Saragossa, whom the emperor, I do not know why, thought he had to make disappear. A log had been buried in his place with great pomp. The whole Earth thought Palafox dead. His own family, his wife were under the same misapprehension. He lived at the top of the donjon of Vincennes. I saw also, under a staircase where he could not hold himself erect, a young German count, a young man of eighteen years of age, accused of having wanted to assassinate the emperor, whom the intercession of the King of Saxony had kept from being shot. He was already sick in that horrible cranny and he died from it.

"At Menestrelle, in the mountains of Savoy, I found a great number of cardinals and other priests. They rightly complained of not being able to

live in that home of the snows. A little further on, in another state prison
(I cannot remember the name), I saw around two hundred Neapolitans
of fairly low rank, among whom however were found some great lords of
the same nation.

"All these institutions were badly kept up and did not offer any safeguard whatsoever. None of the regulations stipulated in the decree legal-
izing state prisons were observed. People were taken away to be put
there; they were left there as long as was wanted. You were taken from
the world and disappeared.

"I know that the state prisoners were very numerous, but I cannot say
the exact number, still more because they were spread among all the prisons of France and my mission, as I have said, only extended to the state
prisons proper."

Inequality of the Burden of Conscription under the Empire

Report on the basis for dividing the contingent of 1809 among departments.
This report, made by the minister of war of the time, was distributed,
by great imprudence, to the Council of State; it was immediately withdrawn. But L. d'Aunay having put his copy in his pocket, this *unique*
example is in his possession and I have copied from the piece itself
(27 March 1853) what follows:

"The intention of the minister is to establish that population alone is
not the only measure to follow in fixing the annual contingent. This number must be raised or lowered for various causes:

"In comparing the population subject to conscription or the number
of men found on the conscription tables to the general population of the
Empire, we find, on average, that the ratio of the general population to
the conscripts of each class is 125 to 1.

"Thus the number of men raised in each department ought to be proportional to its resources, so that the population and the size of each class
of conscripts should be in the same proportion everywhere; but we see
that this relationship is subject to very wide variations: it is 111 to 1 in the
Aisne, 165 to 1 in the Rhone, and 206 to 1 in the Seine. Thus, in basing
ourselves on population to set the departments' contingents, we have imposed on the Rhone and the Seine, where the race of men is in general
weak, a burden almost double that borne by the Aisne, a department
where men are healthy."

After having listed various other causes which must go along with general population, he adds:

"All the other considerations according to which population, taken as the original and general base, needs to be modified, can be assigned to three chief divisions:

1. The kind of men

2. The extent, the nature and needs of the land compared to the population

3. The temperament of the departments

"1. In some departments, almost all men are fit for military service; in others, almost half the species is unable to bear the fatigues of war. If among two departments of equal population, one of which is in the first class and the other in the second, one assigned an equal contingent, it would evidently be unjust.

". . . In all the manufacturing regions where children have a sedentary life not apt for the development of physical abilities, in poor departments where the shortage of labor condemns children to precocious labor, and in places where endemic illnesses persist, rejections for military service are already numerous . . . We conclude that the number of rejections should influence the division.

"2. The size of a department relative to its population, the sterility or fertility of its soil are causes which, it appears to us, ought to be taken into consideration and increase or decrease the number of conscripts to raise . . . If, from land that is rich, fertile, and bears a strong population, we take a certain number of young men every year, it is in a certain way to give new activity to the growth of men. But if we ask for an equal number of recruits from an arid and ungrateful region, we multiply the causes of depopulation and soon the species is threatened with falling into an extreme degree of degradation.

". . . To measure the land and calculate its resources, to evaluate the needs of industry and agriculture; to determine the qualities and habits of the population; to judge the points where it is overabundant and those where it is impoverished; to set the sacrifices which it can make; to indicate the regenerative care which it needs: all this belongs to the minister of the Interior, and soon doubtless we will have information on these subjects as accurate as it is broad. But in awaiting the happy moment, we believe it our duty to beg Your Majesty to allow us to help ourselves with the information which the preceding levies have furnished us.

"3. Moral causes also have a very powerful influence on all the results of the levies and must be taken into consideration. Today as before, almost the whole East and North fly to the colors, without difficulty and even with eagerness. The center of the Empire gives itself up to the call without effort. The West obeys without a murmur. But, in more than one place, the South opposes a resistance which under any other sovereign would be invincible. Shall we employ force and authority to bring all these regions to the same attitude? Or shall we have recourse to prudent modification, to gradual influences? Everything leads me to believe that this latter means is preferable. In attaching ourselves too rigorously to the former, we would increase the number of the guilty and thus insure their impunity.

"Although very convinced, Sire, of the necessity of taking into consideration every one of these causes, I will not propose to Your Majesty to give them all the influence which seems due to them. Some of my observations are not based on a long enough series of facts; others have not acquired all the degree of certainty that time will give them. Furthermore too rapid and too great a change would not be without major inconveniences. Also I have limited myself, in the table of division for 1809 which I have the honor of submitting to Your Majesty, to proposing the modifications which seem to me evidently just and necessary, leaving to experience the task of giving us more certain information."

[Various Reflections]

[On Napoleon Bonaparte's Character]

Bonaparte
One can say that he astonished the world before it knew his name. For, during the first Italian campaign, we see it written and pronounced in various ways; among others, in an ode in praise of him from Year V, titled "Verses on Buonaparté's First Victories," where one finds this verse:

> And you, Posterity,
> Heap your honors on the fortunate *Buonaparté* . . .

Bonaparte—even foreigners had the idea that he should take sovereign power.
M. Mounier reports, in his work titled "On the Influence Attributed to the Philosophes" (Tübingen, 1801, p. 215), that Wieland, as early as the time of the Directory, in the dialogues where he discussed and criticized the system of the Jacobins, argued that in order to put an end to the miseries of France, it was necessary to concentrate all power in the hands of a single man, and that this man ought to be Bonaparte.

Napoleon. His character. Judgments that were made about him.
Speech by Pitt in 1800, cited by Villemain (in his course on eighteenth-

century literature), speech in which Pitt brilliantly analyzes Bonaparte's position and character and predicts that he will be endlessly led from war to war: read this speech. Same lecture by Villemain where he tells that Fox, during the Peace of Amiens, went to see the First Consul and brought back the impression that, content with what he had done, he no longer aspired to anything but a glorious repose, a good young man full of philosophical ideas about the reconciliation of whites and blacks. Go back to the source of this interesting anecdote. Is it in Fox's correspondence?

Villemain's correct and profound judgment about the character of Napoleon's government (p. 313): "It was not force [violent force] which was his usual weapon. The maintenance of order, the regular application of the laws, the avoidance of all useless cruelty, even the desire for justice were his government's general character. But despotism over the will, the destruction of the public virtues at the same time as the *exaltation of courage* on the battlefield, these too were principles and supports of his government."

I have underlined *exaltation of courage*. Note that Napoleon wanted to direct enthusiasm, not forbid it; to eliminate all other great efforts of the soul for the profit of one of them, that which makes one die well in arms. This great genius understood that some high passion is always necessary in order to inspire the human heart, which otherwise falls into gangrene and rots. He would never have imagined wanting to fix all hearts and minds on personal well-being alone.

* * *

Italian or at least Mediterranean side of the emperor's genius . . .

* * *

Indelible impressions of the old regime on this mind so eminently innovative.

* * *

Napoleon treated his generals like the hunter treats his dogs, whom he allows to eat the carcass in order to give them a taste for the hunt.

* * *

What I find most extraordinary among the qualities which this so-extraordinary man possessed is the suppleness, or, to speak the language of science (physiology), the contractile nature of his genius, which allowed it when necessary to extend itself so as to be able to effortlessly embrace the affairs of the world, and then to suddenly contract itself so as to be able to grasp the smallest objects without effort.

[Reflections on the Consulate and the Empire]

[Political Society]

18 Brumaire is an event which had no precedent in the events which came before it, and which has no analogue in the history of our Revolution.

One must not exaggerate the influence that the flaws of the bureaucratic machine exercise over the fate of nations. The chief sources of good and evil are always in the mind which leads it. This truth was then well highlighted. An idea to put at the moment when centralization reconstitutes itself perhaps.

When it is a question of knowing what can or should stop a revolution, it is not the intrinsic strength or greatness of the obstacle which should be considered, but the whole of the circumstances. There are times when a giant is not strong enough to stop the course of a revolution and there are others when a dwarf is more than enough. At the beginning of the French Revolution people thought at every instant that it was going to be stopped, sometimes by this, sometimes by that. Towards the end, people thought it was unstoppable; it seemed that all who wanted to oppose it must be either immediately or soon carried away by the mobility of everything. Double error. To the chapter on the Consulate.

How the same facts seem tolerable or unbearable to the same nation depending on whether they accord with the current of public opinion or oppose it. Bonaparte imposed an additional twenty-five centimes in property taxes upon his arrival in power; people said nothing. People did not turn against him: everything he did was popular. The Provisional Government took the same step in 1848 and immediately fell under anathema. The first one made the revolution that people wanted; the second the one people did not want.

See everything that d'Ivernois said in the pamphlet of 1800 about the First Consul's financial measures.

[Clergy]

To the chapter which will follow the reestablishment of religion during the Consulate. New position of the clergy (Catholic country), zeal for its religious duties, more faith, more Ultramontane, more independent with respect to civil power in religious matters; more servile in civil matters, more deprived of the public virtues, more a stranger to the country's passions and interests, less citizens.

All this due to the same cause: the priest had ceased to be a landowner;

and since he had not become the father of a family at the same time, all the links which attach one to civil society were lacking. A crucial idea to put either at the end of the work or at the beginning, when I say that the Revolution was not directed against religious beliefs.

Paint well how religion regains its dominance in each of the nation's classes as that class is dangerously threatened by the Revolution: first among the upper classes in '93, then the middle classes in '48, the lower classes themselves affected then—or at least all those among the lower classes who had anything—and brought back towards respect and esteem for belief out of fear.

People complain that the Catholic clergy has the instinct to dominate, the thing is true, but not worth noting.

A group is a strong man; and all the passions of the individual man must be found in men associated in this way.

The fact that a group is egoistic and dominant proves that it is well formed and that it approaches the make-up of a man. If the Catholic clergy is above all clergy and dominator, it comes back to individual egoism; it is not because it professes the doctrines of Catholicism, it is because it forms a well-constituted body. Retain the form of the association and change its purpose, you will always arrive at the same results.

[The Intellectual Movement]

Character of literature under the Republic and the Empire. (*Situation of Literature* by Chénier, description of the end of the literary eighteenth century. Read this.)

Villemain says in the next-to-last lesson of his course on eighteenth-century literature: "In this society, which emerged from its ruins under a conqueror's despotic hand, you see literary controversy take up a large part of public attention. Political passions disappear, hide, disguise themselves under the speculative interests of criticism or literature. Dissertations on taste replace the theories that had shaken the world. This conquering nation, mistress of the outside world, was evidently not allowed to have any other discussions, any other public exercise of thought, except controversy over the preeminence of the seventeenth or the eighteenth century. This was the part the master had left to intellectual activity under his empire" (p. 336).

Chénier was charged with making the report on the ten-year prizes; attempt at a hierarchical and official literature, affinity with Chinese literature.

Beneath this artificial literature, the real literature born of the Revolution which reveals itself. Mme. de Staël, M. de Maistre, M. de Chateaubriand.

Reread this piece in extenso when I get to this subject.

Villemain, while forcefully depicting the sterility of this attempt at official and laureate literature, seems to think that a certain literary activity survived political activity. But it is easy to see that literature had become the sole arena where old political enemies could still attack and hurt each other, so that the literary movement which survived freedom was not born of dead political passions, but from the fact that they were still a little alive and took this form.

Villemain says (same lesson or the following one) that Napoleon himself wrote the critical essay in the *Moniteur* about *Corinne* where the praises of Oswald are considered the act of a bad Frenchman. A bitter and spiritual criticism, says Villemain (p. 360).

Read the article in question in the *Moniteur*.

*   *   *

That the means of reviving literary life is not to destroy political life.

It seems that a civilized people, reduced to no longer concerning itself with public affairs, ought to seek out literary pleasures with more ardor. But this is not so at all. One remains as insensitive and infertile in literature as in politics. Those who believe that by taking away from men the greatest objects of their thoughts one makes them more active and more powerful to produce the little that is left for them to do, these people treat the human mind according to the laws of nature. These are steam engines and streams of water which make the little wheels turn faster and better the more their strength has been diverted away from the big wheels. But the rules of mechanics do not apply to our souls. Almost all the masterpieces of the human mind have been produced in centuries of freedom, and if the arts and letters have seemed to take new flight and attain greater perfection immediately after freedom has been destroyed, this has never been sustained. When one closely examines what happened then, one realizes that these absolute governments inherited the strengths, the intellectual energy, the freedom of imagination that free mores and institutions had created. They did nothing but add the sole good they could give, tranquility, to the use of all the intellectual riches which the government they destroyed created, and it sometimes happens then that absolute governments have the appearance of being more fertile than free government. But this is a false appearance, which disappears over time as absolute governments continue to rule over society and make the influence proper to absolute governments prevail. This explains Augustus, the

Medicis, and Louis XIV. The Roman Republic, the Florentine democracy, the feudal freedom which still survived amid the struggles of religion and the Fronde were the different soils which produced the great men who shed luster over what we call the centuries of Augustus, of Leo X, and of Louis XIV. And the proof is to that as the new regimes created by the sovereigns of these times solidified themselves, these claimed effects would steadily disappear, and one fell into the nature of things, that is into the tranquility and sterility of despotism.

*　　*　　*

A wit said, apropos of what he called the literary sterility of the Empire, that the mind was flat there because the circumstances were great. But that on the contrary, when nothing great was happening, minds revived and produced beautiful things. These doctrines will be very consoling for those who live under the present government. But I think they are false. In all times it is freedom alone which has given birth to masterpieces and great actions. It is the great spectacles which are given or which have just been given to the world which suggest high thoughts; it is the shock of great events which fans the torch of human intelligence and makes it cast its greatest light. Mediocrity and political servitude have never engendered anything but literary platitude. Literature was brilliant in Greece when Greece was free, and what has been called the Augustan Century was the century which had seen the freedom of Rome and the conquest of the world. What has been called the Century of Louis XIV was the meeting of minds which were formed in that happy moment when feudal freedom still left traces of the vigor it had given souls, while the human mind had already finished polishing itself. The eighteenth century itself had been a century of independence with regard to the expression of thought; one can even say that it was also a century of greatness; for if the sight of the present then was dull and small, one thought one was discovering an immense and radiant future. It is not even true to say that the Empire was a sterile time; doubtless the writers of that time who sang the praises of the emperor or who enriched themselves in his antechambers, the Mérys and Mérimées of the period, were either very dull authors or at least very second-rate minds. But those who fought the emperor and defended the rights of humanity against him, these have shone brightly. Assuredly, the ten years which produced Mme. de Staël and M. de Chateaubriand were not sterile years. Similarly, for our day one can predict that no intellectual greatness will be left, except among those who protest against the government of their country and who remain free amid universal servitude. If there appear here some great minds, this will not be

because nothing great is happening in the country; but because there will
be found some souls who still retain the imprint of better times (July '53).

[General Reflections. The Heritage of the Revolution]

[Mores and Feelings]

The French Revolution produced or seemed to produce a race of revolution-
aries which was new in the world.

It is true that we have seen a race of revolutionaries come out of the
French Revolution and survive it who seem new in the world, a turbulent
and destructive race, always ready to destroy and unfit to found. A race
who not only practice violence, contempt for individual rights, and the
oppression of minorities but, what is new, profess that it must be so: who
put forth as a doctrine that there are no individual rights and effectively
no individuals, but a mass to which everything is always allowed in order
to attain its ends.

Something analogous has been seen after all great revolutions but there
are special causes this time: 1) The democratic character of our Revolution, which tended towards contempt for individual rights; towards violence since the Revolution had the lower classes as its chief instrument.

2) Its philosophical character, which wanted a theory even for violence.

3) A Revolution which is not limited to a short space of time, but which
has gone on for sixty years, changing only its theater, so that the revolutionary race renews itself constantly and is always found somewhere, with
its tradition, its school. In such a way that for sixty years there has always
been a great school of revolution open very publicly someplace in the
world, where all disturbed and violent minds, men lost in debts . . . go to
educate and instruct themselves.

This is a particular illness, a sort of horror of rules, love of risks or
danger, the combined product of all kinds of passions, errors, vices, mi-
asmas similar to that fever which is born in hospitals and which becomes
a particular and characteristic illness, even though it owes it origin to a
thousand different evils.

[Political Society]

Upper classes enemies of freedom, lower classes friends of license, that is
France.

*   *   *

Back-and-forth marching of our Revolutions, which creates an illusion, if one does not look closely.

At the beginning, invariably a *push* towards decentralization. 1787, 1828, 1848. At the end an extension of centralization.

In the beginning we follow the logic of our principles. In the end, that of our habits, our passions, of power.

In sum, the last word always remains with centralization, which, in truth, fortifies itself in germ even when it is diminished in appearance, for the social ferment, the *individualization* and the *isolation* of the social elements still continues during this time (to develop).

*   *   *

An example, among a thousand, of the way in which the Revolution proceeded with regard to the old regime.

During the old regime, the judges constantly governed and the governors constantly judged. The natural limit of powers was badly fixed and the two spheres, executive and judicial, were often mixed up with one another in many areas. The Revolution has narrowly contained the judge within his sphere, but it has left the government almost as much outside its own as it was then, correcting the abuse which hindered power and preserving the abuse which served it. It has struck down one of the thousand anathemas which hardly cease: it has legitimized and regularized the other.

Thus with everything. The Revolution destroyed from the old regime only what was incompatible with the equality of ranks and the unity of power. It retained all the rest.

What it eliminated and what it left equally show its real character. Always use this instrument to sound its depths.

*   *   *

What is the natural government, and what ought to be the final government, of modern society as the Revolution has created it?

Perhaps at the very end when I will say that if I stop, it is not because the Revolution is over, nor that we know definitively where it leads. Preface perhaps.

Those who have seen the first Republic have told me . . . and although I have not yet reached the usual limits of human life, I have already in my day heard it said four times that modern society, as the French Revolution made it, has finally found its natural and permanent basis, and then the next event proved that people were wrong.

The Empire, we were assured in my childhood, is exactly the government which France needs. Why . . . Say why. I have seen the Empire fall.

In a society like ours, despotism is nothing but an accident, anarchy naturally engenders a despot. A moderate politics, freedom is our natural state . . . The reasons. Thus spoke the publicists and statesmen that I heard in my youth. A little later I saw the government of the Restoration pass away. I heard it said by its conquerors that . . . The reasons. They were still repeating these things when the new Revolution destroyed their work. The Republic which survived them also had its philosophers to show the causes of its duration, and its end . . . Each new government gives birth to its sophists who while it is dying still diligently seek to prove that this government is immortal.

*   *   *

How patriotism is justified in the eyes of Reason and appears to it not only a great virtue but the most important.

When we look at it from a broad and general point of view, patriotism, despite all the great actions which it has motivated, seems a false and narrow passion. It is to humanity that the great actions suggested by patriotism are due, not to that little fragment of the human race closed within their particular limits that we call a nation and a country. At first glance it seems that those moralists, above all among the Christians, who apparently forget duty to country in order to think only of humanity, who forget the fellow-citizen for the fellow-man, it seems, I say, that they are right. It is in fact by taking a detour that we discover that they are wrong. Man, as God has created him (I don't know why), becomes less devoted as the object of his affections becomes larger. His heart needs the particular, it needs to limit the object of its affections in order to grasp the object in a firm and lasting embrace. There are only a very small number of great souls who can inflame themselves with the love of the human species. The sole means which Providence has left itself (given man as he is) to make each of us work for the general good of humanity is to divide humanity into a large number of parts and to make each one of these fragments the object of the love of those who compose it. If every man fulfilled his duty in this (and within these limits the duty is not beyond his natural strength well directed by reason and morality), the general good of humanity would be produced, although little tends directly towards it. I am convinced that we better serve the interests of the human species in giving each man only a particular country to love than in wanting to inspire him on behalf of the human species, which, whatever we do, he will only consider with a distant, uncertain, and cold gaze.

Excerpts from Tocqueville's Research Notes

Plans

First idea of the chapters the book should contain and the basic ideas (Saint Cyr, 1853).

Reread carefully before the final *revision* because the whole *spirit, movement,* and *organization* of the work is seen here better than anywhere else. [In the margin:] This whole notebook is interesting because it contains the first outlines of the book but it only applies to the first volume (1856).

Order of Ideas

First, at the beginning the Revolution seemed like an ordinary event, of ordinary importance. An individual fact analogous to many other individual facts already known to history; coming from minor accidents and capable of being stopped at any moment by minor causes.

[Development in the margin of the preceding:] Where to find some quotations, some distinct facts to support this: what evidence from abroad proves this. Policy of the sovereigns, Young. What diplomatic documents to find? Correspondence of individuals from that period. Works published at the time. Doubtless our foreign agents made reports about what people thought of the Revolution at the courts where they represented us. But how to get knowledge of this correspondence? Chat with Vielcastel, Rivet. Perhaps go directly to Drouyn.

Second, as the Revolution developed; as its terrible and almost satanic character manifested itself internally; as the wild, strange, and monstrous boldness of its principles and its examples appeared; as its efforts seemed to be directed against God himself; as it overflowed its borders like a new Islam, with new ideas, new means, new tactics, knocking down, breaking, trampling over peoples and at the same time winning them to its cause; as these things burst out, people's perspectives changed. The Revolution appeared to be a fact so extraordinary, so inexplicable, that it was super-human. Some saw in it the direct action of Hell; others found in it the dissolution of society; everyone recognized an unknown future for humanity in it, something monstrous which could no longer be stopped. A feeling of horror. A sort of religious terror. Something similar to the state of mind in the Roman world half-submerged by the mounting flood of barbarians. [In the margin of the three preceding lines:] Look for proof of this in the works of the time: M. de Maistre, Mallet du Pan, Burke. The great enemies of the Revolution. Some speeches must have been given in the British Parliament (those of Burke among others) which ought to give a good example of this period. Some Church documents also.

Third, what is the Revolution after all? What does it have in common with the great revolutions which have changed the face of empires? What is new in it? What are its true characteristics?

What is fundamental and what is accidental? What was born naturally and necessarily from the character of this revolution, from its nature, from its purpose, and what came from particular accidents of the times, from one people's character, from previous facts, established opinions, the particular actions of certain men, from the unforeseen turn of certain events?

Examples of these different things: the destruction of the old aristocratic fabric; the foundation of equality: fundamental. Political freedom, the war against religion: accidental.

The Revolution's general character. Its general language. Why. Freedom, an accident, a means, not the purpose of this great social tumult. What came from general causes, what is particular to France. Why it appeared in France rather than elsewhere. This leads to the French causes, to the situation of France, to what prepared a revolution there. Why so violent? Why impious? Role of the French character in this great event. The habits, the antecedents, the history of the nation.

Why it simultaneously attacked government, the social state, beliefs, habits, bureaucracy, language, the things which derived from politics and those which were furthest from it. [In the margin:] There is in all this much of the "French fury," independent of general causes.

The antireligious character of the Revolution seems the most lasting and however is not fundamental. An accident.

The attack on the right of property: accidental. The tendency of the Revolution was certainly to make the right of property weaker vis-à-vis the social power. To make it vulnerable (all its outer defenses having been dismantled) to the social power represented by an assembly or an individual. One can perhaps say that the character of the Revolution, seen in its final consequences, is the weakening and perhaps the destruction of the right of private property. But this is not true if one limits the Revolution's life to the duration of its contemporary period or the period immediately following.

The weakening of power much more accidental than all the rest. On the contrary the fundamental character of the Revolution is to make the social power generally stronger, although changing hands more often. Mirabeau's profound perspective on this. The true mark of genius! Report to the king. [In the margin of the preceding:] The more the master changes, the greater the power, whoever the master is. No more revolutions. A stronger government regardless of the result of revolutions.

Perhaps start by successively rejecting all that is accidental and then arrive at the fundamental, having thus set aside all the accidents: What is the fundamental character of the Revolution therefore?

Then immediately look for why this fundamental Revolution began in France rather than elsewhere.

How to explain the almost unparalleled degree of violence of the Revolution?

Democratic revolutions are always more violent than others. How this one simultaneously stirred up, excited men in every possible way at the same time; and then! The French fury.

But why from the first day this bloody character, unsettled, despising rules, precedents, morality, the idea of law, always intemperate. Constantly? There are very complicated causes of this phenomenon which must be sought out and analyzed: The French character. The low civilization of the lower classes, in the heart of the nation that was apparently the most civilized. Corruption on top. Philosophical irreligion.

Notes on Germany

[Questionnaire]

In the German old regime, what was the position of the nobility?

Did it form a *closed* aristocracy, that is one which could only be entered by birth?

Did it have considerable privileges such as:

The exclusive right to certain positions?

Tax-exemptions?

Did it take part in rural government?

Did it have feudal dues and what were the chief ones?

Did it excite violent jealousies and great hatreds?

Political laws. Bureaucratic and urban institutions. Above all rural government.

Did the nobility have an exclusive right to certain positions such as those of officials, for example?

Did it administer justice? Did they have courts?

The division of the land. Was landownership divided? Was the peasant a landowner?

All this must have left traces in the laws of the times, if not in people's memories. Walter.

The situation and relations of classes.

Did the nobility form a closed body absolutely distinct from the rest?

What kinds of rights had it retained?

Did it govern the countryside?

Did it enjoy great feudal dues?

What were the chief of these dues?

Situation of justice and the bodies which rendered it.

Were there still any kind of representative assemblies?

The bourgeoisie.

Was it confined to the towns or did it extend to the countryside?

Did it have tax-exemptions and which ones?

Was it separated from the nobility by different rights or by habits and pretensions?

Was it very hostile to the nobility?

How was it recruited?

Was it composed in very large part, as in France, of public officials? Was the number of petty public positions already very large?

The rural lower classes.

Where were they still bound to the soil?

What feudal dues ordinarily still weighed heavily on them?

Where and in what proportion were they landowners?

The Catholic Church.

Documents, reports on the two years 1785, 1815: Dahlmann, Loebel.

A work of administrative law.

Whom to contact in Westphalia?

Maps of old Germany.

Conversation with M. Walter, 27 June 1854

The German nobility under the old regime. The principle of the German nobility was *birth*. However, the emperor could make nobles and he had made a fairly large number of them. But this only began at the same time as in France, around the fifteenth century, not in imitation of France but as a result of general causes which operated at the same time both here and there.

These nobles of imperial creation never counted for very much within the German nobility, which derived its strength from its territorial possessions.

The emperor even created princes, such as the princes of Thurn und Taxis. But for these princes to take their place on the princes' bench at the diet, they had to have acquired a territorial fief and their rights were often subject to dispute.

Did there exist between nobles of different origin the feelings of contempt and envy which have been noted in France?

Response. I don't think so. These feelings, at least, have not left any traces.

There was also a kind of personal nobility which was given to judicial officials who sat in the higher courts. When Roman law was introduced and began to corrupt or replace Germanic law, it was necessary to put a lawyer beside the noble judge. These lawyers, who soon became the real judges, received personal nobility, that is for their lifetime they enjoyed the prerogatives of nobles and took their place among them, but without transmitting their rank to their children.

Privileges of the nobility. Do German nobles enjoy the most pernicious of the French nobility's privileges, tax-exemptions?

Response: To a certain extent. In feudal times, nobles personally performing military service were exempt from taxation. But since they ceased to make war at their own expense, a tax called the warhorse tax was imposed on them, or they consented to its establishment, whose precise purpose was to replace military service. The land taxes of the German old regime were not significant. Most taxes were indirect. Most of the petty sovereigns, above all in the ecclesiastical states (M. Walter is a Catholic) lived chiefly from the income from their domains. (Here I think I understand that in the assessment and the raising of what little direct taxation existed, the nobles had certain privileges, but that these privileges were insignificant and this kind of tax so insignificant that M. Walter does not think that this ever gave rise to very strong complaints. Nothing similar to the *taille*.) As for a right to employment, court positions, the entry to certain cathedral chapters, belonged exclusively to the nobility. Most positions as military officers, above all in the cavalry. However, commoners were sometimes also found there and even serfs, as we see by Frederick the Great's law code promulgated in 1794, where this situation is foreseen. We saw above that the nobility shared judicial positions with lawyers invested with personal nobility.

Rights to govern (this time I have left aside everything relating to the right to meet in a *Landtag*). I am speaking only of administrative powers exercised individually by nobles in the countryside. Lord's courts existed everywhere. Everywhere they had real power, even though they were dependent on the state for serious cases. Through them and through his other officials the lord had real police power over the countryside. He also exercised great influence over the collective interests of the village. The central government did not get involved in these details.

Second Conversation, 30 June 1854, with the Same [. . .]

The nobility only governed in exceptional cases.

As a general rule it may be said that administrative power was no longer in the nobles' hands. The country was divided into districts: the bailiff, the sovereign's official, rendered justice, controlled the police, governed, as much as then was governed. The community had a kind of town council (elected as I think); the state raised taxes through its officials and even assessed them I think. Such was the general rule. But there persisted exceptions in many cases. From time to time lords who retained their court and who governed their estates' inhabitants were still encountered there. These lords were of two kinds: one was completely mediatized, that is not dependent at all on the Empire. Some others were simultaneously (through an ambiguous position) half mediate and half immediate.

Feudal dues. All the feudal dues existed: there were rights to exclusive ownership of ovens, mills, first sales, permanent payments, corvées both for the lord and the government . . . (Were there also rights to fees on the buying and selling of land?)

But all these things were moderated and regulated by laws and they did not give rise to complaints. (In general M. Walter seems to me to be very tender towards the old regime.) Some of these things still exist on the other side of the Rhine. They have been completely destroyed among us by France.

The peasants were landowners. The peasants were already in large part landowners. Furthermore the custom of the clergy was to rent out its lands on long-term leases, which made the tenant almost an owner. [. . .]

Differences less great between the noble and the commoner. M. Walter claims that in general in Germany the difference between the noble and the commoner was less noticeable, less great, less humiliating than in France. But I don't understand how and this merits confirmation.

Germany more changed in the spirit than the letter of institutions. In general, one can say that in the eighteenth century Germany had changed little in the letter of its institutions from what it had been several centuries before. It was the spirit in which they functioned which was already, everywhere, more or less profoundly changed. [. . .]

M. Walter, 30 June 1854

[. . .] *Bavaria retains more from the old regime than the rest of Germany.* Today Bavaria is perhaps the region of Germany where the old institutions have left the most traces, because it is the only one which the Revolution of 1848 barely touched.

Abolition of serfdom in Mecklenburg. Mecklenburg was the last country of Germany in which serfdom was abolished. It was only abolished in 1820. And it was only abolished in this way: the peasant was allowed to leave his lord's land, but the lord was allowed to take back the land. Everything else could only be the result of a contract between them. The results of this have been the following: Almost everywhere the peasant, needing the land to live, rents it from the lord under the same conditions which were imposed on him in the time of serfdom, so that in fact the only change that the law of 1820 has produced is to have abolished the perpetual character of the tenure of land. Almost everywhere else in Germany, when serfdom or even feudal payments were abolished, the interest of the old lord was more or less sacrificed to that of the peasant.

The remains of medieval institutions abolished in Prussia in 1850. The legislation of Stein and of Hardenberg (1808 and 1811) already took great strides in this direction. Afterwards everything stopped almost completely until 1848, when the chamber of that time (which was overthrown in November of that year) wanted to make all the rest disappear through revolution, without transition and without payments. It did not have the time. Its work was resumed and completed in 1850, but with much moderation. Some feudal dues were abolished without indemnity, others declared redeemable. See notably in this legislation what is relevant to the *lods et ventes* and the ingenious bank system, with whose aid the peasants' liberation was facilitated and through which the peasants were confronted with the state and no longer with their former lords. These arrangements were very different from those through which Austria armed the peasants against the lords in the regions of Russian origin.

Serfdom transformed rather than abolished in Hanover. In Hanover one cannot say that serfdom has been positively abolished, but it has been so moderated and transformed that it is no longer recognizable. However the peasant in Hanover today still cannot marry without the permission of his lord.

In German regions of Slavic origin, serfdom harsher and its traces more visible. There is a portion of German lands, such as Brandenburg, old Prussia, Silesia, which were originally populated solely by Slavs and which have been conquered and in part populated by Germans. In these regions the appearance of serfdom has always been more harsh than in Germany, it has excited more hatred and the traces it has left are more alive.

The lord's court. The chief and universal engine of feudal or baronial government in Germany was also the lord's court, which was called in German the [blank].

It was there that the chief inhabitants of the lordship met with the lord for government and for the settlement of reciprocal obligations.

This court was also the greatest link between the lord and his subjects, the landowner and the serfs. In most German countries these courts or their vestiges still existed at the time of the Revolution. In Westphalia they are still seen in our day.

The Grand Duchy of Berg has been French. Part of Westphalia, the Grand Duchy of Berg, having been given to Murat as an appanage and joined to France, it is one of those German lands where medieval institutions were suddenly and completely destroyed at the beginning of the century. [. . .]

Conversation with M. Brandis, M. Hälschner, and M. Monnard (1 July 1854)

Socialism in Germany. On my question about whether Germany in general, and in particular the banks of the Rhine, were very infected by socialist doctrines, they did not appear to think so, and all three responded no; these doctrines had remained at the level of abstract theory and had hardly penetrated the lower classes. I insisted and said that the lower classes can understand the theory's practical purpose without being concerned precisely with the theory itself; knowing only vaguely that intellectuals had found that the division of one's neighbor's property was no longer theft, but a political action in conformity with right and justice. They persisted in thinking that there was little evil produced in this sense.

What is certain for me, at least, is that their minds have not been struck by that terror of the socialists like those of so many Frenchmen, or rather almost all Frenchmen, of the same status.

Division of the land. These gentlemen were agreed that in the vicinity of Bonn the land was extremely divided. It was thus, they seemed to think, in most of the German regions bordering the Rhine. They said that even at the end of the old regime there was already great division of the land.

Peasant rules of inheritance. In almost all Germany, and above all in the Germany that had remained closest to the Middle Ages, it seems to me from what these gentlemen said that the principle was the indivisibility of inheritances among the peasants. The eldest or youngest son, depending on the region, took all the estate himself and owed only dowries to his sisters (I suppose that this institution derived from the feudal system itself, the lord having a great interest in not having to deal with anyone but the head of a family, which kept the family from becoming a burden on him).

Disorders of the electoral court of Cologne. These gentlemen who, it is true, are Protestants, said that nothing was worse run than the affairs of this ecclesiastical government, which itself was divided, the cathedral chapter often having more power than the archbishop. In this regard the ecclesiastical states were very inferior to the others and this had affected the mores of the people. They also spoke much to me of the disorders of these ecclesiastical courts. At Godesberg, near Bonn, they showed me a great palace which was the archbishop's theater, and nearby, a very beautiful house which the last archbishop had given to his chamberlain.

State of philosophy in Germany. M. Brandis (a professor of philosophy himself) said to me that philosophy, which used to be so popular in Germany and which had seemed to be the chief and most noble occupation of the human mind, was now held in very low esteem; it was even freely ridiculed, and the chief efforts of the mind were directed toward the various sciences.

I asked him if this did not come from that same general intellectual decline which reigned in France. These gentlemen said no; in ceasing to be interested in philosophy, people had not stopped being interested in other things. M. Brandis, furthermore, seemed to reject the influence that philosophy had had over politics. From the school of Hegel (today much criticized) many revolutionaries had been produced, but they were not exactly revolutionaries because they were interested in that philosophy (a subject to return to).

Complications of medieval institutions still existing at the beginning of our Revolution. M. Brandis said to me that in the town of Hildesheim (Kingdom of Hanover) where he was born, in his childhood he had seen five jurisdictions, that of the bishop, that of the cathedral chapter, that of the old town, that of the new town, and a fifth whose name I forget. None of them were dependent on any of the others and they had the most interlaced jurisdictions.

Religion, philosophy, politics in Germany. M. Monnard assured me of two things today: 1) There was a violent intellectual reaction including the universities against all the materialist, atheist, and demagogical doctrines which had come from the philosophy of Hegel. Although the Christian religion had suffered strong assaults, it was still very powerful, however, and seemed to be reviving in minds; it reigned in most universities; at Halle, which had been the most active center of the whole Hegelian school, only sincerely Christian doctrines were now professed. At the University of Heidelberg, where more than anywhere else positive Christianity had been shaken by the abuse of analysis, there were professors who were not only believers but energetically manifested their faith and made active propaganda. It mustn't be forgotten that the Prussian government had first of all favored Hegel's philosophy to the point of oppression of the opposing party, because it was regarded as very favorable to authority, its tendency being to legitimate and to consecrate the existing situation. One then made violent efforts to make it dominate without opposition in all the universities.

2) Regarding politics, he claimed that political spirit was not dead; people retained a deep and strong taste for constitutional freedom and at the first opportunity one would see that the storm of '48 had rather shown the exaggeration of the ultraunitary school than the weakness of the parliamentary school. In general, great intellectual activity once again reigned and was manifested by greater and greater interest taken in all the works of the human mind. Philosophy proper had lost some of its prestige, but it had not at all fallen into the state depicted by M. Brandis. People were no longer so attached to the search for a system of absolute truths, but they continued to be very actively interested in the *history* of philosophy.

Persecution of the Lutheran Church. Situation of the official Church. M. Walter said to me today (4 July 1854) that we had not known what degree of persecution had been brought by the former king against those who refused to recognize his new church and who remained faithful to the old Lutheranism. The press could not speak of it. A certain number of parishes had emigrated to America. It was the present king who issued the Edict of Toleration, which permitted old Lutherans to have their worship legally established, but while treating them as a *sect*. They could have priests, meetings . . . but at their own expense. The churches, the foundations, the very tithes (on the other side of the Rhine where the tithe still exists) belong to their adversaries. In the Rhine province the registration of births and deaths belongs to the magistrates. Everywhere else to the various clergies, according to the religion of the persons whom the records concern.

According to M. Walter the Protestant religion in Prussia depends absolutely on the king, or rather it is the business of bureaucrats, like the rest. The ministry of religion is the real pope. According to him there is even no official representation of the clergy, synod or anything else. According to M. Walter Protestantism in Prussia is so divided, is based so little today on dogma, depends so much on intellectual fantasies, that if one wanted to establish a free government within it, it would fall to pieces.

Philosophy. Like M. Monnard, M. Walter recognizes that there is a strong reaction against all the crazy and anti-Christian systems.

Position of the Catholics vis-à-vis the Prussian government. It seems from all the conversations of M. Walter (who, however, is very conservative and a strong partisan of the king) that the Catholics are in defiance of the government and that, without considering themselves exactly persecuted, they think there is a fund of bad will towards them and a constant habit of favoring their enemies.

Situation of the peasants and their lands in Germany under the old regime. It seems that in Germany three kinds of property and three kinds of status for peasants have always been known. There more or less always had been, and everywhere in eighteenth-century Germany there still were, some entirely free peasants who possessed hereditary property which was not subject to any servitude, feudal or other: *Erbgüter.*

Below the position of the owner of *Erbgüter* were found those who were designated in Germany under the common name, borrowed from the Romans, of the *colonat*. The *colonat* was established in one of two ways: either the small landowner transferred the property of his lands to the lord (doubtless in order to be protected by him), reserving for himself the use of the land and subjecting himself only to making a payment to the lord. Or the lord conceded a portion of his lands to the peasant, retaining their ownership, but transferring their use in perpetuity, in return for a payment.

This is what we know in France under the name *bail à rente*. In both countries one arrived at this point: the abstract right of ownership was separated from use, in one case from the lord, in the other from the peasant. But the *colon* had, moreover, most of the rights of ownership. He could transfer, sell (mortgage?), but if he did not make the agreed payment, the property returned to the lord.

The result of the Revolution and the new institutions has been to give complete ownership to these *colons,* either by eliminating the payment (as happened, I think, in the parts of Germany which were united to France); or by giving the peasant easy means to free himself from it.

Independently of these peasants who owned *Erbgüter* and of these *colons,* there were serfs.

M. Hälschner persists in contradicting M. Walter, insisting that serfdom still existed throughout Germany in the eighteenth century, and notably in the Rhine provinces. He admits only that its characteristics in certain regions had been so weakened that it was pretty difficult to recognize, and that the position of these serfs was often very little different from that of the *colon.* He admits that in this part of Germany serfdom had retained less of its old form than in the provinces of the north, such as Brandenburg, old Prussia, Pomerania, and above all Mecklenburg. He claims only that this followed less the law of latitude than that of the size of the country. In all the little countries the condition of the peasants was worse (doubtless because the lord had remained more the master under a petty sovereign than under a great one). It is thus that Mecklenburg had preserved the forms of the old serfdom more than any of the Prussian provinces by which it was surrounded (8 July 1854).

Frederick destroyed the collective action of the nobles while allowing their individual action to subsist in part. Everything that related to collective government by the nobility, the estates for example, fell into disuse. Frederick himself, who, continuing the work that his grandfather had begun, destroyed almost completely all that remained of the nobility's collective government, left them individually the government of the countryside. He limited himself to establishing means of supervision, and besides, the forms of government varied considerably from one province to another. This powerful sovereign, who was so passionate for government unity, never was so weak as to want administrative uniformity (ibid., 8 July 1854).

Catholicism. Catholic clergy. M. Walter told me today (11 July 1854) that the clergy in this region (the Rhine province) was recruited chiefly from people of the lower classes; however, for some time young people from the nobility whom no earthly interest could call to it had been entering the clergy, which was very fortunate. The Catholic Church is very prosperous, which comes, according to M. Walter, from the fact that it is independent of the state and faced by a Protestant opposition. This has created zeal, ardor, made people count on no one but themselves and increased the education of the clergy to an unusual degree. No famous preachers. In Austria, where people saluted when the Blessed Sacrament passed, the clergy was put to sleep by the feeling of official favor, and nowhere in Germany was Catholicism languishing more than there. M. W. explained the advantages of not being supported by and as a result not being dependent on the state with extraordinary warmth; bishops are chosen by the chapters but the list of candidates is in general secretly agreed on with the government, which, without having the right to include people, had the right to strike them off the list. In general young people who were destined for the clergy received their first education with everyone else in the gymnasium, and did their course in canon law at a university. Afterwards they went to a seminary. There are bishops who fear contact with the spirit of the century, and who are beginning to want to establish Catholic schools, but this is not general and usually the ecclesiastical students take the common courses.

Division of noble property. Peasant proprietors. Resemblance to France. Serfdom still existed in these provinces at least in one of its forms, *Erbuntertanigkeit,* but in fact the situation of the serfs was not very different from that of the peasants who were *colons* and they became difficult to distinguish. I am furthermore assured that in the electorate of Cologne, for example, property was very divided, that a very large number of peasants were landowners, which I attribute chiefly to the state of war and half-bankruptcy in which the nobles had already lived for a very long time, which forced them to constantly sell some small portions of their lands to the peasants, whether for payments or for cash.

I think that in large part the division of property in France had the same causes. This cause itself was produced by the decline of the old institutions. The nobles did not bankrupt themselves thus during the Middle Ages, during the vigor of feudal aristocratic institutions. From this fact arose, in the parts of Germany where it appeared, an ensemble of feelings and ideas which put the populations there much closer to revolution than in the areas where these particular characteristics did not appear.

Indivisibility of peasant property. The indivisibility of peasant property was the general principle in Germany. The son who inherited only had to pay a dowry to his brothers and sisters (ibid.).

Erbgüter. Erbgüter more or less widespread throughout Germany. Nowhere did one see all the land included within the feudal system. Even in Silesia, where the nobility had preserved immense domains which most villages were part of, there were entire villages which were completely owned by the inhabitants and remained free. In certain parts of Germany, as in the Tyrol and Frisia, the general fact was that the peasants owned their land as *Erbgüter*. In the great majority of the country, this kind of property was only a more or less common exception. In the villages where it was found, the owners of *Erbgüter* formed a sort of aristocracy among the peasants (ibid.).

Influence of France over Germany in the eighteenth century. One cannot hide, according to M. Hälschner, that the whole German intellectual movement of the eighteenth century had in large part a French origin. The legislation of Frederick the Great, which has such a modern and revolutionary appearance, was inspired, in large part, by French principles (ibid.).

Inadequacy of local legislation. Landrecht. Although the Landrecht was only supposed to be applied in cases where local laws were silent, it was constantly applied because most local legislation was very incomplete, very inadequate, often limited to a single subject, such as that of Brandenburg which only regulated inheritances. The gaps which had been filled either by Roman law or by general legislation were now filled exclusively by the Landrecht (ibid.).

Ownership and rental. The only forms of possessing land in our day. M. Walter listed for me today (20 July) all the different forms of possessing land in the old feudal world and still on the eve of the Revolution: free property, perpetual use, hereditary lease, limited use, the *colonat* . . . and finally rental. From the moment when the rules of the feudal system were abolished and measures were taken to liberate the land from perpetual servitudes, all these different forms almost immediately disappeared from one end of Germany to the other, leaving in existence only these two: free and complete ownership of the land, and rental.

Indivisibility, inalienability of peasant land. Mr. Walter told me again that the indivisibility of peasant property had been a very common fact in Germany; however, it had never been universal. In many places division was not prohibited. It was chiefly in the sixteenth century, according to M. Walter, and as a fiscal measure to facilitate raising taxes, that legislators had found it more convenient to only have to do with a small number of landowners.

Serfdom of recent origin or at least its harshness greatly increased around the fifteenth or sixteenth century. M. Hälschner told me today (21 July 1854) that in the thirteenth century there were no serfs in the mark of Brandenburg (I strongly doubt it), that in any case their condition had gotten much worse and the number of serfs had greatly increased, firstly because when Roman law became dominant it had introduced the idea of slavery to everything relating to subjection, and secondly when the different rulers had established their undisputed sovereignty over their subjects. Up until then the emperor was a moderating power.

Provincial laws almost never concerned with serfs. Why? He told me also that it was very rare to see provincial laws about the [duties?] of serfs towards lords. Those laws which bore par excellence the name of Landrecht in each state and were made by free men for free men only spoke of the rights and duties of the free. The serfs followed the law of the lordship. One of the greatest differences between them and free men was that free men had the privilege of making their laws with the consent of the sovereigns, while the serfs *received* their law. In seeing the large number of diverse and often contrary opinions which are professed about the old law, and above all about the condition of the agricultural classes in past times, I am led to think that in this regard there were several systems and many things left up for dispute.

Feudal dues. From information gathered on the spot and from people who lived under the old regime, it results that: 1) Serfdom had entirely disappeared from the electorate of Cologne proper. 2) It existed in the duchy of Westphalia, which belonged to that electorate. It existed there in a very mild and very paternal form which the peasant had more to praise than to complain about, since thanks to this institution he was insured against extreme hardship. 3) Taxes were extremely light, the elector living chiefly on the income from his estates. There only existed a single tax, the land tax, which on average was not higher than five groschen (around fifteen sous). 4) There were a large number of villages without a lord and governed directly by the ruler's agents. In places where the nobility existed, its governing powers were very limited. Its position was more brilliant than powerful (at least individually). It had many honors, entered the sovereign's service, but exercised little real and direct power. 5) The government of the electorate was a very limited constitutional monarchy; nothing could be done without consulting the estates, composed of four chambers. All expenses were regulated and overseen by them; all taxes voted. 6) Everyone was eligible for public employment.

Government of the countryside by the nobles. Austria. M. Springer (a young Slav from Bohemia, privatdocent) told me, today, 30 July 1854, that the administrative centralization that for a long time had been established in the hereditary states of the House of Austria had only just been introduced into Bohemia, where up to then the towns had governed themselves and the countrysides were chiefly governed by the lords.

Infallible signs of the great Revolution and how the old society was not viable (10 July 1854).

To get a clear idea on this point it must be recognized that in eighteenth-century society, not only in France, but in all of Europe: 1) Everything which had formed the real life of medieval society, not only its life, but its strength and energy, was precisely what was languishing and dying. The aristocracy of birth, the bourgeoisie, the towns, the guilds, everything which was based on isolation, separation, privilege, even difference . . .

2) Everything which lived, moved, was fertile in this old society was precisely what did not belong to it, what was younger than it and opposed to it. What was politically alive and had fertility, power, was government founded on the principles of common law, equal for all. Beyond the still-general inequality and diversity, it was easily seen that what lived was everything which was contrary to that inequality and that diversity. What was alive in the moral, intellectual order were the ideas taken from that same source, rights, the equality of all, the human species, mildness, tolerance, everything which was most foreign to the ardent but *local* patriotism of the Middle Ages.

3) Still more, things (institutions, forms, precepts) which by nature did not belong more to one order of society than another, to one time than another, were stricken with deadly languor, a sort of senile dementia, from the moment they were combined with those institutions, those old forms. The aristocracy became imbecile, democracy somnolent. Each of these two kinds of government retained, in that bad atmosphere, nothing but the vices natural to their constitutions. Aristocracy, cliques, nepotism, blind obstinacy, egoism. Democracy, corruption, intrigue . . .

Freedom itself, which in that old world had produced prodigies, did not produce anything as soon as it inhabited these old bodies.

The only thing alive was absolute government, which diverged from these old forms, and had a common, equal government placed outside and above all these old institutions, as in Prussia or France. Or else freedom taking on the new forms of common right, the representation of all classes, equality before the law, distinctions founded on wealth and talent not on birth, in the end the new spirit, opposed to that which had reigned, like England. [. . .]

Bureaucratic paternalism. M. Hälschner told me today (27 July 1854), about this, the following:

Formerly the towns were absolutely independent in the use of their revenues. It was only around the middle of the eighteenth century that people thought of submitting them to the state's control. It was through this that they fell into dependence on the state. Most of the towns were indebted. Here above all the old medieval institutions no longer had any life. Freedom here had become the government of a bourgeois clique and the reign of a small egoistic oligarchy. Whether it was this cause or another which served as the pretext, it is certain that in all of Germany, at the period indicated above, in Prussia under Frederick the Great, in Austria under Joseph II, the state seized possession of oversight and the right of authorization. The legal means were taken from Roman law. Townships under Justinian were subject to guardianship and treated as legal minors. These rules were applied to the German towns, in the same way that this same law had been forcibly applied to so many other Germanic and medieval institutions which were naturally opposed to it and that were thus transformed and deformed. In Prussia, towns were henceforward unable to perform any of the chief acts of landowners or even of administrators, without being subject to obtaining the state's authorization. In most of them an agent of the state was placed on a permanent basis (I have forgotten his name), charged with overseeing what went on. The authorizing power was this bureaucratic body, half administrative, half legal, which was then called [a blank] and which has become the *Regierungsrat* of our provinces. Things went on thus until the reforms of Stein in 1808.

As for the rural communities, they still remain subject to the laws which we have seen, that is they are still chiefly directed by the lords.

One sees that, although this was centralization in germ, it was still far from being as complete and as concerted as centralization was at the same period in France.

Justice. If I have properly understood what M. Hälschner told me on this subject (which I need to have explained to me more), this is the result: The lord's court remained the ordinary court up to the end, with a vast jurisdiction over all cases, justice being rendered in the name of the lords or the towns. In Prussia no efforts were made to reduce the extent of this justice, to attract cases to the king's courts, to subject it to appeal in all cases, in a word to make it an insignificant and miserable exception amid the judicial system.

The way that was taken was to subject these courts more and more to the state's inspection, to rules given by the state. Thus, for example, the lord could still name the judge, but the judge had to have passed the state's examinations; once named, he could not be removed or at least could only lose his position after a hearing. In the end the lord's judge has almost become a royal judge. Despite this, see how internally the nobility still retained its administrative power. [. . .]

[4 AUGUST, 1854]

Manner in which the Landrecht replaced provincial laws and customs. M. Hälschner told me today (4 August 1854), among other things, these: In theory the Landrecht allowed all local laws and customs to continue. In fact, it happened that everywhere local legislation was not recent and very precise, it had little by little fallen into decay; gradually, and without the legislator doing a thing, the Landrecht spread and was applied in most cases. The customs existed, but most often they had already been half-forgotten and by preference judges applied the Landrecht.

Merit of the Landrecht. There are two separate parts in the Landrecht. There is the part which has a political character, such as that which establishes the status of persons, the status of properties such as the old political constitution of Europe had created . . . All this part has almost entirely disappeared. But beyond this there is the part which regulates the relations of men with each other according to the ideas of the civil law. This has remained. It has real merit. But to understand this merit it is necessary to make a detour. One of the great merits of Frederick's code, according to M. Hälschner, was to be partly liberated from the tyranny of Roman law and on many subjects to partly return, more than had been done for a long time, to the ideas of Germanic law.

The first draft of the code, the Codex Fredericanus, written by Chancellor Cocceji, was nothing but a reproduction of the Pandects [that is, of Justinian's codification of Roman law.—Trans.]. Frederick abandoned this draft and had the present code written. There would doubtless be a great picture to draw of the influence of Roman law on the destiny of the modern world from a political perspective, and how Roman law worked to simultaneously introduce into the world *democracy* and *servitude.* It has done more towards this, to disorganize, disjoint, and finally to destroy the old society of Europe, to create centralization and equal dependence, to replace turbulent freedom with orderly and tranquil servitude, than the sovereigns themselves.

What Roman law has done in Germany, it has done almost everywhere except in England. everywhere it has perfected civil society, and everywhere it has tended to degrade political society. [. . .]

Conversation with M. Hälschner (16 August 1854)

Administrative trials. Absolutely unknown under the German old regime. All disputes with the government, all those which arose about a contract with the government, all trials were judged by the courts and followed the rule of law. Even today only by imitating France have we created something which resembles administrative law, the judicial competence of the bureaucracy is extremely limited. It does not extend at all to decisions about contracts. It must be specially expressed. It is an exception. The ordinary courts are the rule. There are not even, in truth, administrative courts. It is the minister who judges the case specially withdrawn from ordinary justice, or (in rare circumstances), the cabinet as a whole. For example, when it is a question of setting a pension, the disputed question which arises on this occasion is decided by the cabinet.

To know which questions are supposed to be judged exceptionally in this way, one addresses oneself to a special body, composed half of bureaucrats and half of judges, which is called the court of competence.

Immunity of public officials. Also unknown in old-regime Germany (I am not so sure of having really understood this). Have it explained to me again.

Guarantee of public officials against the government. In Prussia for about ten years the principle has been established that no official can be fired without the judgment of an administrative court. Only the lowest class of officials (the officials named by department heads) can be fired arbitrarily. 1848 did not bring any exceptions to this rule. All the compromised officials who had not been tried were retained. This must have great consequences. Reflect on it and look for them.

[5 August 1854] *Venality of offices.* Venal offices were not absolutely unknown however. In Germany some petty rulers had introduced a few, but in small numbers and in the unimportant parts of public administration. The system was only followed on a large scale in France.

If a revolution was necessary to destroy the old society and introduce the new. One of the things which it is most interesting to establish in Prussia and that one sees best there is how the old regime could destroy itself and transform itself peacefully without revolution, the old construction sag without breaking. Do not lose this perspective from sight.

The Allgemeines Landrecht had already done much in its time. It destroyed nothing, but it moderated, regulated, or limited almost everything.

But would this have taken place without the French Revolution? Was it not thanks to the violent revolution in France that the old society was able to transform itself little by little in countries outside France? A question to examine.

Notes on Blackstone and England

Is it not extraordinary that:

1) The freest society in Europe at its historical point of departure was founded on, and in theory continued to be based on, a principle that the least free European societies do not accept at all and which has no resemblance to anything but the principle (still contested) that we have found in Algeria.

2) English feudalism led precisely to the theory that extreme democracy planted in the heads of our modern socialists, and even had exactly the same formula: the state alone is an owner. The proprietor is only a user.

3) Finally, the country in Europe where it was most impossible to apply this maxim was the only one where it was legally accepted.

It could be said of England in the eighteenth century and can still be said of it today what was said of France before the Revolution: the land must be liberated.

The tithe, nonredeemable payments on land (I think), dues, services, the difficulty of selling in certain cases, payments to individuals due after changes of ownership, all these charges, all these impediments appear in Blackstone's work. Although the majority of these were doubtless more restrained by law and custom, less frequent than was the case in France, it is nonetheless permissible to say that at least a portion of the state of things that seemed to merit the Revolution in France, that in the eyes of respectable people made it necessary and justified it, could then and could still be cited by the English. This has not prevented England from becoming the place in the world where material prosperity and, in particular, agricultural wealth are greatest. These impediments to the use of landed property, which to us seem unbearable, seem to be barely noticed by our neighbors. The different feelings which a similar situation gives rise to are explained, in part, by the following:

1) In England landed property has always been very little divided and becomes less and less so, while in France the number of small landowners was already immense in '89. Burdens of this nature are much more unbearable to the small proprietor who suffers from them more, and who understands the reason for them less, than to the large landowner.

2) In England these payments benefit a landowner who can be anyone; in France, [they] were to the almost exclusive profit not merely of a class, but of a caste. [Who] is the man who today, even in France, would think it terrible that a field he had bought which was crossed by a right of passage to the neighboring field would remain such while in his hands? The leftovers of the feudal system are seen this way by the English.

What above all appears very clear from all this is that what we have called the liberation of the land does not in itself have the economic importance that we have given it. It is the circumstances in which this happens which makes it more or less burdensome and above all more or less unbearable. From which it results that by destroying the privileges of caste, without touching the rights of property, we would have been able to attain the same end.

Consequences to draw from the preceding study.

If one reads carefully what Blackstone says of the feudal system in England, one remains convinced, despite some efforts by the author, as was his custom, to combine some Saxon institutions with it, that we have under our eyes the same identical institution as that which was known in France; perhaps more complete and more systematic, because it had been introduced all at once and by the most advanced feudal people of the period, the Normans.

At the beginning everything is similar:

All land is directly or indirectly held as a fief from the king, and the maxim "no land without a lord" is better established than in France itself.

The land is divided into fiefs, which are only granted under the condition of military service and of presence at the lord's court of justice.

The possessor of the fief is subject to certain monetary or personal payments to the lord. These are the wardship, the marriage due, the relief, the aid . . . even the names are no more changed than the things.

Below the barons possessing fiefs and owing military service can be found free tenants, that is *free* men who hold their lands by a contract with the baron, no longer on condition of military service, but for services of another kind or for rent: these are the "sokemen," the commoners possessing fiefs, the holders of lands paying the *cens* in our feudal laws. Below these are men attached to the land, sellable with it, to whom the lord gives solely according to his pleasure, without a contract, small portions of land to farm which with time became properties in "copy-hold," which was established by being recognized by the baron's court. These are our people in *mainmorte* who became peasants owing feudal dues and deriving their right from the lordship's *terrier*.

On both sides, ownership of land was combined with the right to judge; or as we would have said in our feudal style, justice is attached to direct ownership.

Perfect parity at the origins. The differences are found in the consequences and all these differences can be summed up in a single one, but one which is immensely important and fruitful. Out of this system there came, in France and throughout Europe, a *caste,* in England there came out of it (and this very early on) an *aristocracy.* The holders of fiefs, the men who owed military service, instead of holding themselves apart and forming a sort of large family, little by little mingled with the commoner fief-holders and, later on, even with those who had copy-hold. The tenures remained distinct, but everyone was able to acquire them and, in acquiring them, to take rank in the hierarchy. The very name of commoner ended up being unknown. From the beginning of the seventeenth century, the commoner fief ("free socage") had become as honorable as the knight's fief, and as it was subject to fewer burdens, it was possible, with the consent and even by the action of the large landowners, to make it the universal form of ownership. How did this change happen in England above all, among all the countries of more or less Germanic origin? At what time period? How did birth cease to be a real boundary between classes? I don't know.

This would be a very interesting point to clear up, because it is crucial, so crucial that for me everything which today is characteristic of England, political freedom, decentralization, in a word self-government [Tocqueville here uses the English "self-government"—Trans.], results from it.

It is to *caste* that one must attribute the fact that throughout the continent, more or less, society ended up finding itself composed of a body and a head more and more separated from one another, time and the progress of civilization constantly tending to make the head weaker and the body stronger.

It is because of caste that the situation enabled the monarchy, introducing itself between the two parties, to use one successively against the other, to establish absolute power on the ruins of feudal freedoms.

It is for this reason also that it was necessary, everywhere, to have royal officials, royal intervention, finally centralization. From the moment when the old aristocracy became or remained a *caste,* it was inevitable that the king was obliged to become an administrator, local government being intolerable, given the situation of society, when exercised by a caste, and once that caste was pushed aside, the elements of a good government lacking. Local government is only practical, can only produce the expected effects and attach hearts and minds to its continuance, when it is exercised by the population represented by all the educated, rich, honored, respected people who are to be found.

[In England,—Trans.] for a very long time, to be the descendant of an old family, which is doubtless an advantage which increases all others, does not however give any particular right, or even a social claim. The people who have what we in France call "birth," within the class of gentlemen [Tocqueville uses the English word "gentlemen" here—Trans.], only enjoy that kind of advantage which for example among the French aristocracy is given by an historic name: an ornament within equality.

The feudal system in England. What it has become. How it was transformed. How in England the sale of fiefs to commoners brought about the confusion of ranks among the wealthy. How the opposite cause produced the opposite effect in France.

I am first of all led to believe that at the beginning, it was much less the fact of birth than the possession of property which constituted nobility. I believe strongly that after a little while the possession of property must have given families noble standing, and later birth, even independently of property, became a great distinction and a great advantage. Then it became necessary to have noble birth in order to be able to acquire and possess a noble property (one could thus define this sort of property as political property). But what is incontestable is that in France as early as the twelfth and thirteenth centuries a certain number of fiefs found themselves in the hands of commoners. This property in part substituted for birth and classed the owner within the feudal hierarchy, although at an inferior rank, since until the ordinance of Blois which forbade this (article 258), commoners possessing fiefs bore the title of squire. Those who worked most effectively to prevent all landed proprietors from becoming members of the same group in this way and from forming an aristocracy instead of a caste were the kings, who for financial reasons, as early as the thirteenth century, thought of raising a special tax on commoners possessing fiefs. In order to give this tax a base they had to make very sure that the possession of fiefs by commoners would never produce the same effects as their possession by nobles. Furthermore the collection of the tax of franc-fief was enough to make the acquisition of fiefs by commoners extremely rare.

I think that the opposite causes have greatly contributed to making all landowners in England into a single class, and to founding an aristocracy there instead of a caste. I think that among the English, caste, if it ever existed in such an exclusive manner as among us, was gradually disorganized by the purchase of noble lands by wealthy commoners, who took rank among the nobility, so that little by little the influence, the importance given by birth were transferred to landownership, even without birth. Political freedom, the custom of assemblies, made this transformation easier than in France, common business transacted by the interested parties naturally bringing people together and tending to combine all those who had common interests. The absence of monetary privileges attached to noble estates when owned by nobles, and of monetary burdens weighing on noble estates when owned by commoners, ended up abolishing this distinction between nobles and commoners, while allowing the political power and social influence, in a word the privileges, of the class of the wealthy and in particular of the possessors of landed wealth to persist.

Similarity and Difference of the Revolutions of 1640 and 1789

SIMILARITIES

1) An effort, instinctive and at the same time theoretical and systematic, towards freedom, civil and intellectual emancipation demanded as an absolute right. Through this, not only are the two revolutions related, but they are both part of the great movement of the modern human mind, and are but the effects of the same cause.

2) An effort, but in extremely unequal degree, towards equality.

DIFFERENCES

1) Even though both revolutions had freedom and equality as goals, the immense difference between them was that the English Revolution was made almost solely for freedom, while the French Revolution was made chiefly for equality.

2) The multitude, the lower classes proper, did not play the same role in the two revolutions: they played a leading role in the French Revolution.

They were almost always secondary in the English Revolution, which was not only begun but led by a large section of the upper or middle classes, aided by the organized power of the army. The English Revolution used old powers while extending them, rather than creating new ones.

3) The third difference is that the French Revolution was antireligious, while the English Revolution, when closely examined, was more religious than political. When one sees the ease with which Charles I faced down his enemies so long as he was only confronted by political passions, the roughness and intermittence of those passions which, more general than the others, were at the same time weaker and less tenacious, the necessity for the leaders of the political parties to call religious passions to their aid, against their will, in order to fight, one finds oneself doubtful when deciding if, without the religious complications, England would have let itself be carried along by the current which at that time was leading all Europe towards absolutism. The service which the English Revolution rendered.

Notes on Russia

Constitution of the Agricultural Class in Russia

Some notes taken on M. Haxthausen's work. It is a very interesting book, very badly written, by a mind without breadth and without justice, but very interesting because of the details that it gives for the first time about the Russian peasantry (the chief aspect in my *opinion* and never observed in Russia (October 1853)).

Rural organization of peasants belonging to the crown.

Three separate associations:

1) The village.

2) The commune, which is often composed of several villages and is called *sel'skoe obshchestvo* (rural commune).

3) The *volost'*, which seems to me analogous to the canton.

The village is directed by an official called the *starosta* elected by the peasants themselves.

The commune or sel'skoe, by an official called *starshina*. He is elected by the delegates of the villages.

The *volost'* is presided over by the *golova*. He is again elected by the peasants; but he needs to be accepted and confirmed by the governor.

All these officials are paid (vol. 1, p. 15).

Above this level of people with the status of slaves who are free as to the choice of their leaders, or syndics, as one would have said in old

France, there is no longer any trace of elections nor of any kind of freedom. It is easy to see that even these slaves owe their electoral right only to their own servitude, that is to the little interest that is attached to them and to the strict dependence in which they are kept, which deprives the voters and the elected of even the possibility of using the right conferred on them.

Centralization. A village does not need authorization to gather the money necessary to build a church. Only when the sum is collected is it necessary to obtain a plan and an architect from the government. All construction must be approved in advance by a committee residing at St. Petersburg (vol. 1, p. 72).

"In the Russian government, documents are even more important than in Prussia. But, in essential matters, in matters relating to education, to zeal, to the order and honesty of employees, this country has remained very behind" (vol. 1, p. 83).

See how this immense, minutia-full and paper-loving centralization is compatible with an almost barbarous situation. Imagine what centralization must be when combined with serfdom, that is uniformity in political condition and immobility and identity in social condition. It is enough to make one die of boredom thinking about it.

Modern birth of serfdom in Russia.

Formerly serfdom properly speaking did not exist. There was only the class of servants who bore the name of serfs. The peasants were free to change their residence and only inhabited the nobility's lands as renters. The lease only had a year's duration and they often changed places at the end of the year. To prevent this mobility, the various princes among whom the land was long divided ordered that the peasants, while retaining the right to change their master, could not leave the limits of their principalities. When later the sovereigns of Moscow destroyed all these individual principalities, by the ukase of Czar Boris Godunov of 21 November 1601, the peasants lost this ability to change place and were attached to the soil. But they still remained personally free, although placed under the authority of the landowners. Later on, under Peter I, they became almost by chance and only de facto (for there was no formal edict) completely serfs (vol. 1, p. 95).

Coming destruction of serfdom.

"In our day, no one with any sense will contest the fact that it is impossible to maintain serfdom in its present form for very long. Everyone knows it in Russia. But how to get there without producing a revolution? This is the question of the day" (vol. 1, p. 103).

This is still more significant in that the author is not a very strong enemy of the present system and finds much good in it. His assertion furthermore is still better proved by all that results from his book, among other things: the weakness of the old nobility, those who still live on their lands and share the peasant's ideas and mores; its substitution by or its transformation into government agents having no point of contact with the agricultural class, the absenteeism of all the large landowners, and as a consequence of these things, the *obrok*. The *obrok* is an arbitrary tax on the peasant's individual worth, a system which is simultaneously more oppressive than the old system of payments in corvée labor and at the same time allows the ability to change places, to act on one's own, to sometimes enrich oneself, a system simultaneously oppressive and *educational*. Finally, despite the fact that the oppression and isolation of the agricultural class is greater than before in certain respects, an ordered and civilized government which spreads the ideas of modern civilization without knowing it and often without wanting to, which permits the easy movement of serfs with the *obrok*, facilitates ease, assures the security of property and persons, establishes fixed rules . . . finally gives people those things which make them miss those still lacking.

Common property, constant changes of owner.

It can be seen from this book that, in the villages, even land is not possessed individually, even by renters. Every ten or fifteen years the commune makes a new distribution of all the land to individuals among the different families of the village. This is how things were done during the last partition (this was written in 1842): The whole territory of the commune is divided into perfectly equal lots insofar as possible, the number of portions being calculated to be equal to the number of people or families. Once this preliminary partition is made, the plots are distributed by lottery. At the peasant's death, his portion returns to the commune. Since Peter I (that is for 130 years) there have been eight partitions of all the land. The government makes sure that these revisions are made, because at each revision it assures itself of the population and of all that it needs to know in order to regulate conscription and taxation (vol. 1, p. 119).

Here assuredly is the perfection of democratic society, and the phalansterians have imagined no more, land divided into equal portions always remaining equal, and chosen by lottery! What a unique and frightening spectacle, sixty million men simultaneously changing their property and their place every ten or fifteen years!

The author says that the peasants have a great deal of repugnance for this operation. But it is necessary so that the division is equal and the absence of property continues. The parts would soon cease to be equal and ranks would be created within the agricultural class if families remained in possession of the same lot.

Napoleon in the cabin of a Russian peasant.

"In all villages of any size in northern Russia I found, in every peasant's house, Napoleon's portrait. No name, no historical personality is as well known and as popular among the lower classes of Great Russia. During the War of 1812, he was the object of implacable hatred which inflamed every heart; at present, popular imagination has made of him a mythic hero, a fabulous and sublime being."

Develop this picture which has strangeness and greatness (vol 1, p. 188).

Republican feeling of the Russians.

This society of slaves vis-à-vis the government reveals the mores of free men internally. Free choice of government, passive obedience by the individual to the common decision.

A peasant permitted himself, contrary to the rules of the commune, to surround his meadow with an enclosure. The commune decided that the enclosure would be destroyed and that the execution of this decree would take place at the moment of our passage. The commune decided it, our coachman said to us, without adding a single word of praise or blame, such was his great respect for the decision of the commune (vol. 1, p. 224).

Weakness or absence of bourgeois elements. Preponderance of the peasant class.

In the government of Vologda, composed of 741,000 inhabitants of whom 40,780 inhabited 13 towns and 700,220 inhabited 11,160 villages, there were thus only $\frac{1}{17}$ who belonged to towns and of that number barely half were bourgeois. Thus, in truth, the bourgeoisie formed $\frac{1}{34}$ of the population, the nobility $\frac{1}{213}$, the clergy $\frac{1}{67}$. The peasants made up $\frac{56}{59}$ of the entire population. Of this latter number $\frac{3}{7}$ were serfs and the rest free (vol. 1, p. 231). Let us note that:

1) The author calls free the crown peasants who, in fact, were hardly different from serfs and who made up about 400,000 individuals out of this total of 740,000 souls.

2) There do not seem to be any bourgeois in the countryside.

3) Finally the immense number of villages and in consequence the extreme dispersal of the population.

This is from the census of 1838.

Land held as domaines congéables *in Russia.*

In some districts of northern Russia, there exists a class of peasants called *Polovniki* who are truly tenants of *domaines congéables,* that is who cultivate the land in return for half the produce, the land belonging to the landowner and the house and animals to the tenant (vol. 1, p. 245).

Uniformity of centralization and slavery.

This *colonage* is only a very small exception and, according to the author, is tending to disappear. In Great Russia, more than six times as large as Germany, we see only a single and unique set of customs; there is neither dialect nor patois, everyone speaks the same language. No country of Europe presents a more homogeneous population. But in return one finds there neither originality nor spontaneity (vol. 1, p. 269).

This uniformity which dates from very far back is a very unusual fact which is difficult to take into account. There is something here which seems very different from what ordinarily occurs in the rest of Europe and even in the world. It must be that the unity of the government in fact dates from long ago and for another thing that there existed:

1) A racial unity unknown elsewhere.

2) Very frequent communication of individuals despite the barbarism and serfdom. Nothing proves better that in fact the Russian peasant has always been a little nomadic and very much a traveler, but does this come from his nature or from his country, from his race or from his plains and his snows? What is certain is that after or even along with the American peasant, the Russian peasant is the one who is least attached to a place, to a profession, who most easily changes himself to all new things . . . a striking similarity in the spectacle which unfolds at the two opposed extremities of civilization!

Power of the spirit of association in these small slave societies.

Just as we see here the spirit of free peoples with a common will, we often find here extraordinary examples of the spirit of association and its marvels. At Moscow the author visited a hospital containing eight hundred sick people, founded and maintained by members of a religious sect composed of peasants. Who are, after all, the founders, he said? Some simple Russian peasants whose intellectual culture did not approach that of a German peasant and who did not receive any help from the government (vol. 1, p. 340).

What ought to astonish is that the government lets them do these extraordinary things. There are a thousand other examples in this book of the peasants' ability to associate and to do very considerable things through association.

Religious movement among the serf and agricultural class.

Just as there reigns a certain spirit of free citizens in the heart of this class, there reigns a true movement of ideas with regard to religious matters which does not seem to be seen in the higher classes. Nothing is more interesting than this part of the book: we see here a prodigious sectarian movement, religious enthusiasms . . . It is, I think, without human example to see such a sight uniquely enclosed within the lowest class and disturbing the base of society in all ways without the movement coming from higher up or influencing the upper classes, and without even, so to say, being perceived higher up, or disturbing anyone in the least!

One of the consequences of this phenomenon is a coarseness, an absurdity, sometimes a singular violence in these sectarian theories, thus governing and developing themselves only among the lower classes.

A thing no less extraordinary! The clergy seems almost as foreign to this movement as the bourgeois and nobles. It is true that this Russian clergy seems to me to be as little clergy and as much *official* as one could imagine. Never has religion seemed to me to have given birth to less intellectual movement among those who are its interpreters.

NOTES RELATING PRIMARILY TO BOOK TWO OF THE FIRST VOLUME

Drafts and Notes Taken at Tours, 1853–1854

[The Welfare State]

Poor Tax. As early as the sixteenth century, at the same time as this means of helping the poor was established in England, it was attempted in France. The ordinance of Moulins of 1566, article 73, and the Declaration of 1586 order that cities, towns, and villages be required to feed and maintain their poor. I have seen in Turgot that he has recourse to a true poor tax in Limousin during a food shortage. As a consequence in 1770 the idea of generalizing this concept and making its application permanent went through the ministers' heads (this was the period when they ferociously punished the beggars, who responded: either let us beg, or give us bread). A decree of the Council of 7 January 1770 authorizes several parishes of the Generality of Orléans to tax themselves for this purpose, but I think that this was still in case of a request by the parish. Here, I see a priest of Iseure, in the diocese of Tours, who writes the minister to ask him to authorize a tax on individuals in the parish, both lay and ecclesiastical, possessing property in parishes where they do not live and from which however they draw considerable income. The sums coming from this tax will be put into the hands of the syndic or the most notable inhabitant in order to be distributed to the poor. This priest paints the most horrible picture of the hardships of the countryside (in this year above all, a year of food shortage). Despite this food shortage they had been overburdened with the salt tax this same year. Another priest, from Neuilly Pont-Pierre, writes similarly in the same year to the minister: I would like to be authorized to tax the said lords both lay and clerical (they possess more than three quarters of the land) for the aid of the said poor.

We also see from this correspondence that in cases of hail or bad weather, losses, floods . . . it was to the government that all eyes were turned and to it that one held out one's hand. However, the government did almost nothing to come to help in these cases of hardship and was itself the cause or the accomplice of much of the evil, but people saw nothing but the government above them, and if it did little, others did nothing. It was not feeling for and recognition for what it did which already made it into providence, it was the solitude which reigned around it in the governmental and bureaucratic spheres.

Charity workshops. From a certain point of view one can define charity workshops as the Bastille applied to the lower classes. [. . .] Not only were the *funds* of the charity workshops fixed by the controller-general, but the details of the use of these funds had to be communicated to him and approved by him. This can be seen in a letter by the intendant of Tours (26 July 1786), who refuses to change the destruction of a workshop because this destruction appeared on a report already approved by the minister. Note the date. As we approach the Revolution, government improves in a sense (an improvement much more apparent than real) because arbitrary actions by the intendant are reported to the minister, but without any real further safeguard for the citizens. Administrative centralization begins in France with the generality. Afterwards it is contracted little by little into the government's hands. [. . .]

Priests. Their interventions about roads.

We see from the files of the charity workshops of 1786 that the greatest number of requests for road repairs were made by priests, either in their own name or in the name of their parishioners. Most of them offer their own money. The priests were the only *gentlemen* ["gentlemen" in English—Trans.] who lived in the countryside. I have not found a single request from a commoner landowner. All the requests are from priests or noblemen, to which must be added a very small number of communities, which again are impelled by a noble or a priest. Even to *request* and even to take care of the village roads public life is nonexistent . . .

[Subsistence]

General observation. This whole correspondence, which is immense during years of food shortage like 1772, happens between the controller-general (Terray) and the local agents, intendants, subdelegates . . .

No visible action by the landowners, in any form whatsoever, or by the inhabitants to help themselves by themselves. The government alone acts, either well or badly (if not, the municipalities of the towns, which most often are not elective; perhaps, however, they are elective in Touraine more than elsewhere). All eyes are turned towards the government. An immense empty space between it and the lower classes. Preparation for the Revolution first of all (the revolutionary measures of the maximum and others were born from the memories and habits of the old regime), and then for what we see today. [. . .] The whole generality seems like a nest where the babies cry together to their mother to come and bring them some food.

The privileged classes help little.

Letter from the prior of the Jacobins of Laval who refuses (11 March 1772) to let grain be stored in the cloister without being paid rent. We see from a second letter that they submit to new orders, doubtless more commanding: "We will execute the orders of Your Greatness with the most perfect obedience." Insensible to the hardship of the lower classes, pliant towards authority.

The welfare state.

I have made your letter public, says the subdelegate. The inhabitants bless and thank God for the tutelary angel which he has sent them. They beg you to continue your protection of them. [. . .]

Riots.

We see from all these documents that as soon as fears of food shortages occurred, and they happened very often, riots were very frequent throughout the countryside. I have not heard of any riots for the past six or eight days (says the subdelegate of Angers in 1771), people are beginning to calm down. For the past month, says another, the insubordinate have presented the daily spectacle of a rising, either by the sound of the tocsin or the tumultuous assemblies from which it results, and if order is not restored, thefts and murders occur . . . Habits which amidst absolute government prepare people for the Revolution. We see that the difficult thing is to give the people a common passion; as soon as they have one, the form of government does not stop them from acting, from uprising immediately. People go immediately from a sort of imbecile obedience to an insurrection which is no less imbecile. The same cause for the two effects. Giving an account of a riot where the mounted police had been forced to flee after having killed two men, the subdelegate of Angers writes: It is necessary to make some examples, there are many areas where we can no longer make any pickup of grain no matter how small, without running the risk of being attacked, this mutinous spirit seems to have become general. A succession of riots: this is 1789 minus the revolutionary spirit proper.

[*Conscription.*]

Absence of safeguards. We already see here the very developed seed of our present conception, and the explanation for the ease with which conscription was established when the following bad aspects of the old regime were taken away: 1) Arbitrariness in forming the list of those who should participate in the draft lottery and, in any case, inevitable confusion. 2) The possibility of being drafted up to age forty if one was a bachelor, from sixteen to twenty if one was married. 3) The two operations of lottery and revision mixed up in great confusion. 4) Never a *formal decree* for liberation. 5) Very great arbitrariness about questions of knowing if by being absent the young man was trying to evade the draft or not. 6) No replacements. Not even replacements made by the parish (in order not to harm recruitment for the regular army). 7) Finally, worst of all, the unequal weight of the draft, because of the multitude of privileges which exempted people from it. 8) None of the safeguards that today come from the council of revision.

Material means of order.

A remark applicable to all branches of the public bureaucracy, to the draft from the eighteenth century and perhaps before, is the abundance of material means of order invented by the paper-pushers of the offices. We already find printed tables of all kinds for various authorities to fill out with columns, alignments, in effect the whole apparatus of modern bureaucracy.

[. . .] *Harshness of old-regime laws when it comes to the poor.*

1757. I find several excerpts of verdicts from the Council of War which condemn deserting draftees to perpetual service in the galleys. On the other hand, we see from the enormous number of deserters and those who do not return from leave that the law only struck from time to time and as if by chance. This is the whole old regime. Terrible laws which are not enforced.

[Prisons]

A lettre de cachet, *1785.*

Done by the authority of the king, dear and good friend, we mandate and order you to receive in your monastery the lord St. Pierre de Tailly, and to keep him there until a new order on our part, in return for the sum of 600 livres which you will be paid. Do not object for such is our good pleasure. Given at St. Cloud, 2 October 1785. Signed Louis. Further down, signed by the Baron de Breteuil. To our dear and great friend the superior of the cordeliers of the Ile Bouchard.

This is truly arbitrary power, naked and leaping before the eye. However, when one looks at it closely, we see that it was not the exercise of this power, rarely put into effect, hindered or made odious by publicity, which most prepared the soul of the nation for what we see, but the petty and hidden administrative despotism which made itself felt in everything, everywhere and every day. It was not tyranny, it was *paternalism* which made us what we are. Freedom can take root and grow in the former, it cannot either be born or develop itself in the latter. Despotism can create liberal nations, paternalism can only make revolutionary and servile peoples . . .

[Municipal Constitution]

REPORT MADE BY THE MUNICIPAL OFFICIALS OF LA FLÈCHE IN
RESPONSE TO A LETTER FROM THE INTENDANT, *1765*

1) Formerly the inhabitants all assembled in order to give their votes. The difficulties presented by such an assembled multitude, without order, without distinctions of estate, were later recognized. The method of assembling through deputies was chosen. Thus the election by estate and by deputy, the molecular fractioning of the electoral body, was a modern fact.

2) Two assemblies, one general, the other of notables. We have seen this above. The general assembly took place once a year to name the municipal officials.

3) Although the foundation edict of 1615 does not say whether the municipal officials should be elected by the general assembly or the assembly of notables, the custom has always been to use the general assembly. This custom *was in accord with the popular spirit of the ancients.* [. . .]

[4] What to do in the future: the general assembly has the advantage of combining all views. We have always seen the municipal offices at La

Flèche awarded to merit and reputation. One can also say, in favor of the lower classes (this means the groups and guilds of artisans), that their desire has always been to elect those most worthy. They desire the good but sometimes make mistakes because of intrigue. In the assemblies the artisans have the majority over the notables.

Election by the notables also has some problems because of professional, party, or friendly [feelings—Trans.], which can influence the voting. But they cannot be fooled or intimidated like the lower classes.

Conclusion. It would doubtless be nicer to preserve for the lower classes the consolation of choosing the officials who command them, but since one cannot be sure that intrigue will not be involved, it would be better for the maintenance of good order and public tranquility to refer to the assembly of notables about these questions.

Thus here this poor lower class is deprived, by the advice of these bourgeois (the government was less egoist than they were, I think, and did not want to accede to their wish), here it is deprived of an age-old freedom which, in the opinion of the bourgeois, they had never abused, or of a *consolation* as they call it.

Here is the real French bourgeoisie, narrow, egoistic, and when it cannot govern solely by itself, preferring a master. What it was in 1764, it is in 1854.

[This deliberation provoked in response a petition from the lower classes addressed to the intendant asking that the right of the lower classes to elect officials be maintained.]

Letter from the subdelegate on this occasion, 1765. The intendant, receiving these contradictory wishes, asked for a *secret* opinion from his subdelegate, who was, from what I see, more the royal attorney at the presidial court and, insofar as I can judge, a man of real merit: he brought together the *six best citizens* of this town in conference: these are the lawyers and judges. These six best citizens agreed that in the future only assemblies of notables should be held, not the notables all together, but deputies elected by each of the groups of notables spoken of above.

What seemed to them most difficult about the question was the ranking of precedence. They invent several reasons for not wounding the vanity of these people, so that these others not feel too much pain, a precaution which is necessary so as not to make everyone boycott the assemblies at city hall.

Nothing was more apt to sharpen, excite, increase French vanity and personality than these innumerable little compartments in which almost identical people were placed, and where the ordering was always disputed. What also seemed very difficult to them was to know if the presidial court ought to have several deputies or only one. As for the question of taking away the lower classes' electoral rights, that did not seem to bother them at all.

This did not prevent the six best citizens from recognizing once again that the artisans, who made no claim to be mayor, allowing themselves to be led by instinct or by feeling and only consulting their common interests, usually made wise choices. Each group of notables, however, wanted to have the mayoralty, so that if the nomination was annual, the mayor would change every year, which would be bad. In consequence of this, if the notables alone were charged with choosing the mayor, as they asked, the duration of his term of office should be made longer. In consequence of all this, their opinion was that the intendant should *reject* the inhabitants' request.

After having passed on the advice of these six best citizens, the royal attorney gave his own opinion, which was that the old general assembly ought to be preserved in three cases. Firstly, for the election of the municipal officials, in order that all citizens should have the satisfaction of being governed by men of their choosing. Secondly, for the establishment of new taxes, because it was hard on the artisans to pay sums which had been imposed by those of their fellow-citizens who were in general the least interested in the question (this in fact is what makes the proceedings of these notables still more remarkable, that they were giving themselves the right to establish taxes which the lower classes almost alone would have to pay). Thirdly, for loans.

Finally, says this decent man, it is not a spirit of criticism which makes me speak thus, I think it is very useful to society in general to give the least citizen a part in affairs. If we do not pay any attention to the lower classes, if we despise them, we take feelings away from them, we debase them, and from then on no more emulation, no more honor, no more honesty. Through this we take from society perhaps the greatest and the best of its supports. This good man was named *Chaubry.*

Municipal Constitution of Tours.

Information taken from a letter of the intendant to the minister accompanying a plan for a letter patent for Tours [1764].

The intendant's observations on the abuses which reign in municipal government.

No official ever pays attention to business. Everyone avoids taking care of town business under the pretext of his personal affairs. If a commission is named by the bureau for the examination of some matter, one soon recognizes its neglect.

Poor use is made of the town's income. The expenses are badly understood. The officials are in complete ignorance of the formalities to be observed. Recently a tax collector, whom they trusted, ran off with 30,000 livres.

The means to remedy this unfortunate state of affairs would be to give the royal attorney some appointments to compensate him for the time he would spend on the town's business, and for this official to be charged with examining and reporting on these matters.

In the assemblies of the executive committee there have always been disputes that sometimes go so far as indecency. Opinions are almost never free. This comes from the despotic authority that the mayor gives himself, to the unreasonable point of throwing out the door anyone who has an opinion different from his own.

Finally, the meetings are constantly disturbed by the claims of the officials of the chief local court (the presidial) who want to be able to participate without having any right to do so.

With regard to the general assemblies, it is proposed here (in the plan for the letter patent attached) to reform them, as had been done for the town of Angers, and to limit their participation to the election of municipal officials.

Through the exaggeration and ill will which then, as now, existed in the government proper towards anything outside it that was still alive, and notably against all independent local life, we can draw from this several pieces of information. We see here:

1) This plague of collective government, which returns in such a deplorable manner in the first attempts of the Revolution. The absence of an idea that is so simple (the only modern innovation), an official charged with all the administration proper, alongside a purely deliberative body. We see that no one in particular here is in charge of government and responsible for it. The mayor is really nothing but the president of the assembly. The royal attorney only has the general duty of making motions and overseeing the course of affairs. Special commissioners must be named constantly. The intendant's idea for the new role to give the royal attorney comes close to our present idea of a mayor, without completely realizing it.

2) Even though the abuses about which the intendant complains were caused in large part by what I have just said, we see that at the same time this creates a really oligarchical situation in the town government, a little bourgeois aristocracy or rather a little irresponsible clique which in fact runs local

affairs. People who only want, naturally, the honors and privileges of the position without its burdens.

3) Finally we see the distance from popular participation, even one so indirect as the assembly of notables, although this is the chief remedy for the problem about which the intendant complains. For in order to get good government there is no middle way; it is necessary either that the government create, oversee, and destroy agents at its whim, or that it be the people.

[Agricultural Societies]

NOTE TAKEN ON THE COLLECTED DELIBERATIONS AND REPORTS OF THE
ROYAL SOCIETY FOR AGRICULTURE OF THE GENERALITY OF TOURS, *1761*

Government initiative and official organization.

Although it was only a matter of agriculture and of a society of land-owners discussing questions of rural economy among themselves, an association which created neither profits nor privileges, we see that it was the government which conceived the idea; it was the government which chose its membership, the government which made up its regulations (the intendant presided over most of its meetings); it was, certainly, the government which authorized it. Things happened exactly as they would happen in the democratic society of our time. However, there were then families, individuals, groups, which would have been able to take the initiative. But on the one hand, everything was already sufficiently concentrated in the government's hands for it to be jealous of everything outside itself which gave signs of collective life. Furthermore the nobility, ornamented with so many privileges which made it hated, was at the same time so deprived of real power and influence that each of its members, separated from one another, did not even conceive of the idea of meeting with others or of becoming the center of any common action by themselves. Completely analogous to the little democratic units of our day, they looked only to the top, in order to find not just the form but the signal, whether from a minister or from an agent, in the very things which were most closely related to local and individual interests.

A final characteristic of this agricultural society of 1761, one which makes it completely like those in our day, is that it was also composed in its immense majority either of public officials who knew nothing of agriculture, or of landowners and lawyers who doubtless did not understand very much about it. The real cultivators were almost entirely absent.

The agricultural societies were established by a decree of the Council of 24 February 1761; all these societies were supposed to be uniform and directed by the same regulation. One would say, again, just as in our day.

Notes on Turgot

It is much less through the evil committed by arbitrary [power—Trans.] than by the good it produces that one may judge the extent of arbitrariness, because one hides the evil and on the contrary highlights the good.

The intendant's omnipotence with respect to the taille. Where one sees clearly the power for ill that an intendant had in this matter is in seeing in Limousin what Turgot could do for good. He eliminated the head tax on wool-bearing animals, he exempted those over seventy and parents burdened with children, he was very careful to promptly give aid and accord tax abatements in case of loss of livestock, in cases of hail, flood, freeze . . . he promised the parishes to lower their taxes by an amount equal to what they spent on roads.

Complete Works, vol. 1, p. 66. *Mémoires sur sa vie.*

Sad condition of the rural population. Turgot, who preferred monetary contributions for roads to the corvée, did not dare suggest the former *for fear that the government would use the funds raised for the roads for other purposes* (ibid., p. 76).

The monetary privileges of the upper classes kept growing, while their power constantly decreased. It was only in the seventeenth century that the roads began to be made by corvée, that is, solely by the lower classes and especially the lower classes of the countryside. Thus, if one bases oneself chiefly on the economic ideas of the times, it was the classes for which the roads were made which did not contribute anything (I say classes, for here the bourgeois of the towns were as privileged as the nobles and the clergy), and the classes who thought they had no interest in the roads' condition who were, solely, burdened with their upkeep.

In Limousin, Turgot found himself obliged to take the money needed for roads from the proceeds of the taille, so that the privileged would not complain; he limited his effort to distributing the burden equitably among the lower classes, without daring to have it bear upon those classes above them.

He later provoked violent complaints when, as a minister, he tried to have the upper classes bear the burden. "The upper classes," says the author, "seeing the roads they used made by the lower classes exclusively, had ended up becoming accustomed to believe that expenses for public works should not concern them" (pp. 77–79).

The intendants especially charged to govern the Third Estate. It was the Third Estate whose administration was particularly given to the detached commissioners of the Royal Council. This explains why these posts were never filled by great lords, rarely by real nobles, and were always considered secondary despite the immensity of the powers which flowed from them.

Corvées for the passage of troops. Every time that troops changing garrisons crossed the country, it was necessary that the corvée (always the peasants) supply them with a great number of wagons (I do not know if this was to transport the men or the baggage at the rear of every unit, which was then enormous). In Limousin this necessitated gathering a considerable number of carts and cattle from far afield for this service. Turgot greatly aided the region in creating a company for this service (paid for, no doubt, by the taille); the service was better done and did not cost a quarter of the loss caused by the army, which crushed the parishes near the roads, usually at harvest time (ibid., p. 99).

Corvée for towing. Independently of the old corvées, people tried to introduce new ones. Some people who had gotten the contract to supply wood for the navy demanded corvée labor to tow their boats on the Charente River. Turgot made this annoyance cease, *because it was determined* that the navy had not at all required that this wood be towed by corvée (ibid., p. 102).

Conscription. When Turgot arrived in the province, half the young men ran away to the woods to avoid the draft lottery. The other half, to get back the runaways and have them declared eligible, pursued them arms in hand. Guns were used and often blood flowed. The measures that Turgot took to prevent this (ibid., p. 105).

Cruel situation of the taille collectors. The only rights that the people had been left were very burdensome and odious to them. Hardly any elections were allowed except to choose the collectors. This post caused the despair and ruin of those who were successively burdened with it. Most of them, not knowing how to either read or write, could not make any regular calculation or mark the sums they received on their roll in the required manner, and yet they were personally responsible. This burden bankrupted almost all the families of a village one after another. M. Turgot remedied this evil by employing the taxes ordinarily given to the collectors of several villages to create a sufficient salary for a real tax collector, bonded and instructed (ibid., p. 107).

Extent of administrative justice. Powers of the intendant. Many trials relating to the administration of the tax farms (that is relating to indirect taxes) were judged first by the intendants and on appeal by the Royal Council (ibid., p. 171).

Offices for sale. The four positions of intendant of commerce were venal offices (ibid., p. 175).

Venality was a particularly detestable system when applied to administrative functions, for which only election or nomination is appropriate.

During the whole of the old monarchy, despotism struggled with greed in the kings' minds, the one being the sole counterweight to the other. Their despotism made them tear positions away from the nobility or from popular election, and their greed led them to sell them for money, thus despite their intentions creating safeguards for a sort of freedom, but at the expense of good administration and good order.

Inequality of burdens. Weight on the peasants. The relationship between taxation and income from land was only nominal. The little properties belonging to the lower classes were rigorously taxed. No lands of the great, no domain of the nobles, of the magistrates, nor of the rich was taxed at its just rate. The lands of the clergy were not taxed at all (ibid., p. 193).

Government paternalism growing as the Revolution approaches despite the winds of freedom which begin to blow: product of the perfection of the art of government and of equality. The reformer Turgot is at the same time very much a centralizer. Not only does he not decrease government paternalism, he increases it while improving it. Towns could not borrow without the authorization of the Royal Council and the intendant's permission. Turgot had the Council render a decree (24 July 1775) that towns could not borrow except when assigning special funds for repayment (ibid., p. 257).

Small example, but the general idea is true and must be used.

The intendant more and more the king's sole representative in the provinces. Consequence of the political decadence of the nobility. Nullity of the governors. We see in the ordinances of Louis XIV that the governors of provinces (still great lords) live in their province and the ordinances charge them with many details of government (notably the draft). Under Louis XVI the governors are still exclusively great lords; but not only do they no longer reside in their provinces, they cannot even travel to their province without an express order from the court. It has become an honorific title, a sinecure provided with enormous salaries: this is characteristic.

The king's sole representative is a stranger to the province and ordinarily a bourgeois or at least an ennobled man, the intendant, whose powers constantly grow, diversifying and becoming more detailed. He is, furthermore, required to reside in the province. A characteristic of the progress of time (ibid., p. 266).

Rapid progress of France at the approach of the Revolution. Prosperity increased every year; manufactures, commerce improved daily and in a progression so rapid that in twenty-seven years the population increased by four million (ibid., p. 313).

The Revolution did not happen because of this prosperity, but the temperament which would produce the Revolution, that active, unquiet, reforming, ambitious temperament, the democratic spirit of new societies, began to inspire all things and, before momentarily turning society upside-down, was already enough to move it and develop it.

Powers of the intendants in tax questions. According to the edict of August 1715, as maintained by various edicts of the Council, all disputes which might arise about the creation of the tax-rolls for the taille were judged by the intendant, with right of appeal to the Council.

The royal declaration of 30 September 1761 stated that these functions no longer existed and that this sort of dispute was to be judged first by the local courts and on appeal by the Tax Court (vol. 4, p. 5).

Real taille, personal taille. The *real taille* was similar to the property tax of our day in that it struck the owner of the land, whoever he was, *in exact proportion to the value of the property.* It differed only in this: not all properties were subject to this tax, some properties did not pay anything. But the properties subject to the real taille paid, whoever the owner was. The privilege belonged to the land and not to the individual. The tax was therefore well established where it was applied, but it did not apply everywhere. Furthermore the real taille was the exception; it existed in only a few provinces, chiefly in the south of France. The *personal taille* was the general rule. It bore not directly on the land but on its presumed product, the usual income that it produced. It was the tenant farmer or sharecropper who was bound to pay it in its entirety. This tax was and had to be triply odious because:

1) It grew in proportion to the industry of the *tenant* or small landowner, whom it deprived of some of his interest in enriching himself.

2) It was by nature variable and arbitrary: variable since it changed according to whether the taxpayer did good or bad business; arbitrary, since there was nothing certain to base it on, above all in regions where large farms did not exist and where rents could not serve as a certain and fixed measure.

3) It was unequal in reality even more than in appearance. In reality, for the noble who farmed himself was exempt from it; in appearance, since it

was from the purse of the tenant or the sharecropper alone from which the money came. The latter did not see that in reality this money came from the landowner's pocket, since the tenant or sharecropper necessarily paid him less in proportion to what the taxes took. But this was not seen or was badly seen by the tenant and the sharecropper, and did not even exist for the very numerous class of peasant proprietors, or small non-noble landowners; these saw themselves struck by the weight and vexations of the taille, while the nobleman, their neighbor and sometimes as poor as themselves, paid nothing (ibid., [vol. 4,] p. 32).

Decline of France at the end of the seventeenth and beginning of the eighteenth centuries. Turgot, in 1762, says: "It is certain that Limousin and Angoumois have lost much of their wealth. The inhabitants formerly drew considerable profits from their land and industry which allowed them to easily bear the state's burdens. It is very probable that the surcharges occasioned by their former wealth have contributed to their present poverty more than anything else" (ibid., p. 52).

Gradual increase of the taille. Difficulty of paying it. Since the beginning of the century, the total taille in Limousin had increased by 700,000 *livres.* The roll of 1762 exceeded that of 1761 by 11,758.

The taille collector of Limoges had a deficit of more than 360,000 *livres.* The others were in proportion. It seems that the generality was over a million *livres* in arrears (ibid., p. 58).

Feudal dues. What Turgot calls manorial taxes. It would be useful "to rescue the lower classes from the continual vexation caused them by manorial taxes, franc-fiefs, exchanges, dues, hundredth-penny . . ." (ibid., p. 95).

I do not know if Turgot is speaking here only of the manorial taxes on the king's domains.

Jurisdictions. The ordinary judges are the local courts with appeal to the parlements; in tax questions, the district courts and the Tax Court (ibid., p. 97).

Rivalry between the government and the courts. This passion is found in even Turgot's mind. He complains that in the preamble of an edict where the king acceded, very rightly, to the complaints of the courts in tax questions, he paid them compliments instead of having the air of spontaneously giving what had been taken from him (ibid., p. 99).

In general Turgot, with the particular character of his great qualities of heart and mind, seems to me the father of the bureaucratic race that we know (however, he is a father very superior to his children): taste for order, for uniformity, for equality under the bureaucracy's thumb; hostility against all privileges and in general against everything which hinders a well-intentioned administrator: public virtue extended so far as to want a government that is just, equal, active, foreseeing, well intentioned, and participating a little in everything, but not so far as to conceive of or desire a free government. The ideal of the bureaucrat in a democratic society subject to absolute government. Nothing more.

Turgot demands on behalf of the intendant the power to make up the list of offices. Vices of municipal government in the towns. Incompetence of the tax collectors in the countryside. Experience had shown that in towns where the taille was arbitrary, it was very badly distributed by the municipal officials, who formed a small oligarchy (officeholders who had bought their positions), almost always controlling the choice of their successors. The power to make up the lists of officeholders was necessary in the towns to avoid cliques and in the countryside to avoid the ignorance and incompetence of the tax collectors. The declaration of 15 April 1715 formally recognized this right of the intendants (ibid., p. 120).

Government of the countryside. "The usual way the community assembles is a real fiction. A notary presents himself at the church door at the end of the service; almost all the peasants leave; among the few who remain, two or three give their opinion, the others do not say anything and usually the notary makes the discussion come out the way he wants it" (ibid., p. 121).

Turgot seems to indicate that in Limousin this was not only the way the community's decisions were taken with regard to its affairs, but also with respect to naming the syndic.

It would be a useful thing to prepare the inhabitants of the countryside for municipal government, a very desirable thing, but one which does not seem to be very near fruition (1764), and which must be preceded by several changes not only in the tax code, but still more in several civil laws (ibid., p. 125).

Turgot is evidently speaking here of a permanent, organized municipal government; the absence of such a body did not prevent parishes from having public business, community assemblies, and an agent called the syndic.

The bourgeois class itself deserting the countryside. Why? It is collecting the taille which changes almost all landowners into urban bourgeois (bourgeois landowners of course, since noble landowners had nothing to fear from the collection of the taille). "A collector is one of the most unfortunate individuals you can imagine, continually exposed to seeing himself dragged to prison, continually forced to pay advances for which he is repaid slowly and only after costly and painful efforts. He spends two or three years running from door to door. Neglecting his own business, he falls in debt and usually finds himself ruined. In provinces of small farms, being taille collector is evaluated as the loss of three or four hundred livres." If this sum were raised from everyone, it would still be considered a very heavy burden; "but, passing one after another to each well-off family, whom it completely bankrupts, it is a thousand times more burdensome. Who is the man who, being able to avoid this misfortune by moving his family to a town, would not do it?" (ibid., p. 125).

The flight from the countryside of all well-off commoner landowners resulted, furthermore, from the fact that in the towns the bourgeois was not isolated and had high status, while in the countryside, it was he whose interests and self-esteem bore the weight of the privileges and position of his neighbor, the petty noble.

The assessors and collectors of the taille were supposed to be chosen by the parish. But this was an illusion. The collection was too burdensome for anyone to want to be charged with it. Far from choosing, it was necessary to draw up a list according to which everyone did it in turn (ibid, p. 128).

Other fiscal reasons which led commoner landowners in the countrysides to leave. A cause particular to Limousin: in this generality the taille remained personal, that is it was only imposed on the taxpayer's residence. However a third of the taille was based on the land itself. As a consequence of practical difficulties which I don't understand very well, the owner, by moving to a town, was relieved of his portion of this third which was distributed among those who remained in the parish (ibid., p. 38).

Unequal positions of those who raised the taxes. "It is very strange that raising the royal taxes is a stroke of good luck for those who don't take any pains over it, and ruin for those who really do all the work" (ibid., p. 130).

In the first category, Turgot doubtless placed the receivers-general, and in the other, the collectors.

The privileges of the nobility in tax matters created by fraud, where they did not exist by law. Almost all the omissions, all the false evaluations (with regard to taxes common to all the orders), were made in favor of the owners of fiefs. Those who paid the taille were generally taxed pretty exactly, because the taille-rolls were surveyed and because real estate and houses are hard to hide. But in regions of small farms, the lords' income was for the most part paid in kind, and these rents were easy to hide; and often the debtor did not dare declare it, despite the interest that he had as a taxpayer, because the lord could always ruin him (ibid., p. 137).

Particular cause of the rural population's complete subjection to the lord in certain provinces. In certain provinces, rents in grain were collective among all the tenants of the same parcel of land, so that the lord could ruin a tenant in a moment by suing him for all the others' debts. "It happens that the peasants are always in the situation of trembling before the lord" (ibid., p. 139).

Difficulty of establishing a real municipal government with the remains of feudalism. Turgot rightly says, with regard to the preceding, that such a situation offered a great obstacle to be overcome for the establishment of a real municipal government (ibid.).

This remark should be generalized: the government of men had certainly been taken away from the lord, but he had remained a man so superior to all the others, master of so much influence over the fortune of a multitude of inhabitants through what remained of the constitution of feudal property, that it was very difficult to establish, opposite him and independent of him, any kind of parish government. One did not want to give the municipal government to him; it could not be given to anyone else. The countrysides found themselves, in fact, without any real government.

Inconveniences of burdens on petty positions. Paralysis of administration. The royal attorneys of the district "do not, with respect to the taille, carry out the tasks imposed on them by the regulations at all. In general, a man who in order to enjoy a few privileges has bought an office which is neither very honorable nor very lucrative does not voluntarily take on work which he can avoid through simple negligence. A man whose position cannot be taken away and who has nothing to gain or lose, whether he works or not, chooses the latter" (ibid., p. 151).

The intendant's power in matters of taxation. We see in the plan for an edict (1764) for improving the raising of the vingtième (a plan which was a great improvement and was never put into effect) that all requests for elimination or decrease which will be made for reason of accidents, losses, or other causes will be decided by the intendant, who is required only to render monthly accounts of his operations to the controller-general of the finances (ibid., p. 164).

The division of taxes among parishes is decided by the intendant alone in the presence of officials from the finance office, officials from the district, and the receivers of the taille (ibid., p. 189).

Turgot assures us that abuses were very rare. However, he himself cites the example of M. d'Orsey, intendant of Limousin, who arranged for the parishes of which he was lord to be discharged from their tax obligations.

Impossibility of a good apportionment of taxes among the parishes. The apportionment is always badly done because "we lack the means to know the parishes' ability" (ibid., p. 189).

Precautions are taken with regard to the nobility, even when it is subject to equality of taxation. I find in a plan for an edict of July 1764 which tends to create equal taxation some provisions which, all the while eliminating the inequality, retain a separate position for the nobles, who, in each district, are treated as a separate taxable body and are taxed in the presence of their power base (ibid., p. 192).

Crushing weight of taxation. Amid the inequalities and disparities of all kinds which characterized the old regime, there were provinces which succumbed beneath the taxes. Among these was Limousin. Turgot says: "In this province the king draws more than the owner from almost all land, that is more than half and sometimes two-thirds of the net product" (ibid., p. 256).

The peasant of Limousin reduced almost as low the peasant of Hindustan. "Poverty is such in this province, and perhaps in others of small farms, that on most properties the tenants do not have, after all deductions are made for the charges they bear, more than twenty-five to thirty livres to spend per year per person (I do not say in cash, but counting all that they consume in kind from what they have harvested). Often they have less, and when they absolutely cannot exist, the master is obliged to supplement it" (p. 274). Turgot attributes this (ibid.) excessive poverty in large part to the extent of the taille and, also, to the inequality of its division, and adds: "Some landowners in the end have been forced to recognize that their so-called privilege was much more harmful than useful to them, and that a tax which had completely bankrupted their tenants had fallen back on them in its entirety. But the illusion caused by self-interest badly understood, supported by vanity, was sustained for a long time and was only dispelled when things had reached such an excessive state that the owners would no longer have found anyone to cultivate their land if they had not agreed to contribute along with their sharecroppers to the payment of a portion of the tax. This custom began to be introduced in several parts of Limousin, but the proprietor only went along with it when he could not do otherwise."

Extent of the lands of the privileged. Their proportion compared to that of the commoners. According to the tax-rolls of the vingtième, the proportion of properties belonging to nobles and the privileged in relation to the properties belonging to those who pay the taille is 7 to 13 (ibid., p. 290).

Feudal dues. Their extent. "Feudal dues form, in this province, the largest part of the income of the lords" (who, however, as we have just seen, already possessed more than half the land as property; ibid., p. 290).

Privileges of the nobles with regard to taxes. 1) According to the custom of the Generality of Limoges, one-third of the tax on agricultural property was charged to the landowner. When the landowner was a noble, he was exempt from it, and this third was divided among the other taxpayers (the bourgeois escaped this third, in part, by going to the towns).

2) Most nobles farmed some lands themselves, their meadows, their woods, their vines, and all these properties escaped even the tax on agricultural property.

3) Finally, even with respect to the vingtième, feudal dues were not taxed (ibid., p. 291).

Corvée for troop transport. Its inconveniences. Its harshness. (P. 200.) Turgot paints the following picture of the inconveniences and rigors of the corvée when used to transport military baggage, which after reading the files does not seem exaggerated to me:

1) Its first inconvenience was the extreme inequality of a very heavy burden. "It falls entirely on a small number of parishes, who are exposed to it by their unfortunate geographical position." The transport, however, was not done for absolutely nothing: they were paid twenty sous per horse (but much too little as he shows later on). Days of five, six, and sometimes ten and fifteen leagues, three days to come and go. The payment given the owners was only one-fifth of the expense they bore.

2) The time of the corvée, almost always summer, that of the harvest.

3) The oxen were almost always overloaded and often sick for a long time afterwards, to the point that a great number of owners preferred to pay fifteen or twenty livres rather than furnish a cart and four oxen.

4) Inevitable disrepair in the equipment.

5) Violence of the military. The officers almost always demanded more than they had a right to. They required the drivers by force of threats and blows to harness riding horses to carriages at the risk of laming them. The soldiers climbed on the already heavily loaded carts; other times, impatient with the slowness of the oxen, they pricked them with their swords, and if the peasant wanted to complain, he was covered with blows (ibid., pp. 375ff.).

You'd think you were in Algeria!

Parish syndics. It is the syndics (the lord never appears in anything, nor for anything) who organize the transport corvées, like all the others; which they do very badly, given their incompetence (ibid., p. 378).

Large and small farms; tenants; sharecroppers; influence of the two systems on the effects of the taille. Turgot says that the regions of small farms form at least four-sevenths of the kingdom (ibid., p. 265).

To speak more precisely, in the regions of large farms or of tenant farmers, the tenant, in making his lease, knows that the taille is his expense. He makes his calculation accordingly. He pays less to the landowner when he pays more to the king. The taille falls in its entirety, in effect, on the landowner and can be raised without harming agriculture (at least that which is not paid by the landowner himself, which is very often the case, even under the old regime). The tenant can only be hurt when the taille is raised during the duration of the lease and until the lease has been redrawn as a consequence.

In regions of small farms or sharecropping, things were different (ibid., p. 271).

I cannot understand very well the reasoning, furthermore very abbreviated, that Turgot goes through in order to explain how taxation crushed the sharecropper. It seems to me that the sharecropper, being a poor devil, a true worker, in charge of cultivation without a lease, in no position to calculate and to impose his conditions like the tenant farmer (who is a true industrial entrepreneur), also cannot in fact easily shift to the landowner the tax established on cultivation and has to be much more hurt and crushed by it.

Privileges. Extension of the system of privilege to everything. An edict of the Council of 30 July 1743 accords to a cotton-fabric manufacturer at Limoges the exclusive privilege to manufacture in the town of Limoges and at a distance of ten leagues from it, for twenty years, and for the duration of the privilege an exemption from lodging soldiers, from the poor tax, from being taille collector, from being syndic, and from other public burdens, all these being based on the taille. At the expiration of their privilege in 1763, the manufacturers ask for its continuation and are not able to obtain it (Turgot says that it was no longer official policy to give exclusive privileges). The manufacturers then ask for at least the perpetual maintenance of all the other privileges, and, furthermore, patents of nobility, exemption from the vingtième on industry and exemption from all customs duties on their fabric inside the kingdom and on export, and finally exemption from duties on the manufacturing material that is used (vol. 5, pp. 168ff.).

Conscription. Exemption from conscription. There are no grounds for refusing this exemption to workers in manufacturing. This exemption is included in a large number of decrees by the Council in favor of manufacturing (ibid., p. 190).

Intendant. Arbitrary powers with respect to conscription. "Intendants are free to give exemptions that they think useful to commerce and, in consequence, I have allowed all masters or entrepreneurs in manufacturing who employ skilled workers to enjoy personal exemptions. I also think it just to exempt, in each trade, some leading workers" (ibid., p. 190).

Exemption from the tutelle and curatelle. "It is a very astonishing thing with what ease this privilege has been given out, not only to favor useful establishments, but to ornament a swarm of little posts which are more harmful than useful, invented for fiscal reasons. It is enjoyed even down to the most petty employees of the tax farms." It had become the style (p. 191).

Administrative jurisdiction. Turgot, sending the minister a plan for an edict from the Council which maintained the manufacture spoken of above in certain of its privileges, took care to add: "His Majesty orders that all disputes which may arise from the execution of the present decree, its circumstances, or consequences will be brought before the intendant to be judged by him, saving right of appeal to the Council" (p. 200).

Thus, not only was administrative jurisdiction continually created

1) by evocation, and

2) by foresight and in advance in a large number of matters,

but the principle that I thought was modern, that the government alone ought to judge trials that arise in consequence of its acts, is simply the principle of the old regime.

Outfit of a regiment on the march. Military system before the Revolution. From what Turgot says about the corvée for military transport, we see what a mass of objects a regiment dragged in its trail, how many horses and carriages it was necessary to furnish the officers and soldiers (vol. 4, pp. 375ff., and vol. 5, pp. 243ff.).

Venality of nobility, a major cause for the end of all industrial careers. The town of Angoulême, which ought to be very commercial, is not: it is probable that one of the chief causes is the ease with which all moderately well-off families acquire nobility. As a consequence, as soon as a man makes his fortune in trade, he hurries to leave his trade in order to become a noble. The capital which he has acquired is soon dissipated in the leisured life attached to his new estate (ibid., p. 265).

Old-regime laws about paying interest on loans. Their consequences.

The laws which forbade moneylending with interest, regardless of the interest rate, still exist at the end of the eighteenth century.

Turgot teaches us that even in 1769 they are still observed in many areas; these laws persist, he says, although often violated. The town judges accept the interest contracted without alienation of capital, while the ordinary courts reject it and impute it to capital. We see, in effect, bad-faith debtors at Limoges suing their creditors [Tocqueville wrote "debtors" again by mistake] in the criminal courts for having loaned them money without risking their capital (ibid., pp. 278ff.).

Independently of the effects that this legislation could not fail to have on commerce and on the industrial mores of the nation in general, it had a great effect on the division of land and its tenure. It multiplied perpetual payments, both agricultural and nonagricultural. It led the former landowners, rather than borrowing for their needs, to sell small portions of their estates in return for a price partly in cash, partly in perpetual payments; which greatly contributed on the one hand to dividing the land, on the other to overburdening small landholdings with a multitude of perpetual payments.

Administrative justice. Evocation. We see how the government's doctrine with regard to evocation emanated from the Council, which told Turgot to evoke before it lawsuits by the debtors of Limoges against their creditors (of which I spoke above), given that there was every reason to fear that the judgment that would be given [by the ordinary courts— Trans.] would be dictated by the rigorous spirit which had inspired the legislation on loans at interest, which would enable the accusers' plot to triumph ([in the margin:] centralization).

Turgot refused to take official jurisdiction over this affair by an edict of attribution, not because this attribution of judicial powers to administrative authority seemed repugnant to him in theory, but because of particular reasons (ibid., p. 351).

What made the attribution of judicial powers to the intendant a little less monstrous than such attributions would be to the prefect is that the intendant was always a master of requests representing the Council or, as they said, *detached* in the provinces.

We see it was really only a question of a civil trial that it was merely thought useful to the public interest to have decided in a certain way.

Government action against individuals, almost unlimited in law. Independently of the utility that there was in having the debtors of Limoges lose their lawsuit, Turgot implies that it would be very desirable to be able to punish them. But the thing could not be done judicially, since they had done nothing but ask for the application of laws that had not been repealed. Therefore they could only be punished by way of authority and by the government, and it will be up to the wisdom of the Council to decide if the direct authority of the king ought to intervene to punish the disturbers of the peace (ibid., p. 354).

Administration of the countryside. Absence of administration. Curates. The rural areas were so deprived of administrative organization, and so empty of intelligent men who could or wanted to concern themselves with administration, that for this purpose Turgot drew as much as he could on the clergy (pp. 364ff.). "He regarded the curates," says his biographer, "as his natural subdelegates, and said that we were very fortunate to have in every parish a man who had received some education."

Is it not characteristic that this sought-after man, for lack of a better, was the curate and not the lord?

Turgot addressed himself to the clergy to learn about the loss of animals (he sent them printed forms for this purpose with the *detailed* instructions that today we give mayors).

He charged them to send him the requests of those of their parishioners who had something to ask of him (p. 369). He invited the curates to make known to individuals certain articles of his ordinances which it was useful for them to know (p. 377), or certain precise provisions of the law that he indicated to them (p. 378).

Administrative and legislative powers of the parlements. Interlacing of powers. On 17 January 1770, the Parlement of Bordeaux ordered the merchants of wheat, tenant farmers, bailiffs, landowners, and tithe holders of the provinces of Limousin and Perigord to bring to market every week a sufficient quantity of wheat for provisioning. On 19 February 1770 the Council annulled this edict, not because it was outside the parlement's competence, but because it was dangerous (ibid., p. 383).

Another decree of the same year (a year of shortage) ordered that in each parish assemblies be held every two weeks, to which ecclesiastics, lords, and the most distinguished bourgeois would be invited, in order to advise upon the means of helping the poor, giving them work and feeding them until the harvest, through contributions from which no order of citizens would be exempt (p. 386).

If someone refused to contribute, the local judge was authorized by the decree to render an ordinance to force him to do so. If there was an appeal under pretext of excessive taxation, the appeal would be brought before the seneschal (the ordinary court, I think; ibid., p. 430).

Thus, the parlement not only created governmental bodies for administrative purposes, but ordered the raising of taxes.

Turgot only intervened to regulate the execution of the decree, and since the decree came from an ordinary court, he recognized that the invitation to assemble, in places where there were judicial officials, should be made by those officials.

The lord appears for the first time in a bureaucratic act. Turgot, in his instructions during the food shortage of 1770, indicates that in the parishes the invitation for notable inhabitants to meet should be made in the name of the curates and lords. The curates (it is even said later on that it is the curate who should convoke the assembly, where there are no judicial officials, ibid., p. 427) should preside because of the charitable purpose of the institution (p. 390).

Subdelegates. Poor foreigners should be expelled from the country; they go from subdelegate to subdelegate, each one stamping their travel papers and providing them with travel expenses per league (p. 401).

Immense power of the intendant. In the circular instruction published by Turgot with regard to the establishment of charity offices during the food shortage of 1770, he says: "Independently of the tax decrease which is customarily given during apportionment (that is to say during the annual division of the taille among the parishes of the province) to communities which have attempted to undertake public works at their own expense (such as paths, road work useful for commerce, those which doubtless have a utility not just for the village or parish), a reduction which reduces their expense almost by half, the intendant further proposes more ease in getting part of the necessary money in advance, until the taxes are in" (ibid., p. 410).

The intendant buys rice and has it distributed in the countryside (ibid., p. 418).

Contempt that people in France have always had for foundations and the will of the dead. "There are some parishes in which foundations have been created to distribute a certain quantity of grain annually to the poor. Various decrees of the Council have combined several of these foundations with the neighboring hospitals, but they still exist in several parishes." If a permanent charity office is created in these parishes (according to the rules given by the circular for provisional offices during the food shortage), this would perhaps be a means to engage the Council to allow these foundations to exist rather than combining them with the hospitals (p. 421). This makes clear not only that what I said above about the contempt for foundations when the living were not in a position to defend the will of the dead, but also about the insufficiency and quasi-absence of any parish organization.

Absenteeism. "The great number of absentee rural landowners," says Turgot in his circular on charity offices in 1770, "may make one prefer the way of a proportional division among all the rich (that is to say a tax) to the way of purely voluntary offers" (ibid., p. 427).

Always the same refrain, the abandonment of the lower classes. [In the margin:] lower classes.

Begging, the arbitrariness of rules in this regard; this is the only concern people had about the poor classes. Instruction from the Council to have all beggars arrested and sent to places of detention, even those with families (vol. 6, p. 2).

It would have been better to decrease their number by abandoning the lower classes to poverty less.

Intendant. His regulatory power. Decree by Turgot which, departing from the principles set forth in the Council's instruction mentioned above, regulates everything that should be done. This simultaneously combines the prefect's decree and regulation by the public administration (ibid., p. 3).

The uselessness of the lords and syndics. Bureaucratic use made of the curates. To make certain that the orders and instructions given in each parish to assure the subsistence of the poor have been executed, it is neither the lord nor even the syndic that the policeman should ask, it is the priest (ibid., p. 4); to know who are the bad subjects, beggars, insolent or stubborn people, the priest (ibid., p. 5).

Intendants. Immensity and unlimited character of their powers above all in cases of crisis. During the food shortage of 1770 we see Turgot render an ordinance (February 1770) to *require* the owners of landed estates to provide for the subsistence of their sharecroppers (which no law demanded of them; p. 8). This ordinance states at the same time the harshness and uncaringness of a large number of landowners who, seeing that the harvest is small and wheat very expensive, get rid of their sharecroppers at the risk of seeing them *die* of hunger (emphasis in Turgot's letter).

Cause of anger of the lower classes against the upper classes encouraged by the upper classes. In the preamble to this ordinance, Turgot does his utmost to highlight the insensitivity and injustice of the landowners towards these poor: "*at the time when hardship has struck them, they exhaust them by the most difficult work, in order to make their employers' property profitable, who owe all that they possess to their labor*" (vol. 6, p. 9).

We see clearly that no one has yet heard anything about Babeuf or socialists, and upper-class people think they can make rhetoric against one another in front of a deaf and impotent audience.

As a consequence, Turgot orders that landowners "will be required to keep and feed until the next harvest the sharecroppers and tenants whom they had on 1 October 1769, as well as their families, on pain of being required to furnish, in money or in kind, the expenses of the parish for the subsistence of four poor people for each one of their sharecroppers whom they have let go" (ibid., p. 11). The syndic, taille collectors, and chief inhabitants are charged to prevent the violation of the ordinance, and the subdelegates, to keep them under control (ibid.).

Another ordinance (1 March 1770) by Turgot which *orders* the landowners and inhabitants of the Generality of Limoges to provide for the subsistence of the poor until the next harvest (ibid., p. 13).

(I do not understand this ordinance very well, it seems to me to make double use of the charity offices—provided with the ability to make charity obligatory—that the decree of the Parlement of Bordeaux had created at the same time and that Turgot had established; see vol. 5.)

This ordinance says that a general assembly for charity composed of the notable inhabitants and landowners will be convoked. This assembly should be convoked by the *syndic in charge or he who will be named by the subdelegate to take his place.* The assembly will only be held in the presence of the priests, lords, and judicial officials and in cooperation with them. If there are disputes about the validity of the deliberations of these assemblies, it is for the subdelegates to decide and, if necessary, to have new assemblies held in their presence (p. 25).

Do not forget that this whole ordinance relates to a critical and temporary situation.

If the *syndic* neglects to convoke the assembly, the priests, lords, or judicial officials will be authorized to hold said assemblies (p. 14).

Nothing proves better than this the legal incapacity of the lords in the administrative affairs of their parish, since they are not called upon when the syndic defaults.

The syndic convokes the assembly, but it is the priest who presides over it (p. 15). It is true that it is a question of public charity.

Intendants. Their powers. In this same ordinance we see the intendant, without seeking a decree from the Council or a decree by the parlement, require all well-off inhabitants, owners of lands, tithes or payments, to help the poor. He states the way in which the tax-rolls will be created for this purpose. This list will next be sent to the subdelegates, who will make it *executive* by virtue of the power that the intendant gives them for this purpose (p. 20). (It is the subdelegates who issue orders for decrees of seizure or the establishment of liens; ibid., p. 31). The intendant orders that those who refuse to pay the tax thus established will be required to do so by an order of seizure or a lien (p. 23). Disputes over the tax-rolls will be brought before the subdelegates (agents of the intendant and not of the state) save for appeal to the Council (p. 24). But the protest will not be heard until the tax is paid (p. 25).

It is when unlimited and arbitrary authorities want to do good that we really understand all there can be of the unlimited and arbitrary in their action, because here they are not even limited by fear of public opinion and popular resistance.

Administration of the parishes. Turgot, in the circular to his subdelegates (3 March 1770), counts on the priests to make his ordinance known and to notify the syndics to convoke the assemblies. If the priest is not disposed to take on the burden of directing the operations for the aid of the poor, he must be replaced by engaging the lord or some notable persons in his stead (ibid., p. 29).

Subdelegates. "You will see," Turgot says to them in his circular, "that all the disputes which may arise because of my ordinance, everything that may require the intervention of authority, will depend entirely on you" (ibid., p. 30).

Intendants. What they could dare. Turgot, during the food shortage of 1770, went so far as to make an ordinance to dispense with the execution of several general tax laws (ibid., p. 37).

Parlements. Often exercised legislative power. Harshness and indifference of the upper classes towards the lower. During the food shortage of 1770 the lords and noblemen who owned rents in grain (almost all their property consisted of this) demanded either the grain due or its value in cash at the exaggerated prices which grain then had. The Parlement of Bordeaux made a decree which declared that rents would not be required, for lack of grain, except at the prices of 1769 (ibid., p. 61).

We see:

1) That nothing is more legislative than this decree. Also the Parlement of Bordeaux took its pretext from a royal declaration of 8 October 1709 which, said the parlement, authorized it to act thus in special cases. The parlements only claimed *de jure* the power to make police regulations, which was related to legislation without being entirely the same thing.

2) How *the regulatory decree* rendered by the parlement violated the principle of contract, for, if wheat had been very abundant and cheap, the share-

cropper would have profited by this abundance and this drop in prices, just as he suffered from scarcity and rising prices. It was the risky part of his contract.

3) How in this society where one habitually abandoned the lower classes to oppression and hardship, from time to time one came to their aid by means that were violent and really revolutionary. A bad education from two directions.

Importance of payments from land and feudal dues to the nobles' wealth. How these payments burdened all land. Payments in grain are set on almost all the inheritances of this province (Perigord, Limousin; (ibid., p. 62). Turgot says in his works: "I must observe that these kinds of payments are of a very different importance in most southern provinces than in the rich provinces, such as Normandy, Picardy, and that region. In these latter, the chief wealth of the large landowners consists in the production of the lands themselves, which are combined in large farms, whose owners receive large rents. There the feudal dues of the largest landholdings are only a very modest part of the income, and this article is regarded almost as honorific. In the least wealthy provinces, cultivated according to different principles, the lords and gentlemen possess almost no land themselves; inheritances, which are extremely divided, are burdened with very large rents in grain for which all the tenants are collectively responsible. The rents often absorb most of the profit of the land and the lords' income is almost entirely composed of them" (ibid., p. 63). *An irregular but all-powerful means of oppression, the unlimited power to bankrupt after the power to govern is taken away.*

Taxes. Their height. "To return the taxes of the province of Limousin to the same proportion as those of other provinces, that is so that they do not pay the king more than a third of their total income or a sum equal to half what the landowners receive, it would be necessary . . . (ibid., p. 72).

The editor adds in a note on page 144 that "the direct taxes on commoner lands and even on land leased from lords, including the taille, the capitation of those who pay the taille, the other taxes we call accessory taxes, and the vingtième, took a third of the income, or half the owners' profits. People regarded it as the general principle that the land tax took this third of the income. It was on this basis that M. Turgot calculated the financial advantages that the government would find in protecting free commerce in grain." Besides this direct tax, there were also the tithes, the aids, the salt tax, the stamp taxes, the sales taxes, the tolls, and the customs barriers (I add the feudal dues). The Constituent Assembly stated in principle that the land tax would not exceed a fifth of the income.

Thus a third of the total income and half what the landowners received was the tax considered proper and normal, that to which Turgot makes no objection. This is the tax of the Hindus.

Poor condition of the lower classes in Limousin. The lower classes are accustomed to pay for their food at nine francs for a setier [old unit of weight—Trans.] of rye at Paris and, even at that price, they find rye too expensive and content themselves with living for much of the year on chestnuts and buckwheat porridge (p. 74).

Why sharecroppers in one place, tenant farmers in another. The landowners in the sharecropping provinces would like nothing better than to find those agricultural entrepreneurs we call tenant farmers, but they do not find any. Why? Is it a difference in the fertility of the land? No, "the plains, from Poitiers to Angoulême, a portion of Berry, Touraine, Perigord, Quercy, are certainly at least equal in fertility to the lands in the Paris region." However agriculture has never been lucrative enough for the miserable sharecroppers to accumulate the capital necessary to make advance payments, or for people with capital to think of investing it in this way. The reason is that produce does not have the same value in provinces in the interior of the kingdom as in provinces in the vicinity of the capital and maritime markets. What seems odd is that Turgot does not seem to suggest roads as a remedy (although they are the sovereign remedy), whether because this point of view was not that of his times, or because he was absorbed in thinking about free commerce in land, which he treats in the manner of the following excerpt: "It is certain that large farms have extended themselves in provinces where they formerly did not exist, since in Beauce farms still retain the name of 'shares,' although there are no longer any sharecroppers." Agriculture by sharecropping is no longer known in England and it is beginning to disappear in Scotland (ibid., pp. 204ff.).

Intendants; their duties and powers. Turgot writes his letters on the grain trade during a month-long voyage which he made during the winter in his generality, doing the work that was called the *apportionment,* that is the division of taxes between districts, subdelegations, and parishes; examining en route what public works would be useful or necessary, whether for general communication or for reason of local circumstances which might require the placement of charity workshops (note by the editor, ibid., p. 292).

We see:

1) The intendant, beyond all the powers of the prefect, had immense powers relative to taxation which prefects do not have at all or only have in part.

2) The habit acquired by the *lower classes* of seeing everything done by a single man, to expect everything from him and to obey his will in everything, preparation for the Revolution and for that which would follow it.

Conscription. The intendant's arbitrary power. It would perhaps be useful at present to limit oneself to making only minor changes in the ordinance (1773) by continuing to leave interpretations that local circumstances might make necessary to the intendants (ibid., p. 401).

All the ordinances rendered up to the present about conscription have not resolved any of the difficulties (he lists a great number of them); each intendant in his generality has followed the course that circumstances seem to demand (ibid., p. 407).

Conscription presents a labyrinth of details where the government loses its way without being able to avoid mistakes and injustices (ibid., p. 408.).

The extreme difficulty of dividing among the different communities the number of men asked for from the province, which constantly varies (ibid., p. 402).

Repugnance of the population for this service which can be judged by the great number of those who evade it by flight. Experience has proven that many of those who flee permanently escape pursuit (p. 405). Conscription is one of the heaviest burdens presently imposed on the rural inhabitants (ibid., p. 408).

Exemptions. "The exemptions from the draft lottery which we have been forced to grant and to extend, from the gentleman down to his valet, do nothing but make the burden doubly cruel by making it ignominious, making it felt that it is only reserved for the lowest classes of society" (ibid., p. 414).

Turgot finds this system of exemptions natural and even just. It derives necessarily, he says, from the constitution of the army. The low pay of the soldier, the way in which he is housed, clothed, fed, his extreme dependence, finally the kind of society with which he lives, would make it very cruel to take anyone but a member of the lower classes (ibid.).

What is remarkable is that among the hardships of the soldier's lot, Turgot himself does not put the impossibility of advancement, which however is the only one which makes the profession intolerable for the man from the well-off and well-brought-up classes. The idea of this possibility doesn't even seem to present itself to his mind.

With this constitution of the army (which was nothing but a necessary result of the constitution of society itself) there was only one tolerable system, that of volunteer enrollment, and it was thus that things happened up until Louis XIV. Then military service was made obligatory without changing anything in the army's constitution, which put a new and very heavy weight on the lower classes. I seem to recall that Frederick, when creating conscription, had introduced some improvements. Further, some of his subjects were still serfs and military service was freedom for them.

What characterizes the lower classes in France is civil freedom and property on the one hand, and on the other hand the weight of all social expenses, monetary charges paid to the rich, abandonment by the educated classes, government arbitrariness and subjection: that is landownership, which could make the privation of everything else that was missing unbearable, and the best preparation for revolutions.

At each draft lottery the inhabitants of the countryside dispersed and led a wandering life in order to flee the draft. At the end of their leave they hurried to quit the army (ibid., p. 417).

"Repugnance for conscription was formerly so widespread among the lower classes of this province that each lottery was the signal for the greatest disorders in the countryside, and a sort of civil war among the peasants, some of whom sought refuge in the woods where the others went to pursue them arms in hand . . . The murders, the criminal proceedings multiplied . . . When it was a question of assembling the battalions, it was necessary for the syndics of the parishes (this function of the syndics explains why in 1787 the new syndics were indignant at being subjected to the same duty—papers of the Hôtel de Ville) to bring their draftees in escorted by mounted police" (ibid., p. 424).

Turgot says that he has brought these disorders partly to an end by various measures, of which the chief one was to authorize voluntary enlistments, which permitted either the parishes or the lottery class to buy a man and send off one who wanted to go.

Inequality. Diversity. The Generality of Amiens was subject to very heavy duties on brandy, those of Paris and Soissons to very light duties. What is striking, when we study bureaucratic rules under the old regime, is not only the privileges and inequalities, but still more the diversity which is found everywhere, even where inequality is not. This is why a study, in no matter how much depth, never allows one to affirm any rule as general. Is it not bizarre that, beneath this variation greater than anywhere else, the work of democratic unity was more advanced than anywhere else!

Government. Syndics. Intendants. In a great epidemic which took place in the south of France, the government, then directed by Turgot (1774), took detailed measures and even pretty violent ones against the scourge. In an edict of the Council (18 December 1774):

1) The intendants must name agents to verify the extent of the sickness in the countrysides.

2) The agents give statements in the presence of the syndics.

3) The animals pronounced ill must be killed on the spot, with the intendant charged to have the owner paid a third of the value of the animal if it had been healthy.

4) The intendant must give a detailed account of all operations to the controller-general.

5) Five hundred livres fine imposed on the owner who hides a sick animal (vol. 7, p. 87).

It was only in 1774 that the sale of meat was made legal at Paris during Lent (ibid., p. 92).

Sales taxes of the towns. A letter by Turgot to the controller-general (1772) shows that the towns, in order to create a tax, were first obliged to obtain an edict from the Council, and then obtain registered *letters patent* (ibid., p. 391).

Oppression of the lower classes by the bourgeoisie. "As the right to levy a duty is always granted at the request of the municipal councils (which were no longer elective but made up of the purchasers of offices), and since the government, busy with everything else, has almost always adopted without examination the tariffs proposed to it, it has happened almost everywhere that by preference foodstuffs consumed by the lower classes have been burdened; if, for example, duties have been levied on wine, care has been taken to impose them only on wine consumed in bars and to exempt the wine imported by the bourgeois for their consumption; similarly, all the foodstuffs which the bourgeois have brought in unprocessed from their country estates; it is thus that those who profit most from the common expenses of the towns are precisely those who contribute nothing or almost nothing to them; and that the expenses are paid for by those who do not have wealth and whose poverty prevents them from buying wholesale, or paid by the inhabitants of the countryside, whose produce burdened by duties is always sold less profitably" (ibid., p. 394).

Turgot, having become minister (28 September 1774), in a circular to the intendants reproduces the same idea: "In almost all the tariffs there reigns a great vice: it is the injustice with which almost all the bourgeois of the towns have found the means to free themselves from contributing to the common expenses, so that they are borne by the lowest-ranking inhabitants or by the poor of the countryside" (vol. 7, p. 36).

Turgot, father of centralization. Instead of being led to the idea that it was necessary to give some weight to this very mistreated lower class, so that little by little it would be in the interest of even the upper classes to hear its complaints and take care of it, Turgot thought only of returning all powers relating to the right to levy sales taxes to the intendant of each province. The intendants would give their opinion about the more or less great utility of these collections relative to the needs of the towns which enjoyed them; those which it might be advantageous to eliminate, those with which they might be replaced. They would suggest new plans for tariffs and the minister would decide (ibid., p. 396).

Intendants. Correspondence with all ministers. Like prefects, the intendants, representing the government as a whole, correspond with all ministers. The ministry with which Turgot corresponds most frequently is that of finance; first of all because the most frequently used, most difficult, and most important powers of the intendant are financial, and secondly because the controller-general was then concerned with a swarm of administrative business with which the minister of finance today does not concern himself, which is now the affair of the minister of the interior. But we find letters from Turgot to the chancellor with regard to matters relating to justice, such as decrees rendered by the parlement or other jurisdictions.

Idea of privilege and permission, which is combined with the idea of commerce and industry. Declaration of 26 December 1774 which exempts from the stamp tax letters containing permission to establish manufactures, forges, glassworks, tileworks, and other similar establishments (p. 96).

Administration, intendants, their powers. Syndics.

Fines replacing loss of office. Nothing better shows the immense power and arbitrariness given to intendants than the new procedures introduced for the collection of the taille in the Generality of Paris by M. Bertier, intendant, during the years 1772, 1773, 1774, and 1775 (see also the notes in the Hôtel de Ville), an operation that in 1775 was validated by letters patent (ibid., p. 105).

Chief means authorized by the letters patent and given in the instruction by Turgot which is attached to them:

1) The commissioners of the taille (named, I think, by the intendant) go to the parishes in the month of April.

2) The syndics, warned eight days in advance, are required to be there under pain of a twenty-livre fine pronounced by the intendant.

3) The community is assembled at the sound of the bell and the commissioners make a general inquiry about the condition of the parish.

4) They then receive each taxpayer's declaration in the presence of the syndic (we see here and in a thousand other cases that the syndic, like the mayor, is the agent of the government at the same time as the agent of the community; only the government has a hold on him through fear of fines and penalties and not always through fear of loss of office). There follow many other dispositions in order to set the taille at the best possible figure, without self-interest, given the proximity of the Revolution (ibid., p. 108).

The condition of the lower classes worsens amid general progress, the tax system becoming more oppressive for them. The regulation of the taille of 1600, by Henry IV and Sully, made the inhabitants of parishes collectively responsible for the payment of the taille, but, in those times, the parish chose a certain number of men, to whom the name of assessors was given, who did the service of assessing, dividing the tax according to reason and conscience. There were also named by majority vote one or several well-off individuals who were charged to assess the tax-roll decided on by the assessors of the collection of the tax of *deniers* (p. 125).

Since then, it was the tax collectors themselves who were charged with the division of the taille and who became at the same time assessors and collectors. According to article 13 of the declaration of 9 August 1723, the intendants had to choose the collectors among the most highly taxed under the taille and to name them to office in parishes where no nomination had been made or where the inhabitants were insufficient to make the collection.

The royal declaration of 3 January 1775 (requested by Turgot) gave new force to the declaration of 1723 (ibid., p. 136). See much other information on the collectors scattered throughout my notes.

As a result, since the collector was required to be responsible for the whole of the collection, the only rule he followed in the division was to tax those who paid best; thus a sure means of seeing one's taxes raised next year was to pay them well this year. Every peasant was thus always busy hiding his wealth. Afraid of devoting himself to his work, he avoided all enterprise, all acquisitions, for fear of giving the tax collector a hold over him and of creating a pretext for increasing his tax. From this, the countryside was impoverished in most of the *pays d'élection,* where the taille remained personal and arbitrary (ibid., p. 125).

The assessors and collectors were always chosen by the parish, the parish always had to be responsible for their administration. This was first established in 1597 for Normandy and then extended to the whole kingdom by the regulation of 1600. Today, cases of bankruptcy and fraud by the collectors are still very frequent, above all in poor provinces. In this case, we make the four most highly taxed people in the parish responsible; this harshness, which is very unjust, is at the same time very harmful to Your Majesty: the four most highly taxed are usually the most intelligent, the most hard-working people in the parish. If these precious men are put in prison because of a default that they could neither foresee nor prevent, all their work is suspended. Every year there are a certain number of the wealthiest and most capable farmers who, without it being their fault, are ruined (ibid., p. 131).

As we discover, in seeing such barbarous and absurd rules perpetuate themselves, it is a question of the particular interests of a weak and ignorant class, which the educated and powerful classes do not deign to concern themselves with even to improve the regulations.

Turgot proposes to abolish the measures against the most highly taxed and to tax the whole community to cover the deficit. He states that the old procedure was based on a form adopted during the recovery [from the Wars of Religion—Trans.] which no longer applies today, and that the appearance of harshness and injustice might then have seemed connected to a principle not wholly lacking fairness. The idea of having the governed participate in government and to use them for this purpose is an idea seemingly absent from Turgot's head. [Note in the margin:] His whole system, such as he imposed it through the royal declaration of 3 January 1775, consists of affirming and reinforcing the power of the intendants to name the collectors to office and to have the whole community made responsible for the sums which the collectors have not raised or have wasted. It is up to *the intendant's wisdom* to decide if the whole missing sum should be raised in a single year.

To do good for the citizens without their participation is his theory, like that of all modern bureaucrats (even the best).

Separation and isolation of the lower classes from all the others. The establishment of a special tax on the lower classes and the predominance of this tax in France (for the tax itself was seen in many other countries) was one of the great causes of the unique isolation of the lower classes under the old regime; in societies still little perfected, the greatest and almost the unique subject of public administration is the fixing and raising of taxes. Since the chief and for a long time the only direct tax was the taille, and since the taille only affected the lower classes, not only were people in the upper classes not involved with it, but this gave them the idea that it was beneath them to be involved with public administration in the countryside. That was the business of the syndic, not the lord. With time and civilization, government became more complicated and more diverse, but this fact remained. Further, several of the new purposes of administration continued to be irrelevant to the upper classes, or were fixed on the lower classes alone, such as conscription in 1648 (I think), the use of corvées for the highways, all were the business of the syndic and not of the lord. The lord thus ended up by occupying an elevated position in the parish, useless and unconnected with everything which surrounded him. Everything was run more or less well by the those poor devils the syndics, who had the real power and were at the same time very despised and very badly treated on all occasions.

The intendant himself was an official of great power given very little respect. He was the governor of the lower classes. A great lord and often a simple noble would not want to get involved in this work. The intendant was a commoner or at most a newly ennobled man.

It was not only the tailles and the other taxes solely on commoners which brought about this state of affairs, but the absence of any representative institutions and the constant action of the monarchy, systematically isolating the lower classes from all who were above them.

Manner in which Turgot speaks of the rural lower classes in 1774. In the preamble to the royal declaration of 5 January 1775 (I do not know if this preamble remained secret), "In most of the kingdom rural villages are composed of poor, ignorant and brutal peasants, incapable of governing themselves" (ibid., p. 124). He was right, but whose fault was it?

The vingtième. The vingtième is a fixed proportion of each taxpayer's income which is directly set by royal authority, according to the information obtained about the income by the directors, controllers, and others charged with fixing this tax. There is no collective responsibility among the taxpayers here (ibid., p. 212).

Today's gross receipts tax on business seems to me largely analogous to this.

Public administration. Aid for the poor not raised and administered locally, as in England, by the educated classes of society, but given by the central government and delivered by its agents. Progress of centralization amid the diversity and privileges of the old regime. The king decided (Turgot's ministry) that each year funds would be granted the various provinces to help the worst-off inhabitants of the towns and countryside, by creating work for them. The intendants had to state the needs, justly divide the funds which were granted, fix the sum for each district, the number of workshops, the kind of work of each workshop, and the place of work (ibid., p. 241).

We are here transported at a single bound into all the processes and procedures of the modern bureaucratic system, even taken to its absurdities and excesses, attempting with still imperfect means what cannot be done well today. Entering into a minutiae of detail which nothing since has been able to surpass, and whose execution it would be equally impossible for the central government of today to supervise. But what to do when the lower classes are ignorant, poor and lazy, and when the rich and educated classes hold themselves apart? It is true that Turgot, no more than anyone else, has no idea of calling on these latter.

The subdelegates will be charged with the supervision of the workshops and with the general oversight of this operation (ibid., p. 246). Given the impossibility of finding a large enough number of agents capable of methodically executing these operations, one must content oneself with seeking reasonable men who . . . (ibid., p. 254). (This whole instruction must be reread to see what immense detail it enters into and all the various duties which it imposes on the subdelegates.)

Administrative employment of the clergy, sign of democracy. Throughout this instruction for the establishment and government of charity workshops in the countryside, Turgot, as in several other circumstances, makes great use of the priests. When the aristocracy is destroyed, indifferent, or absent, and when the government has not yet the skill or the time to replace them with its own agents everywhere, the priest, who by birth is from the lower classes and by education above them, is a tool which naturally presents itself to the government. See the instruction given to all the clergy of the kingdom with regard to grain riots (ibid., p. 281).

Extraordinary criminal jurisdiction. Provost's courts. Some troubles having taken place in 1775 with regard to grain, a royal declaration (5 May 1775) requested by Turgot deprived the parlements (who, it is true, from what it seems, had shown a bad disposition) of jurisdiction: "Given that it is necessary that examples be made rapidly, that for this purpose the kings our predecessors established provost's courts, which are chiefly intended to secure the safety of the highways, to repress popular outbreaks, and to judge excesses and violences committed openly by force . . . at Paris and in all places where the said excesses have been committed, the persons arrested or who will be arrested are to be sent before the provosts-general of our mounted police, to stand trial without further appeal, and the verdicts rendered at their trial to be executed in conformity with the ordinances. Trials already begun had to be transferred to the provosts' clerks. We forbid our courts of the parlement and our other judges to take jurisdiction over them" (ibid., p. 275).

All the safeguards, delays . . . of justice introduced even in administrative procedures and applied to secondary interests or to guard property; summary justice, without safeguards, without mores as soon as it is a question of politics and the lower classes. A bad education for the nation, both through the slackness of the government, which constantly permits people not to obey the laws at all, and then at certain times through its violence and arbitrariness.

"All those who previously left their parish without possession of an attestation of their good life and conduct, signed by their priest and by the syndic of their community, will be pursued and judged before the provost as vagabonds" (ibid., p. 291). These are the bad examples which are the most dangerous, given by good people and for the purposes of public welfare.

Regulation. Contempt for acquired rights and easy violation of contracts by the government. Reims had a sales tax which was farmed out. The king, based on Turgot's report, ordered that during the eight days preceding and following his coronation, this tax would not be collected (it was understood that there would result from the coronation a very large income for the tax-farmer which he should not have counted on; ibid., p. 292). This violation of the contract soon put the tax-farmer into all kinds of difficulties and required him to use all kinds of inquisitorial means. The tax-farmer complained that during the time the tax had been suspended, people had been able to bring provisions into town which made the sales tax unproductive. It was therefore necessary to render an edict of the Council (29 May 1775) to order household inspections for the purpose of checking inventory, chiefly among the wine merchants (ibid., p. 302).

We complain that the French lower classes do not have a feeling for the *law,* for *rights.* Where would they have gotten it? When honest people, in order to do good, as well as scoundrels in order to do evil, combine to prevent these ideas from being born or to make them weak and confused.

Administrative justice. Origins of the arbitrariness to which many rights were subject. Because almost all industry was considered a privilege, a royal concession:

1) Under the pretext that what the authorities had conceded they could take back, change, regulate, many rights were without safeguards and were abandoned to bureaucratic arbitrariness.

2) Since the origin of these rights was administrative, the judgment of disputes relating to them was claimed by the government.

Example of these two things: All transport services, stagecoaches, carriages, and other public conveyances were the subject of concessions and privileges. "His Majesty having recognized that it was important to provide for the various inconveniences introduced into this part of the public service, whether with regard to the operation of said establishments or with reference to the disputes which may arise concerning them, orders that:"

"1) (Edict of the Council of 4 June 1775) all those provided with concessions or privileges, entrepreneurs or owners of said carriages, stagecoaches, transport services, will be required to send a copy of their titles, leases, prices, and special regulations to the secretary of state having in his department the supervision of carriages, to be confirmed by the king in his Council, when His Majesty judges convenient.

"2) All disputes and trials which daily take place between contractors and entrepreneurs concerning the execution of leases, and the merchants, drivers, travelers and others, in almost all the provinces of the kingdom, will be brought before the lieutenant-general of police in Paris, and in the provinces before the intendants, saving appeal to the Council" (ibid., p. 342).

Another example: The Council's edict of 24 June 1775 concedes to all artisans or workers who have the right, by rank or profession, to work in iron and steel, the right to polish works in steel. All disputes which may arise on this point (other guilds can bring suits based on the exclusive right to polish steel belonging to them) will be judged by the Council, jurisdiction over such trials being forbidden the ordinary courts (p. 355).

Supervision over roads given to the intendants. Jurisdiction over matters relating to the paths taken by roads constructed by the order of His Majesty, whether for the alignment of buildings built alongside these roads, or for their demolition in case of danger, is given by the edicts and regulations to the bureaus of Finance, with appeal to the Council (p. 374).

Ease with which contracts are changed and acquired rights effected. Following the correct principle that the towns' sales taxes and the fees charged in markets should not weigh on necessary foods, above all in times of food shortage, the Council's edict of 3 June 1775 suspended the collection of these payments in all towns, limiting itself to deciding that in principle an indemnity would be paid to contractors of the taxes (p. 340). We already see in full, in the legislation of this time, the contempt and envious hatred by democracies for all individuals whose rights harm the public, or for those who can make money, even legally and after a contract, at the public's expense.

Exception in favor of the lords. When it is only a case of taxes received by the towns, and the finances of the latter, the government doesn't bother about it at all. But when it is a case of similar taxes collected, even in times of food shortage, on grain in rural markets for the profit of the lords, the government takes care to explain in a new edict (20 July 1775): "His Majesty wishing to stop the effects of an interpretation (the very natural treating of rural markets like those of towns) harmful to the owners, whose fees will not cease to be collected when His Majesty has explained his intentions, both on their elimination and on the indemnity which will be due them . . . maintains their collection." The sales tax was a new and collective property created by the government; the taxes on rural markets were old and hereditary properties, the only ones really respected during the old regime (ibid., p. 376).

Government action affecting the tax-farmers of the towns. In suspending the towns' sales tax with respect to grain, the Council's edict says: "His Majesty has reason to believe that when the towns examine their income and expenses, they will find, by savings and decreases in useless expenses, the means of making this suspension permanent without having recourse to taxes of another kind" (ibid., p. 342).

[All that which follows, up to the end of Tocqueville's notes on volume seven of Turgot's work, is derived from Turgot's "Report to the King on Municipalities" (1775).]

Striking contempt for tradition and ancestral wisdom. Confidence in one-self. Absence, even among practical men (Turgot had been in government twenty years), of the idea that what exists has reasons for existing and can-not be changed except slowly and cautiously. "We have used much too much, in serious matters, this custom of deciding what we ought to do by the examination and example of what our ancestors did in times we our-selves consider to be times of ignorance and barbarism . . . It is only necessary to understand well the rights and interests of men (one would say that they don't have passions) . . . The rights of men in society are not founded on their history, but on their nature. There can be no reason to perpetuate unreasonable decisions" (ibid., p. 388).

One would not be astonished at finding this among the writers, among the philosophes, but in an intendant!

This contempt for past facts and for existing facts did not come only from a mental defect particular to the times, but also because people did not have a feeling for the good which the old institutions had done and the well-being which they had produced. The dream of a golden age could not present itself to the French mind.

Idea of a revolution absent from minds. Even the idea of disobedience, of resistance absent. "Your Majesty, as long as he does not depart from justice, can regard himself as an absolute legislator and count on his good nation to execute his orders" (ibid., p. 389).

This good nation had however already made the Jacquerie and the massacres of the Maillotins, of St. Bartholomew's night, and the League! But 180 years of repose and passive obedience had made people forget history, even among the educated. None of the little upheavals of freedom had made them imagine the possible effects of a large one. Among free peoples, one often fears revolutions when they are not to be feared; in absolute governments, one still does not fear them on the eve of the day when they are going to happen.

What is most resistant and most permanent in human things is national temperament. We did not know this.

Impossibility of really knowing what is going on in the lower classes when they are not left the means of making it known themselves. "The ministers cannot promise Your Majesty to really know the nation's situation, its needs, its abilities; the intendants can hardly do better, even the subdelegates named by the intendants can only understand it very imperfectly, for the little area confided to their care" (ibid., p. 389).

What Turgot says here, in a general way, is true above all of the lower classes. There is so little real contact between them and the upper classes, that when the lower classes do not have the means of making known their mind, their needs, their passions, their interests, through elections, intermediary bodies, local powers, the upper classes can touch them for centuries without ever penetrating them and be as ignorant of what is really going on in their minds as if they were separated by the entire diameter of the Earth.

Division of the nation into not only distinct but separate orders, which substitutes the spirit of class for public spirit. Absence of local bodies producing a similar effect among the lower classes who are not separated from each other by the spirit of class. The former hold themselves apart, the latter do not have any occasion to meet. "The nation is a society composed of different orders, badly united, and of a lower class whose members have very few social links with one another. Where, as a result, almost no one is concerned with anything except his personal interests; almost [no one] takes the trouble to fulfill his duties or even to understand his relations with others" (ibid., p. 391).

The government obliged to do everything; what results from this. Habit of the governed to expect everything from it; what the consequences are. "In this perpetual war of claims and enterprises that reason and mutual knowledge have never regulated, Your Majesty is obliged to decide everything himself or through his agents. We wait for your special orders to contribute to the public good, to respect the rights of others; sometimes to make use of our own rights." (This necessity for government to get involved in anything being created in the upper classes or the lower in the complete absence of local institutions: good idea to expand.)

Assuredly it could not be better said in our own day, and this picture, made eighty years ago, seems based on the national appearance of today. So much has this great Revolution, which changed everything's place, form and aspect, left us, *at bottom,* the same as we were.

The tax collector considered the common enemy. Law with the appearance of violence. We regard "the exercise of authority for the payments necessary for the maintenance of public order as the law of the strongest which there is no other reason to accept except for powerlessness to resist . . ." (ibid., p. 392). "One would say that Your Majesty is at war with his own people."

Isolation of each individual. "There is no point of visible common interest. The villages, the towns whose members are thus disunited no longer have any relationships among themselves in the districts they belong to. They cannot agree on any of the public works they need" (ibid., p. 392).

Pay close attention to the fact that political society is without links but civil society still has them, which Turgot does not seem to realize. People were linked to one another within classes, there even remained something of the close link which had existed between the class of lords and the lower classes. Although this existed in civil society, the results made themselves indirectly felt in political society. The men thus linked formed irregular and disorganized masses, but recalcitrant under the hand of power.

The Revolution, breaking these social links without establishing political links in their place, simultaneously paved the way for equality and servitude.

Sterility of provincial freedom in the old regime; or, on the constitution of certain provinces with estates. These assemblies "being composed of

orders whose claims are very diverse and whose interests are very different from one another and those of the nation, these estates are still far
from being able to perform all the good desirable for the provinces in
whose government they take part . . . These provinces, however, feel
less necessity for reform." They prided themselves on their constitution
(ibid., p. 393).

*The democratic unity of the nation transparent across the differences and
inequalities of legislation.* Towards the end of the eighteenth century, the
real and democratic unity of the nation was felt so well across the prodigious inequalities and diversity of details and superficial matters, one felt
so much that differences of class were no longer anything but appearances, or at least facts without substance, that the idea of general legislation presented itself to all minds and appeared in all the reform projects
of the times.

A century before, it would not have occurred to the most adventurous
minds; the material for such an idea, if one can speak thus, was lacking.

*Basic idea of the [Napoleonic—Trans.] University in Turgot. Action of
the state, centralization of this action, its uniformity. Has all the administrative genius of our day. Teaching become secular.* The first of all the reforms proposed by Turgot is public education. His system, which is, in its
definitive form, the one Bonaparte completed, is the following:

1) A national executive committee, which would direct the academies,
universities, high schools, elementary schools.

2) Unity of direction and uniformity of method: this council would supervise all regulation of education, it would have textbooks written and require their use.

3) A schoolteacher in every parish

4) The secularization of primary-school instruction passing from the
Church to the state. This last point is not said in explicit terms, but follows
from all the preceding.

*Illusions of Turgot and his times about the effect of education directed
by the state.* We see that all the Revolution's ideas, right or wrong, are
here: the idea that a nation's mind is a kind of dough that the state has the
right to knead from a certain single and uniform point of view of which
it is the sole judge; democratic contempt for individual rights in educational matters and for individual originality, contempt for the past and
the present, the idea of the *blank slate* presenting itself to all minds, in
the very midst of the complication and interlacing of all old and apparently powerful institutions. Finally, unlimited confidence in this kind of

intellectual medicine. "I dare say to you, Sire, that in ten years your nation will be unrecognizable, and that by education, by good mores, by enlightened zeal for your service and for that of the fatherland, it will be infinitely above all other peoples. The children who are ten years old now will then find themselves men prepared for the state, devoted to their country, submissive to authority not through fear, but by reason, helpful towards their fellow citizens, accustomed to recognize and to respect the law" (ibid., p. 399).

An old-regime village. "A collection of huts and of inhabitants no less passive than they" (ibid., p. 400).

It is still exactly that.

The functions of local governments according to Turgot:

1) Apportioning the taxes.

2) Advising about public works and local roads especially necessary to the village.

3) Supervising the regulation of the poor and their aid.

4) Knowing the relations with neighboring villages and the larger public works of the district, and in this respect presenting the wishes of the parish to the authorities (ibid., p. 401).

There does not appear here either the administration of common property or schools, or the duties of the municipal government as government agent in certain cases, except for the apportionment of taxes.

Absence of local government. "These duties, indispensable for the good management of every village's business, cannot be fulfilled by the present *syndics* who have no authority, nor by the *subdelegates,* who have too many villages under their jurisdiction to know them well in detail; the *commissioners* of the taille and the *controllers* of the vingtièmes have neither right nor title nor interest in meddling in roads, or with police, or with the poor" (ibid., p. 402).

Division of the land. "The natural division of inheritances divides what was barely sufficient for a single family between five or six children." The children and their families no longer live off the land. Beyond farming they devote themselves to trade, to domestic service, to all the means of earning a salary (ibid., p. 407).

Imperfect civilization of the rural population. State of the roads, absence of common life. "In the present state (1775) the streets and roads of most villages are impassible. Whatever the poverty of the countryside, it is less the money which is lacking than public spirit, than a way to assemble, notify, carry out the inhabitants' wishes" (ibid., p. 419).

The treasury jealous of local resources. The state halting civilization for fear of decreasing its income from taxation. "We formerly had the bad policy of forbidding localities to tax themselves to build the public works they might be interested in. The reason why we opposed the particular expenses of the villages was fear that it would then be more difficult for them to pay their taxes. This reason was as bad as it was ignoble; for it is clear that the villages, in doing what they recognized to be for their own advantage, would be better-off and as a result would increase their ability to pay" (ibid., p. 420).

Thus, not only was the agricultural class isolated from the other classes, but one also kept the homogeneous elements which composed it isolated from one another!

Monetary privileges. The greatest obstacle to all common life. The greatest cause of the division of men in France. The greatest difficulty experienced by Turgot in his plan for local government was born of the monetary privileges of the nobility and the clergy (the nobility exempt from the taille and its accessory taxes, the clergy from that and, furthermore, from the capitation tax and the vingtièmes). This forced him to create three local assemblies in each parish:

1) A *small assembly* where one would consider only the division of the taxes to which the Third Estate alone was subject.

2) A *middle assembly,* for the division of taxes common to the Third Estate and the nobility (in this case the clergy would not appear).

3) A *great assembly* for business to which everyone, Third Estate, nobility, clergy, had to contribute (when it was a matter of works of particular concern to the parish or the supervision of the poor. It is thus that at the Hôtel de Ville I learned about the affair of the repair of the church of . . . , an affair which I saw end up in a tax-roll where the lord was taxed like the laborer in exact proportion to his ability; ibid., p. 429).

Tax privileges. What most divided classes. Of all privileges, those which keep people most separate from each other are monetary privileges. An aristocracy can have the exclusive right to govern, to fill public offices, it can even take part of the income of the other classes under the form of monetary dues or feudal payments. If equality of taxation remains, all citizens have a constant need of getting together and acting together in a matter in which they are all strongly and equally interested, which can be enough, if necessary, to keep a common link among them. On the contrary, if all privileges were destroyed except those of taxation, this single inequality would be enough to keep classes far apart, because they could never unite in the discussion and decision of the business which interests them most and which comes up most frequently.

I am so convinced of this that I think that if, even under the old regime, parish affairs had been more in common, if the spirit of material improvement had been more developed in the countryside and less compressed by the government (half through lack of interest, half by a detestable and absurd policy), that if in these kinds of affairs all the inhabitants of the parish (without exception) were obliged to contribute, this alone would have been enough to bring the classes together despite the privileges with regard to *state taxes* which divided them.

Role of the nobility and clergy in agriculture. The two privileged classes had reserved to themselves most of the pasture, as the property most easy to exploit. More than eighty percent of the pastures of the kingdom belonged to them (ibid., p. 424).

The aristocracy and clergy without privileges in the towns. The old monarchy itself had established that in towns where there were still municipal councils, or in the assemblies of notables called for certain important matters in these towns, "the nobles and ecclesiastics will not vote separately as distinct orders, but uniformly as the leading notable citizens." The edict of 1764 which was the existing law was essentially in this spirit (ibid., p. 432).

Illusions about the future. "We should not fear that the respect due these privileged groups, who furthermore have wealth and honors on their side, will ever be lost" (ibid., p. 433).

Turgot's system for the establishment of rural government. In summary, Turgot's plan can be summarized thus:

1) No municipal council properly speaking.

An assembly (or several when it was a question of the division of taxes) composed of:

    a) All those in the parish who have a net income of 600 livres;

    b) Representatives named by small groups, who, by uniting, represent 600 livres of net income (Turgot calls these *fractional citizens*). These assemblies, according to Turgot, will not be very large.

2) A mayor or syndic elected annually, neither named nor confirmed by the king, but whose distinction *will only be honorary and will carry with it only the right to see to good order, to present the deliberations, and to count the votes* (p. 435).

The idea of the separation of executive and deliberative power; of an assembly deciding on measures and of an official charged only with their execution, these ideas which seem so simple to us, were absent from the heads of all the French of that time, even, as we see, from those of the administrators who could so easily have seen them. People seemed to understand only two systems: an administrator deciding and executing without a council and according to his own views; an assembly which simultaneously deliberated, decided, and acted. This latter system was that of the estates; it was that of the provincial assemblies attempted by Necker in 1778 and generalized in 1787: it was again applied, so to say naturally, by the Constituent Assembly to the executive power—habits, ignorance, and mistakes previous to the Revolution and which had enormous effects on it and on the whole destiny of the nation.

3) A clerk to keep the registers, also elected.

4) An elected official or deputy to the local assembly for the region, of which we will speak below.

One should note that:

1) Turgot's municipal organization is democratic or at least anti-noble since it only introduces the nobles and priests into the municipal assembly as notables, and does not give them any separate role. *These assemblies are not estates* (p. 432).

2) From another point of view, this municipal organization is very aristocratic since it bases *all* rights on wealth alone and makes the property threshold very high (600 livres of income).

3) It does not foresee anything about the relations of the village thus constituted with the central power, probably because it allows all the principles of bureaucratic paternalism to subsist, and also because it does not foresee that the village, thus constituted, would present difficulties to the authorities that the old system would not allow one to foresee.

Absolute power makes everyone deteriorate: the vulgar man in giving him the soul of servitude, and superior men in depriving their minds of the experience that freedom gives.

Municipal powers of the towns. "All towns already have a sort of municipal government: what we call a provost of merchants or a mayor, aldermen, syndics, magistrates, consuls, or some other kind of municipal officials. In some towns, these officials buy their places as individuals; in others, they are named by Your Majesty without payment; in others, several subjects are elected from whom Your Majesty chooses; in others, election is sufficient. In certain ones, these officials have a term of office; in others, they are for life; in others, hereditary." The only uniformity is a regulatory spirit, which tends to isolate each town, very busy with its own

interests often badly understood, very inclined to sacrifice the local countryside and villages to them . . . "You have often been forced to repress
this constantly usurping and despotic tendency which is characteristic of
the town" (ibid., p. 436).

We see that Turgot does not note the system of municipal officials
holding their positions through venal offices, except in *some towns*.

I think however, to judge from the edicts, that this must have been the
most common case. But, in all cases, what seems most certain is that nowhere did *municipal life* really exist, it was never derived from the masses
and never exercised with some freedom. Turgot seems to believe that it
was still too free: first of all, because he has the bureaucratic mind, and
next because the little bit of local spirit that existed had taken the exclusive and narrow character of a clique.

Turgot's plan for urban municipalities. Same ideas as for the rural ones:

1) Houses as the base for the property qualification, like land in the countryside. *Direct* vote given to those with 600 livres of income or house rent as
in the rural communities.

2) No representative body properly speaking. The assembly of citizens, a
very small assembly because of the property required and because of the
complicated system of fractional citizens. In small towns, this assembly is
authorized to elect a municipal council; in large towns, it is required to; in
the very big towns, it will only choose candidates among whom the king will
choose and, furthermore, the police there will be controlled by a magistrate
named by the king.

3) The same municipal assembly, as in the villages, will further elect a
deputy for the higher assembly (ibid., pp. 435ff.).

Turgot's plan for regional municipalities.

1) Composed of persons elected by the municipal assemblies of parishes
and towns. One deputy for each community.

2) Their functions, very similar to those of [today's—Trans.] councils of
arrondissements (although superior), consist in the division of taxes between
parishes and towns, which takes place in two sessions, the first concerned
with making the plan for the division, the second with applying what the
provincial assembly [today's General Council of the Department] has decided. The privileges in tax matters require, here as in the parish municipal
assemblies, that there be created within the regional municipality a little assembly for the commoners, a middle assembly for commoners and nobles,
and a grand assembly where everyone will vote together.

Independently of the division of taxes between localities, the regional
municipality [would]:

1) Control those roads which were of only regional interest and require all parishes to contribute to them.

2) Name a deputy to the provincial assembly to make known the region's wishes (ibid., p. 450).

Turgot's system for provincial assemblies. Composed of delegates from the regional assemblies.

Its functions:

1) Division of taxes among the regions.

2) Public works.

3) It would elect a deputy to the grand municipality or royal municipality (ibid., p. 460).

On the royal municipality. Composed of one deputy from each provincial assembly.

Its functions:

1) Divide the taxes among the provinces (those which the state needs being set by the king and declared by him or his minister at the opening of the assembly). "The king will include in this budget the value of the public works he has judged appropriate to order and will then leave the assembly perfectly free to decree by a majority of votes such other public works as it judges useful, and to give the provinces such help or such aid is it would like, at the charge of dividing the necessary taxes among the other provinces of the kingdom" (ibid., p. 464).

We see that the assembly only has the right to divide the taxes the king asks for and that its own power only begins afterwards.

General character of the whole system.

1) All deputies paid (except in the parish).

2) All sessions limited (that of the royal municipality to six weeks).

3) The regional assembly could choose its deputy to the provincial assembly outside itself, the latter, likewise, its deputy to the royal municipality.

4) All these assemblies have the right to ask the king to make reforms that they think would be useful. If, by some unlikely chance, the municipal assemblies did not proceed to ask for these reforms (this was not to be feared), "You would be no less able to make them on your own sole authority, for, once again, these municipal assemblies, from the first to the last, are only municipal assemblies and not at all *estates.* They can inform, but they have no authority to oppose the indispensable operations required for the reform of your finances" (ibid., p. 478).

5) The parishes, regions, provinces can communicate and correspond with each other in order to arrive at common decisions.

Observations on this whole system:

1) The difficulties in execution that could arise between the different local assemblies and the government's administrative power do not seem to be noticed at all.

a) We do not know to what extent the assemblies will be free to act, to make works and expenses, to adopt measures without the authority of the state.

b) Who will execute the plans that they have conceived and how?

c) No government representative appears in them; the intendant is never once mentioned, a striking omission on the part of a former intendant. However, the real local government is given to them: all the internal business relating to taxation, public works, mutual aid, the charity necessary in the parishes, regions, even provinces, would be expedited by the people who would know most about it, and who, deciding about their own affairs, would never have to complain about the authorities (ibid., p. 480).

2) Even the place of the government as government, that is as executor of general laws, is not noted in this system.

3) The system is applied only to the *pays d'élection* and not to the *pays d'états*. This can work when it is a question of parish assemblies, regions, and provinces. But for the royal municipality, how? What would the representation of only around two-thirds of the kingdom mean?

4) But what is confounding (if Turgot has revealed his whole plan) is that he thinks he is making an administrative reform chiefly destined to facilitate the reform of taxation and its proper division, and that he does not recognize that he is starting an immense political revolution which changes the state's constitution from top to bottom. The assemblies of parishes, regions, provinces will become political bodies of which no one had any idea up to then; the royal municipality, which will feel itself to be the representative of all or of the largest part of the nation, cannot long be reduced to dividing a tax it does not vote on: a reform so limited and so timid if one considers its purpose, so unlimited, so bold at the same time, if one considers where it leads. What confounds is to see Turgot decide so quickly about a plan so new, whose consequences could be immense, having so little digested its ideas, and proposing its immediate adoption, if not for the current year, at least for the year after, as if it was only a question of a simple administrative reform that one could make without solemnity. Finally, what confounds is the confidence and tranquility of mind with which he ends his report, saying:

"At the end of a few years, Your Majesty will have a new people and the first of peoples. Instead of the corruption, laxity, intrigue, and greed that I have found everywhere, Your Majesty will find everywhere virtue, disinterest, honor, and zeal. It will be common to be a man of good will;

your kingdom, linked in all its parts, which will mutually support each other, will seem to have multiplied its strength by ten. It will become more beautiful every day like a fertile garden; Europe will look at you with admiration and your people will love you with tangible adoration" (ibid., p. 482).

Eighteen years later, Louis XVI was killed and the Revolution did what we know, and left us as we see ourselves.

To get an idea of the political inexperience of the nation at the moment of this great crisis, of the profound ignorance of *humanity,* of the needs, passions, vices, weaknesses inherent in human nature and as unalterable as it, an ignorance which is still more striking in that century of science and philosophy than ignorance of laws and maxims (for the study of man was the great study of the times, and it seemed that it could best be pursued by speculative philosophers); if one wants to get an idea of the nation's contempt for the past and the experience of other peoples, of its vain and confident pride in itself and in its ideas, the greatness of what we were about to do, the superficiality and incompetence of those who undertook it, one should not look at the development of all this in the crowd, but consider it in the eminent men and the *practical* men of the times, such as Turgot. We then remain astonished at seeing such an unusual and frightening occurrence in the history of the human mind.

Financial state of the towns. Result of the absence of free and representative institutions. Turgot says, very rightly, in this regard: "The pretext that Louis XIV used for destroying the towns' municipal freedom was the poor administration of their finances." This same fact, which persisted and got worse, was attributed by Turgot with much more reason to the absence of local freedom: "Most towns today are considerably indebted, partly through the funds they have loaned the government, and partly because of the expenses, the embellishments that municipal officials who control other people's money and have no account to make to the owners nor instructions to receive from them have multiplied with the view of making themselves known, sometimes of enriching themselves" (ibid., p. 446).

Note that, while the towns were thus bankrupting themselves, bureaucratic paternalism over them was equally if not more complete than in our day.

Tailles. Reforms considered by Turgot.

1) Elimination of the taille for laborers who did not own any land and did not engage in commerce.

2) Elimination of the taille on agricultural production, and of the per-

sonal taille, keeping only the real taille, which would no longer be based on the furniture or tools of the farmers, but only the value of the land itself (ibid., p. 470).

Centralization. Regulation. Decree of the Council of 7 August 1775, which made all stagecoach service on the highways a public service conducted directly by the state, also reserving to the authorities the right to establish similar stagecoach service on intersecting roads and the right to set prices for tickets by decree of the Council. Formerly the service had been provided, I think, partly by the state, partly by privileged companies. Privileges or the state, the old regime only thought of these two conditions for industry. The idea of free competition seems unknown to it (ibid., vol. 8, p. 14). The same for ferries and boat services, decree of the Council of 11 December 1775 (ibid., p. 103).

Irregular tax payments by high officials and great lords. Decree of 30 December 1775, which indicates a means, by deduction from salaries, of covering the arrears due from the princes, dukes, marshals, crown officials, knights and officers of the Order of the Holy Ghost, of the chancellery, the finance officers, and the farmers-general (ibid., p. 129).

"We see," says a note by the editor, "that these great and notable personages, who were certainly not among the nation's poor and who were only taxed very moderately by the capitation tax, did not pay it at all or only paid it with great delay, that there were people who had been ten years in arrears."

Harmful, oppressive regulation of industry growing over time as it should have been disappearing. The sale of glass windows had always been free until 1711. At that time the use of square panes was substituted for diamond-shaped panes. Glass not then arriving at Paris in sufficient quantities, a decree was rendered on 11 August 1711 which regulated the number of baskets of glass which the glass masters of Normandy had to furnish and fixed their price. The Parlement of Rouen made a similar decree to require squares of glass to be furnished at Rouen at fixed prices; this state of things was only destroyed by Turgot, 12 January 1775, with great opposition from the Parlement of Paris (ibid., p. 132).

Intendants, Subdelegates. Syndics. Rabbits. Decree of 21 January 1776 for the destruction of rabbits. The syndics and the inhabitants harmed complained to the intendant; he had his subdelegate proceed to fix the damage, and the syndic could require, in the presence of the officials of the captainry and the intendant's delegate, the destruction of the rabbits (ibid., p. 135).

The considerations and dispositions of this decree came from Louis

XVI himself, who showed it to Turgot, saying: "You think I don't do any work myself?" Poor and excellent king who, on the eve of such a great revolution, made reforms about rabbits, precisely seventeen years to the day before he was to mount the scaffold!

Abandonment of the lower classes. The safeguard of registration not existing for taxes which affected them. Those who paid the taille had long been subjected to the corvée without protest by the courts (ibid., p. 151). These courts so proud of their prerogatives, so ready to exaggerate them, who would not have suffered any pecuniary charge whatsoever to be laid upon the upper classes without a registered edict, let the corvée be introduced or increased without saying a word: that only affected the lower classes.

One might thus at most destroy the corvée by edict, says Turgot, but since a tax affecting everyone would have to be substituted for it, the privileged as well as others, a new law was necessary (ibid., p. 152).

Weight of the corvée. I dare assure you, by experience of the harm which the corvée has done in the province that I governed, that there is nothing else so cruel on the lower classes (ibid., p. 152).

The vicinity of Paris always better taken care of than the rest of the kingdom; opinion more powerful there than elsewhere. Never had anyone dared establish the personal corvée in the vicinity of Paris. There one was limited to requiring carts for the transport of material, a corvée always less burdensome than one which required workers. The latter was so hard that, if one had tried to establish it in the vicinity of the capital, it would have excited such a strong protest that the king would necessarily have shared the public indignation. But what happened in the provinces always made less impression (ibid., p. 153). This extended to a thousand other things, and, in general, we can say that when one wants to really appreciate the vices of the old regime, it is not on the vicinity of Paris that one must concentrate.

Taxes levied on all landowners regardless. In the *pays d'élection* there only existed two kinds of these: 1) the vingtièmes; 2) local taxes such as those whose purpose was the repair of churches or rectories, or other expenses useful to the inhabitants of a parish or of a certain area (ibid., p. 155).

This explains why in the affair of Ivry (papers of the Hôtel de Ville) the nobles and clergy who were landowners in the parish fought like devils against the local priest and spoke in the name of the inhabitants. The vingtième was common to the nobles and the lower classes, but not to the

Church; among the direct taxes it was only the capitation which really struck everyone. But the capitation was not a land tax.

Local taxes. We see from the preceding that local taxes were occasional and rare events (this alone proves the imperfect state of civilization and the complete absence of free mores and life). These exceptional cases were not regulated by any general law, says Turgot, as to the mode and rules for their division. This division was usually made by the authority of the intendants, or by persons chosen from among the inhabitants (the case at Ivry), or even most often by the subdelegates, so that (if this tax was generalized by substituting a road tax for the corvée) the vague announcement that the road tax would be combined with the local taxes presented the mind with a disturbing arbitrariness (ibid., p. 157).

See to what degree local political life, which is nothing else but freedom, is narrow in this old regime! Common works and the local taxes that they require were very rare; when these rare cases presented themselves, the community was consulted, but not called upon to vote, the government deciding; and finally the division was made arbitrarily by this government. The occasion for common action, the means to regulate it, everything is missing.

Viability in 1776. We can judge this by the care Turgot took to indicate that the road tax established in place of the corvée could never be increased to more than 10 million (ibid., p. 159). Find out the present figure.

Guild masterships. Abuses of masterships. Turgot alerts the king to the report by M. Albert on the abuses reigning in the guilds of Paris and asks him to read it (ibid., p. 172). Where can this report be found?

Corvées. Their origin. "I think," says Turgot, "that the use of corvées dates from the last years of Louis XIV, and that we first made use of them in provinces where the circumstances of the war required that the roads be promptly made passable. It was used as a means of ordering the local peasants because one did not have the time to look for contractors and set up workshops and, still more, because one lacked money. Afterwards, the intendants of these provinces, wanting to repair roads judged essential in a more durable fashion, used this means that they had found convenient and that they thought cost nothing. The example of the first intendants was followed by their neighbors. The controllers-general authorized it; but it was only really established by the instruction sent to the intendants in 1737 by M. Orry. It was not, by far, without murmurs from the lower classes and without repugnance on the part of a great number of administrators" (ibid., p. 182).

See the unhappy condition of the lower classes in France; the progress of civilization which everywhere else lightened their burdens, here made them heavier: the burdens which weighed only on them increased when everywhere else one was led toward equality of burdens; the increase of roads increased their problem; and this increase happened in a century when society became more democratic and was no longer even inclined to patiently bear the old inequalities. The feudal corvée decreased, the national corvée replaced it; it was during the reign of [king x] that the greatest number of roads were opened or made usable (p. 182).

What a country is without public freedoms and without local institutions. "I have often seen M. de Trudaine, as well as M. Orry his predecessor, want to substitute taxation for the corvée, but be stopped by fear that a tax would be diverted from its object and that the lower classes would end up bearing both the tax and the corvées" (ibid., p. 185).

There was no abuse so obvious that, even in 1776, it was not defended by great persons. See, in this part of Turgot's works all the objections posed by Chancellor Miromesnil to the proposition to abolish the corvée and substitute for it a tax paid by all landowners, that is by all those interested (ibid., p. 185).

Road funds. Privileges. The resources for making roads were of two kinds:

1) The larger was the corvée, for all large works which required only labor.

2) The smaller was taken from a general tax whose product was put at the disposition of the Road and Bridges Corps to pay for skilled work.

The privileged, that is the chief landowners, that is again those most interested in the roads, did not contribute at all to the corvée, and, furthermore, since the tax for the Roads and Bridges was combined with the taille and levied like it, the privileged were therefore again exempt! (ibid., p. 193).

Ensemble of the advantages of the privileged with regard to taxes.

Chancellor Miromesnil having denied or minimized the inequality of burdens, Turgot opposed to him the following picture which summarizes the whole subject:

1) The privileged "can have exempted from all taxes associated with the taille a farm of four plows in extent, which ordinarily bears, in the vicinity of Paris, two thousand francs in taxes."

2) The same privileged pay absolutely nothing for the woods, pastures, vines, swamps, enclosed lands which belong to their château, of whatever extent they may be. There are districts whose principal production is in pasture or vines: then the noble who farms his land is exempt from all tax which

falls to the burden of the taille-payer, a second advantage of the noble which is immense.

The great evil produced by these financial privileges was still less their revolting injustice and the hatreds they suggested than the separation in which they kept the two classes (the upper and lower), the absence of common affairs, of common interests, of combined action which followed from this, of mutual need; no *purse* to defend in common.

3) "The nobles pay absolutely nothing but the vingtième for their feudal dues, feudal tithes, and all the profits of the fief; these objects which are very little in the vicinity of Paris in distant provinces absorb a very large part of the net income of the land." (In this, as in all the rest, the vicinity of Paris, which was one of the great centers of the Revolution, less *crushed* than the rest, so true is it that it is not oppression alone, which one resents, but what makes it more or less seen and felt, which brings about revolutions.)

4) "In the provinces where we have tried to establish the taille proportionally, we have thought of dividing the tax between the landowner subject to the taille and his tenant or peasant: for example we have made the tenant or peasant pay half the taille on the land under the name of *agricultural taille,* the other half paid by the landowner under the name of *property taille.* From this it has resulted that, in these provinces, the nobles, beyond the exemption which they enjoy on what they farm themselves, also enjoy exemption from half the taxes on the land they lease out" (they escaped from the property taille because this only struck the non-noble or taille-paying landowners).

5) The *indirect* advantages of the nobles with regard to the capitation tax are very great. "The capitation is an arbitrary tax by its nature; it is impossible to divide it among the totality of citizens other than blindly. We have found it easier to base it on the rolls for the taille, which were found ready-made. We have made a special roll for the privileged, but since these defend themselves and the taille-payers have no one to speak for them, in the provinces the capitation of the former has been reduced little by little to an excessively low sum, while the capitation of the latter is almost equal to the base of the taille; another result is that all the privileges which the lands of the nobles enjoy bring with them a proportional privilege for the capitation, although according to its institution this latter tax should be divided among all by reason of their wealth" (thus where there is equality in law, it escapes in fact).

6) Particular and particularly crushing inequality in regions of sharecropping: sharecropping and the custom of dividing the harvest in half between the landowner and the peasant had been introduced at a time when the taille had not been established. "It is probable that then this custom was advanta-

geous to both parties; that the landowner received from his land a sufficient profit and that the peasant could live and maintain his family with some ease. It is evident that when the taille and all the taxes came to fall on the head of this unfortunate sharecropper, all equality in the division was broken and he was forced into the greatest poverty. His ruin has been more or less complete depending on the various degrees of fertility of the land, depending on the greater or lesser expense that cultivation requires, according to the greater or lesser value of the produce. In some provinces, notably Limousin, the poverty of the cultivators is such that despite the law and the privileges, it has been necessary for the landowners, even privileged ones, to voluntarily consent to pay part of the taxes due from the peasants in order to find labor, and thus to correct the harshness of the law." But it must be observed that in this case the landowner limited his liberality "to the exact point necessary for his land not to remain fallow, and thus he leaves the peasants all the burden the latter can possibly bear without falling into despair and inability to work."

7) "The tenant farmer and the peasant alone being on the tax-roll, it is against them alone that lawsuits can be directed and they who bear all the expenses, seizures . . . finally this brings with it the vexation and abuses of the collection of a very large tax, often badly divided and raised on the portion of the population whose ignorance and poverty deprive them most of the means to defend themselves."

8) It is said that in regions of tenant farming, the lease is made with the taille included; but "it is notorious that the taille experiences constant variations, much more in increases than in decreases. As soon as there is a war, one makes the taille-payers bear the tax known under the name of utensils or winter quarters." The corvée varies. The increased charges which happen during the course of leases, for which no law authorizes the tenant-farmer to be compensated, upset all his calculations.

Diversion of local taxes by the royal treasury. M. de Miromesnil, the defender of the corvées and all the old abuses against Turgot, himself recognized the abuse by which the government often made taxes intended for the particular needs of towns or provinces go into the royal treasury (ibid., p. 211).

History of the monetary privileges of the nobility. The situation of the lower classes worsened in France as society improved and civilization grew. This part of Turgot's works is very interesting, it is a debate before the king through reports, led on one side by Turgot and on the other by M. de Miromesnil, the chancellor (1776). Miromesnil argued that to touch the monetary privileges of the nobility was to change the constitution and shake the monarchy, Turgot showed that these privileges no longer had any basis and that by destroying them one was returning to the ideas which had been current in the monarchy before their birth.

"It has never happened in any country," Turgot says, "that anyone has imagined making a deliberate proposal to give the richest class the right not to contribute at all to the state's expenses. This happened in France no more than elsewhere. Far from being exempt from taxes, the nobility was, on the contrary, alone charged with rendering justice and military service. This double obligation was attached to the possession of fiefs." Under Charles VII we began to raise a permanent and paid army; it was at this time that the taille was established in a permanent fashion.

(Since the purpose of the paid troops was to dominate the nobles or at least to do without them, it was completely natural that to get through the transition, it was not from the nobles that one asked for the money to be used against them.) Further, the nobility was not exempted from personal service for this reason for a long time. It was difficult to ask for his time and his money from the same man.

The new tax was given the name of the taille, which immediately dishonored it by assimilating it to the contributions that the lords raised in certain cases from commoner vassals. In certain southern provinces only, exemption from the taille was given only to the property possessed by the nobles, without being attached to their person, which made the taille real and not personal, which over the course of time effaced the debasing character of the taille, the nobles finding themselves subject to paying it because of non-noble property that they had acquired, and the commoners being exempted from it in the same case; the privilege was transported from the individual to the land.

After having established the taille in order to acquire a permanent and paid army, it was extended for a thousand other purposes. [Note in the margin:] "To the immense expenses for the upkeep of armies are joined those for fortresses, for the artillery, for the navy, the expenses for the protection [of the colonies] and of trade, those for internal improvements of all kinds, finally the enormous weight of the public debt" (p. 232)

(We thus arrived, in the middle of Louis XIV's reign, at a time when all public expenditures were paid for by the lower classes and when the nobility did not pay any tax. This was the system's high point. But not, in fact, the most oppressive moment, because public expenditures were still limited and the nobility still rendered some *government services,* which passed as the indirect payment of certain taxes. Here comes Louis XIV, who, while for the first time establishing certain taxes on the nobles, increased the mass of taxes so much that while approaching equality one didn't feel any better.)

It was only after the exhaustion from the war which preceded the peace of Ryswick and during the misfortunes of the War of the Spanish Succession that the capitation tax was first established, then the *dixième*. (Note that in thus taxing the nobility for the first time, the lower classes were not relieved of their burden, but on the contrary it weighed more heavily on them, giving them nothing but the satisfaction, in France, it is true, a very great satisfaction, of seeing one's neighbor as oppressed as oneself. For the new taxes—the capitation and the *dixième*—weighed on both the privileged and the taille-payer.)

Today the tax privilege that was justified on the basis that the nobles alone were obliged to serve is combined with the privilege the nobles have of only serving if they want to, for the nobles and even their servants are not subject to the draft laws (p. 232). Thus there is no longer any reason for the reduction, but there would be reason for an extra tax.

The nobles' privilege becoming the privilege of the rich. As a result of the ease with which nobility is acquired for money, "there is no rich man who does not immediately become noble. So that the class of the nobility includes the entire class of the rich, and the cause of the privileged is no longer the cause of the distinguished families against the commoners, but the cause of the rich against the poor" (ibid., p. 234).

Thus the privilege of ennoblement, which was a real privilege for the Third Estate, was again at the expense of the lower classes.

Military expenditures in France. The military expenditures of France were almost five-sixths of the total military expenditures of Austria and Prussia (ibid., p. 237).

Regions of the real taille. Languedoc, Provence, Dauphiny, and part of Guyenne (ibid., p. 239).

Power that the clergy still possessed, 1776. When Turgot proposed to replace the corvée by a tax on all landowners, he declared, with regret, that he did not dare include the clergy and its properties in this tax. The thing is very just however, he says, but it would excite strong protest and one should not start two quarrels at the same time (ibid., p. 244).

How many illusions, on the very eve of the Revolution, the privileged orders still had about their strength!

Monetary privileges of the clergy greater than those of the nobility. How ecclesiastical landowners were nevertheless taxed. The "free gifts" of the clergy were never at the level of what they should have been to equal the taxes the nobility paid. If the *tithes* had become heavy, it was because we had had the weakness to allow the clergy to pay for its free gifts by loans, which threw on the ecclesiastics who were the successors of those who seemed to make a free gift the burdens that the members of the clergy who prided themselves on their gift ought to have borne (ibid., p. 248).

Democratic and revolutionary preaching by the king. We read in the preamble of the edict which abolished the corvées (1776): "The weight of the corvées falls on the poorest part of our subjects. The landowners, almost all privileged, are exempt from it or contribute to it only very little. However, it is the landowners to whom the roads are useful, by the value which they give the production of their lands. It is neither the peasant nor the day laborer who are made to work on the roads who profit by them . . . How could it be just to require contributions from those who have nothing of their own, to force them to give their time and their labor without salary! To take from them the only resource they have against poverty and hunger, in order to make them work for the profit of citizens richer than they!" (ibid., p. 281).

We see that we had arrived at being unable to conceive that the lower classes existed not only as something to exercise power on, but as an unorganized force! The idea, not of a revolution, but of an obstacle, of disturbance coming from this source, was in no one's mind. The rights and interests of the lower classes were discussed in front of the lower classes as if they had neither eyes nor ears, like certain great ladies undressed in front of their domestic servants, not counting them as men. We see here, further, the monarchy following its old tactic of opposing the privileged classes with the lower classes and making itself their loud advocate against the privileged classes, without seeing that times had changed, forces had been displaced, and the danger no longer came from above but from below.

Guilds; communities of workers. Edict which abolishes them (February 1776) basing itself on *natural right.* History of the guilds contained in the preamble of the edict. The communities, first a classification of workers in the towns; then workers of the same type made into communities properly speaking, which created regulations and tended to obtain a separate government and exclusive rights, which the kings freely gave them in return for payment (for almost all the great institutions of the monarchy had financial expedients as origin). The edict of 1581 gave this institution the extent and form of a general law. The edict of April 1597 aggravated the preceding edict still more. The edict of March 1673, by ordering the execution of the two preceding edicts, added to the number of communities already existing other guilds previously unknown . . . "Some persons have ended up going so far as to claim that the right to work was a royal right that the sovereign could sell and that subjects ought to pay for" (ibid., pp. 330ff.).

This whole edict is a preparation for the Revolution. It democratized industry by breaking the connections which suffocated every profession, it did not replace that organization with any other. In place of the supervision the guild exercised over its members, it substituted only the supervision of the state. It gave the example (*for the public good,* an example that much more dangerous) of the sudden, general, and complete destruction of old institutions which had created many interests, habits, and rights. It showed that democratic contempt for collective existences, collective property, which the Revolution would push so far.

In general, we can say that all the ministers who succeeded one another during the old monarchy had equally joined in taking away from the nation the idea of right, respect for that which had been legally created, and had done their best to suggest in advance the idea that individual existences which could not defend themselves were nothing, and should never be obstacles to the state's action. Above all this is seen in all that was done about venal offices, which were constantly created and destroyed for financial reasons, thus periodically turning upside-down the situation of a multitude of individuals.

Centralization. Absence of intermediary powers. "His Majesty reserves it to his Council to determine, according to the accounts which will be given of the importance of the various roads (roads were to be divided into four classes, from highways to village roads), into which class each road should be put and what should be its size"; edict of the Council of 6 February 1776 (ibid., p. 372).

Centralization already wanting to do what was superfluous, when it could not do what was necessary. Decree that there would be sent to the provinces 2,258 boxes of remedies to be distributed annually to the poor inhabitants of the countryside (ibid., p. 376).

Medicines sent from Paris to purge the poor sick person in a village of Lower Brittany! What an administrative farce! What complete absence of an intermediate government! Still, this was a kind of progress. The monarchy had extinguished or forbidden the creation of all powers which could govern the localities, and, since for a long time it was incapable of governing them itself, there was not, in truth, any public administration, above all in the countryside.

Impediments to commerce. Privileges. The owners of vineyards situated in the district of Bordeaux have the right to forbid the sale and consumption in the town of Bordeaux of all other wine except that of the district (p. 409). The wines of Languedoc do not have the right to go down the Garonne before the Feast of St. Martin, nor to be sold before the first of December. Those of Perigord, Agenais, Quercy, and the Haute Vienne cannot arrive at Bordeaux before Christmas. In a multitude of localities this is the way things were. But nowhere, says the preamble, still of the same edict, is the abuse pushed so far as at Marseille, where one inflicted corporal punishment on those who introduced foreign wine into the town's territory, where foreign ships could not even provision themselves with wine except with the local product, *their health certificate* being refused until they had proven that they were in compliance with this rule! All this in an edict which does not go back any further than 1717. One didn't want to permit foreign vessels to consume at Marseille wine which they had brought from elsewhere . . . In the southern provinces the reciprocal prohibition of drinking wines called foreign had become an almost universal custom (p. 414); edict of April 1776, which abolished all these exclusive rights (ibid., pp. 406ff.).

Notes on the Cahiers

[Cahiers of the Clergy]

Press.

All districts attribute to the press the decline of morals and demand some kind of repression. Some (we are not told how many), ask that the system of censorship be continued. Most only demand serious repressive laws (p. 14).

Absolutely nothing is said about *newspapers*. It is only a question of *books*. Nothing shows two things better: that at that time the power of newspapers was unknown; and the great power of books, a fact which is sufficient in itself to show certain intellectual habits and a society still led by the educated classes. In our day it has sufficed to destroy the freedom of newspapers in order to have nothing to fear from the freedom of the press. Books can be disdained. The sign of a great social revolution and a great intellectual revolution.

Freedom of the Church. Councils.

I am sure that the situation into which the Church of France had fallen in the eighteenth century, which was in some respects miserable and disorganized, was due in part to the absence of freedom. That the bulk of the Church was faithful is proven by the persecution it was able to defeat. The abuses which reigned among the clergy is [*sic*] proven by the cahiers. The Catholic clergy, had they possessed the freedom they alone would have enjoyed, would certainly have been more intolerant and more oppressive, but better organized and more influential over mores and ideas, which would have been a great good.

The old regime did not and could not have had that terrifying and Machiavellian idea of a free clergy amid a submissive nation, a clergy owing its freedom only to power, using it in the interest of power as much as in its own, and taking for its maxim "omnia serviliter pro dominatione" ["all things slavishly for the sake of domination," from Tacitus, *Histories*, 1.36, about Otho and his behavior after becoming emperor—Trans.].

Religious intolerance. Only thirteen districts ask that the nation retain the right to tolerate all religions, but not permit the public exercise of their worship. The majority protest against the edict of November 1787 in favor of non-Catholics, and ask that it be revoked or weakened.

Nothing shows better to what extent intolerance is natural to Catholicism, a profound part of its mores. Some of these priests who demanded intolerance didn't believe in anything, and all of them, in perfect accord with the current of the times, were led, as we will see, towards all the liberal and reforming ideas . . .

Public education. Uniformity demanded. Always this idea of the state as the maker of men.

It must be noted here: 1) The Church's blindness (born of its spirit of domination), which made it believe that in making the state the all-powerful regulator of public education it would reign forever through its hands. 2) All the ideas of centralization and tyranny which reigned in the mind of this nation which was going to overthrow everything in freedom's name. 3) In a word, the revolutionary spirit, even in the least revolutionary class. The Convention had only to take and apply the clergy's ideas for its purposes. Isn't this characteristic! Where is real support for the freedom of the individual among this people ready to revolt against all authorities? Let someone show it to me!

Vote by head or by order. The unanimous wish of the clergy seems to me to be that people vote by order when there are separate interests and by head when there are common interests. Several formally note that one ought to vote by head on tax questions (p. 105). Thus the vote by head already practiced in the provincial assemblies was already accepted in part by the clergy for the Estates-General . . .

Oppression of curates by bishops.

The edict of 15 December 1698, interpreting the edict of 1695, allowed a bishop to have a curate, vicar, or other member of the clergy against whom there were complaints temporarily imprisoned in his seminary. It is asked (I don't know by how many districts) that in this case the bishops be subjected to legal forms (p. 170).

Read these edicts. This Louis XIV had such an instinct for despotism! Being unable to absolutely destroy the independent strength of the clergy as a group (the last who could hold out against him), he at least destroyed all this body's freedoms and put it entirely into the hands of a few men whose master he certainly hoped to be . . .

Intervention of the state invoked in questions of church discipline. Uniformity of the liturgy.

Many problems result from the diversity of holidays, rituals, and catechisms. It would be desirable that all these things be made uniform throughout the kingdom. The Estates-General should take this point into consideration (p. 13).

See how minds were ready for the ideas which brought about the Civil Constitution of the Clergy!

Liberalism of the clergy. Reforming spirit. Fear of arbitrariness, belief in the nation's rights, democratic theories, hatred of exceptional courts and administrative law in general . . .

The idea of the necessity and utility of a constitution returns constantly, and is as present in the clergy's minds as in those of the rest of the nation. Several districts even say (p. 121) that the constitution ought to be first of all and without exception voted on before proceeding to any consideration of taxes. The desire for the enunciation of abstract principles and general systems is no less visible among the clergy. Here is a sample: it will be stated that the sovereign power exists for the sole purpose of the happiness of all, that it cannot fulfill its function properly unless the nation is consulted on everything which interests it, and that as a consequence national assemblies are essential to government (p. 113). Note also that *divine right* properly speaking is never found in the cahier of the clergy, rather it is the *primitive* right of peoples which is invoked, as in the above citation and a thousand others. Another example. The nation has the *right* to assemble for the exercise and preservation of its rights, to freely choose its deputies who will pronounce on laws, subsidies, and other objects concerning the general government of the kingdom in its name (p. 117) . . .

All demand that no one should be deprived of his freedom or forbidden to appear in an arbitrarily determined place. No man should be arrested except by order of a competent judge and interrogated within twenty-four hours, because there cannot be any freedom for the nation if that of individuals is not inviolable (p. 121).

A true and beautiful principle, well-expressed. How far from it we are, good God! What immense backwards movement in the last sixty years! . . .

All ask that municipal officials be elected (p. 172). That towns and communities be *returned* through the right to freely choose municipal officials (ibid., p. 130).

It is interesting to see these two intellectual bases of the French mind in 1789. A superficial one born from liberal instincts and from theories which contain (in unarticulated form, it is true) ideas about decentralization. The other deep, based on habits, mores, the past, the social state, where all the ideas of centralization are contained and which remains despite all the movements of the mind . . .

Every farmer should be allowed to defend his property against the assaults of pigeons (p. 295). Lords should be required to destroy the wild game which, conserved for their pleasure, becomes the scourge of the countryside (ibid.). Several other cahiers too long to transcribe demonstrate the same spirit and the same bitterness of peasants who have become priests. Further on we will see the nobility attack the abuses of the clergy just as avidly. The two orders had not yet learned to make common cause . . .

Important general remarks.

In reading these cahiers of the clergy one is struck by the advantages to be found in the system of an unpaid but landowning clergy.

What gives the clergy of 1789 so much civic spirit, what makes them so sensitive to abuses, so respectful of rights, so irritated by arbitrary power, is, it cannot be doubted, property. We thought we were making the clergy dependent by taking its property away from it and giving it a salary; we thus created a clergy which was no longer part of civil society, which no longer felt any of the passions, needs, interests of civil society; for all these things, when we look at them closely, originate in property. We created a clergy which was doubtless dependent on the government, but which no longer belonged to the nation and which even served the government with the soul of a government official, in everything which did not touch the Church's interests that is, and with an unchangeable servility regardless of who was master. Another effect: with regard to the Church greater dependence on the Pope, something less national, even in the portion of nationality permitted by Catholicism.

When the clergy is celibate, as in the Catholic Church, the only means of attaching it to the country and to civil society is to make it a landowner.

[The Cahiers of the Third Estate]

General remarks.

The notes I have already written on the cahiers of the clergy and the nobility ought to shorten my work here. For it is clear that all the liberal innovations—the philosophical ideas, safeguards for property and persons, the rights of the nation, the elimination of abuses and old institutions—asked for by the privileged had to be demanded, still more strongly, by the Third Estate.

Here, before going into detail, general remarks suggested to me by reading the cahiers of the Third Estate:

1) Almost *complete identity* of general ideas about social questions with the general ideas proposed by the first two orders, above all by the nobility, and even, in fact, in specific ideas, at least as long as it is not a question of particular privileges relating to one of these orders, in which case the commoners go farther than that order on that particular point. In summary, it is absolutely the same mind, and the only difference is in the greater or lesser logic applied to drawing conclusions from principles.

2) Not the least trace of any sort of attachment whatsoever to any local customs or personality. Not one appeal to precedent. Not one memory of the past. We only find a feeling of this kind in ONE cahier from Brittany. Except for that, this France still divided in fact into so many jurisdictions, local laws, political customs, local rights . . . seems as unified as the France of our day, where the lines between the departments are invisible, nothing is seen but a single mass, a single mind, a single law. The Revolution was radically complete on this point, before it began.

3) A spirit more radically and effectively democratic than in the cahiers of the nobility, but less suspicious of power, less republican.

4) The old regime already so condemned that no one any longer takes the trouble to prove that it must be destroyed. They are only concerned with what should be put in its place.

5) Little interest in the lower classes proper, and above all in the rural poor. People certainly ask, along the way, for all the reforms concerning them, but without showing that passionate feeling for their griefs and sufferings that we meet with, for example, in certain responses given by the parishes of Touraine, in 1788, to the requests of the intermediary commissions.

Notably they pass over the taille, the intolerable abuses of its collection, abuses little felt by the bourgeoisie but overwhelming for the peasant. What is striking above all about the taille is that it does not weigh on the privileged orders as on everyone else. I do not know if the cahiers of the other orders do not show greater interest in the rural poor than these cahiers, drawn up by men who were close to those poor. In sum, we feel that it is still the bourgeois and not the peasant who is speaking.

6) That which is underlined above all and highly colored are the abuses which harm the industrial classes, commerce, the urban middle classes.

7) As in the cahiers of the other orders, all taxes are disputed, contested, criticized.

8) Little trace and even no trace of struggle between laymen and clergy over the question of public education.

9) The same idea, much more amplified even than what has already been encountered in the other two orders' cahiers, that the state must be involved in everything, participate in everything, encourage, create, forbid . . . Furthermore this is less astonishing than on the part of the other orders, who were the government's rivals. But even they, decentralizers by their passions and often by their ideas, were unfailingly led towards centralization by their needs and habits.

10) Regarding the military, not more and perhaps less anarchic than the nobility.

11) Encouragements for domestic business, restrictions against foreign products: characteristic of all the demands of the Third Estate.

12) Hatred of privileges with regard to trade and industry as much and more than in all other questions.

[General Remark on Book Two]

The external greatness of France was favored by centralization.

My subject was to find the causes of the old regime's death. This naturally led me to study in particular its ills, from which it came about that, without wanting to, I have created something that resembles a diatribe against it.

Pay attention to this when retouching the picture. Add, when the occasion naturally presents itself, those *true* traits which can improve its appearance.

Example:

1) In the chapter on centralization, make it understood that this same work of concentrating power, amalgamating all parts, forming homogeneous and compact bodies, which prepared us first for the Revolution and then for

servitude, at the same time resulted in making France, at the very moment when its example was being imitated throughout the continent, mistress of Europe; and making Paris the school of civilization. For these same things which make states unstable strengthen them at a given time; the same government which prevents peace from bearing all its fruits and freedom from peacefully establishing itself, at a given point in time is very favorable for war, and gives the first who possesses this strength an immense advantage over all others. The greatness of Louis XIV and the Revolution were produced by the same cause, and when I think of all the advantages which it has given us in relation to Germany and the conquests of the seventeenth century, what astonishes me is not what we did then, but that we did not do more. We ought to have conquered half of Europe if we had properly employed the army which we had first known how to create.

2) In the chapter on the kind of freedom which reigned during the old regime, note better that if the French had known absolute power, they had never known servitude and never displayed its spirit.

NOTES RELATING PRIMARILY TO BOOK THREE OF THE FIRST VOLUME

Notes on the Elder Mirabeau

What is most interesting about reading the works of the Marquis de Mirabeau is to see ideas born of equality, which will bring about social revolution, penetrating despite the man among the crowd of aristocratic prejudices, pride, and aristocratic insolence which fills his head. There they take on the bizarre and unexpected shapes given by a place so poorly prepared to hold them.

Nothing is more unusual than this invasion of a feudal mind by democratic ideas.

"Report on Provincial Estates"

The report appeared in 1750; republished with *The Friend of Humanity* in 1758. Here I find this idea of Julius Caesar's: "The mass of humanity is made to serve a few . . ." I do not know when or where Caesar expressed this thought, which was especially appropriate for the chief of the democratic party in a slave society . . .

Page 81. Remarkable picture of local government in the pays d'états. Here are free institutions and free mores! What is it that in the public eye diminishes both this government's purpose and the people who take care of it, and renders almost ridiculous even the power that it exercises? The absence of a free national government, the natural culmination of local freedom. It is only political freedom which enhances local government and gives it greatness. The idea of making freedom live only at the bottom, without putting it on top, is as absurd as that of making it live above without also putting it below.

Aristocratic jealousy against the rich. "Two things," says the Marquis de Mirabeau, "attract respect: birth and employment. One could add wealth to this list, but only in times of anarchy. Everywhere, in a well-regulated state, the wealthy have the benefit merely of the peaceful enjoyment of ease and the pleasures of life, never of deference" (p. 89). A noble of the fourteenth century would not have said this. An English nobleman of the eighteenth century would not have said it either. In the first case the nobleman was rich. In the second case, the rich man became a noble. This is the natural and necessary order. Lasting separation between nobility and wealth is a chimera which after a while always ends up in the destruction of the former or in the combination of the two . . .

See the way their defender spoke of the lower classes. The Marquis de Mirabeau, summarizing his book, formulates this maxim: "The lower classes, like beasts of burden, deserve their fodder"; and "the most harsh and most self-interested policy must take care of the poor" (p. 252).

What the Marquis de Mirabeau took from his birth, from the traditions of his class: the idea of nobility, less as aristocracy than as caste. "The sovereign may admit to the corps of nobles those new men who have distinguished themselves by military service; but if he claims that his patent can give this distinction for other kinds of services rendered, and claims that his patents have any other effect than to register the beneficiaries as notables in such and such a profession, he violates a *law of title,* that is 'a constitutional law,' one that is beyond his control" (p. 44). Thus nobility is a right derived from power alone, wealth is secondary; it is not at all necessary for nobility. The Marquis de Mirabeau even has a sort of permanent anger against the rich, which suggests ideas to him that are almost socialist, like this one: "private wealth is nothing but a violation of the rights of the group. In consequence wealth alone marks rank with the colors of injustice . . ." (same, p. 54). The nobility is in his eyes above all a military caste. He freely gives other classes a considerable role in government proper, law, administration, finance.

His ideal is a conglomerate society, never any mixing of estates.

What the Marquis de Mirabeau took from his century and from the physiocrats. The equality of man recognized and preached amid the principles of social inequality, which leads him to this axiom: "Never a mixing of estates and always a joining of feelings" (p. 5). He uses the word "fraternity," which became sacred forty years later, although he alters it, it is true: "fraternity, with the commandment of a right of the first-born for the nobles" (p. 7).

A single power, but not arbitrary. Unity of fixed rules always observed.

No general right recognized for men to govern themselves by themselves. Enlightened self-interest, which obliges the sovereign to take care of the poor and the little people.

Necessity of interesting people in the public welfare, encouraging them to bring some of the feelings they have for private property to the common good.

Property the foundation of everything.

Religious tolerance, which, however, he combines with the prohibition of all public worship except Catholicism.

Distinction between basic laws, what could be called the nation's constitutional laws, which he calls laws of *title,* and secondary laws, incidental or particular: the former, fixed and unchangeable, derive from the unanimous agreement of the nation . . . It is the nation alone which can alter laws of title (p. 40). The nation has nothing to say about all the other laws, which are, in truth, government in action.

Idea of the omnipotence of the government to transform men to its taste.

No tax farms; elimination of indirect taxes. All others raised by the localities themselves.

Only indirect taxes are burdensome. The land should bear the tax directly.

Freedom of internal and external commerce.

No creation of offices or privileges for sale; no loans.

Regeneration in laws, habits, and regulations.

The king can make reforms without any danger.

The king, says the Marquis de Mirabeau (part 3, p. 87), in reality reigns over life and property, but still more over opinions: "In no other times have all the circumstances contained in this definition been found united in the government's hands as they are today in France, in whatever state of society may have existed" (1758). "The entire nation seems to have identified its interests, its glory, and finally its ideas of all kinds in a single person, the king. Justice, administration, finance, commerce, jobs, artillery, towns, villages, hamlets, lands, people, all belong to the king . . ."

All this was written thirty years before the Revolution. He uses this argument to prove that the government can attempt anything, without risk, with regard to improvements. What confidence given by, on the one hand, these 150 years of submission and, on the other, the progress of royal authority and the absence of all political experience! Seen from a certain angle the picture of the century is accurate; the progress it signals real. Only one must put, instead of the king, the government, the state. The greater, more extensive, more detailed influence of the government on business and even on ideas, this is true. But this was a sign of centralization and democracy, not of stability.

We see, in all this and in many other traits that I could add:

1) That the Marquis de Mirabeau gropingly accepted the modern ideas that can be found at least in germ in most of the ideas he expresses. He often combined them with all kinds of intellectually heterogeneous elements, ideas taken from other sources.

2) That the realization of almost all the ideas he took from his contemporaries would have made absolutely impossible the application of his own ideas, which he took from his education and his memories.

The French way of colonization; national character. "A governor," says the Marquis de Mirabeau, "and an intendant, both claiming to be master and never agreeing: for form's sake, a council. Gaiety, loose morals, frivolity, vanity; great rogues, very rarely honest men, often discontented, and almost always useless. In the midst of all this, heroes made to bring honor to humanity, and a lot of ordinary people occasionally capable of heroic actions. The theft of hearts, so to speak, and the talent for friendship with the natives of the country. Great beginnings, never completed. The taxes which squeeze the sapling and are already attached to its branches. Monopoly in all its state; voilà our colonies" (p. 126).

You'd think you were looking at Algeria. The only thing lacking is the bustling and sterile activity of the civil administration.

Colony of Canada. "The land," says the Marquis de Mirabeau, "was excellent in its production, the sea more full of fish than any in the world, the fur trade brand-new and so abundant that one could not help but be successful. They acted like good Frenchmen: they saw it all and immediately went on further to see if there wasn't something better still. There were seven of them. One remained in Newfoundland and said: "Despite this fog I will stop here, and all the fishing is ours." Two stopped in Acadia, and soon fought with each other, because they were too crowded. The other four went to Quebec, one of whom went on by the best road in the world to establish himself at Hudson Bay; two others, to pass the time, went upriver for twenty-five, thirty, or forty days, talked pidgin with the natives, asked them for news, swindled them as best they could, and made war alongside the first natives who asked them to without asking them why, just to amuse themselves. They threw up four earthen walls that they called "forts" everywhere it seemed to them a lot of people assembled, and above all they planted large stakes on which they took care to write in charcoal: "Done by order of the king" (ibid., p. 126).

A charming piece and, beneath its humorous tone, full of truth and depth.

Notes on the Physiocrats

"Administration provinciale," by Letrosne (June 1853), One Volume in Quarto, 1779, Published or Said to be Published at Basel without the Author's Name

Idea about the book and the author.

The original idea of *provincial assemblies* was very well expressed by Mirabeau (the elder) in 1750, reprinted in 1758, forming volume four of the duodecimo edition of *The Friend of Humanity*.

One might note that the idea was picked up by the Academy of Toulouse. It is characteristic of the times and the country to see such questions fall into the academic domain and there become just a very small part of the *literary politics* which was characteristic of eighteenth-century France . . .

Creation of offices.

"In 1688, under the pretext of regulation and because of need, a large number of official positions were created in Paris for the ports, docks, shops, markets, workshops, to which rights and duties were assigned. The city of Paris gathered together a great number of these offices" (that is, paid for them). In other words, what was going on was this: a certain number of positions were created and people were found to fill them, positions which were not only useless, but positively harmful, and to get rid of this evil the city was required to reimburse the purchasers for the money they had paid the royal treasury. Can one imagine a more barbaric means of raising a tax, and is the Turks' avarice any worse?

Multiplicity of offices.

"The kings had encouraged vanity and put it into play by multiplying innumerable offices under all possible pretexts. In 1664, according to the calculation Colbert had made, there were 45,780 offices in the kingdom . . ."

Why has no one ever cited this way of raising money as unusual and, I believe, unique evidence of our nation's vanity, a way of raising money which I think was used only in France, and which never failed to be effective, even though the government constantly gave these offices out and took them away, often to the purchasers' detriment?

Give a good example of this frenzied desire for government positions, so old in France, which was born in the middle class of the old regime, and which, independently of the vanity I have spoken of above, was constantly encouraged by the injuries to one's self-esteem to which France's unnatural social and political state gave rise. The middle class, which used to have only this petty pleasure with which to restore its self-esteem, has retained this passion for government jobs while changing its position, and remained a beggar while becoming sovereign.

Local tolls.

Finally, independently of the king's local rights, there were the tolls of the towns, the lords, the abbeys, those who held indentures, for example the fee of "passae" which the abbey of Fontevrault received one month of the year, and the very considerable charges that the indenture holders received on everything that entered the Loire river from outside.

It must be noted: 1) That among these old-regime abuses, the most numerous and most striking perhaps were those which were encountered along the length of the Loire, and which were daily suffered by those populations who alone fought against the Revolution. One proof, among a thousand others, that it is less the weight of the abuse than the state of mind which makes it more or less felt. The circumstances which brought about this situation in this West, still so burdened by feudal shackles, were that the classes were not at all divided in the countryside as they were elsewhere, the peasant had not been abandoned in isolation. 2) That many of the payments received for the profit of individuals had certainly been established in return for services, the upkeep of bridges, roads, docks . . . and from this point of view were not any more hateful than those received by railroad companies or anything else. But several payments had continued even though the obligation, in whole or in part, had ended. In England, individuals harmed by these fees would have addressed themselves to the Royal Court of Bails to have the collection declared *without cause* (see my notes on Blackstone). However, in England, one would certainly have had much more real respect than in France for the inviolability of contracts, for acquired rights, for antiquity, and much more real consideration on the government's part for the aristocracy. But that was a government of freedom and publicity. Strong because it was free, it always spoke in the name of all to each; it was easily master of unreasonable individual claims, because those claims did not dare produce themselves in the light of free discussion. The French government was simultaneously absolute, secret, and fearful. The French government had no real consideration for the aristocracy, it much preferred the lower classes, who seemed easier to make obey than the aristocracy, but it feared the aristocracy very much. [. . .]

Due of franc-fief. "This is a fee which eliminates the absolute inability of a commoner to own a noble estate" (p. 216). "This fee which at first was demanded only once in a lifetime, and not after an inheritance, later became a cruel tax" (p. 217).

When I see all the taxes founded on an unequal basis in France, or shifted to one, and the infinite nonfinancial consequences which they have had, I quickly conclude that the visible origin of the evil was that the kings, not wanting to ask the nation for the money they wanted (as had long been done in all Europe, and always in England), yet wanting it, had been reduced to 1) establishing a host of taxes without appearing to do so, and 2) establishing those taxes which were obvious on the least-resistant classes. Try to find out at what time voting on taxes disappeared in the various countries of Europe. I think that France was the country where it disappeared first. At least, at the beginning of the seventeenth century, during the Thirty Years War, voting on taxes was still seen throughout Germany, and was very respected by the rulers. Ferdinand, the tyrannical conqueror of Bohemia, took away its freedom of religion in 1620, but respected political liberty and the vote of the taxes. [. . .]

False idea that the reformers themselves had of England and the effects of political freedom.

"The situation of France is infinitely superior to that of England" (p. 282) (in 1780! . . .). "France has so many more advantages, because the king has all the authority necessary to undertake a reform that will change the state of the country in an instant, while in England this reform will always be prevented by internal divisions" (same page).

What ignorance! England then was already more prosperous than we are even today. What inexperience of practical politics to believe that a Revolution as immense as that which Letrosne was asking for could be made all at once by a single man, without risking turning the whole society upside-down! What incredible and naive confidence in himself! What revolutionary desire for enormous reforms made all at once! French nature in its philosophical state . . .

Absolute absence of public life in the pays d'élection. The nation does not exist in the *pays d'élection*. Society there has no part in the impulses which are given to it (p. 319).

Letrosne finds this bad, but always, with him as with all physiocrats, we see that he wants social and bureaucratic reforms much more than political freedom. All these men visibly fear assemblies, for fear of being hindered in carrying out their plans of reform. For them the ideal would be to take control of the sovereign power and to use it freely to reshape the social base. They have hardly any more idea of rights than the government itself, and thus already possess the true revolutionary temperament.

Provincial government.

Letrosne's system for provincial government (p. 317ff.) is so similar to the project submitted by Turgot to the king in 1776 (I think), that it is impossible not to see that Turgot took Letrosne's ideas or that Letrosne copied Turgot's work. The same general ideas, the same details, the same ignorance of the size and danger of what they are undertaking, the same taste for the system of the blank slate. Notably Letrosne wants to change all the territorial divisions, not limit himself to any of the divisions which existed in his time. He changes the names of territories, he destroys the unity of the parish, for, he says, "everything among us seems to be made by chance. When it is a question of a new institution it seems we should look for the best" (p. 331).

Letrosne is a peaceable magistrate, a friend of order, justice, religion, and even fairly respectful of acquired rights. And this man sitting tranquilly behind his desk draws up plans for changes which contain a great Revolution that he doesn't see at all. When I see this immense contempt for what had previously been done, for the past and the present, in men whose position and temperament are conservative, and when I compare this with what Blackstone showed at the same period, I conclude that this must not be attributed merely to a difference in national character, to a particular trait of the French mind of the time, but that the results of the work of the actors in the two countries had been radically different, in England all in all excellent, France, all in all, detestable. The secondary and accidental causes acted on this basis but should not permit it to fall from sight . . .

Philanthropic nonsense. Utopian dreams which were mingled with the plans of the constructive but speculative and literary minds of the time.

Among the uses which Letrosne finds for the electoral system are these: A man who has brought up and taken care of an orphan will have the right to vote without owning any property. He who has given a cow to poor farmers will have a vote. He who gives a dowry to a poor girl judged to have well deserved it, the same (p. 348).

The electoral system is, in fact, the best means of linking classes and men to one another, but for more general and less sentimental reasons . . .

Guild masterships. Growing abuses of the royal tax system. Fought by the assemblies.

Look well at the origin of all the abuses of the old regime, you will find almost everywhere the kings' taxes. Their desire for money was still more harmful than their desire for power, or, to put it better, the one was born from the other. Their love of arbitrary power prevented them from having recourse to assemblies, and the absence of assemblies forced them to cheat with the taxes and to remove them as much as possible from the rich and the strong. Look again and you will see that at the beginning all the abuses were fought by the assemblies, and would never have been established or would have ended up being reformed if the rule of the assemblies had been established.

Squandering of the towns' revenues.

We see that paternalism in no way prevented the towns from getting into debt. Which does not prevent historians and, I believe, M. Thiers, from accusing local freedom and the absence of centralization of the debts which hobbled a great number of towns at the outbreak of the Revolution, so great is ignorance of the old regime, even among those who have written the history of its destruction. Letrosne (who, moreover, is not very far from paternalism and like his colleagues no great friend of local freedoms, and who can barely conceive of the idea of a *right* of towns, as of individuals, to dispose of themselves within the limits of not harming others) correctly remarks, however, that the real guarantee against urban profligacy would be the obligation to have new expenses ratified by an assembly of citizens, and to require the towns to show at the same time the resources for new expenses, through taxes representing the capital expense or interest.

Public charity.

"The poor are assisted in towns by the efforts of priests and charitable ladies. This resource is completely absent in the countryside; in the countryside there is nothing but distributions of bread made by the tenant farmers in districts where the farmer is a little better-off, distributions which are made at his door, which require the poor to beg" (p. 530). "Begging is an absolute necessity in the countryside, above all during the winter. The most recent means which we have employed, a very harsh and expensive means, is to imprison those who beg" (same page).

This illustrates well the abandonment of the countryside by the landowners. Under a free government, private charity would have been more active, since the presence of landowners among the population would have been more frequent and their interest in helping the poor greater, and furthermore a system of public charity would have been created. I am more and more of the opinion that we cannot avoid doing something of the kind. Humanity and public health make a law of it.

French character.

Our nation is kindly, gay, charming, and full of attachment for its sovereign (p. 545). In 1780!

Means of destroying the tithes.

We see how revolutionary ideas were in the philosophes' heads before they reached the demagogues'.

Letrosne proposes to eliminate the tithe, which is unjustly received by bishops, chapters, abbeys, and benefices (which according to him made up half of the total), without compensation, these tithes having obviously been usurped. He proposes the destruction of the rest, but charges the state to pay the priests (p. 555).

Illusion about the power of governments.

"A government makes men whatever it wishes. It leads them astray, it corrupts them, it improves them and returns them to order, according to its own intentions and the means it employs" (p. 561). "In this century the sovereign authority can do everything for the happiness of society" (p. 634).

This is the eighteenth century in a nutshell. Unlimited confidence in reason and the government's actions. An idea not only of the eighteenth century, but of France, born of inexperience and the sight of absolute government. Faith in reason has been extinguished by experience, but the idea of the government as creator and safety net has remained.

Louis XIV's financial robbery.

"One has only to look at the consequences of Louis XIV's operations on the royal domains, and one will see there the game of a landowner who makes money on everything; who sells at very low prices and baits his trap with advantageous conditions; who then retraces his steps and imposes new taxes; who proves by all his actions that one can have no confidence in him, so that when buying from him at the lowest price one still does not know if one has paid too much. He not only fails to keep the most formal promises, but even incorporates in his financial operations objects which do not belong to him, as when in 1692 he establishes by edict that all land held in *franc-alleu,* whether by noble or commoner, belongs to the crown. A principle formally rejected by many provincial law codes."

It is a striking thing to see this principle that all land belongs to the king, which in England was introduced in the most distant part of the feudal past [see Tocqueville's notes on Blackstone—Trans.], established for the first time in France in the seventeenth century, by an absolute power already aspiring to the socialist theory of our day.

It must also be noted that not only did royalty not destroy the lords' judicial jurisdiction in these domains; rather it sold judicial jurisdictions that it possessed and increased their number by dividing them. Thus itself increasing, at its pleasure (for fiscal reasons), the greatest abuse which remained from feudalism, when this abuse had nothing inconvenient for it, but only for the public.

One should note, finally, the sale of financial privileges, which is also a great and voluntary aggravation of the greatest abuse of the old regime. It is striking here because it is done wholesale, but it never ceased to be done in individual instances, by creating offices or selling nobility. The operation consisted, in its final form, of making a citizen pay a certain sum of money in order to be exempted from paying taxes, and then earning back his share of the taxes by making all the other citizens pay it, so that one received both the sum paid for the tax-exemption and the tax itself.

Ideas before 1789 about the way to destroy feudalism.

The idea of violent and uncompensated destruction is not expressed by anyone before the Revolution.

Quasi-impossibility of the destruction of feudalism in the author's eyes (1780). "This event must be relegated to the class of reforms which are more to be desired than hoped for" (p. 570). "The elimination of feudalism is a good almost impossible to hope for" (p. 570) [actually p. 571].

Is it not striking that these same reforming and adventurous minds who expected all kinds of illusory results from the imminent Revolution did not believe in the one result which it was sure to have!

The liberation of the land.

"Personal servitude has been abolished. But the servitude of the land has remained. It is less prejudicial but it is a servitude; it is a fetter on property and a burden which it must bear" (p. 625).

See the notes on Blackstone for what there is of truth and exaggeration in this great interest in freeing the land. I do not know if in England the old feudal payments were irredeemable, but weren't they? There the result of this was chiefly properties that were bought and sold commercially with an obligation which was incorporated in the sales price and rent and which did not hinder the *use* itself, which is the main point.

ANTILIBERAL TENDENCIES OF THE PHYSIOCRATS

Mercier de la Rivière (born in 1720, died in 1793 or '94), friend of Quesnay and one of the leading writers of his school, in his various works and in particular in the most famous of all, or rather the least unknown, *The Natural Order of Political Societies,* shows himself simultaneously very reformist and very much the enemy of political freedom. He makes great distinctions between "arbitrary despotism" and "legal despotism," that is despotism which governs "according to the rules of essential order" (i.e. the rules given by the author) in conformity with reason . . . Given this, he is strongly of the opinion that the legislative power should be exercised by a single man as executive, that all counterbalances are dangerous. This derives from a mixture of illiberal desires and stubbornness on the system-maker's part. He claims to prove, which is true, that the interest of the sovereign is the same as that of the rest of society. As soon as this demonstration has been made, there is no longer anything to fear from then on; "the ideas according to which we have imagined the system of counterweights" (the representative system) "are chimerical."

The abbé Baudeau, born in 1730, died around 1792, one of Quesnay's disciples, the author of a multitude of little writings on behalf of the physiocrats' doctrines; chief director of the "*Ephémérides,*" the physiocrats' most famous journal.

Once again this is a political theorist in the Chinese style, a great admirer, like Quesnay, of China: the state "is nothing, properly speaking, but a large family. Public authority is nothing but the duty and the right to provide for education, for protection, for universal administration." Once this is well understood, the best thing is to leave the state very free in its movements. The whole modern French idea, a mixture of revolution and despotism, is already here.

The sovereign must be able to exercise this paternal authority by himself and through his agents at all levels. But who then is to prevent him from abusing his authority? The greatest geniuses have exhausted themselves trying to resolve this problem. The author succeeds without difficulty in showing two means, one, to facilitate the exercise of authority: a truly efficient system of collecting public revenue. The second, to prevent the abuse of authority, is general education, from which results universal opinion, which will make everyone understand, both sovereign and subjects, that power and freedom, rather than opposites, are cause and effect (ibid., p. 754).

It is uniquely to prevent the sovereign power from abusing its strength "that all the republics, ancient and modern, which were devoted to the political counterbalances or counterweights that we also call intermediary powers were instituted." All these inventions characterize "mixed" states which are neither arbitrary despotisms (which the author does not want), nor the physiocratic monarchy (which he advocates) (ibid., p. 777).

Struck by the evil which abuse of authority has brought, men have invented a thousand means, totally useless, "and have neglected the one truly effective means, which is public education, general, continual, just by essence, part of the natural order of benevolence" (p. 777). What a literary gallimaufry, in place of real knowledge of men!

Chapter titled "Analysis of Mixed States Compared to the Physiocratic Monarchy," in which the author notes the three great prejudices which regulate all the institutions of these mixed states, *i.e. counterweights, political bodies, fundamental laws* (ibid., p. 783). There follows a long list of the inconveniences and dangers of political bodies and the eternal war among political parties (in mixed states) to conquer legislative power (p. 787). It would make M. Troplong envious.

"The holders of supreme authority should be organized (in the physiocratic monarchy) in such a way that everything is related to a common center, to an intelligence, to a prime will which combines all means and which directs them towards the general goal of universal education, protection, and administration. It is this unity which properly defines a well-regulated state (the physiocratic monarchy). It is this intelligence, this single and unique will which includes everything which acts for good or evil in the state: it is this will which controls, more or less directly, all the holders of authority, in the three areas of instruction, protection, and administration" (ibid., p. 797).

We see, the commentator rightly says, that the system of centralization adopted by all the governments that have followed one another since the Revolution is simply borrowed from Quesnay's doctrine.

I add here that Baudeau had also foreseen the style of government, and that his book is written in the French of bureaucratic circulars.

At the end of all these beautiful things, China, as usual, could not fail to be found. In fact there follows, on page 798, I don't know what nonsense about Chinese institutions in which the author seems to me to chiefly admire three things: 1) An authority which is not directed by laws proper, but by the evident and necessary order that we can consider nature's own desire, the eternal law. 2) A single supreme will throughout the state which directs all the works of social art. 3) A bureaucratic mandarinate governing under this will and teaching and fixing the characteristics of this necessary order, of this eternal law. So, the author ends up saying, the Empire of China is, through the education of the intellectuals who govern it, the state most closely approaching the true theocracy which I call the physiocratic monarchy (ibid., p. 799).

When we read the works of Abbé Baudeau closely (and I could say as much of many others), we see that it is not exactly liberal intentions in their essence which are lacking. He wants all rights to be respected, as well as property, individual freedom. Beneath everything in Baudeau's book there is even an idea that is true and more liberal than that which serves as the base of all free states, the idea that there is a general and unwritten law above all particular laws that the sovereign may make and to which obedience is due before all others.

It is the physiocrats' practical conclusions, their means of execution which, contrary to their will, tend only to the subjection of human will and thought.

Letrosne is, after Turgot, the most illustrious member of the physiocratic school. In my analysis of his chief work and of Turgot's work, see the remarks which show how to a lesser degree they demonstrate the same tendencies I have just noted and which are those of the whole school. These common tendencies can be attributed chiefly to:

1) The spirit and pride of the mathematical mind, which makes one want to impose the acceptance of all these ideas as a whole, without going through the work of submitting them to the examination and choices of political bodies.

2) The absolute lack of practical experience of free institutions, of intermediary powers, of local life, and the perception of the good effects which result from them. England itself (badly known, furthermore) had not yet furnished the striking arguments on behalf of freedom that it has furnished since. Free institutions produced effects there which were internal, invisible to foreigners; their fertility and their greatness had not yet manifested themselves externally.

3) The detestable constitution which took the place of free institutions in France, the privileges of castes and classes. The annoying or impotent oppo-

sition of the parlements, the outdated forms of local freedoms in the *pays d'états.*

All these things had done damage, in the physiocrats' eyes, to free institutions themselves, to the theories of counterweights and safeguards, of "checks" [original in English—Trans.].

The pride and absolute spirit of makers of systems, complete inexperience of free institutions, experience of the bad institutions which took their place.

These ideas of the physiocrats did not have great influence on the French Revolution proper, for even though some of their ideas had entered into intellectual circulation and had largely contributed to shaking the old regime, their persons were not popular in 1789 (as Dupont de Nemours notes in his long letter to Say); but they are nonetheless very worthy of being studied. They bring to light the ideas which, born naturally and peacefully from the nation's state of mind, institutions and mores, from its education, its history, from what was most powerful in the impressions and memories of the old regime (before it was violently shaken and thrown outside itself by the revolutionary movement), were to combine with all the new institutions and remain the permanent basis of our political instincts. We were dislodged from this base (only in part) by the need to use freedom to destroy the old regime, but we returned to it seemingly naturally as soon as the old regime was destroyed.

What is also very interesting is to follow what I have called the illiberal tendencies of the physiocrats, what we may call the natural tendencies of the nation of their time, into the systems which seem most opposed to them, with whose aid the Revolutionaries proper, those of 1789 and the following years, wanted to found what they called freedom.

There is a great deal to be taken from this study to explain the history of the Revolution, its different phases and its real products.

First of all, one must start with the French mind as the old regime made it, that is its opinions, desires, and natural tendencies (represented well enough by the physiocrats) in questions of government, and then follow the action and transformation (never the destruction) of these first elements in all that has happened afterwards.

Notes and Variants

All remarks by the editor appear in italics. Works cited by the editor appear in italics, underscored. Tocqueville's own words, and those of the authors he cites, appear in roman type, underscored only to indicate Tocqueville's own emphasis or underscoring. The translator's occasional remarks are in italics within square brackets and identified as such. For further details on the organization of Tocqueville's notes, see the "Introduction" and "Note on the Manuscript" to this volume, and the last section of the Introduction to volume one, "Tocqueville's Files, Manuscripts, and Proofs,"—Trans.

Page 27, line 2

The very first outline of the plan for Tocqueville's book on the French Revolution, dated 26 June 1853, is found in Folder K (research notes relative to The Old Regime): First chapter, "General Description of the Revolution." Chapter 2, "The Republic on the Inside." Chapter 3, "The Republic from the Outside." Chapter 4, "How Near the End of the Republic France Was Ready to Accept a Master." Five, "Eighteen Brumaire."

Page 27, line 15

In the margin of the last two paragraphs: We are still too close to the events to know the details (this seems odd, but it is true), the details are made known only by posthumous revelations and are often unknown to contemporaries; what contemporaries know better than posterity is the intellectual movement, the general passions of the times, whose last shudders they still feel in their hearts or minds. They know the real relationship between the leading personalities and among the chief facts, among the great historical masses, which contemporary onlookers perceive better than posterity does. Posterity ought to write the history of the details. Contemporaries are better placed to trace its general history, the great movement of facts, the current of thought, which men placed too far away no longer have any idea of, because these things cannot be learned from memoirs.

Page 27, line 27

This text, preserved in a folder of File 45B AA, shows Tocqueville's hesitations about the point of departure for his book about the Revolution. A note sketched on some pages filed together with the text returns to this problem:

We say that the Revolution began with the fall of the Bastille. It was already made then. To prepare myself to discuss this first chapter, concentrate strictly on the period indicated:

   1. Transcripts of the provincial assemblies

   2. Same of the electoral assemblies

   3. Pamphlets, newspapers of the times (the latter in very small number)

   4. Documents of the time from the meeting of the Estates-General to the Constituent Assembly

What was the deficit *[in the government's budget—Trans.]*? This was the central point around which all revolutionary aspirations briefly united.

The struggle of the parlements is the incident from this period which most merits study. Unfortunately, transcripts of the various writings which deal with this struggle are lacking to me. Perhaps this should lead to a special chapter titled "How the Parlement Which Thought It Was Still a Power Suddenly Discovered That It Was No Longer Anything; Why." Or perhaps make all this part of a whole, a symptom of the not merely reformist but new nature of the imprudent, democratic, demagogic Revolution.

Perhaps it would be better to start only with the Estates-General? The first volume already shows all the preceding, even if it doesn't go into it in detail.

Page 28, line 32

Note on a page attached to this text:

After the general picture of the state of minds stop at this last characteristic, that in everyone's eyes it was a question of the transformation of the human species, of accomplishing an immense change in the destinies of humanity. The Revolution's soul must be sought here and not elsewhere. Here is the spring which made the old French monarchy and all the old powers of the world leap into the air; here is what combined honor with the crimes of scoundrels, greatness with the lives of the miserable, and made devotion penetrate even the most egoistic hearts. This is what must be imagined and pictured if one wants to see the Revolution in its true light.

Never would purely individual calculation, purely personal passions, greedy desires, personal interests, have suggested such efforts. These passions never make great things, no matter how violent they are.

Page 28, line 39

Note on a page attached to this text:

How we fell suddenly from the old regime into the Revolution.

The period of time that I ought to include in this is from the first Assembly of Notables up to the fall of the Bastille. From that moment not only was the Revolution made; it already had its chief characteristics: the intervention of the lower classes; popular violence; Paris-master; cruelty; a Revolution not only democratic, but demagogic. To this can be attached as symptoms individual powerlessness, the impossibility of civil war . . . *[A revolution made—Trans.]* not only in the lower classes' interest, but by the lower classes.

On this subject Tocqueville had envisaged a previous chapter whose outline is preserved on a page put in a separate folder with the inscription:

Should this chapter be written? Should it be put at the beginning of volume two? The advantage of this chapter would be to explain once and for all about the character of Louis XVI and the court as a contingent cause.

Better perhaps to throw this in another chapter than to thus dogmatically place it separately; stop for a moment and say: at the sight of this trifling and incompetence one might doubt that a Revolution could have been avoided.

If the old regime could have fallen without a Revolution.

I think that nations, like individuals, are the chief makers of their fate. But I believe that certain mistakes once committed, certain errors once conceived, lead to consequences that are almost inevitable. Man is free to choose his path, he is free to walk with a different step, but . . .

Assuredly, there has never been anything in the world more incompetent than Louis XVI's government; nothing more appropriate than seeing this unfortunate sovereign bring about, by his virtues as well as his weaknesses, a violent and subversive revolution. In all history there has never been a more miserable spectacle than seeing the pettiest thing under the sun, that is, the mind of the salon, put in charge of conducting one of the greatest things ever seen, that is a Revolution which tended not only to change all the conditions of a vast empire but to overturn the entire surface of the civilized world and establish human societies on a new basis . . . All this might make one believe that the Revolution could have been avoided in 1789. But I am convinced that given the men of that time with their ideas, their passions, their inexperience, their indiscipline . . . taking them as a whole, it was virtually impossible to avoid a complete catastrophe. This is not at all meant to say that if the nobility and the clergy had acted differently during the previous two centuries, or even if the monarchy had been better represented, we would not have been able to last thirty years longer before sliding into a democratic monarchy without falling into demagogy.

In the margin of the text: The question would certainly be very interesting, but it would interrupt the train of thought, which after having stopped for a long time at the preliminaries needs to run on towards the facts. This chapter would seem like a second preface.

Another, later folder bears the same title with the note: Chapter 0. Perhaps one should make a chapter of this in the second volume? To look at (1856).

Page 29, title of chapter 1
On the folder bearing the title and containing the pages of this chapter:

A sketch barely outlined although very painstakingly written. Redo all this at one go.

The Rubbish file for these drafts contains a general note about this chapter: General flaw of this piece. In the beginning it seems like it is trying to paint France and the rest of Europe simultaneously. In reality, it doesn't talk about France, and should not talk about it, since my whole first volume was employed in painting the preparation for the Revolution in France. This can't be interesting, and can't avoid seeming repetitive unless it paints the state of mind outside France. Therefore it is necessary to say something like this at the beginning:

"Several of the things that I previously said about France ought to be extended to Europe as a whole."

Page 29, line 6

On the state of mind in Germany, Tocqueville consulted chiefly his friend Circourt (see their correspondence in OC, *v. 18, in 1852 and 1857), but in July 1854 he also read a book by Sarah Taylor (1793–1867), wife of John Austin and aunt of Henry Reeve (first translator of* Democracy in America *into English), titled* Germany from 1760 to 1814 *(London, 1854). At Bonn in August 1854 Tocqueville had spoken with various professors and notably with Löbell, professor of German History and Literature. After these conversations he noted the following (File 44-2):*

General idea. On the whole, we can say that this general intellectual disturbance, this secret revolt against the institutions of the past, this feeling of future instability which characterizes Germany in the period preceding the French Revolution, this is spread throughout all German literature and should not be sought in one book in particular. It is the atmosphere they all breathe. The works of Goethe's youth, for example, strongly bear its imprint. G. de Berlichingen, Werther, and yet another whose title I don't recall.

Page 29, line 17

In the margin of this sentence: Never was humanity as proud of itself as in that time. One can say that man believed in his own omnipotence then. People were proud of civilization, of the progress of science. When people weren't confined within the space of the present moment and the limits of their own country, they dreamed of all kinds of wonders and immense happiness for the human spirit. On the other hand, never had people more felt the flaws of their own time and country.

A separate page attached to the manuscript develops the same idea: One finds traces of the same state of mind in all of German literature: philosophy, history, poetry, even novels show it. All intellectual works take such a distinct imprint from it that it marks all books in a way which makes them different from the work of all other times. All the memoirs of those days which gave birth to so many memoirs, all the letters which have already come to light, are so many witnesses of a state of mind so different from ours that it requires nothing less than such numerous and certain proofs to attest it.

Assuredly, never was humanity more proud of itself than at this moment; one can say that since the beginning of the world it is the only period in which man almost believed in his omnipotence.

One example among a thousand: a pamphlet on the sect of the Illuminati, 1789. It is written in a fairly heated and inflated style, but gives the basic ideas: each year brings forth discoveries or revives a lost idea, man has almost extinguished the lightning bolt in the hands of Jupiter; the human mind frees itself from its prejudices . . . Folder AA, p. 23.

Page 29, line 26

The text indicates here: "Quotations, Folder AA, p. 31." We add the five following paragraphs, up to "It must not be believed . . . ," according to the research notes Tocqueville referred to.

A marginal note adds: Here cosmopolitanism, a new word taking the place of patriotism, love of humanity replacing the love of country. Find the passage from Lessing. See also Folder AA, p. 7.

A separate sheet, after the pages giving the text, contains several quotations relative to this paragraph:

Aspiration for change. Idea of a catastrophe.

Jacobi, Woldemar: "it seems that we are on the eve of a great change."

Forster writes to Jacobi (1779): "Things can't stay the way they are. All the signs announce it, in the learned world and in the theological and political worlds. As much as my soul has until now desired peace, so much does it desire to see this crisis arrive, on which it has built great hope.

To his father (1782): "Europe seems to me on the point of a horrible revolution. In fact the whole thing is so corrupt that a bleeding could well be necessary." See v. 2, p. 286.

Page 30, line 3

Friedrich-Heinrich Jacobi, Woldemar (1779, 2 vols.). French translation by Vandelbourg, 2 vols., Paris, Year IV, v. 1, pp. 154–55.

Page 30, line 10

Jacobi, Woldemar, pp. 277–78. The exact quotation reads: "Such has been the fate of all the forms of humanity which are known to us: all have destroyed themselves and we live in the midst of their ruins; a monstrous chaos which everywhere presents the image of death and corruption."

Page 31, line 5

Left blank in the text.

Page 31, line 11

Tocqueville notes here: Quotation from Perthes. Folder AA, p. 9. See also the quotation and what is to be derived from Haüsser, Folder AA, p. 29.

The text breaks off. At the bottom of the page are some indications of what should follow:

Literary life, polite society

Then, head in the clouds

Literary revolution in Germany

A traveler around the world

German school

Illuminati. Supernatural things.

American Revolution

England not escaping from this sort of universal epidemic. It merely felt it in its own particular way.

On the next page:

At the end of this whole picture, suddenly double back on myself: What is all this? Is it a situation without a cause? A pure caprice of the human mind?

How this confused uneasiness in the human mind suddenly became a precise and definite political passion in France.

How this passion at first was the love of freedom.

How the upper classes felt it first and began the Revolution.

Page 31, line 11

The reference is to a dialogue between the publisher Frédéric-Christophe Perthes (1772–1843) and Stolberg. In 1856 Tocqueville read Perthes' biography, written by his son, the jurist Clemens-Theodor Perthes, Friedrich Perthes Leben nach dessen schriftliche, und mündliche, Mittheilungen aufgezeichnet von Clemens-Theodor Perthes (3 vols., Hamburg and Gotha, 1848). The quotation is found in v. 1, p. 178. On Perthes, see Tocqueville's excerpts below, and on the duration of the taste for destruction, see the quotations from Haüsser cited below.

Page 31, line 30

Summary of Perthes' life, Friedrich Perthes, v. 1, p. 58.

Page 31, line 30

In the margin of the paragraph: Paint all this well. Some citations if possible. This can give the picture life.

In the Rubbish file: At the point where I depict the society of that time: The spectacle of this society was after all, in spite of all the errors and absurdities of the times, one of the greatest humanity has ever presented. There was a strong movement which pulled all men (beyond the lower classes) above petty interests, petty individual passions, and the routine of business, and led them to the study of general truths: people apparently were ashamed of being concerned only with themselves or even with their own country, they wanted to think of humanity as a whole, to work for its perfection.

"We believed then," says Perthes, "that by becoming very educated we could become perfect."

At the heart of the commercial city par excellence, Hamburg, among the very people who ran businesses, this ardent and disinterested intellectual activity, this taste for high subjects of conversation, this passion for ideas reigned. One saw there men of letters, philosophers, artists as well as businessmen, thus discussing above all politics and philosophy. Eminent men of different kinds met: people debated endlessly the greatest problems of the individual and society, they got excited, they fought (all this applies to 1794 but it is the tail end of an old movement).

One of the richest citizens of Hamburg (Sieveking) gathered all these elements at his country house and created a great center for the whole intellectual movement. Around his wife every evening there were seventy or eighty guests among whom the greatest questions of the times and of all time were discussed in conversation.

I dare state, says Forster's wife, that then (1774) the bourgeoisie and the young nobles, without excepting the Catholic countries of Germany, had more intellectual life than today . . .

Alas! How little those born at the end of a long revolution resemble those who began it!

Page 31, line 39
In the margin of the paragraph: Very different from the men of our day, who resemble the mercenary who, tired from the day's work, returns home without wanting to think of anything but his dinner and his bed.

Page 32, line 1
Marginal note: Reread the translated page of Forster's correspondence and put part of it into the text. Folder AA, p. 17.

Page 32, line 8
In 1857 Tocqueville read Forster's correspondence published by his wife, Thérèse Huber: Johan-Georg Forsters Briefwechsel. Nebst Einigen Nachrichten von seinem Leben (Leipzig, 2 vols., 1828–29). Forster (Johan-Georg Adam), 1754–1794, a German naturalist, had accompanied his father, who was attached as a naturalist to Cook's second expedition in 1772, and published an account of that voyage (A Voyage Round the World in His Britannic Majesty's Sloop 'Resolution,' Commanded

by Capt. James Cook, During the Years 1772, 3, 4, 5, London, 1777). Tocqueville is
inspired here by a fragment of the biography written by Thérèse Huber (v. 1, p. 60),
from which his notes give the following translation:

Forster was, when he came to Germany in 1774, the first traveler around the
world whom the educated world had met personally. Today, when we have seen
so many famous men, read so many scientific ideas, and when the educated public has reached a kind of satiation, we cannot have any idea of the interest and
curiosity with which Forster was met in every town where he stopped . . .

He was thus received by educated Germany with avid curiosity, with goodwill,
and even with enthusiasm. Sovereigns lured him to them; the nobility invited him,
the bourgeoisie pressed around his feet. For the scholars themselves his conversation had incomparable interest: for Michaelis, Heyne, Herder, and other men
who sought to penetrate the secrets of the past and the history of the human
species, Forster seemed to open up sources from the primitive world, by making known those peoples of the South Seas who had not been educated by any
kind of civilization, and revealing a nature on which the power of man had not
yet been exercised. In the few years that Forster then passed at Kassel, a well-
brought-up man never passed through that place without trying to meet the famous Forster. When he traveled to Vienna, he excited the same kind of eagerness
in Bohemia and Austria.

Basedow (1723–1790) was a German theologian and educator who founded the
Philanthropinum at Dessau in 1774, a boarding school for children from six to six-
teen years old and also a teacher-training institute. In the same year he published a
manual of elementary education. Tocqueville notes that according to Schlosser (Ge-
schichte des Achtzehnten Jahrhunderts, v. 7, p. 33) he had been excommunicated in
1768. Michaelis (Johann-David), 1717–1791, a German philosopher and orientalist;
Heyne (Christian-Gottlob), 1729–1812, a German philologist and antiquarian; Her-
der (Johann-Gottfried), 1744–1803, the famous philosopher.

Page 32, line 37

A note from Folder AA makes this idea concrete:
Secret societies preceding the Revolution.
In truth, only the Illuminati had this character.
The Freemasons are much older.
The Swedenborgians (who, in truth, are not a secret society, although they
ended up getting mixed up with them) date from the beginning of the century.
Rosicrucians; what exactly is meant by this word? I find in Bouillet's dictionary
that this sect goes very far back, at least to the seventeenth century. They claimed
to penetrate the secrets of nature. It is chiefly before the Revolution that they are
spoken of, without my being able to define very well what occult secret is meant
by it; there is a grade within Freemasonry that bears this name.
Kabbalists go back to the Jews.

Disciples of Paracelsus from the sixteenth century.

Martinists go back to the middle of the eighteenth century, to the Spaniard Martin Pascalis and St. Martin.

Illuminati. These are the ones who above all the others are relevant to my subject, even though all the others at least revealed themselves during this period, and acted powerfully and participated in that vague and unquiet disturbance which preceded the Revolution, when this unique spectacle presented itself: 1) Belief in all kinds of folly developing amid the decline of religious belief, people believing in all kinds of invisible supernatural influences . . . except God;

2) The time when all the sciences became more positive, more founded on the precise examination of facts, was the same time when everything that had been most vague, most inexplicable, least founded on experience and reason developed and troubled minds most.

Swedenborg (1688–1772), theosophist; Martinez Pasqualis (d. 1779), of Portuguese Jewish origin, made disciples among the masons of Paris, Bordeaux, Toulouse, and Marseilles; Louis Claude de Saint Martin (1743–1803) is one of his disciples.

On the Illuminati, Tocqueville's research notes show signs of his consultation of:

—Marie-Nicolas Bouillet, Dictionnaire universel d'histoire et de géographie, Paris, 1842.

—An anonymous brochure on the sect of the Illuminati from 1789.

—Grégoire, Histoire des sectes réligieuses qui depuis le commencement du siècle dernier jusqu'à l'époque actuel, sont nés, se sont modifiés, se sont éteints dans les quatre parties du monde, Paris, 1810, 2 vols., republished in 1814.

—Mounier, De l'influence attribuée aux philosophes, aux francs-maçons et aux Illuminés sur la Révolution de France, Tübingen, 1801.

—Mirabeau (comte de), De la monarchie prussienne sous Frédéric le Grand, 4 vols., London, 1788. Volume 3 contains a section devoted to secret societies, which was written in collaboration with the German major Jacques Mauvillon.

—Friedrich Christoph Schlosser, Geschichte des Achtzehnten Jahrhunderts und des Neunzehnten bis zum Sturz des französischen Kaiserreiches, 7 vols., Heidelberg, 1843–48.

Page 33, line 11

Marginal note: It was not the crowd, not the lower classes who surrendered themselves to these follies; intellectuals and scholars believed in alchemy, the visible action of demons, the transmutation of metals, the appearance of spirits; dreams were the delight of princes above all. Forster, from Kassel, wrote to his father in 1782: There is an old French adventuress here who makes spirits appear to the landgrave: he is vain enough to think that the devil would take the trouble to tempt him in person. With her she has a Frenchman who exorcizes demons from the possessed; he presses their stomach and thus chases them from place to place until they are finally forced to clear out. The great kings have some rascals of the first order at their courts, Cagliostro, the Count of Saint Germain, Mesmer; for lack of better the petty princes content themselves with ridiculous little magicians.

Page 33, line 22

This paragraph ("In our day it is poor workers . . . ") is found in the manuscript after "were close" (page xxx), preceded by another paragraph, circled and bearing the following note in the margin: Eliminate I think this general idea, and limit myself to the particular fact which follows. In this case move it to page 7. *We follow Tocqueville's note in changing the organization. The circled paragraph reads as follows:*

What must be well noted is that this deep uneasiness, this violent and confused intellectual disturbance that I have just described was not at all noticeable among the lower classes, who, however, bore most of the weight of the abuses. These classes were still calm and silent. Thus it was not the poor man who upset himself about his condition with feverish ardor, it was the rich man. The movement only began in the upper reaches of the bourgeoisie.

Page 33, line 25

Adam Weishaupt (1748–1830), professor of Canon Law at Ingolstadt, in 1776 founded there the order of the Illuminati, which in 1784 was banned by the Bavarian government.

Page 33, line 28

In the margin: The founder of the secret society of the Illuminati was a professor of canon law. Refer to Folder AA, pp. 26 and 22.

Page 33, line 38

Heinrich Steffens, philosopher and literary writer (1773–1845), <u>Was ich erlebte</u> *(Breslau, 1840–44). Tocqueville here quotes v. 1, p. 78, then pp. 79–80.*

Page 34, line 6

The manuscript breaks off. In the margin: Translate the piece. *We substitute the passage below according to the research notes.*

Page 35, line 6

In the Rubbish, a first draft of this passage: All Europe resembled an encampment which wakes before dawn, stirs about chaotically, and heads off in every direction until the sun finally rises and shows the road that is going to be taken.

Page 35, title of chapter 2

At the top of a note for review in the folders, Tocqueville notes: A picture of the subject of the chapter, a quotation to be made from the correspondence of

Mme. de Staël: at the end of the old regime we had the freedom that excited, not that which satisfied (a good sentence). *The manuscript refers to a research note (Folder 45B YY) which is more developed and also influenced by the reading of an article by A. Geoffrey, "Madame de Staël ambassadrice, avec des papiers inédits," Revue des deux mondes. 1 November 1856, pp. 5–43:*
  Movement of the public mind at the beginning of the Revolution:
  1. First, a powerful general desire for reforms, class passions violent but latent, vague, without any precise goal, not conscious of themselves, and as if asleep in the social and political immobility. It is the end of the old regime, the point where I stopped. Here is where Illuminism should be put, after 1 and before 2, it is one stage further on.
  2. But in 1787 (*in the margin:* this sudden passage from vague disturbance to more precise passions is nowhere better marked than in the correspondence of Mme. de Staël with Gustavus III [*King of Sweden—Trans.*] from 1786 to 1789; Revue des deux mondes, 1 November 1856, p. 27). The letters before '87 are full of little anecdotes about the court, mostly very frivolous, and show only the vague ideas and passions of the times, the hatred of abuses, philanthropy.
  In 1787 the style suddenly changes. For the past six months public affairs have so much occupied all Paris, she says, that not only have they been the sole subject of general interest, but personal events themselves, I believe, have been more rare and no one wants to do something unusual at a time when no one would notice it. *The text continues:* this spirit of opposition, of novelty, of malaise, took on fixed and precise practical form. It passed from a state of vague opposition to a precise struggle. It attached itself strongly to certain people and certain things: it is the hatred of certain ministers, the passionate desire for certain men; it is above all war on the court, a still vague word which conceals the entire old regime.
  3. In the discussions about their constitution which preceded the Estates-General, class hatred, class jealousy suddenly took on precise shape and immediately showed extreme violence. The basis of people's emotions appeared, the real and fundamental character of the Revolution came to light.
  4. Then came '89 and the cahiers. In the presence of this great object, for a moment souls calmed and elevated themselves. Then class hatreds, class jealousies seemed to be forgotten for a moment, so that we could think of nothing but the greatness of what we were about to do, the beauty of the future that we were about to prepare together. Then there broke out those disinterested, generous feelings, that spirit of mutual sympathy which is astonishing. We held out our hands to each other from far away and in darkness. As soon as daylight came and we were close to one another we found ourselves face to face, and we grappled with each other.

Page 35, line 19
  Note by Tocqueville in the margin of the paragraph: But why is it that the hatred of despotism was produced first? A question which comes to mind, to which it

would be very important to be able to give a satisfying response immediately, in a few words. It was the only political passion which could be used by the upper classes, which only shifts the difficulty: for then, why did the upper classes start?

I think this happened because:

1) In the kind of discomfort that was universally felt, the thing about which it was easiest to agree was war on the political power that preserved everything which annoyed everybody.

2) Because the nobles and the rich who felt this discomfort more than anyone else could naturally show it only in this fashion.

All this is very metaphysical and not striking enough to be put at the beginning of everything this way, and furthermore pretty difficult to contain within the bounds of one or two sentences.

Page 35, line 26

On a separate page in the manuscript of chapter 3, another version: If I am asked how it happened that the Revolution started among the classes which suffered least from society's flaws, or even profited from them, I will respond that these classes themselves obeyed the general spirit of the times; but they took from it the only thing which they could use, opposition to the political power.

Page 35, line 31

In the margin of this sentence: Say something about the composition of the Notables.

Page 35, line 31

A note (Folder 45B 10) taken from L'Histoire parlementaire de la Révolution française, *by Buchez and Roux (40 vols., 1843–40), v. 1, p. 480, states the composition of the Notables:*

1) About 9 peers of France; 2) 20 nobles without rank; 3) 8 state councilors; 4) 4 masters of requests; 5) 10 marshals; 6) 13 bishops or archbishops; 7) the first presidents of the parlements, about 18; 8) various other magistrates, attorneys-general, or presidents of royal courts; 9) the municipal officials of the leading towns, about 22; 10) the deputies of the *pays d'état,* about 12 (Burgundy, Languedoc, Brittany, Artois); altogether about 125 or 135 people including the princes of the blood and the magistrates who were not first presidents.

In the margin: An assembly too numerous to be an effective council, without enough authorization to be a support.

Tocqueville's chief source for this chapter is the book by Abbé Jean-Pierre Papon, Histoire du gouvernement français depuis l'assemblée des notables tenue le 22 février 1787, jusqu'à la fin de décembre de la même année, *London, 1788, which Tocqueville judged:* well done and on the government's side, a rare thing at that time *(Folder 45B).*

Page 36, line 7
Variant sketched in the margin: These princes, great lords, these bishops, these rich bourgeois.

Page 36, line 17
First version: the reformers. *Interlinear correction:* their adversaries.

Page 36, line 21
In the margin of this paragraph: Paint the opponents well, I think, and prepare for the piece by a section containing this idea: For a long time already all the discomfort that was felt seemed to be summed up in discontent with power, and to transform itself into a spirit of opposition.

Page 36, line 23
First version: elected assembly. *Interlinear correction:* representatives of the country.

Page 36, line 26
In his research notes (Folders 45B, 45BB):
Collected Errors of Louis XVI: The list of them is immense, but it is useful to summarize a few of the chief ones.
1787. 1) When he decided to call a national council to his assistance, under the name of Notables, that is to address public opinion, not to understand that what was needed was not popular measures to propose but a popular minister to present them. The ABC of the science of government in a free state. He chose Calonne, and after he served to make the enterprise fail, he got rid of him, losing simultaneously the profit of the appeal to the people and the profit of absolute power he still held in his hands.
2) Gathering an assembly to ask its advice about finances, he did not get ahead of all the demands for information that it could have made and thought that it would help him fill a deficit whose extent he did not want to show them. O inexperience!

Page 36, line 28
In the margin, under the title:
Proof of this is the different measures proposed in conformity with the modern spirit and that of the Revolution which, however, were rejected with popular support.
End if possible by introducing here the piece on the provincial assemblies, so characteristic of the period's profound ignorance. I doubt if this will be possible without breaking the flow.
The sole purpose of this chapter is to highlight the spirit of this first period,

the struggle against the government, the love of political freedom, the hatred of absolute government and arbitrariness. It must run towards this goal.

Page 36, line 32
In the margin: What I am missing are sufficient ideas about what happened in this first Assembly of Notables.

Page 37, line 4
In the margin: Check this and the rest.

Page 37, line 9
A note in a file of diverse ideas (Folder 44.2) details this: How in 1787, when still in the midst of monarchy, the Assembly of Notables (notables and government together) tore up the whole old fabric of the monarchy in the edict on provincial assemblies. All without having the appearance of doing it and above all without realizing it.

Page 37, line 20
Report by Calonne, 7 March 1787, nonliteral quotation taken from Abbé Papon, Histoire du gouvernement français, *pp. 36–7.*

Page 37, line 33
In the margin of the paragraph: Check this.

Page 37, line 33
Nonliteral quotation from the committees taken from Papon, Histoire du gou-vernement français, *p. 23.*

Page 000, line 000
In the margin: Here perhaps a short development of the idea.

Page 39, line 6
A research note (Folder 45B YY) gives a chronology:
Different grounds on which the struggle between the government and the par-lements successively took place.
It is important to give a foreshortened picture in order to clearly understand the groups of facts:
1) First of all, after the first meetings of the Notables, all the parlements, I think, opposed the stamp tax and the land tax.
2) When after its exile to Troyes the Parlement of Paris agreed to accept the vingtièmes in their new form, several other parlements (the majority I think), not accepting this attitude, refused to register these vingtièmes.

3) Further, the edict on provincial assemblies that the Parlement of Paris and the <u>majority</u> of the other parlements accepted gave rise to violent resistance in some parlements, above all that of Bordeaux and that of Dauphiny.

4) In the month of November 1787, there occurred the royal session for the loan, after which the Duke of Orléans was exiled and two members of the Parlement of Paris arrested. Almost all the parlements took the side of the Parlement of Paris and made violent protests about the particular facts and about <u>lettres de cachet</u> in general.

5) Siege of the Palace of Justice in May 1788. Capture of d'Eprémesnil, the great event of this struggle, but which could not lead to the intervention of the other parlements, because of the coup d'état or <u>lit de justice</u> of 8 May which immediately followed.

6) Following this coup d'état, which sent all the parlements on vacation and after which all the palaces of justice were militarily occupied, an explosion of fury in all the parlements, taking place irregularly in special assemblies.

Page 39, line 10
In the margin: This is only good with respect to language.

Page 39, line 33
In the margin, an idea of the following paragraph: A new motor had just been installed in this old machine of government and was going to give it a jerkier motion than it had ever had.

Page 40, line 6
The edicts of 17 June 1787 are in question here. Tocqueville lists them in his research notes:
  1) Free trade in grains
  2) Edict for the conversion of the corvée into a money payment
  3) Provincial assemblies
  4) Land tax
  5) Stamp tax
The parlements accepted the first two without opposition, the third with amendment, they refused the last two.
In its remonstrances of 16 July 1787, the parlement rejected the stamp tax and demanded an account of income and expenditure. The remonstrances of 24 July, referring to Charles V and Henry IV, demanded the meeting of the Estates-General. After having attempted to impose the registry of the edicts by a lit de justice on the sixth of August, the king had to exile the Parlement of Paris to Troyes on the fourteenth, and then to have the edicts registered by the Tax Court and the financial chamber, which provoked their protest and that of the provincial parlements.

Page 40, line 7
In the margin of this paragraph: What makes this idea original is the contrast
of old forms and new spirit.
This is what one must try to spotlight.

Page 40, line 23
The research notes (Folder 45B YY) analyze the events of July–August 1787.
In what and how the parlement exceeded its powers and reason. What made
it popular despite this. July 1787.
With regard to the stamp tax the parlement asked that it be given the accounts
of income and expenditure.
This exorbitant claim was exactly what made it popular.
What must be well noted here is that while ardently supporting the parlement,
the public understood perfectly that this body was going beyond its powers. The
public was very aware of the personal passions and narrow views which led the
magistrates to act. It covered them with applause all the while blaming them and
despising them in petto. And as soon as the circumstances were different, the
opinions people arrived at during this same struggle in which the parlement was
their champion served to overturn it.
I have often seen this in politics, in assemblies and in masses: not only do those
who are pushed by a torrent of opinion not realize that it is what they are doing
that is approved and not they themselves; that the act they support is important
and not them; but they do not realize that what supports them so strongly diminishes them and will be imputed as their crime when the real object of public
passions is attained or forgotten.
Difficulty of resistance for the king. Almost impossible. How from the minute
when people took seriously the doctrine that the laws needed to be communicated to the parlements, freely registered by them, and for this registry discussed,
debated in their midst as if in a political assembly—not only certain laws, like
tax laws, but all laws, not only the general principle of the laws but their details
of execution, that is all of government—in a word as soon as the legislative power
found itself, in effect, shared between the parlements and the king—government
was much more difficult with them than with a single assembly. The action of all
these bodies was not only powerful but absolutely irresistible, for one could neither intimidate them, nor win them over, nor dissolve them as one could have
done with a grand assembly. The difficulty was to give this whole machine the
same impulse, but once that was done, it was less easy to stop and break than any
other; for, independently of the power of each of these bodies, they rallied all the
lower jurisdictions, and all those who were in any respect whatsoever attached to
the justice system, which created an immense mass capable of crushing any government beneath its weight.
Faced by the parlement's resistance, the king had the edicts of 17 June registered

by a lit de justice *on 6 August 1787. Here is how Tocqueville comments on this session (Folder 45B, BB):*

The king's propositions were not only good, but in the interest of the lower classes (examine them if I want to treat this subject in more depth, as well as all the transcripts of the parlementary sessions). However, in this first struggle popularity was not on the king's side, but on that of the parlement. Two lessons to be drawn from this:

1) The first lesson is that in politics we are always very wrong to judge the impression an action will produce by its intrinsic value, whether for good or evil. Its influence depends chiefly on the circumstances in which it is taken, and above all on the person from whom it comes. This is why politics cannot be a science or even an art. We do not find any fixed rules here, not even that to please people one must do what is useful to them. When the circumstances as a whole make a power popular one accepts even harm from it voluntarily. Unpopular, even its benefits wound.

2) The second lesson is how hard it is for one who is the object of popular favor to see what is really behind an event and the real sources of the power which is thus put at his disposal.

The parlement thought it could fight the king by virtue of its constitution, its antiquity . . . by everything which had been its roots and strength in former times. It did not realize that it no longer had any roots and was an old tool, whose only strength came from the hand which used it. Fundamentally people did not have any consideration for the parlement, they used it while expecting better. The parlement thought it was participating in one of those struggles whose course or, to put it better, whose routine was known. It did not see that it was participating in something in which it was only a little insignificant incident. The parlement calculated that what made it strong was the old favor it enjoyed, while its strength came to it by chance from a state of public opinion which was not only not favorable to it, but which was positively hostile to it as to all old institutions. How many times in my own day have I seen the same play performed by other actors on a smaller stage!

There followed a rebellion by all the parlements which is analyzed in the notes (Folder 45B-BB):

General remark. The impossibility of governing.

As long as the parlements only used registration in very rare cases, for extraordinary things or for corrections or modifications of detail, one could govern with them, and they were a dike which was irregular but useful, which hindered abuses of power without preventing its exercise.

But from the moment when the right of registration was understood as:

1) A means to be exercised equally by the thirteen parlements.

2) A means to be used in all matters which could give rise to any government whatsoever.

3) A means of running things that became daily and usual, requiring simultaneously the discussion of the measure and its means of execution, I say that from
then on government was not only difficult, but absolutely impossible.

To govern and administer with thirteen assemblies, all with particular points
of view and composed not of administrators or of simple citizens, but of judges,
was impossible. This could only be practical when dealing with only one parlement, that of Paris, and finding it willing to consider registration only a matter of
form, remonstrances the rare exception, and above all to limit its field of action
by a sort of tacit agreement.

Page 40, line 31

Note in the margin: Gather and accumulate here, in order to present them all
at once, all the new theories presented by the parlements throughout the struggle;
as much as possible clothe them in the revolutionary words already used; finally,
make the philosophy of the eighteenth century show through clearly, and note
the republican spirit showing its head through the old monarchical tatters.

Page 41, line 2

In the margin of this paragraph: The actors using the same language without
realizing that this time the play is different and the audience changed.

Page 41, line 18

The research notes (Folders 45B-BB) develop this point:

Inflated language. The inflation of feelings, the exaggeration of words, the
incoherence and extravagance of images, the quotations from antiquity . . .
which characterized revolutionary language were already in the nation's habits
of speech.

People were not allowed to be calm about anything. Passion itself, which was
at the bottom of people's hearts, was furthermore in most cases, even among
those who hardly felt it, a necessary common bond, and as a result people were
not allowed to speak of anything simply, expression always had to go a great deal
beyond the idea or the feeling to be expressed.

It is a striking thing, further, that the magistrates' style had always been an
exaggerated style. It always struck the target it was aiming at with violence and
seemed to want to compensate for the usual fruitless result of its remonstrances
by the violence of its words.

*Tocqueville gives some examples of the parlements' emphatic language in his
notes taken on official documents in January 1857:*

24 July '87. Remonstrances: a sharp lesson given to the king.

The general style of these remonstrances is to give a pretty rude lesson to the
king, both in form and substance. One cannot say that this is absolutely new. The
parlements had often used, even under the most powerful kings who had preceded Louis XIV, language whose firmness went as far as rudeness. But for one

thing the king, established amid solid and uncontested institutions, could tolerate this language; further, the same parlement which spoke to him so crudely and scolded him was his chief support against powers he feared far more: the nobility and the Church. Thus the king was not angry to see the parlement take this independent tone, which increased the strength of the tool in his hands.

There was thus established a kind of tradition of frank speech, of bold and even exaggerated style when speaking to the king, which was connected neither in the king's mind nor in the nation's, nor even in the parlement's, to corresponding acts; it was a sort of useless noise authorized by custom. The king allowed himself to be spoken to by his parlement and took in good part things which would have appeared high treason to him from an assembly of nobles or from a great lord.

These habits from an old feudal society, transported into a democratic society where the lower classes were going to play the leading role, instead of producing useless noise could not fail to make a revolution. In our day there is no sovereign power, even in the freest state, which could allow language like the language the Parlement of Paris spoke to the king in the decrees I am analyzing to be spoken to it without a conflict or a revolution beginning. In the conduct and language of the parlement there was an anachronism it did not perceive, but which the result would suddenly demonstrate.

Here are the most significant of the examples analyzed by Tocqueville relative to the provincial parlements in 1787:

Parlement of Toulouse. 27 August '87, on the occasion of the exile of the Parlement of Paris. I think that up to the present this is the one whose language is the most violent and least mixed with old formulas of respect and praise, which are sometimes combined in such a ridiculous way in the manifestos of the other parlements. (*In the margin:* In general, the others say to the king, almost in these words: You have governed very badly; you have let your subjects be devoured by courtiers and tax collectors. You want to subject them and take away their essential rights, but you are nevertheless the best king and above all you have the best heart of all kings. These contrary assertions are often so close to one another that from the first one can jump without any intermediary into the second.) I do not know if in revolutionary periods and after civil wars anyone has ever spoken a more revolutionary language. Far from being astonished that such language brought about a revolution, we should admire the power of the old institutions, which allowed such language to be spoken for a long time without overthrowing any authority whatsoever. I claim that today there is no government in Europe strong enough to bear anything like it: "The nation must be saved from the oppression which threatens it; the people tormented by the tax collectors' exactions are at the last extremity, taxes already take three-quarters of France's income." . . .

Parlement of Brittany . . . More traditional character of the violent language of the Parlement of Brittany. This parlement certainly asks for the Estates-

General by virtue of absolute principles, but the language is less abstract, all the passions of the day covered by infinite citations of precedents and texts of old ordinances and old authors.

Parlement of Bordeaux. 8 August '87 . . . Clever partisan language, which is used in this decree by the parlement in order to deprive the king of the popularity which belonged to him by right when it was a question of the provincial assemblies: the plan for provincial assemblies is based on an excellent idea, but in the minds of those who wish to establish them today it could well be merely a trap hiding a tax-collecting institution and a later tax increase. Return to this idea in the decree of 7 September '87: The measure is good in itself but coming from a plundering minister must be suspect. The people may suspect that the purpose of the provincial assemblies is to acquire exact knowledge of every individual's income and not to decrease the total taxes, and that one proposed to tax those funds which paid less rather than help those who paid too much. It is difficult to imagine an appeal in worse faith to the people's blindest and most avaricious passions.

A separate page in the same folder states the synthesis:

General remarks suggested by the reading of the various documents of this year.

Nothing which spreads a feeling of equality in all these writings, and several which show contrary feelings. See notably the Parlement of Grenoble.

How this violent language with regard to taxes became common: 1) No link between those who established and raised the taxes and those who paid them. On the contrary, struggles and chronic and hereditary jealousies between these two kinds of people.

2) The tax collectors freely considered by the king himself as a third party whom one could allow to be insulted without any consequences, a kind of scapegoat to give public opinion to distract it from the real authors of the taxes.

3) The struggle with the government was a chronic situation. The language used with it a sort of accepted language. One couldn't say today a quarter of what the parlement said between 1787 and 1789 without bringing about a violent revolution.

Not only the same ideas, but the same words: taxes are always catastrophic. The actions of the authorities against the parlement threw it into consternation. Never less than this.

Since the government had been created by continuous and very great force of action combined with great respect for old forms and great freedom left to language from time to time, one could find arguments everywhere in our history: actions on the side of power, maxims on the side of freedom.

Page 42, line 4

In the margin of the development which begins here: Here, I think, the piece on provincial assemblies (it interrupts the flow of facts since it talks about agreement in the middle of a piece intended to show struggle). Nevertheless, it contains a characteristic very necessary to highlight, for nothing shows better how deep political ignorance was, and how the <u>involuntary</u> disorganization of society was its consequence. Since this is an appetizer, it can only be done as a vivid contrast; also, just when I make the struggle's <u>violence</u> most visible, show this <u>unconscious</u> agreement.

From this point of view, the place I want to give this piece is not the best chosen, since the last phase of the piece, which would follow, indicates a kind of agreement between the government and the parlement to attack the <u>tax-farmers</u>.

Page 42, line 19

In his research notes (Folder 45B-BB) Tocqueville gives the following analysis of the royal project for provincial assemblies presented to the Notables of 1787:
1) <u>Elective assemblies</u>
2) Elected every three years
3) Taken from all estates without distinction

These assemblies will be elected in their first degree in the rural parishes and the towns, at the second degree in districts containing a certain number of parishes and towns of the area combined, and at the third degree at a meeting of the whole province so that there will be three kinds of assembly:
1) Parish and municipal assemblies composed of property owners
2) District assemblies composed of deputies from towns and parishes
3) Finally, provincial assemblies whose members will be delegated by the districts

We see that this plan left the old regime behind completely, brusquely throwing society onto a new basis. It was a radical destruction of the entire old order of things such as the Middle Ages had created it and whose traces survived. To prove this: it was the country's entire government without the nobility and clergy. When we see the king, without anything forcing him to, put forward such a plan, we must conclude:
1) To what point the old society was dead within people's minds without their realizing it.
2) How natural it was that all the ideas created with respect to the Estates-General were produced.

Next, studying the composition of the parish assemblies, Tocqueville notes: According to the plan, it was necessary to have an income of 600 livres to vote in the parish. This was <u>aristocratic</u> but no longer <u>noble</u>. Those who did not have 600 livres could join <u>together</u> until that sum was reached in order to name a representative. It is absolutely Turgot's plan, without any trace of new ideas.

Page 42, line 27

In the margin: In this old struggle a very characteristic novelty of this period is the king discussing the origin of powers, the rights of the monarchy . . . instead of the matter in question.

Page 42, line 35

Variant of this passage sketched in the margin of the sentence which follows:
One side attacked a power that it didn't want to destroy, the other established
only hateful rights which it did not want to use. A dangerous game on both sides.

Page 42, line 35

After aristocracy: At the same time as the government spoke this new language,
it went to the weapons of the old despotism to look for the least used and most
offensive to the spirit of the times. After having allowed his rights to be disputed
in front of him, the king tried to take them back with violence. He himself had
opened the orators' mouths, he wanted to punish them for having spoken. The
arrest of the two chief speakers was ordered, and what is very characteristic of
the spirit of the moment is that one of these tribunes was a noble by birth and
the other was an abbé.

This passage is eliminated by a marginal remark: Perhaps take another road to
3 arrive at the session at the Palace *[of Justice—Trans.]* and say without transition:
"While . . ." *Tocqueville here confuses the member of parlement Honoré-Auguste
Sabatier de Labre with the "abbé" Sabatier, writer, opponent of the philosophes,
who furthermore was not a member of the parlement.*

Page 43, line 5

*Tocqueville is referring here to the meeting of 19 November 1787 when the king,
having been constrained by the resistance of the parlements to recall the Parlement
of Paris (20 September) and withdraw the two contested edicts, attempted to have a
loan registered without wishing to make his promise to call the Estates-General
specific. In his research notes on the abbé Papon's work, pp. 231ff., Tocqueville comments thus:*

The king himself becomes a theoretician.

Here the king, entering the dangerous ground of political theory, has his chancellor establish that he is an absolute monarch, even though he consents to allow
his laws to be debated before him.

Then he allows everyone to talk for seven hours. Discussed in front of him are
all the theses most contrary to his power, and often in violent terms. After which
the king does not have the votes counted, but orders the registration. Finally he
promises the Estates-General for 1791. He leaves and the next day orders the exile
of the Duke of Orléans, and two magistrates who had spoken violently are carried off to prison. One could not combine more mistakes:

1) To have a government measure debated before a great assembly, when one
knows that it will be violently attacked and badly defended, is to range against
oneself all the inconveniences of government by assemblies without any of its
advantages.

2) To have the very principles of government debated and to attract minds to
this subject or let them be attracted is still more absurd.

3) After having invited people to speak freely (sic), to put them in prison without trial and with harshness is to show despotism, which was already the black beast of the Apocalypse in the nation's eyes, in its most odious and least justifiable form.

4) Finally, to promise the Estates-General without assembling them was to strangely misunderstand the course of human passions once excited, and particularly those of the French.

It is superfluous to say that although the parlement was rebellious, in this situation it was more and more popular despite this and in part because of it (p. 259).

After the failure of this session, on 20 November the king exiled the most virulent of the orators: the Duke of Orléans, Freteau, and Sabatier.

The whole nation interested in the imprisoned magistrates. We see well how the spirit of freedom and the hatred of despotism and authority was the spirit which then inspired the entire nation, so that everyone felt himself injured by the harm done to the personal liberty of two men. This is the very soul of political freedom, but it inhabited the body of France only by chance and for a moment (p. 264).

Page 43, line 7
First version: the least hateful. *Interlinear correction:* the least feared.

Page 43, line 11
In the margin of this paragraph there is an outline of the development which follows:
Gradation of the attempts at constraint:
1) One exiles some members individually
2) One exiles the parlement as a body
3) One has two of its members imprisoned
4) Finally one takes away its chief powers, acts without its participation

Page 43, line 13
Doubtless writing, as was often the case, without his notes, Tocqueville here combines two different events: the exile on 20 November of the Duke of Orléans, Freteau, and Sabatier; and the arrest on 6 May 1788 of Duval d'Eprémesnil and Goislard de Montsabert, leaders of the parlementary opposition. The confusion probably comes from the fact d'Eprémesnil is noted by Abbé Papon as one of the leading speakers during the session of 19 November 1787.

Page 43, line 14
In the margin: This must be told in order to show how the established powers acted so as to teach the people how to overthrow them. I have noticed a hundred times that the success of measures has much less to do with the good-

ness of the measures in themselves than with the popularity enjoyed by those who take them.

Page 43, line 25
In the margin: The difficulty and danger of what I do here is that I cannot enter into the narrative of events enough to interest the reader in the facts, and yet the little that I do go into the story slows down the idea.

Page 43, line 35, after "cede"
Crossed out: We were then in the shortest days of the year.

Page 44, line 4
The parlement had declared the two councilors who had taken refuge in its midst "under the protection of the law." In fact, it was only at eleven o'clock on the morning of the sixth that d'Eprémesnil gave himself up.

Page 44, line 20
In the margin: It is absolutely necessary to speak of the union of all the parlements and to paint the whole judicial riot before getting to the other classes; this is necessary:
   1) Because it is the natural order of the facts and the ideas which derive from them.
   2) Because the May edicts will be inexplicable without this . . . It is absolutely necessary to speak about the May edicts. It is a base which cannot be dispensed with to build the rest of the ideas on.
Tocqueville did not continue with this project.

Page 44, line 20
On 8 May 1788 the king imposed the registration of the six edicts prepared by the chancellor Lamoignon. The edicts immediately provoked the resistance of the parlements and the provincial estates. In his notes Tocqueville showed the already revolutionary character of these edicts, imposed in the last lit de justice *of the monarchy (Folder 45B-BB):*
How the king fully entered into the spirit of the times and even the Revolution's own path yet could not become popular.
   1) The law brought closer to suitors—An organization similar to today's yet unable to achieve popularity:
      A) county courts (the presidials) whose jurisdiction was increased;
      B) District courts which would judge criminal trials as courts of last resort and civil trials concerning less than 20,000 livres;
      C) the parlements for trials exceeding 20,000 livres and for the special cases of the privileged.

We see that these are our courts of first instance and our contemporary courts of appeal. (*In the margin:* On 25 September 1788, the parlement having met for the first time, the advocate-general Séguier criticized the edicts before it and in particular this one, against which he raised the most illusory objections, considering as impractical what has always taken place with the greatest of ease since 1789. Curious to read and perhaps useful to say.)

The parlement, which was allowed to continue to exist while having its jurisdiction reduced, was evidently a superfluity that was maintained in order not to attack the sovereign courts too violently, but it was a useless piece which ought to disappear from the system when it was convenient.

2) Elimination of all exceptional courts and the return of all disputes judged there to the presidial courts, the district courts, or the parlements, depending on the importance of the issue.

This immense reform was in conformity with all the new ideas with regard to the simplification and unity of justice. It destroyed a multitude of venal offices, another wish that was universally expressed.

It was essentially liberal since it returned all disputes in which the government was concerned to the ordinary courts.

This side struck contemporaries less than us, because the exceptional courts being composed of people who were equally independent and irremovable, they only saw in them the inconveniences of a bad system of justice, where we see above all the action of a one-sided judicial system.

Moreoever, we do not see that the edict affects that part of administrative justice exercised by the intendants and the Royal Council.

3) Reform of the Penal Code.

a) Sentences of death will be followed by a delay before their execution, a delay during which one could always appeal to the king.

b) The use of the culprit's seat, which dishonored an unconvicted accused, eliminated.

c) Judges required to justify criminal arrests.

d) Torture abolished.

e) Payments given to acquitted defendants.

All this strongly demanded by public opinion, all in the spirit of the new times, all realized since, except the last point.

4) Reduction of the number of positions in the parlement. This was the natural result of the decrease of its business. The king correctly states that the principle of irremovability concerns only individuals and cannot prevent the elimination of positions.

Precautions taken to make the position of those whose jobs are eliminated less difficult: positions repaid immediately, right to succeed to vacancies. There is absolutely nothing here that anyone except the parlement could complain about.

5) Establishment of a supreme court. This is the most direct blow at the par-

lements. Registration and consequently the right of remonstrance are taken away from them and given to a single body where they had considerable representation, but which nevertheless took political power out of their hands.

Motivations in accord with the spirit of the times. The reasons the king gave were excellent and in conformity with the secret passions of the times, the unity and uniformity of the law. Nevertheless, people saw in the reforms only the triumph of absolute government. This measure had several problems:

A) It struck the entire magistrature as well as the Parlement of Paris.

B) However, it allowed the parlements to subsist.

C) It was useless if one really intended to call the Estates-General. It was an immense useless disturbance, for the arrival of the Estates-General would eliminate resistance by the magistrates.

D) Finally, it created a single and very powerful body which, in certain circumstances, could have been a very great threat.

6) All the parlements prorogued: justice suspended throughout the kingdom. It was impossible to take a more effective measure to simultaneously upset and damage all classes and strike all imaginations.

The Estates-General should have been called immediately.

Page 44, line 23

In the margin: separation of powers, equality of taxation.

Page 44, line 30

In the margin of the draft of this passage: Two ideas must be distinguished:

1) The action of the parlements in opposite ways, as when it was a question of the edict on provincial assemblies.

2) The centralized action of the parlements. All having not only the same spirit of resistance, but claiming to be only the separated members of the same body.

The Parlement of Paris tacitly considered the political director of the others.

Thus resistance was everywhere. It was a body where one didn't know where to find the head to strike it.

Show that this judicial riot was particularly dangerous, which brings me to the May edicts.

Page 45, line 12

In the margin of a first version of this passage, circled: It is very necessary 1) to read La Fronde by M. de Saint Aulaire; 2) to look again at the remonstrances of 1770 (I am sure that there will be several new ideas through comparison with these periods). *The final version of the paragraph is on an added page.*

Page 45, line 17

In his research notes (Folders 45B, CC) Tocqueville remarks:

<u>Unanimity and monotony of the parlementary resistance:</u> What makes it use-less to summarize the individual remonstrances of 1788 is that they come from <u>all</u> the parlements, they <u>all</u> have the same purposes, <u>all</u> say the same thing and <u>all in</u> the same tone. Whoever has read the remonstrances of the Parlement of <u>Paris</u> has read them all . . . Nothing shows better 1) how similar position and profes-sional education can make a single group out of different ones; 2) how all the different parts of France were already homogeneous, ideas similar, rights not much different, local spirit destroyed, since nowhere does one sense appear, even confusedly, anything particular to a province, unless there is something Breton which still remains embedded even in the general ideas which are expressed in Brittany.

Commenting later on about the remonstrances of the Parlement of Normandy of 8 June 1788, Tocqueville notes: <u>In this last struggle the parlements make much more use of traditional arguments than before.</u> The parlements, beside them-selves because of the violent and personal attack they are subjected to, use all the arguments they can think of pell-mell. Having to defend <u>themselves</u>, they are forced to go back to arguments which all have a traditional origin: old customs, acquired rights, precedents, provincial privileges . . . arguments they could avoid making when they fought on the ground of taxation or of individual freedom. It results that in a struggle begun with popular support and popular arguments, they ended up using the least popular arguments. Their origin and their particu-lar situation is stronger than their general ideas and comes back to dominate them. *In the margin of this paragraph:* These bold innovators, says the Parlement of Normandy, who have dared to present the fatal plan of returning all things to a system of <u>unity</u>, who reject the diversity of ranks, of privileges, of provinces' individual rights, the diversity of customs . . . Those who were beginning the Revolution announce as a great crime what was the Revolution's own purpose, and was going to be this Revolution's final effect.

Page 45, line 23

In a circled paragraph: Pay attention now to what is said throughout the coun-try at the same time. Everywhere the same ideas appear expressed in exactly the same way. So that what at first appears to show only the unity of the judiciary demonstrates the prodigious unity of the nation. *In a marginal note to this para-graph:* All this takes the mind away from the rapid track on which the writing must make it run. *The text continues with a first draft of the paragraph which follows, whose final version is found on an added page.*

Page 45, line 30

In the margin: Note to consult. Already, I think, eighteen years before, during the war between the parlements and Louis XV, the same attempt had been made and the union of all the parlements of the kingdom attempted, and I think in part accomplished (carefully check the history of this first act).

But before 1770, nothing like it had ever been seen in France, because nothing like it could come out of the institutions, the mores, and the ideas of those times, amid the diversity of each province's laws and the dissimilarity and separation of interests.

Page 45, line 32

First version: parlements "attacking like a crowd, aiming like a single man." *Present text in an interlinear correction.*

Page 46, line 2

Marginal note: An idea to highlight and which leads to the picture which follows.

Page 46, line 13

In the margin of this paragraph: Perhaps instead of this, after having painted this resistance by the parlements, simultaneously multiple and united, go right to this: Each parlement thus formed a point of resistance to which all the orders of each province came, to find support to hold firm against the action of the central power.

The other movement is worth more, I think. The sentence here is good, but put it elsewhere.

Page 46, line 33

First version: the bourgeoisie. *Interlinear correction:* other classes.

Page 47, line 2

On this opposition by the nobility, the clergy, and the Third Estate, see the excerpts from political pamphlets in the appendix to chapter 5.

Page 47, line 16

In fact the last assembly of the clergy of France was held from 5 May to 5 August, at the convent of the Grands-Augustins in Paris.

Page 48, line 3

In the margin: Good enough and true.

Page 48, line 22

In the margin: All kinds of writings; perhaps reserve the depiction of this literary flood until the following period.

Page 49, line 4

Now, let us for a moment close our ears to the sounds of these tumultuous noises, which come from all the middle and upper classes of the nation, in order to listen for a while to the muffled noise which begins to arise from among the lower classes. *First version, correction on a separate page.*

Page 49, line 13

First version: The lower classes were at first seemingly strangers to what the upper classes did, and seemingly indifferent to the noise that was made above their heads. They listen, they look, they are astonished at the sight, they seem to be more interested than angry, but as soon as they start to act, one perceives that a new spirit moves them; when the triumphant magistrates return to Paris, the people, who had done nothing to defend the judges arrested at their seats, assemble tumultuously to celebrate their return. *Corrected text in the margin.*

In the margin of the first version under the correction: In certain provincial towns, when they wanted to arrest the judge, the lower classes gathered and resisted. *It was doubtless in order to take this reservation into account that Tocqueville limited the analysis of the rural lower classes.*

Page 49, line 15

Word missing.

Page 49, line 28

Variant sketched in the margin: Took up again its old weapons, but to use them with a wavering hand whose blows were strong enough to irritate, not powerful enough to kill.

Page 49, line 39

In the margin: Perhaps find means to introduce here the picture of the machinery of government functioning <u>all by itself</u>: its agents continuing their little jobs in the same way, in the same spirit, making their plans

Page 49, line 39

In his notes on the pamphlets of 1788 which appeared after the edicts, Tocqueville gives several examples of these progovernment brochures, of which the following are the most characteristic:

"Advice to Ladies," *a pamphlet which responds to the "Very Humble Remonstrances of the Women of France," where the women demand their right to govern the state.* Between 8 May and September 1788. One of those brochures doubtless put out by the government to influence high society.

Pretty interesting and unusual in showing how high society, fashion, women had entered into opposition. The author enters a salon where there are four charming women, a great lord, a clergyman, some bourgeois (all the personnel of an old-regime salon). These women preach national freedom. We remember the first assemblies on the Champs de Mars . . . The young clergyman wants to support the monarchist party. The great lord attacks him first, then the three marquis go down. Then, all reserve is lost and all the women together attack the clergy-man, who, treated as a traitor and a vile slave, is obliged to flee as fast as he can. The author rightly says to the women: But don't you know that what you are asking for is the destruction of your own power! Do you want, instead of being the arbiters of all things, to be reduced, as in England, to the department of tea? Business, honors, everything is in your hands. If that Anglican sap which is fer-menting in people's minds pushes us into the depths of politics, in middle-class fashion duchesses will be transformed into mothers of families, and will become pure reproductive machines . . . *(p. 9)*.

What proves this society's incurable frivolity, is that all these things (which seem to be said in order to prove what is wrong with the existing regime) secretly are said in order to show its advantages.

"Demand of the Third Estate to the King." After the edicts of 8 May *(1788, n.d., 8 pages)*. Anonymous. One of the brochures attributed to an author subsi-dized by the court.

Remarkable in that at this period of 1788 it presents the only trace of the class passions which fill all the year's end, and it is the government and its agents who fire up and excite class passions.

In this writing one tries to prove that what motivates the parlement is a ques-tion of privilege. They want to keep the right not to pay taxes. One tries to dem-onstrate that it is really a question of a formidable alliance between the military nobility and the judicial nobility in order, under the banner of freedom, to con-tinue to subject and humiliate the Third Estate, which the king alone defends and wants to help. That indeed reform is necessary, but directed by the king and the Third Estate against the privileged orders. A premature attempt, but well worthy of being considered, through the union of democracy and absolute power to destroy privileges and aristocracy to the profit of absolutism. An attempt re-peated so often and so successfully since.

Page 50, line 1
In the margin: Do an animated but brief account of this incident.

Page 50, line 3
In the margin:
Special situation of the province.
The *taille réelle.*
The old estates.
Grievances between the classes previously perhaps stronger than elsewhere. But for a moment all particular passions silenced by the common passion.

Page 50, line 5
First version: Made together, but tumultuously. *Interlinear correction:* sepa-rately and independently.

Page 50, line 9
A blank. The provincial estates of Dauphiny had been suspended by an edict of July 1628.

Page 50, line 10
A blank. Vizille is situated about ten miles south of Grenoble.

Page 50, line 13
On the events in Dauphiny, see the appendix to chapter 3.

Page 50, line 35
In his research notes (Folder 45B-BB) on the abbé Papon's book, Tocqueville comments:
The king surrenders. Could he have resisted?
The king ends up by giving in for the most part. On 17 September the parlement agreed to register an extension of the vingtièmes, which might seem to approach the land tax it had not wanted to accept. The king on his part recalled the parlement, withdrew the stamp tax and the land tax . . .
If the king wanted to stay the king of the old monarchy, this is what he could not do at any cost. Once this moment had passed, all kinds of concessions were necessary, unless there was a change in public opinion. But arrived where he was, and with opinion excited the way it was, could the king have resisted? I doubt it. We don't take enough account in human affairs of the power of resistance of an opinion which is not armed, but is universal. Because resistance may not seem considerable on any particular point and is seemingly invisible; it nevertheless exercises such general pressure then, makes itself felt so much, over the whole extent of power simultaneously, if one can speak thus, that it becomes irresistible. It is like the excessive thinning of the air, which even though invisible nevertheless makes itself felt over the whole surface of the human body and reduces the strongest man to inertia. If one really wants to take public opinion into account, we will see that even the most stable and best-armed government cannot execute its will without the aid or at least the sympathy of part of the nation. Only a conqueror at the head of a foreign force can escape this law. But in 1787 the king had no one on his side. All the new passions were ardent against him; all the interests which favored his power were blind to the threat. He was alone. It would have been easier to resist violently after the summoning of the Estates-General and after the Constituent Assembly, when a large party was already opposed to the Revolution, when the Revolution had shown its character, than in 1787. Napoleon said that it was still possible on 10 August 1792. I am led to believe it.
Opinion was so unanimous and so general in 1787 that while recognizing the defeat of royal power, people accused the parlement of weakness and the desire to sacrifice the public cause to its ease.
On a separate page: At the place where I show the king surrendering, make it

clear that this time it was not a matter of concessions on details. It was absolute government that was being given up. One agreed to share the government and pledged this to the country by finally seriously accepting the Estates General.

All this is necessary, among other things, in order to make it understood in the following chapter how the parlement, which was only a weapon against absolute power, immediately became nothing once that power was defeated.

Page 51, line 2

First draft sketched on a page from the Rubbish file: Surely in the whole history of human affairs, that history so full of errors and stupidities, nothing was ever met as incompetent as and more stupid than the government of King Louis XVI.

However, having reached this position (amid the struggle of all classes against him) it must be recognized that there was nothing left for him to do but surrender.

Page 51, line 23

On a separate page of the manuscript: To put after having shown the king's defeat. Doubtless at the end of chapter 3:

Among the authors who write at the end of the year 1788, one often finds these words: things happened this way under the old regime and before the revolution. This astonishes us, we are not used to hearing about a revolution before 1789. In fact, if we consider the acts which the year 1788 announced and the political innovations it gave birth to, we discover that such a considerable change in the relationship between classes and the government of the country had not occurred for centuries. Therefore it was in fact a very great revolution, but one which would soon be lost in the immensity of the revolution which was going to follow, and thus disappear from history's sight.

On another separate page: Idea to put perhaps after the defeat of the royal power. Chapter 4: This defeat of the royal power before the class struggle had begun eliminated the only chance that that struggle could be moderated and end in a compromise. For the royal power alone could impose a compromise and, having lost its prestige, it had become incapable of succeeding in doing so.

Page 51, line 31

The paragraph which follows has been changed according to a note in the manuscript: here place that which is found on the page of the last chapter.

Page 51, line 31

The arrest of d'Eprémesnil and of Goilard de Montsabert, and then the edicts of 8 May 1788, provoked both the protests of the parlements and popular riots, above all in Béarn, Brittany, and Dauphiny. On 8 August, Brienne had to suspend the supreme court and promise the meeting of the Estates-General for 1 May 1789. The king replaced him with Necker on 26 August, and annulled the reforms of Lamoig-

non, who resigned on 14 September. On 23 September, the courts were recalled to their duties, and from the twenty-fifth the Parlement of Paris marked Brienne and Lamoignon with infamy as authors and supporters of the laws of 8 May. Tocqueville took his information on this latter episode chiefly from Linguet's pamphlet, "France More English Than England; or, Comparison between the Indictment at Paris on 25 September 1788 against the Royal Ministers, and the Trial at London in 1640 of Count Strafford, Prime Minister of Charles I, King of England, with Reflections on the Imminent Danger with Which the Enterprises of the Judiciary Threaten Individuals and the Nation" (La France plus qu'anglaise; ou, Comparaison entre la procédure entamée à Paris le 25 septembre 1788 contre les ministres du Roi de France, et le procés intenté à Londres en 1640, au comte de Strafford, principal minstre de Charles premier, Roi d'Angleterre, avec des réflexions sur le danger imminent dont les entreprises de la Robe menacent la nation et les particuliers), Brussels, 1788, a pamphlet "written with very remarkable style, great talent, and some profound and prophetic views." *Tocqueville notes:* "in Linguet's eyes, the most probable result is the triumph and definitive despotism of the parlements over everyone. The book is written with fury to prove this. Linguet didn't know that at the moment when he wrote these lines the parlements existed only as history. Their time was over" *(Folder 45B CC).*

Page 52, line 10

In the margin of this paragraph: So that his popularity took no more time to disappear than was necessary to travel comfortably from the coast of Brittany to Paris in 1788.

Page 52, line 15

The manuscript bears here:

All the courts of this district appeared in person or by representatives before it and said to it . . . the clergy . . . the university itself came in robes and square bonnets to nasally intone its homage in bad Latin. *In the margin:* Picture the parlement itself treating them like a king. *Up to "the court's good will" [page 53, line 27] the text has been supplemented from Tocqueville's research notes from Folder 45B BB,* Struggle of the parlements in 1787. Notes taken on the official documents *(January 1857).*

Page 53, line 37

On Dauphiny see the appendix to chapters 3–5. In Folder 45B CC Tocqueville describes the events of Bordeaux according to the "Account of What Happened at Bordeaux When the Parlement and the Tax Court Returned to Their Duties, on 20, 21, 22, and 23 October" (Récit de ce qui s'est passé à Bordeaux lors de la reprise des fonctions du Parlement et de la cour des Aides, les 20, 21, 22 et 23 octobre 1788), written by Jean François Aymard Martin de la Colonie, doyen of the Grand Chamber, councillor of the Parlement of Bordeaux since 1733:

The people unhitch the first president's carriage; they carry it to his apartment. The oldest member of the parlement (councillor La Colonie), nearly ninety years old, cries out : "My children, teach this to your descendants so that this memory will preserve the fire of patriotism." This man had spent his first youth under Louis XIV. See what changes in ideas and language can do among a nation during one man's lifetime!

The magistrates who had wanted to obey the king were hooted, the first president addressed a public reprimand to them.

On the town square a dummy dressed as a cardinal was burned, which didn't stop the clergy from chanting a Te Deum.

The parlement, when registering the edict which recalled it, took care not to recognize any of the legal acts which had taken place in its absence, and naturally gave a right to appeal to all those who had been given final judgments by the superior courts.

In the same folder Tocqueville put some notes on the celebrations at Troyes in September 1788 at the news of the reestablishment of the Parlement of Paris, which had been exiled to Troyes the previous year. The source utilized is the "Account of What Happened in the City of Troyes, Capital of Champagne, with Regard to the Reestablishment of the Courts" (Relation de ce qui s'est passé dans la ville de Troyes, capitale de la Champagne, au sujet du rétablissement des Tribunaux).

We saw illuminations, firecrackers, shouts . . . M. de Lamoignon was paraded in the form of a black goose, Cardinal Brienne as a purple goose. They booed all those who had helped the king in this campaign. The town was full of little poems, for the intellect and literature joined in everything then. A certain canon, at whose house d'Eprémesnil had been lodged during the parlement's exile, put four Latin verses under glass in honor of the great man:

> exilio magnus, legum sed major amore
> D'EPRÉMESNIL renovat gaudia nostra redux
> *[Great in exile but greater in the love of the laws*
> *D'Eprémesnil renews our joys—Trans.]*

What did d'Eprémesnil and the canon think six months later?

Page 54, line 5

Tocqueville's research notes (Folder 45B CC) give a few examples of this:

How the triumphant parlement buried itself with its own hands. *[In the decree of 25 September 1788, the parlement]* decided that "the king will be begged to call the Estates-General under the forms of 1614."

The movement of opinion which would put the parlement in its place had already begun two months before. After 5 July 1788, the time when the king convinced the nation that it was really going to have the Estates-General, and by turning attention to the composition of that assembly put all classes into confrontation with each other, from that time on the affair of the parlement began to become secondary and the real mother passion of the Revolution, the passion of class which the parlement did not represent, overshadowed the struggle with royal power, which others would represent better than the parlement.

Violent attacks immediately follow the applause. The decree in which the considerations given above are found is dated 25 September 1788. I find an anonymous brochure of the twenty-eighth, three days later, where it is said that the supporters of faction "defame" the parlement because of it. Why so many clamors against it, cries the anonymous defender? Why so many insidious suppositions? *(p. 8)*.

Because up until now you have accidentally been a tool of the dominant passion and now you get in the way of a new one.

Unheard-of rapidity of the parlement's unpopularity.

The same act which reopened the Palace of Justice to the parlement set d'Eprémesnil free. We recall the dramatic scene of his capture, his words in the style of Regulus, the audience's tears, the immense popularity of the martyr. He was imprisoned on the Sainte Marguerite islands, I think. The order for his freedom arrives, he comes running; at first he is treated like a great man along his route; as he advances he finds himself less illustrious; when he arrives at Paris no one pays any attention to him any more except to make fun of him. To go from triumph to ridicule it only needed the time necessary to do 150 leagues by carriage.

5 December 1788. Failed effort by the parlement to become popular again.

France is flooded with pamphlets in which not only is the parlement no longer praised, but where people run it down and even turn its liberalism against it, where some revolutionaries show themselves more royalist than it: "These are judges who understand nothing of politics. Fundamentally, they only wanted to dominate and used the people for that.

"They are in agreement with the nobility and the clergy and are as much the enemies of the Third Estate as the others, that is to say enemies of almost the whole nation; they thought that by attacking despotism they would make people forget this. By demanding the nation's rights, they made them questionable, these rights born of the social contract, in order to give them the false appearance of a voluntary concession . . ." (pamphlet attributed to Servan, "Commentary on the Parlement's Decree," London, 1789).

Linguet, in a violent pamphlet, insulting but often full of truth, calls them a company of judicial nobility who usurp the right to call themselves the representatives of the people:

Who has authorized them to call themselves the people's interpreters? They have never been anything but the king's officers.

The parlement is a judicial aristocracy; what the people are asking for is a supreme authority, dominant, sole, which will defend them against the schemes of bishops, generals, and judges.

It is because of the treason of the courts, through the self-interested cowardice with which they let certain rights be substituted in place of the people, that the people have lost the rights that they claim for themselves today (p. 13).

The parlements have gotten the Estates-General, to their very great surprise and their very great regret. For the right of registration so abusively extended, so tyrannically applied was going to escape from them; they were going to go back to the narrow and obscure circle of their natural functions.

What greater abuse than their existence? The right to judge, to dispose of the property, the life, the honor of men, sold like the cloth from which their symbolic robes were made . . . Your title is to represent the king; at war with the king, what are you?

No more despotism either by a judicial aristocracy or by the ministers (p. 26). In this writing all kinds of ideas which it didn't have are attributed to the parlement, and the very words which made it popular and powerful three months before are turned against it.

The king, the gentle Louis XVI himself, was pleased to let them know how they had fallen into nothingness. I have nothing to say to my parlement about its requests. It is with the assembled nation that I will plan the dispositions proper to consolidate public order and the prosperity of the state forever.

One cannot imagine anything more disdainful. This time the remonstrance is hardly repeated.

Tocqueville is using here an anonymous brochure, Sur l'arrêt du 25 septembre 1788, 28 September 1788, 8 pages, and Glose et remarques sur l'arrêté du parlement de Paris, du 5 décembre 1788, an anonymous brochure attributed to Joseph-Michel-Antoine Servan by Barbier, from which he cites very freely several sentences from pp. 38–41, and the Observations sur le nouvel arrêté du Parlement de Paris en date du 5 décembre 1788, Brussels, 1789, by Linguet. Nonliteral quotations from pages 3, 5, 13, 21, and 26.

Page 54, line 8

Histoire de mon temps: Mémoires du chancelier Pasquier, Paris, 1893, v. 1, chapter 2. Tocqueville frequented the salon of chancellor Pasquier (1767–1862) and entered into historical discussion with him after the publication of The Old Regime (see his letter to Ampère, 7 January 1857, OC, v. 11, pp. 359–60). He doubtless learned things from Pasquier's then-unpublished memoirs.

Page 55, line 11

See Tocqueville's research notes (File 45B, Folder CC): D'Eprémesnil attacked after having been adored: in a pamphlet titled "Warning to the Public (and Chiefly to the Third Estate) from the Commander of the Prison of the Sainte-Marguerite" (Avis au public [et principalement au Tiers Etat] de la part du commandant [du château] des isles Sainte-Marguerite), all d'Eprémesnil's aristocratic and parlementary opinions are attributed to an insane person who has escaped from the islands and is using his name. *This pamphlet of 10 November 1788 is attributed by Barbier to Servan.*

Page 55, line 11

First version: When hatred of absolute government had become the sole and general feeling of the French, the parlement seemed to everyone the route for the country to take. Everything that people had most disliked, its spirit of domination, its pride, its prejudices, was for a moment the nation's own weapon; one used its passions, one sheltered oneself behind its vices. *Crossed out:* we perceived that the venality of the judiciary was what prevented the venality of the individual judge. *Final version added at the end of Tocqueville's manuscript.*

Page 55, line 13

First version: thought itself sure of being able to defend its rights itself. *Interlinear correction:* no longer had need of a champion.

Page 55, line 17

The research notes (45B) contain a more detailed analysis of the parlements' discredit:

How could the parlements, who saw that they were popular despite all these egoistic ideas and doctrines contrary to the spirit of the times, not have believed themselves to be a real force with deep roots? How could they have divined that what made them popular came in part from the hatred people had for the very institutions which they represented or defended, a hatred that, by a unique combination of circumstances, found the parlement momentarily useful to its cause?

How the parlements were never more powerful, more enterprising and apparently deep-rooted than at the moment when they were no longer connected to anything. This is interesting, because it is a story repeated at the beginning of many other revolutions.

Never, during the five hundred years since they came into existence, had the parlements used such haughty language to the king as in 1787, spoken more as rivals, often as masters, or grasped for such legislative power. Never had the parlements established in a manner more authentic, more formidable and more new, the doctrine that all of them together made up a single body, of which the Parlement of Paris was merely the head, such that every one of them had the right to deliberate on all the acts of the government in all of France.

And yet the parlement no longer had any foundation anywhere. After having been the great weapon of royal power against the aristocracy, provincial spirit, and the Church, it was only an embarrassment and hindrance for the monarchy. It had become a tool that was too heavy, too defective, and too dangerous to manipulate for the uses it had previously had; there was no longer any relationship between its power and its purpose.

The institution was no less outmoded in the people's view. The whole new social and political situation that the parlement itself had contributed to creating, all the ideas which were naturally created by or artificially drawn from this situation, were against a body of judges who bought the right to render justice, who rendered it hereditarily, whose members possessed individually or as a group all kinds of privileges, and finally combined with the judicial functions proper to them political functions which were not theirs. But this same change in conditions, laws, and ideas which made the parlement a badly made tool in the king's eyes had spread a vague wish for novelty, the desire for change, a spirit of independence, and desire for control in the entire nation, which, from all sides, pushed people to resist authority.

This new and irregular power of opinion found in the parlement the only tool which it could use; it seized it not so that the parlement would become powerful, not because it was the most popular body, but because it was the only body in France which remained sufficiently organized, sufficiently large, and sufficiently strong to fight royal power and upset the constitution which people wanted to overturn.

As soon as it was possible to create an instrument of resistance more appropriate in origin, ideas, and constitution to the new passions, this old institution which had only been good for shaking up all the others was brought down as if by its own weight, without anyone even needing to put a hand on it, so to speak, through the common hatred; and thus a giant who a moment before had had a hundred arms, and who for ten months had made the air resound over the whole surface of France, suddenly became enfeebled and died without even the strength to sigh.

Page 55, chapter 5 title
This chapter is written based on notes taken on the official documents and the pamphlets of 1787, 1788, and 1789, filed in Folders BB, CC, DD, and EE of File 45B.

Page 55, line 30
The last Estates-General had been held in 1614, a hundred and seventy-five years previously.

Page 56, line 4, after "result"
The text here leaves three dots. In the margin: Text of the edict folder CC 115. *We add according to the folder mentioned.*

Page 56, line 10
The edict of 5 July 1788, reproduced in the Recueil des anciennes lois françaises, *v. 28, pp. 601–4. In his notes (Folder CC), Tocqueville comments thus:* Use this characteristic, it depicts the political education of France. It succeeds in giving an idea of the prodigious and really amazing incompetence of the poor unfortunates who were going to have to direct such an immense movement. Furthermore, it is through this that the movement, which up to then had been liberal, sud-

denly took on its real character, and from a struggle against despotism became a struggle between classes.

Page 56, line 20
In the margin: Perhaps paint the character of these various writings in a sentence.

Page 56, line 20
In the margin: Start with the writings, then the local authorities, then the groups, then the classes.

Page 56, line 26
Word missing.

Page 56, line 27
Here are inserted five pages of notes and planning sketches:
Show that at first the Third Estate only asked for a place.
Then wanted to have the first place.
Then wanted to be alone and here the violence became unheard-of.
Finish I think by examining these questions myself, at least if I do not find a means to put it in the account, which would be better.
Clearly disentangle the positive demands relating to the form of the Estates-General and summarized in two points: 1) the doubling of the Third; 2) the vote in common. Talk about all the ideas of reform or revolution which were joined to these demands or expressed on the occasion of these two demands.
First the class war in all its phases.
Then discussion of the chief points in question.
Finally the decisions of the king which close the chapter.
Where should the electoral campaigns go?
The salient trait of this chapter is the war that broke out suddenly and violently among classes which had just fought united. Full light must be shed on this point and it must be kept in the spotlight. Perhaps paint it first in its general form, then go to the two particular points on which the class war concentrated, which two points in reality are only two sides of the same idea: doubling of the Third, the vote in common.
The agitation about the cahiers must certainly follow or accompany this picture, probably be part of it.
The writing of the cahiers for a moment turned people's eyes away from royal power inwards towards the center of class. This was done not for a purpose but in order to gain time, figuring that while the nation devoted itself to the innocent pleasure of speaking and writing about the composition of the Estates-General, it would let its masters breathe for a moment.
This brings me to the king's decision deciding the means and leaving the ends

vague. After having inflamed hostile passions, he prepared the battlefield in advance, and of all battlefields the most dangerous since here it was a question not of an individual success, but of deciding supremacy on all points. This will lead me perhaps to reflections about short levers. *[On short levers see p. 63—Trans.]*

The most difficult thing is to put in many of the accessory traits which it is necessary to show throughout this picture of class war: profound ignorance of the practical science of government in the century when political theory was studied even in bedrooms . . .

No idea of: the need for counterweights, the necessity of maintaining a certain balance between classes, the importance of safeguarding acquired rights (even when these rights would be condemned). The most educated and most numerous portion of the Third Estate went right by these truths without seeing them. The most interested and most impassioned of the privileged did the same . . .

A note on a separate page states: Radicalism of the moderates. Highlight this well, it is above all through this that we can get a picture of the general ideas which were current. Furthermore it is the most original way of tackling the subject.

Page 56, line 30

The words "around five months" were added by Beaumont, the manuscript leaving a blank in the text, and in the margin the note: "the king gave in on the . . . September, and it was finally on . . . that the voters." Tocqueville did not have time to check the dates of the elections. He dates the king's surrender to the recall of the parlements on 20 September, although in fact the king had already retreated on several occasions, notably on 8 August by dismissing Brienne, and on the twenty-fourth by dismissing Lamoignon.

Page 56, line 33, at "furious speed"

Tocqueville bases himself here on a file of petitions and requests printed at the end of 1788 (Folder 45B CC), containing: Requête du tiers état de la ville de Bourg; Lettre écrite au Roi par les officiers d'un grand nombre d'élections du ressort de la Cour des Aides de Paris; Protestation de la noblesse de Bourgogne; Requête au Roi des habitants de la ville de Lyon; Délibération des habitants de Saint-Jean-de-Losne; Délibération des habitants de Châtillon-sur-Seine; Pétition des citoyens domiciliés à Paris. Tocqueville concludes thus:

How, after having read all these pieces, and measured the real intellectual abyss (bridged only by oratorical precautions and good feelings) between past and present, between what existed and what was wanted, between the viewpoint of the nobility and clergy and that of the rest of society; how, I say, not to see that the Revolution was inevitable, or rather that it was made in advance. (In the first part of the year this intellectual basis was hidden, it appeared suddenly during the second half of the year. Fundamental idea.) What strikes me is less the class passions which inspire this whole polemic, the jealousies, the grievances, the struggle of opposing interests which are seen here, than the base of opinions (and it is always to this that one returns and which makes the final result of revolutions). Those very individuals who testify the most regard for privileges, for special rights, consider these rights and these privileges absolutely unjustifiable. Not only those which were exercised in their times, but any special rights or privileges of any kind. The very idea of a balanced and tempered government, that is to say a government where the different classes which form society, the different interests which divide it, act as counterbalances, where men weigh not only as units, but by reason of their property, their patronage, their interest in the general good . . . All these ideas are absent from the minds of even the most moderate (in part, I think, even from those of the privileged), and are replaced by the idea of a mass composed of similar elements and represented by deputies who are the representatives of numbers and not of interests or persons. Penetrate into this idea and show that the Revolution was there still more than in the facts, that it was virtually impossible that ideas being such, the facts were not pretty close to what we have seen them to be.

Independently of the passions, there was an idea of society and government, a notion that was peaceful, disinterested, cold, which was fundamentally established in all minds and which was not the product of passions, even though it came to their aid and was enough to create them and produce effects as violent as they did.

First the painting of interests and passions, then perhaps of opinions.

Page 57, line 10

In his research notes on the pamphlets of the year 1788 (45B CC), Tocqueville returned on several occasions to this substitution of Rousseau for Montesquieu:

Theoretical and learned politics in 1787 and 1788. Montesquieu in 1788, and afterwards Rousseau. A general remark to make in reading all these writings. At all periods, it is pure theory that we call upon. But in 1787 and 1788, it is above all Montesquieu among the theoreticians whom I see quoted; in '89 and afterwards, Rousseau.

Apropos of the pamphlets on the composition of the Estates-General, in the same file:

What is law? A convention made between the members of society for their mutual happiness. Always the idea of the social contract. The more I read this polemic, the more I perceive that this doctrine of Rousseau's was, of the philosophes' ideas, the one which had penetrated the nation's mind most deeply and had the most influence on its conduct.

In the appendix, see on this point notably Tocqueville's notes on the pamphlets by Roederer, "On Representation in the Estates-General," 8 November 1788, pp. 82–83, and by Lacretelle, "On the Convocation of the Estates," 1788, p. 84.

Page 57, line 11
Circled: Amid all the abuses of the French old regime, the institutions of England seemed outdated and insufficient.

Page 57, line 15
See the analysis in the appendix, notably of the brochures by Sieyès and Rabaud-Saint-Etienne.

Page 57, line 17
In the margin: All this should be mingled with and padded with short and decisive quotations. *See below the notes Tocqueville took on these pamphlets.*

Page 57, line 28
In the appendix, see Tocqueville's analysis of Sieyès's "What Is the Third Estate?" Tocqueville is referring here to a famous passage from it (p. 11 in the 1789 edition): "Why don't we send them back to the forests of Franconia, all these families who maintain the crazy claim to be the descendants of the conquering race, and to have inherited their rights?"

Page 57, line 31
On a sheet of fragmentary drafts of this passage at the end of the manuscript: People only differed as to numbers. Some said they were one hundred thousand, others . . . All agreed in thinking that they formed only a small foreign body that we could not tolerate except in the interest of public peace.

Page 57, line 31
This remark is inspired by the reading of the pamphlet <u>Suite de l'écrit intitulé les Etats généraux convoqués par Louis XVI</u>, n.d., 41 pages, attributed to Target. Target counts 400,000 clergy and 500,57 nobles, to whom he opposes the 23,000,000 men of the Third Estate (p. 7). On this brochure see Tocqueville's notes below, p. 104.

Page 57, line 36
On a separate sheet at the end of the manuscript: When I get to the period of class war, show well that a kind of fear of dissolution reigned. It was not only the bourgeoisie who made war on the nobility, it was the petty nobility against the great, the lower clergy against the higher . . . until the Revolution simplified divisions and put the various occupants of the same social compartment together.

Page 58, line 22
At the end of the manuscript Tocqueville puts "various pieces relating to the chapter and written in pencil in my notebook" of which one refers to this passage: In speaking about the difficulty the nobles had in defending themselves from the

application of theories which they accepted in principle: They were not far from believing themselves that the inequality of ranks was nothing but a kind of deformity which the aging social body had contracted, and which time and their interests alone made respectable.

Page 58, line 22

On this inability of the nobility to defend itself see the analysis in the appendix of the "Report of the Princes of the Blood presented to the King" of December 1788, and the polemic engendered by this report, as well as the analysis made of the "Report to the King in Favor of the French Nobility by a Patrician Friend of the People," by the Marquis de Gouy d'Arsy, 1788, p. 96.

Page 58, line 36

First version: The habit of despising those whom they spoke to. *Interlinear correction:* of being the first.

Page 58, line 37

Marginal note: Here and before putting in the discussion of the systems of doubling the Third and the common vote, put the divisions within the attacked parties, depict the spirit of rivalry and contention introduced among even those who were isolated, the nobility against the clergy, the clergy against the nobility, the little nobles against the big ones, the curates against the bishops . . . make a satirical picture drawn from the cahiers.

Page 59, line 13

On the estates of Languedoc, see Tocqueville's appendix to the first volume of The Old Regime and the Revolution.

Page 59, line 17

In the file of fragments from the Rubbish file for this chapter:
What had prevented the doubling of the Third and the vote in common from producing a change in the province's social and political constitution (*circled in the margin:* Human institutions ought never to be judged in themselves, but only relative to the space in which they have to act and to temperaments. The same law produces one effect applied to a part of the empire and another when applied to the empire itself.):

1) The representation of the bourgeoisie, which made its deputies a small number of aristocrats and privileged bourgeois.

2) The representation of the nobility [*sic*], which was made up of bishops who were almost all nobles, furnished almost no support to democratic feelings.

3) The fact that this happened in a particular province, the aristocracy weighing there with all the weight which it had in the kingdom.

In Languedoc the doubling of the Third and the vote of all the orders together in a single assembly had not had any result other than to assure the bourgeoisie a greater part in the administration of affairs without giving it the power or even the desire to govern alone. *In the margin:* It will be very difficult to get something out of the comparison with Languedoc, because the reasons which made it that doubling and the common vote there did not have the effects that one should expect from them, when applying the same system to the whole country, are too numerous and too detailed.

The text continues: But the same law which created only minor changes in the government of a province could not fail to produce a sudden and complete revolution if applied to the whole country.

Page 59, line 25
In the margin of this paragraph:
The Third could not fail to have the majority.
It could not fail to want to abuse it.
And dominating a single sovereign assembly, it could not fail to make not a reform, but a revolution.

Page 60, line 15
In the margin of this paragraph: Perhaps entirely give up this piece, which is debatable and dangerous, and limit myself to showing the folly of the king, who of all means chose the worst.

Page 60, line 21
On a separate page at the end of the manuscript, without reference to the text: The government of the old regime was organized in such a way as to easily defeat individual resistance, but its constitution, its precedents, its mores and those of the nation hardly allowed it to govern with the majority against it.

Page 60, line 30
First version: an idea of the conditions of a free and ordered government.
Interlinear correction: of what he wanted to do and had seen the consequences of his ideas.

Page 60, line 32
The manuscript here has " . . . "; the text is supplemented according to the research notes.

Page 60, line 36
Tocqueville, without quoting literally, here summarized an essential idea of chapter 28, pp. 258ff., of the Nouvelles observations sur les Etats généraux de France, published by Mounier in 1789. On this brochure see Tocqueville's notes below, pp. 107–11.

Page 61, line 1

Marginal note: Perhaps here put a portrait of M. Necker. One needs to be very sparing of these, but the importance of the man and the moment can justify it here.

In the margin of the following page: The traits of this man are so effaced that it is difficult to see his appearance distinctly.

Page 61, line 1

The Royal Council of 27 December 1788 had decided that each district would have a number of deputies proportionate to its population, without prejudice to the question of voting by head, which was left to the decision of the Estates-General. File 44-2 contains an analysis of the report made to the king in his Council by Necker, according to the pamphlet "Result of the Royal Council Held at Versailles, 27 December 1788 (Résultat du Conseil du Roi tenu à Versailles le 27 décembre 1788), 26 pages, 1788:

Vote by head left undecided.

This question (which is the chief one in all constitutions) is treated like a simple matter of internal order, a question of regulations which naturally belonged to the Estates-General and which the king ought to leave them to decide. Can one imagine a more profound ignorance of the importance of the question in itself, and above all of the importance that it had at the time? All that Your Majesty can do, says this report, is put the Estates-General in a position to make one decision or the other. What finally makes this document miserable is that this neutrality on a question so crucial is not even sincere. We see that the whole tendency of the report is to push for the vote by head.

Chimerical idea that the Third Estate if it was equal in numbers would still be threatened by the domination of the other orders. That this would be said by a newcomer in a partisan spirit, this is conceivable. But in the prime minister's mouth, the error is much too great. If they vote by head, says Necker, there would still remain with the first two orders all the ascendancy born of their superior rank and of the various graces of which they are the depositaries . . . He bases himself on what had happened in former times and in assemblies of estates like the estates of Languedoc, where the Third Estate equaled the other two orders. As if in the eyes of a politician what happened in a period of submission and in one corner of the country, with regard to petty local affairs (without even speaking of the composition of the Third Estate in those particular estates), could be compared with what might happen when war was declared between the orders and when we were going to deal with questions which concerned their very existence.

"The cause of the Third Estate will always have public opinion for it and it is sustained by all minds capable of leading those who read or who listen" *(p. 11).* Where thus is the danger that the Third Estate even when equal in numbers will be dominated by the other orders?

On this decision see also the analysis in the appendix of the anonymous pamphlet "Observations on the Report Made to the King by M. Necker."

Page 61, line 11

Between parentheses in the text: "here consult Burke's piece in my first notes." Nothing indicates what piece Tocqueville was alluding to. In the margin of the sentence: [the King] saw this truth but only through a haze, [the truth] that absolute government needed a certain kind of class war.

Page 62, line 1

Marginal note: soften a fall?

Page 62, line 5

In the margin, a draft variant: The leading classes, feeling royalty add its weight to that of the Third Estate, would have despaired of retaining their domination and would have fought only for equality. They would have gotten used to the idea.

Page 62, line 16

See the appendix to chapters 3–5 above, p. 69.

Page 62, line 27

In the margin, the draft of an outline:

1) Minds had been given all kinds of new ideas, all kinds of hopes had been born, all kinds of passions had been excited.

2) Class war had been set alight in advance.

3) The material strength of the Third Estate had been increased, after its hopes had been raised and its passions inflamed.

Page 63, line 11

First version, not crossed out: A king whose only virtues were those of an ordinary man. *A second version follows immediately afterwards and is used in the text.*

Page 63, chapter title

A note in the file "Drafts" (November and December 1856) marks the point of departure for Tocqueville's thinking:

The proceedings of the cahiers, nothing more proper to sum up grievances and produce the Revolution. However, done a hundred times without this. But institutions are above all what the times make of them.

What more free than this process? What even more free and more manly in this absolute monarchy than a *lit de justice,* that solemn debate before throne and nation? Who can in what we call our orderly society even give an idea of such a spectacle?

At the bottom of the folder which contains this chapter's pages, Tocqueville notes:

There are in this little chapter some important things which it would be very annoying to lose. It prepares the mind for the peasants' insurrection and the burning of the châteaux after the 12 July . . . But perhaps it breaks the flow of ideas because it changes the setting for the reader. Just before we were among the educated classes; here we find ourselves among those who are not, and the following chapter returns us to the former.

In the margin, added later: Response. In substituting the idea of a <u>revolution</u> for the <u>revolutionary passion,</u> and in postponing the fall of the Bastille, the famine, and the economic crisis until what follows, I think that chapter 6 doesn't break the flow.

Lower down: I have never been able to make anything satisfactory out of the winter of 1789 and yet this accident of nature was a great political event.

Page 63, chapter title

For this chapter Tocqueville used chiefly his notes on Mounier's pamphlet, "New Observations on the Estates-General," 1789 (see below), and on the history by Buchez and Roux and the notes he took in the archives in June 1857 on the documents relating to the electoral assemblies of 1789 (Folder 45B EE).

Page 63, line 33

Suspension points in the manuscript. Text supplemented from Tocqueville's research notes.

Page 63, line 33

On this chest see Mounier, "New Observations on the Estates-General." See below, p. 108.

Page 64, line 1

First version: the entire population. *Interlinear correction:* each and every.

Page 64, line 25

Variants sketched in the margin:

People thought merely of modifying institutions, they were changed from top to bottom . . . and while apparently only modifying old institutions one made something *[new—Trans.]* out of them.

Medieval customs were not changed at all, one only enlarged them. One did not create new freedoms, one only extended some very old freedoms to new classes, to a new people.

Page 64, line 25

The research notes in Folder 45B CC state the novelty of this universal participation:

How the idea of the universal vote found itself everyone's natural idea in 1789.

This ultrademocratic idea occurred to everyone because of the division of the nation into orders whose limits were perfectly and definitively traced, that is because of facts removed as far as possible from democracy.

The idea of political privilege was attached to the class, not to the individual who belonged to it. In the interests of each class it seemed natural and necessary that each individual was consulted about the common interest. This was everybody's idea, which no one fought. The Third Estate of a village was in a situation subordinate to that of the lord and the curate and had separate taxes and interests. But when it was a question of those taxes and those interests, no one doubted that the least peasant had a voice to be heard.

Tocqueville had found in Mounier the remark about the ultrademocratic character of the writing of the cahiers. See below, p. 108.

Page 64, line 25

Analyzing Luchet's pamphlet, "The Contemporaries of 1789 and 1790; or, The Opinions Debated during the First Legislature with the Chief Events of the Revolution" (Les contemporains de 1789 et 1790; ou, Les opinions débattues pendant la première législature avec les principaux événements de la Révolution), 3 vols., 1790, Tocqueville notes: Pretty good phrase by a peasant reported by Luchet, in his history of 1789. A peasant when asked what he wanted from the Estates-General responded: The elimination of pigeons, rabbits, and priests. The pigeons eat our wheat when it's sown, the rabbits when it's growing, and the priests when it's harvested." *(Folder 45B EE).*

Page 65, line 21

In the margin: This whole thing a painful draft.

Page 65, line 27

Variant on a separate page: When in the midst of a worried and famished family, in the presence of a half burnt-out fire, in a bare room, the poor man thought about his situation, it seemed to him still more cruel than he had imagined; and it was at this moment that people came to ask him to look for the cause of his problems and to tell his grievances.

Page 65, line 27

Tocqueville finds the hostility to the large landowners, "symptom of the spirit of the times," in the pamphlet by a certain Pelletier, "The Regeneration of France; or, Essay on the Reform That the Estates-General Should Make" (La régénération de la France; ou, Essai sur la réforme que les Etats généraux ont à faire), 1789:

The smallholders disappear, the large landowners grow; the more the land is divided, the better it is cultivated. The author, without citing any facts, it is true, and in the style of an orator, complains that small landholdings are disappearing, to be absorbed into big ones which are becoming limitless. One would say that the author was writing in England. The fact is very false for France.

Like all his contemporaries (not excepting, I think, the large landowners) he also has the idea that large landholdings are bad for agriculture and that the more the soil is divided, the better it is cultivated, a notion that what had happened in France, because of the abandonment of the countryside by the large landowners, explains and justifies.

This notion of political economy has strikingly followed the spirit of democratic passions, and has come greatly to the aid of the hatred of the rich, so well represented by the author *(Folder 45B EE).*

Page 65, line 36

Without being able to study it precisely, Tocqueville had noted the importance of the grain crisis while reading the 1788 correspondence of the ministry of the royal household in the archives in May and June of 1857 (Folder 45B CC): As we advance into the winter of 1788–89, we see in this correspondence the agitation about the means of subsistence which disturbs the lower classes and sets them in motion throughout France: the ferment happens in all markets; from all sides come flocks of people, troops of armed beggars who come from the countryside. These same symptoms had existed a hundred times before without revolt. They have since almost always been the forerunners of revolution. There was thus already in the society of 1789 a latent situation which would suddenly produce this new fact which has remained permanent. Understand this and show it.

A later note from File 44-2 returns to this subject:

Food shortage, commercial crisis in the winter of '88–'89. One of the most effective secondary causes. To study in depth on my return to Paris in March '58 and to place, I think, before the insurrections, whether at Paris or of the peasants. There was nothing more decisive among the secondary causes of the Revolution than the winter of '89. To which it should be added, in fully analyzing the stagnation of trade and industry as a consequence already of the general feeling: what was then called an embarrassment of trade, what we call a commercial crisis today.

This point to be well researched. Very important. New. But to whom and to what documents to address myself? (Perhaps Lanjuinais.)

Perhaps make a short chapter separate from the writing of the cahiers on the food shortage and the industrial crisis. Don't force myself to find a link between the writing of the cahiers and these points here. The link is in the very nature of the subject, the mind makes it more easily than it could be described.

Page 66, chapter title

The cover of the Rubbish file bears the crossed-out line "last chapter of the first book," which is a trace of the plan implying a second book. On the cover of the folder containing the definitive text:

This was the great tidal wave of '89 which continued on afterwards and whose last ripples have persisted until our own day.

A very necessary nuance to point out is that, except for the agreement, most of the feelings that I depict were not born at the moment, but prepared long in advance, and above all that most do not end with the moment.

At the head of the Rubbish file of this chapter, a more detailed text about Tocqueville's intentions:

What is it that I want to paint?

Is it the general élan of souls which produced the French Revolution, and has driven on this great tidal wave of ideas and feelings whose last ripples have persisted to our own day?

The conviction that it was a matter of regenerating France and changing the world, the fervor which was born from the conception of this great plan, the devotion to this great cause, the contempt for private interests and individual well-being that it would suggest to millions of men.

Or is this not just a particular moment, a special accident of this great movement of souls?

This solemn moment when people were going to pass from speculation to practice, from the preparation to the event, from words to deeds, the time when the French, ready to launch themselves on this immense voyage, had a clear and close view of the work they were going to undertake, stopped, calmed themselves, came together and made a supreme effort to try to understand each other, to forget their particular interests in order to concern themselves only with the greatness and beauty of the common enterprise. *In the margin:* The apparent and sincere rapprochement of classes is the chief sign, but it is only a sign of this admirable effort of souls to prepare themselves by devotion to the great cause, by the spirit of abnegation, of sacrifice, for the task that they were going to undertake. The contempt for material well-being, for ruin, for life, is only its final effort.

The whole chapter must be based on this sole idea.

The text continues: Moment of a moral grandeur unequaled in history.

Page 67, line 3

Marginal note: Perhaps develop this.

Page 67, line 6

In the margin of this sentence: Idea badly expressed but good and certainly to be put here.

Page 67, line 12

This sentence is added in the margin, followed by ". . ." and a notation: (perhaps).

Page 67, line 19
Marginal note: Perhaps stop short here and say: class interest seemed to abstain for an instant (poor, but the movement perhaps good).

Page 67, line 21
In the margin: Perhaps already said in the first volume?

Page 67, line 22
From the Rubbish file: The upper and educated classes did not yet have any of those cowardly fears which since then have so often abased them below the lowest and most uneducated ones. They were ignorant then of the humble feeling that we call fear. For a long time they had not feared . . .
On the same page of the Rubbish file in the margin: People were not only proud of their country. They were proud of themselves. The old construction of society had made of each profession, each class, a little stage on which . . .
In the ranks of the nobility and the bourgeoisie there was no one, whatever his rank, who did not believe that he had a certain part to fill, a certain place to occupy, and spectators to judge his attitude and his acts. The little theaters were already half overturned, but each person kept the idea that he had a part to play, a personality to display, and brought to this great theater which had just opened . . .
No one yet had the idea of sinking himself in the crowd, or the cowardly hope of hiding himself there. Everyone believed themselves to have a rank to maintain and an honor to guard.
On a separate page of the Rubbish file, the same opposition of past and present:
To the chapter where I speak of the great movement of '89. After having painted the nation's unlimited pride and its confidence in itself . . . say: that we were far from those times when the government's chief support would come from fear of what the nation would do to itself, the contempt for itself that it would have . . . *An isolated note in File 43 K returns to this point:*
On the energy of the weak when it comes to hatred. Without having lived among men for a long time, one cannot imagine what a peaceful, timid, but implacable and, if need be, cruel hatred weak and flabby souls can harbor against what annoys them, frightens them, or only requires them to make an effort. All the energy which is left them secretly contracts and concentrates itself in the ability to hate.

Page 67, line 27
The sentence has been supplemented here from the Rubbish file.

Page 67, line 31
In the margin: Make all this precise without worrying about terms of money.

On an isolated sheet in the Rubbish, a draft of a more precise analysis: And if there were met then some orator who had dared to say to the <u>bourgeoisie</u> . . . (I am afraid of diminishing the picture by mentioning a particular class, even though this one is well-chosen. In order to keep the greatness of the picture it is better to stay within the general idea of the nation, which would have been indignant if someone had dared tell it that the great Revolution it dreamed of in the end was going to limit itself to establishing a new society that was egalitarian and enslaved).

Page 67, line 36
In the margin: In several districts, the three orders made war on each other; but in almost all, one suddenly saw born a concord that was far from expected.

Page 69, line 4
Tocqueville's notes refer at this point to a "first glance at the chapter" in his research notes (45B YY):
Men, in general, only bring ardor, persistence, and energy into affairs where their personal passions are involved. But their personal passions, however strong they may be, never push them either very far or very high, unless they become greater in their eyes and are legitimated by some great cause useful to the whole human race which is combined with them. It is the honor of our nature that we need this stimulant. Combine the passions born from personal interest with the goal of changing the face of the earth and regenerating the soul, and only then will you see what people can do.
This is the history of the French Revolution. What it contained of narrow views and personal egoism made it dark and violent, what it contained of generosity and disinterest made it powerful and great, irresistible.
On an undated page from File 44 (I), Tocqueville notes: <u>To the last chapter of book 1</u>: We must make haste to speak of these proud virtues of our ancestors; for our contemporaries, who are already incapable of imitating them, will soon no longer even be in a position to understand them.

Page 69, line 14
The principles of the new government by provincial assemblies announced in the edict of June 1787 had been developed in particular regulations for each generality which appeared between 23 June (Châlons-sur-Marne) and 4 September 1787 (Grenoble). The provincial assembly of Dauphiny met on 1 October 1787, but a decree by the chamber of annulment of the Parlement of Dauphiny on 6 October 1787 forbade it to meet. On 15 December the court confirmed by 28 votes to 8 the prohibition of the assembly, and the Parlement of Paris and the ministry had to order the leaders of the resistance to Versailles.

Page 71, line 5

Tocqueville comments here on a pamphlet titled "Dialogue on the Establishment and Formation of Provincial Assemblies in the Generality of Grenoble between Monsieur M., Councillor of the Parlement of Dauphiny, Member of the Chamber of Annulments of 1787, and Monsieur N., Inhabitant of the Baronies" (Dialogue sur l'établissement et la formation des Assemblées provinciales dans la généralité de Grenoble entre M. M*** conseiller au parlement de Dauphiné, membre de la chambre des vacations de 1787 et M. N***, habitant dans les baronies), 1787, 159 pages. This anonymous pamphlet, favorable to the reform, was written by the comte de Virieu, a liberal aristocrat and syndic of the first two orders in the parlement. The pamphlet reacted to the edict of 6 October; in it an inhabitant of the barony, the author's spokesman, talks with a councillor of the Parlement of Dauphiny (see Jean Egret, Le parlement de Dauphiné, Grenoble, 1948, v. 2, pp. 170–89).

Page 71, line 26

After the edicts of May 1788, the members of the Parlement of Grenoble had issued an edict of protest on 20 May. On 7 June 1788, they received lettres de cachet; the Duke of Clermont-Tonerre, lieutenant-general of the province, had to face a riot during which roof tiles were thrown at the troops. Following this "Day of the Tiles" the members of the parlement left the town on 12 June. On 14 June Mounier gathered 101 notables in the meeting room of the Grenoble city hall. On 21 July, with the resigned consent of the marshal de Vaux, who had entered Grenoble on 14 July with dragoons, a new assembly met at Vizille with 491 representatives from the three orders (165 nobles, 50 clergy, 276 from the Third Estate).

Page 71, line 32

"To the King. Humble Supplication of the 41 Corps and Communities of the Town of Grenoble" (Au Roi. Supplient humblement les quarante et un corps et communautés de la ville de Grenoble), 5 pages in octavo, 25 May 1788. See Jean Egret, Le parlement de Dauphiné, pp. 220–21.

Page 72, line 13

Doubtless the "Letters of a Lawyer of Dauphiny to an English lord" ("Lettres d'un avocat de Dauphiné à un Milord anglais"), by Achard de Germane, published around 20 June. But the affirmation of the separation between Dauphiny and the kingdom of France is frequent in the pamphlets of the time.

Page 72, line 14

Report from the city government, 20 May 1788. See Jean Egret, Le parlement de Dauphiné, p. 220.

Page 72, line 22

During the meeting of 14 June the three orders of the city of Grenoble had begged the three orders of the different cities and towns of the province to send deputies to Grenoble. On 1 July the lieutenant-general published an ordinance forbidding the mayors and aldermen to convoke unusual assemblies. On 6 July an edict of the Royal Council annulling the decisions of 14 June was posted. These measures remained without effect. Tocqueville correctly notes the weakness of popular participation. Only 194 of the 1212 parishes participated in the movement (see Jean Egret, La prérévolution française, Paris, 1962, chapter 6).

Page 73, line 7

Barnave's pamphlet was distributed from the eighth of June and was a great success. See Jean Egret, Le parlement de Dauphiné, v. 2, pp. 252–54.

Page 74, line 21

On the assembly of Vizille of 21 July 1788, Tocqueville's notes remain factual, like the notes taken on the transcripts of the general assembly of the three orders of Dauphiny at Romans on 10 September 1788. The pamphlet analyzed here, "The Secret Exposed; or A Circular Letter to the Parlementary Aristocracy of Dauphiny," published in July 1788 (15 pages), is also attributed by Jean Egret to a prominsterial member of parlement. See Les derniers états du Dauphiné, Grenoble, 1942, p. 19.

Page 74, line 32

"Twenty against One; or Decree Proposed to the Third Estate of Dauphiny" (Vingt contre un, ou Arreté proposé au Tiers Etat de Dauphiné), 32 pages in octavo. Pamphlet attributed to Berger de Moydieu, opponent of the parlement which had expelled him, and a progovernment pamphleteer. In his preface the author accuses the parlement of having distributed 50,000 livres in order to have pamphlets written.

Page 76, line 37

In response to the assembly of Vizille, a decree of the Council of 2 August had ordered the meeting of a preliminary assembly at Romans, where the Third Estate would have representation equal to the two other orders and would propose to the king the future constitution of the Estates of Dauphiny. This assembly was held from 10 to 28 September and wrote a draft constitution. In the "Letter Written to the King" (Lettre écrite au Roi), 14 September 1788, the orders, after having denounced the "chaos of the feudal regime" (p. 2), make an elegy about the freedom of ancient times: "the free concession of the taxes was established naturally between the people, owner, and the king, administrator. This right was constantly exercised by the national assemblies" (p. 3). There follows the examination of the "magnificent constitution" of feudal times.

Page 78, line 15

See the "Letter Written to the King on Behalf of the Orders of the Province of Dauphiny about the Estates-General" (Lettre écrite au Roi pour les ordres de la province du Dauphiné sur les états généraux), 8 November 1788, 16 pages. On 14 September the estates had proposed a "Plan for the Formation of the Estates of Dauphiny" (Plan pour la formation des états du Dauphiné): 144 representatives (24 from the clergy, 48 from the nobility, 72 from the Third Estate) elected for four years, empowered to apportion taxes and to order public works. They had asked for new laws to be examined by the provincial estates before their registration by the parlement. It was this disposition which had been rejected by the Royal Council on 22 October, to which responded the meeting of a new assembly of the three orders from 2 to 8 November, which reaffirmed the project in its original form.

Page 78, line 25

"The authority of the laws is never more respectable than when it protects the rights of nature," p. 8.

Page 78, line 33

"Observations on the Letter of the Estates of Dauphiny to the King about the Estates-General" (Observations sur la lettre des états du Dauphiné au Roi sur les Etats généraux), 8 November 1788, 47 pages. The author describes himself as an "obscure citizen" (p. 2).

Page 79, line 8

The author writes that "the Third Estate has more than nineteen-twentieths the weight of its two competitors" (p. 14).

Page 79, line 29

Pamphlet, 8 pages in octavo. The estates of Dauphiny, meeting from 1 December 1788 to 17 January 1789, decided on Mounier's motion to give the deputies to the Estates-General orders requiring them to leave if they did not vote by head and with the three orders united. See Egret, Les derniers états de Dauphiné.

Page 80, line 20

These remarks are inspired by the "Observations on the Principles of the Constitution of the Estates of Dauphiny to Use for the Estates-General" (Observations sur les principes de la constitution des états de Dauphiné pour servir aux états généraux), no date, 1788, 87 pages, a pamphlet probably written by the lawyer Lenoir-Laroche; see Egret, Les derniers états de Dauphiné, p. 30.

Page 81, line 6

Tocqueville chiefly comments in these notes from File 45B, CC, on issue number 4 of the Moniteur put out by Condorcet, Brissot de Warville, and Clavière. Basing themselves on the authority of Locke and Montesquieu, the authors call for respect for the ancient and constitutional rights of the privileged (p. 5), who are called upon to contribute to the common tax burden; they ask for a regeneration of the com-

mons, voting by order in the Estates-General, and the creation of a mixed govern-
ment in the English style (p. 32).

Page 81, line 24
    Tocqueville's notes on Volney's violent pamphlet (Folder 45B CC) end with a
long quotation of the attack against the parlements, which are full of "an esprit de
corps which is not that of the nation" (pp. 10–11).

Page 82, line 18
    Count Pierre Louis Roederer, "On the Deputation to the Estates-General" (De
la députation aux Etats généraux), 8 November 1788, 88 pages. It is interesting that
Tocqueville was so severe about a pamphlet which pleads in a very elaborate fash-
ion for the protection of minorities and for educating people about their interests
through the participation of all in political affairs (Folder 45B CC).

Page 82, line 32
    In the margin: Beautiful sentence! Spirit of the Laws *[by Montesquieu—*
Trans.], book II, chapter 6.

Page 83, line 4
    Roederer, who refuses to consider property the sole source of devotion to one's
country, tries to show that the dispersal of inequalities of wealth, of birth, and of
power in eighteenth-century society makes freedom dear to all and not only to the
aristocrats alone, as Montesquieu thought. It is in this context that he attempts
(p. 70) to minimize the importance of the nobles' privileges; according to him they,
like commoners, are subject to the salt tax, tolls, vingtièmes, and some other taxes.

Page 83, line 7
    Lacretelle, "On the Convocation of the Coming Meeting of the Estates-General
in France" (De la convocation de la prochaine tenue des Etats généraux en France),
1788, 50 pages. According to the author the work was begun on 13 October 1788.
Tocqueville's notes on it are filed in Folder 45B CC.

Page 84, line 3
    "Advice to the French on the Country's Safety" (Avis aux français sur le salut de
la patrie), by Jérome Pétion de Villeneuve, 1788, 254 pages. The Postscript on page
225 shows that the work was finished after Necker was called to office on 26 August.
Tocqueville dates the completion of the work to the discussion of the notables about
the form of the Estates-General, thus to November 1788 (Folder 45B CC).

Page 85, line 23
    In the margin: The idea of the balance of powers has never seduced me (p. 92).

Page 86, line 2

Tocqueville made this remark on decentralization again when briefly analyzing, in the same Folder 45B CC, the "Essay on the Constitution and the Function of the Provincial Assemblies," (Essai sur la constitution et les fonctions des assemblées provinciales) by Condorcet, 1788: Condorcet like all the men of that time (except perhaps Baudeau the physiocrat) are [sic—Trans.] all enemies of administrative centralization; it is mores, not ideas, which created it. All, while wanting to take the rights of sovereignty away from the provinces, or not give them any, gave the provinces great freedom for the administration of their affairs and in general respect local freedom.

Page 86, line 33

In the margin: "A day will come when all men will be governed by the same laws and will live as happily as their situation permits . . . The project of perpetual peace is no longer impractical today" *[p. 69].* (Written at the moment when one of the longest and most violent wars of modern times was about to begin!)

Page 87, line 17

On the first page of his notes, Tocqueville writes: My copy is bound in Morocco leather and belonged to the former royal library and perhaps to the king's personal library; it bears, separately from the coat of arms of France, the crowned Ls.

Page 87, line 27

Note in the margin: The universal principle which should serve as guide to the Reformation of the laws is equality (p. 178).

Page 89, line 2

"Consideration on the Interests of the Third Estate by a Landowner" (Considération sur les intérêts du tiers état par un propriétaire foncier), 1788, 107 pages. Tocqueville used the re-edition of 1826, in octodecimo, which also includes the "Question of Public Law: Should Votes at the Estates-General Be Counted by Order or by Head" (Question de Droit public: Doit on recueiller les voix dans les états généraux, par ordre ou par têtes de délibérans?), analyzed after this, and the "Commentary on the Decree of the Parlement of Paris of 5 December 1788" (Commentaire de l'arrêté du Parlement de Paris du 5 décembre 1788), notes in Folder 45B CC.

Page 93, line 35

Mémoire des princes, présenté au roi, edited by M. de Montyon, 1788, 14 pages. This report provoked a polemic in December 1788. Beyond the pamphlets discussed here, Tocqueville also analyzes in Folder 45B CC the "Response to the Report of Some Princes of the Blood"; the "Letter on the Princes' Report"; "Letter to the Count of Artois"; "The Last Word of the Third Estate to the Nobility"; the "Report for the French People" (76 pages), all by Joseph Cerutti (Réponse au Mémoire de quelques princes du sang; Lettre sur le mémoire des princes; A monsieur le comte d'Artois; Le dernier mot du Tiers à la noblesse; Mémoire pour le peuple français). *Tocqueville finds:* Throughout the polemics of this period great enthusiasm shown for the king and opinions very favorable to his authority. This is the character of this <u>moment,</u> different from the preceding moment and the one which will follow.

Tocqueville also notes that: what is characteristic of the nation and the times is the special irritation which is caused by the clause of the "Report of the Princes" which says that "every author makes himself into a lawgiver, eloquence or the ability to write without study and experience seems sufficient title to decide about the constitution of the state." This bites to the quick, more than all the rest. People come back to it constantly, responding with bitterness, often with fury.

Page 94, line 27
Abbé Morellet, "Plan of a Response to a Report known as the Report of the Princes" (Projet de réponse à un mémoire répandu sous le titre de Mémoire des Princes), 21 December 1788, 51 pages (analyzed in Folder 45B CC). The abbé Morellet, friend of Turgot, Diderot, d'Alembert, Malesherbes, here defends the double representation of the Third Estate.

Page 94, line 31
Page 12: "It is evident that a great nation, writing its constitution, may declare that there will not be among them either a nobility or distinct orders."

Page 95, line 12
Notes from Folder 45B CC. Gabriel Brizard (1730–1793), called Abbé Brizard although he had not been tonsured, was put on a proscription list because of the publication of this pamphlet.

Page 95, line 24
Mémoire pour le peuple français, 1788, 76 pages, attributed to Joseph Cerutti (Folder 45B CC). Joseph Antoine Joachim Cerutti (1738–1792), after having left the Jesuit order in 1768, joined the Duke of Orléans' faction at the approach of the Revolution. His "Report" had great success. A supporter of Necker and Lafayette, he became more radical in 1790 and was a deputy from Paris to the Legislative Assembly, 13 September 1791.

Page 95, line 33
See p. 35: "What therefore is political freedom or a free government? One where all forces are combined in such a way that each of them has the strength which is proper to them, and the rules which are useful for them."

Page 95, line 38

Tocqueville here paraphrases page 58: "You fear that the leaders of the multitude will attempt to lower the rank held by the nobility and the clergy; but they secretly hope to mount there one day themselves, or let their descendants mount there, and they will be very careful not to degrade their most brilliant opportunity for the future: among them several already think they are nobles, and the rest count on becoming nobles. If they are at your feet because of their opinion, they are also there because of hope."

Page 96, line 6

Notes from Folder 45B CC. Louis Henri Marthe, Marquis de Gouy d'Arsy, born 1753, decapitated 23 July 1794, admirer of Necker, elected deputy to the Estates-General 2 April 1789.

Page 96, line 28

Notes from Folder 45B EE: The author in a very long historical section denounces the monopolizing of the tithes by the monasteries as early as 847.

The workers, i.e. the curates, reduced to living from occasional fees.

Page 97, line 22

"Salutary Advice to the Third Estate on What It Was, What It Is, and What It Can Be, by a Savoyard Lawyer" (Avis salutaire au Tiers Etat sur ce qu'il fut, ce qu'il est et ce qu'il peut être par un jurisconsulte allobroge), 1789, 63 pages. This pamphlet is attributed to Joseph-Michel Antoine Servan (1737–1807), advocate-general at the Parlement of Grenoble.

Page 98, line 10

Tocqueville's notes (Folder 45B EE) were taken on the third edition.

Page 98, line 10

Marginal note: Born in 1748. Forty-one years old. Vicar-general at Chartres. Agent of the diocese at the assembly of the clergy. Named member of the provincial assembly of Orléans by the king. Elected to the Constituent Assembly not by the clergy but by the Third Estate of Paris.

Page 98, line 12

Note in the margin: Works by the same author at the same time:

1. "Essay on Privileges" (Essai sur les Privilèges), 1788 (November).

2. "Plan of Deliberation for the District Assemblies" (Plan de délibération pour les assemblées de baillages), March 1789.

3. "Recognition of the Rights of Man and the Citizen," (Reconnaissance des droits de l'homme et du citoyen), July 1789.

Page 104, line 31

The pamphlet commented on here (Folder 45B EE) is the continuation of "The Estates-General Convoked by Louis XVI," 75 pages. Guy Jean Baptiste Target (1733– 1807), a famous lawyer, was a deputy to the Estates-General from the city of Paris in 1789. On a separate page Tocqueville notes: A good sentence by Target: "In politics the big mistakes come when one has the mores of one's own time and the principles of another."

Page 105, line 10

Target argues for a number of deputies based on the amount of taxes paid more than on population: "In every society, those whose stake is greater feel a stronger desire to conserve it and to assure prosperity for it" (p. 1). The political order needs to base itself on the interests of individuals: "we will not have citizens at the end unless we start by admitting calculators," he writes (p. 3).

Page 105, line 12

On Mounier's book, later than, but read by Tocqueville before, that by Target, see the following note.

Page 107, line 5

"New Observations on the Estates-General of France" (Nouvelles observations sur les Etats généraux de France), 1789, 282 pages, by M. Mounier, secretary of the estates of the province of Dauphiny (notes from Folder 45B CC).

Page 110, line 35

Note in the margin: This certainly took place in 1484 at the estates of Tours under Charles VIII. But I do not know if there is proof that it had happened this way previously, I think so. But very certainly this was not done afterwards. *Tocqueville is commenting here on chapter 29 of Mounier's work.*

Page 111, line 16

Notes from Folder 45B CC. Jacques-Pierre Brissot, called Brissot de Warville, 1754–1793, early on gave up a judicial career for literature. He had lived in London in 1779 and 1787, and in 1788 went to the United States to think about the abolition of the slave trade there. He would be elected deputy from Paris to the Legislative Assembly on 13 September 1791 with the support of the Jacobins. In chapter 20 of the work analyzed here, Brissot proposed that the Estates-General convoke the nation to name a convention of men to write the constitution (p. 257). This was to follow the American example and to deny the Estates-General the right of giving a constitution to France. This Americanophilia caused Brissot's failure at the elections of the spring of 1789.

Page 117, line 3
Notes from File 45B, Folder YY

Page 118, line 10
Notes from File 44. The Journal de Paris, *a daily, appeared throughout the Revolution. Tocqueville's notes bear on the period 1 January–4 May.*

Page 121, line 3
Notes from File 44. The Journal historique et politique de Genève, *edited by Mallet du Pan, was a weekly which appeared from 5 January 1788 until 29 December 1792 in Paris. Tocqueville's notes bear on the period January–May 1789.*

Page 122, line 4
Tocqueville had as a neighbor in Normandy a member of this family, Count Gaston de Blangy, owner of the château de Saint-Pierre-Eglise.

Page 122, line 31
In the margin of the title: All this sketched out.

Page 122, line 31
Notes from File 44.1, started in June 1858.

Page 122, line 37
Notes from File 43.3. In the Constituent Assembly 151 lawyers had been elected, thus 23 percent of the deputies, and 218 owned a legal office. A total of at least 322 had studied law. See Edna Lemay, "La composition de l'assemblée constituante," Revue d'histoire moderne et contemporaine *(July–December 1977), pp. 341–63.*

Page 123, line 20
Notes from File 44.2. These notes relate to the Correspondance de MM. les députés des Communes de la province d'Anjou, avec leurs commettans relativement aux Etats-Généraux tenans à Versailles en 1789, *Angers, 1789. Tocqueville took notes on volume 1 (27 April–24 July 1789) on two occasions.*

Page 124, line 8
Marie Etienne Populus, born in 1736 and executed in 1793, lawyer, only made brief speeches on 27 May, 6 June, and 11 July in the period analyzed here.

Page 125, line 2
Proposition of M. Coroller de Moutier at the session of 25 May, Correspondance, *pp. 55–56.*

Page 125, line 11
On 25 June, 47 deputies of the nobility, led by the Duke of Orléans, came to join with the Third Estate.

Page 125, line 39
A blank in Tocqueville's manuscript.

Page 129, line 8
Martin Dauch, deputy from the district of Castelnaudary.

Page 130, line 13
Note in the margin: M. de Talleyrand only came on 26 June (242).

Page 132, line 35
Note in the margin: When the parlement sent its compliments at the same time as it sent a deputation to the king, the Assembly complained that the deputation had not made an address to it too.

It is the king who asks the Assembly to forbid a great deputation from Paris, 16 July.

Page 134, line 3
On 17 July, at St. Germain-en-Laye, the crowd had murdered a miller. On the day after at Poissy the intervention of a deputy of the National Assembly barely saved the tax-farmer Thomassin, accused of hoarding. The bishop of Chartres on his knees asked for mercy for Thomassin and offered to take him to prison himself. The account of this action to the Assembly by Le Camus led M. Goupil de Préferne to ask the Assembly to vote thanks to the Bishop of Chartres and his colleagues.

Page 134, line 23
Page 464: "an outraged people has spilled blood, he says. Well, was this blood so pure then?"

Page 135, line 1
Notes from File 44.2.

Page 135, line 17
File 44.

Page 136, line 8
Notes taken at Tocqueville in May 1858 on the pamphlets from series Lb 39 of the Bibliothèque Impériale and grouped in File 44.1. Tocqueville had also read some pamphlets from June and the beginning of July 1789, notably the "Account of What

Took Place at the Abbey of St. Germain on the Night of 30 June" (Relation de ce qui s'est passé à l'abbaye Saint-Germain, le 30 juin au soir), a pamphlet from 1 July; "Account of the Liberation by Force and the Voluntary Return of the French Guards in the Prison of the Saint-Germain Abbey" (Récit de l'élargissement forcé et de la rentrée volontaire des gardes françaises dans la prison de l'abbaye Saint-Germain), by Marie de Saint Ursin, undated; "Where It Hurts Us: A Song for Everyone, Accompanied by Interesting Notes" (Où le bât nous blesse: Chanson à la portée de tout le monde enrichie de notes intéressantes), July 1789; "The Orator of the Palais Royal Should Be Whipped: By an Old Observer, a Patriot of the Palais Royal, Who, for Seventy-One Years, Has Had the Honor of Being a Member of the Third Estate" (Le coup de fouet à l'orateur du Palais Royal, par un vieux observateur, patriote du Palais Royal, qui, depuis soixante-onze ans, a l'honneur d'être du tiers état), undated. Tocqueville notes: First revolution. The soldiers' hesitation or refusal to participate. Incitement to revolt . . . revolutionary violence which precedes the armed struggle . . . one flaunts being a member of the Third Estate as in '48 being a worker."

Page 136, line 25

La chasse aux bêtes puantes et féroces qui après avoir inondé les bois, les plains, etc., se sont répandues à la cour et à la capitale, 1789, 31 pages. The pamphlet establishes a "special list of those proscribed by the nation, with a notice of the punishments to be inflicted upon them for contumacy."

Page 137, line 21

The revolution of 1688 replaced James II with his daughter Mary and his son-in-law William. In 1842 Tocqueville had written "Some Notes on the Revolutions of 1688 and 1830" about it. There he opposed the aristocratic character of the English revolution to the troubles and democratic demands which characterized revolution in France: After 1688, England remained deeply aristocratic and monarchical. The men who had made or adopted this Revolution wanted a royal power more or less limited, but no one wanted to destroy it. The lower classes always remained in silence and shadow *(OC, v. 16, pp. 560–61).*

Page 138, line 16

Tocqueville's bitterness comes from the attitude of the clergy, who, after having rallied to the Republic, burnt incense before the image of Louis Napoleon Bonaparte. See his letter to Corcelle of 13 May 1852, OC, v. 15, t. 2, p. 55.

Page 138, line 22

"National Verdict Rendered as a Last Resort by the General Committee of the Dietines at the Palais Royal at Paris" (Jugement national rendu en dernier ressort

par le comité général des diettines du Palais Royal à Paris) (excerpt from the register of the committee of the dietines from 14 July to 25 August 1789).

Page 138, line 26

The Sepoy Revolt had broken out in India in May *1857*. Delhi was taken on *11* May by the insurgents, who massacred Europeans. On *15 July* European women and children were massacred at Cawnpore. Tocqueville was horrified by the violence. See his letter to Beaumont of *17 August 1857*, <u>OC</u>, v. *8*, t. *3*, p. *496*.

Page 138, line 35

"Second Discourse on French Freedom, Pronounced on *31 August 1789*, in the Parish Church of Saint Margaret, in the Presence of the Three Combined Districts of the Faubourg Saint-Antoine" (*Second discours sur la liberté françoise, prononcé le 31 août 1789, dans l'église paroissiale de Sainte-Marguerite, en présence des trois districts réunis du faubourg Saint-Antoine, 22 pages. In his analysis of the pamphlets from the beginning of 1789 (File 45B EE) Tocqueville had analyzed the pamphlet <u>La Religion nationale,</u> 300 pages, by Abbé Fauchet, already noting in Abbé Fauchet the alliance of a Catholicism "not very liberal towards Protestants" and "socialist doctrine"*: Nothing shows better than this book the disorder in the ideas of the times, the mental confusion and incoherent doctrines, until finally events pushed everyone down the slope towards which his chief interests directed him. *The abbé Fauchet, constitutional bishop of Calvados in 1791, deputy in the Legislative Assembly and the Convention, opposed the condemnation of Louis XVI and was executed in 1793.*

Page 138, line 37

Abbé Fauchet accuses the "concealed aristocrats who hide among us" (p. 2), "the hydra of the aristocracy" (p. 6), of spreading unworthy suspicions against the leaders.

Page 139, line 4

"Jesus Christ is nothing but the divinity as fellow-citizen of the human species. Catholicism is nothing but the Assembly, the community, the unity of brothers, faithful to the fatherland of the Earth, in order to raise ourselves together to the fatherland of Heaven" (p. 21).

Page 139, line 27

René-François Lebois, "Letter of the Lower Classes to M. Necker about the High Price of Bread" (*Lettre du peuple à M. Necker sur la cherté du pain*), Paris, undated, 7 pages.

Page 139, line 34

24 August 1789, 7 pages.

Page 140, line 11

In the margin of the first two headings: "excerpts made in May '58." The notes on Bailly's correspondence were taken from the French Manuscripts of the Biblio-

thèque Nationale, number 11.696–697. The notes on the transcripts, from French Manuscripts 11698–11703. They are collected in File 44.

Jean-Baptiste Gouvion (1747–1792) had served under Lafayette in the United States and had been chosen by him as major-general of the national guard.

Page 142, line 15

In the margin: Judges seditious the address from the district of the Cordeliers presided over by Danton.

Page 142, line 16

Note in the margin: They note among other things the insults that some frenzied writers permit themselves against the municipal government and those who compose it.

Page 144, line 3

Tocqueville's notes on the registers of the minister of the Royal Household (Archives Nationales, series O 485 and 486) collected in File 44, bear principally on February and the following months, and notably on the grain riots of April and May, the fear of brigands, and the organization of the bourgeois militia.

Page 144, line 15

Tocqueville had already made this reflection on the precociously revolutionary character of Brittany in 1853 while reading the cahiers of grievances of Rennes. See volume one of The Old Regime and the Revolution, *pp. 362–63.*

Page 144, line 35

Notes collected in File 44 on the grain riots and the "Great Fear" of July. Tocqueville writes "pays d'états. Various subjects; new folder. M." It relates to series M of the archives nationales (M 664 papers seized at the Tuileries on the beginnings of the Revolution in the Paris region and M 668–669, "Decisions, Reports, and Correspondence on the Troubles and Insurrections in the Provinces, 1789–1799").

Page 145, line 17

Louis-Bénigne-François Bertier de Sauvigny, assistant to the intendant of the Generality of Paris (1768–1776), then intendant himself after 1776 until his murder on 23 July 1789 in Paris.

Page 147, line 24

In the margin: Read for the chapter where I speak of the unanimity of the cahiers.

Page 149, line 6

In the margin: The bourgeoisie wanting political rights, the lower classes some material benefit.

Page 150, line 23

Note in the margin: At the beginning of the Constituent highlight not only the famous names then unknown, but the names which suddenly became famous to be immediately forgotten, Bouche, Populus, Lacoste . . .

On Populus, see above, p. 435. Charles-François Bouche (1737–1795), member of the Parlement of Aix, elected to the Constituent Assembly, spoke there frequently, notably on questions of the discipline of the Assembly. From 1791 to 1795 he sat on the appeals court of Paris. The marquis Lacoste de Messelière (1760–1806), deputy of the nobility of Poitou, favorable to the vote by head, was among the 47 members of the nobility who joined the Third Estate by 25 June.

Page 155, line 8

A blank in the manuscript.

Page 156, line 25

In the margin: See in Mounier the humiliation of the Assembly, almost as great as that of the king during this ill-fated night! *See "Defense of M. Mounier's Conduct," below, p. 160.*

Page 157, line 30

Notes collected in File 44.1. Mounier, De l'influence attribuée aux philosophes aux francs-maçons et aux illuminés sur la révolution de France, *Tübingen, 1801. Tocqueville also used his notes on these works for chapter 1 of book 1, "agitation of the human mind."*

Page 157, line 31

On this portrait see the use Tocqueville was thinking of making of it, on p. 163 below.

Page 158, line 5

Like Mounier, Rabaud was accused of participating in secret assemblies with Mme. de Polignac. Cf. Mounier, De l'influence attribuée aux philosophes, *p. 103.*

Page 158, line 8

Mounier alludes to the "Daily Headline; or The Result of What Happened Yesterday at the National Assembly" (Point du jour; ou, Résultat de ce qui s'est passé la vieille à l'assemblée nationale), *a daily published by Barère from 19 June 1789 until 1 October 1791.*

Page 158, line 11

Roland de La Platière, "Letters Written from Switzerland, Italy, Sicily, and Malta in 1776–1778" (Lettres écrites de Suisse, d'Italie, de Sicile et de Malte en 1776–

1778), Amsterdam, 1782, 6 vols., reprinted in 1801. The passage mentioned is found in volume 5, letter 28. He was in fact the husband of Mme. Roland.

Page 159, line 10

"Considerations on Governments, and Chiefly on That Which Is Suitable for France" (Considérations sur les gouvernements, et principalement sur celui qui convient à la France), *by M. Mounier, member of the committee charged with work relating to the constitution, Paris, 1789, 54 pages.*

Page 159, line 11

Note in the margin: In the following work, Mounier says that this pamphlet was written around the seventh or eighth of August 1789. *The pamphlet was published on 16 August 1789.*

Page 159, line 23

In the margin: Highlight well this change of meaning.

Page 160, line 24

Mounier notes that only the eldest sons of noble families entered the peerage and that they therefore did not form a separate class. The peers "ought therefore to be considered as hereditary magistrates, established for the maintenance of the constitution" (p. 37).

Page 160, line 26

"Description of M. Mounier's Conduct in the National Assembly and the Reasons for His Return to Dauphiné" (Exposé de la conduite de M. Mounier dans l'Assemblée nationale et des motifs de son retour en Dauphiné), *Bordeaux, 1789, 96 pages.*

Page 162, line 14

On 6 October Mirabeau had rejected the deputies going to the king in the name of the "dignity" of the Assembly. Mounier replied that it was a sacred duty to help the king in danger. Mirabeau and Barnave then proposed to form a delegation to accompany the king to Paris. Mounier lists the mistakes committed then: "to have refused to go to the king, and this under the pretext of preserving its own dignity, at the moment when the king's habitation had just been soiled by the most horrible crimes; to have kept silent about so many crimes; to let the king leave accompanied by the murderers of his servants and by a militia led astray by factious men who had raised the standard of revolt, who had forced their chief to lead them to the king's and the National Assembly's seat with all the gear of war . . ."

Page 162, line 31

All these notes are taken from File 44.

Page 162, line 31

Notes of June 1858. See below, chapter 7, the draft of the ideas stated here. Tocqueville's bad temper here is directed towards the Caesarists who made the First and Second Empires the necessary heirs of the Revolution.

Page 162, line 33

In the margin of the first paragraph: To the principles of '89.

Page 163, line 33

In a separate page of remarks on the "Correspondence of the Deputies of Anjou," Tocqueville had noted: We see that his power over the Assembly was not established all at once. In the correspondence of the deputies of Anjou (very revolutionary, however), we see that in the session of 16 June, M. de Mirabeau made a speech in favor of the chamber of the Third Estate taking the title of representative of the people, and that this speech seemed ranting. "People complained loudly and several voices were raised to interrupt him" (*[v. 1,]*, p. 163).

File 45A also contains several notes relating to the beginnings of the Constituent Assembly on the work published under Mirabeau's name, "On the Prussian Monarchy under Frederick the Great; with an Appendix Containing Research on the Present Situation of the Chief Countries of Germany" (De la monarchie prussienne sous Frédéric le grand; avec un appendice contenant des recherches sur la situation actuelle des principales contrées de l'Allemagne), 8 vols., London, 1788:

Anticentralizing character of the beginning of the revolution.

Mirabeau never called the government functionaries, in his work on Prussia, anything but the salaried.

To put in chapter 2 or chapter 3 when I show the opposition spirit of the nobility and enmity for bureaucrats: the phrase "the salaried" frequent in Mirabeau's mouth.

Timidity of the greatest reformers when they start to work. Mirabeau in his work on Prussia, published in 1788 or '89, speaks at length about the necessity of going ahead with prudence and with consideration and slowness.

To put perhaps in chapter 7 to better paint this kind of terror which overtook the most carried-away souls at the moment of action. I have not sufficiently described this feeling in chapter 7. True and good to take up; the kind of terror which overtakes the strongest souls when one is finally going to begin a plan, even the best thought-out.

Necessity of a nobility or at least of a body of landowners participating in government. Mirabeau, his opinion on this point, in his work on Germany: only independent watchmen can stop despotism. Perhaps in the principles of '89.

The author, who defined "the salaried" as those who traded their bodily or intellectual strength like the farmer trades his products, the manufacturer his creations" (v. 3, p. 249), in fact constantly employs the term in volumes three and following, along with that of "wage-earners," in order to designate the employees of the Prussian state. This contempt for "the salaried" of the finances or of justice in particular is part of the central thesis of the book, which is a vibrant defense of the freedom of commerce and industry. The economic liberalism also explains the prudence with regard to reforms which would be engaged in by the state.

Page 163, line 33

In the margin: This portrait can only come during the Constituent Assembly.

Page 163, line 36

In the margin: This cannot come during the first book: the Revolution is not yet launched.

Page 164, line 7

All these sketches of plans, written on separate pages, are grouped in File 44.

Page 164, line 15

The title is found on a folder, and a piece of paper contains the remarks which follow.

Page 164, line 24

Tocqueville's notes on foreigners' feelings are scattered among several files:

—The notes on Heinrich Steffens's work, Was ich erlebte: Aus der Erinnerung-niedergeschrieben, 1 vol., Breslau, 1840, taken in July 1858, and those on the work by Heinrich Campe, Briefe aus Paris zur Zeit der Revolution, Brunswick, 1790, taken in June–July 1858, are filed in the papers on The Old Regime, File 43, Folder M, "Foreigners' Judgments on the Revolution."

—The notes on the work Friedrich Perthes Leben nach dessen schriftliche, und mündliche, Mittheilungen aufgezeichnet von Clemens-Theodor Perthes, 3 vols., Hamburg and Gotha, 1848, are classed in the papers for the continuation of The Old Regime (File 45, Folder AA, "Vague Intellectual Disturbance Which Preceded the Revolution"). Tocqueville read this work in 1856 and used his notes for chapter 1 of his unfinished work. See above.

—The notes on Ludwig Haüsser's book, Deutsche Geschichte vom Tode Friedrichs der Grossen bis zur Gründung des deutschen Bundes, 4 vols., 1854–57, taken during Tocqueville's trip to Germany in 1854, are found in File 43, Folder Q (papers on The Old Regime). Tocqueville had used chapters 4, 5, and 6 of book 1 of Haüsser's work relative to the social and political situation of Prussia for the notes published at the end of his work. On Haüsser, see The Old Regime, v. 1, pp. 330–31.

—The notes on the book by G.-H. Pertz, Das Leben des Ministers Freiherrn vom Stein, 1849–51, are taken from the article by Saint-René Taillandier, Revue des deux mondes, 15 November 1852, and filed in the papers for The Old Regime, File 43, Folder K. Tocqueville read Pertz's work himself in February 1857 (see his letter to Monnard, 1 February 1857, OC, v. 7, p. 358).

We publish these notes here not according to the chronological order of the writ-

ing but according to the period on which they bear. Beyond the notes published here Tocqueville took notes on the correspondence (for the years 1788–89) of Johann von Müller (volume 16 of his Sämmtliche Werke, Tübingen, 1810–19). These notes only include fragmentary quotations.

Page 164, line 27
Heinrich Steffens, man of letters and philosopher (1773–1845).

Page 166, line 9
Joachim-Heinrich Campe (1746–1818), German educator, disciple of Basedow. The National Assembly would give him the title of honorary citizen on 6 September 1792 for his works for children and the creation of a pedagogical institute near Hamburg in 1777. In France Campe was considered the representative of enlightened pedagogy. His "Lettres de Paris" were first published in the Journal de Brunswick. Tocqueville here uses the first letter and the beginning of the second (pp. 1–32).

Page 168, line 5
Marginal note: The armed bourgeois clashed with the old French Guards, now called soldiers of the fatherland, over who would better maintain public peace and order, not by the bayonet, but through requests and friendly warnings; and the means were perfectly sufficient to maintain hundred of thousands of inspired men within the bounds of order and morality (p. 31).

Page 168, line 16
Friedrich Christoph Perthes (1772–1843), after studies at Leipzig entered the Hoffmann publishing firm at Hamburg in May 1793, before founding his own publishing house. He entered into relations with intellectual Europe and in 1810 published a review called the Vaterlandisches Museum where the German patriots were collected. He took an important part in the Romantic and national movement.

Page 168, line 21
By the Peace of Lunéville of 9 February 1801, Austria ceded the left bank of the Rhine and recognized French domination over northern and central Italy; Austria retained Istria, Dalmatia, and Venetia. Ratisbon, which was the seat of the Imperial Diet from 1645, had been mediatized to the profit of Archchancellor Dalberg in 1806, before being annexed to Bavaria in 1810.

Page 168, line 23
By "Eugénie," The Life of Perthes means the play Die natürliche Tochter ["The Natural Daughter"—Trans.] (April 1803), which Goethe several times called by the title "Eugénie."

Page 171, line 6

Adam Gottlob Detlef Count von Moltke (1765–1843), schoolmate of Niebuhr, lived at Nütschau near Segeberg in Holstein. He had people call him "citizen Moltke" out of enthusiasm for the revolution. From 1815 to 1823 he played a large role in the efforts of the nobility of Schleswig-Holstein to obtain a constitution.

Page 171, line 39

Johann von Müller (1752–1809), a historian of Swiss origin who successively served the Landgrave of Hesse, the Elector of Mainz, Emperor Leopold of Austria, and Frederick-William the King of Prussia, before rallying to the Napoleonic cause.

Page 173, line 16

An allusion to God.

Page 175, line 23

By the Treaty of Pressburg in December 1805, Austria, isolated, abandoned its Venetian possessions, including Istria and Dalmatia, and its lands in southern Germany. This upheaval allowed Napoleon to force the German princes to leave the Holy Roman Empire and form a Confederation of the Rhine under his protection (12 July 1806).

Page 176, line 11

Tocqueville here translates the word "Wissenschaft" [in English, "science" or "discipline"—Trans.] as "literature."

Page 176, line 36

The Vaterländisches Museum ("Patriotic Museum"), published by Friedrich Perthes from spring 1810 until the end of the year. Schlegel would take up the mantle by publishing the Deutsches Museum at Vienna from 1812 to 1813, which also defended a patriotic vision of literature and art.

Page 177, line 39

Tocqueville here cites or comments on two fragments from volume two of Haüsser's work, pp. 422ff., then p. 331.

Page 179, line 4

Tocqueville's reference is inexact. The work by Görres in question is Resultate meiner Sendung nach Paris im Brumaire, des VIII Jahres, Koblenz, Year VIII. Joseph von Görres (1776–1848), a liberal Catholic German publicist, born at Koblenz, went to Paris in 1799 at the head of a republican embassy asking for the annexation of the left bank of the Rhine. Disappointed by the Terror, he later became one of Napoleon's opponents alongside Arndt.

Page 179, line 30

Saint-René Taillandier, "le baron de Stein," Revue des deux mondes, 15 No-
vember 1852, pp. 708–755. The article is a review of the biography of the Baron vom
Stein published by G.-H. Pertz in four volumes, Berlin, 1849–51. Henri-Frédéric-
Charles, Baron vom Stein (1757–1831), named minister of public works, of com-
merce, and of the customs by Frederick William II in October 1804, then prime
minister of the King of Prussia from October 1807 to November 1808, had taken
from the principles of a revolution which he detested the principles of his own
reform. Later Stein took an active part in the struggle against Napoleon until
1815.

Page 179, line 31

All these notes are taken from File 44.

Page 180, line 8

The Mercure britannique, a bimonthly publication by Mallet du Pan (August
1798–March 1800).

Page 180, line 31

See on this point the portrait of the French above, p. 68. Tocqueville had noted
during the Crimean War that the French peasants' lack of enthusiasm for going to
war did not prevent them from showing great courage during the fight. See his letter
to Mme. Swetchine, 6 October 1855, OC, v. 15, t. 2, p. 263.

Page 180, line 34

Tocqueville had already compared revolutionary proselytism to the expansion of
Islam in chapter 3 of the first volume, "How the French Revolution Was a Political
Revolution Which Acted Like a Religious Revolution, and Why." He had found
this comparison in the Mémoires et correspondance of Mallet du Pan. See the notes
on this work, taken in the spring of 1852, below, pp. 121–23. On the propaganda of
the Revolution, a page from File 44 gives "books mentioned by M. de Circourt: Bar-
ruel, Histoire du jacobinisme, 5 vols. in octavo, Hamburg, 1800; Mémoires de Cus-
tine to show the revolutionary propaganda which preceded the French armies in
Germany."

Page 181, line 5

Armand Lefebvre, "Soulèvement de l'Allemagne après la guerre de Russie. York
et Stein.—Le cabinet de Berlin et le cabinet de Vienne," Revue des deux mondes,
1 January 1857, pp. 5–64.

Page 185, line 2

Notes from File 44, dated from 1850 to 1852.

Page 188, line 30

On the men to consult, see below, p. 237 (conversation), and pp. 250, 252 (chapter on the Empire).

Page 189, line 2

In the margin: Histoire du directoire *by Fain. M. Fain was secretary to the Directory. Incomplete, but good to read. A single volume. On another page of the same file (44) Tocqueville notes: Ask for again at the library of the Institute, when I come back to the Consulate and the Directory, the following volumes that I thought I had to return after having borrowed them, but without having read them, in December 1852:*
  1. Histoire du directoire, *2 vols., Year IX, 1801*
  2. Mémoire sur le consulat par un conseiller d'état *(Thibaudeau), 1799 to 1804*
This allows us to date the indications of method to December 1852 at the latest.

Page 189, line 5

Jean-Barthélémy Hauréau (1812–1898), at first close to the republicans, took over direction of the "Courrier of the Sarthe," a newspaper which supported Beaumont [Tocqueville's friend, and member of the French lower house under the July Monarchy—Trans.], from 1830 to 1845. In 1848 he sat on the left in the Constituent Assembly. A scholar, in the same year he became conservator of manuscripts at the Bibliothèque Nationale, was dismissed after 2 December [1851, date of the coup d'état by Napoleon III—Trans.], but introduced Tocqueville to his successor. He was to write a very positive review of The Old Regime *in* L'Illustration *of 17 July 1856.*

Page 191, line 5

The files of the Tocqueville Archives contain two folders. One, bearing the note "Rubbish from the first two chapters done at Tocqueville in 1852. End of the First Republic," contains ten pages of sketches written on both sides; the definitive text of forty pages in folio, written on one side only, is in a folder bearing the title "How the Republic Was Ready to Accept a Master," and on an interior folder the note "good pages for a chapter of the second volume of the work on the Revolution." In the margin of the first paragraph, crossed out: "This chapter will follow the one on the victories and their causes."

Page 191, line 30

On a separate page of the Rubbish and bearing the note "should this be put here?":

Its entire reign was nothing but tempered anarchy. A disturbed situation which properly speaking was neither revolt nor obedience, and during which the citizens ended up being disgusted with public affairs without being able to devote themselves usefully to the care of their own personal affairs. The nation no longer wanted anything but rest, and its government could never find it a quiet place in which it could.

Page 192, line 17

Since Fructidor, Year V, the royalists had been subject to close watch, and Jacobinism was on the upswing, but the Republic no longer had any authority. After having annulled the election of Treilhard to the Directory, on 30 Prairial, Year VII (18 June 1799), the Councils forced Merlin de Douai and la Revellière-Lépeaux to resign from the Directory. They were replaced by some obscure former members of the Convention, Gohier, Roger Ducos, and Moulin. On the regime of terror instituted by the law of 24 Messidor (12 July 1799), see above, p. 192.

Page 193, line 17

Tocqueville underlined this sentence in view of a future revision. There is found here in the manuscript a circled paragraph: This deadening of passions, this slackness of mores did not show itself only in the impossibility of executing revolutionary laws, but also in the choice of punishment. For the scaffold one substituted deportation, a punishment often harsher than death, but which one didn't see being applied and which, while satisfying hatred, spared people the inconvenient sight of pain.

Page 193, line 19

The Jacobin Club was reopened at the beginning of the month of July 1799, then closed on the order of Sieyès on 13 August (26 Thermidor) 1799.

Page 193, line 30

First version: suddenly. *Interlinear correction:* little by little.

Page 194, line 7

Marginal note, circled: The roads are becoming impassable, assured the minister of the interior in 1799, the costs of levying the tax intended for their upkeep have entirely absorbed its income.

Page 194, line 15

Tocqueville put in File 44 some notes taken on the files of "General Police" at the National Archives, notably on the weekly bulletins of the general police from 20 to 30 Fructidor, Year VII, which analyze the correspondence received from the civil and military authorities of the departments (Archives Nationales AF III 47, dossier 172). See also below, pp. 197–98.

Page 194, line 36

Circled marginal variant: Paris slept, but it was a painful sleep and troubled by bad dreams.

Page 195, line 26

Circled: This internal revolt of hearts was enough to paralyze public power at a time when it was not provided with a living organism of its own.

Several times in our day we have seen the bureaucracy survive the government which directed it. While the great powers of the state were either overthrown, or disorganized, or languishing, the secondary powers nevertheless continued to firmly and regularly take care of business. We were in revolution, but not in anarchy.

The reason for this is that today, in France, the bureaucracy proper forms within the state, in a way outside the sovereign, a separate body which has its special habits, its own rules, its agents who belong only to it, so that for a while it can present the phenomenon of a body which walks after its head has been cut off. This is Napoleon's work. We will see how, in constructing this powerful hierarchy, he simultaneously made revolution among us easier to make and less destructive.

Nothing similar existed at the time of which we speak. The old authorities were destroyed, without anything really having taken their place. Like the nation the bureaucracy was incoherent and disorganized, without rules, without hierarchy, without traditions. The Terror had been able to hold these badly made and badly joined springs together; terror having become impossible and public spirit lacking, the whole machinery of power fell to pieces all at once.

In the margin of the circled text: All this, which is good, ought, I think, to be kept for another place. Here the flow of ideas is broken by it.

Tocqueville developed the same idea in a note from File 43, Folder K: Perfection of the bureaucratic machine built by Bonaparte proved by the ease with which it functions in the weak hands of mediocre rascals like those who rule us today, almost as well as it could work under the impulse of the greatest minds. It produces its work independently of the value of the worker. Never was this phenomenon produced more obviously than at this moment, and never has government seemed more within the abilities of the first-comer who arrives to grab the crank which makes the machine go.

Centralization is pretty similar to those Barbary organs which play their tune just as well in the hands of the first idiot who comes along as in those of Paganini, which even a blind man can play, and which even a one-armed man can play as well as anyone once he has put the hand which remains to him on the crank.

See also Tocqueville's notes on Thibaudeau, below, p. 213ff.

Page 195, line 27

For the end of great passions is always sad. After a determined ardor there follows a weak and vague emotional disturbance. From time to time, however, habit still leads one along the roads where passion used to run, the appearance of love survives love itself. The words remain the same when already the souls freeze. The French had loved freedom passionately, or rather they had believed they loved it; they loved it no longer. After having lent liberty a thousand imaginary qualities, people no longer saw its real charms. People were only aware of its difficulties and dangers. The truth is that for ten years freedom was what we had least encountered in this Revolution made in freedom's name. *Rubbish. The page stops here.*

In the margin: This is good, but in another place where I will show this mockery of freedom.

The idea is partially taken up again on p. 197.

Page 196, line 17
Tocqueville here uses the work done at Tocqueville in 1852 on the profits gained from the Revolution, which he also uses in the following chapter (see below, p. 201ff and note) and in chapter 1 of the second book of The Old Regime and the Revolution, *"Why Feudalism Was Hated by the People in France More Than Anywhere Else."*

Page 198, line 4
Tocqueville here paraphrases a passage from July 1799 of the Mémoires *of General Lafayette, v. 5, p. 66.*

Page 198, line 22
The calendar of festivals as it was set in Year IV included five moral holidays: youth, old age, marriage, gratitude, and agriculture; five great commemorations, 14 July, 10 August, 1 Vendémiaire, 21 January, 9 Thermidor; to which was added the festival of the sovereignty of the people. See Mona Ozouf, Festivals and the French Revolution, *translated by Alan Sheridan, Cambridge, Mass., 1988.*

Page 198, line 23
In his notes in File 44, on the documents in the National Archives relating to the Directorial regime in Year VII, Tocqueville judges François de Neufchâteau severely: The stupidest intellectual who ever took part in politics. He is an old scoundrel who thinks he can rejuvenate himself by taking on the airs and words of youth. *His circulars:* could be cited as models of revolutionary style surviving through its flowery and bloated tone after the revolutionary period. The last thing that a party changes is its language. Why? *asks Tocqueville.*

Page 198, line 31
Marginal note: Check the date.

Page 199, line 8

In the margin: Should this be put in the text?

On an intercalated page in the final manuscript: As a sign of the times, put someplace around here how it was accepted that one could speak of France with contempt, of its vices and the moral weaknesses of the nation (at the Bibliothèque Nationale see cahier written in Year VII). What a fall from the heights of limitless pride of 1789, and from the dogma of unlimited perfectibility. *This commentary was inspired by the reading of Joseph Michaud's pamphlet, "Les derniers Adieux à Bonaparte victorieux" (1799, see below, in the chapter on the Consulate and Empire)*

Page 199, line 22

On the powerlessness of the press, see above, the notes on the Mercure britannique, p. 228 and note.

Page 199, line 22

Marginal note: Perhaps develop here, based on that original idea by Michaud in his *Adieux à Bonaparte* (cahier of the year VII, collected at the Bibliothèque Nationale), that style becomes more exaggerated as the minds of the listeners and readers become more incredulous. Since one knows that people will always discount a lot, one is obliged to overdo.

A sentence containing this idea and coming after what is already found on the page would go well. One would have to cite Michaud's name.

Page 200, line 27

Crossed-out marginal addition: and whose instincts are almost always worth more than its morals. *Below the crossed-out passage:* This would indicate the contrary.

Page 200, chapter title

The final text, written on only one side of the folio pages at the end of the preceding chapter, is in a folder bearing the chapter title. Some pages of bibliographical notes in the Rubbish file are relevant to this chapter. In them are found some brief mentions of the Mémoires of Lafayette, 3 vols., which are one of the chief sources of this chapter, and the Mémoires of Thibaudeau.

Page 201, line 6

Circled marginal note: The point will possibly and even probably be treated in one of the chapters which will precede this one. But in doubt treat it here.

Page 201, line 19

The mass of confiscated goods was so enormous that the state could not get rid of them except very slowly, even though they had been divided into very small parts and sold at very low prices. Thus as long as the Revolution lasted the number of irreconcilable enemies of the old regime regularly increased every year; what I say about the purchase of confiscated lands should be extended to many other advantages that people received from the Revolution, some in jobs, others a rank in the state, these some rights, those importance in their village, new advantages, each day more widespread or better enjoyed and whose possession seemed incompatible with a return to the old regime.

Page 201, line 29

In the Rubbish file (reading notes): Address of the Directors to the People (17 Fructidor, Year VII, a little before 18 Brumaire) summarizes well all the hatreds and all the fears that the return of the old regime would bring forth.

How France wanted the monarchy, but not the king. Ch. 2. 20 *(reference to Lafayette's memoirs).*

Page 202, line 3

Marginal addition topped by the word "perhaps": The same causes produced the same phenomenon at the end of the Empire, the situation of the workers improved amid our disasters.

Page 202, line 5

Citation from the Mémoires of Mallet du Pan, v. 2, p. 262: "the workers earned as much and more than in 1790."

Page 202, line 8

Marginal note: Pamphlet titled "On the Causes Which Have Brought About the Usurpation by General Bonaparte and Will Bring About His Fall" (Des causes qui ont amené l'usurpation du général Bonaparte et produiront sa chute). London, 1800.

Page 202, line 9

Tocqueville here uses the work done at Tocqueville in 1852 on the profits gained from the Revolution, for which he assembled the material in Folder O (Preparatory files for the work of 1856). For this work he had consulted two liberal economists who were his colleagues at the Institute about the rise of salaries and the decline of the price of wheat: Hippolyte Passy (1792–1880), several times minister under the July Monarchy and the Second Republic, and Adolphe Blanqui (1798–1854).

Page 202, line 9

In the margin of the paragraph, circled: Speak in depth with Passy, Blanqui, and all those who are concerned with such matters about this question of salaries at different periods. Only say things recognized by science.

Page 202, line 12

Sentence broken off. Marginal note: Try to get an idea of 1) the extent of the confiscations, 2) the extent of the profits for the agricultural class, and put the summary of this work into the text.

Page 202, line 17

Sentence broken off. Marginal note: If possible say in the text 1) the approximate amount of these different charges, 2) by what and when they were replaced.

Page 202, line 23

See Tocqueville's notes on his American trip in Oeuvres, Pléiade edition, v. 1, pp. 57–58, conversation of 27 August 1831 with Mr. Neilson.

Page 202, line 32

Marginal note: Try to get an approximate idea, if this is possible, which I doubt, of the state of indebtedness of the agricultural class at the outbreak of the Revolution.

Page 202, line 34

Marginal note: If possible put this question clearly and give my proofs.

Page 203, line 1

Marginal note: Where can I find information about this?

Page 203, line 7

Marginal note: Take well into account what happened then, in order not to be either vague or exaggerated.

Page 203, line 11

This number is left hanging in the air. Assure myself of the exact number by looking at the accounts. But are they trustworthy?

Page 203, line 21

Mallet du Pan, Mémoires, v. 2, p. 154.

Page 203, line 24

Jacques-Henri Meister, "Recollections of My Last Trip to Paris" (Souvenirs de mon dernier voyage à Paris), Year V, p. 48. See above, pp. 220–21.

Page 203, line 39

See Tocqueville's Recollections, part 2, chapter 5: Following the examples of the past without understanding them, *[the revolutionaries of 1848]* foolishly imagined that it was enough to call the crowd to political life in order to attach it to their cause, and that to make people love the Republic, it was enough to give them rights without procuring them profits, *OC, v. 12, p. 116. Tocqueville thus explains the defeat of the revolutionaries at the elections to the Constituent Assembly.*

Page 204, line 13
In the margin, circled: Do not neglect the moral and intangible reasons which attached people to the Revolution. The satisfaction given to reason, to the opinions formed throughout the whole eighteenth century on questions of justice, of equality, of social principles.

Page 204, line 24
Quotation from the Mémoires of Mallet du Pan, v. 2, p. 207.

Page 204, line 24
In the margin of this paragraph: Should this be included?

Page 205, line 17
Montlosier, "On the Effects of Violence and Moderation in the Affairs of France" (Des effets de la violence et de la modération dans les affaires de France), London, 1796. Tocqueville here combines various passages of the third letter of this short treatise.

Page 205, line 20
Marginal note: We see from a report made in 1798 on the state of the émigrés' debts by Bergerat, head of the bureau of liquidation, that the debt of the émigrés in the department of the Seine *[that is, at Paris—Trans.]* alone equaled the mass of all the other debts left by the émigrés from all the other departments combined, because all the great landowners of France lived at Paris. Nothing shows better than this fact how this nobility had ceased to be an (political—*crossed out*) aristocracy to become only a select social circle, and abandoned real power for the honor of the court.

Page 205, line 23
In the margin, circled: Exile had taught them resignation and industry in poverty, but it hadn't given them political good sense: exile doesn't give good sense to anyone and takes it away from many.

Page 206, line 3
In the margin, circled: Look in Mallet du Pan for the particular facts that I have noted and put several of them in the text.

Page 207, line 20
Marginal note: "Journey of a German to Paris and Return through Switzerland" (Voyage d'un Allemand à Paris et retour par la Suisse).

Page 207, line 37

The army is always the last place in the nation where the ideas and desire for an ordered freedom comes to light. When they are found there, one can be sure that they have penetrated everywhere else. *This is a first version, not crossed out. The final text of the end of the paragraph is on a different page.*

Page 208, line 13

In the last moments, the approach of this decisive crisis seemed so obvious that even the amusements of Paris were disturbed. Towards the end of Fructidor, that is to say about two months before 18 Brumaire, among many little rhymes this notice is found in a journal of literature and fashion (Le Mois, Fructidor, Year VII), where the frivolousness, fears, and the ridiculous taste of the times are well displayed: "We will not have any more articles about fashion," says this journal, "until the crisis is over. Until then, it is fear and worry that seem to have taken control of the amiable Frenchman." *An addition on a separate sheet noted in the margin:* This perhaps in a note?

Page 208, line 14

In the margin, circled: The present situation cannot last. Letter by Lafayette. April '99. A counterrevolutionary crisis can't be forestalled except by a patriotic crisis very soon. It is impossible for the present state of things to last. Ibid., October 1799.

Page 208, line 25

Correspondance et relations de J. Fiévée avec Bonaparte, 1803 à 1813, published by the author, 3 vols., 1836. The quotation is found in volume 1, p. 161. Tocqueville added the words "in the depths of the Bourbonnais." In reality Fiévée was then in Champagne. Joseph Fiévée (1769–1839) was involved with the royalist party after Thermidor and had had to take refuge in the provinces after Fructidor. He later rallied to Bonaparte, to whom he sent very counterrevolutionary secret reports. Master of requests at the Council of State in 1810, prefect of the Nièvre in 1813, he was set aside under the Restoration because of his ultrareactionary positions.

Page 208, line 25

Marginal Note: Introduction, p. clxi.

Page 208, line 33

The notes grouped under the heading "general fatigue" (pp. 208–23) and placed in File 44 can be dated to the spring of 1852, thanks to two references after the title to Mallet du Pan's work. See below. At that time Tocqueville envisaged a single large "second chapter" about the Republic internally.

Page 209, line 8

Tocqueville is alluding firstly to the events of the year 1795 (Year III): the decree of 5 Fructidor had declared that the electoral assemblies must choose two-thirds of the new deputies from former members of the Convention; on 13 Fructidor (30 August) a decree stated that if this proportion was not reached, the re-elected conventionnels would increase their number by co-optation. The constitution of the Year III including this provision was ratified by a large majority, but on 13 Vendémiaire (5 October) 1795, Barras and Bonaparte had to put down a royalist insurrection at Paris, and the elections which began on 20 Vendémiaire (12 October) elected chiefly moderates among the former members of the Convention, while the new third was composed above all of royalists or Catholics. The elections were not annulled, but the difficulties of the Directory were to lead to the coup d'état of 18 Fructidor.

Page 209, line 24

Thibaudeau, Mémoires sur la Convention et le directoire, 1824, 2 vols. In 1848 Tocqueville himself had been a member of that honest and powerless third party, composed of sincere supporters of the Republic who tried to defend it against Bonapartists and royalists.

Page 210, line 1

The notes grouped here under the heading "Movement of the Revolution" are scattered throughout File 44. They date from various periods: the first paragraph, from its link with the first plans of 1852 and its insertion into a folder of pages from this period, is doubtless the first account of Tocqueville's thought. The following ones are later.

Page 210, line 22

The head of this paragraph bears the note: To the chapter on the progress of France under Louis XVI. Probably in brief, *which seems to indicate that it initially belonged to book 3 of the first volume of The Old Regime.*

Page 211, line 6

See on this point the chapter in Democracy in America titled "Why Great Revolutions Will Become Rare."

Page 211, line 19

Tolosan, "Report on the Commerce of France and Its Colonies" (Mémoire sur le commerce de la France et de ses colonies), 1789.

Page 211, line 24

See below, p. 216.

Page 212, line 36

Karl Vogt (1817–1895), naturalist, had lived in Paris in 1844–47 before returning to Giessen, his native town, as professor of zoology. A radical, friend of Bakunin, in 1848 he was elected to the Frankfurt National Assembly. Stripped of his teaching position in 1850, he became a professor at Geneva, where he defended materialism and Darwinism. Tocqueville took these notes on his arrival at Bonn where he studied contemporary Germany at the same time as the old regime.

Page 213, line 14

The allusion to recent events leading to the coup d'état (p. 214) allows us to date these notes from File 44 to 1852, at the very beginning of Tocqueville's historical work. Antoine-Clair, Count Thibaudeau (1765–1854), elected to the Convention, Montagnard, had voted for the death of Louis XVI. On 9 Thermidor he took part against Robespierre. Elected to the Five Hundred, neutral on 18 Fructidor, not re-elected in Year VI, he was an accomplice in the coup d'état of Brumaire, and became prefect of the Gironde then councilor of state, and a count of the Empire, in 1809. Proscribed under the Restoration, he returned to France after 1830, and rallied to Napoleon III who made him a senator. Tocqueville is here commenting on his Memoirs on the Convention and the Directory.

Page 213, line 32

Letter written from Bern to the abbé de Pradt on 28 September 1794 by an unidentified émigré, describing France after Thermidor.

Page 214, line 2

Volume 2, chapter 12, "religions and priests."

Page 214, line 12

After the elections of Year V, marked by royalist success, the legislative body was divided: the pro-Directory party, like Boulay de la Meurthe or Chénier, defended revolutionary measures; the constitutionnels, *like Portalis and Thibaudeau, rejected proscriptions; the members of the Club of Clichy, whom Thibaudeau calls "white Jacobins" (p. 173), detached themselves from the* constitutionnels *and leaned towards royalism. The Club of Clichy is compared by Tocqueville to the "rue de Poitiers" under the Second Republic, which included the royalists, whether Orléanist or Legitimist, like Thiers, Berryer, Molé, Guizot, and Falloux. The slang of the times called them the "Burgraves" in memory of the ridiculous and solemn old men of Victor Hugo's play by that name (1844).*

Page 214, line 21

On 28 Messidor (16 July 1797) the Directory had dismissed the ministers Cochon, L'Apparent, Petiet, and Benezech and named Talleyrand to Foreign Affairs, Hoche to War, and François de Neufchâteau to the Interior. In order to intimidate the opposition, Hoche, who commanded the Army of the Sambre and Meuse, had nine thousand men march towards Paris, under the pretext of a transfer of troops towards

Brest for the purpose of an expedition to Ireland. This episode marks the first victory of the "left" directors Reubell, La Révellière-Lépeaux, and Barras against Carnot, a republican become a conservative, and Barthélémy.

Page 214, line 33

The eighteenth of Fructidor (4 September 1797) is here compared with 2 December 1851. The preparation for the two coups presents some similarities: General Saint Arnaud, named minister of war on 27 October 1851, had affirmed his respect for legality to the Assembly on 17 November, at the very time when he was preparing the coup d'état. The disunion between the Mountain and the party of order prevented the Assembly from resisting Louis Napoleon Bonaparte.

Page 214, line 37

Tocqueville is commenting here on the laws of exception of 19 and 22 Fructidor (5 and 8 September 1797) against émigrés who had returned to France or royalists, on the one hand, and against refractory priests, on the other. Sieyès wanted the expulsion of all nobles, which would have realized the threat announced in 1789 in his work What Is the Third Estate? *Only civic exclusion was pronounced. But more than a thousand priests were arrested, of whom 263 were sent to the prisons of Guyana. An isolated note in File 43, however (notes preparatory to the work of 1856), nuances the judgment brought here on the terror which followed 18 Fructidor:*

Why, according to Sir F. d'Ivernois, the proceedings in France's revolutionary crises gradually became milder, the comparative mildness of 18 Fructidor, the absolute mildness of 30 Prairial, Year VIII.

This comes about, according to the author, because each party having acquired the experience that the Revolution was a wheel that always turned (the expression is mine and not his), the various parties had tacitly accepted the maxim that it was necessary to spare the defeated. The horror of the Terror, the weakening of enthusiasm, the enervation of passions, in a word the absence of a cruel public to facilitate cruelty, counted for much in this result. However, d'Ivernois's remark is just. *Crossed out:* The party leaders had something of the spirit of the Italian Free Companies *[mercenary soldiers—Trans.]* who . . .

On d'Ivernois, from whom Tocqueville had read excerpts in the Mercure britannique *in 1852, see below.*

Page 215, line 12

Until 18 Fructidor the representatives on mission contented themselves with a tricolor scarf. After 18 Fructidor, writes Thibaudeau, "the representatives of the people were given the senatorial purple, as we take from the kings after their death all the ornaments of royalty. A miserable vanity which did not keep the corpses from rotting or the names from being forgotten! We gave the Directory the clothing of chivalry or of feudalism, and the Councils that of Greece or Rome." The coats were seized at the frontier by a mischievous trick of the Directory against the Councils.

Page 215, line 24

In the margin: Good. Fifth Chapter. 18 Brumaire.

Page 216, line 9

Notes from File 44 on the work of Mallet du Pan, <u>Mémoires et correspondance de Mallet du Pan pour servir à l'histoire de la Révolution française</u>, collected and put in order by A. Sayous, Paris, 1851, v. 2. Tocqueville had read this work in the spring of 1852. See his letter to Beaumont of 23 June 1852, <u>OC</u>, v. 8, t. 3, p. 53. Jacques Mallet du Pan, a Swiss political writer (1749–10 May 1800), close to Voltaire and then to Linguet, became a royalist in 1789. Sent by Louis XVI in 1792 to the German princes to push them to intervene in France, he then had to flee the French armies and in 1789 settled in England, where he founded the <u>Mercure britannique</u>.

Page 216, line 13

In the margin: This power, he says, which has succeeded at the phenomenal task of organizing disorganization and combining the strengths of despotism with those of anarchy (p. 39).

Page 217, line 40

In the margin of the preceding sentence: It spread and propagated itself by arms and by opinion, like Islam. In one hand they held the saber and in the other the Rights of Man (p. 135).

Page 218, line 11

In the margin of this paragraph: Insurrection against the old world, the old society, everywhere the same goals, giving rise everywhere to the same passions and the same ideas, as all the passions of freedom rose up at the same time against the common yoke of Catholicism. What did this come from? What was there that was really new about the event? From where did this energy of expansion come? To research, to analyze in depth.

Page 218, line 18

Quotation in fact of a statement by Mallet du Pan to the abbé de Pradt.

Page 219, line 5

Tocqueville is commenting here on pp. 164ff. From very early on he had considered the emigration a mistake: "We would doubtless have liked it better to see the émigrés not leave France at all, if necessary to bury themselves under the debris of the monarchy they wanted to defend," he wrote in an indictment of February 1828. <u>OC</u>, v. 16, p. 46.

Page 219, line 12
Quotation from a letter by Mallet du Pan to the Count de Sainte-Aldegonde, 28 January 1796, v. 2, p. 207.

Page 219, line 31
The Army of Italy, under the command of general Bonaparte, had won its first victory in the upper plain of the river Po at the battle of Montenotte, 12 April 1796.

Page 219, line 39
Zurich, 1797. Notes from File 44, without date. The work is by the Zurich writer Jacques-Henri Meister (1744–1826), who lived in Paris for the last twenty years of the old regime and had been Diderot's friend.

Page 220, line 26
Note in the margin: The east, from the Swiss or German frontier to Paris.

Page 222, line 32
Tocqueville here is summarizing and using the expressions found on pp. 123–26.

Page 223, line 1
Notes placed in File 43, Folder K, of "Various Ideas." This file was organized after the completion of the first volume of The Old Regime *and includes notes from before 1856. Published in April 1796 and directed against the reactionaries, Constant's pamphlet, "On the Strength of the Present Government of France and the Necessity of Supporting It" (De la force du gouvernement actuel de la France et de la nécessité de s'y rallier), tried to demonstrate the necessity of rallying to a Republic that was as yet very little rooted in opinion. Beyond the passages cited, in this pamphlet Tocqueville could find the denunciation of the "terrorists," "this new race which seems to come out of the abyss to rescue and devastate the earth, to break all yokes and all laws, to make freedom triumph and to dishonor it" (p. 32). The expression "new race" is taken up by Tocqueville. See below, p. 260.*

Page 223, line 16
After the partial elections of April 1797, the counterrevolutionaries had conceived the hope of taking power peacefully. The coup d'état of 18 Fructidor was followed by the exceptional laws of 19 and 22 Fructidor, which condemned royalist and refractory priests to exile or capital punishment and muzzled the press. Constant, who had participated in the planning for the coup d'état, judged this return of the Terror necessary to save the regime. See his speech of 30 Fructidor to the constitutional circle, Ecrits et discours politiques, *Paris, 1964, v. 1, pp. 115–28.*

Page 223, line 24
"On Political Reactions," a pamphlet of 1797 whose preface is dated 10 Germinal,

written to defend the Directory. The work contains one of the oldest examples of the adjective "liberal" to describe political moderation. The passage analyzed by Tocqueville is found in chapter 5.

Page 223, line 31

Notes from File 44 on the Mercure britannique; ou Notices historiques et critiques sur les affaires du temps par J. Mallet du Pan. *Like the notes on Mallet du Pan's correspondence, they date from 1852. Tocqueville took notes on volumes 2, 3, and 4 (December 1798 to December 1799).*

Page 224, line 35

Like the preceding ones, these notes are taken on number 14, 10 March 1799. This issue contains an excerpt from the work by Sir Francis d'Ivernois, "Historical and Political Description of the Losses Which the Revolution and the War Have Caused the French People in Population, Agriculture, Colonies, Manufactures, and Trade" (Tableau historique et politique des pertes que la Révolution et la guerre ont causées au peuple français dan sa population, dans son agriculture, ses colonies, ses manufactures et son commerce). *Sir Francis d'Ivernois (1757–1842), a Genevan lawyer, had to go into exile after 1782. Taking refuge in England, he was a friend of Bentham. Although a naturalized English citizen, he represented Geneva at the Congress of Vienna. He was the author of numerous works on the financial history of France during the Revolution and the Empire.*

Page 226, line 2

The quotation is taken from number 18 (10 May 1799): "On Several Comparative Differences between the Present Period and That of 1792, Relative to the State of France and Europe."

Page 226, line 4

In the margin of this sentence: Profound phrase to retain.

Page 226, line 30

Number 19, 25 May 1799: "Transfer of the Pope to Briançon: General Conduct of the French Republic towards the Pontiff and His States."

Page 226, line 34

Number 23, 25 July 1799, "Some Remarks on the Attempted Revolution at Paris Last Month."

Page 227, line 24

On Michaud see below, p. 467.

Page 227, line 27

In returning to the river metaphor which was familiar to him, Tocqueville para-

phrases here a passage of the article cited above from the issue of 25 July: "all deceive themselves equally, as before them the constitutionnels, the Brissotins, the Dantonists, the Terrorists, the Thermidorians, the Vendémiarists deceived themselves, as until the end all the successive factions will be wrong, reduced to basing their support on the back of roaring waves, constantly reproducing this contrast between measures and their results, and trapped inside a circle all of whose radii lead to confusion" (v. 3, p. 396).

Page 227, line 39
   Reflection on the article "France: Situation of Affairs and Parties in This Republic since the End of August," number 26, 10 October 1799.

Page 228, line 20
   Commentary on the article "France," number 27, 25 October 1799.

Page 228, line 23
   Commentary on the article "France: Continued Discussion on the Events of the Month of November; Character, Means, Actors, and Consequences of the Latest Revolution," number 30, 10 December 1799.

Page 229, line 1
   Notes from File 44. All the notes which follow are taken from this file but without being grouped in the same folder there nor, generally, dated. Tocqueville worked on the Directory in May 1852 at Tocqueville, then took up these histories again after the appearance of his first volume in 1856.

Page 230, line 20
   Notes from May 1852, taken at the National Archives.

Page 231, line 3
   48 pages long. Grégoire reported on a 72-day visit to his diocese.

Page 231, line 25
   Honoré Riouffe (1764–1813), man of letters, Girondin, had been arrested at Bordeaux on 4 October 1793 and imprisoned at the Conciergerie [at Paris—Trans.] until Thermidor. Rallying to Napoleon, he would begin a career as prefect in 1804. Tocqueville here refers to the indulgence for the Terror in the name of "circumstances," whose expression is found as early as Thermidor and then in the liberal historiography of Mignet or Thiers and among the republicans.

Page 232, line 4
   Notes from May 1852 taken at the National Archives (AF III 7).

Page 232, line 5
On 28 Messidor, see above, p. 457.

Page 233, line 5
After the military occupation of Paris during the night of 17–18 Fructidor (4 – 5 September 1797), as early as the morning of the eighteenth a proclamation was posted by the three members of the Directory announcing that a royalist plot had been eliminated. In the following days what could be gathered of the Councils voted the exclusion of 177 deputies, the deportation of 65 persons including Carnot, then in flight, and Barthelemy, and annulled the elections of the judicial and executive branches in numerous departments. The press was muzzled. The right-wing opposition was struck down and the majority of the Councils overthrown with the soldiers' aid.

Page 233, line 21
"Aux Républicains," by Hilarion Puget, Marquis de Barbentane, 1754–1828. Allied to the Orléans, he was a substitute deputy from the nobility of Paris in 1789, in 1791 served as a general in the south of France, was sent to the army of Italy then to that of the Pyrenees as lieutenant-general, but was dismissed at the end of 1793 as an aristocrat, saved by 9 Thermidor, reattached to the army in 1797, then put on half-pay in 1798. Hostile to the Directory and to Bonaparte, Puget presents himself as "a true republican," a stranger to faction, in order to obtain his recall to the army.

Page 233, line 29
Compte-rendu par le citoyen Grégoire au Concile national des travaux des évêques réunis à Paris, 1797.

Page 234, line 14
In the margin of this last paragraph: See in this writing an interesting address by Toussaint-L'Ouverture to his army, reminding it to think of God in the most simple and noble style, and declaring that it is God who has been the source of their success (p. 36).

Page 234, line 24
Pie VI et Louis XVIII, conférence théologique et politique trouvée dans les papiers du cardinal Doria traduite de l'italien, by J. M. Chénier, Year VI, 1798.

Page 234, line 28
Du système suivi par le directoire exécutif, relativement à la république cisalpine; et quelques détails sur les derniers événements qui ont eu lieu dans cette république par le citoyen Ed. Bignon, ex-secrétaire de légation en Helvétie, et près de la République cisalpine, Paris, Year VII. An addendum indicates that the pamphlet was finished during the first days of Fructidor. Edouard Bignon (1771–1841), joined the navy

and then the army in 1793 in order to avoid prison. Named by Talleyrand in Year VI to the Swiss legation and then the following year to Milan, after the entry of Austrian troops into Milan he published the pamphlet cited here in order to denounce the Directory's negligence.

Milan had been occupied by French troops in May 1796. During Bonaparte's stay in Egypt (July 1798–August 1799) war rekindled between the Directory and the rest of Europe. The pillage and the Directory's blundering policy increased Italian hostility to the French, who had to leave Milan in April 1799.

Page 235, line 5

In the margin: All the generals who have followed Bonaparte have wanted to march in his footsteps (p. 19). Berthier had dismissed the leading magistrates of an allied republic and had replaced them at will.

Page 235, line 31

Le Mois, an historical, critical, and literary journal . . . by a society of intellectuals, Year VII to Year VIII. The fashion magazines then occupied an important place through their satire on mores. Interestingly, Tocqueville does not seem to have consulted the most famous of Le Mois's contemporary journals devoted to fashion, the Journal des dames et de modes (Year V–1839), nor did he leave notes on La décade philosophique, created in the Year II by Guinguené.

Page 235, line 31

The first page ends here. The continuation is found in the same File 44 but separated from the beginning.

Page 235, line 34

Created in 1829 by Emile de Girardin and de Lautour-Mézeray, La Mode, journal of elegance, after 1830 became a virulent legitimist organ which had some talented contributors like Balzac.

Page 236, line 26

Tocqueville here nuances the statement of Mme. de Staël in Literature Considered in Relation to Social Institutions (1800). Chateaubriand's work The Genius of Christianity (1802) presented itself as a response to Mme. de Staël. Chateaubriand attributed to Christianity the characteristics of modern literature that Mme. de Staël had attributed to perfectibility. The success of Chateaubriand's book marks the beginning of a religious renaissance.

Page 237, line 7

Notes placed in File 44 in a folder bearing the title "Period which followed the Terror. Ideas about the Revolution, the Directory, interesting conversations." Mathieu-Louis Count Molé (1781–1855), auditor then master of requests (1806) at the Council of State, under the Empire was prefect of the department of the Côte d'Or (1807–1809), director of the Roads and Bridges Corps (1809–1813), then minister of Justice (1813). He was several times a minister under the Restoration and the July Monarchy. He appreciated Tocqueville, who was related to him. François-Marie-Charles Count de Rémusat (1797–1875), linked to Molé from childhood, publicist, minister in 1840 and under the July Monarchy deputy for twenty years from the Haute Garonne and then again in 1848, was simultaneously close to the doctrinaires and to Thiers. Molé, Rémusat, and Tocqueville, all three opponents of the Empire, at that time saw each other regularly, notably at the Académie Française.

Page 237, line 11
    Prosper de Barante, Histoire de la Convention nationale, Paris, 6 vols., 1851–53; Histoire du Directoire de la République française, Paris, 3 vols., 1855.

Page 237, line 29
    Delécluze, Louis David, son école et son temps, souvenirs, Paris, 1855.

Page 237, line 36
    In the margin: Are these not truly the rapid, irregular, anarchic movements of the sea, right after the storm?

Page 238, line 19
    Molé had had numerous conversations with the emperor. He had given a vibrant elegy of the emperor in his response to Tocqueville's reception speech at the Académie Française, 21 April 1842. See Mélanges, OC, v. 16, pp. 270–80. Rémusat was the son of Augustin-Laurent de Rémusat, advocate-general at the Tax Court of Provence before the Revolution, chamberlain of Napoleon and superintendent of the Imperial Theaters under the Empire. Rémusat's mother, Claire Elisabeth Jeanne Gravier de Vergennes, was a lady-in-waiting to Joséphine.

Page 238, line 32
    In the margin: "This building is sad," said Roederer to the First Consul, just settled in the Tuileries.
    "Like greatness," responds the other.
    Oeuvres du comte P. L. Roederer publiées par son fils, v. 3, 1854, which contains chapters titled "Personal Relations with the First Consul" and "Personal Relations with the Emperor."

Page 238, line 32
    In 1837 Charlotte de Sor had published the Souvenirs of Armand-Louis Augustin Caulaincourt, Duke of Vicenza, followed in 1845 by a Suite des souvenirs.
    Etienne-Denis Duke Pasquier (1767–1862) had served Napoleon and then the Restoration before being named chancellor in 1837. Tocqueville had relations of long standing with him and consulted him for the preparation of The Old Regime.

Page 239, line 5

Undated notes. Like all the notes which follow without contrary notation, these remarks are preserved in File 44. This conversation, which is grouped with information furnished by Le Peletier d'Aunay and Passy, seems to date from Tocqueville's earliest work. On Molé see also above, p. 465, on the conversation of 3 April 1855.

Page 239, line 6

A.-C. Thibaudeau, <u>Mémoires sur le Consulat, 1799 à 1804,</u> 1827.

Page 239, line 20

Molé, prime minister from 1836 to 1839 and related to Tocqueville through the Lamoignons, had affectionate relations with Tocqueville, which didn't exclude reservations on Tocqueville's part. In 1837 Molé wanted to promote Tocqueville's election at Valognes but Tocqueville's feelings were rubbed the wrong way. Molé, elected to the Academy in 1840, supported the candidacy of his young cousin and received him under the cupola on 21 April 1842, but the reception speech showed the divergence between Tocqueville, very critical towards Napoleon, and Molé, an admirer of the emperor. Returned to private life by the Second Empire, Molé here expresses a point of view much more critical than in 1842.

Page 239, line 25

<u>"Evénements des 18 et 19 Brumaire, an VIII et jours suivants; ou Répertoire historique des faits, rapports, discours, opinions, lois, proclamations, lettres ministérielles et autres pièces authentiques concernant l'ajournement des deux conseils, la création et l'exercice du pouvoir des commissions législatives, l'établissement et l'exercice du pouvoir des trois consuls de la république française et les changements introduits dans le gouvernement français par suite de l'exécution de la loi du 19 Brumaire,</u> by Rondonneau.

Page 242, line 36

In 1800 J. F. Michaud published two pamphlets, "Les adieux à Buonaparte" and then "Les derniers adieux à Buonaparte," the pamphlet cited here, which was written in June 1800 and went through several editions. The purpose of the two pamphlets was to destroy the republicans' illusions and above all to show the fragility of Bonaparte's regime, founded on a usurpation and thus forced to have recourse to war and then to the fear that France was surrounded by powerful enemies. Michaud contrasted the strength of Cromwell's regime, which based itself on a vigorous country endowed with firm religious beliefs, to the tottering bases of Bonaparte's domination. Joseph François Michaud (1767–1839) acquired notoriety under the Restoration as a Christian writer and ultraroyalist journalist. Historian of the Crusades, he was also editor-in-chief of <u>La Quotidienne.</u> Since Michaud's pamphlet is cited in Tocqueville's notes on Mallet du Pan (see above, p. 227), which date from June 1852, we can date this work to the beginning of 1852.

Page 244, line 2

Marginal note: A politician who wants to use certain ideas, passions, prejudices, or vices which are found in a party, in order to produce a general result different from that which the party itself intends, in fact can use only this class. If one can put it this way, he can only seize the party by the tail.

Page 244, line 26

Discours prononcé dans le Temple de Mars, par Lucien Bonaparte, ministre de l'Intérieur, le 25 Messidor an 8, pour la fête du 14 juillet et de la Concorde. Lucien Bonaparte here affirms: "the inexorable hand of centuries pushed the throne towards destruction" (p. 2); "18 Brumaire finished the work of 14 July 1789" (p. 10), and he calls for the formation "of conservative feeling" (p. 5).

Page 244, line 35

Mémoires, correspondance et manuscrits du général Lafayette, Paris, 1837–38, 6 vols. Tocqueville's notes bear on volumes 4 and 5 (from the end of the Directory to the end of the Empire). The edition had been prepared by Francisque de Corcelle, Tocqueville's friend, who like Gustave de Beaumont had married a granddaughter of Lafayette. Tocqueville reread this work in 1858 in order to study the Americans' opinion about the Revolution (see his letter to Corcelle, 10 June 1858, <u>OC,</u> v. 15, t. 2, p. 218).

Page 247, line 30

In the margin: There is nothing new in the world (transition to get there).

Page 247, line 34

A note in the same file states:
To the chapter on the Consulate and the Empire.
As soon as you see a despot appear, count on it that you will soon meet a lawyer who will learnedly prove to you that violence is legitimate and the vanquished are guilty. Put somewhere the Troplong who inevitably appears beside the despot. *Raymond Théodore Troplong (1795–1865), counselor at the Court of Appeals and peer of France in 1846, author of numerous legal treatises, after the coup d'état of 2 December 1852 was named president of the Council of State. His obsequiousness towards authority also made him one of the favorite targets of Victor Hugo in* <u>Les Châtiments</u> *("The Chastisements").*

Page 248, line 30

In the margin of the paragraph: <u>Gibbon.</u>

Page 248, line 30

This text from January 1853 is inspired chiefly by the reading of Charles Merivale, <u>A History of the Romans under the Empire,</u> *London, 1850–51, 3 vols. During his research for* <u>The Old Regime and the Revolution</u> *Tocqueville had also read Gib-*

bon's *History of the Decline and Fall of the Roman Empire,* 8 vols., London, edition of 1848.

Page 250, line 8
Cours de littérature française professé par M. Villemain, Tableau de la littérature française au Moyen Age,, 1830, v. 1, p. 56.

Page 250, line 13
Marginal note: Tacitus, Annals, I, 2.

Page 250, line 13
Tocqueville then read the five reports sent to the Academy of Moral Sciences on the subject proposed in 1852 by the Morals section, "to research the history of the various systems of moral philosophy which were taught from antiquity to the establishment of Christianity. To make known the influence which the social circumstances in which they were formed might have had on these systems and that which they in their turn exercised on the ancient world." See Mélanges, OC, v. 16, pp. 221–25.

Page 250, line 18
Marginal note: Tacitus, Histories, IV, 3; Cuncta principibus solita decernit senatus *[The Senate decrees on everything usually done by the emperors—Trans.].* Ulpianus and Gaius, Frag. I, D. de Constit. princip., LL, Gaius Inst. (or Justinian), 1, 2, 3, 6.

Page 250, line 19
In the margin, crossed out: How to go through the papers of the ministry of the police of those days? The great point would be there.

Page 250, line 22
Anne Jean Marie René Savary, Duke of Rovigo (1774–1833), had presided in 1802 over the execution of the Duke of Enghien; close to Napoleon, on 3 June 1810 he succeeded Fouché as minister of police and made terror reign.

Page 250, line 26
Napoleon had had a road passable by carriages made through the Mt. Cenis pass, and rebuilt the hospice, where he established some monks in 1801.

Page 251, line 29
In 1808 José de Palafox y Melci (1776–1847) put himself at the head of the population of Saragossa, which was revolting against Napoleon. He victoriously repulsed a first siege, then was taken prisoner during a second and taken to Vincennes where he remained captive from April 1809 to December 1813.

Page 252, line 7

A decree of 3 March 1810 had officially reestablished the state prisons and ordered an annual inspection of the prisons by councilors of state. In 1814 these prisons contained around twenty-five hundred prisoners.

Page 252, line 16

Since 21 March 1802 Dejean had been minister of war. Conscription had been established by the law of 19 Fructidor, Year VI (5 September 1798) proposed by General Jourdan. Every year a contingent was called, which at first was set by the Legislative Body and later by imperial decree, and after 1805 divided among the departments by the prefects and subprefects. An instruction of 11 Vendémiaire, Year VII (2 October 1798) had organized councils of revision.

Page 252, line 36

Marginal note: Which means, I imagine, that relatively more of the <u>strong</u> population had been lost in one of the departments than the other; but if to eliminate this inequality between departments the contingent from the Aisne had been increased, one would have ended up making more human beings leave and die from one department than the other, which would have been an inequality still more shocking. Is this it?

Page 253, line 11

Note in the margin: That is you have more right to die in your bed when you are weak than when you are strong.

Page 253, line 23

Note in the margin: Comparison taken from the art of cutting wood.

Page 253, line 32

Marginal note: That is the levy must become arbitrary; and the only reason to submit to it, <u>equality,</u> will disappear.

Page 253, line 35

Note in the margin: We see that we are still at the first step. Judge what this must have been in 1813!

Page 254, line 24

In the margin: By Cubières. Sold at Marchand, house of equality.

Page 254, line 24

Michel Cubières de Palmezeaux (1752–1820), prolific dramatist and poet, author of civic hymns.

Page 254, line 30
On this work by Mounier, see above, p. 440.

Page 255, line 8
Cours de littérature française, given in 1828–29, Tableau du XVIIIème siècle, 1829, 4 vols., 19th lesson, v. 4, pp. 259–60.

Page 255, line 10
Words omitted in the manuscript, replaced here in accordance with Villemain's lectures.

Page 255, line 17
Nonliteral quotation from the 23rd lesson, v. 4, p. 373.

Page 256, line 25
From the beginning of the Consulate, Bonaparte was faced with grave financial difficulties and had to take emergency measures. Similarly, in order to avoid bankruptcy the provisional government had decreed on 17 March 1848 that 45 centimes of additional direct taxes would be collected [that is, that property taxes would be increased—Trans.].

Page 256, line 29
D'Ivernois, "On the Causes Which Brought About General Bonaparte's Usurpation and Which Are Preparing His Fall" (Des causes qui ont amené l'usurpation du général Bonaparte et qui préparent sa chute), London, 1800.

Page 257, line 24
This analysis of the virtues of the landowning clergy of the old regime is developed in The Old Regime and the Revolution, book 2, chapter 11, pp. 173–74.

Page 257, line 25
A letter to Corcelle of 13 September 1851 attributes the return of minds to religion in 1848 to two causes: to the fear of socialism, which has momentarily produced an effect on the middle classes comparable to that which the French Revolution previously produced on the upper classes; secondly, to the rule of the masses, which, for the present at least, has returned an influence they have not had for sixty years to the Church and the landowners, and which, in truth, they no longer possessed even sixty years ago; for then their influence was a reflection of power, while today it comes from the very bowels of the lower classes *(OC, v. 15, t. 2, p. 48).*

Page 257, line 38
The decennial prizes had been instituted by an imperial decree of 24 Fructidor, Year XII (10 September 1804), and the first distribution took place in 1810.

Page 257, line 38
Marie-Joseph Chénier, "Presentation to His Majesty the Emperor and King in His Council of State of the Historical Report on the Situation and Progress of Literature"

("Présentation à sa majesté l'Empereur et Roi en son conseil d'Etat du rapport historique sur l'état et les progrès de la littérature"), 27 February 1808. The text was republished several times after 1815 under the title "Historical Picture of the Situation and Progress of French Literature since 1789" ("Tableau historique de l'état et des progrès de la littérature française depuis 1789").

Page 258, line 13
The action of Mme. de Staël's novel <u>Corinne ou l'Italie</u> (3 vols., 1807) takes place in the Italy of 1795. Mme de Staël, favorable to Italian independence, did not leave any role for the French, which discontented Napoleon.

Page 258, line 14
In fact it relates to the preceding lesson in Villemain's work.

Page 258, line 16
The whole development which follows is found in File 43 for the volume of 1856, Folder K.

Page 259, line 32
Joseph Méry (1798–1865), Bonapartist, made himself known in 1831 by a pamphlet against the Périer ministry titled <u>Nemesis</u>. A very prolific author who collaborated with Nerval in the theater, he composed collections of poems, novellas, over twenty novels, and opera librettos. Tocqueville had long been friendly with Mérimée, a relationship which Mérimée's friendship for the imperial family had weakened.

Page 259, line 39
In the margin of the last four lines, crossed out: La Rochefoucauld. History of Port-Royal. Lesage. *Tocqueville is doubtless alluding to the three first volumes from Port-Royal by Sainte-Beuve, published in 1840, 1842, and 1848.*

Page 260, line 3
The texts which follow, up until p. 262, are located in the preparatory file for the first volume of <u>The Old Regime,</u> in a folder of diverse ideas dating from 1852–53.

Page 260, line 24
This text may be compared with the contemporary passage in Tocqueville's <u>Souvenirs,</u> part 2, chapter 1, <u>OC,</u> v. 12, p. 87, "and here is the French Revolution starting again, for it is always the same."

Page 261, line 4

On the reform of the provincial assemblies in 1787 see The Old Regime, *book 3, chapter 7: "How a Great Administrative Revolution Had Preceded the Political Revolution, and the Consequences That This Had." The Martignac ministry, named in 1828, had two projects of reform of communal and departmental government presented to the chamber in 1829, which were not adopted. Tocqueville's father had at that time published a pamphlet favorable to decentralization, "De la charte provinciale," Paris, 1829. In 1848 legitimists and republicans allied to demand a reform of internal government, notably during the debate on the constitution of 18 October 1848.*

Page 261, line 16

On the intermingling of justice and administration see The Old Regime, *book 2, chapter 4, "How Administrative Justice and the Immunity of Public Officials Are Institutions of the Old Regime." Already in 1846 Tocqueville had insisted on both the continuity and the rupture of the Revolution with the old regime in matters of administration in his report on Macarel's course of administrative law (OC, v. 16, pp. 185–98).*

Page 261, line 28

One can read a similar text in the Souvenirs, *part 2, chapter 1, OC, v. 12, p. 87. The experience of the Second Republic confirmed Tocqueville in the conviction that the form of government was of little importance. See Tocqueville's letter to Beaumont, 27 August 1848, OC, v. 8, t. 2, p. 31: "At bottom, what France wants is not such or such a form of government, it is a stable and regular government."*

Page 262, line 12

Text placed in File 44 of diverse ideas relative to the second volume.

Page 262, line 37

In the margin of the last sentence: True idea, which can be fruitful, but badly explored here.

Page 262, line 37

Tocqueville here develops an idea about patriotism already present in Democracy in America, *OC, v. 1, t. 2, chapter 6, subsection on "Public Spirit in the United States."*

Page 263, line 22

Charles-Louis de Viel-Castel (1810–1887), director of political affairs at the Quai D'Orsay from 1849 to 1853, also published historical studies in the Revue des deux mondes, *notably an "Essai historique sur les deux Pitt" reprinted in 1845–46.*
Jean-Charles Rivet (1800–1872), prefect of the Rhone and then deputy from the

Corrèze from 1839 to 1846, elected to the Constituent Assembly then councilor of state under the Second Empire, became an administrator of the Western Railway. He was one of Tocqueville's most faithful friends.

Edouard Drouyn de Lhuys (1805–1881), minister of foreign affairs in the Barrot cabinet of 20 December 1848, replaced by Tocqueville in June 1849 and named ambassador to London, was again minister of foreign affairs for a few days in January 1851, then from 1852 to 1855 and from 1862 to 1866.

Page 265, line 31

Tocqueville's interest in Germany was old, since he had planned a first trip in 1837, at the time of the writing of volume two of Democracy in America. "Absolute governments are for me a terra incognita," he wrote to Reeve, 21 November 1836 (OC, v. 6, t. 1, p. 36), "and every day I realize that some idea of them is necessary for me." Absorbed by political life, Tocqueville had to give up this plan. A first trip to Cologne, Frankfurt, and Bonn (9–24 May 1849) was interrupted by the negotiations for the formation of the Barrot ministry, which took office on the second of June. Tocqueville could only realize the planned research trip in June 1854. He stayed at Bonn from 19 June to 19 August 1854, before spending a month at the baths of Wildbad in Württemberg, until the seventeenth of September, for his wife's health (see Karl-Joseph Seidel, "Tocquevilles forschungsaufenthalt in Bonn 1854," Rheinische Vierteljahrs-Blätter, 41, 1977, pp. 283–97).

Tocqueville made two files on Germany: one for the first volume of The Old Regime, which was essentially about eighteenth-century Germany and its social constitution, titled "Work on Germany done in Germany in June, July, August, and September 1854"; the other file, for the book on the Revolution, groups documents on the intellectual movement of the eighteenth century and the effects of the Revolution in Germany, documents assembled both during the course of the first volume and afterwards.

For the first volume, beyond the Bonn professors who gave Tocqueville bibliographic information, Tocqueville's chief informants were Circourt and Mrs. Austin (1793–1867), the author of a book on Germany, Germany from 1760 to 1814, published in London in 1854, on which Tocqueville took notes in August 1854. Bibliographic references to German works by Tocqueville, or in his friends' handwriting, are numerous, but Tocqueville also read the following works in French: Mme. de Staël, De l'Allemagne (1813), from which he cites an excerpt in his notes on the separation of classes, from chapter 2 "on the mores and character of the Germans," and Saint-René Taillandier, Etudes sur la Révolution en Allemagne, Paris, 2 vols., 1853.

Although Tocqueville had to cut short this trip because of his wife's illnesses, and for this reason was unable to do any archival research, we may say that this trip was essential because of his reading of published works and the meetings he had. Tocqueville would have liked to go to East Prussia, where the old regime seemed to him to be more alive. However, the stay in the Rhineland constituted an excel-

lent introduction because of the synthesis at work there between French ideas that twenty years of French occupation had spread and the influence of Prussia to which the Rhenish lands had been given on 10 February 1815 by the Congress of Vienna. Tocqueville, although he had read the work of the Catholic social conservative Reichensperger, Die Agrarfrage (1847), above all met liberals whose thought seemed close to his own. From 1 October 1853 until his departure for Germany at the beginning of June 1854 he read the Kölnische Zeitung, the newspaper of the German liberals, where the work of Frederick the Great and the reform era of Stein and Hardenberg were exalted, but from the liberal perspective of an English-style constitutionalism. Tocqueville could also find in this journal the desire for self-government ["self-government" in English as often in contemporary German— Trans.] opposed to centralization in the French style. At Bonn he could encounter the chief thinkers of this political current: Moritz von Bethmann-Hollweg, Kruse, the director of the Kölnische Zeitung, and above all the professors of the University of Bonn whose influence was great: Dahlmann, Brandis, and more than any other Hugo Hälschner, who commented on several legal works for Tocqueville. Hälschner, who had made himself known by publishing Die preussische Verfassungsfrage und die Politik der rheinischen ritterbürtigen Autonomen in 1846, had in this work sought to rebuild the political structure on the principle of Selbstverwaltung [self-government—Trans.], representative institutions serving as the reinforcement of the state's power. Tocqueville also had occasion to read or hear about the works of the great historians of the time, who were generally pro-Prussian because Prussia seemed to them the only power capable of uniting Germany: Schlosser, Haüsser, Ranke. Tocqueville had Circourt send him the table of contents of Ranke's work Neun Bücher Preussischer Geschichte (3 vols.), and in his preparatory notes Tocqueville announced his intention to read Heinrich von Sybel's Geschichte des Revolutionszeit von 1789 bis 1795, and to meet the author, but it does not seem as if he put this plan into operation. Tocqueville certainly found himself at Bonn during a period when liberalism had been in retreat since Frederick William IV had refused the crown which the Frankfurt Parliament had offered him on 3 April 1849, and afterwards followed a resolutely conservative policy. At Bonn, Tocqueville nevertheless encountered a whole liberal political ideology based on a moral doctrine inspired by Kant, and close to the ideas presented in The Old Regime: the rejection of a liberalism defining itself, as in France, only by the limitation of power and the defense of the individual; the primacy of law; freedom defined as obedience to laws in whose creation the citizen had participated, the combined defense of the power of the state and of self-government. This encounter with contemporary Germany also gave Tocqueville historical information on the society of orders, towards which the Bonn professors looked with a very critical gaze, distancing themselves here from the tradition of historical rights. On Rhenish liberalism see Jacques Droz, Le libéralisme rhénan, 1815–1848: Contribution à l'histoire du libéralisme allemand, Paris, 1940.

    From the notes on Germany (Folder Q) we give solely the ideas and conversations, which recall Tocqueville's method in the United States. Tocqueville himself noted on the folder of these conversations: In these notebooks [. . .] are found ideas and perceptions which even though suggested by Germany are only a little or not at all related to it, but to my work in general.

Page 265, line 32

Tocqueville moved this questionnaire, written on three folios, into his Rubbish file. Datable to 1854, it allows us to understand the leading lines of the conversations which follow and may be compared with the lists of questions Tocqueville drew up during the preparation of Democracy in America.

Page 265, line 33

A paragraph separate from the discussion of the nobility is inserted here: Taillandier stops at 1847.

How to know what happened in Prussia immediately before the Revolution of February? Where to find even the narrative of the agitations and revolutions of Germany in 1848? Does there exist a summary of those times in German? *In the margin:* Reden und Redner des ersten Preussischen Vereinigten Landtags, Rudolf Haym, Berlin, 1847, cited by Taillandier.

Page 266, line 36

Friedrich Christoph Dahlmann (1775–1860), historian, one of the distinguished figures of Rhenish liberalism, was a member of the Frankfurt National Assembly in 1848, where he was one of those who offered the German Imperial Crown to Frederick-William. Dahlmann later participated in the work of the Prussian Upper House in 1849–50 and in the Erfurt Parliament (1851), and then, discouraged, returned to his academic position at Bonn. Johann Wilhelm Loebell (1786–1863), professor of history and German literature at Bonn from 1829.

Page 267, line 1

Ferdinand Walter (1794–1879), professor of law at the University of Bonn, had been a member of the Prussian National Assembly at Berlin from May to December 1848, where he sat on the right wing, and a member of the Upper House from February 1849 to January 1850.

Page 267, line 12

Since 1650 the family of Thurn and Taxis had borne the title and coat of arms of Counts of La Tour and Valsassina, and was elevated to the rank of Princes of the Empire in 1695.

Page 268, line 16

Marginal note: All this is crucial for me, but still so confused that I don't know how to reproduce it.

Page 270, line 23

Crossed out: This is not particular to Germany. One finds this manorial court in all the old documents of medieval France. Traces of it still exist in England. The complete disappearance of this institution in France, several centuries, I believe, before the Revolution, should be considered I think one of the chief causes which made the division deeper between the lord and his vassals, and in general between the different classes, and made the old regime more hateful than anywhere else (specify).

Page 270, line 24

Napoleon had given Joachim Murat the principality of Berg (capital Düsseldorf) when making it a grand duchy in 1806. Ceded in 1808 by Murat to the still-minor eldest son of the King of Holland, the grand duchy was governed directly by Napoleon until it was given to Prussia by the Congress of Vienna in 1815.

Page 270, line 29

Christian August Brandis (1790–1867), professor of philosophy at Bonn since 1823, a specialist in Greek and Roman philosophy, friend of Victor Cousin.

Hugo Philipp Egmont Hälschner (1817–1889), professor of law at Bonn from 1847 until his death, and a specialist in criminal law (according to Droz, he had the emperors Frederick and William II among his students, he published in 1846 on the constitutional question in Prussia, and he was one of the Rhenish liberals grouped around the Kölnische Zeitung; see Droz, Le libéralisme rhénan, chapter 6). Like his teacher Dahlmann he was favorable to an organic conception of the state founded on the principle of self-government, and to an English conception of freedom. Tocqueville spelled his name in varying ways, we correct.

Charles Monnard (1790–1865), by origin from the Vaud, in Switzerland, and leader of the liberal party at Lausanne, had lost his position as professor of French literature at the Academy of Lausanne (1816–45) for political reasons. He then became professor of Romance languages at Bonn (1846–65).

Page 270, line 33

Taking notes on the book by Saint-René Taillandier, Tocqueville remarked: Nothing seems more interesting to me than the role played by philosophy in Germany, more original and more particular in the general appearance of human affairs. It is above all for the last sixty years that this phenomenon seems to me to present itself. Is this true? Why? Represented above all by four great names: Kant then Fichte then Schelling then Hegel. First left in freedom by the sovereigns who saw in it only an intellectual study; then favored and become an official organ of the government in Prussia; then the object of fear and persecution when it got close to reality. The *Halle Annals* were suppressed in 1841. The Young Hegelian school, exiled from Berlin, retreated to Saxony and published the *German Annals* at Leipzig. Still a power, it is according to Hegel and through the doctrine called

Young Hegelian that German philosophy emerging from its ineffable intellectualism fell into matter and affairs with an extravagance unprecedented even in France . . . *From the preparatory notes.*

Page 272, line 19

In the margin of this sentence: He considers the country of Baden (above all because of the proximity of Heidelberg) as the country of Germany where Christianity is weakest.

Page 274, line 5

Marginal note: The relative position of the lord's property and the peasant's property was perpetual and could not change.

Page 275, line 22

Crossed out: M. Hälschner, with whom I spoke today (11 July 1854), persisted in saying that . . .

Page 275, line 25

Crossed out: He admitted that chiefly in the provinces; *marginal correction:* I was assured.

Page 275, line 27

Crossed out: which he attributed; *interlinear correction:* which I attribute.

Page 277, line 24

Crossed out: Today (19 July '54) I saw an old man of eighty-four years, President Wurtzer, who was a public official under the last elector, an Austrian archduke, and even attached to his personal service. His conversation confirms everything which M. Walter told me. He affirms; *marginal correction:* it results.

Page 278, line 10

This text was not filed by Tocqueville in chronological order. It is found in a file ("Notes, ideas, questions") of documents from July 1854, placed after the documents from August 1854.

Page 278, line 25

In the margin of the two preceding paragraphs: A good chapter to do on these ideas while developing them. To show that even in England, what was alive, despite appearances, was not exactly the institutions of the Middle Ages, it was a contrary spirit which had been able to introduce itself into them without destroying them. For example, the principle of an aristocracy based on wealth and talent, not on birth, replaced caste.

Page 278, line 30

Marginal note: It was destroyed everywhere. A very remarkable sign. It was not destroyed during the vigor of medieval institutions.

Page 279, line 4

Hälschner was here commenting for Tocqueville on title 8, section 2, of the All-gemeines Landrecht. Tocqueville's notes on the Landrecht bear the imprint of many discussions on different points with Hälschner. Tocqueville returned to the progress of centralization with regard to administrative organization in Prussia in his notes taken in August 1854 on A. Büsching's book Erdbeschreibung (1791), which he read with Hälschner's help: We see . . . to what point we were more advanced in France than Germany along the path of the absolute destruction of all secondary governing powers, the isolation of individuals, the abandonment of any common action, and centralization. What difference between the Landrat and the intendant's sub-delegate! Before Frederick the Great no taxes were farmed out. Frederick the Great farmed some out. But we see that the indirect taxes were raised by a royal bureaucracy. Moreover, Frederick's tax farms excited so much public hatred that they were destroyed by his successor. See the limits of Frederick's genius in public administration, and how he even marched in reverse of the movement of education. *Preparatory notes. Further on Tocqueville notes:* In the eighteenth century, in Prussia as in France, the bureaucracy proper is dispersed, but its chief functions are put in the finance ministry. There is no ministry of the interior yet. This centralization is not finished. The police do not belong to any ministry, they are still entirely in the hands of the courts and intimately joined to justice whether royal or baronial. *The book by Anton Friedrich Büsching, theologian and geographer (1724–93), of which Tocqueville only read the part about Prussia, gives an especially large place to statistics and social and political organization. But Tocqueville's notes are more the reflection of Hälschner's commentaries than of Büsching's rapid descriptions.*

Page 280, line 27

Here there appears a first version very close to the final text of the last two paragraphs of the note on Roman law on pp. 247–48.

Page 281, line 19

In the margin of this sentence: How administrative justice had to be created in France from the political powers possessed by our parlements and from their dominant position. Good idea to develop. One did not need to have recourse to this means in countries where the courts were always half-dependent.

Page 281, line 25

Tocqueville was attentive to the growing resemblances between Prussia and France. In his preparatory notes he writes:

Guarantee of public officials. Administrative justice. I see in the Kölnische Zeitung of 16 January 1854 that the Prussian chambers have just voted the judicial guarantee of public officials and administrative justice. The journalist adds: the political principles of Germany (Principien deutschen Rechtstaates), which in England are still in full vigor and which up to now have preserved a considerable position in Prussia, are going to be sacrificed to the French Moloch of bureaucratic dependence. *Tocqueville comments further on:* The minister of justice spoke in favor of this law in exactly the same way that a French minister would have done. We do not wish to show distrust of the judicial system, on the contrary. We are only acting in the interest of the principle of the division of powers . . . always the same nonsense.

Page 281, line 33

This conversation about venal offices, on a separate sheet of paper, was not filed in chronological order by Tocqueville.

Page 281, line 36

This paragraph is a marginal correction introduced by a circled note: To chapter 10. How all the evils of the old regime came from the tax system. *It replaces a circled first draft:* very little known in Germany. Only in a few places and for a few unimportant positions. Introduced by some petty rulers (doubtless in imitation of France) in order to make money. This is what Bluhme and Hälschner told me today, 5 August 1854. I see that this system hardly existed on a large scale anywhere except in France.

Look for the differences which could have come from this. I already see one of them: the bourgeoisie more independent and more proud in France, although not loving positions any less than in Germany. Venality was a great administrative evil; a great good from this particular perspective.

Friedrich Bluhme (1792–1874), professor of the history of law at Jena (1820), Halle (1823), Göttingen (1831), and then Bonn (1843), after having published a study Die Ordnung der Fragmente in den Pandectentiteln *(4 vols., 1821), specialized in Germanic law.*

Page 282, line 11

*During the old regime England represented the archetype of liberalism, opposed to the archetype of despotism incarnated by France, as Seymour Drescher has shown (*Tocqueville and England, *Cambridge, Mass., 1964). Tocqueville's sources for comparing France and England are chiefly Blackstone, Burke, and Young, who are frequently cited or commented on in* The Old Regime, *as can be seen in the "Notes and Variants." From Young, Tocqueville took only factual information. The notes on Burke also consist chiefly of quotations with commentary, of which a list can be found in* OC, *v. 2, pp. 334–42. Tocqueville's only general judgment on Burke bears on the* Reflections on the Revolution in France:

In sum, this is the work of a mind in itself powerful, and provided with those notions of practical wisdom which are acquired, so-to-speak without thinking about it, in a free country. We see in him, to a supreme degree, the superiority which the practice of [freedom] gives for judging the scope of institutions and their short-term effects. This same effect makes a farmer of good sense like Young so superior, in this regard, to an inexperienced man of genius like Mirabeau. Thus Burke is admirable when he judges the details of new institutions, their immediate effects, the countless errors arising from the new reformers' philosophical presumption and inexperience. He foresees several of the great dangers of the future. But the general character, the universality, the final scope of the Revolution which is beginning, completely escape him. He remains seemingly buried in the old world, the English part of that world, and does not understand the new and universal thing which is happening. He does not yet see in the Revolution anything but a French accident; he does not perceive anything but the strengths the Revolution is taking away from France, and does not see the strengths it will give her. In this work his already furious hatred for our reformers (for he senses that it is his old world that is being attacked, without yet seeing that it is going to fall) is mingled in this work [sic] with a supreme contempt, not merely for their villainy, but for their foolishness, their ignorance, their impotence. Later this hatred, stronger and stronger, is combined with terror and with the kind of respect that one has for great abilities used for doing evil. These are rogues, he says in 1792, but the most terrible rogues the world has ever known.

Only Blackstone's work was really the subject of a sketch, although Tocqueville did not have a high opinion of the author, as he explained to Nassau W. Senior, in a letter of 2 July 1853 (OC, v. 6, t. 2, pp. 160–61):

Following your advice, I have read or rather reread Blackstone (I had already studied him twenty years ago). As for the impression he makes on me, it was the same both times. Today, as then, I permit myself to judge him (if one can say this without blasphemy) a poor enough mind, without intellectual freedom or real breadth of judgment, in a word a commentator and a legist, not what we understand by the words jurisconsult and statesman. Further he has a mania for finding everything old admirable, to an extent sometimes laughable—he makes everything he thinks good in his own time derive from the past. I am led to believe that if he had had to write about England's agricultural production, rather than concerning himself with English agricultural institutions, he would have found that beer might well originally have come from grapes, and that going back to the venerable sources of antiquity, one discovers that hops came from the vine; a product that has degenerated a little, it is true, from the wisdom of the ancestors, but still respectable. One cannot find an excess more opposite from his French contemporaries, for whom it was enough that a thing was old for it to seem bad.

The notes published here were taken in June 1853 and collected in Folder L on

Blackstone's work, Commentaries on the Laws of England, *first published from 1765 to 1769. We give here only the general ideas this work inspired in Tocqueville, on which see also Tocqueville's note, to p. 284, line 18.*

Page 282, line 27

Marginal note: To which must be added the difficulty of sale arising from the immense expenses necessitated by the sale of land to individuals, a hindrance unique to England.

Page 284, line 18

Marginal note: One can see, as in the preceding note on Blackstone, that like us at the beginning landownership subject to the cens, the commoner fief (free socage) was considered a base, ignoble form of ownership; that only the knightly fief gave honor, privileges, power.

Page 284, line 21

Marginal note: Just as in certain provinces of southern France, all those who acquired ownership of noble estates, even if they were commoners, were not subject to the taille on those estates, the privilege belonging to ownership, not to the owner.

Page 284, line 22

Marginal note: Commoner *[Tocqueville uses the English word—Trans.]* has no analogy with "roturier" *[the French word here translated as "commoner," despite the validity of Tocqueville's distinction, for reasons analogous to those Tocqueville himself presents below for the use of "gentleman"—Trans.],* A commoner can be the son of a peer. This only means that he does not belong to the nobility *[Tocqueville uses the English word—Trans.],* which, itself, is only the nobility which belongs to the House of Lords.

Judge social revolutions by revolutions in language. "Gentleman" loses the meaning of the French "gentilhomme" to take on the more general meaning of a man belonging to the upper classes, little by little even to the educated classes. In the fate of the word lies the whole fate of the people which speaks the language in which it is found. Today the idea of "gentilhomme" cannot be expressed in English. I defy anyone to find in that language [a word] or even a paraphrase which can render it. The single word which served this purpose has so much lost its original meaning that it would not be understood with the idea that we attach to it. The English, speaking of persons of the social position of "gentilhomme" in France, are forced to use an improper word because of the impossibility of finding another. For, note (and this is no less significant) that no French word has taken on the meaning of the word "gentleman," the caste word "gentilhomme" has ceased to be used, and the word "gentleman" or an analogue, an aristocratic word, has not been created. It requires a paraphrase. The whole history of the two nations is here.

Thus, neither "roturier" nor "gentilhomme" has an analogue in the English language. I do not know if roturier ever had one, but "gentleman" is certainly from the source from which "gentilhomme" arose and has had, without doubt, the same meaning. The English dictionary translates "roturier" as "man of the people," which is nonsense, for a "roturier" was often a millionaire.

Page 285, line 23

This note, which appears in Tocqueville's research notes in Folder L, is inspired by both Blackstone and volume five of Thomas Babington Macaulay's History of England (1849–1861).

Page 285, line 30

Marginal note: The *Encyclopédie* cites only two acts, one of 1265, the other of 1282, which forbade commoners to acquire fiefs (both from the end of the thirteenth century). Only some Customary Laws, such as those of Maine and Artois, contain this prohibition. But the customs are from the fourteenth or fifteenth century.

Page 286, line 23

This text is scrawled in pencil on four sheets of paper folded into the shape of a small notebook which also bear a discussion about the colonization of Algeria (certainly from 1841), some accounts, and the beginning of a report to the Academy of 1841 on the treatise on Roman Law by Lebastard Delisle. Beaumont dated it to Tocqueville's first trip to England in 1833; more probably it is from 1841. Furthermore, Tocqueville developed the parallel by a comparison between 1688 and 1830 written in 1842. See OC, v. 16, pp. 558–61. The manuscript was re-filed by Beaumont in File 45 B (continuation of The Old Regime). Tocqueville came back to the English Revolution in 1853 when reading volume five of Macaulay's History of England.

Page 287, line 15

The end is missing.

Page 287, line 18

Notes found in File 43 of The Old Regime, Folder Q. August, baron von Haxthausen (1792–1866), first studied agriculture in the Prussian provinces, and sat for agriculture in the Prussian ministry. At the request of the Russian government, from April to November 1843 he made a great trip through Russia, from which came his "Studies on the Internal Situation of the National Life and Rural Institutions of Russia" (Etudes sur la situation intérieure de la vie nationale et les institutions rurales de la Russie), 2 vols., Hanover, 1847–52. Very antiliberal, Haxthausen's book was however at the time the most detailed study on the Russian peasantry, and Tocqueville selected elements from the work useful for comparison with France.

Page 288, line 6

This political remark is by Tocqueville himself.

Page 288, line 11

Compare this with the story of the repair of the bell tower and rectory of Ivry in Tocqueville's notes to The Old Regime, *v. 1, pp. 278–80.*

Page 289, line 13

"I could not help being extremely surprised in learning that at Nizhni-Novgorod all the personnel of a pretty good troupe of actors that I had just seen, actors, singers . . . were serfs," paying the obrog tax, attached to the soil (v. 1, p. 271).

The painter who painted the interior of the church of St. Isaac at Saint-Petersburg (a distinguished painter), M. Osip Semionowitsch Serebriakoff, whom I visited, belonged as a serf to M. de Bezobrazoff of Moscow (v. 1, p. 286).

Haxthausen admired a charming young woman to whom he said that she was one of God's most beautiful creatures. She responded I am only the daughter of a peasant who is still a serf (v. 1, p. 90).

Page 289, line 19

Haxthausen shows the replacement of the nobility, bankrupted by the adoption of Western tastes, by a class of parvenus. Tocqueville, in insisting on "absentee-ism," introduces a parallel with the condition of the French peasant. [See The Old Regime, *v. 1, book 2, chapter 12, "How, Despite the Progress of Civilization, the Condition of the French Peasant Was Sometimes Worse in the Eighteenth Century Than It Had Been in the Thirteenth," pp. 180–92—Trans.] The obrog was a tax varying according to the age, health, and extent of land possessed by the peasant, which partially substituted for corvées. Conscious of the evils of serfdom, Nicholas I had attempted, without great success, to regulate relations between masters and peasants by the decree of 2–14 April 1842.*

Page 291, line 24

Haxthausen insists only on the specificity of the "slav nationality," while Tocque-ville takes up here the famous parallel between America and Russia which ends the first volume of Democracy in America.

Page 292, line 3

Chapter 11, v. 1, pp. 298ff.

Page 292, line 17

For the first six chapters of the second book of The Old Regime, *Tocqueville based himself chiefly on the work he did on the* archives *of the Generality of*

Touraine in the present series C in 1853–54. We present here the most elaborated notes and drafts grouped in File 43, Folder H. Tocqueville also read a large number of printed works on the functioning of intendancies. We present below his notes on Turgot's works, read in 1853 [in addition, his notes on intendant d'Aube's report may be found on pp. 339–42 of volume one of this edition.—Trans.].

Page 292, line 19

Excerpt from a folder examined on 5 July 1853 titled: Letters from the Controller-General to the Intendant 1781, 1782, 1783.

Page 292, line 29

In the hope of averting the influx of beggars into large towns, the Edict of Moulins of February 1566 (article 73) had ordered "that the poor of each city, town or village will be fed and maintained by the inhabitants of the city, town or village of which they are natives and inhabitants, without their being able to leave and beg for alms elsewhere than at the place where they were born." The same ordinance had instituted an obligatory poor tax, but it was only collected irregularly. The eighteenth century would take up again the concern for the regulation of the poor, notably by the declaration of 3 August 1764 on vagabonds, and the edict of the Council of 21 October 1767 on beggars' barracks. The measures led to an extreme brutality which Tocqueville denounced and which Turgot as intendant of Limousin made efforts to alleviate. Under the ministry of Abbé Terray in 1770 the necessity of collecting the poor tax had been reemphasized and an instruction on charity work on 11 October 1770 had created charity workshops financed by the towns and the state in order to help the poor to live. See Camille Bloch, L'assistance et l'Etat en France à la veille de la Révolution, Paris, 1908, and Thomas McShay Adams, Bureaucrats and Beggars, New York, 1990.

Page 294, line 3

Excerpt from a folder examined 2 August 1853 titled "subsistence." Tocqueville particularly used the correspondence of the controller-general Terray (22 December 1769–6 May 1774) with the subdelegate of Angers, Charles-Jean-Poulain de la Marsaulaie (Tours archives, C 94–95).

Page 295, line 12

Excerpt from two folders examined on 12 September 1853 and titled "Milices." Tocqueville's commentary on the absence of safeguards is inspired by an ordinance of the intendant of Tours, Charles Pierre de Savalette, in 1750, repeating previous ordinances (Tours archive, C 48).

Page 296, line 3

Excerpt from a folder examined on 1 October 1853 titled "Prisons."

Page 296, line 24

The chief file about this subject created by Tocqueville is titled "Constitutions of the Municipalities of Touraine, Anjou, and Maine" and dated 30 November 1853. It is derived from two files presently in the archives of the department of Indre et Loire, catalogued as C 328 and C 329. These files contain documents relating to the edicts of 1764 by the controller-general Laverdy, which reorganized the municipal life of towns of more than forty-five hundred inhabitants. The purpose of these edicts was to unify the composition, designation, and powers of the municipal governments, and destroy the excessive influence of the great bourgeois families. As early as November 1771, Terray revoked Laverdy's edicts and reestablished the old venal and hereditary offices. Before issuing his edicts, Laverdy had asked the intendants to institute a major inquiry on the functioning of municipal institutions in all the town councils.

On the folder of his notes Tocqueville writes: Some of the most important and instructive work that I have done in the Tours archives, which has made me aware not only of the towns' constitutions, but of the constitution of the middle class which inhabited them. *It was purely archival work, done firsthand, with the exception of a few notes on the government of the town of Tours before Louis XI, taken from volume 2 of the* L'histoire romaine *by Cheruel.*

Tocqueville studied the municipal constitutions of the towns previous to the edict of 1764, as they were revealed by the intendants' and subdelegates' inquiries, and notably those of the towns of Sillé, Tours, Amboise, Laval, Le Mans, La Flèche, Mayenne, Angers, and all the little towns of the generality in 1764. Tocqueville paid special attention to the composition of the general assemblies and the assemblies of notables, to their powers, to the progressive replacement of elected bodies by privileged cliques, to statistics on the population, to the creation and repurchase of offices which unbalanced the towns' budgets. From these studies Tocqueville derived two leading ideas: First of all the primacy of fiscal considerations in the organization of the state: Almost all the abuses were born of fiscal expedients, and the towns, among others, were treated as usurers would the sons of the family on whose passions they speculated. No elevated and general perspective. Nothing but the idea to make money *["to make money" in English.—Trans.].* Secondly, the effects of the fractioning of the electoral right could not fail to undermine the principle of election and to create little oligarchies from these sham popular elections. [. . .] Do not forget this when describing communal freedom under the old regime. We see that everyone had his group for his only audience and was responsible only to it, two reasons that destroyed all zeal since the motives of pride and fear were eliminated.

The excerpt presented here relates to the municipal constitution of the town of La Flèche. The mayor and aldermen had presented a first report in 1764 demanding that the general assembly (which in the edict of 1764 replaced two previous assemblies, a general assembly and an assembly of notables) be composed only of notables. This was to exclude the artisans from the town's government.

Page 297, line 25

Gaspard-César-Charles Lescalopier, lord of Liencourt, councillor at the Parlement of Paris (1727), master of requests (1733), intendant of Montauban (1740–1756) and then of Tours from June 1756 to October 1766.

Page 298, line 32

René André Chaubry (1718–1785), royal prosecutor at the district and presidial court of La Flèche in 1751, named subdelegate at La Flèche by the intendant of Tours, Lescalopier, 29 November 1763. In 1778 he became a royal secretary, and auditor in the chancellery at the Parlement of Grenoble.

Page 300, line 10

Excerpt from a folder of notes on agriculture examined in May 1854.

Page 300, line 18

By a circular of 22 August 1760, the controller General Bertin had invited the intendants to create agricultural societies on the model of the one founded in Brittany in 1757. At Tours, from October 1760, the intendant recruited members and prepared regulations for the society which was established by a decree of the Council of State sent on 24 February 1761, and served as a model for other societies. The society had three sections, at Tours, Angers, and Le Mans, of twenty persons each, and the intendant had the right to be present at all meetings as a royal commissioner. See Emile Justin, Les sociétés royales d'agriculture au XVIIIème siècle (1757–1793), Saint-Lô, 1935.

Page 301, line 2

Tocqueville next analyzed the society's criticism of the taille, of the burden of perpetual payments, of the due of franc-fief, and then concludes with the development on p. 366.

Page 301, line 3, Turgot title

These notes were taken by Tocqueville on the Oeuvres de M. Turgot, ministre d'Etat, précédées et accompagnées de mémoires et de notes sur sa vie, son administration et ses ouvrages, 9 vols., edited by Dupont de Nemours, Paris, 1808–1811. Tocqueville's citations are not always exactly faithful to the letter of the text; however, we have only noted the passages where he departs from the spirit of the text in question. These notes are preserved in Folder B. In places the manuscript has in the margin indications of chapters where Turgot's remarks could be used.

Anne Robert Jacques Turgot, baron de l'Aulne (1727–1781), intendant of Limoges in 1761, applied his theories of reform, close to those of the physiocrats, in dividing the taille more justly, in eliminating the corvée, and in encouraging agriculture. In 1774, at the advent of Louis XVI, he was named secretary of state for the navy and then controller-general of finances. He introduced free trade in grain (1774), eliminated guilds, masterships and journeymen (1776), and the corvée, but popular resistance and the hostility of the parlements and the queen led Louis XVI to dismiss him in 1776.

Although he saw in Turgot the precursor of the centralizers of the nineteenth century, Tocqueville respected Turgot: he and his school are those "who in the eighteenth century represent best the Revolution's real spirit and see most clearly how equality of conditions could lead to the centralization of power. Turgot, moreover, is infinitely superior, both for his elevation of soul and for the breadth of his mind, to all the others" (letter to Corcelle, 31 December 1853, OC, v. 15, t. 2, pp. 88–89).

Page 301, line 22

In the margin: The custom of making the royal roads by corvée was less than a century old, that of making landowners of all orders contribute to the expenses required for the upkeep of roads was as old as the monarchy.

Page 302, line 39

In the margin: I say the usual courts. I am not speaking of the exceptional courts of the evocations.

Page 303, line 18

In the margin: It is not Turgot who says this, it is he who writes his history in 1811. A remark equally applicable to all the preceding.

Page 304, line 12

From the beginning of the text to the end of this paragraph, Tocqueville's notes relate to Dupont de Nemours's introduction in volume one. The notes which follow are taken on volumes 4, 5, and 6, dedicated to Turgot's administrative work in the Generality of Limoges, and on the reports and short pieces written by him during this period (1761–1774).

Page 304, line 29

In the margin: It could not even have any relationship whatsoever with the land like the taille in the towns, which was based, I do not know how, on presumed wealth.

Page 304, line 38

In the margin: We know that in most of the southern provinces the taille was real, that is to say it was not divided except by reason of the lands which each taxpayer possessed and the income corresponding to them. It was imposed on the sites where the property was situated and it was the land which was responsible for it. There were no exempt lands except those which, during the creation of the cadaster, had been recognized as noble or those which belonged to the Church. Most of the other provinces were subject to the personal taille, which bore equally on the income from land and the profits of industry. Since in these provinces it was less the land which was responsible for the tax than the person to whom it belonged, or the fruits that it produced, it was thought necessary to order that all lands belonging to the same owner would pay at the residence of that owner (ibid., p. 74).

The real taille presupposed a cadaster, for the intrinsic value of the land being the only measure of the tax, and this value hardly being subject to change, the idea of a cadaster, that is of a list made once and for all of the value of the lands, presented itself naturally.

Page 305, line 11

In the margin: Turgot does not say this in a vague and general way . . . There follow details about all the products of industry *[and]* agriculture, and their vicissitudes.

Page 309, line 17

In the margin of this paragraph: I think I am right, after all the details which I have just described, to state that the taxes, in the Generality of Limoges, amounted in general to 48 to 50 percent, and that the king drew as much from the land as the owners. In wartime, this mounted much higher (p. 297).

Page 312, line 40, after "consequences"

Crossed out: The laws recognized by the court on questions of interest on money are bad. Our legislation is in conformity with the rigorous prejudices against usury. The strict observation of these laws would be destructive of all commerce; also they are not observed rigorously. They forbid all interest without alienation of capital. It is a notorious fact that there is no commercial town where most commerce is not based on money borrowed without alienation of capital.

Page 313, line 12, after "tenure"

Crossed out: and these effects make one think strongly of the Revolution.

Page 313, line 18

Crossed out: great interest in a Revolution. To develop further.

Page 319, line 18, after "honorific"

Note crossed out in the margin: See, however, how the payments are often considerable in Normandy and judge the extent of the thing in the south.

Page 319, line 29

Incomplete sentence: "It would require an effective decrease of more than 700,000 livres, of which half was from the taille and the other half from the taxes accessory to it" (v. 6, p. 72).

Page 322, line 1

Marginal note: On the contrary, in Turgot's time, the ordinances forbade replacement or the choice of a paid volunteer which the communities made in order to exempt others; in order, doubtless, to make the enlistment of regular troops (who were recruited only by voluntary enlistment) easier.

Page 322, line 30

The notes which follow are mostly taken from volumes 7 and 8, which cover the period of Turgot's ministry.

Page 323, line 1

Marginal note: At the same time as it tried to destroy the epidemic, the government gave high subsidies for the importation of animals in the provinces. Subsidies paid on the certificate of the buyer, certified by the subdelegate (ibid., p. 142).

Later, the epidemic continuing, troops were marched in, boundaries set up, the stables and animals visited without exception. Sick animals were immediately killed. The stables were purified, all this under the supervision of the intendants and subdelegates (p. 169).

Page 323, line 19

In the margin: Abandonment of the lower classes even by the government, contrary to the opinion that in France the government has been the guardian of the lower classes. The truth is that the government was only concerned with the bourgeoisie, almost never with the lower classes, and always from an egoistic perspective with regard to both.

Page 324, line 21

This remark bears on volumes 5 and 6, that is on Turgot's activity as intendant and not as minister.

Page 324, line 32

See Tocqueville's notes of April 1853, "Examination of the papers of the Generality of Paris. Hotel de Ville, File 43A I." The notes on Turgot containing two references to this scrutiny on pp. 403, 406, and 420 are therefore later.

Louis Bénigne François de Bertier de Sauvigny, born in 1737, master of requests at the Royal Council, was assistant to his father at the intendancy of Paris in 1768, filled all its duties when his father was promoted the to presidency of Maupeou's parlement in 1771, and received the title in September 1776. He had a general cadaster established between 1771 and 1776, eliminated the corvée of manual labor, limited and regularized military service. He was killed on 22 July 1789 in front of the Hôtel de Ville at Paris.

Page 325, line 18

Sic. Turgot writes: "one also named, by majority vote, one or two well-off individuals who were charged to collect the money, according to the tax-roll drawn up by the Assessors, and pay it into the treasury of the Royal Tax-Receivers."

Page 327, line 25

Turgot is more balanced: "It is much more easy for the government to say to the communities: 'I need this sum of money; arrange it as you like, or as you can, provided that I get the money that I ask of you,' than it is for communities composed of poor, ignorant and brutal peasants, as they are in most of the kingdom, to effectively arrange to divide a very heavy burden with exact justice and while taking account of a swarm of exemptions established by the innumerable regulations whose detailed knowledge would require all a man's time for study, and whose ignorance exposes the unfortunate peasant to overburden his fellows and himself, if he pays attention to unfounded exemptions; or to bear, along with his community, ruinous lawsuits, if he refuses to respect legitimate exemptions."

Page 331, line 24

Mémoire au Roi sur les municipalités, sur la hiérarchie qu'on pourroit établir entre elles, et sur les services que le Gouvernement en pourroit tirer, v. 7, pp. 387–484.

Page 334, line 5

Tocqueville truncates the quotation: ". . . in whose government they take part. Perhaps it is unfortunate that these half-measures exist. The provinces which enjoy them feel the need for reform less." Turgot's project consisted of giving a good constitution to the pays d'élection, so that the pays d'état would agree to change their form.

Page 336, line 27

Left blank in the text. Doubtless the Church of Ivry.

Page 341, line 34

Marginal note: "All this could take place this year as well as at the beginning of next year; but it would only be in the first days of October of the latter, after all the harvests had been collected and known, that the municipal electoral assemblies could be held" (ibid., p. 472). We see that the difficulty related to the fact that the harvests were or were not made before putting the plan into execution.

Page 344, line 6

Here begins the examination of the Mémoire sur les projets d'édits proposées au Roi, v. 8, pp. 150–77.

Page 345, line 26

Here begins the examination of the Observations de M. le Garde des sceaux sur le projet d'édit proposé par Turgot, pour la suppression des corvées; et résponses de ce ministre, v. 8, pp. 178–262.

Page 345, line 29

In the margin: Forty years ago the corvées were generally established (this was written in 1776), and a much longer time ago they had been put into effect in several provinces (ibid., p. 204).

Page 346, line 25

In the margin the following lines: Indirect privileges with regard to taxes: difference in collection. Turgot also makes a picture of this which I have reason to believe accurate according to the evidence.

Page 349, line 3

Marginal note: If you want to have an idea of all the futile reasons that could be given to maintain the nobility's privileges with regard to taxes, one must read the statements of Chancellor de Miromesnil.

Page 353, line 18

Folder C, notes of October 1853. Tocqueville is taking notes here on the Résumé général; ou, Extrait des cahiers de pouvoirs, instructions, demandes et doléances, remis par les divers baillages, sénéchaussées et pays d'Etats du royaume, à leurs députés à l'assemblée des Etats Généraux, ouverts à Versailles le 4 mai 1789, 3 vols., 1789. The cahiers of the clergy are summarized in the first volume. In the published text Tocqueville used only his notes on the cahiers of the nobility. See vol. 1, The Old Regime and the Revolution, p. 294 and note.

Page 353, line 30

Most of the cahiers simply ask that the unlimited freedom of the press be circumscribed. Tocqueville seems to be commenting here particularly on the cahier of Troyes (Résumé, p. 17): "If the Estates General believe that freedom of the press is a consequence of individual freedom, let there at least be established punishments for the authors of books contrary to religion and good mores." Tocqueville contrasts this liberalism with the subjection of the press by the decree of 17 February 1852, which gave the government the ability to suspend newspapers and even to close them permanently as a measure of national security.

Page 354, line 15

Examination of the ninth section, "On non-Catholics." The edict of Versailles of 19 November 1787 had established the legal existence of Protestants, while excluding them from judicial offices, government jobs, and all positions involving public education.

Page 356, line 28

In the margin: Good idea to follow and extend. All this analysis of the cahiers proves it. Get a good deal out of this when I say that the war on religion and the resistance of the clergy are an accidental and particular fact, and that the new state is neither naturally opposed to religion nor naturally attacked by the clergy.

Page 357, line 3

In 1857 Tocqueville would continue his interpretation of the cahiers of the Third Estate while reading the cahier of the Third Estate of Amiens (Folder E.E. 45B):

Cahier of the Third Estate.

Vote by head. The deputies should withdraw if the majority of the Third Estate decides to do so, if the vote by head is refused.

Thus the collision was announced in advance! What abominable imprudence by the government thus warned to have let it break out! Moreover, it would have happened a moment later whatever had been done.

Exceptional courts and administrative courts.

In the old regime one must distinguish carefully between these two things. The exceptional courts often were harmful to the good administration of business, but most often they were not stained with the vice which today is inherent to exceptional courts and which they bring to mind, partiality in favor of the government or the administration. These courts were also most often as separate from the administration proper and its particular spirit as were the parlements.

What I call administrative courts are those which put justice into the hands of the administration itself, like the intendant or the Council, also the provost's office although it was inconvenient, but its institution and its spirit were essentially governmental and repressive.

In the cahiers one always asks for the elimination of administrative courts but not always for that of the exceptional courts. *More or less complete reform of justice, one of the most widespread ideas among the three orders:* This does not vary except in emphasis but is found in all the cahiers. It is striking that these ideas and feelings had sprouted so well even amidst the enthusiasm which the parlements had just inspired and perhaps even (if one could have seen into the bottom of hearts) because of the facts which gave birth to this enthusiasm. These secret and unexpected works often take place in people's minds.

Decentralizing tendency: We see at this time that every time one took away a right, a privilege from individuals, it was not as in our day to give it to the state, but rather to some intermediate bodies. For example, one destroys the venality of offices. This was to give the office either to individuals or to the provincial assemblies at least insofar as to who could be a candidate.

All demand that no one may be arbitrarily deprived of his liberty or forbidden to appear in a certain place. That no one may be arrested except by order of the competent judge and interrogated within the next twenty-four hours, given that there cannot be freedom for the nation as long as the freedom of individuals is not inviolable (p. 121).

A true and beautiful principle well-expressed. How far from it we are, good God! What an immense backwards movement from sixty years ago!

Page 358, line 28

Folder K. The text is preceded by the remark: Ideas to look at again during the final revision in order to weave them in, if there is a place, in the chapters already written.

Page 359, line 18

At Tours, in July 1853, Tocqueville read Eugène Daire's Collection des principaux économistes (1846) and then, shortly afterwards, the Eléments de la philosophie rurale (1 vol.) and L'Ami des hommes (2 vols.) by the elder Mirabeau, and the Journal économique for the year 1752 (see Tocqueville's letter to Beaumont, 1 July 1854, OC, v. 8, t. 3, p. 132). It was not the physiocrats' ideas which interested him, but what they showed of the revolutionary mind, from which Tocqueville's insistence on the radicalism of their political position without any examination of the details of their proposed economic reforms. Mirabeau was "a very intelligent and original man, but strongly colored by old feudal prejudices," "well-acquainted with the universal scope of revolutionary ideas, which to a certain extent influenced him as well," explained Tocqueville to Nassau Senior on 15 February 1854 (OC, v. 6, t. 2, p. 409). For this reason Tocqueville put particular emphasis on him.

Tocqueville's notes were taken on L'Ami des hommes, 2 vols. divided into 6 parts, Avignon, 1756–58. Tocqueville's handwritten manuscript is lost. All that remains is a copy by Beaumont preserved among Tocqueville's research notes, which we follow here. Tocqueville had also read Mirabeau's book on the Prussian monarchy but judged it poor, and his notes are lost (see his letter to Corcelle from the château de Tocqueville, 11 March 1857, p. 385).

Page 359, line 29

The Mémoire sur les états provinciaux, which appeared anonymously in 1750, constituted the fourth part of L'Ami des hommes.

Page 359, line 33

This description is found on pp. 79–81 of volume 2.

Page 360, line 10

Ami des hommes, Mémoire sur les états provinciaux, t. 2, pp. 89–90: the quotation is shortened: ". . . of deference, except in one circumstance too unusual to have consequences: I mean services to the country and to individuals, as much by good employment as by example."

Page 360, line 28

Nonliteral quotation.

Page 361, line 1

This quotation and the following are taken from the Dialogue entre le surinten-

dant d'O et L.D.H., published in v. 2 of L'ami des hommes, *a dialogue on "frater-nity" between a superintendent for whom the lower classes are a beast of burden and the "friend of humanity."*

Page 361, line 4
Nonliteral quotation.

Page 361, line 35
L'Ami des hommes, *t. 1,* Traité de la population, *part 3, p. 87. The quotation is inexact: "in whatever state or society which may have existed."*

Page 362, line 21
L'Ami des hommes, *t. 1,* Traité de la population, *part 3, p. 126. Inexact quotation: "very active great rogues, honest people often discontented."*

Page 362, line 26
L'Ami des hommes, *t. 1,* Traité de la population, *part 3, p. 127.*

Page 363, line 10
De l'administration provinciale, et de la réforme de l'impôt, *Basel, 1779. Research notes, Folder D.*
Letrosne (1728–1780), after studying law, in 1753 was named royal attorney at the presidial court of Orléans, where he remained for twenty years. Very soon linked with the physiocrats, from 1765 he wrote in Le journal de l'agriculture, du commerce et des finances, *and then in the* Ephémérides du citoyen. *A shorter first version of the work that Tocqueville is commenting on here had been written in response to a competition launched in 1775 by the Academy of Toulouse on the creation of provincial governments. Tocqueville made only a very partial reading of Letrosne: he was not interested in the propositions for tax reform, but only in the denunciation of the old system and the means for its destruction (book 9), one proof among others that it was not the ideas of the physiocrats which interested Tocqueville, but the radicalism of their critique and their haste to destroy.*

Page 363, line 24
Nonliteral quotation from book 3, chapter 6, p. 164.

Page 363, line 34
Quotation from book 3, chapter 9, p. 187.

Page 364, line 17
Tocqueville here summarizes book 3, chapter 9, pp. 188–89.

Page 365, line 10
Nonliteral quotations.

Page 365, line 31
Nonliteral quotations.

Page 366, line 2

Tocqueville here summarizes a discussion in book 5, chapter 2, "that provincial government is the only means of interesting the nation in the reestablishment of political life." But he radicalizes Letrosne's position, which does not refer to the division of interests and makes of representation above all the means of producing national unity, but does refer—like Tocqueville—to Malesherbes's authority to defend the right of representation. Thus p. 322: "It is of the essence of every civil body, of every society, to exist either by the meeting of its members, or, if it is too numerous, by that of their representatives. To take from a nation the right of having representatives is to dissolve it, it is to reduce it to no longer being a civil society."

Page 366, line 11

Fifth book: "on the form of a provincial government" pp. 315ff. Letrosne here discusses the reform, division, and collection of taxes. He proposes to institute in each capital of a generality a provincial council of landowners named for life, and a provincial assembly of landowners named for two years; in each lesser town a district council composed of landowners named for life, and in each district a community with a general assembly and a committee.

Page 366, line 23

Letrosne ends his discussion of distinctions among the orders thus on p. 330: "Moreover, a philosopher who is creating a plan at his leisure looks for what seems to him to be the absolute best. The administrator who gives orders is often forced to content himself with the best possible, and to have regard for obstacles in opinion, to contradictions and to circumstances. Let us hope that if we introduce into these assemblies the distinction among the three orders, the clergy and the nobility will make it a duty and an honor to forget the claims and privileges of their body, if the good of society demands it." We see that his taste for a blank slate is not absolute.

Page 367, line 18

Commentary from book 9, chapter 9, "on urban taxes."

Page 368, line 2

Nonliteral quotations from book 9, chapter 11.

Page 369, line 32

Letrosne's prudence comes from the feeling that feudalism is inseparable from the monarchy. Here is the context of the quotation, p. 570: "I find that the greatest obstacle to the abolition of feudalism is that it is part of property and that it forms an inheritance. In this regard it is respectable. I do not see any means to destroy it except to allow those who pay dues, and vassals, to redeem the freedom of their inheritances at a price which would be determined without the suzerain lord being able to object. Since feudalism ends in every direction with the king as its sole center, it would be required that the king set the example, by breaking the chain and accepting the redemptions. But this operation is dependent on so many things, and would be so long-term in its execution, that it must be relegated to the class of reforms which are more to be desired than hoped for."

Page 369, line 39

Nonliteral quotation (p. 625) taken from the Dissertation sur la féodalité dans laquelle on discute son origine, son état actuel, ses inconvénients, et les moyens de la supprimer, *published as an appendix to the work* De l'administration provinciale.

Page 370, line 11

For Mercier de la Rivière, Baudeau, and Quesnay, Tocqueville used the collection made by Eugène Daire, Collection des principaux économistes, *Paris, v. 2, 1846.*

Mercier (1720–1793 or 1794) in 1747 had acquired the office of councilor of the Parlement of Paris, which he gave up for the position of intendant of Martinique. On his return he linked himself with Quesnay, whose ideas he supported as early as 1767 in the best-known of his works, L'ordre naturel et essentiel des sociétés politiques, *which Tocqueville comments on here.*

Page 370, line 24

Tocqueville is commenting here on the Première introduction à la philosophie économique; ou; Analyse des états policés, *1771, pp. 657ff., in Daire's collection.*

Page 370, line 31

*Marginal note: "*Introduction à la philosophie économique, *1771. Daire's collection, v. 2, p. 670."*

The quotation is truncated. Baudeau makes a lengthy elegy of ancient Egypt and Mesopotamia, and of modern China (pp. 680–81) with its Wall, its Grand Canal, its dikes, bridges, machines. In China he admires an enlightened government, mother of public and private prosperity.

Page 371, line 34

The commentator is Daire, Collection des principaux économistes, *p. 797.*

Page 373, line 13

First letter from Dupont de Nemours to Say, in Daire's collection, pp. 394–416. Tocqueville is referring here to p. 410.

THE END

Index

This index covers the Introduction as well as Tocqueville's text, including the Notes and Variants. Years as entries or subentries (e.g., 1787, 1848) are alphabetized as if they were spelled out (i.e., under S or E).

Absolute government, absolutism. *See also*
Despotism
aristocracy and, 13, 14, 46
bourgeoisie and, 47
bureaucracy and, 306
civilian, 51
class unity destroys, 13, 50–51, 388, 419
confidence in government, 368
cult of, 8, 15
degrades people, 338
democracy and, 105, 163, 191, 404
do not fear revolutions, 332
fearful, 365
freedom and, 41, 420
hatred for, 35
inherit free intellectual life, 258
judiciary opposed, 39, 406, 411
Louis XVI and, 51, 387, 396, 406
modern, 278, 285
prepares revolution, 294
radicalism and, 13, 16, 17
reform seen as, 400
revolution appropriated, 15
socialism and, 369
temporary, 105
Tocqueville finds in archives, 15
Tocqueville unfamiliar with, 473
universe of, 16
Algeria, 282, 310, 362, 482
Allgemeines Landrecht (Prussian Civil Code), 276, 277, 280, 282, 478
America, American, United States. *See also*
American Revolution; *Democracy in America*

Brissot and, 111–13
constitutions, 102
emigration to, 272
France more democratic than, 85
influence replaces English, 86
lawyers in, 123
manage class interests, 15
not cited, 80
parallel with Russia, 291
theories' different effects compared to
France, 163
view of Revolution, 10, 18
American Revolution, 19, 33–34, 84, 111, 380
Amiens, 255, 322
Ampère, Jean-Jacques, 6, 7, 9, 410
Anarchy
army and, 180, 358
Caesarism and, 16
centralization and, 186, 449
Constituent Assembly created, 118
despotism and, 262
Directory as, 191, 193, 194, 198, 214, 447
18 Brumaire and, 240
Estates of Dauphiny as, 50
France, 140, 151
Illuminati, 33
National Assembly and, 134, 161, 162
Paris, 126, 138, 141, 144, 169
Revolution as, 14, 186, 206
Terror and, 210, 231
wealth and, 360
Anjou, 96, 123, 124, 126, 134, 146, 442, 485
Aristocracy, aristocratic. *See also* 1789, 4 August; Assembly of Notables; Caste;